Second Edition

P9-DEQ-143

Nonprofits &
GOVERNMENT

Collaboration & CONFLICT

THE URBAN INSTITUTE PRESS
Washington, D.C.

THE URBAN INSTITUTE PRESS
2100 M Street, N.W.
Washington, D.C. 20037

Library of Congress Cataloging-in-Publication Data

Nonprofits and government : collaboration and conflict / edited by Elizabeth T. Boris and C. Eugene Steuerle.--2nd ed.
    p. cm.
    Includes bibliographical references and index.
    ISBN 0-87766-732-2
    1. Nonprofit organizations--United States.   2. Administrative agencies--United States.   3. Public-private sector cooperation--United States.   4. Democracy--United States.   I. Boris, Elizabeth T. II. Steuerle, C. Eugene, 1946–
    HD62.6.N64 2006
    361.7'63--dc22   2006025103

Printed in the United States of America

10   09   08   07   06   1   2   3   4   5

Nonprofits &
GOVERNMENT

Edited by
Elizabeth T. Boris and C. Eugene Steuerle

Also of interest from Urban Institute Press:

Property-Tax Exemption for Charities, edited by Evelyn Brody.

THE URBAN INSTITUTE is a nonprofit, nonpartisan policy research and educational organization established in Washington, D.C., in 1968. Its staff investigates the social, economic, and governance problems confronting the nation and evaluates the public and private means to alleviate them. The Institute disseminates its research findings through publications, its web site, the media, seminars, and forums.

Through work that ranges from broad conceptual studies to administrative and technical assistance, Institute researchers contribute to the stock of knowledge available to guide decisionmaking in the public interest.

Conclusions or opinions expressed in Institute publications are those of the authors and do not necessarily reflect the views of officers or trustees of the Institute, advisory groups, or any organizations that provide financial support to the Institute.

CONTENTS

FOREWORD

M uch has changed since the first edition of *Nonprofits and Govern-ment: Collaboration and Conflict* came out in 1999. There are roughly 230,000 more nonprofit organizations operating today. Unlike today, it wasn't possible to get a PhD in philanthropic studies or to study the nonprofit sector as an undergraduate in numerous American colleges and universities. Warren Buffet hadn't yet made history by tendering the biggest philanthropic gift ever and bestowing it on a foundation. In 1999, the budget was in surplus; today, growing deficits threaten government's ability to sustain the country's social safety net, the failure of which could overwhelm the nonprofits that fund or deliver social services. When the first edition was published, the stock market was soaring; its subsequent tumble depressed both endowments of and the contributions to nonprofits. Nor had the aftermaths of such earthshaking events as September 11th and Hurricane Katrina demonstrated beyond doubt how much nonprofits and government need to work together during emergencies.

This book was revised in part to take account of these developments and in part to reassess the fundamental forces shaping the nonprofit sector and its interaction with government. While the environment has changed, the important questions remain the same: What types of organizations make up the nonprofit universe? How are nonprofits financed, governed, and regulated? How do government spending and tax policy affect the nonprofit sector? Why are government and the public holding nonprofits more accountable? What burdens and opportunities does new information on nonprofits create? Why are some nonprofits converting to for-profit organizations? How can cooperation between nonprofits and government be enhanced and conflicts minimized? And how does the nonprofit scene here differ from that in other countries?

The answers to these questions are of more than academic interest. As contributors to this volume note, nonprofits account for almost 6 percent of the U.S. gross domestic product, own about 5 percent of private sector net worth, and engage over 9 percent of working adults. They touch the lives of hundreds of million people here and abroad.

The sector's challenges are immense. Social service providers and advocates must deal with sweeping changes as the U.S. population ages, the share of federal funds available for discretionary services shrinks, and needs grow. Educational institutions are sailing in uncharted waters as they try to educate diverse populations for rapidly changing workforce needs. Hospitals, clinics, and other nonprofit health care providers face increasing numbers of uninsured patients. Nearly all nonprofits face new administrative challenges, as regulations, tax laws, and public social programs change while budget constraints tighten.

Nonprofits' diverse roles, constituents, and beneficiaries make generalizations about the sector's relationship to government both fascinating and difficult. This new edition of *Nonprofits and Government* approaches the sector from many vantage points, which is the best way to see overlapping spheres in constant motion and occasional collisions. Buttressed by rigorous scholarship, a solid grasp of history, and practical ideas, this 360-degree assessment should free discussion of the nonprofit sector's relationship to government from both wishful and insular thinking.

Robert D. Reischauer
President
Urban Institute

PREFACE

Nonprofit organizations and government try to address many of the same societal problems, but not always in the same ways. Their relationship has long been both symbiotic and adversarial, with events and opportunities continually coloring or governing their interactions. The sectors can cooperate on one issue while butting heads on another, continuously prodding the other to do more and do it better.

The 1999 edition of this book was the first comprehensive, research-based inquiry into the collaborative and conflicting relationship between nonprofits and government. Since then, researchers have brought this relationship into sharper focus and deepened our understanding of its impact on organizations, governments, and the public. This revised edition adds new insights and data on the scope and nature of nonprofit–government interactions. We explore how government regulates, facilitates, finances, and oversees nonprofit activities, and how nonprofits, in turn, try to shape the way government serves the public and promotes the civic, religious, and cultural life of the country.

Highlights of this second edition include new material on trends affecting nonprofit–government interactions and new chapters by Janelle Kerlin on the roles of U.S. international nonprofits and Woods Bowman and Marion Fremont-Smith on how state government finances and regulates nonprofits.

Major government trends include increased pressures on discretionary spending in the federal budget and rapid growth in health spending—both greatly influence nonprofits' finances. Trends in the nonprofit sector include growing reliance on fee-for-service revenues, increasing organizational transparency and visibility, and mounting demand for improved accountability, effectiveness, and coordination among charities and between government and charities for disaster relief. Congressional hearings on abuses by and regulation of charities are part of the changing political landscape, as is growing concern about the political use of charities in the wake of campaign finance reform. Understanding the forces affecting nonprofits and their relationship with government is the impetus for this new edition. It is our hope that this volume will make collaboration more productive and reduce needless conflict.

ACKNOWLEDGMENTS

A book of this nature is impossible without the contributions of many individuals. The editors are especially grateful to the authors for their excellent contributions and tolerance of our editorial suggestions, to Amisha Chaudhary for her extensive editorial and bibliographic assistance, and to William Bradbury for his thorough and professional editing.

INTRODUCTION

NONPROFIT ORGANIZATIONS IN A DEMOCRACY—ROLES AND RESPONSIBILITIES

Elizabeth T. Boris

Nonprofit organizations are a vital force of civil society, distinct from both government and business. Nonprofits are like government in some of their goals, but they are different in others. Through both collaboration and conflict, they shape and are shaped by government policies and funding. Nonprofits have in common that they are voluntary and self-governing, may not distribute profits, and serve public purposes as well as the common goals of their members. These organizations are even more diverse than the terms typically associated with them: nongovernmental organizations, civil society, philanthropic sector, tax-exempt organizations, charities, voluntary associations, civic sector organizations, third sector organizations, independent sector organizations, nonprofit organizations, and social sector organizations.

This introduction provides a broad overview of nonprofit organizations and their finances, the roles they play in society, and their relationships with government—themes the following chapters examine in detail.

"Nonprofit" is the generic term used in this chapter and in this book to describe organizations that make up the "nonprofit" sector,[1] distinct from the government and business sectors. The nonprofit sector includes religious congregations, universities, hospitals, environmental groups, art museums, youth recreation associations, civil rights groups, community development organizations, labor unions, political parties, social clubs, and many more. Nonprofits play prominent social, economic, and political roles in society as service providers, but they are also employers and advocates. Their numbers and economic impact have grown recently as they increasingly contract with government to deliver a variety of services, particularly health care. This relationship is usually collaborative. As advocates, however, they lobby for and against government policies that affect their constituencies or interests, often invoking conflict.

Nonprofits also play less visible but vital roles that are captured under the rubric of "civil society"—fostering community engagement and civic participation, and promoting and preserving civic, cultural, and religious values. These roles are usually financed though giving and volunteering rather than fees and contracts, and can involve either collaboration or conflict with government, although they typically fall outside direct government purview.

The service provision and economic dimensions of nonprofit activities tend be better documented than their contributions to democratic pluralism. Scholars are increasingly, however, exploring the central role that formal and informal nonprofits play in creating the glue that holds communities together and the avenues they provide for civic participation and a robust civil society (O'Connell 1999; Putnam 2000; Skocpol and Fiorina 1999; Verba, Schlozman, and Brady 1995).

Voluntary associations strengthen and add to the prosperity and success of democracies. They help build the networks of trust and reciprocity, the social capital that allows democratic societies to function effectively (Putnam 1993; Walzer 1995). Cooperative activities bring together people with divergent opinions who learn to work together on issues of mutual interest or for the common good. Citizens participate in democratic governance by joining together to accomplish public purposes, voice their concerns to government, and monitor the impact of business, government, and nonprofit activities on the public. Nonprofits also promote and defend values and competing visions of the public good, and they harness altruism and public and private resources to serve those who need assistance. All of these activities require the freedom to associate, deliberate, and act in the public sphere—freedoms constitutions and laws guarantee. Inevitably, however, competing values and interests often produce conflict. Also inevitably, where public resources are directly or indirectly involved, government regulation and oversight follow.

The interaction between government and nonprofit organizations in civil society is complex and dynamic, ebbing and flowing with shifts in social and economic policy, political administrations, and social norms. Because nonprofits are heterogeneous, they reflect sharp differences as well as common aspirations. Their impacts can be positive or negative, antagonistic or conciliatory, depending on their activities as well as the perspective of the analyst. Of course, speaking about nonprofits in the aggregate invites overgeneralization—obscuring the huge variation and diversity of nonprofit roles, contributions, and inter actions with government. Similarly, misconceptions of the scale and financial capacity of nonprofits relative to government lead to unrealis tic expectations of what these institutions can do, as well as to misconceived public policies that lean too little or too much on them. Partly to avoid these perils, this book analyzes the relationships of nonprofits and government in myriad detail.

DEFINITION AND REGULATION OF NONPROFIT ORGANIZATIONS

Nonprofits in the United States are defined and regulated primarily under the federal tax code. They are self-governing organizations that do not distribute profits to those who control them and are exempt from federal income taxes by virtue of being organized for public purposes. Regulation of nonprofits is fragmented; there is no central U.S. government agency that focuses solely on the oversight of nonprofits. At the national level, the Internal Revenue Service (IRS) is the primary regulator of nonprofits and is charged with determining their legitimacy as tax-exempt entities and overseeing their activities. State governments oversee and regulate nonprofits that operate in their jurisdictions, and the Federal Election Commission regulates nonprofits engaged in federal elections. (See chapter 4 for a discussion of rationales for tax exemption, the impact on activities, and the value of preferential tax treatment for nonprofits. Chapter 5 provides an analysis of state tax exemption and regulation, and chapter 10 discusses regulation of advocacy and political activities.) A legal framework based on tax definitions and enforcement is not the norm for regulating the nonprofit sector in other countries (see chapter 12).

All U.S. nonprofit organizations with annual gross receipts of $5,000 or more, except religious groups, are required to register with the IRS.

Organizations with revenues (gross receipts) of more than $25,000 are required to complete and file an annual IRS Form 990; all private foundations must file IRS Form 990-PF. These forms are public docu-ments that provide the basis for federal and state oversight of nonprofits and the only financial data on nonprofits required to be publicly available.[2]

Nonprofit organizations that serve broad public purposes and are organized for educational, religious, scientific, literary, poverty relief, and other activities for the public benefit are eligible to apply for charitable status under section 501(c)(3) of the tax code. Charitable status permits organizations to receive tax-deductible contributions, an important incentive to encourage donations. Religious congregations, however, do not have to apply for charitable status; they have it. Charitable nonprofits serving broad public purposes account for the majority of tax-exempt organizations, and are the focus of most chapters in this book. Membership organizations, such as labor unions, recre-ation clubs, credit unions, and political parties, are also tax-exempt but receive less attention here.

Even within the charitable portion of the nonprofit sector, nonprofits are extremely diverse. They vary greatly in mission, origin, structure, size, sources of revenues, and financial means. They are accountable to multiple constituencies—board and staff, members, donors, clients, volunteers, funders, and the public.[3] Public confidence and trust are crucial to their success, yet the public has limited understanding of the scope and operations of nonprofits. Lack of transparency, particularly about the use of donated money, and scandals of any type negatively affect the whole sector, often leading to public outcry, congressional inquiries, and new regulatory proposals.[4]

Nonprofits' diversity confounds attempts to explain them through some overarching theory (although see chapters 1, 9, and 12 for dis-cussions of theories of the government–nonprofit relationship). Researchers have made progress in measuring the scope of the formal organizations (Weitzman et al. 2002), but less has been accomplished in measuring the informal groups, coalitions, and religious organizations (Smith 2000). There is also a dearth of information on the direct and indirect impacts of nonprofit groups on society.

SCOPE OF NONPROFIT ORGANIZATIONS IN THE UNITED STATES

The nonprofit sector in the United States is dynamic and has grown significantly in recent decades. Although characterized by a great diver-sity of organizations and activities, resources are concentrated in a small number of organizations, while activities are fragmented and vary in scale and by geographic area. In total, nonprofits have assets of approximately $3 trillion and expenses of $1.3 trillion. In economic terms, the nonprofit sector represents 6 percent of national income and employs over 9 percent of the labor force (excluding volunteers). (See chapter 2 for a comparison of the resources of the nonprofit sector and government and a breakdown of nonprofit revenues by source.)

There were approximately 1.8 million tax-exempt nonprofit organizations (including congregations) in 2004, up from fewer than 1.3 million in 1989. This 39 percent increase (table I.1) may be somewhat exaggerated by nonprofits failing to file statements of their demise.

Among the 1.5 million nonprofits required to register with the IRS because they had more than $5,000 in gross receipts in 2004, were over one million "charitable" 501(c)(3) organizations eligible to receive tax-deductible contributions. This group includes operating public charities (such as hospitals, universities, and soup kitchens) as well as supporting organizations (such as private and community foundations) that provide resources to other nonprofit organizations. Congregations are charitable organizations that are not required to register with the IRS, although many do.[5] The total number of charitable organizations registered with the IRS more than doubled between 1989 and 2004 and rose from less than half to about two-thirds of all registered nonprofits.[6]

In this period, small charities, many recently created, grew more quickly than charities overall. Defined as organizations with between $5,000 and $25,000 in revenues, they represented about 62 percent (631,000) of 501(c)(3) charities in 2004.[7] The information on these small charities is limited because they do not have to file the yearly IRS Form 990 that tax-exempt organizations with $25,000 or more in gross receipts must submit.

There are probably millions more small formal and informal associations (with less than $5,000 in revenues) that are not required to register or report to the IRS. Recent research is attempting to document the prevalence of these small and often volunteer-led organizations, as well as the many nonprofits that should be registering with the IRS but are not (Gronbjerg and Paarlberg 2002).

In addition to the charitable organizations, approximately 138,000 public-serving social welfare organizations are tax exempt under IRC section 501(c)(4). Most of these organizations may not receive tax-deductible gifts; many elect to do substantial lobbying and advocate for specific issues.[8] Along with public charities and congregations, they are considered a key component of the independent sector, as defined in various editions of the *Nonprofit Almanac* (Weitzman et al. 2002).[9] Unlike charities, the numbers of social welfare organizations are declining.

Other types of tax-exempt organizations primarily serve their members; for example, business leagues, social and recreational clubs, war

Table I.1. Number of Nonprofit Entities in the United States, 1989–2004 (numbers in thousands)

	1989 Number	1989 Percent	1993 Number	1993 Percent	1998 Number	1998 Percent	2004 Number	2004 Percent	1989–2004 % change
Total private nonprofit organizations	1,262	100.0	1,386	100.0	1,526	100.0	1,758	100.0	39.3
Tax-exempt orgs. Registered with the I.R.S.	993	78.7	1,118	80.7	1,273	83.4	1,541	87.7	55.2
Total 501(c)(3) charitable organizations	464	36.8	576	41.5	734	48.1	1,010	57.5	117.8
Total public charities	422	33.4	527	38.0	675	44.2	934	53.2	121.4
Reporting with financial data	138	10.9	172	12.4	228	14.9	303	17.2	119.6
Out-of-scope organizations[a]	0.5	0.0	0.5	0.0	0.6	0.0	0.4	0.0	–20.0
Reporting public charities	137	10.9	171	12.3	227	14.9	303	17.2	121.2
Operating[b]	124	9.8	152	11.0	201	13.2	263	15.0	112.1
Supporting[c]	13	1.0	18	1.3	26	1.7	39	2.2	200.0
Mutual benefit[d]	0.5	0.0	0.6	0.0	0.6	0.0	0.6	0.0	20.0
Nonreporting	284	22.5	355	25.6	447	29.3	631	35.9	122.3
Private foundations	42	3.3	49	3.5	59	3.9	76	4.3	81.0
501(c)(4) social welfare organizations	141	11.2	142	10.3	140	9.1	138	7.9	–2.0
Other registered tax-exempt organizations	388	30.7	400	28.9	400	26.2	392	22.3	1.1
Religious congregations not registered with the IRS[e]	269	21.3	268	19.3	253	16.6	217	12.3	–19.3

Sources: The Urban Institute, NCCS Core Files, Public Charities, Public Charities and Private Foundations, 1998, 1993, 1998, 2004; Internal Revenue Service Data Book, Publication 55B, 1989, 1993, 1998, 2004.

[a] Includes governmental or supporting government entities (such as public colleges), organizations located in another country, and organizations whose location could not be determined.

[b] Includes organizations that engage in a variety of activities, producing information, delivering services and products to their members and the public.

[c] Includes organizations that primarily collect funds and distribute them to operating organizations.

[d] Includes organizations that primarily provide services to members and customers.

[e] Authors' estimates, see "Note on Data Sources" in this chapter.

veterans' organizations, nonprofit cemetery companies, labor unions, benevolent life insurance associations, and credit unions (table I.2). Donations to these organizations are not tax-deductible, although earnings on their assets are often tax exempt. Their numbers have not grown since 1993, and they are a declining proportion of the nonprofit sector. While these groups potentially contribute to the social fabric of the country, we know most about the "charitable" 501(c)(3) organizations and the social welfare 501(c)(4) organizations that make up the

Table I.2. Tax-Exempt Organizations Registered with the IRS, 2004

Section	Description	Number
501(c)(1)	Corporations organized under act of Congress	116
501(c)(2)	Title-holding corporations	7,144
501(c)(3)	**Charitable and religious**[a]	**1,010,365**
501(c)(4)	Social welfare organizations	138,193
501(c)(5)	Labor and agriculture organizations	62,561
501(c)(6)	Business leagues	86,054
501(c)(7)	Social and recreation clubs	70,422
501(c)(8)	Fraternal beneficiary societies	69,798
501(c)(9)	Voluntary employees' beneficiary associations	12,866
501(c)(10)	Domestic fraternal beneficiary societies	21,328
501(c)(11)	Teachers' retirement funds	16
501(c)(12)	Benevolent life insurance associations	6,716
501(c)(13)	Cemetery companies	10,728
501(c)(14)	State-chartered credit unions	4,289
501(c)(15)	Mutual insurance companies	1,988
501(c)(16)	Corporations to finance crop operations	21
501(c)(17)	Supplemental unemployment benefit trusts	462
501(c)(18)	Employee-funded pension trusts	2
501(c)(19)	War veterans' organizations	36,141
501(c)(21)	Black Lung trusts	33
501(c)(22)	Multiemployer pension plans	—
501(c)(23)	Veteran's associations founded prior to 1880	2
501(c)(24)	Trusts described in Section 4049 of ERISA	4
501(c)(25)	Holding companies for pensions and other entities	1,285
501(c)(26)	State-sponsored, high-risk health insurance organizations	11
501(c)(27)	State-sponsored workers' compensation reinsurance organizations	9
501(d)	Religious and apostolic associations	141
501(e)	Cooperative hospital service organizations	38
501(f)	Cooperative service organizations of operating educational organizations	1
501(k)	Child care organizations	3
501(n)	Charitable risk pools	1
Total		1,540,738

Source: Internal Revenue Service Data Book, Publication 55B, 2004.

Note: Exempt subsections change over time according to IRS regulation. Farmers' cooperatives (1,400 in 1998) are no longer reported in the Data Book.

[a] Some 501(c)(3) organizations, such as churches, integrated auxiliaries, subordinate units, and conventions or associations of churches, are not included because the IRS does not require that they apply for tax exemption.

majority of formal nonprofit organizations. We focus on them because of their public-serving nature.

TYPES OF ORGANIZATIONS

The National Taxonomy of Exempt Entities, developed by the National Center for Charitable Statistics,[10] classifies all nonprofit organizations and demonstrates their variety (Stevenson 1997). It includes 9 major groups, 26 categories, and over 400 subcategories.[11] The major groups are

- Arts, culture, and humanities (e.g., art museums, historical societies)
- Education (e.g., private schools, universities, PTAs)
- Environment and animals (e.g., Humane Societies, the Chesapeake Bay Foundation)
- Health, hospitals (e.g., nonprofit hospitals, the American Lung Association)
- Human services (e.g., Girl Scouts, YMCA, food banks, homeless shelters)
- International, foreign affairs (e.g., CARE, the Asia Society, International Committee of the Red Cross)
- Public societal benefit (e.g., Rockefeller Foundation, the Urban Institute, civil rights groups, United Ways)
- Religion-related (e.g., interfaith coalitions, religious societies, congregations)
- Mutual and membership benefit (e.g., nonprofit credit unions, labor unions, fraternal organizations)

Among the 262,897 charitable operating nonprofits that report financial information to the IRS, environmental, education, and religion-related organizations increased most rapidly, while the number of health organizations grew much more slowly (table I.3). In terms of numbers, however, human services added the most organizations (53,768), increasing by 119 percent from 1989 to 2004. Education and religion-related organizations also grew significantly, probably due to the increase in charter schools and faith-based providers.

FINANCES OF NONPROFIT ORGANIZATIONS

Nonprofits vary tremendously in resources and capacity. Almost all nonprofits, however, benefit financially from their tax-exempt status,

Table I.3. Growth in Nonprofit Organizations by Type of Service, 1989–2004

Type	1989	1993	2004	Change	1989–2004 % change
Arts and culture	13,817	16,961	30,009	16,192	117.2
Education	16,939	22,240	44,133	27,194	160.5
Environment and animals	3,305	4,639	11,077	7,772	235.2
Health	23,039	26,892	33,355	10,316	44.8
Human services	45,156	58,267	98,924	53,768	119.1
International	1,196	2,347	5,216	4,020	336.1
Public and societal benefit	8,352	11,548	19,408	11,056	132.4
Religion related	5,764	7,478	16,488	10,724	186.1
Not classified	6,119	2,073	4,287	−1,832	−29.9
Total	123,687	152,445	262,897	139,210	112.6

Source: The Urban Institute, NCCS Core Files, Public Charities, 1989, 1993, 2004.
Note: Only operating public charities are included (see table I.1 for definition).

and charities additionally benefit from the incentives that charitable income tax deductions provide to donors.[12] Most nonprofits are extremely small entities with meager resources that operate locally with modest budgets and volunteer labor. Some organizations, however, are large and professional, with hundreds of employees and many millions of dollars in expenditures; nonprofit resources are concentrated in these large organizations, largely hospitals, universities, and multipurpose service organizations.

Nonprofit revenue sources include fees for service, government and foundation grants, individual and corporate donations, income from special events, member dues, investments, revenues from commercial ventures, and miscellaneous other sources. Direct government grants are less important than fee-for-service income, which is the dominant source of revenue for the sector in aggregate terms. Government provides significant amounts of fee income, both directly and indirectly, although it varies significantly by type of organization. Fees involve payments for services provided (including, for example, individual payments for tuition), government contracts through Medicare and Medicaid, and government or private vouchers for job training or child care. According to Steven Rathgeb Smith, Medicaid is a driving force in the growth of government funding of nonprofits. (See chapter 6 for a discussion of the mechanisms government uses to finance social services and the impacts these funding mechanisms have on nonprofit activities and operations.)

The resources of charities are highly concentrated in the largest organizations. Only 4 percent (10,513) of all operating charities (those health, education, arts, etc. organizations required to register and report to the IRS) have $10 million or more in expenses. These large organizations are professionally staffed and account for 83 percent of the $947 billion in expenditures and almost 82 percent of the $1.6 trillion in assets of operating charities.

In contrast, about 43 percent of organizations (112,921) have expenses of less than $100,000 and represent only 0.5 percent of the total expenses for operating charities in 2004 (figure I.1). These smaller organizations are largely volunteer run with minimal, if any, paid staff. Because large organizations and the tremendous resources deployed in the health sector drive aggregate financial statistics, such statistics fail to reveal a great deal about the majority of organizations in the nonprofit sector.[13]

Health and educational institutions dominate the finances of the nonprofit sector. Almost 57 percent of the revenues and expenses of public charities are in health-related organizations. Hospitals make up

Figure I.1. Nonprofit Finances by Total Expense Level, 2004

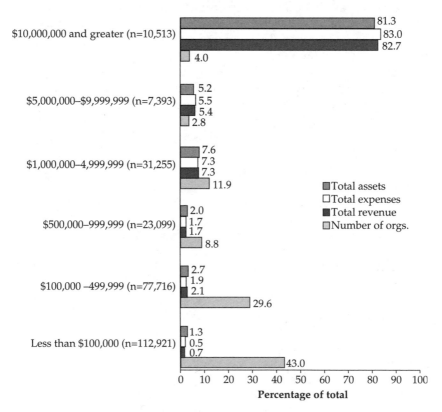

Source: The Urban Institute, NCCS Core File, Public Charities, 2004.
Note: Only operating public charities are included (see table I.1 for definition).

about 1 percent of organizations, but 45 percent of expenditures and 33 percent of assets. Private higher education accounts for about 0.5 percent of organizations but almost 11 percent of expenses and 24 percent of assets. Human service organizations, in contrast, account for almost 38 percent of operating charities but less than 14 percent of expenses and about 12 percent of assets (see figure I.2). Human service organizations tend to be smaller organizations, and their financial status is often quite weak.[14]

Figure I.2. Nonprofit Finances by Type of Activity, 2004

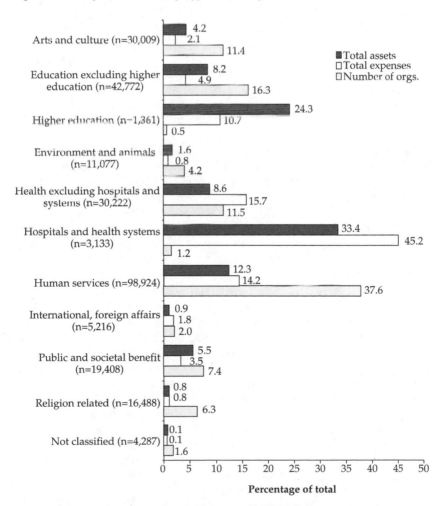

Source: The Urban Institute, NCCS Core File, Public Charities, 2004.
Note: Only operating public charities are included (see table I.1 for definition).

Significant nonprofit assets are held by endowed foundations that make grants to nonprofits. Private grantmaking foundations are 501(c)(3) organizations created by an individual or a family (60,031) or by a corporation (2,596) to fund other, mostly nonprofit, entities over time.[15] Community foundations are endowed public charities that raise money from individuals to benefit a city or other geographic area. Together, these organizations had approximately one-fifth of the assets of the charitable sector (excluding religious congregations). The number and assets of philanthropic foundations grew significantly over the past decade. The more than 67,000 foundations had an estimated $510 billion in assets in 2004 and made about $32 billion in grants. Resources are concentrated in the largest 50 foundations, which held over a third of foundation assets in 2004 (Lawrence, Atienza, and Barve 2005; Renz, Lawrence, and Atienza 2006).

In chapter 3, Abramson, Salamon, and Steuerle explore how federal budgetary priorities affect both the need for nonprofit services and the revenues available for providing those services. They estimate that 82 percent of federal funding for nonprofits (primarily for hospitals, nursing homes, and some social service providers) is from Medicaid, Medicare, and Temporary Assistance for Needy Families (TANF) programs.

While hospitals and higher education have long relied on fees, commercial fee-for-service income is increasingly important for other types of charities. Recent analyses show that, in 1982, commercial revenues for nonprofits (excluding hospitals and higher education) accounted for 48.1 percent of nonprofit revenue and, by 2002, had grown to 57.6 percent.[16] Increasing reliance on fee-for-service income from government and other sources inevitably affects the character and operations of many nonprofits (see chapter 6). As government contracting with nonprofits increases, some fear the commercialization of nonprofit service providers, even as government continues to be the dominant, if indirect, funder. Competition for clients and for government contracts—among nonprofits and between nonprofits and businesses—has led to more business-like marketing strategies and management practices. In addition, the Charitable Choice provisions of welfare reform designed to permit congregations to compete for government contracts enhances the resources of religious providers while potentially creating competition between secular nonprofits and religious congregations (see chapter 7). Involving congregations in fee-for-service government contracts raises concern about government involvement in religious affairs and loss of independence for faith-based providers, who presumably will have to respond to government demands for transparency and accountability in the use of resources and evidence of successful programs.

The uncertainty of sole sources of revenues has helped to fuel the search for resource diversification. Opportunities for commercial ventures and social enterprise have increased as new entrepreneurs enter the sector and businesses seek ways to use charities to enhance their marketing and visibility and expand their client bases. These market forces lead to greater concern for efficiency, the financial bottom line, effectiveness, and program outcomes.

Foundations are also stressing organizational effectiveness and measurement of outcomes in the nonprofits they fund.[17] Yet, funders are generally reluctant to make grants for operating support—which permits organizations to strengthen their infrastructure; most foundations prefer to support specific programs and often do not provide overhead costs. Of course, notable exceptions, such as Venture Philanthropy Partners and the Edna McConnell Clark Foundation, among many others, make significant capacity-building grants. However, a growing number of charity monitoring organizations base their ratings on low overhead and fundraising costs (efficiency) rather than results attained (effectiveness), thereby discouraging organizations from investing in strengthening their internal operations, a necessary ingredient for effectiveness.[18]

REGIONAL VARIATION

Numbers, types, finances, and growth of charitable nonprofit organizations vary by state and region. Obviously, the numbers of nonprofits tend to increase with population. California, Texas, and New York have the most charitable nonprofits. Similarly, the growth rates for nonprofits tend to be higher in states with rapidly growing populations. Density of nonprofits across the states, however, varies widely and tells a different story. Sparsely populated states have among the highest density of nonprofits. Vermont, for example, had a density of about 23 organizations per 10,000 people in 2004, and Montana with almost 16, compared with just under 7 for Texas, more than 10 for New York, and almost 9 for California. There are 9 nonprofits per 10,000 people nationally (figure I.3).

The Northeast has proportionately more arts, culture, and humanities organizations; the Midwest more human services; and the West more environmental groups. The Northeast, with about one-fifth of the population, is home to almost a quarter of nonprofits that account for nearly 30 percent of the expenditures of the sector, while the South, with 31 percent of organizations, accounted for 28 percent of expenses (table I.4).

Some areas have higher rates of giving and stronger civic and nonprofit infrastructure than others. Wealthier areas have larger numbers of nonprofits that provide amenities such as recreation, private schools, and art activities (Wolpert 1993). Cultural, political, economic, and

Figure I.3. Number of Nonprofit Organizations per 10,000 Residents, 2004

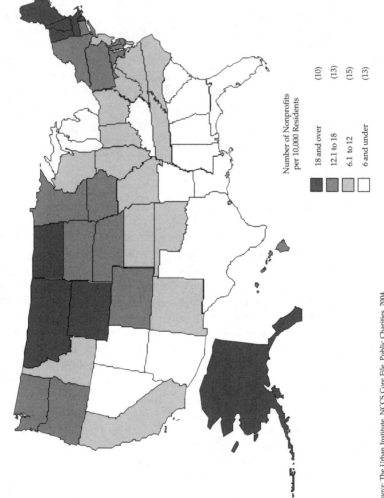

Number of Nonprofits
per 10,000 Residents

■	18 and over	(10)
■	12.1 to 18	(13)
▨	6.1 to 12	(15)
□	6 and under	(13)

Source: The Urban Institute, NCCS Core File, Public Charities, 2004.
Note: Only operating public charities are included (see table I.1 for the definition).

Table I.4. Total Number and Expenses of Nonprofit Organizations by Region, 2004

Region	Organizations	Percent	Expenses ($ millions)	Percent
Northeast	59,825	22.8	272,807	28.8
Midwest	60,052	22.8	223,361	23.6
South	81,881	31.1	264,181	27.9
West	60,734	23.1	185,435	19.6
U.S. Territories	405	0.2	1,587	0.2
Total	262,897	100.0	947,371	100.0

Source: The Urban Institute, NCCS Core File, Public Charities, 2004.
Note: Only operating public charities are included (see table I.1 for definition). Regions follow the Bureau of the Census definition.

historical factors all affect the types of organizations and their financial strength in each region (for California, see Gammal et al. 2005; for Indiana, Gronbjerg and Allen 2004; New York City, Wolpert and Selcy 2004; Pittsburgh, DeVita et al. 2004; Washington, D.C., Twombly and Auer 2004).

State policies and federal devolutionary policies that fund programs and people based on financial status, as well as the local capacities of nonprofits, sometimes magnify regional differences. Because the fiscal capacities of states and cities vary widely, projecting how future shifts in governmental priorities and spending on charitable organizations will affect nonprofits is difficult. Some policies increase resources available to nonprofits, while other policies increase the number of people who need services. Certain programs, like faith-based initiatives, may benefit some types of organizations and not others. Government financing decisions seldom, if ever, affect all nonprofits equally.

An infrastructure of associations at the local, state, and national levels provides a voice for nonprofits in the policy process, seeking to affect funding decisions on the one hand and trying to enhance nonprofit capacity, conduct research, educate nonprofit managers, and encourage collaboration on the other (Abramson and McCarthy 2002). This infrastructure, dating generally from the early 1980s, has had significant, if rarely documented, impacts on the nonprofit sector.

The portrait of the nonprofit sector that emerges is one of disparate groups, thinly and unevenly spread across the states, with a great range of missions and activities. Although their increasing economic strength raises their visibility as a whole, most are community-based, modestly funded, and not well known outside of their neighborhoods. Despite the increase in numbers of nonprofits in recent decades, they are still only a small proportion (less than 8 percent) of all business, government, and nonprofit entities in the country.

NONPROFIT ACTIVITIES

A great diversity of activities matches the wide variety of nonprofit organizations. Nonprofits produce and display art, culture, and music; generate knowledge through research and education; protect consumers, the environment, and animals; promote health; prevent and treat diseases; provide basic social services, such as housing, food, and clothing; promote international understanding; provide international aid and relief; create community social and economic infrastructure; advocate for and against public policies; provide services and funding to other nonprofit groups; transmit religious values and traditions; provide solidarity, recreation, and services to members and others; and educate and register voters, as well as many other activities.

This laundry list gives some sense of the difficulty of defining and describing the nonprofit sector. It also makes clear that voluntary organizations do many things that governments and businesses also do. There are no sharp boundaries among the sectors; in fact, there is increasing concern about the blurring of boundaries, particularly with regard to commercial activities. However, some activities (such as religious worship, membership activities, and the monitoring of government) are almost exclusively accomplished in the nonprofit sector, and other activities (such as museums, botanical gardens, and zoos) are more likely to be undertaken by nonprofits than by government or business. Some activities are more evenly divided between government and nonprofits (such as providing social services), while others (such as primary education) are largely a government activity. Business and government also sometimes collaborate or cooperate with nonprofits in providing, for example, low-income housing and disaster relief.

Nonprofits have a long history of pioneering programs that other sectors subsequently take over. Nonprofits popularized primary education, kindergartens, and disease control, which government then took over when demand outpaced nonprofit providers' ability to supply services. Businesses picked up recreation programs that nonprofits pioneered and developed the programs into profit-making enterprises. Nonprofits are often lauded for being flexible and innovative, a source of ideas for improving society; those ideas transcend sectors.

Collaboration with government, however, is frequently difficult for both partners. Experiences with disaster relief in large-scale tragedies, such as the attacks of September 11, the Asian Tsunami of 2004, and the hurricanes of 2005, reveal the strengths and weaknesses of nonprofits and of their collaboration with government. Nonprofits are quick to respond and galvanize volunteers and donations, but their capacity varies in different regions of the country and the world. They are flexible problem solvers, but weak on long-term logistics and coordination with other nonprofits and government, although coordinating mechanisms were improved after the attacks of September 11 (Foundation Center 2004; Goldman 2006). But importantly, given their relative size (see chapter 2), they cannot compensate for weak government leadership or inadequate government responses in large-scale disasters.

Some nonprofits have the characteristics of business corporations or of government programs, and a small proportion of organizations do change from one type of organization to another.[19] Governments set up nonprofit corporations, such as the Corporation for Public Broadcasting, to carry out public programs. Nonprofits may create profit-making subsidiaries (which pay taxes on earned income) to subsidize their charitable activities, a trend that appears to be accelerating (Steuerle 2001). They also engage in social enterprises that directly use market activities as part of their missions; for example, nonprofits may train youth in business practices by employing them to manage a nonprofit-owned ice cream shop (Dees 1998; Kerlin 2006; Skloot 1988).

The interaction of nonprofits with the business sector affects their relationship with government. A few nonprofits give up their tax-exempt status when they can accomplish their missions more effectively as business corporations or when economic incentives, government policies, or the need for capital make it profitable for them to become businesses. The conversion of nonprofit hospitals to for-profit businesses is one example. Conversions raise questions about whether it is in the public interest for businesses to take over hospitals and other services, but as long as the assets are reserved for charitable purposes and some form of community service is maintained, the current barriers to conversion seem minimal. Scholars' efforts to discern whether program outcomes are different depending on whether organizations operate as nonprofits or for-profits suggest that the nonprofit form adds value, but the results are not definitive (Gelles 1993; Gray and Schlesinger 2002, Schlesinger and Gray 2005). Some members of Congress, however, are particularly interested in the rationale for permitting nonprofit hospitals to compete with for-profit hospitals when donations are a minor portion of their revenues and charity care is a small part of their services.[20] John Goddeeris and Burton Weisbrod discuss the policy implications of the conversion of organizational form in chapter 8, "Ownership Forms, Conversions, and Public Policy." They note that higher education is likely to be the next area of for-profit conversions.

The sometimes overlapping and complementary nature of the three sectors may seem inefficient at times, but it provides flexibility and adaptability. Public-serving activities are not restricted to government but can be undertaken through multiple avenues. Diverse populations with different tastes and requirements can create entities to meet their perceived needs. Government can contract with nonprofits to provide

d health services without expanding the government work-
.v.cc. social entrepreneurs can implement their visions through nonprofit organizations, and the alternatives they develop sometimes find
their way into the public or business sectors.

ROLES OF NONPROFIT ORGANIZATIONS

Why do nonprofits exist? Scholars answer that question in different
ways depending on their disciplines and orientations. Economic theories include the notions of "market failure," "government failure," and
"nonprofit failure," to explain the public services nonprofits deliver
and the partnership of the government with the nonprofit sector in
financing public services.

Market failure is based on the concept that there are desired services
or collective "goods" that do not have sufficient potential for profit
to attract business providers. Market failure is also precipitated by
insufficient information on the quality of services, which may lead
consumers to turn to nonprofit providers, which are perceived as trustworthy because they do not have a profit motive. Similarly, government
failure implies that government will not provide certain public services
for reasons that may include the cost or the limited constituency that
desires the service (Hansman 1987; Weisbrod 1988). Nonprofit failure
explains the nonprofit–government partnership as a consequence of
the public demanding services best met by nonprofit provision but
requiring government financing. In this theory, nonprofits are the preferred providers of services, and government action becomes necessary
because nonprofits are unable to meet perceived needs (Salamon 1995).
Dennis Young reviews economic theories of the relationship of nonprofits and government in chapter 1. Lester Salamon uses slightly
different terms for a similar analysis applied to the international context
in chapter 12.

In contrast to economists, political scientists tend to stress the role
of the nonprofit sector in terms of providing avenues of civic participation and representation of interests in the pluralistic political system
of a heterogeneous society. Nonprofit groups aggregate diverse values
and interests and represent them to the political system through political advocacy and lobbying of the government (Berry 1984; Berry and
Arons 2003; Boris and Krehely 2002; Douglas 1987; Verba et al. 1995;
Warren 2002). Roger Lohmann builds on the idea of the commons as
the civic arena in his book on the nonprofit sector (Lohmann 1992).

The government–nonprofit relationship in the political sphere is
delineated in part by the constitutionally guaranteed rights of free
speech and association and in part by the limits on using dollars subsi-

dized by the charitable tax deduction for advocacy, lobbying ar
lar types of political activities (Fremont-Smith 2004; Reid 2003). (
occurs when government and nonprofits disagree on the boundaries
of permissible efforts to influence government policies and engage in
political activities.[21] (See chapter 10 for a discussion of regulations
affecting nonprofit advocacy and the implications of campaign finance
reform for the political use of charities and other types of nonprofits.)

Interdisciplinary approaches to studying nonprofits provide valuable
alternative perspectives. Communitarians view voluntary associations
in organic terms, as the precursors of government and the market and
thus as among the most basic social relationships that connect people
and create communities. Those relationships became more complex
over time and evolved into the state and the market (Etzioni 1993).
Robert Putnam and others use the concepts of social capital and civil
society in a basically communitarian framework (Putnam 1993;
Walzer 1995).

Scholars also look to the civic history of the United States—the
suffrage, antislavery, and child welfare movements, for example—and
to the religious roots of charity, altruism, and social justice to explain
the giving and volunteering that characterize involvement in nonprofit
organizations and rights-oriented social movements (Friedman and
McGarvie 2003; McCarthy 2003; O'Connell 1997; Payton 1988; Skocpol
1995; Wuthnow 1991).

Each approach reveals a different aspect of the roles of nonprofits,
and thus their relationship with government. A civil-society approach
examines the role of nonprofits in generating the social capital that
links people to their communities and to others. A political analysis
highlights efforts to influence the political process and create social
change. An economic perspective looks at the creation of income, jobs,
and knowledge, as well as service provision and economic development, often in collaboration with government. A values perspective
helps explain the roles of nonprofits in alleviating poverty and promoting and maintaining religious, ideological, cultural, and artistic values
and beliefs, activities that sometimes lead to conflict with government.
The chapters in this book reflect the richness of these approaches.

Social Capital

Nonprofit organizations, regardless of origin, create networks and relationships that connect people to each other and to institutions quite
apart from the organization's primary purposes. Research by Robert
Putnam and others suggests that relationships such as those fostered
by choral societies, bowling leagues, and other community associations

build the trust and cooperation essential for the effective functioning of society, politics, and the economy (Putnam 1993).

Despite growing professionalism in the nonprofit arena, most nonprofits still facilitate relationships and connect people to each other and to the constituencies they serve. Members and volunteers are critical to the success of many nonprofits. Volunteers serve in governance capacities on boards of directors, in staff management and service positions, as fundraisers, and in many other ways. Volunteers bring expertise from business, government, and the community to bear on local, national, and international problems. Volunteers enhance civic engagement and spread expertise; people of various backgrounds learn about the needs of their communities and others, and act together to solve them. Volunteering also harnesses the enthusiasm of the young and old and adds meaning to their lives. People involved in youth groups, churches, and other voluntary activities when young are more likely to give, volunteer, and be engaged in civic life as adults (Hodgkinson and Weitzman 1996). Recent research finds those who participate in the arts are more likely to give, volunteer, and be active in civic affairs (Ostrower 2005; Walker and Scott-Melnyk 2002). Those who are involved in their communities are also more likely to be healthy and happy (Seligman 1991). Other research shows that political and civic engagement is related to feelings of efficacy (Pew Research Center for People and the Press 1997).

Civic Activities

Many nonprofit efforts inform and influence domestic social and economic policies as well as international affairs. Much public policy activity involves nonpartisan research, writing, evaluation, and demonstration projects. Some groups try to influence executive agencies, others, the legislative branch. Think tanks and universities conduct research and evaluations and make that information available to policymakers through publications, news media, forums, and individual conversations (Boris 1999; Boris and Krehely 2002). The role of the nonprofit policy expert is changing, however, as some think tanks strive to gain visibility for their ideas and take on the role of advocates with ideological agendas, which calls into question their expertise and credibility (Rich 2004).

Grantmaking foundations and other nonprofits try to influence public policy by demonstrating the efficacy of alternative approaches to economic development, population issues, or hunger (Hess 2003). They may conduct experimental programs, evaluate the results, and communicate them to public authorities. Foundations may also promote policy agendas indirectly. For example, foundations financed the conservative think tanks that provided much of the intellectual capital for the Reagan and Bush administrations (Covington 1997; Rich 2004).

Nonprofit advocacy groups try to educate the public and encourage individuals to contact their representatives directly or to sign petitions for or against certain positions; they promote voter registration and inform voters. Jeffrey Berry maintains that public interest citizen groups have been very effective at setting and influencing the congressional agenda (Berry 1999). Some nonprofits also try to influence public policy through demonstrations, sit-ins, parades, and boycotts.

Political Activities

Certain types of nonprofits are involved more directly in politics, and some develop multiple organizational structures to permit them to be involved in a variety of ways. They might have a 501(c)(3) charity to provide services and collect tax-deductible contributions, a 501(c)(4) social welfare organization to lobby freely for policies that serve their constituencies, a 527 organization to engage in electoral politics through independent issue advocacy, and a political action committee (PAC) so they can be involved in partisan political campaigns. These structures are a direct result of government regulation of political activities (Reid and Kerlin 2003). Elizabeth Reid, in chapter 10, discusses nonprofits as politically active organizations, highlighting the representative and participatory functions of nonprofit advocacy and the regulations that guide and constrain such activities.

Some of the most profound social changes of this century have been promoted through a combination of research, public education, advocacy, legislation, and litigation fostered by nonprofit organizations. Those nonprofits usually work in coalitions, sometimes in collaboration with government and business interests and sometimes in conflict with them and with other nonprofits. For example, civil rights groups, working with religious and other organizations, attacked racial segregation in this country through direct action, lobbying, advocacy, litigation, and public education. Environmental groups used research, public education, advocacy, and litigation in their pioneering efforts to reduce air and water pollution and protect the environment and wildlife. Mothers Against Drunk Driving used a variety of tools, including public education, to create a major change in the public perception about the consequences of drinking and driving. Anti-smoking groups fostered research and used the results to educate the public about the negative impacts of tobacco smoking on health.

Not all advocacy is designed to introduce change. Groups all along the political spectrum may aim to conserve or protect the values that they espouse, or try to prevent the erosion of values they cherish or advantages they enjoy. The National Rifle Association, for example, promotes gun ownership and lobbies against legislation that would limit an individual's right to own guns. The American Civil Liberties Union defends individuals' rights and litigates against legislation that it believes threatens freedom of speech and other liberties guaranteed in the Constitution and the Bill of Rights.

Advocacy can be contentious work, as nonprofits may face direct and indirect opposition from other groups, business interests, and government agencies. Success for some causes may mean failure for others, and some outcomes may not be widely perceived as positive for society. For example, pro-choice organizations use public education, advocacy, and litigation to protect a woman's right to control her reproductive choices, while anti-choice groups use the same tools to limit access to abortions because of those groups' religious and ethical values. Neither side accepts success for the other as a positive outcome for society. In California, anti-tax groups successfully collected signatures and put on the ballot measures to cut public spending, while other nonprofits attempted to counter these efforts and save certain public programs. Similarly, groups successfully organized to overturn affirmative action in that state despite other groups' opposition. In these types of cases, each side perceives the other as undermining their core values and beliefs, often leading to rancorous public discourse.

Highly charged and partisan public communications, declining participation in voting and membership in civic groups, along with low levels of trust in government and other institutions, are arguably indicators that the civic base of the U.S. pluralist democracy is eroding, although this view is not universally held. Of perhaps greater concern is whether there is a participation gap in the United States, particularly among poor people, typically women and minorities, who are not as involved in politically active organizations as others and often do not have the resources, opportunities, and skills to make their needs known in the political system (Berry 1999; Burns, Schlozman, Verba 2001; Skocpol 2003; Verba et al. 1995).

A countervailing trend is the extensive use of the Internet for communication, information sharing, fundraising, and mobilizing people for causes and political activity. Electronic advocacy can mobilize communities of interest to contact legislators quickly and inexpensively. The impact of the Internet in linking nonprofits via e-mail, blogs, discussion groups, and web sites has permitted them to partner more effectively and to reach more people, both nationally and internationally. The Internet has also increased the ability of nonprofit constituents and members to interact and affect the policies and practices of their organizations. Recent elections revealed the power of such groups as Moveon.org, Civic Action, and Focus on the Family in mobilizing liberal and conservative voters, respectively.

Religious, Cultural, and Artistic Activities

In chapter 9, Robert Wuthow illustrates that the most deeply felt controversies over values are played out in the nonprofit sector—around religious beliefs, artistic expression, personal responsibility, individual rights, and the separation of church and state. Nonprofits express conflicts over competing values long before they reach the political system. These conflicts may be positive when they promote the dialogue and deliberation that are healthy for democracy. In extremely divisive cases, like racial segregation and access to abortions, conflicts can involve legislative and judicial battles at the national, state, and local levels over long periods of time.

The impact of religion on American society is deep and enduring. Religious organizations serve the spiritual needs of their members and promote and preserve the group's religious doctrines and values. Social and health services, crisis care, and advocacy activities may supplement sacramental and membership-serving activities, such as child care and counseling (Chaves 2002; Cnaan 1997; Hodgkinson and Weitzman 1993; Printz 1997; Wuthnow 2004). Religious congregations also impart civic skills to members who learn to organize and collaborate for common ends. Black churches, for example, are well known for their efforts to mobilize members to vote and for their political work, particularly around ending segregation and promoting civil rights (Harris 1994). Some religious denominations are vocal in opposition to birth control, abortion, gay marriage, stem cell research, and teaching evolution. Religious congregations are also among the most forceful advocates for peace, social justice, environmental protection, and policies that protect immigrants and the poor. The IRS, however, does scrutinize political speech in religious organizations to determine if they are engaging in prohibited partisan campaign activities by endorsing candidates who share their values.[22]

The separation of church and state in the United States involves an ongoing debate with a long evolution. Historically, however, the religious charities' receipt of government revenues for services provided to the general public is well established (Hall 1982). Government-funded social service provision by nonprofits affiliated with Catholic, Lutheran, and Jewish faiths, for example, has been widespread. Such groups accepted limitations on proselytizing when providing government-funded services and did not provide preferential services to their members.

More recently, under federal Charitable Choice and faith-based initiatives, congregations and affiliated religious service providers are permitted to compete for government contracts to deliver social services that have religious content and display religious icons. The resulting partnership between government and congregations is a contentious issue that has raised the separation of church and state in policy debates (Wuthnow 2004). (See chapters 7 and 9 for discussions of the policy issues.)

Most religious entities fall outside of the government regulatory framework for nonprofit organizations. Houses of worship and closely aligned entities enjoy the benefits of tax exemption and deductible contributions but are not required to register or report to the IRS. Many do report, however, and the number is increasing, partially in an effort to create a formal structure to qualify for faith-based funding initiatives. Government funding requires accountability, and some fear that monitoring contracts and performance will involve the government too deeply in the affairs of religious bodies. Congregations that desire government funding often set up separate charities to segregate finances, avoid potential conflicts, and protect their sacramental activities from government involvement.

Arts and culture are embedded in community life and are reflected in worship, education, celebrations, and much more. Through arts and culture, we transmit group memory, celebrate ethnic and national identity, and interpret the past. The arts enhance our quality of life and generate economic benefits and much more for communities (Jackson 1998). Government support of the arts raises questions about the types of art that deserve public support and standards of morality and decency that may offend some people but not others. (See chapter 9 for a discussion of the controversy surrounding funding for the National Endowment for the Arts.)

Service Provision

Nonprofits of all types provide services they may offer to the community, special populations, members, governments, businesses, or other nonprofits. As service providers, nonprofits overlap with business and governments, for example, in education and medical care. They may be contractors for governments and businesses (providing preschool programs or drug abuse treatment), be collaborators with governments (maintaining national and regional parks or preventing diseases), or act in lieu of government (providing accreditation or protecting consumers). As government has contracted out more services, the nonprofit's share of the workforce has increased by roughly the amount that government employment has decreased (see chapter 2).

With more government money at stake, it is not surprising that nonprofits find themselves competing with for-profit providers (U.S. Congress 1996).[23] The effects, including the adoption of business practices, are felt not just internally but by donors and clients. Nonprofits often find that competition means that they must market, actively attract clients, and report on their outcomes and impacts (see chapter 6).[24] These changes can be positive but may affect the way donors view nonprofits and clients experience them. A pervasive bottom-line orientation may inadvertently affect even nonprofits that do not have government contracts or commercial revenues; it may increase efficiency but could also undermine charitable service missions.

Government may turn to nonprofits to undertake activities that require reaching local populations with culturally sensitive materials or to avoid building up staff for short-term projects. Nonprofits provide a way for governments to devolve programs either directly or through state and local authorities and provide services without incurring government salary scales and bureaucratic red tape. In chapter 7, Carol De Vita and Eric Twombly summarize current research on devolved federal programs and the impact these policies have on nonprofit organizations. The authors also document the lack of resources of the smaller, nonprofit human service providers.

Nonprofits also interact with and provide a variety of services directly and indirectly to the business sector. They collaborate with businesses in promoting quality of life in areas where firms operate. Donations to and contracts with cultural organizations, child care, and recreation groups underwrite amenity services that attract and hold corporate employees, thereby helping to maintain the community's tax base. Support through gifts and contracts also enable universities to undertake research, develop technology, and train current and future employees (and public servants). Environmental groups help level the playing field for socially responsible behavior by demanding, for example, that all competitors within an industry clean up pollutants. Collaboration between voluntary groups and businesses develops when industries benefit from the educational and advocacy campaigns of nonprofits, as in disease prevention and anti-smoking campaigns that assist insurance companies.[25]

Nonprofit business associations provide information, research, and advocacy services for member corporations. These associations monitor the health of industries and the impact of legislation and regulation on corporate activities. They may provide low-cost insurance or cooperative buying opportunities. Similar nonprofit associations provide such services for groups of nonprofits, health related nonprofits, philanthropic foundations, colleges and universities, symphonies, museums, and others.

State and local governments directly and indirectly fund nonprofits to provide services and also oversee the activities of nonprofits and their fundraising to ensure that the public is given accurate information and not misled by false claims and illegal operators. Woods Bowman and Marion Fremont-Smith describe state financing and regulatory systems in chapter 5. They also show the prevalence of Medicare and Medicaid funds in government contracting with nonprofits.

Economic Impacts

As mentioned earlier, nonprofits make significant contributions to the U.S. economy as employers and service providers. Their assets represent at least 5 percent of net worth (excluding churches), as Steuerle and Hodgkinson report in chapter 2. Millions of people serve as volunteers, further expanding nonprofit resources. This economic role, however, is disproportionately concentrated in the largest organizations and in certain sectors, especially in hospitals, private universities, and multipurpose organizations like the American Red Cross, Catholic Charities, and others. More than one-third of nonprofit employees work in hospitals.

Nonprofits provide the entry point into the labor force for many women and minorities. About two out of three workers in the nonprofit sector are women. Employment is often at lower-than-market wages and without health and retirement benefits. Major nonprofit hospitals and universities anchor whole inner-city neighborhoods or small towns with employment opportunities, services, and amenities like arts, culture, and recreation opportunities. They contribute to public coffers by paying payroll taxes, while employees pay both income and payroll taxes.

Because nonprofits generally do not pay property taxes or sales taxes, they may be perceived as a drain on the local economy (Borowski and Gaul 1993; Brody 2002b). Some large nonprofits, including foundations, make payments in lieu of taxes (PILOTs) to city governments to help cover costs of services. Major cities, including Baltimore, Boston, Detroit, Indianapolis, Minneapolis, Philadelphia, and Pittsburgh, have developed programs to solicit PILOTs from nonprofits (Leland 2002).[26]

Regional studies of nonprofits reveal their significant economic contributions to local economies and are being used to grab the attention of policymakers as nonprofits attempt to negotiate for policy influence and revenues. A study of nonprofits in the Washington, D.C., metro region revealed a sector second only to the federal government in its employment. The 7,614 organizations raised over $33 billion and spent $29 billion in 2000 (Twombly and Auer 2005). They employed over 11 percent of the region's private workers, generating approximately $9.6 billion in wages, or over 10 percent of the region's total in 2003 (Salamon and Geller 2005). In New York City, active nonprofits accounted for more than $50 billion in expenditures in 2000 (Wolpert and Seley 2004). In Baltimore, nonprofits generated full-time equivalent jobs for 18 percent of the workforce and $5.4 billion in economic activity. The Baltimore City government received an estimated $41 million in "piggy-back" state income tax, real estate tax, and sales tax revenues traceable to spending by nonprofits, their vendors, and employees (Maryland Association of Nonprofit Organizations 1997).

International Trends

Nonprofits that operate across national borders, as well as nonprofits that work within other countries, are growing both in numbers and influence. International nongovernmental organizations (INGOs) are active in human rights, economic development, disaster relief, disease prevention and treatment, environmental protection, conflict resolution, and many other fields. They often act in concert with national governments, and multinational and international institutions, although conflicts are also common. Contracts with governments are becoming more prevalent and disaster relief and recovery have become high profile issues. The Internet has transformed the ability of INGOs to collaborate, advocate, and raise money. They are linked in global networks that have huge potential to monitor and affect public policies.

U.S.-based international nonprofits receive the bulk of their resources from contributions, but government support is a growing proportion of their revenues. About a fifth of their financing is from U.S. government grants, chiefly through the United States Agency for International Development. As U.S. foreign policy goals change, funding levels change. These organizations do not always fully agree with U.S. government policy, however, so they strive to preserve their ability to undertake independent action. They are potent advocates on a variety of issues, from development and family planning to environmental protection. (See chapter 11 for a discussion of government relationships and financing of U.S. INGOs.)

Many countries have long-standing, expansive nonprofit sectors that play economic, social, and political roles like those in the United States. In some cases, governments provide more significant support and permit more engagement in the policy process. The extent of government use of nonprofits to provide social and health services sometimes obscures the nature of some welfare states. Lester Salamon's research illuminates the extensive scope and economic impact of nonprofits and the variation in nonprofit–government relationships in countries around the world. (See chapter 12 for a discussion of the comparative trends in government–nonprofit relationships in developed and emerging economies.)

NEGATIVE IMPACTS

Nonprofits, of course, have the potential for negative as well as positive impacts on society and are subject to the failings of the people who lead them. Regulations are often designed to protect the public from malfeasance but are often hard to monitor. Many types of negative behaviors are not easily regulated in the first place. Some effects are obvious: nonprofits can be a divisive and fragmenting influence in the political system. They may undermine political parties (or support them). Well-funded groups can manipulate public opinion, promote ideological positions, or have a disproportionate impact on public policy, all without revealing their funders. Politicians may use nonprofits to attract donations or bestow favors on cronies. Low-income populations may be at a disadvantage in the policy process because they may not have access to groups that can represent their interests. Although the evidence is mixed, nonprofits may have an edge over businesses in the same markets because of their tax-exempt status.

Other potentially negative consequences are not as obvious. The use of nonprofits by governments to deliver services may separate governments from accepting responsibility for services funded, thus undermining popular support for public financing of programs or promoting cynicism toward nonprofits if programs fail. Nonprofits can provide a "cop out" for political leaders who wish to curtail government responsibilities. Wealthy communities can also use nonprofits to provide for their own needs, while neglecting to provide tax revenues for public education and other public health and human services for low-income residents.

CONCLUSION

We must understand the variety of roles the nonprofit sector plays before we can thoroughly explore its relationship with government. Because the spheres of activity that nonprofits and government undertake intersect in so many ways, the nature, scope, and impacts of nonprofits are sensitive to changes in public policy.

Nonprofit and government interactions are multifaceted in a civil society. Simplistic assumptions about what nonprofit organizations can do and how they affect society may lead to public policies that are ineffective or have unintended negative consequences both for the organizations and for society. The remaining chapters in this volume describe many dimensions of these interactions.

We hope that this book will increase understanding and provoke ideas about how to improve the dynamic relationship between nonprofits and government.

ACKNOWLEDGMENTS

The author is indebted to Jennifer Auer, Amisha Chaudhary, Kendall Golladay, and Tom Pollak for their assistance with the data, and to Gene Steuerle, Dan Oran, Joe Cordes, and Linda Lampkin for their suggestions and comments.

NOTE ON DATA SOURCES

Data Sources

Data used in this chapter are compiled by the National Center for Charitable Statistics (NCCS) at the Urban Institute. These data are derived from the Forms 990 that nonprofits are required to file with the IRS. NCCS creates research data sets and summary tables from IRS data and provides them to researchers and the public at http://nccs.urban.org. The most comprehensive data set, National Center for Charitable Statistics/GuideStar National Nonprofit Data Base, was developed in collaboration with GuideStar and is available to researchers on request. Forms 990 and 990 PF can be viewed at http://www.guidestar.org and http://www.foundationcenter.org. Data on private and community foundations are also available on the Foundation Center's web site.

Religious Congregations

Estimates of the number of religious congregations are from *The New Nonprofit Almanac and Desk Reference* (Weitzman et al. 2002), which reports approximately 344,000 congregations in 1989 (number imputed from 1987 and 1992), 343,000 in 1993 (number imputed from 1992 and 1997), and 354,000 in 1998. The 2004 estimate of 330,000 congregations is from Hadaway and Marler (2005). These figures were adjusted to exclude congregations that have registered with the IRS and so are already accounted for in table I.1. An estimated 113,000 congregations registered with the IRS in 2004, based on an analysis of organizational purpose in the 2004 IRS Business Master File.

NOTES

1. We use the term nonprofit sector to mean all nonprofit organizations.
2. Forms 990 are public documents that provide financial data—assets, revenues, expenses, etc. They are available for inspection on the web sites of GuideStar and the Foundation Center. Research databases with financial information based on Forms 990 are available at NCCS.

3. For a through discussion of nonprofit accountability see Brody (2002a).

4. See for example, the white paper from U.S. Congress, Senate Finance Committee (2004), "Senate Finance Committee Staff Discussion Draft, Tax Exempt Governance Proposals," June 22. The proposals in this document led to a sectorwide effort to address the proposals and develop recommendations that nonprofits could accept. The Nonprofit Panel, convened by the Independent Sector, formed working groups to draft and discuss recommendations for strengthening nonprofit transparency and governance. The results were published in Panel on the Nonprofit Sector (2005).

5. The number of congregations in the United States is estimated at about 330,000 (Hadaway and Marler 2005). About 113,000 register with the IRS, although they are not required to do so. See the section "Note on Data Sources."

6. Most congregations are not included here because they are not required to report to the IRS, although many do. See note 5 and table I.1.

7. Charities with between $5,000 and $25,000 in gross receipts must register with the IRS, but they are not required to report their finances on Forms 990. In table I.1, they are under the heading "nonreporting."

8. While 501(c)(4) organizations are commonly referred to as advocacy organizations because they are permitted greater freedom to lobby and conduct issue advocacy, and if they are membership organizations, they may issue partisan communications to their members (see chapter 10). Organizations in this category include a mix of organizations that serve public purposes but are deemed not to be eligible for tax-deductible contributions.

9. *The New Nonprofit Almanac and Desk Reference* (Weitzman et al. 2002) defines the independent sector components to include all 501(c)(3) charities, including congregations, and 501(c)(4) social welfare groups.

10. The National Taxonomy of Exempt Entities (NTEE) was developed by the National Center for Charitable Statistics (NCCS) and is currently used by the IRS and many researchers to classify nonprofit organizations. See http://nccs.urban.org for a description of the categories.

11. NTEE originally had over 600 categories that were consolidated into approximately 400 when the IRS began to use NTEE to classify organizations.

12. Each of these tax benefits has a cost to government of revenues foregone, in effect a subsidy that in tight financial times may become a source of controversy, for example, the Senate Finance Committee actions to limit the deductibility of car donations to the actual revenue realized by charities will cut government costs. Measuring the cost to the government and the benefit to nonprofits is possible; more difficult to measure is the benefit to society.

13. Salamon shows a similar picture for Germany in table 12.1.

14. De Vita and Twombly discuss the financial vulnerability of many human service organizations in chapter 7.

15. Here we focus on grantmaking foundations as defined by the Foundation Center, rather than all foundations reported in table 1.1, which include operating foundations and organizations that have lost public charity status for failure to meet the public support test (Lawrence et al. 2005).

16. Analysis by Kerlin (forthcoming).

17. Grantmakers for Effective Organizations has a membership of 500 that seeks to increase nonprofit effectiveness. See also the Human Interaction Research Institute database of capacity-building programs supported by foundations (http://www.humaninteract.org).

18. See Wing et al. (2004) for a discussion of nonprofit overhead and fundraising costs; also see Fremont-Smith and Cordes (2004).

19. See table 8.1 for a summary of conversions of post-secondary schools to and from nonprofit status.

20. Defining the public service or charitable activities that nonprofit hospitals must undertake to legitimize their charitable status has proven to be difficult and controversial. A hearing before the House Ways and Means Committee in 2005 explored the issues surrounding charitable status for hospitals (among others). A report by the Joint Committee on Taxation set out the issues (U.S. Congress, Joint Committee on Taxation 2005).

21. Chapter 4 argues that nonprofit tax exemption may be a government attempt to respect the sovereignty of the nonprofit sector: government takes a hands-off approach to taxing, and nonprofits are required to be hands off in terms of advocating for government subvention.

22. To counter this limitation, Representative Walter Jones introduced a bill in the U.S. House called the Houses of Worship Free Speech Restoration Act of 2005.

23. Todd J. Gillman, "Health Clubs Hit YMCAs' Tax Breaks," *Washington Post*, June 30, 1987.

24. The Government Performance and Results Act requires contractors to report on outcomes (see chapter 7).

25. Gene Steuerle and Joe Cordes are editing a volume on nonprofits and business that will examine the policy and practical issues in nonprofit–business relationships.

26. After a series of stories in the *Philadelphia Inquirer* criticized nonprofits for not contributing to the city's coffers, the city of Philadelphia required payments in lieu of taxes from the larger nonprofits within its jurisdiction (Borowski and Gaul 1993).

REFERENCES

Abramson, Alan J., and Rachel McCarthy. 2002 "Infrastructure Organizations." In *The State of Nonprofit America*, edited by Lester M. Salamon (299–330). Washington, DC: Brookings Institute Press.

Berry, Jeffrey M. 1984. *The Interest Group Society*. Boston: Little, Brown, and Company.

———. 1999. *The New Liberalism: The Rising Power of Citizen Groups*. Washington, DC: Brookings Institution Press.

Berry, Jeffrey M., with David F. Arons. 2003. *A Voice for Nonprofits*. Washington, DC: Brookings Institute Press.

Boris, Elizabeth T. 1999. "The Nonprofit Sector in the 1990s." In *The Future of Philanthropy in a Changing America*, edited by Charles Clotfelter and Thomas Erlich (1–33). New York: The American Assembly, Columbia University.

Boris, Elizabeth T., and Jeff Krehely. 2002. "Civic Participation and Advocacy." In *The State of Nonprofit America*, edited by Lester M. Salamon (299–330). Washington, DC: Brookings Institute Press.

Borowski, Neill A., and Gilbert M. Gaul. 1993. *Free Ride: The Tax-Exempt Economy*. Kansas City: Andrews and McMeel.

Brody, Evelyn. 2002a. "Accountability and Public Trust." In *The State of Nonprofit America*, edited by Lester M. Salamon (471–98). Washington, DC: Brookings Institution Press.

————, ed. 2002b. *Property Tax Exemption for Charities*. Washington, DC. Urban Institute Press.

Burns, Nancy, Kay L. Schlozman, and Sidney Verba. 2001. *The Private Roots of Public Action*. Cambridge: Harvard University Press.

Chaves, Mark. 2002. "Religious Congregations." In *The State of Nonprofit America*, edited by Lester M. Salamon (275–98). Washington, DC: Brookings Institution Press.

Cnaan, Ram. 1997. "Social and Community Involvement of Local Religious Congregations: Findings from a Six-City Study." Paper presented at annual meeting of ARNOVA, Indianapolis, Indiana, December 4–6.

Covington, Sally. 1997. "Moving a Public Policy Agenda: The Strategic Philanthropy of Conservative Foundations." Washington, DC: National Committee for Responsive Philanthropy.

Dees, J. Gregory. 1998. "Enterprising Nonprofits." *Harvard Business Review* (January): 55–67.

De Vita, Carol, Eric C. Twombly, Jennifer Auer, and Yuan You. 2004. "Charting the Resources of the Pittsburgh Region's Nonprofit Sector." Washington, DC: The Urban Institute.

Douglas, James. 1987. "Political Theories of Nonprofit Organization." In *The Nonprofit Sector: A Research Handbook*, edited by Walter W. Powell (43–54). New Haven: Yale University Press.

Etzioni, Amitai. 1993. *The Spirit of Community: Rights, Responsibilities, and the Communitarian Agenda*. New York: Crown Publishers, Inc.

Foundation Center. 2004. *September 11: The Philanthropic Response*. New York: Foundation Center.

Fremont-Smith, Marion. 2004. *Governing Nonprofit Organizations: Federal and State Law and Regulation*. Cambridge: President and Fellows of Harvard College.

Fremont-Smith, Marion, and Joseph Cordes. 2004. "What the Ratings Revolution Means for Charities." *Emerging Issues in Philanthropy* Seminar Series. Washington, DC: The Urban Institute.

Friedman, Lawrence J., and Mark D. McGarvie, eds. 2003. *Charity, Philanthropy, and Civility in American History*. Cambridge: Cambridge University Press.

Gammal, Denise L., Caroline Simard, Hokyu Hwang, and Walter W. Powell. 2005. "Managing Through Challenges: A Profile of San Francisco Bay Area Nonprofits." Stanford: Stanford Graduate School of Business.

Gelles, Erna. 1993. "Administrative Attitudes and Practices of For-Profit and Nonprofit Day Care Providers: A Social Judgment Analysis." Paper presented at annual meeting of ARNOVA, Toronto, October 28–30.

Goldman, Karen Kunstler. 2006. "Nonprofits and Disasters: Experience of New York State on 9/11/2001." *Emerging Issues in Philanthropy Seminar Series: After Katrina*. Washington, DC: The Urban Institute.

Gray, Bradford H., and Mark Schlesinger. 2002. "Health." In *The State of Nonprofit America*, edited by Lester M. Salamon (65–106). Washington, DC: Brookings Institute Press.

Gronbjerg, Kirsten A., and Linda Allen. 2004. "The Indiana Nonprofit Sector: A Profile." Bloomington: School of Public and Environmental Affairs.

Gronbjerg, Kirsten A., and Laurie Paarlberg. 2002. "Extent and Nature of Overlap between Listings of IRS Tax-Exempt Registration and Nonprofit

Incorporation: The Case of Indiana." *Nonprofit and Voluntary Sector Quarterly* 31(4): 565–94.

Hadaway, C. Kirk, and Penny Long Marler. 2005. "How Many Americans Attend Worship Each Week? An Alternative Approach to Measurement." *Journal for the Scientific Study of Religion* 44(3): 307–22.

Hall, Peter Dobkin. 1982. "Institutions, Autonomy, and National Networks." In *Making the Nonprofit Sector in the United States*, edited by David C. Hammack (174–87). Bloomington: Indiana University Press.

Hansman, Henry. 1987. "Economic Theories of Nonprofit Organization." In *The Nonprofit Sector: A Research Handbook*, edited by Walter W. Powell (27–42). New Haven: Yale University Press.

Harris, Frederick C. 1994. "Something Within: Religion as a Mobilizer of African-American Political Activism." *Journal of Politics* 56: 42–68.

Hess, Gary. 2003. "Waging the Cold War in the Third World: The Foundations and the Challenges of Development." In *Charity, Philanthropy, and Civility in American History*, edited by Lawrence J. Friedman and Mark D. McGarve. New York: Cambridge University Press.

Hodgkinson, Virginia, and Murray Weitzman. 1993. *From Belief to Commitment: The Community Service Activities and Finances of Religious Congregations in the United States*. Washington, DC: Independent Sector.

———.1996. *Giving and Volunteering in the United States*. Washington, DC: Independent Sector.

Jackson, Maria-Rosario. 1998. "Arts and Culture Indicators in Community Building: Project Update." *Journal of Arts Management, Law, and Society* 28(3): 201–5.

Kerlin, Janelle A. 2006. "Social Enterprise in the United States and Abroad: Learning from Our Differences." In *Researching Social Entrepreneurship*, edited by Rachel Mosher-Williams. ARNOVA Occasional Paper Series, Volume 1, Number 3.

———. Forthcoming. "Nonprofit Commercial Revenue: A Replacement for Declining Government Grants and Private Contributions?"

Lawrence, Steven, Josefina Atienza, and Asmita Barve. 2005. *Foundation Yearbook: Facts and Figures on Private and Community Foundations*. New York: Foundation Center.

Leland, Pamela. 2002. "PILOTs: The Large-City Experience." In *Property-Tax Exemption For Charities*, edited by Evelyn Brody (193–210). Washington, DC: Urban Institute Press.

Lohmann, Roger. 1992. *The Commons*. San Francisco: Jossey-Bass Publishers.

Maryland Association of Nonprofit Organizations. 1997. "The Baltimore City Nonprofit Sector: A Study of Its Economic and Programmatic Impacts in the City of Baltimore." Report prepared by the Jacob France Center. Baltimore: University of Baltimore.

McCarthy, Kathleen. 2003. *American Creed: Philanthropy and the Rise of Civil Society, 1700–1865*. Chicago: The University of Chicago Press.

O'Connell, Brian. 1997. *Powered by Coalition: The Story of Independent Sector*. San Francisco: Jossey-Bass Publishers.

———. 1999. *Civil Society. The Underpinnings of American Democracy*. Hanover: University Press of New England.

Ostrower, Francie. 2005. "Motivations Matter: Findings and Practical Implications of a National Survey of Cultural Participation." Washington, DC: The Urban Institute.

Panel on the Nonprofit Sector. 2005. "Strengthening Transparency, Governance, and Accountability of Charitable Organizations: A Final Report to Congress and the Nonprofit Sector." Washington, DC: Independent Sector.

Payton, Robert L. 1988. *Philanthropy: Voluntary Action for the Public Good*. New York: American Council on Education/Macmillan Publishing Company.

Pew Research Center for the People and the Press. 1997. "Trust and Civic Engagement in Metropolitan Philadelphia: A Case Study." Philadelphia: Pew Research Center for the People and the Press.

Printz, Tobi J. 1997. "Services and Capacity of Faith-Based Organizations in the Washington, D.C., Metropolitan Area." Paper presented at the annual meeting of ARNOVA, Indianapolis, Indiana, December 4–6.

Putnam, Robert D. 1993. *Making Democracy Work: Civic Traditions in Modern Italy*. Princeton: Princeton University Press.

———. 2000. *Bowling Alone: The Collapse and Revival of American Community*. New York: Simon and Shuster.

Reid, Elizabeth J. 2003. "In the States, Across the Nation, and Beyond: Democratic and Constitutional Perspectives on Nonprofit Advocacy." Washington, DC: The Urban Institute.

Reid, Elizabeth J., and Janelle Kerlin. 2003. "More than Meets the Eye: Structuring and Financing Nonprofit Advocacy." Annual Conference of the American Political Science Association, Philadelphia, Pennsylvania.

Renz, Loren, Steven Lawrence, and Josefina Atienza. 2006. *Foundation Growth and Giving Estimates: Current Outlook*. New York: Foundation Center.

Rich, Andrew. 2004. *Think Tanks, Public Policy, and the Politics of Expertise*. Cambridge, U.K.: Cambridge University Press.

Salamon, Lester M. 1995. *Partners in Public Service: Government-Nonprofit Relations in the Modern Welfare State*. Baltimore: Johns Hopkins University Press.

Salamon, Lester M., and Stephanie Lessans Geller. 2005. "Nonprofit Employment in the Greater Washington Region." *The Business of Doing Good in Greater Washington: How the Nonprofit Sector Contributes to the Region's Economy*. Washington, DC: The Nonprofit Roundtable of Greater Washington.

Schlesinger, Mark, and Bradford H. Gray. 2005. "Why Nonprofits Matter in American Medicine: A Policy Brief," *Nonprofit Sector Research Fund*. Washington DC: Aspen Institute.

Seligman, Martin E. P. 1991. *Learned Optimism: How to Change Your Mind and Your Life*. New York: A.A. Knopf.

Skloot, Edward, ed. 1988. *The Nonprofit Entrepreneur: Creating Ventures to Earn Income*. New York: Foundation Center.

Skocpol, Theda. 1995. *Protecting Mothers and Soldiers: The Political Origins of Social Policy in the United States*. Cambridge: Harvard University Press.

———. 2003. "Diminished Democracy: From Membership to Management in American Life." Norman: University of Oklahoma Press.

Skocpol, Theda, and Morris P. Fiorina. 1999. *Civic Engagement in American Democracy*. Washington, DC: Brookings Institution Press.

Smith, David H. 2000. *Grassroots Associations*. Thousand Oaks: Sage Publications.

Steuerle, C. Eugene. 2001. "When Nonprofits Conduct Exempt Activities as Taxable Enterprises." *Emerging Issues in Philanthropy Series*. Washington, DC: The Urban Institute.

Stevenson, David R. 1997. *The National Taxonomy of Exempt Entities Manual.* Washington, DC, and New York: National Center for Charitable Statistics and Foundation Center.

Twombly, Eric C., and Jennifer Auer. 2004. "A Portrait of Nonprofits Serving Children in the Washington, D.C., Area." Fast Facts Series No. 2. Washington, DC: The Urban Institute.

———. 2005. "The Size and Scope of the Nonprofit Sector in the Greater Washington Region" and "The Financial Scope of the Nonprofit Sector in the Greater Washington Region." In *The Business of Doing Good in Greater Washington: How the Nonprofit Sector Contributes to the Region's Economy.* Washington, DC: The Nonprofit Roundtable of Greater Washington.

U.S. Congress. 1996. "Government-Supported Unfair Competition with Small Business." 104th Cong., 2d sess., July 19. Washington, DC: U.S. Congress, House Committee on Small Business.

U.S. Congress, Joint Committee on Taxation. 2005. "Historical Development and Present Law of the Federal Tax Exemption for Charities and Other Tax-Exempt Organizations." Washington, DC: U.S. Congress, Joint Committee on Taxation. http://www.house.gov.jct/x-29-05.pdf.

U.S. Congress, Senate Finance Committee. 2004. "Senate Finance Committee Staff Discussion Draft, Tax Exempt Governance Proposals." Washington, DC: Senate Finance Committee. http://www.finance.senate.gov/hearings/testimony/2004test/062204stfdis.pdf.

Verba, Sidney, Kay Lehman Schlozman, and Henry E. Brady. 1995. *Voice and Equality: Civic Voluntarism in American Politics.* Cambridge: Harvard University Press.

Walker, Christopher, and Stephanie D. Scott-Melnyk, with Kay Sherwood. 2002. "Reggae to Rachmaninoff: How and Why People Participate in Arts and Culture." Washington, DC: The Urban Institute.

Walzer, Michael, ed. 1995. *Toward A Global Civil Society.* Providence: Berghahn Books.

Warren, Mark. 2002. *Democracy and Association.* Princeton: Princeton University Press.

Weisbrod, Burton A. 1988. *The Nonprofit Economy.* Cambridge: Harvard University Press.

Weitzman, Murray S., Nadine T. Jalandoni, Linda M. Lampkin, and Thomas H. Pollak. 2002. *The New Nonprofit Almanac and Desk Reference.* New York: Jossey-Bass Publishers.

Wing, Kennard, Mark A. Hager, Patrick M. Rooney, and Thomas Pollak. 2004. "Special Issues in Nonprofit Financial Reporting: A Guide for Financial Professionals." Washington, DC: The Urban Institute.

Wolpert, Julian. 1993. "Patterns of Generosity in America: Who's Holding the Safety Net?" New York: Twentieth Century Fund.

Wolpert, Julian, and John E. Seley, with Ana Motta-Moss. 2004. "Nonprofit Services in New York City's Neighborhoods: An Analysis of Access, Responsiveness, and Coverage." New York: The New York Cities Nonprofits Project.

Wuthnow, Robert. 1991. *Acts of Compassion: Caring for Others and Helping Ourselves.* Princeton: Princeton University Press.

———. 2004. *Saving America.* New Jersey: Princeton University Press.

1

COMPLEMENTARY, SUPPLEMENTARY, OR ADVERSARIAL? NONPROFIT–GOVERNMENT RELATIONS

Dennis R. Young

From time to time, public policymakers in the United States take an oversimplified view of the nonprofit sector and its relationship with government. In the 1980s, the Reagan administration argued that as government cut back on expenditures for public services, the nonprofit sector would simply fill the vacuum through volunteer efforts and charitable contributions (Bremner 1988; Salamon 1995). In the 1990s, House Speaker Newt Gingrich expressed a similar view in his *Contract with America*, while members of Congress proposed the infamous Istook amendment, which would have curtailed lobbying by nonprofit organizations receiving federal funds (U.S. Congress 1995). More recently, nonprofits such as the NAACP and other social justice, environmental, and advocacy organizations have complained that they have been sub-

ject to government harassment (at both the federal and state levels) as
a result of their taking positions on issues (Cohen 2004; Schwinn 2001;
Strom 2005) and, in response to the terror attacks of September 11,
2001, new governmental restrictions and oversight practices have constrained or intimidated many charities (Odendahl 2005). At the same
time, government's reliance on nonprofit services appears to be increasing as policymakers expand the role of faith-based institutions in delivering social services (Farris, Nathan, and Wright 2004) and place heavier
reliance on nonprofits in responding to national and regional emergencies (Williams 2005). These cases illustrate a limited view of appropriate
nonprofit activity as narrowly circumscribed, service-producing
organizations running largely on voluntary resources and having a
narrowly restricted role in public policy formation.

Policymakers on the left have made similar errors of oversimplifica-
tion, disparaging private philanthropy and implicitly extolling governmental solutions to public needs:

Philanthropy remained in bad repute in liberal and radical circles
throughout the 1930s . . . Eduard C. Lindeman . . . whose *Wealth
and Culture* (1936) was a study of the operation of one hundred
foundations during the 1920s, offered an economic interpretation
of modern philanthropy: it was disintegrating capitalism's way of
distributing, in its own interests, wealth which could not be spent
on luxuries, was not needed for reinvestment, and could not
profitably be employed for speculation. Foundations, and by implication, all large-scale benefactions, denoted the development of
a rudimentary social consciousness in the donors, but they also
represented the donors' determination to control social thought
and expression. (Bremner 1988, 152)

The reality of government–nonprofit sector relations in the United
States is far richer and more complex than such narrow views suggest.
Nonprofit organizations interact with government in several different
ways, and these patterns of interaction vary over time and among
different fields of service. In various contexts, nonprofits have served
as privately supported supplementary service providers of public
goods, as complementary partners with government in public service
provision, and as advocates and adversaries in the process of public
policy formulation and implementation. Often, two or three of these
roles are manifested simultaneously.

In this chapter, we consider the theoretical underpinnings of these
three modes of government–nonprofit relations. Various strands of
economic theory pertaining to nonprofit organizations illuminate the
circumstances under which we can expect nonprofits to fulfill different

roles vis-à-vis government—supplementary, complementary, and adversarial. These three theoretical modes of government–nonprofit relationships are first explained and then applied as conceptual screens for examining the history of government–nonprofit sector relationships in the United States, from colonial times to the present. We show that each theoretical cut reveals new insights into the complex relationships between nonprofits and government, and that no one view suffices for a full understanding.

Finally, we consider how alternative views of government–nonprofit relations can inform the present debate on the roles of government, nonprofits, and business in the United States. Recent developments, including governmental retrenchment and devolution, privatization of public services, restructuring in the business sector, commercialization in the nonprofit sector, demands for greater public accountability of nonprofit organizations, and new emphasis on government funding of faith-based institutions, have dislocated current patterns of government– nonprofit sector relationships. Government no longer takes comprehensive responsibility for social welfare, expects more from nonprofits, and has become more focused on its abuses; corporations have become more narrowly strategic in their philanthropic programs; substantial new private wealth has been created among business entrepreneurs; and nonprofit organizations have become more competitive and market-oriented in their quests to remain financially viable and to address growing social needs, and at the same time more aware of their need to be accountable to the public for their performance and behavior (Independent Sector 2005b). This shuffling of institutional conditions leaves open to question how the sectors will continue to divide responsibilities and work together toward solving social problems and meeting public needs in the future. Our review of the history of government–nonprofit relations through the three theoretical lenses suggests that a new "social contract" between government, nonprofits, and business must emerge if public needs are to be met.

STRANDS OF THEORY

Different strands of economic theory support alternative notions of the nonprofit sector as supplementary, complementary, or adversarial to government. (This taxonomy is similar to that postulated by Najam [2000] for relations between government and nongovernmental organizations internationally.) In the supplementary model, nonprofits are seen as fulfilling demand for public goods left unsatisfied by government. In this view, the private financing of public goods can be expected to have an inverse relationship with government expenditure. As government takes more responsibility for provision, less needs to be raised through voluntary collective means.

In the complementary view, nonprofits are seen as partners to government, helping to deliver public goods, and are largely financed by government. In this perspective, nonprofit and government expenditures have a direct relationship with one another. As government expenditures increase, they help finance increasing levels of activity by nonprofits.

In the adversarial view, nonprofits prod government to make changes in public policy and to maintain accountability to the public. Reciprocally, government attempts to influence the behavior of nonprofits by regulating their services and responding to advocacy initiatives. The adversarial view does not posit any specific relationship between the levels of nonprofit and governmental activity. For example, nonprofits can advocate for smaller or more efficient government operations or they can advocate for new programs and regulations that would increase government activity.

Figure 1.1 depicts the three views of government–nonprofit relations. As shown, the two sectors work separately, in parallel, in the supplementary mode. In the complementary mode, their activities are connected and coordinated with one another. In the adversarial mode, they oppose one another, each attempting to change the other.

Figure 1.1. Three Dimensions of Government–Nonprofit Relations

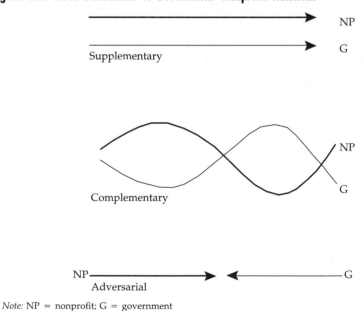

Note: NP = nonprofit; G = government

The three perspectives are by no means mutually exclusive. Non-profits may simultaneously finance and deliver services where the government does not, deliver services financed or otherwise assisted by the government, advocate for changes in government policies and practices, and be affected by governmental pressure and oversight. For example, Kramer (1981) observed that nonprofits' reliance on public funds to deliver services did not necessarily constrain their advocacy activity. Recent research by Chaves, Stephens, and Galaskiewicz (2004) has reinforced this conclusion.

Moreover, while the three views frame our discussion of non-profit–government relations as if nonprofits and government are distinct entities, in fact the boundaries are often blurred. For example, the governing boards of some nonprofit community development agencies have members appointed by government officials, and many state universities and public libraries incorporate private fundraising associations or foundations within their structures. To a certain extent, such hybrids can be understood as forms of government–nonprofit collaboration vis-à-vis the complementary view of nonprofit government relations. More generally, however, we abstract from the messy detail of the real world in the following discussion and proceed under the assumption that government–nonprofit boundaries can be recognized without undue difficulty in most instances.

In the same vein, we note that the three analytical views developed here all derive from rational choice models in the economics tradition. Other schools of thought—for example, behavioral and sociological theory—also have much to contribute to the understanding of institutional relationships, such as those between government and nonprofit organizations, as well as to an appreciation of the limitations of the economic approach. (See Powell and DiMaggio [1991, chapter 1] for an excellent discussion of these issues.) Since the first edition of this book, the supplementary–complementary–adversarial model has been applied in a number of different contexts, including a comparison of nonprofit government relations in different countries (Young 2000), changes in the relationships between nonprofit social service agencies and government following welfare reform (Reisch and Sommerfeld 2003), and in a textbook on nonprofit theory, management, and policy (Anheier 2005).

Nonprofits as Supplements to Government

The thesis that nonprofit organizations provide collective goods on a voluntary basis was first advanced by Burton Weisbrod in his seminal work on government failure (Weisbrod 1977). The basic premise is that citizens have individual preferences about the levels, qualities, and types of public goods they desire and how much they are willing to pay for them. Governments decide on the level of public goods provided based on citizens' preferences and are constrained by equity considerations and bureaucratic procedures to tax and to offer public goods in a uniform way (Douglas 1987). Given democratic voting and policymaking procedures, governments follow preferences of the median voter or of a dominant political coalition (Buchanan and Tullock 1962) in choosing those uniform tax rates and levels, types, and qualities of services. If citizen preferences are not homogeneous, some citizens (e.g., those whose preferences vary substantially from the preferences of the median voter) will be left unsatisfied, either paying for and receiving more (of various) public goods than they want, or paying less and receiving less than they want. Citizens in the latter group are presumed willing to provide additional (supplementary) levels of public goods for themselves and others by mobilizing on a voluntary collective basis through the nonprofit sector.

Weisbrod (1977) points out that nonprofits are not the only solution to the problem of public goods provision where the preferences of the citizenry are heterogeneous. Citizens may instead purchase various private market substitutes for public goods (e.g., guard dogs to supplement public policing). Moreover, where multiple local political jurisdictions exist, as they do in the United States, people may move to communities where tax rates and public goods best match their preferences (Tiebout 1956). However, these solutions all have limitations. Exercising mobility is costly. Political jurisdictions package multiple public goods together so citizens cannot make perfect matches between communities and personal preferences for services and taxes. And private goods are usually imperfect substitutes for public goods. Hence, substantial room is left for nonprofits to supplement government services.

In light of this theory, we can expect substantial variation in nonprofit sector–government relationships among fields of activity. In areas such as the arts, where citizens' preferences vary widely, private nonprofit provision can be expected to be substantial. In areas such as policing and defense, where preferences may be relatively homogeneous, we can expect the nonprofit role to be less substantial. In areas such as social services, where citizens' preferences can be volatile, we can expect nonprofit provision to respond to ebbs and flows of public sentiment and consensus.

The supplementary model also suggests an interesting dynamic when people's preferences change over time. In particular, nonprofits can view public decisions to expand the role of government in areas they traditionally serve as a threat. Commenting on government activism in the 1960s, for example, Bremner (1988, 184) notes:

To some observers, government intrusion into areas formerly the preserve of voluntary activity comprised a more serious threat to philanthropy than internal rivalries.

Alternatively, however, the supplementary view also illuminates the notion that private action is often intended to prod government into action. For example, the Ford Foundation's Public Affairs Program in the 1960s funded demonstration programs "addressing education and delinquency in the slums and mobilizing the electoral strength of minority communities" (Bremner 1988, 187).

Nonprofits and Government as Complements

Lester Salamon (1995) has been the principal advocate for the view that nonprofits and government are engaged primarily in a partnership or contractual relationship in which government finances public services and nonprofits deliver them. (In chapter 2, Steuerle and Hodgkinson show how much the government has increasingly contracted out to nonprofit institutions, affecting the relative employment in each sector over time.) Aspects of the economic theories of public goods and of organizations help clarify the rationale behind this thesis. In the former category, the theory of collective action advanced by Mancur Olson (1965) highlights the phenomenon of "free riding" when people attempt to provide collective goods on a voluntary basis. Where the good to be provided is "nonrival" (i.e., can be consumed by one party without reducing the amount available to others) and "nonexcludable" (i.e., the good cannot be made available to one party without making it simultaneously available to others), then people have the incentive to avoid contributing to its provision but to consume it once others provide it. As a result, a voluntary collective effort will not support such goods at efficient levels. Large groups with relatively homogeneous preferences (no one party is tempted to provide a good on its own) exacerbate the problem of free riding.

Solutions to the public goods problem include social pressure (e.g., appealing to conscience and peer to peer solicitations), tying together of private incentives with public goods support (e.g., bonuses given to members of public radio stations), and coercion (e.g., using the police power of the state to collect taxes). This last solution suggests government should finance public goods, either directly or through tax incentives, while not necessarily delivering them.

Economic theory of organizations, specifically aspects of the theory of the firm and transactions cost theory, helps illuminate why, in many instances, it may be more efficient for government to delegate delivery of services to private organizations (e.g., nonprofits) than to deliver those services itself. Coase (1988) addresses the question of why an organization (business firm) would choose to carry out a (marginal) transaction through the market rather than internally. For example, why might a firm contract out for a particular task rather than hire or direct its current employees to do it? One part of Coase's explanation is that as an organization gets larger, the costs of administering additional transactions (enlarging the bureaucracy) rise. At some point, it becomes cheaper to contract outside rather than expand work internally; that is, there are diminishing returns to management as well as differences in direct production costs inside versus outside the organization. Such an explanation appears relevant to government provision of public services (Gronbjerg 1997). Complaints about the cost and inefficiencies of public bureaucracies are common. Despite the costs of arranging and monitoring external contracts, it may be cheaper for governments to contract out for certain services than perform them internally. In addition, private suppliers may have lower labor costs if they are not unionized and may be better able to exploit economies of scale for certain services by producing them for more than one jurisdiction. (See Ferris [1993] for a comprehensive discussion of government's decision to contract out.)

Governments do not always try to minimize their production costs. (See Niskanen [1971] for one explanation.) Assuming that they do sometimes try to reduce costs, however, the Coase argument helps explain why governments sometimes contract for service delivery with private suppliers. However, this explanation does not distinguish between nonprofit and for-profit contractors. Another aspect of transactions costs theory pertains to the information an organization requires in order to carry out a market transaction efficiently. In the case of public services, two aspects related to the quality of services delivered appear relevant. First, government may choose to contract out, not only because it is cheaper but because it may be unable to differentiate its services in response to the heterogeneous preferences of its citizens. There would be too much information to gather in order to do so. However, by contracting with nonprofits that are knowledgeable about the individual communities in which they are based, government can overcome the information problem and, within limits, allow those delivery agents to customize their services to local constituents.

To a certain extent, such differentiation would be possible if government contracted with for-profit businesses as well, so long as those businesses were community-based or conscientious about monitoring their customers' preferences. However, without its own data, how could government verify such responsiveness? Here another aspect of the transaction cost literature comes into play in favor of nonprofits: nonprofits operate under different incentives than for-profits. In particular, they do not face the same imperatives to skimp on quality, renege on promised service, or lower the costs of production by homogenizing services in order to increase profits (see the discussion of contract failure, below). Hence, government presumably faces lower monitoring and contract enforcement costs associated with ensuring differentiated, responsive community services by contracting with nonprofits rather than with for-profits.

Steinberg (1997) points out that the arguments for nonprofits as less costly contractors for government are subject to a number of caveats and subtleties associated with donor reactions to government financing, the internal motivations of nonprofit agents, the level of competition, and the structure of the contracts themselves. Indeed, many nonprofits employ substantial paid staff who can be expected, as in any organization, to capture, in the form of additional wages or other benefits, some of the value-added their organizations produce. Certainly this is a concern of donors, government overseers, and nonprofit sector leaders (Independent Sector 2005b; Jensen, Kerkman, and Moore 2005; Wolverton 2004b). Nonetheless, Steinberg concludes that

> Nonprofit organizations deserve some preference in bidding because they provide benefits to the government (reduced opportunistic behavior and reduced transaction costs of negotiating, monitoring, and enforcing a contract) that cannot be enforceably written into a contract with for-profits. (Steinberg 1997, 176)

In all, the theory of public goods coupled with the theory of transactions costs provides a plausible explanation for why government and nonprofits often engage in a complementary relationship in which government finances and nonprofits deliver services. This relationship is more likely to be observed in areas such as social services where free riding is a significant problem, where direct public production is likely to require a large bureaucratic operation, and where differences in local preferences favor some differentiation of services to alternative locales and consumer groups.

Finally, a curious but historically important variation of government–nonprofit complementary relationships is where the government and nonprofit sector roles are reversed in terms of financing and service delivery. Interestingly, throughout U.S. history, government has often been the recipient of private largesse for carrying out public projects, such as the construction of public monuments or the establishment of state or national parks (see below). A theoretical explanation of such behavior seems more consistent with the supplementary than complementary view but with a slight twist: private parties raise funds for activities that public demand does not support. Moreover, the private givers find it more efficient (given the costs of private supply) to "contract" with government for their production rather than produce the goods themselves. (This occurs, for example, when the projects represent marginal additions to public sector operations and private supply would have to start from scratch, or when the government is expected to assume a larger proportion of the costs eventually.) Additionally, the public values these activities, accepts implementation within the public domain, and may indeed contribute to their financing. In this sense, private financing of governmental projects needs to be understood through both the supplementary and complementary lenses.

Nonprofits and Government as Adversaries

To date, economic theories have not explicitly addressed the advocacy role of nonprofits in public policy or the role of government in controlling nonprofits. To a certain extent, nonprofit advocacy and government pressure on nonprofits can be understood through the complementary lens of nonprofit–government relations. Often, nonprofits and government are collaborators in passing legislation or changing public attitudes. Similarly, government sometimes undertakes to encourage, prod, and stimulate private, voluntary activity in support of social goals. But advocacy activity suggests a third way of characterizing the relationship between nonprofit organizations and government— as adversaries in policymaking and service delivery.

Bits and pieces of economic theory help illuminate the adversarial relationship. On the issue of nonprofit advocacy, Weisbrod's (1977) theory of government failure is helpful again. In heterogeneous jurisdictions, where minority views are not well reflected in public policy, minorities will organize themselves on a voluntary collective basis not only to provide public services for themselves but also to press government to serve their interests and communities more adequately. In the basic Weisbrod model, government would have no incentive to respond since it simply follows the preferences of the majority. However, more nuanced analyses of public choice that allow for logrolling, vote trading, and the concentration of minority efforts on particular issues, demonstrate that organized minorities can be effective in having their public policy concerns addressed (Buchanan and Tullock 1962). Such minorities mobilize through voluntary associations or interest groups, becoming an important component of the government– nonprofit sector constellation of relationships.

The Weisbrod model is also helpful for understanding how advocacy leads to new public services. Initially, only a minority of voters favor proposals for new programs, which therefore are not immediately adopted by government. A minority of citizens may promote the idea through advocacy and demonstrate its efficacy with voluntary contributions. Nonprofit think tanks may play a role in such efforts (e.g., see Hall 1994) or, as noted above, foundations may fund demonstration projects (e.g., see Bremner, 1988). Such promotional efforts may secure pilot funding from government. Eventually, the concept may be proven and receive the support of a majority; then the government may undertake full scale provision.

Economic theory is also helpful for understanding why government is moved to oversee nonprofit behavior and performance, and sometimes to press nonprofits to change. In particular, the theory of contract failure first developed by Henry Hansmann (1980) postulates that nonprofit organizations are chosen as efficient vehicles for delivering services where there is a condition of "information asymmetry" between consumers and producers that would allow a profitmaking firm to exploit consumer ignorance to its advantage. Nonprofits are seen to be more efficient in this circumstance because the nondistribution constraint, as Hansmann argues, or the internal governance structure of nonprofit organizations, as Ben-Ner (1986) suggests, reduces the incentives and opportunities for nonprofits to cheat consumers; this makes them more "trustworthy."

Why then, if nonprofits are more trustworthy, does government need to regulate nonprofits? Two reasons are implicit in the theory of contract failure. First, the trustworthiness of nonprofit organizations depends in part on the credibility of the nondistribution constraint and the integrity of the nonprofit governance structure. These, in turn, must be policed, which is the government's role. Government must ensure that the nondistribution constraint is observed (see Young 1983) and, to ensure nonprofits' trustworthiness, that appropriate principles are followed for constituting governing boards.

Second, contract failure may be seen as a broad phenomenon subject to a variety of approaches and solutions including licensure, accreditation, competition, and other means. Utilization of nonprofits is one weapon in the arsenal and not necessarily a perfect or complete solution to the problem. Nonprofits also violate the trust put in them on occasion and some of the same oversight mechanisms that government uses to oversee for-profit providers in various markets can be applied to nonprofits as well.

It is interesting to return to Weisbrod's (1977) model in the context of the nonprofit advocacy role and explore its implications for government behavior. If nonprofits advocate for minority positions in the policy arena, it follows that government may react by defending majority interests. One form that reaction may take is an attempted restriction of nonprofit advocacy. In the guise of regulation, government can become the adversary of nonprofits in the policy arena. Debate over the Istook amendment in the 1990s, the various deliberations leading to the restrictions on foundations in the 1969 Tax Act (see Bremner 1988; Hall 1994), and the provisions in the Federal Housing Finance Reform Act of 2005 to restrict funding of housing groups that participated in nonpartisan election-related activity (Independent Sector 2005a) may be partially understood in this light.

Finally, it is worth observing that nonprofits and government may oppose one another for the simple reason that these parties independently pursue objects whose impacts are felt differently by the two parties. For example, public sector initiatives to reduce taxes and simplify the tax code, although not intended to harm nonprofits, could do so. In such instances, the actions of the government reflect Weisbrod's model of public sector decisionmaking in which the majority approves what it sees as a public good, and the minority (nonprofits) opposes what it sees as a public bad. Alternatively, some nonprofits may support public goods whose benefits are confined to the nonprofits' own narrow constituencies, such as sufferers of a rare disease, where government judges the opportunity costs of support (relative to other uses of funds) to be too high.

Interactions and Transitions

We have recognized that government and nonprofits may relate to each other via all three modes simultaneously. In addition, government and nonprofits influence each others' behaviors in ways that involve more than one of these modes. The best example of this involves tax policy. By decreasing income tax rates, for instance, government reduces revenues that might be available to finance nonprofit services in a complementary relationship. At the same time, the lower tax rates can suppress giving, discouraging nonprofit activity in a supplementary mode, as well as increasing nonprofit adversarial activity aimed at restoring lost government financing. Similarly, other types of incentives such as tax credits or loan guarantees may be viewed nominally as government policy encouraging nonprofit activity in a supplementary mode, while in effect they are similar to a direct government expenditure. Indeed, the term "tax expenditure" is used to describe this ambiguous form of government support (Gronbjerg and Salamon 2002).

The faith-based initiative of the George W. Bush administration illustrates another subtle interplay of the modes of nonprofit–government relations. While it promises to expand the complementary relationship of government with religiously based social service providers, it threatens to undermine longstanding government support of nonprofit social services, leading to greater reliance on the supplementary form of nonprofit social service provision (see Formicola, Segers, and Weber 2003).

It is noteworthy also that changes in the political environment can lead to changes in the relationships between government and certain nonprofit organizations whose missions align differently with different political administrations. For example, faith-based institutions and pro-life advocacy organizations may move from supplementary or adversarial to complementary relationships with government when a conservative political regime comes to power, while other nonprofits, such as those in the arts or environmental conservation, may shift in the reverse direction. These changes help institutionalize the values of incoming administrations by bringing resources to activities and policy positions that the current governing coalition favors and drawing resources away from nonprofits associated with the previous regime (see Evans, Rueschemeyer, and Skocpol 1985).

HISTORICAL PERSPECTIVES

The supplementary, complementary and adversarial theories, taken as a cluster, show the complexity of nonprofit–government relationships. These are not mutually exclusive ways of understanding those relationships but rather overlapping models that each capture important elements. History may be examined in layers by asking sequentially, what does each model reveal about the nature of government–nonprofit relationships as they have evolved over time in the United States?

We proceed by reviewing, through each of the three theoretical lenses, the history of the nonprofit sector in the United States at various stages—colonial times, the early republic, after the Civil War, the late 19th and early 20th centuries, and modern times—as documented by several contemporary nonprofit sector scholars. History is examined here in a necessarily cursory fashion through secondary and tertiary sources. This approach does not do justice to the work of serious nonprofit historians, but it does suggest researchers can use the proposed theoretical framework to understand government–nonprofit relations and how they change over time. We hope it partially addresses Hall's (1992, 109–10) complaint that

> The shortcomings of the social sciences have stemmed primarily from their ahistoricity and their tendency to fragment and thereby distort the continuum of collective action.

Finally, it must be acknowledged that the concept of nonprofit as a sector is a modern construct that we must impose somewhat awk-

wardly to analyze earlier historical periods. Like the blurring of boundaries between sectors in the modern era, the ambiguity of institutional
definitions requires a certain amount of license in making historical
observations.

History Through the Supplementary Lens

Examining how nonprofits have attended to collective needs unad-
dressed by government help us appreciate the roles of government
and nonprofit organizations in the United States:

> Americans had a long experience in founding voluntary agencies
> to perform tasks which individuals could not accomplish alone
> and which public bodies, for one reason or another, were not able
> to undertake. (Bremner 1988, 176)

While documentation is spotty, nonprofit activity supplementing
government clearly predates the U.S. republic. A review by Lohmann
(1992, 121–22) suggests that colonists brought with them religious-
based traditions of mutual aid:

> Scottish immigrants to Boston formed the first ethnic mutual aid
> society in 1657, initiating a trend that continues today for virtually
> every ethnic, racial, or nationality group. . . . A French religious
> order founded the first American orphanage in New Orleans in
> 1718. . . . Residents of Williamsburg, Virginia and Philadelphia
> founded early mental hospitals.

Lohmann (1992, 122) goes on to note that

> New England Puritans, Virginia planters, and Dutch colonists in
> New York and New Jersey all adopted church-based relief commit-
> tees as the basis of colonial welfare systems. Only gradually did the
> New England Puritan towns move to civil welfare administration.
> Although religious voluntary associations date from the earliest
> settlement of New England, more secular associations of charitable
> and mutual aid societies, fire brigades, lodges, and professional
> societies emerged later, mainly in Boston.

O'Neill (1989, 25) emphasizes the point that religion dominated what
we now think of as the nonprofit sector in colonial times and the early
period of the republic:

Religion was by far the most important part of what would come to be known as the nonprofit sector. Arts and culture organizations were nonexistent, health care was primitive and family based, formal education was far less extensive than it is now, social services were minimal, and somewhat frowned upon, and there was nothing even vaguely resembling grantmaking or international assistance organizations. As far as the incipient nonprofit sector went, religion was virtually the only game in town.

Interestingly, while religion and government were sometimes intertwined during the colonial period, specifically in New England and the South, O'Neill argues that the diversity of religious beliefs in the colonies ultimately made necessary the separation of church and state, hence reinforcing the development of the nonprofit sector as supplementary to government:

What started to emerge almost immediately in the English colonies was the notion that allegiance to one country, culture, language and tradition could coexist with sharp diversity in religious ideas and practices . . . the English colonists simply had to deal with the fact of religious diversity; the economic, political, social, and military realities of the New World left them no choice. It was principally this variety of religious experience in colonial New England that prepared the way for religious liberty. That idea and reality, in turn, played a critical role in the development of the American third sector, since organized religion not only was a major part of the sector but also spawned much of the rest. Without religious diversity and state neutrality toward religion, the American nonprofit experience would have been very different. (O'Neal 1989, 26–27)

Bremner (1988, 48) notes that in the early period of the republic, private initiative in higher education was a particularly important area of nonprofit activity as a supplement to government:

The field of higher education, neglected by the federal government and very poorly supported by the states, gave philanthropists their greatest opportunity for service. A nation growing rapidly in population and wealth possibly needed more colleges than the twenty-odd in existence at the start of the century.

O'Neill (1989, 72–73) describes one of many examples where privately based initiatives ultimately led to adoption by government in the first half of the nineteenth century:

In 1813 . . . Quakers . . . founded the first private psychiatric hospital in the United States. . . . With a revolutionary set of practices, the Quakers released the insane from their chains, gave each a private room with a window, allowed them to walk around the wooded grounds and work in the hospital gardens, and made caring conversation the basis of treatment. When the State Lunatic Hospital at Harrisburg was opened in 1851, the Pennsylvania General Assembly declared that the quality of care should be the highest and should be based on the Quaker model.

In the 19th and 20th centuries, the traditions of self-help, both religious and secular but largely separate from government, continued to be very important:

Most nineteenth century U.S. residents immigrated from cultures with broad repertoires of associational and common practices. . . . Culturally, these immigrants were already armed with many organizational skills. . . . From the start these skills were used in organizing fire companies, mutual aid societies, local governments, and an array of other associations. . . .

During much of the nineteenth and early twentieth century, fraternal organizations serving both civic and quasi-religious functions were an important means of social integration for the middle and lower classes, particularly in predominantly rural areas . . . (Lohmann, 123)

Bremner (1988, 85) observes that "The twenty-five or thirty years after the Civil War seemed, to Americans living at the time, an era of stunning achievement in all fields of philanthropy." Nielsen (1979, 14) claims that the late nineteenth and early twentieth century was the period in which private initiative peaked in its prominence:

. . . in the last decades of the nineteenth century and the first decades of the twentieth century, many Third Sector institutions— in addition to the churches—developed private sources of support and simultaneously an ideology of separateness which affected the policies of both private agencies and government.

The surge of private, nonprofit initiative supplemental to government in this period was fueled by a combination of new and enormous private, concentrated industrial wealth and political progressivism stemming from industrialization, urbanization and immigration. According to Hall (1992, 39):

. . . the use of private nonprofit organizations grew enormously in the last decades of the nineteenth century. Big business and private wealth underwrote the growth of universities, libraries, hospitals, museums, social-welfare organizations, professional societies, and private clubs. At the same time, the middle and lower classes supported labor unions, mutual-benefit societies, fraternal organizations, volunteer fire companies, building and loan associations, and even cooperatively owned nonprofit businesses. Growing awareness of urban poverty among the middle and upper classes encouraged the establishment of charitable organizations of every sort, ranging from traditional funds for the relief of the sick, poor, and disabled to new forms nonprofit activity, such as settlement houses and charity organizations. . . . No less important than the private organizations directed to the reform of society was the rise of new kinds of cultural organizations whose primary constituencies were the rich. The establishment and professionalization of museums and symphony orchestras . . . played a major role in recasting the nature of urban culture.

Andrew Carnegie's *Gospel of Wealth* was influential in this period and supportive of the concept of philanthropy as a substitute for government programming:

According to the gospel of wealth, philanthropy was less the handmaid of social reform than a substitute for it. Wise administration of wealth was an antidote for radical proposals for redistributing property and a method of reconciling the poor and the rich (Bremner, 1988, 102)

The role of women was especially important in creating voluntary associations that addressed social needs in this era of weak government:

While wealthy businessmen such as John D. Rockefeller and Andrew Carnegie lavished massive donations on growing crops of foundations, universities, museums, and think tanks created in the corporate image of their business ventures, women—even very wealthy women—continued to build their own organizations through an economy of time, rather than cash. . . . [These] voluntary associations were unusually influential in weak governmental systems, such as that of the United States in this era . . . (McCarthy 1997, 145–146)

Of great long term significance in this period was the invention of the modern foundation which institutionalized the ability of private interests to fund nonprofit sector activity in a focused manner:

> Credit for establishing the first foundation of the modern type—
> an open-ended endowment devoted "to the good of mankind,"
> which carried out its charitable purposes by giving money to insti-
> tutions rather than operating them, and which entrusted decision-
> making to staffs of experts . . . went to Margaret Olivia Slocum
> Sage, the widow of Wall Street buccaneer Russell Sage. . . . Mrs.
> Sage decided to establish a philanthropic trust "elastic in form
> and method to work in different ways at different times" for "the
> permanent improvement of social conditions." (Hall 1992, 47)

As Hall notes, the Russell Sage Foundation was followed by the major
foundation initiatives of Andrew Carnegie, John D. Rockefeller and
other industrial giants. These initiatives were but one aspect of a
broader strategy of "welfare capitalism" that allowed private initiative
and wealth to underwrite a variety of programs supplemental to government's own efforts:

> Sometimes welfare capitalism involved direct corporate subsidies
> of charitable organizations, as with the massive support by the
> railroad industry of the Young Men's Christian Association
> (YMCA). . . . Companies also contributed to the creation of parks
> and playgrounds, schools, and libraries . . . (50)

Other institutional innovations, including the community foundation
and the community chest also emanated from the era of business and
private social activism in late 19th and 20th centuries, as means to
coordinate the development and allocation of private resources to community needs (Hall 1992, 51).

While much of the 20th century witnessed the growing role of government in the provision of public services of all varieties, supplemental
provision by nonprofit sector institutions persisted and grew. Early in
the depression of the 1930s, for example, President Hoover put perhaps
undue emphasis on charity as a substitute for potential government
relief. Partially as a consequence, charity fell into some public disrepute
between the 1930s and the 1960s (Bremner 1988). But measurements
made since then (in the 1980s) of the size and scope of the sector
reveal the substantial character and continued growth of churches,
foundations, trade and professional associations, and other subsectors
that support themselves without government help and that provide
collective goods essentially supplemental to those of the government
sector. Indeed, the number of foundations has grown rapidly over the
course of the past quarter century, along with the real value of assets
they hold and the allocations they dispense.[1] Moreover, the measured
part of the supplemental nonprofit sector may represent only a fraction

of the total picture. If David Horton Smith (1997a) is correct, quantitative research has missed a substantial fraction of the grassroots organizations that provide self-help, communal, relief, and other services, essentially on a volunteer basis without significant exchange of funds, and supplemental to government. These organizations trace themselves back further than formal nonprofits and have been part of the American scene since the beginning (Smith 1997b).

Finally, the late 20th and early 21st centuries seem to manifest a resurgence of the supplemental model, not just in the United States but internationally. Weisbrod (1997, 542–43) notes

> . . . the growing importance of nonprofits everywhere, as population migration and the flow of information through television and computers have the effect of magnifying diversity in country after country. . . . This growing diversity of societies is bringing, everywhere, retrenchment of government and increased reliance on the nonprofit sector.

Developments such as the growth of venture philanthropy by newly minted billionaires, the extraordinary public policy initiatives of modern-day Rockefellers and Carnegies such as Bill Gates, Ted Turner, and George Soros, and the rapid growth of private foundations, donor-advised funds, and international nongovernmental organizations suggest an era when the supplemental mode of nonprofit–government relations may again become predominant.

The supplementary lens identifies an important component of the history of nonprofit–government relations in the United States. In various contexts, private citizens, rich as well as poor, have often provided for themselves and for others. In some cases, such activity supplements government provision; in other cases, the nonprofit sector creates and supports new forms of collective activity not yet undertaken by government. History shows that such activity is undertaken by minorities, including ethnic and religious groups and business leaders with their own social preferences and agendas, different from the political majority, in a manner that appears consistent with the supplemental theory of voluntary collective action.

Some scholars argue, however, that the supplemental mode of nonprofit–government relations is not usually the dominant stream. For example, Hall (1992) claims that voluntary associations were relatively sparse and subservient to government in the 18th and early 19th centuries. And Nielsen (1979) considers the period of private sector vigor in the late 19th and early 20th centuries an aberration from the more pervasive mode of nonprofit sector–government interpenetration.

Thus, the supplementary lens gives only a partial view, and we need to take another look through the complementary lens.

History through the Complementary Lens

Several scholars, including Hall (1992), Nielsen (1979), Bremner (1991) and Salamon (1987), have observed that governmental partnerships with private philanthropy and nonprofit organizations has been a part of the American scene from colonial times. No less prominent a figure than Benjamin Franklin was a proponent of public/private collaboration:

> His political talents were never better displayed than in his ability to unite public and private support behind municipal improvements. He played a leading part in the establishment of both the Pennsylvania Hospital (1751) and the academy which became the University of Pennsylvania. (Bremner 1988, 17–18)

The case of Harvard University is often cited as the earliest example of public support and nonprofit provision:

> The situation of Harvard College, the oldest eleemosynary corporation in the colonies, illustrates well the anomalous status of all colonial corporations. Although chartered as a corporation, the college was governed by boards composed of ministers of the tax supported Congregational church and government officials sitting ex officio. Although Harvard possessed a small endowment, given partly by benevolent colonists and partly by British friends, it was regarded as a public institution because most of its revenues came from legislative grants and from tuitions and fees. (Hall 1992, 16–17)

Parallel situations characterized Yale vis-à-vis the state of Connecticut (Salamon 1987) and Williams College (Massachusetts), Columbia (New York), and the University of Pennsylvania (Nielsen 1979).

Similar arrangements were found in the health and social services in colonial and post-revolutionary times:

> Early hospitals such as Pennsylvania Hospital, founded in 1752, offered health care for indigent patients with their expenses paid by local or colonial governments. Private institutions for the mentally ill such as the Hartford (Ct.) Retreat and McLean Hospital in Boston used state and local government funds to provide care for indigent mentally ill patients. (Smith and Lipsky 1993, 47)

Governmental involvement and financial support of private, non-profit organizations providing higher education, hospital care, and social services, begun in the early republic, continued unabated through the 19th and 20th centuries. For example, Nielsen (1979) cites Massachusetts General Hospital, Louisville General Hospital, University Hospital in Baltimore, and Natchez Charity Hospital as examples of private, nonprofit institutions established or supported with state government funds between 1820 and 1840. And Salamon (1987) observes that towards the end of the 19th and beginning of the 20th centuries, government support of hospitals and nonprofit social service organizations was fairly common:

> A survey of seventeen major private hospitals in 1889 . . . revealed that 12 to 13 percent of their income came from government . . . [and] a 1901 survey of government subsidization of private charities found that "except possibly two territories and four western states, there is probably not a state in the union where some aid [to private charities] is not given either by the state or by counties and cities." (100–1)

Observers seem to agree, however, that governmental support of nonprofit organizations did not become extensive until the mid-20th century. According to Smith and Lipsky (1993, 49),

> Government funding of private service organizations was not extensive by today's standards. A 1914 survey revealed that "22 states made no appropriations whatever to privately managed charities, fifteen make such appropriations sparingly, and nine place no apparent restrictions on their grants."

In the 1930s, however, the federal Works Progress Administration (WPA) promoted an especially important example of government–nonprofit collaboration in the arts, helping important institutions such as Chicago's Art Institute, the Cincinnati Museum, and New York's Metropolitan Museum survive financially:

> Although Federal One and the Treasury arts program are the most famous examples of Depression Era government patronage, the influence of the WPA extended to local cultural institutions as well, adding a new slant to the practice of third party government. . . . By 1933, the [Metropolitan] Museum's investment income was diminishing as well, generating salary cuts. By 1936, however, staff costs were being offset by workers seconded from the WPA. Clerical staff, carpenters, painters, masons, lecturers, even guards

were provided with support from the public till. (McCarthy 1994, 18–19)

Government–nonprofit collaboration picked up some lost steam in the 1960s:

> The public-private partnership in public service, never dissolved but in abeyance during and for some years after the New Deal, took on new life in the 1960s and 1970s. (Bremner 1988, 210)

And Salamon, writing in 1987, observed that:

> Although government support of the voluntary sector has deep historical roots in this country . . . this support has grown considerably in scope and depth over the past thirty years (p.101)

The magnitude and scope of governmental support and contracting with nonprofits began to grow dramatically in the 1960s because of expansion in federal programs. For example,

> Federal expenditures for social welfare services almost tripled between 1965 and 1970. . . . The federal role continued to expand throughout the 1970s. . . . A big percentage of the increase in public funding of social services was expended through nonprofit agencies. . . . Faced with public pressure to expand social services, particularly for the poor, Congress enacted the 1967 Amendments to the Social Security Act . . . which specifically encouraged states to enter into purchase-of-service agreements with private agencies. . . . A 1971 study indicated that 25 percent of state spending on social services was for purchased services. . . . By 1976 this expenditure had risen to 49 percent. (Smith and Lipsky 1993, 55)

In addition, in 1961, the establishment of the Combined Federal Campaign allowed certain charities to solicit charitable contributions from federal employees (Bremner 1988). In a study of 16 local communities in 1982, government reliance on nonprofit organizations to deliver public services was found to be extensive in social services, housing and community development, health care, and the arts. In each field, more than 40 percent of government expenditures were allocated to private, nonprofit organizations (Salamon 1987). In the arts, the creation of the National Endowment in 1965 was a particularly important element in the developing public/private partnership:

According to Senator Claiborne Pell, who helped to draft the enabling legislation, the notion of using the Endowment "as a catalyst . . . [to] help spark nonfederal support . . . was the key to the entire proposal." With the creation of the NEA, the notion of public/private partnerships emerged full blown. (McCarthy 1994, 15)

International relief was another area where public support of non-profit efforts became important:

The engines of cooperation between public and private sector efforts in overseas aid were the Food for Peace Program, originating in 1954, and the Agency for International Development (AID), founded in 1961 . . . people to people groups such as Catholic Relief, CARE, Church World Service, and the American Joint Distribution Committee distributed 70 percent of the donations. . . . In addition to supplying surplus commodities, mostly food, the government paid the overseas freight costs of clothing, medicine, and other material purchased by or given to voluntary agencies by their members. (Bremner 1988, 196–97)

While the expansion of contractual arrangements between government and nonprofits was dramatic in the 1960s and 1970s, it continued unabated, though modified in form, in the 1980s and '90s and into the new century. In the social services, for example, Smith (2002) cites four particular developments: expanded use of Medicaid to support social services; new federal programs for children and youth, AIDS services, AmeriCorps, home health care, and other services; welfare reform legislation that provided new funding for job training, welfare-to-work aid, and child care; and innovations in the form of federal financing, including tax credits, loans, and tax-exempt bonds. Medicaid payments alone rose from $47 billion in 1980 to more than $142 billion in 1998 (measured in 1998 dollars). Nor has the experience of expanded government financial support for nonprofits been limited to the social services or health care for the poor. Government funding of health care and educational services, broadly construed, have become two of the largest sources of government contracting, for example (see Stewart, Kane, and Scruggs [2002] and chapter 3).

Bremner observes that the modern period of government–nonprofit contracting had its roots in earlier periods in American history:

In some respects, purchase of service agreements marked a return, although on a much larger scale, of the nineteenth-century practice of granting subsidies from public funds to private orphanages,

hospitals, and relief societies. Had advocates or critics of privatization chosen to do so they might have cited examples in earlier
periods of American history when towns, counties, and states
delegated responsibility for the care of the poor and criminals to
private contractors. (Bremner 1988, 202)

The reverse model of private financing and public provision has also
appeared throughout U.S. history. In the early republic, for example,
Stephen Girard made

bequests to the city of Philadelphia for improvement of certain
streets, to the state of Pennsylvania for the development of canals
. . . (Bremner 1988, 39)

Later examples include James Smithson's gift to the federal government
for what became the Smithsonian Institution, Andrew Mellon's gift of
the National Gallery, and Andrew Carnegie's gifts of public libraries
to many communities (Bremner 1988). This tradition is also reflected in
various voluntary campaigns to raise charitable funds for government
monuments, including building the Washington Monument and refur-
bishing the Statue of Liberty; funding drives during and after World
Wars I and II; establishing the Sanitary Commission during the Civil
War to improve conditions in military camps; and financially assisting
government in wartime from revolutionary times to the present era
(Bremner 1988). Indeed, the tradition continues unabated to today:

Private givers further supported their part of the public–private
partnership by contributing to mainly tax-supported institutions
such as state colleges and universities, public radio and television
stations, and public or endowed museums, libraries, parks and
zoos. Nearly every public educational, civic, or cultural institution
cultivated "friends" whose gifts supplemented appropriations
from federal, state, or local government. In New York City in 1987,
twenty public monuments in need of costly repair were put up
for "adoption" by private donors; in Washington, D.C., the
National Park Service, operating on a tight budget, asked private
individuals to donate money to replace aging and dying cherry
trees around the Tidal Basin. (Bremner 1988, 211)

Finally, the complementary relationships of government and nonprofits extend to more subtle instances where government has acted
as an encourager and cheerleader of nonprofit sector efforts. In the
early years of the Depression, for example, President Hoover "enlisted
the services of one hundred leaders of business, industry, finance, and

philanthropy . . ." in the ". . . task of mobilizing and coordinating the charitable resources of the country" (Bremner 1988, 139). National administrations made similar efforts during wartime, and in the 1990s, we have witnessed such efforts as the Points of Light program, initiated by President H. W. Bush and the President's Summit on Voluntarism, under President Clinton, aimed at stimulating volunteerism and engaging business in solving social issues.

The early 1980s was a robust period for government and nonprofits to partner in funding the delivery of public services. Beginning with the Reagan administration, however, policy shifted toward cutting back government funding and encouraging private organizations to take up the slack not only in service delivery but in resource support. Still, funded partnership arrangements between government and nonprofits persisted. With the acceleration of federal devolution in the 1990s, however, funding depended on state and local governments' propensity to compensate for federal budget cuts and to exploit the flexibility of new block granting arrangements to expand and diversify contracts with private providers:

> The federal money machine is turned off. This is not just a fiscal event. It shifts the social policy agenda to others—mainly to state governments—when it comes to defining social needs, determining how to meet them, and deciding who should have the responsibility for doing so. Nonprofit organizations have every reason to be very nervous about these budget reductions. (Nathan 1996, 49)

Indeed, at the turn of the 21st century, whether even the states would have the resources to maintain a robust funding relationship with nonprofits is unclear. Not only has the federal budget been further squeezed (Kotlikoff 2004; Steuerle 2003), but the fiscal outlook for the states had worsened (Bowman 2003). Nonetheless, under President George W. Bush, support for nonprofit services has remained strong, while the administration has pushed for contracting and funding nonprofits in social services through its faith-based initiative and in response to natural disasters such as the tsunami in South Asia and hurricane Katrina. The question is whether this pattern is sustainable, given the simultaneous emphasis on cutting taxes and addressing the federal budget deficit.

The complementary lens reveals a very different overlay of nonprofit–government relations than does the supplementary lens. Through the complementary lens, we see one sector engaging the other in order to get the public's business done together. At various times and places in American history, private philanthropy has been seen as a supportive force, helping finance government work. More generally, government has been the driver, looking to nonprofits as means of delivering mainstream public services under mandates of public policy. This orientation was particularly apparent in the post–World War II period when the federal government allocated massive new funding for social services, health care, education, and the arts, but largely resisted creating or expanding government bureaucracies to deliver those services. In terms of theory, the transactions and production costs associated with contracting with, subsidizing, or creating nonprofits were apparently more reasonable than those associated with administering a greatly expanded governmental delivery system.

While efficacious for government, the partnership model, under which government finances and nonprofits deliver services, may have looked more ominous to nonprofits. As noted, this mode of government–nonprofit relations clearly gained prominence in the 1960s and 1970s. And it would appear nonprofits could hardly have resisted its momentum. Given mandates for expanded public services and facing internal fiscal problems, many nonprofits had the choice of joining the parade or being swept aside:

> As demands for social services burgeoned with the mobilization and social ferment in American cities in the 1960s, traditional agencies experienced pressures from within and without to expand their activities. . . . Federal funding . . . pushed up revenues throughout the sector. . . . The growth of government funding clearly bailed out many financially troubled traditional agencies. . . . With these public funds, agencies enter into a new relationship to government. Agencies which for decades had relied on private contributions or small government subsidies were now primarily dependent on government funds. . . . The traditional agencies had now become instrumentalities of government funding, expanding beyond niches supported by private funds. (Smith and Lipsky 1993, 58–60)

As noted, the momentum of the complementary relationship between government and nonprofits is slowing in the early 21st century because of constrictions in government funding. However, at least two countertrends should be noted. First, in the social services, the George W. Bush administration has sought to expand the scope of complementary relationships to faith-based organizations that previously would not have qualified for government funding (Chaves 2002) and to independent and parochial schools through school voucher programs (Stewart et al. 2002). While these initiatives tend to spread funding among more nonprofits rather than add significant government resources, they represent interesting extensions of the complementary relationship.

Second, government has moved to support nonprofit services in a variety of ways through the tax system (Gronbjerg and Salamon 2002), which, as previously observed, could be considered an indirect form of government partnership with nonprofit organizations.

History through the Adversarial Lens

As nonprofit organizations became more dependent on government funding in the 1960s and 1970s, the nature of the relationship between government and nonprofits changed in other ways as well:

> Historically, government purchased services from charitable organizations and attached few strings beyond those common to many other service purchasers. Today governments contract for whole programs, and even create providers where they otherwise do not exist. There is more contracting today than ever before, and the terms of contracting are more demanding. If in the past government went to the private sector for limited services, today its purchasing power is such that it is often in a position to shape the sorts of services offered by private providers. (Smith and Lipsky 1993, 9–10)

Thus, public funding has been accompanied by greater governmental control and regulation of nonprofits. Some of this regulation derived from failures similar to those that occurred in the profitmaking marketplace:

> During the 1950s, standards of care in some of the traditional service areas started to come under criticism . . . for example . . . systems of adoption placement dependent upon sectarian community agencies. . . . Social welfare advocates attacked the larger traditional agencies for neglecting the needs of the poor and racial and ethnic minorities. Meanwhile, government officials exerted greater regulatory oversight over private social programs, especially on public safety and staffing issues. (Smith and Lipsky 1993, 53)

Another reaction took place in the arts, where government officials sought to censor artistic endeavor and restrict funding for controversial projects:

> Funding issues ceded center stage to ideological concerns after George Bush came to office in 1989. Controversies over funding for photographic exhibits by Robert Mapplethorpe and Andres

Serrano revived in more vitriolic terms the questions of censorship, state control, and ideology that had first emerged in the 1930s. (McCarthy 1994, 21)

While government oversight, regulation, and control of nonprofit sector services grew considerably in the mid-20th century in the United States, it too has long historical roots. The earliest manifestations of government control of nonprofits predate the republic and center on the debate concerning the very existence of nonprofits as corporate entities. In colonial times, the status of nonprofits was unclear. Recall that Harvard College was governed by boards composed of ministers and public officials (Hall 1992). In the early days of the republic, especially prior to the resolution of the Dartmouth College case (see below), government–nonprofit relations differed by state, depending on the state's position on the issue of incorporation of private organizations:

In the South, a forcefully expressed body of anticorporate doctrine began to emerge, largely under the tutelage of Thomas Jefferson. Although favoring the freedom of individuals to associate for common purposes, Jefferson worried that such groups, if incorporated and empowered to hold property, would become the basis for new kinds of tyranny ... he believed that all [organizations]— governmental and nongovernmental—should be restricted in their powers and privileges. (Hall 1992, 22–23)

A crucial turning point was the Dartmouth College case, which

... involved New Hampshire's efforts to take over Dartmouth College. When Jeffersonians took control of the legislature in 1816, they reorganized the college, changed its name, and replaced its twelve member self-perpetuating board with twenty-one gubernatorially appointed trustees and a board of twenty-five legislatively appointed overseers, who enjoyed veto power over the trustees. The president of the college was required to report annually to the governor on its management, and the governor and his council were empowered to inspect the college every five years and report on its condition to the legislature. (Hall 1992, 28–29)

In 1819, in the Supreme Court, Dartmouth College ultimately won its case against the state of New Hampshire to retain control on the grounds that the college's charter constituted a contract between trustees and donors that could not be violated without contravening the Constitution. This set the precedent that has allowed nonprofit corporations in the United States to maintain their corporate integrity without threat of arbitrary governmental intervention.

Still, government regulation of nonprofits continued to evolve. For example, at the time of the Civil War, the U.S. Freedmen's Bureau attempted to discourage duplication in the efforts of voluntary societies devoted to the needs of freed slaves. Several states established state charity boards ". . . to inspect, report upon, and make recommendations for improving public welfare institutions and such private ones as received state assistance" (Bremner 1988, 91).

National emergencies sometimes required unusually heavy control of nonprofits by government. Just prior to World War II, the Neutrality Act of 1939 required "voluntary agencies which wished to engage in civilian war relief in belligerent countries to register with and submit monthly reports to the Department of State" (Bremner 1988, 158). And during World War II, the Roosevelt administration established the War Relief Control Board:

> The board now had the power to control all solicitations for voluntary war relief. . . . It had power to license and withdraw licenses from war relief agencies and, in the interest of economy and efficiency, to eliminate or merge organizations. The board scheduled the various national fund appeals and prevented competing campaigns during the periods set aside for the Red Cross National War Fund, United Jewish Appeal, and War Bond drives. The staff of the Control Board sharply scrutinized overhead costs and made reasonable economy of operation a requirement for continued licensing. (Bremner 1988, 159–60)

In the 1970s, charitable solicitation gained prominence as an issue for state and local governmental regulation:

> Just as conduct of foundations had seemed to require corrections in the 1960s, so, in the 1970s, according to many state and local officials, the activities of charities that solicited money from the public needed to be brought under closer scrutiny. By the end of the decade, twenty states and numerous county and local governments had adopted laws or ordinances limited charity solicitations to organizations that could prove a sizable proportion of the collection went for charitable purposes rather than for salaries and administrative costs. (Bremner 1988, 190).

As Bremner hints in the above quotation, perhaps the most vociferous efforts at government regulation of nonprofits have been directed toward foundations. Here the issue has been the concentration of private power under nonprofit auspices and the public influence of that power. These concerns were apparent in the Jeffersonian era and became prominent again in the late 19th and early 20th centuries with the blossoming of large industrial enterprises and the concentration of private wealth in the foundations of Carnegie, Rockefeller, Ford, and others. It was no secret that these institutions intended to influence public affairs:

> The new foundations, particularly Russell Sage and Rockefeller, were unusual for not only the broad discretion granted their trustees but also their explicit goals of reforming social, economic, and political life. These lofty ends were to be achieved not by direct political action, but by studying conditions, making findings available to influential citizens, and mobilizing public opinion to bring about change. This relationship between academic experts, influential private parties, and government would become the paradigm of a new kind of political process—one based on policy rather than politics. (Hall 1992, 48)

Although concerns about the power of foundations were expressed in the 1930s and '40s, the issue intensified in the 1950s:

> In April 1952, the Select (Cox) Committee for the House of Representatives began an investigation of "educational and philanthropic foundations and other comparable organizations which are exempt from federal taxation to determine whether they are using their resources for the purposes for which they were established. . . ." (Hall 1992, 68)

This began a series of congressional inquiries into foundations, which picked up steam in the 1960s when foundations such as Field, Ford, and others were becoming particularly active on social issues like voter registration, school decentralization, and urban poverty. Ultimately, the 1969 Tax Reform Act put new restrictions on foundations and other tax exempt organizations, largely to curb undesired behavior, such as low pay-out rates and control of large businesses, that might obscure their charitable purposes:

> The 1969 Tax Reform Act created a large number of new regulations for private foundations, mainly aimed at keeping foundations out of politics, preventing them from controlling large business interests, and making them more open and accountable. (O'Neill 1989, 146)

Government efforts restricting foundations can be seen as part of a wider effort to limit advocacy by nonprofit organizations. As Simon (1987) notes,

> The federal tax code limits the channels through which nonprofits can participate in public affairs activities, here defined as "those activities which seek to study, criticize, inform people about, and modify the actions of government at all levels." (90)

In the 1990s, conservatives in Congress made several attempts to pass the Istook amendment that would have banned lobbying by any nonprofit organization receiving federal funding. This issue too has a historical pedigree. As Bremner (1988) recounts,

> Rules against lobbying by tax-exempt organizations . . . went back to 1934 and had been reiterated in 1954 and strengthened in 1969. Efforts at relaxation of the rules began in the latter year when the American Bar Association . . . charged that the neutrality of the tax laws with respect to lobbying had been upset in favor of business interests against charitable organizations. . . . In addition to the fairness issue advocates of relaxation questioned the constitutionality of the restrictions and charged the Nixon administration used IRS audits to harass groups that criticized or opposed its policies. (194)

Indeed, during the 1970s, the pressure from government to suppress advocacy cut a broad swath, extended to grant making:

> During the Nixon administration the tax-exempt status of civil rights, welfare rights, environmental, and antiwar groups, and public interest law firms received censorious attention from the Internal Revenue Service. In 1974 Alan Pifer, president of the Carnegie Corporation of New York, called the situation "paradoxical": foundations were advised they could engage in activities bearing on public policy development but given to understand that it would be unwise to do so. (Bremner 1988, 191)

Nor was the Nixon administration the last in pressing to restrict nonprofit advocacy prior to the 1990s. In the 1980s, for instance, the Reagan administration worked to exclude advocacy organizations from the Combined Federal Campaign (Bremner 1988). In all, through regulations and restrictions, government seems periodically to attempt to restrict the activities of nonprofits and hold them accountable to the public. At the same time, reciprocal efforts of private interests, through the formation and development of voluntary associations, have held government accountable, influenced the direction of public policy, and ultimately protected the nonprofit sector from government attack. Hall (1992) provides a summary of Tocqueville's prescient and still relevant observations in the early 19th century:

> Tocqueville . . . view[ed] private voluntarism . . . as a fundamental part of a national power system . . . at its core there was, as he observed, "a natural and perhaps a necessary connection" between the civil associations and the political associations through which citizens combined to influence the state. And this connection was of no small significance. First, it was the basis for organizing *political* opposition to the power of elected officials. . . . Second, this connection was the basis for formulating the conceptual agenda on which political opposition necessarily had to be based. Tocqueville's belief that the ability of an organized political opposition to diminish the moral authority of the majority came not from its numerical strength, but from the peculiar relation of political and civil associations, through which "those arguments that are most fitted to act on the majority" are discovered in the hope of ultimately "drawing over the majority to their own side, and then controlling the supreme power in its name." (85–86)

O'Neill (1989) ties these developments back to religious diversity in the colonies and the early republic, leading to the First Amendment to the Constitution as a fundamental pillar of the nonprofit sector in its advocacy role:

> [T]he First Amendment, which deals with freedom of religion, freedom of speech, freedom of assembly, and the right to petition government over grievances, can without exaggeration be seen as the Magna Carta of the nonprofit sector in American life. These First Amendment freedoms guarantee not only to individuals but also to groups the right to assemble, speak out, and proclaim values and beliefs. The independence of the independent sector finds its strongest legal support in the First Amendment, including its religious liberty clause. (30)

Since colonial times, social reformers have pushed government to take action or institute programs in such areas as prison reform, help for the poor and homeless, care of neglected children, opposition to slavery and assistance to freedmen, and improvement of schools. Such activity has extended to the improvement of governance itself. In the context of the settlement house movement of the late 19th and early 20th centuries, Bremner (1988) observes,

> A host of voluntary associations were at work or organizing to strengthen the social framework of democracy and to restore and extend the principles of self-government. (109)

Women's movements have been a very important strand of public policy advocacy:

> A growing number of scholars have set about to analyze the connections between activism of women's groups and government policy in the late nineteenth and early twentieth centuries. . . . They have stressed the relationship between women's voluntary associations and the creation of social services and political programs that in the United States culminated in the New Deal and the welfare state. . . . Women's efforts to establish playgrounds, libraries, and public health programs and their activism in state and local government contributed to the development of federal programs like Social Security and Aid to Dependent Children. . . . Their voluntary associations constituted a link between grassroots women's groups and those women who gained national power and recognition, for example, Frances Perkins, the first female cabinet member. These women were able to build on small, local issues to lay the groundwork for the campaigns for social justice that ultimately shaped national policy. (Robertson 1998, 193)

Overall, social action movements, manifested largely though voluntary organizations, have been aimed at changing public policy across a broad spectrum of issues:

> America from the start has been a hotbed of social, economic, religious, and political reformism. . . . The revolution, the Civil War, Populism, Progressivism, and the New Deal have been among the earlier surges. The years since World War II have seen the eruption of a combination of powerful thrusts of dissent and demands for change. The most notable of these have been the civil rights movement, the anti-Vietnam War movement, the student rebellion, the environmental movement, the consumer protection movement, the women's liberation movement, and the movement for greater responsiveness and accountability of institutions, both government and corporate. (Nielsen 1979, 157)

Bremner (1988) notes that the 1970s was an exceptionally active period for advocacy organizations in the United States:

> The same period that saw government and voluntary service agencies working in closer cooperation also witnessed the rise of a great many advocacy organizations monitoring the performance of government and seeking to influence public policy by lobbying, demonstrations, litigation, and empowerment of beneficiaries of social programs. (203)

While Nielsen characterizes social movement organizations as the "soft" part of the nonprofit sector, he acknowledges that the boundary is fuzzy between this part of the sector and the highly structured "hard" service-oriented part of the sector:

> These distinctions are more clear in concept than in practice. Nonprofit organizations do not break neatly into two distinct segments . . . rather they are arranged as points along a spectrum according to the particular mix of service orientation and reformism which gives each its distinctive personality. (Nielsen 1979, 156)

Still, the distinction is important because in it lies a fundamental tension in the contemporary nonprofit–government relationship: how much should organizations that receive tax benefits or direct governmental support be allowed to influence public policy? Despite the different tax-exemption categories—for example, 501(c)(3) versus 501(c)(4)—the near impossibility of segmenting nonprofits neatly into those which do and do not attempt to influence public policy implies an ongoing tension between government and nonprofits that continues today.

Interestingly, the blurring of nonprofit categories in public policy is mirrored by blurring in the commercial sphere as well, and this has ramifications for the adversarial relationship with government. Looking toward the end of the 20th century and the beginning of the next millennium, Weisbrod (1997) predicted

> the increased fiscal pressure on nonprofits will lead them to generate new, more creative forms of commercial activities, and that these new forms will further blur the distinctions between nonprofit organizations and private firms. In the process, I expect reconsideration of many existing public policies regarding nonprofits: their subsidization and restrictions on their freedom to lobby government; to engage in joint ventures with private firms; and to compete with private firms. I also expect increased pressure from government to require nonprofits to disclose more publicly

their compensation of executives, and I anticipate the applicability of antitrust laws to nonprofits to emerge as a political issue. (547)

The congressional attack on foundations in the 1950s and 1960s galvanized foundations and other parts of the sector into unprecedented collective action, first through exercises of self-study via the Peterson and Filer commissions, and ultimately to the organization of Independent Sector, a comprehensive umbrella organization designed to increase public understanding about the sector and to advocate for its interests at the national level. Thus, instead of continuing to present itself in a fragmentary manner, the sector would for the first time speak as one in addressing public policy. That voice has subsequently addressed major national policy initiatives in the 1980s, 1990s, and early 21st century, affecting the welfare of the sector, including the Reagan budget cuts, federal budget cuts proposed in connection with the 1994 *Contract with America*, changes in the tax code such as above-the-line deductibility of contributions by non-itemizers, the proposed flat tax and reductions in tax rates that would reduce incentives to give, the issue of intermediate sanctions for disciplining nonprofits in violation of federal law, restrictions on lobbying and advocacy by nonprofit organizations, and self-regulation of the sector (U.S. Congress, House Committee on Ways and Means 1995).

The adversarial relationship between the nonprofit sector and the federal government has continued to evolve. For example, concerns about corporate governance stemming from scandals in the corporate sector, which led to the Sarbanes-Oxley legislation to hold top management more responsible for corporate misconduct, have spilled over into discussions about the nonprofit sector. With this in mind, instances of nonprofit malfeasance have led to new congressional hearings and a wide-ranging series of discussions in the nonprofit sector on nonprofit regulation and governance (BoardSource and Independent Sector 2003; *The Nonprofit Quarterly* 2005b). In particular, the Senate Finance Committee has vigorously criticized perceived abuses in the sector, such as excessive compensation for top executives and board members, conflicts of interest, inappropriate uses of donor-advised funds, exploitation of charities as tax shelters, over valuation of noncash contributions, and inappropriate expensing of travel and other costs (see Senate Finance Committee 2004). In response, a broad cross-section of stakeholders in the sector, led by Independent Sector, has collaborated with the Committee to devise a set of recommended practices to help the sector police itself and assure government of the sector's integrity. This emerging working partnership hints of an evolution from an adversarial to a complementary relationship (Independent Sector 2005), reminiscent of self-policing frameworks that govern subsectors such as high education, using mechanisms like peer review and accreditation standards and procedures.

Governments have severely challenged nonprofits at the state and local level in recent years as well, especially in connection with property tax exemptions. In the 1990s, challenges to property tax exemptions have been pursued in many states, including Utah, Colorado, Pennsylvania, New York, New Hampshire, Oregon, Maine, and Wisconsin (Salamon 1997). Moreover, state attorneys general are becoming increasingly active in regulating the fundraising and other practices of charities in their states (*The Nonprofit Quarterly* 2005a). Mirroring its efforts at the national level, the nonprofit sector has also mobilized at the state and local levels, especially through state associations of nonprofit organizations which now exist in three dozen states. In an environment of devolution, these associations were intended to give the nonprofit sector a stronger voice in the local policy process, especially in state capitols. The free-rider tendencies that characterize the large and diverse nonprofit sectors at the state and local levels hamper efforts to mobilize these state associations. However, federal devolution initiatives appear to be the same kind of catalyst for organizing nonprofits at the state level that congressional attacks on foundations in the 1960s were for galvanizing collective action by the sector at the national level.

In sum, the turn of the 21st century has witnessed a return to a national debate on accountability of nonprofit organizations. This debate is driven by various forces, including ongoing concerns about the performance and integrity of nonprofits, fiscal pressures from tax cuts, the war in Iraq and natural disasters such as hurricane Katrina, perceived abuses of tax shelters, and continued questioning of the nature of charitable enterprise and justifications for tax exemption. In this contentious atmosphere, there are also signs, however, that this debate is constructive, with the potential to ameliorate tensions between government and nonprofits while increasing self-scrutiny in the sector. Overall, the adversarial relationship between government and nonprofits will continue to manifest itself strongly at multiple levels, and in various forms, into the foreseeable future.

THE CHANGING SOCIAL CONTRACT

The foregoing discussion suggests that, while each conceptual lens offers substantial insight in every period, different views of the nonprofit sector–government relationship have prevailed at different times. The adversarial lens is especially helpful in understanding the early republic, when public and private spheres of autonomy were first being sorted out, and the mid- to late 20th century, when government sought to redress the balance of power of government and private interests. The supplementary lens helps especially to illuminate the late 19th and early 20th centuries, when private interests asserted themselves in providing for social needs. The complementary lens helps explain the post–World War II era, when government sought to address social needs without unduly expanding bureaucracy.

In each period, there appears to have been an implicit, though dynamic, understanding of the relative roles of government, business, and the nonprofit sector in addressing the overall needs of society. Before the period of rapid industrial growth, the "social contract" divided responsibilities between modest government efforts to provide for social needs and multiple, autonomous private efforts. With massive changes following the Civil War, including industrialization and immigration, the private sector—through new social welfare associations and the underwriting of welfare capitalism by the business sector—assumed new levels of responsibility for collective needs. In the mid-20th century, an American version of the welfare state emerged with government, partnered with nonprofit organizations, providing for public needs, not only in human services but in the arts, education, health, environment, and other fields. While public services vary, these chronological patterns are remarkably similar from field to field over the past three centuries (see O'Neill 1989). However, nothing is permanent about the pattern of intersector relations from era to era:

> Relations between responsibilities assigned the three sectors are neither rigidly defined nor permanently fixed but shift from time to time to meet changing circumstances and needs. (Bremner 1988, 216)

Today, in another sea change, the social contract is implicitly being rewritten. However, through the three lenses of government–nonprofit relations, the new contract appears to be incomplete. The principal emphasis appears again to be supplementary, where government takes a relatively passive, fiscally conservative role in public service provision, and the private and nonprofit sectors are expected to move to the fore with new levels of charitable funding and volunteering. However, unlike a hundred years ago, when new industrial enterprise and private wealth grew rapidly, it is not clear what contemporary economic engines are able or willing to power new private initiatives of requisite strength. Certainly, impressive new industrial enterprises now exist, especially in the technology and communications areas, but these are embedded in a highly competitive international economy that leads them to downsize and shed employees rather than take care of them.

And while corporate titans such as George Soros, Bill Gates, Warren Buffett and Ted Turner have given massive gifts, these have been relatively isolated instances; corporate philanthropy generally is becoming more of an exercise in strategic marketing and employee morale building than corporate social responsibility (Burlingame and Young 1996). While there is massive new private individual and corporate wealth, tax reform policy initiatives, such as simplifying taxes, lowering tax rates, and eliminating the estate tax, threaten to undermine rather than strengthen incentives for charitable giving (see Steinberg 1996). However, the growing number of the "super-rich" in America may yet lead to a critical mass of philanthropists who could breathe new vigor into private initiatives that supplement government provision. Moreover, signs are emerging that government itself will develop further measures to encourage charitable giving, such as the Charity Aid, Recovery, and Empowerment (CARE) Act (Wolverton 2004a).

The complementary lens reveals a limited arena of government–nonprofit partnerships. The numbers and variety of arrangements through which government and nonprofits collaborate are increasing—as government seeks ways to squeeze more out of its limited resource base—but such collaboration is no longer of overriding concern, as government, at least at the federal level and possibly at all levels, removes itself from bottom-line financial responsibility for providing public services. Arguable exceptions to this pattern include the current faith-based initiative of the Bush administration, the growing emphasis on tax incentives to encourage private support of nonprofit activity, and the continued growth of spending on health-related services (see Abramson and Salamon 2005).

Viewed through the adversarial lens, the changing social contract is just as troubling. While extolling the virtues of private, charitable initiatives, government seems more willing now both to question the tax exemptions of nonprofit organizations and to constrain the voices of nonprofits where their advocacy activity becomes too politically sensitive. Thus, while limiting its own resource commitments to social needs, government in some instances hampers the ability of nonprofits to function successfully, both in raising resources and in speaking out for those who may be ill-served under a new regime of limited government responsibility. In contrast, however, IRS scrutiny of nonprofit activity has been substantially constrained in recent years, leading even representatives of the sector itself to call for more resources for IRS oversight (Independent Sector 2005)

While the current changes derive from various political agendas and economic forces, the incompleteness of the pending new social contract may be more a matter of inattention than ill intention. Examining the contemporary scene through the three lenses reveals gaps and inconsistencies that need to be resolved through some holistic concept of what the new contract ought to be. What are the roles of nonprofits and government, absolutely and in relation to one another, and what is the social role of business and private wealth? If nonprofits are to assume new levels of public responsibility, how can the resources be mobilized for them to do so? How can they do so if government limits certain tax incentives that encourage giving (such as income and estate tax rates), questions the legitimacy of nonprofit commercial enterprise, and discourages nonprofits' voice in the public policy arena? And if private wealth is to drive new levels of voluntary initiative, how can that wealth be mobilized? In particular, how can businesses and individuals be encouraged to contribute at a level commensurate with governmental reluctance to allocate greater resources to these challenges directly? Or will we live in a society in which great inequalities of wealth and welfare continue to grow, and social problems such as chronic poverty, homelessness, and differential access to basic human services such as health care and education persist?

Nonprofit organizations appear to be caught up in the middle of this perplexing uncertainty over the pending social contract. Contemporary government policy toward the nonprofit sector is inconsistent, at once encouraging voluntarism and private initiative, and at the same time limiting its resource base and voice in various ways. And the role of the economy's largest and arguably most important sector—business—remains anomalous, again largely due to the absence of an overall concept of the social contract underlying public policy. On one hand, business is reducing its explicitly philanthropic efforts. In addition, segments of the business community object to the expansion of nonprofits into commercial arenas, while parts of the business sector expand into areas of health care, social services, and education that once were the more exclusive domains of nonprofit activity. On the other hand, businesses have discovered that partnership with nonprofits is a lucrative marketing strategy, and employee voluntarism is an efficient means of building morale and maintaining good relations in the communities where they are located. Overall, however, the social role of business remains in flux and is not clearly articulated as part of an overall consensual social arrangement.

Benjamin Franklin was a great social reformer driven by his own holistic concepts of society. According to Hall (1992, 19) he helped establish various

> voluntary associations directed to public benefit. These would eventually include subscription libraries, volunteer fire companies, a hospital, and an academy. (Hall 1992, 19)

Franklin also invented bifocals. He knew the importance of using appropriate lenses to see things clearly at different distances. For government–nonprofit relations and the social contract, Franklin might have prescribed trifocals. We need all three conceptual lenses—supplementary, complementary, and adversarial—to bring the issues into proper focus.

ACKNOWLEDGMENTS

The author would like to thank Robert Wuthnow, Kathleen McCarthy, and Waldemar Nielsen for their comments and suggestions on the first edition of this chapter, Elizabeth Boris, Eugene Steuerle, and Betsy Reid for their overall guidance in framing and refining the discussion, and Gardner Neeley for his assistance in checking citations.

NOTE

1. The Foundation Center, "FC Stats: The Foundation Center's Statistical Information Service." http://www.fdncenter.org/fc_stats.

REFERENCES

Abramson, Alan J., and Lester M. Salamon. 2005. "The Nonprofit Sector and the Federal Budget: Fiscal Year 2006 and Beyond." Nonprofit Sector Research Fund, Working Paper Series. Washington, DC: The Aspen Institute.

Anheier, Helmut K. 2005. *Nonprofit Organizations: Theory, Management, and Policy*. London and New York: Routledge.

BoardSource and Independent Sector. 2003. "The Sarbanes-Oxley Act and Implications for Nonprofit Organizations." Washington, DC: BoardSource and Independent Sector.

Ben-Ner, Avner. 1986. "Nonprofit Organizations: Why Do They Exist in a Market Economy?" In *The Economics of Nonprofit Institutions*, edited by Susan Rose-Ackerman (94–113). New York: Oxford University Press.

Bowman, Woods. 2003. "Fiscal Crisis in the States: Its Impact on Nonprofit Organizations and the People They Serve." Washington, DC: The Nonprofit Sector Research Fund of the Aspen Institute.

Bremner, Robert H. 1988. *American Philanthropy*, 2nd ed. Chicago: University of Chicago Press.

Buchanan, James M., and Gordon Tullock. 1962. *The Calculus of Consent*. Ann Arbor: University of Michigan Press.

Burlingame, Dwight F., and Dennis R. Young. 1996. *Corporate Philanthropy at the Crossroads*. Indianapolis: Indiana University Press.

Chaves, Mark. 2002. "Religious Congregations." In *The State of Nonprofit America*, edited by Lester M. Salamon (275–98). Washington, DC: The Brookings Institution.

Chaves, Mark, Laura Stephens, and Joseph Galaskiewicz. 2004. "Does Government Funding Suppress Nonprofits' Political Activity?" *American Sociological Review* 69(April): 292–316.

Coase, Ronald H. 1988. *The Firm, the Market, and the Law*. Chicago: University of Chicago Press.

Cohen, Rick. 2004. "State Officials Are Trying to Hinder Fund Raising by Advocacy Charities." *The Chronicle of Philanthropy* 16(18).

Douglas, James. 1987. "Political Theories of Nonprofit Organizations." In *The Nonprofit Sector: A Research Handbook*, edited by Walter W. Powell (43–54). New Haven: Yale University Press.

Evans, Peter B., Dietrich Rueschemeyer, and Theda Skocpol. 1985. *Bringing the State Back In*. Cambridge: Cambridge University Press.

Farris, Anne, Richard P. Nathan, and David J. Wright. 2004. *The Expanding Administrative Presidency: George W. Bush and the Faith-Based Initiative*. Albany, NY: Nelson A. Rockefeller Institute of Government.

Ferris, James M. 1993. "The Double-Edged Sword of Social Service Contracting: Public Accountability versus Nonprofit Autonomy." *Nonprofit Management and Leadership* 3(4): 363–76.

Formicola, Jo Renee, Mary C. Segers, and Paul Weber. 2003. *Faith-Based Initiatives and the Bush Administration*. New York: Rowman & Littlefield Publishers, Inc.

Gronbjerg, Kirsten A. 1997. "Transaction Costs in Social Services Contracting: Lessons from the U.S.A." In *The Contract Culture in Public Services*, edited by Jeremy Kendall (99–118). London: Ashgate Publishing Limited.

Gronbjerg, Kirsten, and Lester M. Salamon. 2002. "Devolution, Marketization, and the Changing Shape of Government–Nonprofit Relations." In *The State of Nonprofit America*, edited by Lester M. Salamon (447–70). Washington, DC: The Brookings Institution.

Hall, Peter Dobkin. 1992. *Inventing the Nonprofit Sector*. Baltimore: The Johns Hopkins University Press.

———. 1994. "Historical Perspectives on Nonprofit Organizations." In *The Jossey-Bass Handbook of Nonprofit Leadership and Management*, edited by Robert D. Herman and Associates (3–43). San Francisco: Jossey Bass Publishers.

Hansmann, Henry, 1980. "The Role of Nonprofit Enterprise." *Yale Law Journal* 89(3): 835–901.

Independent Sector. 2005a. "Advocacy Rights Threatened by Affordable Housing Legislation." Washington, DC: Independent Sector. http://www.independentsector.org/programs/gr/housingadvocacy.html.

———. 2005b. *Panel on the Nonprofit Sector: Strengthening Transparency, Governance, Accountability of Charitable Organizations*. Washington, DC: Independent Sector.

Jensen, Brennan, Leak Kerkman, and Cassie J. Moore. 2005. "Pay Raises for Charity Leaders Keep Pace with Inflation." *The Chronicle of Philanthropy* 17(24).

Kotlikoff, Laurence. 2004. "Apres Bush . . . Le Deluge?" *The Milken Institute Review* (June): 17–25.

Kramer, Ralph M. 1981. *Voluntary Agencies in the Welfare State*. Berkeley: University of California Press.

Lohmann, Roger. 1992. *The Commons*. San Francisco: Jossey-Bass.

McCarthy, Kathleen D. 1994. "Twentieth Century Cultural Patronage." In *Alternative Futures: Challenging Designs for Arts Philanthropy*, edited by Andrew Patner (1–22). Washington, DC: Grantmakers in the Arts.

McCarthy, Kathleen D. 1997. "Women, Politics, Philanthropy: Some Historical Origins of the Welfare State." In *The Liberal Persuasion: Arthur J. Schlesinger, Jr. and the Challenge of the American Past*, edited by John Patrick Diggins (142–50). Princeton: Princeton University Press.

Najam, Adil. 2000. "The Four-C's of Third Sector-Government Relations: Cooperation, Confrontation, Complementarity, and Co-optation." *Nonprofit Management and Leadership* 10(4): 375–96.

Nathan, Richard P. 1996. "The 'Nonprofitization Movement' as a Form of Devolution." In *Capacity for Change?* edited by Dwight F. Burlingame, William A. Diaz, Warren F. Ilchman, and associates (23–55). Indianapolis: Indiana University Center on Philanthropy.

Nielsen, Waldemar A. 1979. *The Endangered Sector*. New York: Columbia University Press.

Niskanen, William A. 1971. *Bureaucracy and Representative Government*. Chicago: Aldine-Atherton.

The Nonprofit Quarterly, editors. 2005a. "Attorneys General and Nonprofits." *The Nonprofit Quarterly* 12(Special Issue): 44–48.

———. 2005b. "A Survey of Proposals for the Further Regulation of Nonprofits." *The Nonprofit Quarterly* 12(Special Issue): 30–37.

Odendahl, Teresa. 2005. "Antiterrorism Policies Hurt Philanthropy." *The Chronicle of Philanthropy* 17(7).

Olson, Mancur. 1965. *The Logic of Collective Action*. Cambridge: Harvard University Press.

O'Neill, Michael. 1989. *The Third America*. San Francisco: Jossey-Bass.

Powell, Walter W., and Paul J. DiMaggio, eds. 1991. *The New Institutionalism in Organizational Analysis*. Chicago: University of Chicago Press.

Reisch, Michael, and David Sommerfeld. 2003. "Welfare Reform and the Future of Nonprofit Organizations." *Nonprofit Management and Leadership* 14(1): 19–46.

Robertson, Nancy M. 1998. "Kindness or Justice? Women's Associations and the Politics of Race and History." In *Private Action and the Public Good*, edited by Walter W. Powell and Elisabeth S. Clemens (193–205). New Haven: Yale University Press.

Salamon, Lester M. 1987. "Partners in Public Service: The Scope and Theory of Government-Nonprofit Relations." In *The Nonprofit Sector: A Research Handbook*, edited by Walter W. Powell (99–117). New Haven: Yale University Press.

———. 1995. *Partners in Public Service*. Baltimore: Johns Hopkins University Press.

———. 1997. *Holding the Center*. New York: Nathan Cummings Foundation.

Schwinn, Elizabeth. 2001. "Charity's Advocacy Work Under Fire in Complaint." *The Chronicle of Philanthropy* 13(19).

Senate Finance Committee. 2004. "Staff Discussion Draft." Washington, DC: United States Congress.

Simon, John G. 1987. "The Tax Treatment of Nonprofit Organizations: A Review of Federal and State Policies." In *The Nonprofit Sector: A Research Handbook*, edited by Walter W. Powell (67–98). New Haven: Yale University Press.

Smith, David Horton. 1997a. "Grassroots Associations Are Important: Some Theory and a Review of the Impact Literature." *Nonprofit and Voluntary Sector Quarterly* 26(3): 269–306.

———.1997b. "The International History of Grassroots Associations." *International Journal of Comparative Sociology* 27:3–4.

Smith, Steven Rathgeb. 2002. "Social Services." In *The State of Nonprofit America*, edited by Lester M. Salamon (149–86). Washington DC: Brookings Institution Press.

Smith, Steven Rathgeb, and Michael Lipsky. 1993. *Nonprofit for Hire*. Cambridge: Harvard University Press.

Steinberg, Richard. 1996. "Can Individual Donations Replace Cutbacks in Federal Social Welfare Spending?" In *Capacity for Change?* edited by Dwight F. Burlingame, William A. Diaz, Warren F. Ilchman, and associates (57–79). Indianapolis: Indiana University Center on Philanthropy.

———. 1997. "Competition in Contracted Markets." In *The Contract Culture in Public Services*, edited by Jeremy Kendall (161–79). London: Ashgate Publishing Limited.

Steuerle, C. Eugene. 2003. "The Incredible Shrinking Budget for Working Families and Children." *National Budget Issues* No. 1. Washington, DC: The Urban Institute. http://www.urban.org/urlprint.cfm?ID = 8688.

Strom, Stephanie. 2005. "Nonprofit Groups Question Motive for Federal Actions." *The New York Times*, March 31, p. A10.

Stewart, Donald M., Pearl Rock Kane, and Lisa Scruggs. 2002. "Education and Training." In *The State of Nonprofit America*, edited by Lester M. Salamon (107–148). Washington, DC: Brookings Institution Press.

Tiebout, Charles. 1956. "A Pure Theory of Public Expenditure" *Journal of Political Economy* 64(October): 416–24.

U.S. Congress, House Committee on Ways and Means. 1995. "Contract with America: Overview: Hearings before the Committee on Ways and Means." Washington, DC: U.S. Government Print Office.

Weisbrod, Burton A. 1977. *The Voluntary Nonprofit Sector*. Lexington: D.C. Heath and Company.

———. 1997. "The Future of the Nonprofit Sector: Its Entwining with Private Enterprise and Government." *Journal of Policy Analysis and Management* 16(4): 541–55.

Williams, Grant. 2005. "Tax Agency Offers Guidance to Disaster-Relief Charities." *Chronicle of Philanthropy* 16(19).

Wolverton, Brad. 2004a. "Charity Measure Gets New Life in Congress" *The Chronicle of Philanthropy* 16(11).

———. 2004b. "Rethinking Charity Rules." *The Chronicle of Philanthropy* 16(19).

Young, Dennis R. 1983. *If Not for Profit, For What?* Lexington: D.C. Heath and Company.

———. 2000. "Alternative Models of Government–Nonprofit Relations: Theoretical and International Perspectives." *Nonprofit and Voluntary Sector Quarterly* 29(1): 149–72.

2

MEETING SOCIAL NEEDS: COMPARING INDEPENDENT SECTOR AND GOVERNMENT RESOURCES

C. Eugene Steuerle and
Virginia A. Hodgkinson

The role of the nonprofit sector is often compared with the government's role, in no small part because both sectors provide social
benefits to the public. Comparisons between nonprofits and government are also invoked in political debates over whether government
is too large, whether nonprofit organizations should assume greater
responsibility for tackling public problems, or whether nonprofit organizations are failing to separate their political efforts from their charitable, religious, or other nonprofit missions. Closely related to those
political debates is the question of whether growth in government
tends to displace the nonprofit sector, or vice versa.

Addressing these issues requires understanding the resources for
meeting social needs that are available in the nonprofit sector relative

to government. Our focus often will be on nonprofit "charities" that qualify under section 501(c)(3) of the Internal Revenue Code for a tax deduction because they are devoted to religious, educational, charitable, scientific, cultural, health, and similar purposes, and sometimes on the "independent sector"—charities plus civic leagues and organizations operated exclusively to promote social welfare under section 501(c)(4). The nonprofit sector also includes nonprofit organizations such as cemeteries, labor unions, clubs, and other mutual benefit societies.

Social needs here refers to such social welfare functions as health, welfare, and education that both nonprofit organizations and the government have traditionally supported. In the not very distant past, government spent only small proportions of its revenue on social welfare. Today, the majority of public expenditures fall into this category. In recent decades, the percentage of total government spending directed toward social welfare rose as spending on the "physical" side of government—defense, highways, energy, buildings—declined in relative importance (figure 2.1). Defense itself has declined from about 60 percent of federal spending in the mid-1950s to around 20 percent today. Of course, that percentage can only decline so far, and it has witnessed several cycles that included increases in spending for wars such as in Iraq.

Over time, government has dramatically influenced the character of the independent sector. Some debates have focused on greater "devolution" of welfare and health care (Medicaid) responsibilities to the states, others on a stronger federal role, such as for hurricane relief or drug benefits for the elderly. A glance into history quickly reveals that devolution of service responsibilities to the nonprofit sector—whether from federal or state governments—has been occurring for decades. A driving force behind many recent changes in the size and scope of the nonprofit sector has been the use of charities and nonprofit institutions as intermediaries or contractors in providing the services government finances.

In focusing on resources, we do not pretend to provide more than a statistical snapshot of the complex picture of the relative roles of government and nonprofits. Government enforces order and contracts while nonprofit organizations provide individuals and communities with a voice and a means for participation. Those and many other important activities cannot be measured adequately by a simple focus on measures of resources such as budget outlays, contributions, or volunteer time. Nonetheless, examining trends in resources reveals much about how much the public relies on these sectors to meet a range of different social needs, how priorities have changed over time (often by subsector), and the degree to which the two sectors exert

Figure 2.1. Trends in Federal Spending

Federal public assistance spending as a percentage of GDP

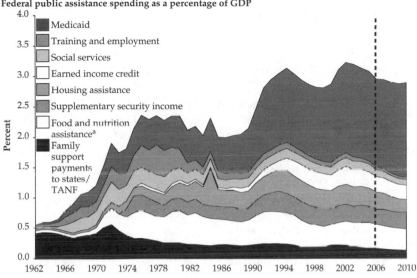

Composition of the federal budget

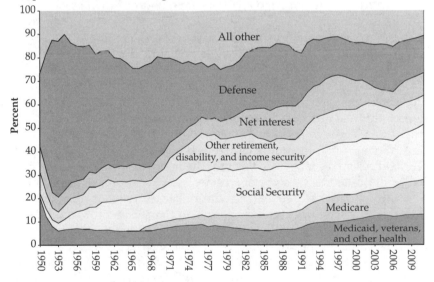

Source: Budget of the US Government, Fiscal Year 2007.
[a] Includes food stamps, child nutrition, WIC, and CSFP.

control over the delivery of social services. By comparing the resources government and nonprofits provide, we can also roughly assess how much their activities complement or substitute for each other.

THE INEVITABLE INADEQUACY OF BOTH SECTORS

Any discussion of resources must recognize that both the nonprofit and the government sectors face limits on their ability to satisfy social needs. Economic scarcity is unavoidable; needs are infinite, but the resources available to satisfy those needs are not. No single nonprofit organization, group of organizations, or government agency can prevent all death, suffering, and pain, or educate each one of us to our full potential. Moreover, nonprofit organizations and the government are merely two institutional means through which individuals act to address a variety of social needs. Despite all the power of institutions, individual efforts at being good parents, neighbors, spouses, friends—and yes, citizens of the state and participants in nonprofit efforts—form the base on which a "civil society" is built.

As noted above, this chapter explores the capacity—measured in terms of physical and budgetary resources—of nonprofits and the government to meet social needs. It is not a philosophical essay on the attributes of a good society. Nonetheless, only by considering the total scope of what we do can we place in perspective the activities of government and the independent sector, and their relationship to each other.

What we accomplish through government and nonprofits is moderate when compared to what we accomplish as individuals, in our households and our workplaces. Why is this important to our inquiry? It is at home and at work that we spend and make use of most of our time, money, and physical resources. Hundreds of billions of dollars' worth of resources may flow through the nonprofit and public sectors, but as important as those resources are, they are small relative to the economy at large. Moreover, the sum of measured economic activity includes only activities involving formal exchanges in the marketplace. Thus, the resource snapshot we present is limited to those formal exchanges, plus some adjustments for volunteer activity.

That the activities of nonprofits and the government are embedded in a larger web of economic and other activities has an important implication. When government expands, it is at least as likely to divert resources from the household and business sectors as it is from the nonprofit sector. Why? There is simply greater room for substitution from sectors with the most resources. Similarly, when the nonprofit sector expands, it often substitutes for activities undertaken in the home or by businesses instead of government. For example, as formal schooling and child-care arrangements have expanded, government and the nonprofit sector have increased their efforts simultaneously. They together substituted for labor that otherwise might have been employed in private business or in home-provided education and child care.

A corollary is that if substitution can take place elsewhere, then the nonprofit sector and government often complement rather than substitute for each other. Expanded or changing government services may create a demand for more nonprofit organizations to act as intermediaries, and conversely, a larger independent sector may demand more government services.

Nonprofit organizations may alternate between complementing and substituting for what government does, depending upon the social needs to be met. Government programs may displace private assistance for old age, for instance, or they may expand the need for new types of organizational assistance to the retired by encouraging more of the population to drop out of the workforce at younger ages, even while improved health means people are living longer and longer.[1]

In any event, we should expect the size of the nonprofit sector or government—whether measured by income produced, assets, workers, or other attributes—to change over time not only relative to each other but also relative to the business and household sectors. The relative "size" will vary in no small part with the efficacy with which nonprofits and government help achieve various goals, including those of greater equity and well-being for parts of the population. Large swings in the relative importance of the independent and government sectors can come about through an expansion of defense needs or of government contracts to nonprofits, through tax revolts, or through the transformation of large nonprofits into profit-making institutions. There is, therefore, no basis for a simplistic view that an ever-growing or ever-declining government or nonprofit sector is somehow good or bad. Swings in relative size may represent either gains or losses to society but are not inherently bad or good because there is no unchanging ideal size for these sectors.

Constraints on Both Sectors

If the challenges of meeting infinite needs with finite resources were not enough, government and nonprofits also face significant constraints on their ability to collect and use resources. Government does not obtain its resources in the same way as nonprofit organizations. Individuals make relatively few contributions to government (although there are exceptions, as in the case of purchases of war bonds and volunteering in public schools). It may appear that government raises resources more easily than do nonprofits because of its legal power to tax. Yet the ability to tax is limited because taxation exacts a variety of costs. The most visible cost is that taxes reduce the income that people and businesses have to spend. Less visible but equally important is the fact that taxes are costly to administer and enforce, and also distort people's economic decisions about working and saving.

The need to treat individuals fairly—which is essential when compulsory forces of the state are at play—can also have the unintended consequence of discouraging experimentation and limiting flexibility in government programs. Norms of fair taxation and equitable distribution of benefits tend to push government toward uniform treatment of citizens in equal situations. But that may also make it administratively difficult to respond to the particular needs of individuals (Douglas 1987; Steuerle et al. 1998).

In contrast, the nonprofit sector often can better respond to individual situations, but seldom in any uniform manner.[2] Such responses depend upon the nature of the organization and the cohesion of community (Wolpert 1993). People often express their generosity through a community or church or other voluntary or citizen association in which they are involved, leaving aside other communities and groups that may have equal or greater needs. The definition of community and church is at once both inclusive (it encourages identity and mission) and exclusive (it excludes those who do not belong and ignores issues to which the organizational mission is not directed). Nonprofit organizations often do not have the time and resources to worry about standards such as equal treatment, so they select on the basis of membership or geography (see, for instance, Printz 1997). Similarly, even when individuals give beyond the immediate family, it is usually to relatives and friends. In 2000, for instance, 52 percent of respondents in a national survey indicated that their household gave an average of $2,137 (4.7 percent of average household income) to assist relatives, friends, and strangers who did not live with them, compared with an average household charitable contribution of $1,620 (3.1 percent of average household income) for the same respondents (Toppe, Kirsch, and Jacobel 2001).

MAJOR FINDINGS

With that background, we now provide some data on the size, capacity, and employment of the nonprofit sector, often comparing it with the government sector or with wider measures of economic output. We start with two caveats. First, one should avoid the temptation to project the future based on the recent past. Some trends we will discuss are sustainable, some are not, and some measures themselves are affected by the interaction between government and the nonprofit sector, especially when the former pays the latter to carry out its functions.

Second, one should not confuse statistical measures of resources with "importance." Resources such as revenues often are counted twice. For example, one dollar of government spending through a contract with the nonprofit sector may result in only one dollar of output to the economy, despite being counted in both sectors' revenues and expenditures.

By the same token, measures of resources can understate the impact of the activities of government and nonprofits. Regardless of size, the presence of a well-functioning government allows individuals to act without fear of repression or anarchy and with trust that legal obligations will be fulfilled. Nonprofits can provide unity within diversity, enhance goodwill in society, and encourage a "civil society," in which social interaction more easily transpires among individuals with their government. Some measures of resources are also incomplete; for example, there is no easy way to account for the added output that is made possible when individuals work for nonprofits at below-market wages.

With those cautionary notes, the following broad conclusions can be drawn about the resources of the independent sector.

The Nonprofit Sector in Relation to the Economy

The nonprofit sector is a large part of the American economy:

- It produces close to 6 percent of national income (excluding the value of labor of volunteers).
- It owns about 5 percent of private sector net worth.
- It employs over 9 percent of the labor force (excluding volunteers).

Figure 2.2 displays these three measures of the size of the nonprofit sector and relates them to other sectors of the economy. As might be expected, the nonprofit sector is much smaller than the business sector, which dominates the production of goods and services. When calculations of output are made, they reflect mainly where production occurs, not who finances it. Thus, federal, state, and local government production in figure 2.2 is much lower than the taxes government collected or expenditures made, which are more than one-third of personal income. Of course, government makes both direct transfers through programs that involve very little outright production, such as Social Security, and indirect transfers by purchasing services, such as health care, from other sectors credited with production. Over the past few

Figure 2.2. The Nonprofit Sector in the U.S. Economy (percent)

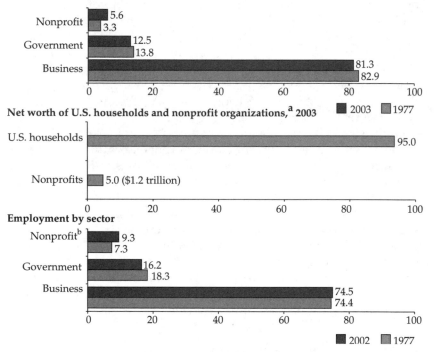

National income by sector

Nonprofit 5.6 / 3.3
Government 12.5 / 13.8
Business 81.3 / 82.9

■ 2003 ▢ 1977

Net worth of U.S. households and nonprofit organizations,[a] 2003

U.S. households 95.0
Nonprofits 5.0 ($1.2 trillion)

Employment by sector

Nonprofit[b] 9.3 / 7.3
Government 16.2 / 18.3
Business 74.5 / 74.4

■ 2002 ▢ 1977

Sources: The Urban Institute, 2005; Board of Governors of the Federal Reserve System, Flow of Funds Accounts of the United States, L.100 and L.100.a, 2005; Bureau of Economic Analysis, NIPA Table 1.13, August 2005.
[a] Excludes net worth of organizations not reporting to government—mainly churches and organizations with less than $25,000 in annual receipts. Measures of assets and liabilities are not calculated in precisely the same way for nonprofits as part of the household sector and for nonprofits standing alone.
[b] Includes full- and part-time nonfarm employment for the nonprofit sector.

decades, government has increasingly spent larger shares of its expenditures and revenues on transfers and produced less within the formal government sector itself.

The nonprofit sector now holds about 5 percent of the combined net worth of U.S. households and nonprofit organizations (business assets are included in household net worth and, therefore, are not counted separately).[3] There are many valuation problems that on net probably cause that estimate to be low; for instance, the nonprofit sector totals shown in figure 2.2 exclude the assets of churches and some small organizations.

Employment by the nonprofit sector, including volunteers, is about 9.3 percent of total employment in the United States. That figure, which has grown over the past few decades, is higher than the sector's share of gross national product (GNP), at least partly because of how national income is measured. It values the output of many services according to consumers pay or what is paid to workers, lenders, and owners. Consider a child-care center in which paid workers might earn less than they could in other jobs. As one consequence, charges for the services of the center will also be lower than they might otherwise be. In effect, the value of the below-market wages accrues to the children and families using the center. But that value will not be counted in national income.[4] The services of a child care working making $5,000 a year who could make $20,000 elsewhere will be counted as $5,000, not $20,000. However, the case should not be overstated. There is some evidence that workers in nonprofit hospitals and private higher education earn as much and sometimes more by working within the nonprofit sector (Leete 2001).

Relative Size of Monetary Contributions to Nonprofits

Although the charitable sector is economically important, charitable contributions are a small share of total income and are dwarfed by the government's social welfare spending. The charitable sector receives about 2 percent of personal income as contributions, about one-twelfth of the government's social welfare spending.

Figure 2.3 shows that charitable contributions are (and, for some time, have been) about 2 percent, perhaps a little less, of personal income. That can be contrasted to social welfare spending supported

Figure 2.3. Government Social Welfare Spending and Charitable Contributions (1965–2004)

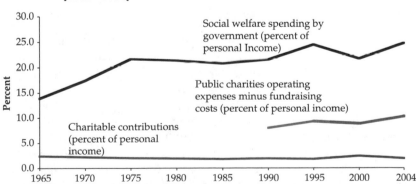

Sources: The Urban Institute 2005. Based on data from the Social Security Administration 2002 Statistical Supplement, Table 3.A3, the Bureau of Economic Analysis NIPA Table 2.1, Giving USA (2004), and the NCCS Core File Public Charities, 1989–2003.

by government at all levels, which has been in excess of 20 percent of personal income since the early 1970s and was close to 25 percent at the beginning of the 21st century. By far, the largest part of that spending is on retirement assistance and health care (social insurance) for the near elderly and elderly, followed by education and public aid.

Outright charitable giving of money has always been moderate relative to households' total monetary resources and assets and relative to the economy's output. For better or worse, that is one reason why government has stepped in to provide many social welfare benefits. Some argue that relying on government distorts behavior and reduces welfare because of the costs associated with enforced taxation and other government actions. Others, however, argue that only government can raise adequate revenues and ensure people who would otherwise ride free—that is, benefit from others' efforts without sharing the cost—pay their "fair share."

No matter who is right, individuals have shown more willingness pay higher taxes than to contribute voluntarily out of their own pockets. That calls into question the notion that nonprofits could take on all social welfare roles if they had to rely upon private contributions. It might be nice to hope that voluntary effort could rise to that level—a very few individuals do give a substantial portion of their income to charity—but no historical precedent for such widespread generosity exists, no matter how much the nation's various religions and mores might espouse the values associated with giving. It is highly doubtful, therefore, that the nonprofit sector could, in the foreseeable future, rely on voluntary giving to take over all or even most social welfare functions, such as providing health care or minimum cash benefits to the elderly, universal education for the young, or widespread opportunity for college attendance.

Growth in Public Welfare Spending

Public social welfare spending, which affects much of the independent sector, has grown rapidly in the postwar period. Between 1960 and today, the share of personal income devoted to public sector social welfare spending nearly doubled, rising from about one-eighth of gross domestic product (GDP) to one-quarter (figure 2.3).

Especially worth noting is the large and significant growth in social welfare spending between the mid-1960s and mid-1970s. Indeed, almost one-third of the federal government's growth in domestic spending over its history, measured relative to the size of the economy, occurred during Richard Nixon's presidency (Steuerle et al. 1998). Public social welfare spending relative to national income leveled off from the mid-1970s to the late 1980s. It resumed its growth in the late 1980s and early 1990s, leveled out, perhaps declined in the late 1990s, and then grew again from 2000 to 2005—with much of the trend due to cycles in the growth of health care spending. Much of that growth at the federal level was accomplished without increases in average tax rates. Peace dividends and the corresponding decline in defense's share of the budget often allowed these shifts toward social welfare spending (see figure 2.1).

Of course, within each period, the story is more complex. At the end of the 20th century, a stalemate between a Republican Congress and a Democratic president led to little expensive new legislation. Revenues increased with a stock market bubble, defense spending continued to decline, and health care spending was temporarily restrained. At the beginning of the 21st century, each of these items reversed. While revenues declined with the stock market bust, a small recession, and a tax cut, spending on war, health care, and almost every domestic spending category increased as a percentage of GDP. It was an unusual and unsustainable period when taxes went down and almost every major spending category went up as a percentage of GDP. By 2005, much larger deficits loomed. With the beginning of the baby boom retirement, this period appeared to mark the end of that free-spending-and-tax-cutting era and the search for more structural reforms.

No peace dividend was available to state and local governments, but throughout much of the post–World War II period, growth in domestic and social welfare spending exceeded the economy's real growth rate. These governments also suffered from the revenue boom-bust-recovery accompanying the late 20th century stock market bubble and 2001 recession, but they recovered in subsequent years. They also continued to face significant liabilities and problems due to the aging of the population, especially in health care.

In the earlier post–World War II period, some state and local growth may have been induced by federal matching grant formulas, which might lead one to speculate that state and local growth in welfare spending could slow in the future if enough federal matching grants are converted into block grants. As Steuerle and Mermin (1997) note, devolution of "welfare" to the states (the conversion of welfare from Aid to Families with Dependent Children [AFDC] to Temporary Assistance for Needy Families [TANF]) initially increased federalization of the financing of cash welfare; that is, the federal government has taken on a bigger share of the total financing. The incentives for states to spend additional money are reduced when matching grants are replaced with block grants, since the state then bears 100 percent rather than only a fraction of the cost of additional spending.[5]

The conversion from AFDC to TANF initially involved a boost in federal funding during a period of both economic expansion and declining welfare rolls. By 2005, there was a trend toward lower state spending on cash welfare as a percentage of personal income and as a percentage of state revenue. In health care, the story is more complex. Under Medicaid and a related health support program for children (S-CHIP), sharing formulas with the federal government so far has meant large and rising portions of state budgets and personal income spent on health care (see also chapters 3 and 5).

Constancy of Private Giving

In contrast to rising public social welfare spending, private contributions have been almost constant as a percentage of personal income. The share of income given to health organizations appears to have declined slightly over the past 20 years, and religious institutions have claimed a declining income share for a longer period of time. More recently, rates of giving among higher-income individuals have fallen.

In 2004, charitable giving stood at 1.9 percent of personal income, slightly below its post-1964 average of 2.1 percent (Giving USA 2005). One needs to be careful here, as there are problems of overreporting and underreporting contributions on tax returns and surveys. Further, changes in survey techniques or audit practices of the Internal Revenue Service (IRS) could produce different types of error over time. Still, the rate of giving today is probably below the levels witnessed in the 1960s and early 1970s.

Individuals, rather than organizations, make most donations (figure 2.4). When one adds up all sources of private contributions from 1989 to 2003, the annual rate of growth in real (inflation adjusted) private contributions equals 3.9 percent (figure 2.5). Giving, however, has shifted among subsectors. Over the same period, private giving to health services increased by only about 2.5 percent per year; thus, its share of the total declined. Contributions to human services, too, have grown more slowly than the total.

Giving by high-income taxpayers follows its own cycle. While the gifts of a few people can dominate this giving (e.g., when a billionaire decides to give sizable shares of his wealth away before death) (see table 2.1), at least one thing is clear. High-income taxpayers' share of total income increased dramatically from 1979 to 2003, reaching a peak during the stock market bubble at the end of the 20th century, but by 2003, still well above its 1979 level. At the same time, this group has experienced many changes in tax law, including lower marginal tax rates (tax rates applying to the last dollars of income). The top tax rate mainly declined over that period, but there were some ups and downs. It dropped from 70 to 50 percent in 1981, to 28 or 33 percent in 1988, back up to about 41 percent from 1993 to 2000, and then fell again to

Figure 2.4. Philanthropic Giving by Source, 2004 (percent)

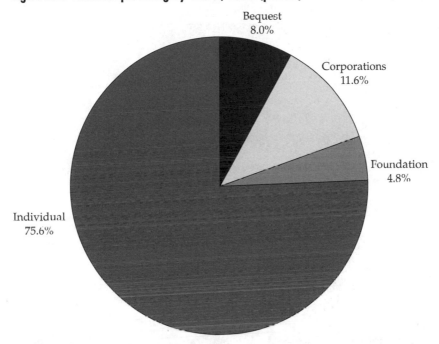

Source: Giving USA (2005).

about 35 percent through legislation passed between 2001 and 2003 (see chapter 3).

Despite modest recent declines in the rate of giving for the population as a whole, giving shows a relative constancy that is surprising in two respects. First, the decline in tax rates significantly increased the net cost of charitable giving, leading many analysts to expect a sharp drop in private giving (see chapter 4). Second, if government spending on social needs displaces private charity, one might have expected the substantial increase in public spending described above to have dis-placed more private giving than it appears to have displaced.

One needs to be cautious when interpreting data from any particular period. Individuals adjust their behavior only gradually in response to a change such as an increase in the after-tax cost of giving. For example, when tax rates change, individuals may take years to fully respond. Randolph (1995) finds that people are much more likely to adjust their giving up or down in response to what they believe are temporary changes in their tax rates, and hence in the after-tax cost of giving, than to changes they believe are permanent.[6]

Apart from changes in tax rates, a further complication is that the greater inequality in income after the mid-1970s has been attributed

Figure 2.5. Annual Rates of Change in Private Contributions, 1989–2004

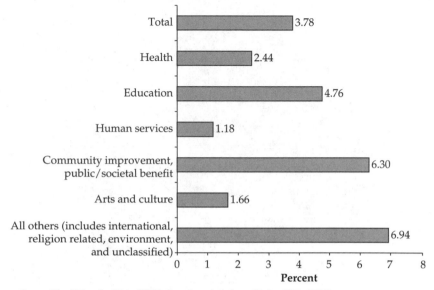

Source: The Urban Institute (2005). Based on data from Giving USA (2005).

to a variety of factors that may separately influence giving. These include an increase in the number of two-earner couples where both spouses earn significant incomes and, at very high incomes, the appearance of a "winner-take-all" economy with large rewards to those who obtain, through publicity or other means, status or unique monopoly-like positions (Frank and Cook 1995).

Moreover, almost all previous estimates of the determinants of giving examine only the supply side of giving, but the demand for giving—for example, the needs of churches and research and educational institutions—may be more invariant (inelastic in economic terms). In effect, if taxpayers respond to lower incentives by giving less, then the demand for giving becomes more pressing and offsets some of the decline in giving that might otherwise occur. That would explain how changes in incentives might shift who gives, while resulting in little or no changes in total giving. Kent Smetters was the first to develop a formal model that predicts behaviors consistent with some patterns we currently see in the data.[7]

Even before the increase in the after-tax cost of giving and shifts in the distribution of income that took place in the 1980s, giving dropped a bit from the higher level in the mid-1960s. Yet it bears repeating that any drop was remarkably small when compared with a growth in social welfare spending of more than 10 percent of personal income between the mid-1960s and the late 1990s.

Table 2.1. Giving and Income of the Top 1 Percent of Taxpayers, 1979–2003

Variable	1979	1984	1991	1994	1999	2003
Number of returns	872,011	950,556	1,033,202	1,063,600	1,155,386	1,207,478
Income	143,712	258,091	437,722	530,634	980,019	858,170
Charitable deductions	4,848	8,555	13,054	17,332	37,337	33,855
Giving as a percentage of income	3.57	3.09	3.10	3.26	3.81	3.95
Top 1 percent share of total income	9.39	11.22	12.75	13.65	19.32	17.21
Top 1 percent share of charitable deductions	14.01	14.14	14.12	16.57	31.44	26.12

Sources: Auten, Clotfelter, and Schmalbeck (2000). Updated January 2006 by Gerald Auten.

Notes: Income is a constant-law definition of adjusted gross income (AGI) based on post-TRA86 law: all long-term capital gains and deductions for IRAs, SECA taxes, health insurance, and moving expenses are added back for years in which they are deductible against AGI. Contributions are the deductions claimed, which include carryovers from prior years and exclude nondeductible contributions in excess of percentage limitations. Dollar amounts are mean values.

If one were to use those data to make a naive case that government social welfare spending displaces charitable giving, it would imply at most that $100 of additional social welfare spending displaces $3 of charitable giving in aggregate. That is consistent with Richard Steinberg's (1996) estimate that the rate of displacement ranges from 1 to 10 percent. A problem with any aggregate estimate, of course, is that the effect may vary over time, by subsector, and even by charity. If government activity displaces one type of charitable effort but enhances another, for instance, the combined effect may show up as no net displacement of total charitable activity even though each separable change may be substantial. People may give less to the poor elderly today, for instance, because there are relatively fewer of them, but they may still give equal shares of their income to poorer classes of society.

Volunteer Time

Contributions of volunteer time significantly leverage the resources available to the independent sector. When contributions of time and foregone earnings are added, donations made to the independent sector are much larger than they appear when only monetary contributions are taken into account.

Volunteer effort is expended largely, if not entirely, in the independent sector portion of the nonprofit sector. Although estimation requires a variety of simplifying assumptions, the value of volunteer effort has been measured as close to the value of cash contributions. As of 1998, the worth of volunteer effort to the independent sector was estimated $124.7 billion, while total giving of money or assets was $131.1 billion, about four-fifths of which is individual giving outside of bequests (Weitzman et al. 2002).[8] One can see this also by comparing the number of paid employees in the independent sector with the number of full-time equivalent volunteers (table 2.2).

Table 2.2. Employment and Volunteering in the Independent Sector

	1977	1987	1992	1997	2002
Paid employees, full- and part-time (percent of labor force)	5.3	5.7	6.6	6.4	6.4
Volunteers, full-time employee equivalent (percent of labor force)	3.1	3.9	4.0	4.7[a]	4.5

Source: Weitzman et al. 2002; Economic Census, 1977, 1987, 1992, 1997, and 2002; Current Population Survey; *Monthly Labor Review,* August 2003 and authors estimates; Giving and Volunteering in the United States, 2001, Independent Sector.

[a] Figure is for 1998.

Note: The volunteer data for 1977–1992, 1997, and 2002 are based on several different sources and may not be completely comparable throughout all years.

Assigning a value to volunteer time poses problems of potential underestimation and overestimation. The time contribution of volunteers is estimated based upon the average wage rate, which is then applied to unpaid volunteer time. Yet many who work for pay in the nonprofit sector also contribute, but in the form of lower wages instead of unpaid time. For example, teachers in many religiously affiliated schools are paid much less than teachers in public schools, but there is no evidence on average that they are less qualified or produce less quality or quantity of educational services. The difference between what nonprofit employees are paid and what they could earn in the private sector is not counted in the estimates of the value of volunteers.[9] On the other hand, many volunteers and low-paid workers in the nonprofit sector enjoy the camaraderie, fellowship, and autonomy associated with their work and may spend part of their time in mutual support rather than, say, production of charitable goods and services. If a food bank uses twice as many volunteers as it would paid staff, for instance, the valuation of their output—and, indeed, whether to count their mutual support as output—is difficult.

That is not to imply that the government does not receive volunteer support. In fact, it typically receives about 17 percent of total volunteer time, primarily from efforts made in conjunction with public schools (Weitzman et al. 2002). Still, the vast bulk of volunteer effort—about 70 percent—is transmitted through nonprofits.

Several issues pertaining to volunteers are not examined in depth here.[10] For example, surveys have noted that certain groups in the population (blacks, young people, Hispanics, other ethnic groups, low-income individuals, and older people) are not asked to volunteer at the same rates as more affluent whites age 25 to 64, thus resulting in lower rates of volunteering among those demographic groups (Toppe et al. 2001).

Comparability of the Two Sectors in Terms of Spending

Measuring resources in terms of total spending brings the relative size of the nonprofit sector and government closer together.

- Spending by nonprofits and government appears more comparable in size, in part because the nonprofit sector is a major contractor or intermediary for both government and for other parts of the private sector.
- Due partly to this contracting, employment by the nonprofit sector as a share of total employment increased by almost exactly the amount as the decline in government employment from 1977 to 2002.

As opposed to spending financed by private contributions, total spending by the nonprofit sector comes somewhat closer in size to that of government (see figure 2.3). What accounts for this magnified measure of nonprofit sector activity? The nonprofit sector does not finance its activities exclusively from charitable donations of money and time; it also charges for many of its activities, especially in such areas as health and education. In turn, the government often works through other sectors to achieve its goals. Perhaps the best examples of government money flowing through nonprofit organizations are grants for higher education and payments for Medicare and Medicaid services.

One of the more interesting and telling recent institutional changes has been the growth in nonprofit sector employment, from 7.3 to 9.3 percent of all employment between 1977 and 2002 (see figure 2.2). Interestingly, that growth is almost of the same order of magnitude as the decline in the government sector from 18.3 to 16.2 percent of all employment. Many government officials like to proclaim their success at reducing the government's size and point in particular to the decline in the direct employment of individuals. In truth, what has occurred in large part is that the government has increasingly paid others to perform the work it finances.

That outsourcing or contracting for services has not simply been a result of "reinvention" of government—for example, finding private garbage disposal companies to displace public employees. Instead, the large growth in government spending for services, particularly health care, that were always "contracted out" dominates the figures. Doctors, nurses, and others increasingly have had to view themselves as service providers for government insurance payments. Their work for the government has in a sense displaced others' work in areas where government activity has declined—defense being the most obvious example for the postwar period, despite increases during the second Iraqi conflict.

Table 2.3 shows the size and growth of revenue sources for various subsectors of operating charities from 1989 to 2003. As the table shows, program service revenues dominate, particularly in health, but also in education and human services. By contrast, program service revenues are relatively unimportant in international affairs, religion-related programs (that report to the IRS), environment, community improvement, and arts and culture. The table also shows that government grants have grown at about the pace of private sector contributions. (Note that private sector contributions do not exactly match charitable contributions reported by individuals, as the former are what charities report on their tax returns and may include contributions not qualifying as charitable.)[11]

It is hard to determine how much these past trends and relationships will continue. The amount that can be produced under government

Table 2.3. Government Grants, Private Sector Contributions, and Program Service Revenues by Nonprofit Subsector (Billions of 2005 Dollars)

Subsector	Government grants, 1989	Private sector contributions, 1989	Program service revenues, 1989	Government grants, 2003	Private sector contributions, 2003	Program service revenues, 2003	Change from 1989 to 2003 (%)		
							Government grants	Private sector contributions	Program service revenues
Total	46.2	58.6	368.5	94.6	125.1	715.8	105	113	94
Arts and culture	2.1	5.0	3.8	3.2	10.0	6.9	50	102	80
Community improvement, public and societal benefit	4.1	10.5	6.8	11.3	21.8	13.5	176	107	98
Education and research	14.8	17.1	64.0	21.2	29.9	97.4	43	75	52
Environment and animals	0.4	1.4	0.8	1.4	4.9	2.2	229	263	191
Health	7.3	10.8	266.9	20.8	22.7	522.5	183	111	96
Human services	15.7	9.5	24.3	54.3	24.2	70.2	118	153	189
International affairs	1.5	2.1	1.1	2.1	7.0	0.8	36	234	−25
Religion related	0.3	2.2	0.8	0.3	4.6	2.3	11	111	187
Addendum: GDP							48		

Sources: IRS Statistics of Income Division Exempt Organizations Sample for Public Charities, 1989; The Urban Institute, NCCS National Nonprofit Research Database, Special 2003 Research Version; Bureau of Economic Analysis, NIPA Table 1.1.6, August 2005.

contracts must, by its nature, be less than the total production in the economy, so the government's growth rate depends upon the economy's growth rate, the corresponding growth rate in government revenues, and what share of those revenues government attempts to spend by contracting out.

Diversity of the Nonprofit Sector

Measures of resources available to all nonprofit organizations disguise the great diversity of the nonprofit sector. The nonprofit sector is diverse and heterogeneous; its characteristics are sometimes hidden when viewing figures on aggregate size, which are dominated by the large health and education subsectors and, within each subsector, by the largest organizations.

There are a variety of ways of disaggregating to get a better view of the nonprofit sector's component parts. Figure 2.6 shows the distribution revenues by different subsectors of the charitable sector. In 2003, health services garnered about 56 percent of revenues, including assets and public support. The international and foreign affairs subsector is relatively small relative to health or higher education, but it has the greatest relative dependence on private sector contributions (table 2.3).

These numbers warn researchers to be careful to distinguish claims made about the entire sector from claims about its various subsectors. What may happen to social services, for example, may be very different from what happens to health services.

Trends in government and nonprofit spending on health care demonstrate the different ways in which shifts in government policy can affect nonprofit organizations. Rising government payments for health have dominated growth in overall spending on health care, and, under current law, Medicare and Medicaid growth are projected to continue to dominate almost all uses of new government revenues (see chapter 3 and Steuerle 2003). But those payments go not only to nonprofit organizations (mainly nonprofit hospitals), but also to profit-making organizations such as doctors' offices. Government recently has put larger shares of its money into doctor services not provided in hospital settings (e.g., by putting money into Medicare Part B, rather than Hospital Insurance or Medicare Part A). Congress has been motivated both to save money (by discouraging expensive hospital stays) and to play games to meet arbitrary budget accounting standard rules. (Medicare hospital payments are paid out of a fund that depends on Social Security Health Insurance taxes and thus is threatened with a shortfall, while Medicare outpatient care is paid mainly out of general revenues, for which no shortfall is measured; switching the location of payment thus allows the trust fund to appear to be more in balance.)

Figure 2.6. Share of Total Funds for Selected Public Charity Subsectors (percent)

Share of total public charity revenues, 1989

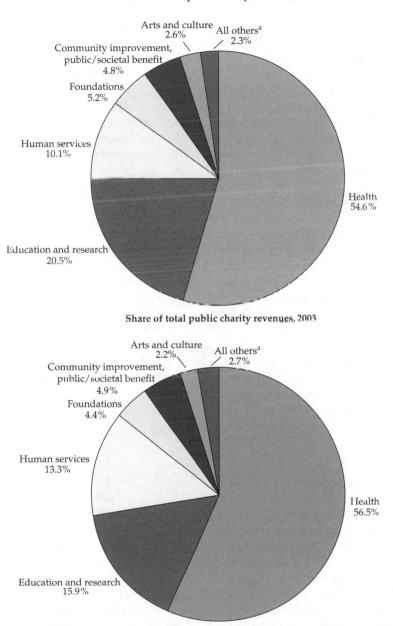

Share of total public charity revenues, 2003

Source: IRS Statistics of Income Division Exempt Organizations Sample for Public Charities, 1989 and 2003.

[a] Includes international affairs, religion related, spiritual develoment, environment and animals, as well as unclassified organizations.

One consequence of a simple shift to outpatient care, even if the same services and personnel are involved, is that fewer funds flow through nonprofit hospitals and more funds flow directly through doctors' offices. Another shift can occur when hospitals move to profit-making status. It does not follow, however, that there will be a net loss in "charitable" activity simply because fewer receipts flow through nonprofit hospitals. Such activity could fall if the charitable contributions or free care given to low-income patients decline when services move out of hospitals into doctors' offices or other settings defined as "profit-making" (for a discussion of the conversion of hospitals from nonprofit to profit-making organizations, see chapter 8).

Finally, nonprofit organizations exhibit a phenomenon common to modern organizational life: the dominance of larger organizations. Among public charities that report information about their finances and operations on the IRS Form 990, organizations with more than $10 million in expenses make up a mere 4.2 percent of total organizations but have 80 percent of the total assets and 82 percent of the expenses. Correspondingly, 79 percent of organizations (those with less than $500,000 in expenses) have only 2.5 percent of the total expenses and 4.5 percent of the total assets (see figure I.1 in the introduction). Indeed, much nonprofit activity may not be reflected here at all. If a group of volunteers organizes and has little or no financing, it may not even establish itself as a legal organization, much less file with any government agency. Note also that subsectors with larger institutions, such as the higher education and hospital sectors, show up with smaller percentages of total organizations than their percentages of total expenses and assets, whereas other subsectors, such as arts and culture or human services, have a much larger share of total organizations than they do of total expenses or assets (see figure I.2).

Conclusion

In recent decades, the government and the nonprofit sectors have often acted more as complements than substitutes in many of activities. When one considers the relatively constant rate of charitable contributions out of personal income and the growth in shares of total output and employment by the nonprofit sector—all of which occurred during a period of rising social welfare spending by government—it is hard to argue that increased government activity has displaced private nonprofit activity in any aggregate sense. Indeed, one of the most important aspects of the modern relationship between the sectors is the way that the government has increasingly turned to the nonprofit sector to serve as an intermediary or contractor in providing many public services.

The combined response to disasters like Hurricane Katrina, whether successful or not, provides only one example of their complementary efforts.

Although more government social welfare spending does not appear to have crowded out nonprofit activity in the aggregate, there has nonetheless been both significant displacement and reorientation of specific nonprofit activities over time. For example, the very large government role in programs for the elderly probably has displaced much cash or housing assistance to the old that would have otherwise occurred. The movement toward foster care helped reduce the use of orphanages. Large government subsidies for health care have probably reduced charitable contributions to hospitals. The expansion of public schooling coincided historically with the decline in the percentage of children attending religious schools. In each of those cases, of course, other factors are also at play, but, clearly, when government meets a need, private efforts often shift focus within the independent sector.

In many cases, what is observed can be better described as "replacement" rather than "displacement." That conclusion follows from the observed constancy of the share of personal income contributed to charitable activities. A constant share of income earmarked for contributions implies that the activities such contributions finance will rise at about the rate of growth in the economy. Since the nature of charitable activities is changing, the further implication is that the public will "replace" support for some "old" activities with support for "new" efforts. In other words, a decrease in the rate of giving to one activity often means an increase in rate of giving to another.

Returning to a point made at the start of this chapter, one should not be surprised to find that what looks like a "crowding out" of nonprofits may represent shifting priorities. Recall that theoretically there is no a priori reason why government activity should necessarily displace nonprofit activity. The two sectors merely satisfy a range of social needs, acting as both substitutes and complements in fulfilling those needs. More government spending on education, for instance, could either substitute for private and nonprofit spending or add to the demand for scholarship funds.

To think that all past trends, whether short or long, will continue would be a mistake. For example, the federal government's social welfare budget may continue to grow faster than the economy, but social security and health care are scheduled to garner the lion's share of that growth. If cash assistance in Social Security grows enough, it may displace other government social welfare efforts that use nonprofit organizations as intermediaries. Within health care, there are significant pressures to subsidize almost any organization that will help to control costs, which could over time include or exclude the nonprofit portion of the sector. If there is less emphasis on hospitals and more on out-patient care, contracts may shift more into profit-making settings. The latter movement could also reduce the relative size of nonprofit hospitals simply because more dollars flow directly to doctors.

As another example, devolution of welfare to the states was initially accompanied by significantly larger amounts of money being spent on child care, job search, and transportation services, even while cash assistance was reduced. Those welfare reform shifts may have temporarily expanded different service roles for nonprofits and public institutions alike, both of which might spend more on early childhood care, education, and career counseling.

Each example illustrates a basic theme of this chapter: the growth of the nonprofit sector, no matter how measured, is likely to vary over time relative to the growth in government and the economy. Whether the consequence is positive or negative cannot be determined without a specific examination of each change, a broad concept of social welfare, and an examination of the combined changes in all sectors—nonprofit, government, business, and household.

NOTES

1. By not adjusting age of retirement as people live longer, yet providing higher levels of annual benefits, Social Security and Medicare encourage individuals to retire for close to a decade longer than they did around 1950. That is, the average individual retires about five years earlier and lives about four years longer. This creates a new and different type of demand for services by individuals who are not "old" by traditional standards.

2. Admittedly, government often makes exceptions to a uniformity standard, but only at the cost of inequity and a disgruntled citizenry. For example, queues, which define who is the "next" eligible beneficiary in a precise legal fashion, are used in housing and other programs even though this process is applied arbitrarily.

3. Household net worth also includes the value of government bonds; because of the large value of that debt, the government sector would show up as a negative value if presented under that set of accounts.

4. Similarly, national income accounts exclude the value of all services and goods produced in the home and not sold in the market.

5. These changes in incentives are not examined here in any depth. On the one hand, removing matching grants may make states more efficient in spending their money. With no match, when they spend a dollar, it costs them a dollar. On the other hand, some argue that fear of having too high a tax rate relative to neighboring states creates a "race to the bottom" where states bow out of providing much social welfare. Still another issue is whether any federal minimum—such as the earned income tax credit, food stamps, and Medicaid might provide—might not already deal with many of these interstate equity and efficiency issues.

6. The expected difference in response is similar to how people might be expected to act if, say, Macy's announced it would offer a 50 percent discount on all purchases made between Christmas and New Year's but offered no discount thereafter. Shoppers could be expected to respond to this "once in a lifetime" chance by shifting purchases of goods they might have made in future years to the "sale year." That would magnify their spending in the sale year and cut into sales in subsequent years. Economists believe that people will respond to temporary changes in tax incentives in a similar fashion. For example, if people have tax rates that in one year are likely to be unusually high, their tax accountants would advise them to shift charitable contributions and other deductions to that year. That produces an exaggerated increase in charitable contributions in the year in which the tax rate is temporarily high (and hence when the net cost of giving is temporarily low).

7. Kent Smetters, "A Free-Rider Explanation of the Charitable Giving Puzzles of the 1980s and an Application to Fundamental Tax Reform," unpublished paper. Another study using cross-section data but a different econometric technique also argues that taxpayer responses to tax rates are much lower than many former studies tended to find (see Bradley and McClelland 1998).

8. Note that these figures relate to the independent sector and are slightly lower than the figures used for employment in the entire nonprofit sector shown in figure 2.1.

9. Note that national income accounting traditionally leaves out most non-market valuation. Adding in the value of volunteer time logically leads to adding in the value of volunteer effort that comes in the form of lower pay, which logically leads to adding in the value of all nonmarket production. Such comprehensive estimation has never been performed.

10. Longer-term forces are not investigated here. It is worth noting, however, how larger societal factors can affect the availability of volunteers. For example, not too long ago, a nation of farmers had limited time and resources to gather in formal volunteer activity even though interfamily cooperation may have been intensive. With urbanization came many demands, often met by generous increases in the volunteer efforts of women who were not always working at paid jobs, but worked instead through the home and volunteer associations. (See, for example, McCarthy 1982 and Scott 1992.) On the other hand, recent decades have seen a greater concentration of work, especially by women, in the formal marketplace and a lesser concentration of work among the many near-elderly and elderly who now typically retire almost two decades before their expected year of death.

11. Congregations and aligned organizations are not required to report to the IRS, although some do. Government grants are as reported on Form 990. Finally, note that private contributions include corporate and corporate foundation gifts.

REFERENCES

Auten, Gerald E., Charles Clotfelter, and Richard Schmalbeck. 2000. "Taxes and Philanthropy Among the Wealthy." In *Does Atlas Shrug? The Economic Consequences of Taxing the Rich*, edited by Joel Slemrod. Cambridge: Harvard University Press.

Bradley, Ralph, and Robert McClelland. 1998. "A Robust Estimation of the Effects of Taxation on Charitable Contributions." Washington, DC: Bureau of Labor Statistics.

Douglas, James. 1987. "Political Theories of Nonprofit Organization." In *The Nonprofit Sector: A Research Handbook*, edited by Walter Powell (43–54). New Haven: Yale University Press.

Frank, Robert H., and Philip J. Cook. 1995. *The Winner-Take-All Society*. New York: Free Press.

Giving USA. 2005. "Giving USA." Center on Philanthropy at Indiana University. New York: Giving USA Foundation.

Leete, Laura. 2001. "Whither the Nonprofit Wage Differential? Estimates from the 1990 Census." *Journal of Labor Economics* 19(1): 136–70.

McCarthy, Kathleen. 1982. *Noblesse Oblige*. Chicago: University of Chicago Press.

Printz, Toby J. 1997. "Services and Capacity of Faith-Based Organizations in the Washington, D.C., Metropolitan Area." Paper presented at the annual meeting of ARNOVA, Indianapolis, Indiana, December 4–6.

Randolph, William. 1995. "Dynamic Income, Progressive Taxes, and the Timing of Charitable Contributions." *Journal of Political Economy* 103(4): 709–38.

Scott, Ann Firor. 1992. *Natural Allies: Women's Associations in American History*. Urbana: University of Illinois Press.

Steinberg, Richard. 1996. "Can Individual Donations Replace Cutbacks in Federal Social Welfare Spending?" In *Capacity for Change: The Nonprofit World in an Age of Devolution*, edited by Dwight F. Burlingame, William A. Diaz, Warren F. Ilchman, and associates (57–79). Indianapolis: Indiana Center on Philanthropy.

Steuerle, C. Eugene, and Gordon Mermin. 1997. "Devolution as Seen from the Budget." Washington, DC: The Urban Institute. *Assessing the New Federalism* Policy Brief A-2.

Steuerle, C. Eugene, Edward N. Gramlich, Hugh Heclo, and Demetra Smith Nightingale. 1998. *The Government We Deserve: Responsive Democracy and Changing Expectations*. Washington, DC: Urban Institute Press.

Steuerle, C. Eugene. 2003. "The Incredible Shrinking Budget for Working Families and Children." *National Budget Issues* No. 1. Washington, DC: Urban Institute Press.

Toppe, Christopher M., Arthur D. Kirsch, and Michel Jocabel. 2001. "Giving and Volunteering in the United States: Findings from a National Survey." Washington, DC: Independent Sector.

Weitzman, Murray, Nadine Jalandoni, Linda Lampkin, and Thomas Pollack. 2002. *The New Nonprofit Almanac and Desk Reference*. San Francisco: Jossey-Bass Publishers.

Wolpert, Julian. 1993. "Patterns of Generosity in America: Who's Holding the Safety Net?" New York: The Twentieth Century Fund Press.

3

FEDERAL SPENDING AND TAX POLICIES: THEIR IMPLICATIONS FOR THE NONPROFIT SECTOR

Alan J. Abramson, Lester M. Salamon, and C. Eugene Steuerle

Government spending and tax policies have a significant impact on the shape and role of the nonprofit sector. Through their spending decisions, state and federal governments affect the scope of societal needs that remain for nonprofit organizations to address. But through their tax and spending decisions, these governments simultaneously affect the resources that nonprofits have available to address these needs. Government decisions affect the level of nonprofit resources because government programs have become an important source of nonprofit revenue and tax policies significantly influence citizen propensities to make charitable contributions.

This chapter examines the impact that federal spending and tax decisions have had on the work of American nonprofit organizations over the past twenty-five years and the likely impact of pending proposals over the next three to five years. As will become clear, the past quarter century has been a period of significant policy change, though the impact of these changes on nonprofit organizations has often been overlooked. By putting these impacts into perspective, this chapter underlines the frequently inadvertent consequences for the nation's nonprofit organizations of decisions often made for completely different reasons.

As reflected in our previous work on this subject (Abramson and Salamon 1986; Abramson, Salamon, and Steuerle 1998; Salamon with Abramson 1981; Salamon and Abramson 1982), several caveats must be borne in mind in interpreting the discussion here:

- First, the focus here is on tax and spending policies only and not on the broader array of impacts that government has on the nonprofit sector through its regulatory, credit, and other programs.
- Second, even among tax and spending policies our focus here is on federal government policies only and not those of state and local governments, though we do track the flow of federal funds through state and local governments and on to nonprofit organizations. One reason for this somewhat confined focus is the absence of comprehensive data on combined state and local spending and its effects on nonprofit organizations. Even to assess the flow of federal support to nonprofit organizations, we have had to develop our own estimates based on detailed scrutiny of program records and other sources.[1] It is worth noting, however, that while state and local social welfare spending increased substantially over the period examined here, the overwhelming majority of this increase (90 percent) went to finance education.[2]
- Third, we use FY 1980 as the "base year" for this analysis even though it was far from the high point of federal spending for many programs of interest to nonprofit organizations. As the year prior to the onset of a significant round of domestic budget cuts in 1981, followed by a series of deficit reduction agreements from 1982 to 1997, 1980 seemed an appropriate basis for comparison, though meaningful budget paring in many budget programs began in advance of this.
- Finally, no independent attempt is made here to assess the changing level of societal needs during the period. Rather, we take the level of need as of our base year as given and measure the extent to which funds are being allocated over time to address these needs. Obviously, if needs decline, reductions in government spending may be justified, whereas if they grow, reductions may be even more problematic.

Although we do not measure the effectiveness of programs or how well resources are matched to needs, it is fairly clear that many needs remain and some have increased over the period we examined. For example, while many improvements in social and economic conditions clearly occurred, the gains for many of the country's disadvantaged populations were limited. For example, as table 3.1 shows, the number of persons living in poverty in the United States increased by 26 percent from 29.3 million in 1980 to 37.0 million in 2004, while the number of children living in poverty increased by 13 percent. Increases also occurred in the elderly population, the number of immigrants, the number of persons without health insurance, and the number of unemployed, although this last number is obviously dependent upon the point in the economic cycle at which it is measured.

FEDERAL SPENDING AND NONPROFIT ORGANIZATIONS, FY 1980–2004

As noted at the outset of this chapter, federal spending decisions affect both the *demand for* nonprofit services and the ability of nonprofits to *supply* these services. The demand effects result from the fact that federal spending affects the level of unmet need in society. For instance, at any given level of need, when federal food stamp spending declines, more needy individuals may turn to nonprofit soup kitchens for assistance. We can refer to these as the *indirect* effects of federal budget decisions on nonprofit organizations.

Because the federal government often finances nonprofit service delivery, however, the same budget cuts that increase the need for nonprofit services can also decrease the ability of these organizations to meet this need. We can refer to these as the *direct* effects of federal budget decisions on nonprofit organizations. Because only a portion of federal spending in most fields flows through nonprofit organizations, the indirect effects are likely to be larger in overall size than the direct effects, but both are important and will be examined here.

To assess these effects, we analyzed federal spending on more than 100 programs in fields where nonprofit organizations are active, such as social services, health, education, income assistance, international development, and the arts. We then analyzed the implications of the resulting spending decisions for the flow of resources to nonprofit organizations through these programs. In this section we examine both of these effects.

Table 3.1. Selected Indicators of Demand for Nonprofit Services, 2004 and 1980 (in millions of persons, except where indicated)

			Change, 2004 vs. 1980	
Program area	1980	2004	n	Percent
Social welfare				
Persons below poverty level[a]	29.3	37	7.7	26
Children below poverty level[b]	11.5	13	1.5	13
Persons 65 and over below poverty level[a]	3.9	3.5	−0.4	−10
Total population[b]	227.7	290.6	62.9	28
Persons 65 and over[c]	25.6	36.3	10.7	42
Persons 85 and over[c]	2.2	4.9	2.7	123
Births to teenagers (thousands)[d]	552.2	415	−137.2	−25
Immigrants (thousands)[e]	531	946	415	78
Education and research				
High school dropouts (thousands)[f]	658	486	−172	−26
Health				
Persons without health insurance[g]	31	45.8	14.8	48
Infant deaths (thousands)[h]	45.5	27.7	−17.8	−39
AIDS deaths (thousands)[i]	12.5	15.8	3.3	26
Income assistance				
Unemployed workers[j]	7.6	8.1	0.5	7
Criminal justice				
Juvenile arrests for drug abuse (thousands)[k]	86.7	133.6	46.9	54
Child abuse cases (thousands)[l]	690.7	906	215.3	31

[a] U.S. Census Bureau. 2005. Poverty Status of People by Family Relationship, Race, and Hispanic Origin: 1959 to 2004. http://www.census.gov/hhes/www/poverty/histpov/hstpov2.html.

[b] U.S. Census Bureau. 2005. Poverty Status of People, by Age, Race, and Hispanic Origin: 1959 to 2004. http://www.census.gov/hhes/www/poverty/histpov/hstpov3.html.

[c] U.S. Census Bureau. 2005. Annual Estimates of the Population by Sex and Five-Year Age Groups for the United States. http://www.census.gov/popest/national/asrh/NC-EST2004-sa.html.

[d] U.S. Centers for Disease Control and Prevention.2005. Number and Percentage of Births to Unmarried Women, All Ages and Women under Age 20 years: United States. http://www.cdc.gov/nchs/data/hestat/prelimbirth04_tables.pdf#04.

[e] U.S. Department of Homeland Security, Office of Immigration Statistics. 2006. *2004 Yearbook of Immigration Statistics*. Washington, DC: U.S. Department of Homeland Security.

[f] U.S. Census Bureau. 2006. Annual High School Dropout Rates of 15 to 24 Year Olds by Sex, Race, Grade, and Hispanic Origin: October 1967 to 2004. http://www.census.gov/population/socdemo/school/TableA-4.xls.

[g] U.S. Census Bureau. 2005. People With or Without Health Insurance Coverage by Selected Characteristics: 2003 and 2004. http://www.census.gov/hhes/www/hlthins/hlthin04/hi04t7.pdf. Data are for 1987 and 2004.

[h] U.S. Centers for Disease Control and Prevention. 2005. Births, Marriages, Divorces, and Deaths: Provisional Data for March 2005. http://www.cdc.gov/nchs/data/nvsr/nvsr54/nvsr54_05.pdf. Initial data for all deaths through 1985.

[i] U.S. Centers for Disease Control and Prevention. 2006. Estimated Numbers of Deaths of Persons with AIDS, by Year of Death and Selected Characteristics, 2000–2004\United States. http://www.cdc.gov/hiv/topics/surveillance/resources/reports/2004report/table7.htm.

[j] U.S. Bureau of Labor Statistics. 2005. Employment and Earnings http://www.bls.gov/cps/home.htm.

[k] U.S. Department of Justice, Federal Bureau of Investigation. 2005. Crime in the United States, 2004. Clarksburg, WV: U.S. Department of Justice, Federal Bureau of Investigation.

[l] U.S. Department of Health and Human Services., Administration on Children, Youth and Families. *Child Maltreatment 2003*, 2005. Data for 1990 and 2004.

Federal Spending and the Need for Nonprofit Services: The "Demand Effect"

As reflected in table 3.2, when expressed in FY 2005 dollars, federal spending on the major federal programs of interest to nonprofit organizations accounted for outlays of $412 billion as of FY 1980.[3] By comparison, total federal expenditures in that year amounted to $1.23 trillion after adjusting for inflation. In other words, approximately one-third of all federal expenditures in FY 1980 went to programs identified here as being especially relevant to nonprofit organizations.

Of this $412 billion in spending, more than half consisted of health care expenditures, chiefly for Medicare and Medicaid, the large federal health finance programs for the elderly and the poor, respectively. Another 20 percent represented income assistance payments, including food stamps, housing vouchers, and welfare aid. Spending for social welfare services and for education and research accounted for another 13 and 10 percent, respectively. Outlays for foreign aid, arts and culture, environment and conservation, and the nonprofit postal subsidy made up the remaining 4 percent.

Aggregate Changes: FY 1980 to FY 2004

Between FY 1980 and FY 2004, overall federal spending on these programs of interest to nonprofits increased rather steadily, from $412.1 billion in FY 1980 to $871.1 billion in FY 2004. Over the 23-year period, FY 1982–2004, inflation-adjusted spending was a cumulative total of $4.2 trillion above what it would have been had FY 1980 levels been maintained (see table 3.2). However, this aggregate picture can be somewhat misleading because it is heavily affected by the inclusion of the two large federal health programs, Medicare and Medicaid, which grew significantly through this period. Outside of Medicare and Medicaid, the cumulative gain was a much smaller $1.1 trillion. And if income assistance, comprised mostly of entitlement programs, is also excluded, the remaining programs experienced a cumulative 23-year gain of only $10.7 billion, or roughly zero percent.

Much of the increase in federal spending outside of Medicare and Medicaid took place, moreover, only in the latter part of the period. Prior to this, federal spending on these programs, after adjusting for inflation, remained below FY 1980 levels. In fact, outside of the major entitlement programs in health and income assistance, federal spending did not return to its FY 1980 level in real dollar terms until FY 1994, as shown in figure 3.1.

Because the country's gross domestic product (GDP) was rising during this period, federal spending on programs of interest to nonprofit

Table 3.2. Federal Spending in Program Areas Where Nonprofits Are Active, FY 1980–2004 (in billions of constant 2005 dollars)

Fiscal Year	All programs		Excluding Medicare and Medicaid		Excluding Medicare, Medicaid, and income assistance		
	Outlays	Change from FY 1980	Change from FY 1980		Change from FY 1980		Federal spending as a percentage of GDP (FY 1980 = 100)
			Amount	Percent	Amount	Percent	
1980	$412.1						100
1982	410.7	–$1.4	–$27.1	–14%	–$28.5	–23%	76
1983	415.7	3.5	–26.6	–13	–33.4	–27	70
1984	420.4	8.2	–27.7	–14	–33.3	–27	65
1985	445.1	32.9	–20.8	–11	–28.7	–23	66
1986	443.3	31.2	–22.4	–11	–31.2	–25	62
1987	443.3	31.2	–25.0	–13	–33.3	–27	58
1988	455.7	43.5	–17.5	–9	–30.9	–25	58
1989	469.0	56.9	–13.3	–7	–29.4	–24	57
1990	494.8	82.6	–3.7	–2	–24.4	–20	58
1991	524.9	112.8	16.3	8	–15.7	–13	64
1992	572.1	159.9	34.9	18	–10.2	–8	65
1993	602.8	190.6	51.7	26	–4.1	–3	67
1994	636.4	224.3	68.0	34	0.2	0	67
1995	665.8	253.6	78.1	39	2.7	2	66
1996	676.0	263.8	75.5	38	1.0	1	63
1997	692.5	280.4	81.5	41	5.4	4	63
1998	689.7	277.6	79.5	40	9.2	7	62
1999	689.4	277.3	87.5	44	15.9	13	63
2000	709.9	297.8	103.3	52	26.6	22	65
2001	746.5	334.4	117.6	59	40.0	33	70
2002	792.5	380.4	147.2	74	56.8	46	76
2003	837.0	424.8	174.6	88	74.4	61	82
2004	871.1	458.9	189.2	95	81.6	67	81
Total	13,704.5	4,225.3	1,120.7	25	10.7	0	66

Source: U.S. Office of Management and Budget. 2005. Budget of the United States Government: Fiscal Year 2006, Historical Tables. Washington, DC: OMB. See also appendix A. GDP = gross domestic product.

organizations outside of health and income assistance slipped steadily during this period as a share of the country's GDP, ending up as of FY 2004 at only 81 percent of its FY 1980 value, as table 3.2 also shows.

Breakdown by Functional Areas

As shown in table 3.3 and figure 3.1, the direction and level of federal spending changes between FY 1980 and FY 2004 varied considerably by program area:

- The *social welfare services* category, which includes the subareas of social services, employment and training, and community development, absorbed the heaviest reductions in federal spending during this period. Spending in these fields remained well below the FY 1980 baseline level of $53.8 billion for much of the 1982–2004 period. In fact, the value of federal spending in this area was a cumulative total of $282 billion lower over the 23 years, FY 1982–2004, than it would have been had FY 1980 spending levels been maintained, although some real increases did finally occur during the latter part of the period. Measured as a share of GDP, in fact, federal spending in this area as of FY 2004 was only 57 percent as great as it was in FY 1980.

  The largest portion of this reduction in social welfare spending came from substantial cuts in federal employment and training program expenditures. As of FY 2004, spending on these programs was 62 percent below what it had been in FY 1980. Significant cuts also occurred in the field of community development. In the social services area spending in real dollars was below FY 1980 levels for much of the FY 1982–2004 period but ended up significantly above the base year by the end of the period. In large part, this increase resulted from increased spending for social services through the Medicaid and Temporary Assistance for Needy Families (formerly Aid to Families with Dependent Children) programs passed in the mid-1990s.
- Federal spending on *education and research* programs grew by 105 percent between FY 1980 and FY 2004.[4] However, this aggregate total disguises important variations in the subcomponents of this field. In particular, spending grew substantially in the fields of elementary and secondary education and research and development. However, it declined substantially for higher education. Measured as a share of GDP, in fact, federal higher education spending as of FY 2004 was less than 60 percent of what it had been in FY 1980. And measured as a share of GDP, overall education and research spending as of FY 2004 was just about where it had been

Table 3.3. Changes in Federal Spending in Program Areas Where Nonprofit Organizations Are Active, FY 1982–2004 vs. FY 1980, by Program Area (in billions of constant 2005 dollars)

Program area	Outlays		Change, FY 2004 vs. FY 1980		Cumulative change, FY 1982–2004 vs. FY 1980 level	FY 2004 outlays as a percent of GDP (FY 1980 = 100)
	FY 1980	FY 2004	Amount	Percent		
Social welfare	$53.8	$63.8	$10.0	19%	−$282.1	57%
Social services	15.7	45.8	30.1	192	191.0	140
Employment and training	21.5	8.1	−13.4	−62	−303.4	18
Community development	16.6	9.9	−6.7	−40	−169.7	29
Education and research	42.9	88.1	45.2	105	126.3	99
Elementary and secondary	14.5	35.0	20.5	142	73.4	116
Higher education	18.5	22.9	4.4	24	−122.9	59
Research and development	9.9	30.3	20.3	205	175.8	147
Health	223.7	518.3	294.6	132	3,246.6	222
Health finance[a]	216.6	494.4	277.8	128	3,177.8	226
Health services	7.2	24.0	16.8	235	68.8	161
Income assistance	75.7	183.3	107.6	142	1,110.0	117
Housing	11.4	37.3	25.9	227	332.2	158
Cash	30.6	84.8	54.2	177	590.4	133
Food	29.2	46.9	17.8	61	176.7	77
Other	4.5	14.2	9.7	215	10.6	164
Foreign aid[b]	11.1	15.3	4.2	37	82.5	66
Arts and culture	1.8	1.7	−0.1	−6	−9.7	45
Environment	1.5	0.4	−1.0	−71	−23.6	14
Other	1.6	0.0	−1.5	−98	−27.7	1
TOTAL	412.1	871.1	458.9	111	4,225.3	141
Total, excluding Medicare and Medicaid	198.2	387.4	189.2	95	1,120.7	95
Total, excluding Medicare, Medicaid, and income assistance	122.5	204.1	81.6	67	10.7	81

Source: U.S. Office of Management and Budget. 2005. *Budget of the United States Government: Fiscal Year 2006, Historical Tables.* See also appendix A.
Note: Excludes federal credit programs.
[a] Excludes Medicare premiums and collections.
[b] Excludes Iraq Relief and Reconstruction Fund.

Figure 3.1. Federal Outlays in Areas of Interest to Nonprofits Excluding Health and Income Assistance, FY 1980–2004

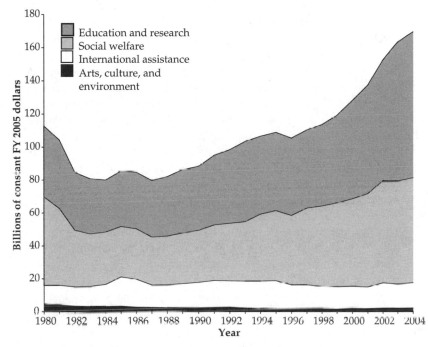

Source: U.S. Office of Management and Budget. 2005. Budget of the United States Government: Fiscal Year 2006, Historical Tables. See also appendix A.

in FY 1980 despite the increases in the elementary and secondary education and research and development fields.

- In contrast to most other areas, federal *health* outlays rose significantly over the FY 1982–2004 period, largely as a result of increased spending for Medicare and Medicaid. By FY 2004, annual health finance outlays were $277.8 billion above FY 1980 levels and absorbed more than twice their former share of GDP. Health service spending also increased substantially over the same period. Taken together, over the 23-year period, cumulative health spending was $3.2 trillion above what it would have been had FY 1980 funding levels been maintained, even after adjusting for inflation.

- Federal spending on *income assistance* also increased during the FY 1982–2004 period, largely as a consequence of automatic expansions triggered by increases in the number of people eligible for assistance under these programs.[5] As of FY 2004, the value of federal spending on housing, cash, food, and other income assistance programs was $107.6 billion, or 142 percent, higher than it had been in FY 1980. Altogether, these programs absorbed $1.1

trillion more in funding over the FY 1982–2004 period than they would have absorbed had FY 1980 spending levels been maintained.

- Spending on *foreign aid programs* also increased during the FY 1982–2004 period. By FY 2004, foreign aid spending was $4.2 billion, or 37 percent, above its FY 1980 level. Even so, this rate of growth lagged behind the growth of U.S. GDP. Measured as a share of GDP, therefore, federal spending on foreign aid as of FY 2004 was only 66 percent of its FY 1980 level.

- Federal spending on *arts and culture* programs fell substantially both absolutely and as a percentage of GDP during this period. Compared with FY 1980, federal spending in this field remained 6 percent lower as of FY 2004. As a share of GDP, federal arts spending as of FY 2004 was only 45 percent of its FY 1980 level.

- In percentage terms, spending on *environment and conservation* programs registered the biggest drop of all program areas between FY 1980 and FY 2004. By FY 2004, real spending for these programs was 71 percent below FY 1980 levels. As a percentage of GDP, environmental spending in FY 2004 was only 14 percent of what it was in FY 1980.[6]

Summary

Federal spending in program areas of concern to nonprofits declined in the early 1980s but subsequently recovered, so that by FY 2004 federal outlays in these areas were 111 percent above FY 1980 levels. However, this overall trend hides the very different spending histories of the various fields. Medicare, Medicaid, and some income assistance programs expanded rapidly throughout much of the FY 1982–2004 period, largely because of rising health costs and, to a lesser extent, legislated changes in federal poverty programs. Excluding these health and income assistance programs, federal spending in the other programs of interest to nonprofits barely budged in inflation-adjusted terms and lost significant ground as a share of GDP. This suggests considerable increased pressures on nonprofit organizations during this period to respond to social and economic needs, especially in areas where federal resources were withdrawn.

Federal Spending and Support for Nonprofit Organizations: The Supply Effect

Changes in overall federal spending during FY 1982–2004 in programs of interest to nonprofits affected not only the need for nonprofit services but also the revenues these organizations received from federal programs and hence their ability to meet this need.

Aggregate Changes: FY 1980–2004

As reported in table 3.4, overall, federal support of private nonprofit organizations grew both in absolute terms and as a share of GDP between FY 1980 and FY 2004.[7] As of FY 2004, federal support to nonprofit organizations was thus 232 percent higher than it was in FY 1980 after adjusting for inflation. Measured as a share of GDP, such support as of FY 2004 was 179 percent of what it had been in FY 1980.

However, these aggregate data mask two strikingly different trends in federal support—one for health and health-related institutions and the other for all other types of nonprofit organizations.

So far as the health institutions are concerned, growth in federal Medicare and Medicaid spending significantly boosted federal support. Between FY 1980 and FY 2004, federal support to nonprofit institutions in the health field more than doubled both absolutely and as a share of GDP.

Outside of the health field, however, federal funding of nonprofit organizations grew much less robustly. In fact, for the first decade or more of this period, such support declined and only recovered in more recent years. By FY 2004, however, support for these other nonprofit organizations stood 95 percent above its FY 1980 level. Even so, measured as a share of GDP, such support was still only 92 percent of its FY 1980 level as of FY 2004.

Breakdown by Program Area

Behind even these broad categories of assistance lie some significant variations by program area, however:

- *Social service organizations*—including agencies that provide day care, counseling, and related services to children, families, the elderly, and others; legal services; and employment and training services—gained a cumulative 23-year total of $52.4 billion in federal support during the FY 1982–2004 period. These organizations sustained significant reductions in federal support during the 1980s and early 1990s. However, expansions in coverage of the Medicaid program coupled with new social service funding made available through the welfare reform legislation passed in 1996 ultimately boosted the income that these organizations receive from federal sources. By FY 2004, therefore, this support

Table 3.4. Estimated Federal Support of Nonprofit Organizations by Type of Organization, FY 1982–2004 vs. FY 1980 (in billions of constant FY 2005 dollars)

Type of organization	Amount		Change, FY 2004 vs. FY 1980		Cumulative change, FY 1982–2004 vs. FY 1980 level	FY 2004 Support as a percent of GDP (FY 1980 = 100)
	FY 1980	FY 2004	Amount	Percent		
Social services	$14.2	$30.0	$15.8	111%	$52.4	102%
Community development	3.4	3.6	0.2	5	−11.0	50
Education and research	11.3	23.7	12.4	109	59.3	104
Elementary and secondary	0.8	2.3	1.5	199	6.0	310
Higher education	5.1	5.5	0.4	8	−35.2	52
Research and development	5.4	15.9	10.4	193	88.4	141
Health	105.8	255.7	150.0	142	1,430.5	234
Health finance	103.4	251.0	147.6	143	1,419.3	240
Health services	2.4	4.7	2.4	101	11.2	97
Foreign aid[a]	1.3	3.1	1.8	134	14.9	113
Arts and culture	0.8	0.8	0.0	−1	−4.3	48
TOTAL	136.8	316.9	180.0	232	1,541.8	179
Total, excluding Medicare and Medicaid[b]	34.6	67.6	33.0	95	134.1	92

Source: U.S. Office of Management and Budget. 2005. Budget of the United States Government: Fiscal Year 2006, Historical Tables. Washington, DC: OMB. See also appendix A.
[a] Excludes Iraq Relief and Reconstruction Fund.
[b] Includes spending on social services funded through Medicaid.

was 111 percent higher than it had been in FY 1980, though it remained barely on the same level as a share of GDP.

- *Nonprofit housing and community development organizations*, by contrast, did not fare as well during this period. These organizations, which are involved in housing, economic development, neighborhood improvement, land acquisition, and historic preservation, suffered significant reductions in federal support during FY 1982–2004, with cumulative losses of $11 billion compared with what they would have received had FY 1980 spending levels been maintained throughout this period. By FY 2004, federal support of community development organizations in real dollars was 5 percent above what it had been in FY 1980, but it accounted for only 50 percent of the share of GDP allocated to these organizations in FY 1980.

- Overall, federal funding of nonprofit *education and research organizations* rose by a cumulative 23-year total of $59.3 billion during FY 1982–2004 compared with what would have been available had FY 1980 spending levels been maintained. However, not all types of nonprofit institutions benefited from this increase. Thus, federal assistance to higher education institutions, outside of student loan and loan guarantee programs, fell by a cumulative total of $35.2 billion during this period. Federal funding of private elementary and secondary schools, which is relatively limited, increased by a cumulative total of $6 billion during this period. By contrast, federal support of private nonprofit research institutions, including private universities, registered substantial increases, rising a significant $88.4 billion during the 23-year period compared with FY 1980 spending levels.

- *Nonprofit health organizations*, as noted above, registered the largest gains in federal support during this period, gaining a cumulative total of $1.4 trillion during the FY 1982–2004 period compared with what they would have received had FY 1980 levels been maintained in real dollar terms. Increased funding of nonprofit hospitals, nursing homes, and other medical providers through the Medicare, Medicaid, and other health finance programs made up the bulk of this increased support. In addition, federal funding of health service providers such as outpatient clinics and social service organizations providing health-related services also rose between FY 1980 and FY 2004.

- *Nonprofit foreign assistance organizations* gained considerable federal support over this period, rising from $1.3 billion in FY 1980 to $3.1 billion in FY 2004. The bulk of this gain came from increased funding of nonprofit contractors from the U.S. Agency for International Development, the largest international assistance program. (See also chapter 11.)

- Federal support of *nonprofit arts and culture organizations*, such as museums, art galleries, symphonies, community arts facilities, and theaters, declined slightly between FY 1980 and FY 2004. Cumulatively, these institutions lost a total of $4.3 billion of federal support over the period.

Summary

In the health, research, social service, foreign aid, and elementary and secondary education fields, federal support of nonprofits registered cumulative increases over the FY 1982–2004 period. However, nonprofits in other fields—community development, higher education, and arts and culture—experienced cumulative 23-year declines over the same period. Because of spending increases in the latter part of the period, however, by FY 2004 federal support of nonprofits was above FY 1980 levels in all areas except community development and arts and culture. Even so, as of FY 2004, the amount of federal support flowing to nonprofits, outside of Medicare and Medicaid, measured as a share of GDP was 8 percent below what it had been in FY 1980.

Not only has the quantity of federal support to nonprofit organizations shifted in significant ways during this period, but so has the form. Most dramatic has been the shift from the use of grants and contracts, which channel assistance directly to nonprofit providers, to the use of voucher-type payments, which channel assistance to nonprofits through the ultimate recipients of services. As of FY 2004, 80 percent of all federal support to nonprofit organizations took the form of such consumer-side subsidies, most of it through the Medicare and Medicaid programs. By contrast, producer-side subsidies constituted the bulk of federal assistance during the 1960s and 1970s.

TAX CHANGES AND CHARITABLE GIVING

Overview: The Connection between Taxes and Giving

Government's impact on the nonprofit sector does not result only from spending policies. Also important are changes in tax policy, and such changes have been extensive in recent years. Tax provisions are important because they affect private giving, an important source of revenue for many nonprofits. As Steuerle and Hodgkinson (chapter 2) reveal, even excluding most religious organizations, which do not have to report, private sector contributions provided more than $140 billion to operating charities in 2003.

Tax rates are important because they influence giving both through the "price" of giving and the income taxpayers have available for gifts. The price of giving is the net, out-of-pocket cost of giving to charity. Generally speaking, the higher the tax rate, the lower the actual price of giving, and hence the greater the incentive to give. Falling tax rates therefore provide less incentive to give. For example, the cost of giving $100 to charity for an individual itemizing deductions and in the 45 percent tax bracket is $55, because the government would have taken $45 of the $100 of the gift anyway if the donor had not chosen to give it away. If the tax rate for this individual falls to 35 percent, however, her cost of making the same $100 gift would rise to $65, because this is the actual amount of spending that the giver would have to forgo to make this gift ($100—$35 in taxes = $65). Conversely, when the tax rate rises, the cost of giving decreases and the incentive to give to charity rises.

Changes in tax policy do not only affect the price of giving, however. They also affect the amount of income people have to spend, which affects the amount they give. One complication in assessing this income effect is that it can be temporary since a reduction in current taxes must be paid for either by cutting government spending or by raising future taxes to pay for current borrowing. Those changes, in turn, have their own income effects that may offset the initial effect.

Also important in shaping the impact of tax changes on charitable giving are expansions and contractions in the income tax base—that is, the share of income subject to taxation. Broadening the base of income subject to tax tends to increase the amount of reported, taxable income against which charitable contributions can be deducted and hence the value of the deduction. It also reduces the number of alternative ways that individuals can avoid tax. Measures that narrow the base and provide new forms of tax breaks have the opposite effect. Moreover, changes in the tax code that add or remove tax deductions other than the charitable deduction can change the relative value of the charitable deduction itself. These changes, too, are therefore relevant to a consideration of the impact of tax policy on charitable giving.

Tax Changes: 1980–2004

As outlined in table 3.5, the 1980–2004 period saw constant revisions of the tax code. Most important for charitable giving, the price of giving was altered as tax rates were first lowered and then raised (though not back to their original levels), and then lowered again. Because net income tax rates were lowered, individuals and corporations had less incentive to give to charity. In addition, a variety of changes were made in such areas as the treatment of gifts of appreciated assets, limits on deductible gifts to foundations, and limits on corporate charitable giving. Some of these changes increased incentives to give; some decreased them. In addition, many tax shelter opportunities were eliminated in the 1980s, making the charitable deduction more attractive as one of the few remaining deductions. However, much base erosion took place after 1988—moving in the opposite direction from base broadening and weakening the relative importance of the charitable deduction. Finally, there were a number of more modest changes, such as the provision and elimination and potential restoration of a charitable deduction for non-itemizers, and changes in the treatment of capital gain property donated to foundations. In the following pages we highlight these changes and their effects.

Economic Recovery Tax Act of 1981

Perhaps the most important of the tax changes affecting charitable giving occurred at the beginning of this period. The Economic Recovery Tax Act of 1981 reduced marginal tax rates by approximately 23 percent between 1981 and the end of 1984. The act introduced indexing tax brackets for inflation after 1984, which automatically prevented tax rates from rising with inflation, as they had over the previous decades. Together these changes dampened incentives to give.

The effect of these individual tax rate reductions on changes in giving is open to some debate. Tax rates had risen dramatically by the end of the 1970s due largely to inflation-related "bracket creep." Thus, whereas the 1981 tax reduction seemed to signal a sharp increase in the price of giving when viewed from the perspective of a single point in time, when viewed with a somewhat longer time horizon they represented for most taxpayers a return to prior levels. The one exception was for the highest-income taxpayers, who did witness a drop in their tax rate from 70 percent in 1980 to 50 percent in 1981 (and lower still in later tax acts, as will be seen).

While inflation-induced bracket creep was eliminated in the 1981 act for years after 1984, moreover, there remained some bracket creep resulting from two factors.[8] First, indexing was provided only for inflation, so real growth in incomes still pushes individuals gradually into higher brackets. Second, the period from the mid-1970s witnessed changes in family structure, such as the growth in the percentage of two-earner families, that pushed numerous families into higher income tax brackets.

The 1981 tax cut also established for the first time a charitable deduction for non-itemizers, thereby increasing their incentive to give. Starting at a very low level in 1982, when only 25 percent of contributions were deductible up to a maximum of $100, this deduction grew until

1986, when 100 percent of charitable contributions were to be deductible with no limit. The 1981 provisions, however, had no allowance for deductions for non-itemizers beyond 1986, and the law was never extended. Because individuals probably lag in response to changes in tax provisions, many economists believe that the full impact of such a deduction, and its ability to increase charitable giving, was probably never fully tested. After all, there was a full deduction for non-itemizers in only one year, 1986.

The 1981 tax act also reduced the incentives for corporate charitable giving. The act significantly increased tax write-offs for depreciation, which allowed many corporations to reduce their taxable income toward zero. A charitable deduction is of little immediate value to a corporation with little or no taxable income. Faster depreciation was later removed but replaced with a lower corporate tax rate, which still reduced corporate incentives to give.

Because of a reduction in the estate tax rate, the 1981 action also made charitable deduction for gifts out of estates less valuable. Changes in spousal inheritance tax also reduced incentives to give. Before 1981, transfers to spouses at death could be taxable; after 1981 spouses inherited estates without tax consequences. In effect, no tax was assessed on the first spouse to die, and it became less important to plan for charitable giving before the death of the first spouse.[9]

Deficit Reduction Act of 1984

The Deficit Reduction Act of 1984 also affected charitable giving, but only slightly. The limit on deductible gifts to private foundations was increased from 20 to 30 percent of income, but limits on giving to charities remained at 50 percent. A new requirement for qualified written appraisals for contributions of property valued at $5,000 or more, excluding property with readily quotable market prices such as stocks and bonds, may have had some minor negative effect on giving. Also in 1984, Congress reinstated through 1994 full deductibility for contributions of appreciated property to foundations that it had limited in the 1969 tax act. This provision was then extended in later acts.

Tax Reform Act of 1986

The Tax Reform Act of 1986 again lowered marginal income tax rates substantially. The top rate was reduced to 33 percent for those with moderately high incomes and to 28 percent for those with the highest level of taxable income. The act reduced the corporate rate from 46 to 34 percent. At the same time, this act attacked a variety of tax shelters and mechanisms by which individuals had been able to reduce taxes through manipulation of portfolios and purchase of tax shelters. Although the rate reduction again pared the tax incentive to give, the reduction in ability to reduce taxes through other means might have increased incentives to give.

The 1986 Tax Reform Act also weakened the incentive to give by increasing the standard deduction that can be taken in lieu of itemizing deductions (including charitable gifts). Again, the effect of this change is exaggerated by looking only at a point in time. The value of the standard deduction had eroded in the late 1970s and 1980s and, accordingly, boosted the number of itemizers significantly. The 1986 act in many ways only restored a balance that had existed in prior years and followed a tradition of many postwar acts. As noted above, there had also been real bracket creep, so that the standard deduction and personal exemptions had generally risen more slowly than real wages.

A further complication introduced by the 1986 act was the establishment of an alternative minimum tax (AMT). This tax essentially creates a second tax base and a second set of tax rates as an alternative to the regular income tax to keep taxpayers from evading tax liabilities altogether through the clever manipulation of tax shelters and deductions. Of special relevance to charities was the addition of unrealized capital gains on gifts of appreciated property to the taxable income base. The rationale for this change was that income on such gains was never recognized for income tax purposes. To allow it to be deducted as a charitable contribution, therefore, created a double deduction. As a simplified example, if one person earned $100 of additional wages and gave that $100 to charity, her taxable income would be $0 thanks to the charitable deduction—the $100 in income would be offset by a charitable deduction of $100. If another person earned $100 in additional accrued capital gains and gave the asset containing those gains to charity (the simplest example would be an asset that initially was almost worth nothing and grew in value to $100), his additional taxable income would equal negative $100 (income would be zero before the deduction, as unrealized capital gains are not taxable, and the deduction would allow $100 to be subtracted from other taxable income).[10]

Omnibus Reconciliation Act of 1990

In the Omnibus Reconciliation Act of 1990, Congress sought to induce more charitable giving by excluding from the AMT for 1991 capital gains on contributions of tangible personal property.[11] Museums, for example, experienced significant declines in gifts during the late 1980s. The change was designed mainly to deal with museums' great difficulty in generating donations of artwork and other collectibles when an AMT might be levied on that amount.

The 1990 act also saw some slight movement toward raising tax rates, thereby increasing the incentive to give. Tax rates were raised directly for a few individuals at the top of the income distribution. The top rate of 28 percent was increased to 31 percent, although some offset occurred through a lowering of an effective 33 percent rate for upper-middle-income taxpayers back to 31 percent.

Some other tax rate increases were imposed, however, in parts of the tax system that provide no charitable deduction. For instance, the Social Security Health Insurance tax rate was increased. The greater the reliance upon such non-income tax sources to generate revenues, the smaller the relative incentive to give. In like manner, within the income tax, there were various backdoor ways of increasing taxes by phasing out the availability of tax breaks as income increased. For instance, when taxes are effectively increased by phasing out the personal exemption as income increases, it is almost identical to a rate increase in that income range. However, there is no charitable deduction available against that rate increase (see also Clotfelter 1987; Lindsay 1987).

Omnibus Reconciliation Act of 1993

In the Omnibus Reconciliation Act of 1993, tax rates for the highest-income taxpayers were raised significantly—from 31 to 39.6 percent at the very top (taxable incomes greater than $250,000) and from 31 to 36 percent at near the top ($140,000 to $250,000 of taxable income for a joint return). The higher rates again increased the incentive to give. The 1993 act also eliminated gains on appreciated property from the AMT tax base, thereby restoring incentives to give away appreciated property. The preference was extended beyond tangible property to include gifts of stock, bonds, and other intangible assets.

To pay for the change in the AMT rules, the 1993 act moved to discourage overreporting of charitable gifts. It required written substantiation from charities for gifts of $250 or more and also tightened the disclosure requirements for quid pro quo contributions, where the taxpayer receives some benefit for the gift made.

Taxpayer Bill of Rights Act II of 1996

As part of a "taxpayer bill of rights," Congress decided in 1996 that certain abuses by charities should not cause outright repeal of their exempt status but instead should lead to penalties and excise taxes called intermediate sanctions. It also increased the responsibility of exempt organizations to provide copies of their annual Internal Revenue Service (IRS) Form 990 returns to the public.[12] As information on nonprofits becomes more accessible, public scrutiny of nonprofit activities is likely to intensify and even revolutionize the sector itself (Steuerle 1998).

Tax Act of 1997

In 1997, Congress enacted the first significant legislative tax reduction since 1981, although its aggregate size was much smaller. Among the more important provisions affecting charities was a reduction in the tax rate for capital gains property and an increase in wealth exempt from the estate tax. The latter was not all that great, especially when compared with increases in societal income and wealth since the early 1980s. The capital gains tax reduction mainly reduced the price of consumption out of capital gains property and, consequently, raised the *relative* price of giving, rather than consuming, such capital for a few individuals.

Economic Growth and Tax Relief Reconciliation Act of 2001

The 2001 act substantially lowered tax rates for individuals, provided for the eventual elimination of the estate tax, and increased the standard deduction, among other tax reductions. As noted, these types of reductions raise the price of giving to charity and reduce the incentive to give, though in the case of the estate tax elimination there is some debate about whether the disincentive to give will be outweighed by the greater amount of wealth heirs will have available to give.

Most of the tax reductions enacted in 2001 were scheduled to end in 2010 (or sooner in some cases), however, creating almost continual debate over making the tax cuts permanent.[13]

Although the 2001 legislation significantly reduced tax rates, it left intact features of the alternative minimum tax that made it likely that millions of additional taxpayers would be caught in its throes, thereby increasing their tax obligations without increasing their incentives to give (because the alternative minimum tax does not consider these deductions). This problem may have the effect of canceling or reducing whatever income effects the other tax changes generated, further exaggerating their potential negative effects.

Job Creation and Worker Assistance Act of 2002

In 2002, Congress enacted legislation that provided a temporary acceleration of depreciation allowances (through an up-front write-off of a portion of capital outlays), leaving corporate taxpayers and noncorporate business owners with lower taxable income initially, and thus making it easier for them to hit the limit on charitable contributions at 10 percent of taxable income. The flip side is that taxable income would be higher in later years, when accelerated deductions were no longer available.

The Jobs and Growth Tax Relief Act of 2003

The Jobs and Growth Tax Relief Act of 2003 accelerated some of the tax reductions enacted in 2001 and extended some of them. Like legislation almost every year or two since, these acts temporarily slowed down (through a temporary increase in exemptions) the rate of increase in the number of taxpayers subject to the AMT. It also temporarily lowered capital gains tax rates to a maximum of 15 percent in the top four income brackets and 5 percent in the lower two, and it reduced the maximum tax rate on dividends to 15 percent. These latter items reduced the incentive to give capital gain property and, to the extent that they lowered total income subject to tax, also reduced the incentive to give out of that income.

Working Families Tax Relief Act of 2004

This act mainly extended some of the tax breaks in the 2001 and 2003 legislation, chiefly applying to lower- and middle-income taxpayers.

Pending Legislation

In addition to the legislation that has been enacted, several pieces of legislation remained alive from prior sessions of Congress. These included a revived, and slightly modified, version of the charitable deduction for non-itemizers and various provisions designed to avoid real or perceived abuses in the charitable sector.[14] The Senate passed the Tax Relief Act of 2005 (formerly S.2020) in November 2005. It contains, among other items, both charitable giving incentives and reforms. Notably, the bill would allow a deduction floor for non-itemizers who report annual charitable contributions in excess of $210 ($420 for joint filers), permit tax-free individual retirement account distributions to charities, and grant enhanced deductions for contributions of food, books, and gifts of literary, musical, artistic, or scholarly compositions. Reforms include strengthening appraisal rules required to claim tax deductions, requiring increased reporting to the IRS, and permitting the IRS to disclose information on tax-exempt organizations to state authorities. Many of these provisions were drawn from similar ones in the CARE Act (S.1780) and the Senate Finance Committee's recommendations on the regulation of charities.

In addition, a Tax Reform Commission proposed major revisions to the tax code that would have eliminated many tax deductions, though not the charitable deduction. It suggested a charitable deduction for non-itemizers and itemizers alike that was quite similar to what was in the Senate bill at the end of 2005. However, the administration declined to put these or other proposals for major tax reform forward in 2006.

Net Effect on Charitable Giving

The overall thrust of tax policy from the 1980s to 2005 thus appears to have weakened the financial incentive for charitable giving. When tax rates were cut in 1981, 1986, 2001, and 2003, the rise in the price of giving was widely expected to cut charitable contributions sharply. This expectation was based on econometric studies predicting that a 1 percent increase in the price of charitable giving would reduce charitable giving by at least 1 percent. These models effectively predicted that giving would fall by 15 percent in response to the rate cuts enacted in the 1986 act and that total giving in the 1980s would be cut by as much as 40 percent as a result of the 1981 act.[15]

These predictions only partially fit the results, however. For wealthy individuals, the after-tax price of giving $1 rose from 30 cents to 69 cents between 1980 and 1991 and then fell back to about 60 cents in 1994 and beyond.[16] Consistent with predictions, giving has dropped significantly at the very high end of the income distribution (see chapter 2), but not by as much as might have been expected. Moreover, outside of that group, predicted drops in giving were not observed. Indeed, as Steuerle and Hodgkinson note in chapter 2, giving as a percentage of income has remained relatively constant in the face of increases in the cost of giving.

Analysts have debated why the predictions of econometric giving models have failed to materialize. Possible reasons include the fact that individuals may adjust to changes both in incomes and tax rates only slowly over time until they are sure that their circumstances have changed permanently. More recent econometric work has also raised questions about the results from earlier econometric studies. For example, the availability of panel data has allowed analysts to examine the behavior of the same taxpayers over several years—how they react to changes that they perceive to be temporary and to those that are permanent. A widely cited study using these data has found that people tend to react less sharply to changes in the price of giving that they believe to be permanent than they do to changes in the price of giving that result from temporary tax changes (Randolph 1995).

One issue of special concern is that all these models predict what happens to giving by individuals while ignoring the possible feedback between donors' behavior and the ability of charities to meet social needs. If givers start to contribute less because incentives are reduced, the unmet needs of charities would rise because support has fallen. These higher needs may reverberate back to induce individuals to give more. As an example, the fixed cost of running a church or a school may be unrelated to the price of giving. If one changes incentives, it could turn out that the taxpayer whose relative cost has gone up will give less and vice versa, but that people in the aggregate will still cover the fixed cost of that church or school. Kent Smetters (1998) made a somewhat similar argument through a model where individuals meet needs according to both the benefits from the charitable activity (a portion of which comes back to the individual, e.g., in better communities in which to live or other "externalities") and the price of giving as set in the tax code. That model yields some hypothetical response rates that can roughly duplicate the historical shift in giving from higher- to lower-income households.[17]

Further complicating the efforts to assess the effects of tax changes have been limitations in the basic data on charitable contributions. Although required reporting on non-cash contributions became stricter in 1985, fewer individuals were audited as the 1980s progressed. As a result, even the amount of charitable giving is suspect because of potential misreporting. Beyond this, the profusion of tax changes during the period covered here very likely confused tax planning. People may respond with lags to changes in incentives, and their behavior is also affected by expectations about the future.

Although giving may not have declined as much as many feared, neither did it rise as fast as some hoped. Some advocates of budget cuts argued, in fact, that declining federal spending would serve as a spur to private charitable giving and would therefore more than offset the effects of federal budget cuts.

The record of the 1980s and early 1990s, when federal spending was reduced below its FY 1980 levels, provides little support for this view, however. Not until 1991 did the growth of giving reach a level where it roughly equaled the cuts in federal spending on programs of interest to nonprofit organizations outside of health and income assistance, but by this time a sizable shortfall had already accumulated. If our measure of recovery is not the absolute level of federal support but the level that would bring federal spending in these fields back to its FY 1980 levels as a share of GDP, the record is even more discouraging. As table 3.5 shows, giving as a share of GDP barely budged until the stock market frenzy of the late 1990s and early 2000s. Even so, the combination of giving and federal spending in areas of interest to nonprofits as a share of GDP remained below its FY 1980 level as of 2004.

Table 3.5. Major Tax Changes since 1980 Affecting Charitable Contributions

Change in incentive to give	Major tax laws and provisions affecting charitable contributions
	Economic Recovery Tax Act of 1981
−	• Reduced individual marginal income tax by about 23% between 1981 and 1984; maximum rate reduced to 50% and capital gains rate to 20%
−	• Top estate taxes rate scheduled to be reduced from 70% to 50%, exempt amounts raised, and a complete marital deduction allowed
+	• Introduced charitable deduction for non-itemizers for 1982–86. Amount deductible rose from 25% of contributions up to $100 in 1982, to 100% of all contributions in 1986
+	• Increased limit on corporate contributions from 5% to 10% of net income (effective 1982)
+	• Allowed deduction for scientific property used for college or university research on its basis plus 50% of the capital gain (previously only for medical equipment)
	Deficit Reduction Act of 1984
?	• Required signed qualified written appraisals for contributions of property valued at $5,000 or more (except securities with prices quoted on exchanges)
−	• Increased penalties for inflated appraisals
+	• Increased limit on gifts to private foundations from 20% to 30% of adjusted gross income
+	• Increased mileage allowance for use of passenger cars in performing services for charities from 9 cents to 12 cents per mile
	Tax Reform Act of 1986
−	• Reduced individual marginal income tax rates by 1988 to range of 15% to 33%, with rate at highest income levels equal to 28%
+	• Reduced opportunities to shelter income
−	• Reduced corporate tax rate from 46% to 34%
−	• Reduced number of itemizers by increasing standard deduction and reducing certain itemized deductions
−	• Capital gains in gifts of appreciated property included as a preference under the AMT
+	• Capital gains tax rates increased by elimination of exclusion; maximum rate equal to 28%
−	• Charitable deduction for non-itemizers allowed to expire
	Omnibus Budget Reconciliation Act of 1990
+	• Excluded capital gains on contributions of tangible personal property (such as art or antiques) from AMT for 1991. Capital gains on stock, real property, conservation easement, etc., still subject to AMT. Exclusion extended to June 1992 in the Tax Extension Act of 1991.
+	• Increased individual income tax rate to 31% and altered bubble rates
−	• Introduced phaseout of itemized deductions for taxpayers with incomes over $100,000. Equivalent approximately to a 0.93% tax rate against which no charitable deductions are allowed
+	• Increased AMT rate to 24%

Change in incentive to give	Major tax laws and provisions affecting charitable contributions
	Omnibus Budget Reconciliation Act of 1993
+	● Raised 31% top rate to 39.6% (36% when taxable income is less than $250,000)
+	● Made permanent the top estate tax rate of 55% (rather than 50% as scheduled as a final drop from 1981 act but continually delayed)
+	● Eliminated from the AMT all gains on appreciated property given to charity
?	● Required written substantiation from charities for deductions of gifts of $250 or more, and increased disclosure requirements for quid pro quo contributions
	Taxpayer Bill of Rights Act II of 1996
+	● Imposed "intermediate sanction"—in lieu of outright removal of tax exemption—on certain self-dealing and excessive benefits for qualified persons
	Small Business Tax Bill of 1996
+	● Temporarily restored, from July 1, 1996, to May 31, 1997, a deduction equal to fair market value for "qualified" appreciated stock contributed to a private foundation
?	● Increased responsibilities of charities to provide copies of tax returns to the public
	Tax Act of 1997
−	● Lowered capital gains tax rate to a maximum of 20% (and for some average-income tax payers to 10%). The maximum rate is lowered again to 18% for property held or owned more than five years and purchased after December 31, 2000.
+	● Temporarily restored again, from June 1, 1997, to June 30, 1998, a deduction equal to fair market value for qualified appreciated stock contributed to a private foundation
−	● Increased the estate and gift tax unified credit from $600,000 to $1 million by 2006. Also allowed an exclusion for some qualified family- owned businesses from the estate tax.
+	● Increased the standard mileage rate to 14 cents per mile for computing charitable deductions
?	● Eliminated certain abuses with respect to charitable remainder trusts
	Economic Growth and Tax Relief Reconciliation Act of 2001 (EGTRRA)
−	● Created a new 10% bracket for low-income households; lowered tax rate from 39.6% to 38.6% for 2001 to 2003 (decreasing to 35% by 2006)
−	● Expanded the size of the child credit to $600 in 2001 and $1,000 by 2010 and made this credit more available to low-income families
−	● Proposed a repeal of the estate tax in 2010; reduced top rate from 55% to 50% by 2002 and 45% by 2009; increased the unified credit exemption amount to $1 million by 2002 and $3.5 million by 2009

Table 3.5. Major Tax Changes since 1980 Affecting Charitable Contributions *(cont.)*

Change in incentive to give	Major tax laws and provisions affecting charitable contributions
	Economic Growth and Tax Relief Reconciliation Act of 2001 (EGTRRA) *(cont.)*
−	● Increased standard deduction for joint filers to between 174% and 200% of the deduction for single filers
−	● Decreased the tax rate on dividend income to 5% for those in the lowest two brackets and 15% for all other brackets starting in 2003
	The Jobs and Growth Tax Relief Reconciliation Act of 2003 (JGTRRA)
−	● Decreased marginal rates, retroactive to 2003, to 10, 15, 25, 28, 33, and 35 percent. Accelerated the expansion of the 10% bracket to 2003 and 2004.
−	● Accelerated EGTRRA's expansion of the child credit to $1,000 in 2004
−	● Accelerated changes in the standard deduction for joint filers in EGGTRA
−	● Lowered capital gains tax rates to a maximum of 15% for taxpayers in the top four income brackets and 5% in the lower two. The 15% rate extends through and the 5% rate drops to zero in 2008.
	Working Families Tax Relief Act of 2004
−	● Applied JGTRRA's extended 10% tax bracket through 2010
−	● Extended marriage penalty relief in JGTRRA and EGTRRA to 2010
−	● Extended higher AMT exemptions through 2005
Proposed Changes Affecting Charitable Contributions and Incentives to Give	
	Tax Relief Act of 2005 (as it passed the Senate in 2005)
+	● Individuals who do not itemize may deduct a portion of their charitable contributions (in excess of $210 for single filers and $420 for joint filers) made after 2005 and before 2008.
+	● Distributions to charities from individual retirement accounts become tax-free (after 2005 and before 2008).
+	● Allow for charitable deductions of food and book inventories and enhance deductions for charitable contributions of literary, musical, artistic, and scholarly compositions
+	● Exclude mileage reimbursements for charitable volunteers from gross income
+	● Institute more stringent reporting requirements for charities and provide funds to the IRS for oversight
?	● Increase substantiation requirements and limit certain charitable donations, e.g., for facades of buildings
+	● Allow the IRS to more readily share information about its enforcement of nonprofits with state charity regulators
+	● Mandate electronic filing of more detailed returns and applications for exemption

The growth of private giving did measure up better against the direct revenue losses to nonprofit organizations during this period, though only partly so. Even with this more limited measure, it was not until the latter 1980s that the growth of private giving reached a level where it drew equal to the direct revenue losses nonprofit organizations sustained as a result of federal budget cuts. And if the measure is a restoration of the level of support nonprofits received from federal sources as a share of GDP, it was not until 1988 that this level was reached. Here again, however, there is no clear relationship between the areas where nonprofits sustained cuts in federal support and those where it enjoyed gains in private giving. One also needs to be careful with the estimate of changes in private giving as a percentage of GDP, because the change from 1980 to 2004 may simply reflect limitations of the data as well as a response to lower rates of inflation if households respond with a lag in their giving to inflation-induced increases in income.

THE FUTURE OF FEDERAL-NONPROFIT RELATIONS

Whereas the period from the mid-1990s to the mid-2000s saw substantial increases in federal spending in fields where nonprofit organizations are active and in federal support to nonprofit organizations after fifteen years of rather severe cuts, at least outside of health, the near-term future promises to see a return to fiscal stringency. Tax cuts, increases in health and retirement spending, and larger debt, combined with a shrinking labor force and growing elderly population, are putting huge pressure on the rest of the budget. Certainly the budget proposals advanced by the president and Congress for the latter part of the first decade of the 21st century suggest some serious belt-tightening for charities and those they serve. Under the president's FY 2006 budget, for example, federal spending on programs of interest to nonprofit organizations outside of health and income assistance would decline 12 percent between FY 2005 and FY 2010, slicing a cumulative total of $71.5 billion out of the resources available to support federal activities in these fields (Abramson and Salamon 2005). This would lead in turn to a 4 percent drop in federal support to nonprofit organizations in these fields, cutting $10 billion out of the income stream that these organizations would receive over this period compared with what they would have received had FY 2005 spending levels been maintained.

How nonprofits will fare on the tax side of the ledger is harder to predict, but with continued talk of income tax cuts, fundamental tax reform (e.g., a flat tax), and tax increases to deal with fiscal imbalance

Table 3.6. Federal Outlays in Areas of Interest to Nonprofits and Private Giving, Excluding Health and Income Assistance, FY 1980–2004

	As a percentage of GDP (FY 1980 = 100)		
FY	Federal outlays in areas of interest to nonprofits[a]	Private giving[b]	Combined federal outlays and private giving
1980	100	100	100
1981	89	103	94
1982	71	100	80
1983	65	98	76
1984	59	93	70
1985	58	84	66
1986	55	94	68
1987	52	88	64
1988	52	89	64
1989	53	98	67
1990	52	98	67
1991	57	101	71
1992	58	105	73
1993	59	105	73
1994	59	99	72
1995	59	93	69
1996	56	96	69
1997	56	115	75
1998	57	119	76
1999	57	126	79
2000	60	147	87
2001	64	147	90
2002	69	148	94
2003	74	150	98
2004	73	139	94

Sources: Data on private giving are adapted from calendar year data in Giving USA (2005). See also appendix A.

GDP = gross domestic product.

[a] Excludes health and income assistance programs.

[b] Private giving to other than health or sacramental religious activities. Includes 20 percent of religious giving; excludes a one-time gift to the arts of $1.3 billion in calendar year 1982.

still in the air it seems likely that further changes are quite possible. Some changes move in the direction of reducing the incentives to give. For example, it seems likely that Congress will increasingly turn toward revenue sources other than the income tax to pay for government or put limits on itemized deductions. On the other hand, some income tax rate increases may also occur, and Congress has moved toward adopting a non-itemizer deduction that would likely increase giving.

Closer scrutiny of charities themselves is also likely to continue and to increase. One potentially revolutionary change—more public scrutiny of tax forms filed by charities—has already accelerated. All this attention, in turn, may well induce charities to find improved mechanisms for monitoring themselves. Depending upon how any or all of these changes are implemented, they could either increase or decrease giving, and they could either improve or reduce the efficiency of giving.

CONCLUSION

Although it has long been clear that the federal government's activities have an important impact on the nation's nonprofit sector, the dimensions of that impact have been difficult for researchers and others to gauge. No ongoing governmental or other tracking system or database follows the flow of funds from government to nonprofit agencies. To fill the gap in understanding of the relationship between the federal government and the nonprofit sector, it has been necessary to formulate our own estimates.

What these estimates suggest is that a significant shift in federal spending priorities occurred in the late 1970s and early 1980s. This shift had a significant effect not only on government's ability to assist citizens in need, but also on the ability of nonprofit organizations to respond to the resulting new demands. What is more, private giving was not able to make up for the resulting shortfalls.

More recently, the federal budget picture loosened considerably in fields of interest to nonprofits, and nonprofits benefited as a consequence. However, the budget squeeze resulting from rapidly rising retirement and health spending and reduced tax revenues now seems likely to choke off this recovery and mark a return to fiscal constraint. In fact, since health and retirement are so much larger a portion of the budget, their inexorable growth, along with the retirement of the baby boomers, suggest a much more stringent period of fiscal constraint. Since the budget situation is unsustainable, reforms may provide some reprieve.

These data highlight the complex relationships that now link the federal government and the nonprofit sector. Although these two sets of institutions at times act as if they were substitutes for each other, to a larger extent they function as partners in responding to public needs. It is hoped that the kind of analysis undertaken here can provide a more secure foundation for strengthening this partnership for the years ahead.

NOTES

This study was supported by funding from the Aspen Institute's Nonprofit Sector Research Fund, Independent Sector, and the Urban Institute. The authors thank Gerald Auten, Virginia Hodgkinson, and Richard Steinberg for comments on earlier drafts of this report. They also thank Michael Brotchner, Michelle Chaffee, Kelly Daley, Brent Dillabaugh, Carole Plowfield, and John Russell for assistance with the research for this report.

1. These estimates were based on detailed examination of programmatic data, scrutiny of existing program evaluations, and extensive discussions with program managers at the federal, state, and local levels. Our estimates of federal support flowing to nonprofits include funds that flow directly from the federal government to nonprofit organizations, as well as federal funds that flow indirectly through state and local government or other entities to nonprofits.

2. State and local spending increased by 125 percent between 1980 and 2002, an increase of some $395.4 billion after adjusting for inflation. Of this total, $355.1 billion was for education (U.S. Census Bureau 1997).

3. We focus here on "outlays" as our measure of spending even though when Congress allocates money to a program, it formally makes an "appropriation" or grant of "budget authority" to the program. Ultimately, however, it is not the grant of budget authority but the actual outlays of money that make the difference on the ground. Also, it often takes well over a year for changes in budget authority to show up as changes in outlays.

4. The guaranteed student loan program, along with other federal credit programs, was excluded from this analysis. Included in research and development outlays is the federal spending on research and development that flows outside the government to public and private nonprofit colleges and universities and to nonprofit research institutes. Intramural government research spending and support of for-profit businesses for research are not included.

5. Federal income assistance programs such as Food Stamps, Supplemental Security Income, and welfare are automatically available to all citizens who meet the programs' eligibility requirements. Because the number of people in poverty or unemployed grew during this period, the amount of spending under these programs also increased.

6. In addition to these programmatic changes, reductions have also occurred in the mail subsidy provided to nonprofit, public, religious, and some for-profit organizations. By FY 2004 the value of this subsidy was reduced by $27.7 billion, or 99 percent below FY 1980 levels.

7. See note 2 above and Salamon and Abramson (1981) for more detail on the estimating procedures for nonprofit revenues from federal programs. Our "nonprofit share estimates" were developed for three points of time—1981, 1993, and 2005—to take account of shifts in program operations and structure.

8. Here is a simple example of bracket creep. A tax system taxes the first $10,000 at a zero rate, the next $12,000 at a 10 percent rate, and all other income at a 20 percent rate. A household with $20,000 of income then pays an average 5 percent tax rate and a marginal rate of 10 percent. Now suppose that its income rises to $25,000 because of inflation, a few years of real wage growth, or a second member of the household entering the labor force. Then the average tax rate rises to 7.2 percent and the marginal rate to 20 percent.

9. Again, one needs to be careful here, as there have also been periods when larger shares of the population have been moved into the estate tax because average individual wealth grew faster than exemption levels in that tax.

10. One difficulty with including appreciated property in the tax base, however, was that there was no change in the treatment of appreciated assets at

death. There, any accrued capital gains are essentially forgiven tax: heirs acquire the assets with no income tax due on past accrued, but unrealized, gains. Accordingly, a person who held an appreciated asset could still forgo the tax on the appreciation and also give cash away to charity during life. That person would still benefit from both the non-taxation of the appreciation and the charitable deduction, just as in the example above. The 1986 law, therefore, actually provided taxpayers a disincentive for giving away appreciated property instead of cash.

11. This exclusion was extended to June 1992, in the Tax Extension Act of 1991.

12. Research databases are available at the National Center for Charitable Statistics. GuideStar and Foundation Center provide data upon request.

13. Some phase-ins and phaseouts were hard to track. For instance, the phaseout of itemized deductions and of the personal exemption—backdoor types of rate increases discussed above—were eliminated, but only temporarily, beginning in 2007 and ending in 2009.

14. The deduction for non-itemizers that was carried forward to the Senate Finance Committee bill and to the proposals of the tax reform commission largely followed a suggestion made by one of the authors (Steuerle) in testimony in 2005 (Steuerle 2005).

15. For example, see Lindsay (1987). See also Clotfelter (1987).

16. See Auten, Cilke, and Randolph (1992).

17. As noted in Steuerle and Hodgkinson (1998), the Smellers model criticizes what he calls "reduced form" equations that do not deal simultaneously with demand and supply of charitable giving. In our examples above, we do not specify precisely what may lead to the demand for giving, allowing even for the possibility that charitable giving may simply be an act of outright generosity, regardless of the benefits derived for the giver. His model formalizes what we have called here (and in an earlier version of this chapter presented to ARNOVA in November 1996) a "demand for giving" into a more elegant model using the economic concept of externalities—gains back to the giver for the charitable activity—as the mechanism driving individual giving.

REFERENCES

Abramson, Alan J., and Lester M. Salamon. 1986. *The Nonprofit Sector and the New Federal Budget*. Washington, DC: Urban Institute Press.

———. 2005. *The Nonprofit Sector and the Federal Budget: Fiscal Year 2006 and Beyond*. Washington, DC: The Aspen Institute.

Abramson, Alan J., Lester M. Salamon, and Eugene Steuerle. 1998. "The Nonprofit Sector and the Federal Budget: Recent History and Future Directions." In *Nonprofits and Government: Collaboration and Conflict*, edited by Elizabeth Boris and Eugene Steuerle (99–139). Washington, DC: Urban Institute Press.

Auten, Gerald E., James M. Cilke, and William C. Randolph. 1992. "The Effects of Tax Reform on Charitable Contributions." *National Tax Journal* 45(3): 267–90.

Clotfelter, Charles T. 1987. "Life after Tax Reform." *Change* 19(4): 12–18.

Lindsay, Lawrence B. 1987. "Gifts of Appreciated Property: More to Consider." *Tax Notes*, Jan. 5: 67–70.

Randolph, William. 1995. "Dynamic Income, Progressive Taxes, and the Timing of Charitable Contributions." *Journal of Political Economy* 103(4): 709–38.

Salamon, Lester M., with Alan J. Abramson. 1981. *The Federal Government and the Nonprofit Sector: Implications of the Reagan Budget Proposals*. Washington, DC: Urban Institute Press.

Salamon, Lester M., and Alan J. Abramson. 1982. *The Federal Budget and the Nonprofit Sector*. Washington, DC: Urban Institute Press.

Smetters, Kent. 1998. "A Free Rider Explanation of the Charitable Giving Puzzles of the 1980s and an Application to Fundamental Tax Reform." Unpublished paper.

Steuerle, C. Eugene. 1998. "The Coming Revolution in the Charitable Sector." *Tax Notes* 17 (Aug. 10): 727–28, 859–60.

———. 2005. "Charities on the Frontline and Making the Best Use of Tax Policy to Help Them." Testimony before the United States House of Representatives Committee on Ways and Means Subcommittee on Social Security and Family Policy, September 13.

Steuerle, Eugene, and Virginia Hodgkinson. 1998. "Meeting Social Needs: Comparing the Resources of the Independent Sector and Government." In *Nonprofits and Government: Collaboration and Conflict*, edited by Elizabeth Boris and Eugene Steuerle (71–98). Washington, DC: Urban Institute Press.

U.S. Bureau of the Census. 1997. *Statistical Abstract of the United States: 1997*. Washington, DC: U.S. Government Printing Office.

Appendix A

NOTE ON DATA SOURCES

I. OVERALL FEDERAL SPENDING DATA

Published sources include the annual volumes containing the president's budget that were released in 1982–2004. In addition, unpublished backup material to the published volumes was obtained from the U.S. Office of Management and Budget (OMB) and the executive departments (e.g., Department of Health and Human Services, Department of Labor).

II. FEDERAL SUPPORT OF NONPROFIT ORGANIZATIONS

Authors' estimates of the share of program resources flowing to nonprofit agencies are based on detailed examination of programmatic data, scrutiny of existing program evaluations, and extensive discussions with program managers at the federal, state, and local levels. "Nonprofit share estimates" were calculated in 1981, 1993, and 2005. For years between these years, the nonprofit share estimate is calculated as the weighted average of the estimates for the two end years. For a more detailed discussion of the estimating procedure, see Salamon and Abramson (1981), pp. 35–80.

III. DEFLATION FACTORS

Deflators for Medicare and Medicaid

Unpublished material from OMB and the U.S. Congressional Budget Office (CBO) on the actual and projected values of the medical services component of the Consumer Price Index (CPI)

Deflators for All Other Programs

Published and unpublished material from OMB and CBO on actual and projected values of the gross domestic product implicit price deflator.

4

TAX TREATMENT OF NONPROFIT ORGANIZATIONS: A TWO-EDGED SWORD?

Evelyn Brody and Joseph J. Cordes

Nonprofit organizations play various roles in civil society: independent, private suppliers of goods and services; agents of the government in delivering services aimed at meeting social needs; and contributors to political life and discourse in a democracy. Nonprofit organizations have come to rely on a variety of special tax rules to secure an important portion of the resources needed to fulfill these various roles. Charitable organizations in particular have long enjoyed a special relationship with the tax collector.

At least since Joseph's proclamation of a land law in Egypt that "Pharaoh should have the fifth part; except the land of priests only, which become not Pharaoh's" (Genesis 47:26), societies have acknowledged the presence of a nontaxable sector. In modern America, the nexus between the government and the nontaxable sector is myriad and complex. Multiple levels of government lay claim to different sources of tax revenue. State and local governments rely primarily on property and sales taxes; the federal government relies primarily on personal and corporate income taxes and payroll taxes. The nonprofit sector embraces a range of mutual, donative, and commercial enterprises, not all of which qualify for exemption under one or more of the foregoing taxes. The government provides supply-side tax subsidies for two specific forms of support for charity: donations and borrowing through bond finance. Both government direct expenditures (see chapter 2) and demand-side tax expenditures (see chapter 5) provide billions of dollars of additional support to social service charities. While the state attorneys general enforce the substantive nonprofit laws, Congress gives the Internal Revenue Service an increasing role in regulating the nonprofit-government border and the nonprofit-commercial border (Simon, Dale, and Chisolm 2006), as well as the financial arrangement between charities and their insiders (Brody 1998a).

A few words on terminology will help focus the following discussion. The public often conflates the terms "nonprofit" and "tax-exempt." Nonprofit entities fall loosely into two categories: charities (including churches, schools, hospitals, and social service organizations) and mutual-benefit organizations (including labor unions, trade associations, and social clubs). While exemption from federal, state, and local taxes is available to most corporations and trusts organized as nonprofit enterprises under state law, so central is the federal tax law's role that nonprofits have come to be known by their designation in the Internal Revenue Code. For example, charities are referred to as "section 501(c)(3)" organizations. Importantly, most of the special tax treatments discussed in this chapter (notably, deductibility of contributions and property tax and sales tax exemptions) extend only to charities, while mutual-benefit nonprofits generally enjoy only income tax exemption. Similarly, "action" organizations (which engage in substantial lobbying) generally qualify for exemption only as section 501(c)(4) social welfare organizations, which cannot offer tax deductibility to their donors. Because of its focus on the tax benefits for charities, this chapter sometimes uses the term "nonprofit" interchangeably with "charity."

Tax exemption confers financial advantages on nonprofit organizations that other providers of goods and services do not enjoy. Tax exemption allows nonprofits to keep much, if not all, of the surplus earned from a range of income-producing activities. In addition, charities have access to several unique sources of revenue: at the federal level, tax-deductible charitable contributions and the ability to issue tax-exempt bonds; at the state level, property tax exemption and sales tax exemption on purchases.

But what the government provides it can also take away—or at least regulate. Tax exemption casts the government in the role not just of benefactor, but also of certifying the legitimacy of nonprofit organizations through requirements for tax-exempt status and regulation of what nonprofits can and cannot do to retain their tax-preferred status.

The special tax treatment of nonprofit organizations and the accompanying tax regulations make up a major set of government policies for the nonprofit sector. As a result, changes in tax policy can be as important to the nonprofit sector as the ebb and flow of government spending. Thus, after summarizing the main tax benefits nonprofit organizations enjoy, we consider a number of questions raised by the tax treatment of nonprofit organizations:

- What is the economic importance of nontaxable status to nonprofit organizations?
- What policy judgments does the current tax treatment of non-profits reflect?
- What strings are attached to receipt of the nonprofit tax exemption?
- How does the existing web of tax provisions and regulations shape the behavior of donors and nonprofit organizations?
- What does the future hold for the tax treatment of nonprofit organizations?

TAX POLICY TOWARD NONPROFIT ORGANIZATIONS

The government acts as a benefactor of the nonprofit sector through the tax code in two broad ways.

First, allowing individuals and corporations to deduct the value of charitable contributions against income and estate taxes provides an important economic incentive for private donors to provide financial support to a wide range of philanthropies. It is widely recognized that allowing such deductions effectively reduces the out-of-pocket cost of supporting nonprofit organizations by an amount that depends on the donor's tax rate. For example, if the tax rate is 25 percent, allowing a tax deduction for charitable contributions cuts the net cost of contributing from $1.00 to $0.75 because the taxpayer gets back a tax deduction that saves $0.25 in tax for every dollar contributed. A deduction has the upside-down effect of having a greater subsidy value to those in the highest tax brackets; moreover, only those who itemize their personal deductions may claim deductions for charitable contributions. The price of giving falls further for gifts of appreciated property, by the capital gains tax that would have been paid had the donated property been sold.[1] The donor may not, however, "zero out" income with charitable gifts.[2]

In addition to deductions that may be taken against income for charitable contributions, the tax code also allows charitable contributions to be deducted against the taxable value of estates. Although this provision is relevant only for a relatively small number of estates that are taxable, in those cases where estate taxes are due, the deduction lowers the after-tax cost of leaving bequests to charities by between 39 and 50 cents on the dollar.[3]

The federal tax code allows nonprofit organizations to devote more financial resources to support their philanthropic missions by exempting them from the obligation of paying corporate or trust income taxes. In addition to the charitable-contribution deduction and entity-level exemption, the federal tax system subsidizes charities by granting them the ability to issue section 501(c)(3) bonds, the interest income of which is exempt from tax. Similarly, states typically exempt nonprofits from state income tax and exempt charities from local property taxes (as well as sales taxes on purchases). Entity-level tax exemption, though quite broad, does not extend to any and all income earned or property owned by the nonprofit organization. In particular, the income must be earned from activities deemed related to the organization's exempt purpose. Since the 1950s, nonprofit organizations have been subject to a federal "unrelated business income tax," which is meant to tax nonprofits on the same basis as for-profit corporations on income earned in a trade or business that is regularly carried on and not substantially related to the nonprofit's exempt purposes (Hansmann 1989; Simon, Dale, and Chisolm 2006). States that levy corporate income taxes usually follow the federal government's lead in this area by imposing their own unrelated business income taxes, and most states require that property be used for an exempt purpose to qualify for property tax exemptions (Brody 2002).

ECONOMIC VALUE OF THE CHARITABLE DEDUCTION, TAX EXEMPTION, AND TAX-EXEMPT BONDS

What is the economic importance of special tax treatment to charities? The accompanying tables provide data bearing on this question.

Charitable Deduction

Each year the Joint Committee on Taxation estimates the cost to taxpayers, in forgone tax revenue, of providing tax incentives to individuals and corporations for contributing to charitable activities (JCT 2006a). As shown in table 4.1, the five-year cost (for fiscal years 2006–2010) of this "tax expenditure" is estimated at $235 billion

From the perspective of nonprofit organizations, what matters, however, is not the budgetary cost of tax incentives for charitable deductions, but the importance of charitable contributions as a financial resource and how much additional giving these tax incentives encourage. That is, taking the 2006 numbers in table 4.1, the charitable-contribution deduction could increased donations by more or less than the $235 billion in foregone taxes over the next five years, depending on how responsive donors are to the tax incentive.

Charitable deductions vary in importance as a resource for supporting nonprofit activities, as set forth in table 4.2 (which is the same as table 2.3). On the one hand, some nonprofits, such as those in health care (most notably hospitals), depend relatively little on charitable gifts as a source of revenue compared with program services revenue. For education and research, and social and legal service organizations, charitable gifts are a considerably more important revenue source. Overall, notwithstanding growth in alternative sources of funding, private contributions remain a significant financial resource for most philanthropic organizations.

How much lower would private contributions be if donations to charity were not deductible? In the case of giving by individuals, which account for more than three-fourths of private contributions (Center on Philanthropy at Indiana University 2005), there is fairly broad empirical consensus among economists who have studied private giving that individual donors are sensitive to the after-tax cost of giving, although there is a range of sensitivity estimates. The middle to high end of the range suggests that increasing (decreasing) the cost of giving by 10 percent decreases (increases) contributions by at least 10 percent. The lower end of the range implies considerably more modest responses, with a (permanent) 10 percent increase (decrease) in the cost of giving leading to only a 5 percent decrease (increase) in contributions (Cordes 2001; Vesterlund 2006).[4]

Table 4.1. Charitable Tax Expenditures, 2006–2010

	Estimated budgetary cost of tax deductions for charitable contributions		
Charitable activity	Corporate tax expenditure (billions of $)	Individual tax expenditure (billions of $)	Total
Education	3.1	32.0	35.1
Health	4.3	21.5	25.8
Social services (i.e., other)	8.7	170.4	174.1

Source: U.S. Congress, Joint Committee on Taxation (2006a).

Table 4.2. Government Grants and Independent Sector Contributions by Nonprofit Subsector, 1989 and 2003 ($ billions)

Subsector	Government grants, 1989	Private-sector contributions, 1989	Program service revenues, 1989	Government grants, 2003	Private-sector contributions, 2003	Program service revenues, 2003	Change 1989–2003 (%) Government grants	Private-sector contributions	Program service revenues
Total	46.2	58.6	368.5	94.6	125.1	715.8	105	113	94
Arts and culture	2.1	5.0	3.8	3.2	10.0	6.9	50	102	80
Community improvement / Public/societal benefit	4.1	10.5	6.8	11.3	21.8	13.5	176	107	98
Education/research	14.8	17.1	64.0	21.2	29.9	97.4	43	75	52
Environment and animals	0.4	1.4	0.8	1.4	4.9	2.2	229	263	191
Health	7.3	10.8	266.9	20.8	22.7	522.5	183	111	96
Human services	15.7	9.5	24.3	34.3	24.2	70.2	118	153	189
International affairs	1.5	2.1	1.1	2.1	7.0	0.8	36	234	−25
Religion	0.3	2.2	0.8	0.3	4.6	2.3	11	111	187

Note: This table is the same as table 2.3.

The responsiveness of corporate donors and of bequests to changes in the after-tax cost of giving has not been studied as intensively as the price sensitivity of private giving. Estimates of the determinants of corporate giving suggest that the responses of corporations to changes in the after-tax cost of giving are similar to the range of estimates reported above for individual giving (Joulfaian 1991). In the case of bequests, some recent research suggests that a 10 percent decrease (increase) in the cost of making a bequest would increase (decrease) bequests by just over 20 percent (Bakija and Gale 2003a, 2003b), although other research again shows a wide variance (Joulfaian 2004, 2005a, 2005b).

Table 4.3 presents some rough estimates of the effect of charitable tax deductions for the case in which donations are assumed to be fairly responsive to changes in the after-tax cost of giving. The estimates are based on applying a factor to total private contributions that assumes (a) that in the case of private donors and corporations a 1 percent increase (decrease) in the after-tax cost of giving would result in a 1 percent decrease (increase) in giving by individuals and corporations and (b) that a 1 percent point rise (fall) in the cost of making a bequest reduces (increases) the size of the bequest by 2 percent. In addition, we assume that individual contributions enjoy an average combined federal-state tax subsidy of 30 percent, that corporations face an average combined federal-state tax rate of 40 percent, and that a typical bequest is taxed at a marginal rate of 45 percent. Taken together, these assumptions imply that if contributions were not tax deductible, private contributions would decline by approximately 30 percent.[5] Applying that factor to the contribution levels shown in table 4.2, one can roughly estimate the decrease in financial resources that nonprofit organizations would experience if charitable contributions were not tax deductible. These estimates, which are shown in table 4.3, suggest that absent charitable tax deductions, the financial resources of nonprofit organizations would fall by amounts ranging from 0.5 percent to just over 20 percent.

At the same time, as noted in the previous two chapters and as discussed below, charitable giving did not drop as sharply in the 1980s as these calculations would portend when the price of giving rose, which has led some analysts (e.g., Randolph 1995) to suggest that giving may not be as sensitive to the price of giving as previously believed. If instead donor responses to changes in the cost of giving are at the low end of the estimated range, eliminating charitable tax deductions would lower private contributions by one third, which would cut the total financial resources of nonprofit organizations by between roughly 0.30 and 7 percent.[6]

Table 4.3. Predicted Effect of Tax Deductions on Financial Resources of Charities

NTEE group	Total private contributions ($ billions)	Predicted change in contributions ($ billions)	Predicted change as a percentage of financial resources (%)
Arts and culture	9.2	2.8	13.4
Education	28.0	8.4	5.9
Higher education	11.2	3.3	4.2
Environment and animals	4.6	1.4	16.5
Health	19.8	5.9	1.2
Hospitals	5.9	1.8	0.5
Human services	33.2	10.0	8.2
International affairs	5.2	1.6	21.1
Public, societal benefits	20.8	6.3	13.3
Religion	4.5	1.3	18.1
Mutual/membership benefit	0.1	0.0	3.3
Unknown	2.2	0.7	4.2
TOTAL	127.7	38.3	4.4

Source: Tabulations are based on digitized IRS 990 data for the fiscal year 2002 from the National Center for Charitable Statistics (2005) and author estimates based on these 2002 data.

Note: Figures do not add to totals shown because of rounding. NTEE = National Taxonomy of Exempt Entities.

Exemption from Corporate Income Taxes

Data tabulated from Form 990 returns (National Center for Charitable Statistics 2005) show that in 2002 charities received just over $ 32 billion in revenue in excess of their expenses (third column, table 4.4). No major grouping of nonprofit organizations was found to have expenses in excess of revenue, although of course some individual charities have suffered deficits.

The size of the nonprofit surplus is sometimes an indicator of the economic importance of the corporate income tax exemption (CBO 1997). The reader should bear in mind, however, that the residual between income and expense that is measured by the *surplus* of a nonprofit organization is not a measure of *profit* as accountants and economists would understand the term. For example, in computing a nonprofit's surplus, donations are appropriately treated as a source of funds. Although donations could, in theory, be counted as a taxable receipt for determining taxable profit, given the stated rationale for organizing as a nonprofit organization, this seems rather unlikely. Similarly, for policy reasons, one might choose not to count "below-market" fees received for providing mission-related services to clients as a taxable receipt. Moreover, as a recent Congressional Budget Office report points out, if the nonprofit surplus were to become subject to tax, nonprofits (and other tax-exempt organizations) might react by reduc-

Table 4.4. Surplus of Public Charities, 2002

NTEE group	Total revenue ($ billions)	Total expense ($ billions)	Surplus ($ billions)	Surplus as a percentage of total revenue
Arts and culture	20.6	19.0	1.7	8.1
Education	141.4	133.5	7.8	5.5
Higher education	79.6	76.2	3.3	4.2
Environment and animals	8.3	7.1	1.2	14.5
Health	499.4	487.6	10.5	2.1
Hospitals	374.3	365.3	8.7	2.3
Human services	122.1	118.4	5.2	4.3
International affairs	7.4	7.3	0.1	1.5
Public, societal benefits	46.9	41.3	4.1	8.7
Religion	7.4	7.0	0.4	5.3
Mutual/membership benefit	1.3	1.4	-0.1	-7.7
Unknown	15.6	14.7	0.9	5.8

Source: Tabulations are based on digitized IRS 990 data for fiscal year 2002 from the National Center for Charitable Statistics (2005) and author estimates based on these 2002 data.

Notes: Figures may not add to totals shown because of rounding. Percentages are calculated using data before rounding. NTEE = National Taxonomy of Exempt Entities.

ing their taxable income by, for example, lowering fees charged for services provided or increasing staff salaries (CBO 2005).

A more reasonable measure of what might be termed the "potentially taxable income" of nonprofit organizations would be the income earned from investments plus profit earned on activities undertaken with the specific intent of earning income to support mission-related activities. This amount is not directly observable from the financial data that nonprofit organizations provide. An estimate of this magnitude can be inferred by adding together an organization's interest, dividend, and net rental income plus capital gains from sales of securities and other assets plus its gross profit on sales of goods (Cordes 2004).

These estimates of nonprofit organizations' potentially taxable income are presented in table 4.5. If one assumes that this income would otherwise be taxed at a combined federal and state rate of 40 percent, tax exemption is estimated to increase the resources of charitable nonprofit organizations by roughly $10 billion in the aggregate.[7]

Exemption from Property Taxes

Table 4.6 presents data showing the value of the tax exemption from local property taxes. Because of the myriad of local property tax rates, it is extremely difficulty to place a precise value on the aggregate value of the property tax exemption. The available data led Cordes, Gantz, and Pollak (2002) to arrive at a rough "order of magnitude" of between

Table 4.5. Potentially Taxable Income of Public Charities, 2002

NTEE group	Estimated potentially taxable income ($ billions)	Estimated income tax savings ($ billions)	Tax saving as a percentage of total revenue
Arts and culture	1.5	0.6	3.0
Education	8.4	3.4	2.4
Higher education	4.7	1.9	2.4
Environment and animals	0.3	0.1	1.6
Health	7.6	3.0	0.6
Hospitals	5.7	2.3	0.6
Human services	3.6	1.4	1.2
International affairs	0.1	0.0	0.6
Public, societal benefits	2.9	1.2	2.5
Religion	0.5	0.2	2.6
Mutual/membership benefit	0.0	0.0	1.4
Unknown	0.3	0.1	0.9
TOTAL	25.4	10.1	1.2

Source: Tabulations are based on digitized IRS 990 data for fiscal year 2002 from the National Center for Charitable Statistics (2005) and author estimates based on these 2002 data.

Notes: Figures may not add to totals shown because of rounding. Percentages are calculated using data before rounding. NTEE = National Taxonomy of Exempt Entities.

$8 billion and $13 billion nationally for the annual value of property tax exemption, or between 1.3 percent and 2.1 percent of the total revenue public charities that filed federal tax returns received. This magnitude may understate the aggregate value to the extent that non-

Table 4.6. Estimated Financial Effect of State and Local Property Tax Exemption

Organization type	Percent with taxable property	Estimated tax savings as a percent of total revenue of organizations with taxable real property		Estimated tax savings of organizations with taxable real property ($)	
		Mean	Median	Mean	Median
Higher education	62	4	2	1,477,483	381,507
Hospitals	70	4	2	1,736,467	515,603
Human service, multipurpose[a]	40	5	2	49,989	13,443
Housing/shelter	58	20	9	63,526	27,576
Museums	44	16	4	133,682	20,181
Performing arts	19	4	2	79,103	10,079
Retirement homes	81	15	6	214,039	80,492
All organizations	33	9	2	203,114	18,529

Source: Table 4.6 in Cordes, Gantz, and Pollak (2002).

[a] Multipurpose human service organizations provide a range of different types of social services.

profit organizations value potentially taxable property at book rather than market value. Moreover, the authors increase this dollar estimate by an additional one-third to represent church-owned real estate. Finally, as discussed below, the authors find wide variation by state and across jurisdictions within states.[8]

Ability to Issue Tax-Exempt Bonds

According to data from the Internal Revenue Service Statistics of Income Division, section 501(c)(3) organizations reported nearly $196 billion in outstanding tax-exempt bonds in 2001 (Arnsberger 2004, 135, table 1). This amount represents an explosion in tax-exempt borrowing. Note that after the Tax Reform Act of 1986 and until the Taxpayer Relief Act of 1997, a charity other than a nonprofit hospital could not have outstanding more than $150 million of section 501(c)(3) bonds. A 1996 study (JCT 1996) reported that in 1992 hospitals issued $13.152 billion in section 501(c)(3) bonds, and non-hospitals (mainly private universities) issued $9.745 billion. The Joint Committee's revenue estimate for the 1997 Taxpayer Relief Act provision repealing the non-hospital cap totaled $798 million over the 10-year period 1997–2006 (JCT 1997). The Joint Committee's latest tax expenditure budget separately reports the value, for the five years 2006–2010, of the exclusion of interest on state and local governments bonds at $8.4 billion for private nonprofit and qualified public educational facilities and at $13.1 billion for private nonprofit health facilities (JCT 2006a).

Indirect Value of Other Tax Preferences

Of growing importance to charities is the indirect benefit from a host of tax preferences that, deliberately or incidentally, stimulate demand for the services that charities provide (see chapter 5). The exclusion from workers' income for employer-provided health insurance has long been one of the largest tax expenditures; while doctors and other proprietary firms benefit, so do the hospitals, which are mostly non-profit.[9] The Clinton-era education tax credits, designed to help keep college affordable for the middle class, immediately made the list of top-20 tax expenditures; many education experts believe that colleges and universities capture the credits' value by charging higher tuition or granting lower internal aid (Brody 1999a). Nonprofit day care providers benefit from the dependent-care credit. Nonprofit housing developers benefit from the low-income housing tax credit. Although the non-profits' share of these subsidies cannot be quantified, for 2005 to 2009 the Joint Committee on Taxation's (2005a) estimates by budget function peg the cost of tax expenditures—aside from the charitable-contribution deduction—at $62.1 billion for education, $21.6 billion for social services (ignoring $231.7 billion for the child credit), and a staggering $609.9 billion for health.

SUBSIDY OR TAX-BASE DEFINING? A SOVEREIGNTY PERSPECTIVE

As the above tables show, the economic values of the special tax treatments for charities increase the resources available to nonprofit organizations for their philanthropic missions.[10] It is tempting to treat these features of the federal and state tax systems as government subsidies to nonprofit organizations as a quid pro quo in recognition of the philanthropic goods and services they provide. As Brody (1998b) has argued elsewhere, however, the underlying policy rationale for tax policy for the nonprofit sector may be better characterized as involving some mix of (1) an attempt to properly measure the tax base and (2) an explicit intent to subsidize nonprofit organizations. Moreover, both of these approaches seem influenced by a historic desire to respect the sovereign boundaries between the nonprofit and public sectors rather than to ascertain the appropriate ability to pay of a taxpayer (either the entity or its donors).

Charitable Deduction

Although Congress did not include a deduction for charitable contributions in the 1913 enactment of the income tax, from its 1917 inception the deduction has been designed to provide a government subsidy to charitable activities through the tax code. Concerned that the high marginal tax rates enacted to finance World War I would deter donations, Congress permitted individuals to reduce up to 15 percent of their net taxable income by charitable contributions. From that point on, the scope of the deduction steadily expanded—to broaden the range of charitable activities eligible for the deduction; to extend the deduction to corporate contributions; and to increase the percentage of taxable income (later, adjusted gross income) that could be deducted annually. The legislative history of these changes reflects a clear subsidy motivation. In the Tax Reform Act of 1969, for example, Congress declared that raising the contribution limit from 30 percent of adjusted gross income to 50 percent (for cash contributions to public charities) would "strengthen the incentive effect of the charitable contribution deduction." (JCT 1970, 75.)

That policymakers view the charitable-contribution deduction as a subsidy is suggested through its treatment as a tax expenditure by both the Treasury Department and the Joint Committee on Taxation.

Tax expenditures—as distinct from provisions that properly measure the tax base—include special income tax provisions "analogous to direct outlay programs," in the sense that the tax expenditure and an equivalent direct outlay or subsidy are considered to be "alternative means of accomplishing similar budget policy objectives" (JCT 2006a, 2).

As discussed more fully below, the subsidy conception of the charitable-contribution deduction appears firmly embedded in debates about fundamental tax reform. For example, some of the recent proposals to replace the income tax with a consumption-based flat tax include, as an express recognition of the desirability of the subsidy, provisions to allow taxpayers to continue to claim deductions for charitable contributions, while those proposals that withhold the deduction do so in a deliberate attempt to measure donors' tax base more accurately rather than to provide a subsidy (see Clotfelter and Schmalbeck 1996; JCT 1996; Price Waterhouse 1997).

Tax Exemption

Nonprofit organizations clearly have more resources to finance their activities because they do not have to pay income taxes, and charities usually can obtain property tax exemption. In contrast to the charitable-contribution deduction, however, the impetus for the tax exemption appears not to have been to provide an economic subsidy to nonprofits. Rather, tax exemption appears to have emanated from an attempt to properly define the corporate income tax base, overlain with a historical desire (at least in the Anglo-Saxon tradition) to avoid government intrusion into a sphere of activities believed to belong to the church and its secular philanthropic successors.

The base-defining rationale is seen most clearly in the treatment of the nonprofit tax exemption in the federal tax-expenditure budget. Notwithstanding its economic value to nonprofit organizations, the federal exemption from corporate income tax is not treated as a tax expenditure:

> With respect to . . . charities, tax-exempt status is not treated as a tax expenditure because the nonbusiness activities of such organizations generally must predominate and their unrelated business activities are subject to tax. In general, the imputed income derived from nonbusiness activities conducted by individuals or collectively by certain nonprofit organizations is *outside the normal income tax base* (JCT 2006a, 7; emphasis added).

In other words, tax exemption does not constitute a tax subsidy because the income from the nonbusiness activities of nonprofit organizations never rises to the level of taxable in the first place.

This explanation, however, begs the question of why nonprofit enterprises' income should fall outside of the normal tax base. For example, why should the income of commercial charities such as hospitals be treated differently than income of their for-profit counterparts for providing similar goods and services (see chapter 8)? The issue broadly applies to any income earned by nonprofits from activities that have a commercial character, even if such activities are deemed to be for the organization's primary tax-exempt purpose. As the proprietary sector makes further incursions into traditionally nonprofit industries (such as higher education and social services), and as charities expand their search for related sources of revenue, pressures on the definition of a normal tax base will increase. (See Ben-Ner and Gui 1993; Brody 1996.)

Even if tax exemption for charities represents a subsidy, exemption rather than direct grants makes for a rather inefficient form of subsidy. Consistent with both the history of the tax exemption and its form, perhaps exemption represents an attempt by the government to respect the sovereignty of the nonprofit sector in much the same way that federal tax rules respect the sovereignty of state and local governments. Although no one would argue that the nonprofit sector enjoys true co-sovereignty with the public sector (because the nonprofit sector lacks the compulsory powers that inhere in a sovereign), tax exemption nonetheless carries with it a sense of leaving the nonprofit sector inviolate, and the very concept of sovereignty embodies the independent power of self-governance.

Indeed, parallels between how the federal government treats local governments and the way in which it treats the nonprofit sector are quite striking. (Even JCT [1996] lumped nonprofits together with state and local governments, without commenting on the juxtaposition.) The federal income tax excludes from gross income "income derived from any public utility or the exercise of any essential governmental function and accruing to a State or any political subdivision thereof" (IRC sec. 115(a)). States and municipalities that borrow may generally issue bonds whose interest is tax exempt in the hands of the bondholders. Payments of state and local income and property taxes are deductible from income, but user fees paid to the government are treated as nondeductible payments for services.

As already described, each of these inter-government tax treatments finds an analogue in the tax treatment of charities. Charities are exempt from the corporate (or trust) income tax, although income from the performance of business activities unrelated to the charity's exempt purpose is taxable. Charities may issue tax-exempt bonds. Contributions made to charities are generally deductible from income. Payments made to a charity for a particular service (such as tuition or for hospital care), however, are not deductible.

A reasonable case can thus be made that the underlying purpose of the tax exemption is not to establish a quid pro quo relationship between government and charities in which charities receive the exemption in exchange for doing particular good deeds. Instead, as explained below, exemption establishes a relationship of co-sovereignty in which government stays out of charities' day-to-day business (by not taxing them) and charities stay out of the business of petitioning government for subvention.

How Tax-Exempt Status Affects the Range and Scope of Charitable Activities

What strings are attached to being able to receive tax-deductible contributions and being treated as tax-exempt?

The range of charities receiving tax-deductible contributions is quite broad. That is, despite the subsidy motive that seems to explain the rationale for the charitable contribution deduction, the government has not, as a matter of policy, tried to target the subsidy to particular uses. (For example, both a pro-life nonprofit and a pro-choice nonprofit can qualify for the tax treatment for charities.) Some might argue that open-endedness follows logically from using the tax code to provide the subsidy, because tax subsidies are harder to target than direct subsidies. Yet many tax expenditures do come with eligibility rules that try to distinguish between activities that merit subsidy and those that don't. (The tax credit for research and experimentation is a particularly good example.) In the case of the charitable deduction, the only real rule is that a nonprofit be recognized as a 501(c)(3) organization.

For charities, one main set of strings are the restrictions on lobbying ← and the prohibition on electioneering, again explainable by sovereignty analysis. These limitations can be viewed as an attempt by the "public sovereign" to tell the other that "your boundaries will be respected as long as you stay on your side of the line—don't engage in overtly political activities." (Organizations exempt under sections other than 501(c)(3) can engage in greater amounts of lobbying, as well as some political activity—but these organizations cannot offer contributors a charitable-contribution deduction, nor, in general, may contributors to these entities claim business expense deductions for amounts used for lobbying and political activity.) Similarly, other rules that determine which commercial activities will be granted tax exemption can be viewed as attempting to police the borders between nonprofit and for-profit organizations (Simon, Dale and Chisolm 2006).

Apart from increasing the financial resources of nonprofits, the charitable-contribution deduction and the income tax exemption affect the range and scope of charitable activities in several ways. The decision to subsidize charitable contributions through a tax deduction, instead of some other means, implicitly favors some philanthropic activities over others.[11] Particular requirements of qualifying for tax exemption also cause nonprofit organizations to act differently than they might otherwise. Lastly, because of its close link to the tax system, the magnitude of the nonprofit subsidy will be sensitive to broader changes in tax policy. (See Brody 1999a.)

CHARITABLE-CONTRIBUTION DEDUCTION

By its terms, the charitable-contribution deduction provides a neutral tax subsidy that is not directly targeted to any particular set of charitable activities. In practice, however, the deduction tends to high-bracket donors (affluent individuals and corporations) with the greatest incentive to give. One reason is that lower-income taxpayers typically do not itemize deductions and hence do not receive a deduction for charitable contributions. In addition, among itemizers, the subsidy increases with the taxpayer's marginal tax rate.

To describe the government's share of donations made, however, does not necessarily describe the additional amount of giving deductibility induces: Depending on why donors give, the tax subsidy could be more or less efficient. If donors are inelastic in their decision to give—that is, if they would give with or without tax deductibility—then the tax subsidy would be wasted. Many theories exist of why people give to charity, and apparently tax considerations are not paramount. A pure altruist cares simply about increasing the charity's output, but a dollar of support from another source (either other private donors or the government) would crowd out the altruist's donations once the level of output was satisfactory. Studies have found incomplete crowd-out, however, implying that donors give either because of continued need elsewhere or out of noninstrumental motives, such as religious, ideological, political, historical, or other social reasons (Steinberg 1989; Vesterlund 2006).

James Andreoni (1989, 1990), dubs donors "warm glow altruists," finding that they enjoy contributing to charitable organizations and get greater satisfaction the larger their gift to the charity. The publicity given to many donations suggests a status theory—either signaling to other donors that a certain level of giving to a particular charity is expected of those in the group,[12] or signaling one's wealth or income to the peer group or society at large (Glazer and Konrad 1996). Under these models, giving may even be excessive. (See, e.g., Salamon [1995] discussing "philanthropic particularism," "philanthropic paternalism," and "philanthropic amateurism.") William Randolph (1995, 2005) has suggested that even high-bracket taxpayers might really just be time shifting—contributing in years when tax rates are highest, rather than changing their lifetime amount of giving. Proposals to improve the efficiency of the tax subsidy for charity include enacting a floor equal to a low percentage of the taxpayer's adjusted gross income under deductible donations (a floor now exists under the aggregate of all the itemized deductions of high-income taxpayers). Proposals to improve the fairness of the subsidy include an above-the-line deduction[13] or substituting a tax credit for the tax deduction. (See Gravelle 2005; Steuerle 2005.)

As a separate matter, if higher-income donors had preferences for giving that broadly reflect those of the population at large, providing an incentive to contribute that increased with a taxpayer's income would not tend to favor one type of charitable activity over others. Indeed, in the parlance of "optimal tax theory," one might argue that targeting the subsidy in this manner would be a cost-efficient way of encouraging giving, because the subsidy would be aimed at taxpayers who, some studies have shown, are more likely to respond to a reduction in the price of giving.

But there is considerable evidence that higher-income donors tend to channel their giving to charities in the arts and, particularly, education (Clotfelter 1992; Havens, O'Herlihy, and Schervish 2006). Thus, providing the subsidy in the form of an itemized deduction—instead of, for example, a tax credit or deduction available to itemizers and non-itemizers alike—skews the subsidy contributions toward charities such as arts and education and away from churches and social service organizations with low-income clienteles.[14]

EXEMPTION AND THE UNRELATED BUSINESS INCOME TAX

The attempt to draw boundaries between exempt and commercial activity can lead to suboptimal social policy. Notably, nonprofit hospitals are entitled to section 501(c)(3) tax exemption, but the returns to capital that nonprofit physician practices earn are not (of course, the government taxes wages earned from both for-profit and nonprofit hospitals). The Internal Revenue Service has been struggling with the appropriate limits on "whole hospital joint ventures" and "joint operating agreements" with proprietary partners (Rev. Rul. 98-15, 1998-1 Cum. Bull. 718; Rev. Rul. 2004-51, 2004-1 Cum. Bull. 974). However, to the extent it makes economic sense for health care to be provided earlier (e.g., preventive care rather than treatment), we inefficiently constrain provision of preventive health care by denying charity exemption.

Moreover, the income tax exemption can cause nonprofit organizations to become more commercial, but the mechanism through which this happens is a subtle one. If nonprofits act as if a tension exists between earning income to finance their primary mission and undertaking their primary mission, then they will only pursue commercial activities when they can earn a premium return. Income tax exemption, though initially granted to respect the sovereignty of the nonprofit sector, creates opportunities for not-for-profits to earn such premium returns (Steuerle 1988).[15]

Limiting the exemption to related activities probably reinforces internal incentives that nonprofits already have to limit their commercial pursuits to areas where excess returns are likely to exist, which involve cost complementarities between the primary mission-related activity and secondary commercial activities (Cordes and Weisbrod 1998).

The requirement that nonprofit organizations pay taxes on income earned from unrelated business activities appears, on its face, to be quite strict. However, the practical operation of the regime can be slippery. First, a particular activity is exempt or taxable depending on the purposes of the entity engaged in it. The Internal Revenue Service from time to time issues such odd rulings as the declaration that a nonprofit cemetery association may sell caskets for burial in the cemetery and use the proceeds for cemetery maintenance without triggering unrelated business income tax (IRS Private Letter Ruling 9814051 [1998]).

Second, nonprofit organizations have sought out perfectly legal ways of shifting costs from their tax-exempt activities to taxable activities to reduce, if not eliminate, tax liability. Because it is easier to shift costs from tax-exempt activities to taxable activities when these activities are complements in production, nonprofit organizations appear to have been somewhat selective in the types of unrelated business activities they have chosen to undertake (Cordes and Weisbrod 1998; Hines 1999; Sansing 1998; Yetman 2001, 2005). Because many unrelated businesses accordingly make use of assets used in or employees devoted to exempt activities, the allocation of dual-use expenses to the taxable activity can minimize net income. Indeed, most unrelated business income tax returns report net losses (Riley 2004, reporting that 38 percent of the charitable organizations filing Form 990-T in 2001 had unrelated business income that was taxable), and the IRS's own regulations limit its ability to reallocate deductions under current law.[16]

In some cases, the combination of tax rules inadvertently solves problems. For example, if a charity has issued tax-exempt bond financing to build the facility, the charity may not use more than 5 percent of the proceeds for a taxable activity; accordingly, to preserve the exempt status of its bond financing, the charity will be loath to overallocate the costs of dual-use assets away from the exempt activity.

EXEMPTION FROM PROPERTY TAXES

State property tax exemption does not automatically follow from Internal Revenue Code section 501(c)(3) status, but rather must be independently obtained (although the 501(c)(3) requirements are often comparable). Many property tax statutes are less developed than the federal income tax regime. In some states, charities can forfeit property tax exemption by using the property, even in part, for an unrelated business, while in other states, the exemption is apportioned. Similarly, in some but not all states, exemption does not extend to property rented out to commercial tenants. Finally, many states adopt various acreage limits for exempt property held by particular types of organizations.[17] Separately, as described below, in some localities, agreements by exempt owners to make "payments in lieu of taxes" have modified the statutory exemption.

Recently, lawsuits and proposed legislation asserting tighter state and local definitions for exemption reflect a growing divergence of federal and state policies on tax exemption and a growing acceptance by the states of a quid pro quo rationale, particularly for health care organizations.[18] See discussion below, in the section entitled "State and Local Initiatives to Limit the Nonprofit Property Tax Exemption."

REMOVING THE CAP ON TAX-EXEMPT BORROWING

The ability of charities to issue tax-exempt debt favors charities that generate a revenue stream sufficiently predictable to support an acceptable bond rating. Moreover, a nonprofit hospital can issue an unlimited amount of 501(c)(3) bonds, and in 1997 Congress removed the prior $150 million cap on non-hospital charities. The ability to issue low-rate debt while earning a market return on investment assets proves irresistible to well-endowed colleges and universities (even some private foundations are bond financing, most often for offices); the arbitrage profits need not be returned to the federal government unless the bond is actually secured by the endowment or investment assets (Brody 1997). The most recently available Form 990 of Harvard University—admittedly an extreme example—reports more than $1.8 billion in tax-exempt debt issued as of June 30, 2004.

LOBBYING AND POLITICAL ACTIVITIES

At the political boundaries of charities, it is worth asking whether the tax restrictions on lobbying and the ban on electioneering have really had much effect, or, rather, have changed the way in which these organizations participate in the political process. Non-charity exempt organizations—such as social welfare organizations, labor unions, and trade associations—operate under looser restrictions. Congress imposes the stricter regime on charities because it does not want tax-deducted charitable contributions to be used for these purposes; however, charities generally view the current lobbying regulations as quite generous, although, with inflation, the dollar limits of the available safe harbor are starting to bind some large charities. The rules do not limit the production of educational position papers and other publications not involving a call to action to contact legislators (IRC sec. 501(h) and Treasury Regulations secs. 1.501(h)-1 through -3). Moreover, in *Regan v. Taxation With Representation* (1983), the U.S. Supreme Court upheld the lobbying limitations against First Amendment challenge because charities can, and often do, establish social welfare affiliates exempt under section 501(c)(4) to conduct lobbying.

In addition, social change can sometimes instead be advanced through the other branches. Neither public-interest litigation nor contacting the administrative branch and its agencies (for example, about rule-making) constitute lobbying under the tax rules.

Finally, political campaign activity more often results in settlement and a fine than permanent revocation of exemption.[19] However, the IRS made headlines in 2004 when it initiated more than 100 investigations of charities (notably the NAACP) for election-year campaign activities (U.S. Treasury Inspector General for Tax Administration 2005). (See also chapter 9.)

As a separate matter, charities that conduct international grant-making at times come into contact with rules designed to prevent the sponsorship of terrorism. In December 2005, following substantial criticisms from the charitable sector, the Treasury Department released revised voluntary guidelines that, while they "do not supersede or modify legal requirements, they [do] promote the development of a risk-based, transparent approach to guard against the threat of diversion of charitable funds for use by terrorists and their supporters" (U.S. Treasury 2005, 2).

Relying on the Tax Code: A Not-So-Mighty Fortress

Because most subsidies to nonprofit organizations arrive in the form of tax incentives, changes in the tax code can affect the financial value of such subsidies. Important recent and/or current examples of such changes include changes in tax rates, the tax treatment of estates, and the tax treatment of capital income; attempts to better target charitable incentives; and proposals for fundamental reform of the income tax.

Changing Tax Rates

Consider recent dramatic changes in marginal (e.g., last dollar) income tax rates that directly affect the subsidy value of the charitable-contribution deduction. Legislation enacted in the 1980s slashed the top individual tax rate from 70 percent to 50 percent (in 1981) and 28 percent (in 1986). The top rate subsequently increased, to 31 percent in 1990 and to 39.6 percent in 1993. Finally, the 21st-century Bush tax rate cuts have been fully phased in, reducing the top rate to 35 percent. As more taxpayers are subject to the alternative minimum tax, however, the value of the charitable deduction will be set by the 28 percent (or the lower 26 percent) alternative minimum tax rate. In addition, in a move to simplify the tax system for more individuals, Congress deliberately reduced the number of itemizers by increasing the standard deduction in various years.

Especially in the 1980s, there was concern that large rate cuts, which significantly increased the after-tax cost of giving, would adversely affect contributions. Surprisingly, however, studies found that expectations of drastic contribution falloffs failed to predict taxpayer response; donations increased overall and at every income level except the highest, where the fall in donations was smaller than predicted (Auten, Cilke, and Randolph 1992; Clotfelter 1990).

The Estate Tax

Similar studies have been made of the impact on giving of reducing or eliminating the estate tax. Repealing the estate tax altogether would have offsetting effects on charitable bequests. On one hand, estates that were previously taxable would have more assets that could be distributed to both heirs and charities; this "wealth effect" would tend to increase charitable bequests. On the other hand, estate tax repeal would increase the cost of making a bequest from the current average of $0.45 to $1.00. This "price effect" would have the opposite effect, reducing bequests. The empirical evidence indicates that the price effect would be stronger than the wealth effect, so that one estimate is that the net effect of abolishing the estate tax would be to reduce bequests by between 22 and 37 percent, or by between $3.6 billion and $6 billion per (Bakija, Gale, and Slemrod 2003). (See also CBO 2004.)[20]

Tax Treatment of Capital Income

Changes in the effective income tax rate on capital income can also affect the relative value of the nonprofit income tax exemption. After all, subsidies to private businesses in the form of tax credits can have unintended effects on nonprofits. In the 1980s, for example, in the first wave of tax reform under President Ronald Reagan, certain sectors of the business community actually enjoyed *negative* income tax rates through the combination of accelerated depreciation and investment tax credits on new equipment (JCT 1982). In this setting the relative advantage resulting from the *zero* tax rate conferred by the nonprofit exemption was eroded. An implication was that during this period, nonprofits had less incentive than before (or after) to seek out related commercial ventures as a source of income.[21] Some might be pleased with this effect on the ground that nonprofits should be discouraged from expanding their financial resources by undertaking businesslike activities. Yet the relative reduction in the value of the corporate income tax exemption also may have caused nonprofits to avoid pursuing some legitimate opportunities for exploiting cost complementarities between their primary activity and ancillary profit-making activities. Nonprofits should also have found it financially more attractive to engage in nonexempt income-producing activities because these benefited from the investment tax incentives provided to for-profit businesses.

Lastly, from colonial times, the states have also granted exemptions to infant business industries,[22] a practice enjoying a resurgence as states deliberately choose the tool of property tax exemption to entice business relocation.[23] Like the case of negative tax rates, such property tax abatement programs have the effect of reducing the relative advantage that nonprofits enjoy from the local property tax exemption. In addition, to the extent that such tax abatement programs shrink the local property tax base, local governments may look to other sources of revenue, such as limiting the nonprofit property tax exemption. To some extent, nonprofits might be able to defend the exemption by contending that removing it will encourage mobile nonprofit organizations to move, thereby costing jobs. But the fact that nonprofit organizations do not pay other taxes, as for-profit businesses do, may somewhat weaken that argument.

Targeting The Tax Subsidy

The fact that tax incentives for charitable giving tend to favor certain charities over others has also not been lost on policymakers. In the late 1990s, Republican proposals to grant additional tax credits for contribution to charities that primarily serve the poor attempted to better target the tax subsidy that the charitable deduction is intended to provide. The charities, however, closed rank, thwarting the attempt to treat anti-poverty philanthropy as more worthy of public support

by asserting that they do not know the income levels of their beneficiaries. In addition, Congress might selectively repeal tax exemption for
particular institutions, such as hospitals, continuing the trend to identify overly commercial activities as candidates for taxation (JCT 2005a).

As a separate matter, the Joint Committee on Taxation (2005c)
recently described three alternative proposals to limit the deduction
for donations of appreciated property: (1) allowing a deduction for the
contributor's basis only (or fair market value, if less); (2) allowing a
fair market value deduction only for publicly traded securities; and
(3) allowing a fair market value deduction for both publicly traded
securities and assets used in the charity's conduct of its exempt purpose.
Notably, the Joint Committee raised an additional efficiency concern:
that, other things being equal, a charity would prefer a gift of cash to
a gift of property to be sold.[24] A similar basis-only deduction rule that
existed temporarily under the alternative minimum tax suggests how
costly such targeted rules could be to charities.[25]

Effects of Proposals for Fundamental Tax Reform

The ongoing debate about federal tax reform offers some clear examples
not only of continued support for providing, and in some cases extending, tax incentives for private giving, but also of how some elements
of the nonprofit subsidy can be at the mercy of broader trends in
tax policy.

Although the variety of proposals for tax reform that have been
offered in recent years can overwhelm the casual observer, several
broad models have emerged for consideration at various times in the
public debate about reforming the income tax: (1) a simplified version
of the current personal income tax, (2) variants of a personal consumption tax, (3) the value-added tax, and (4) the national retail sales tax.
The possible effects on charities of these four types of proposals were
first analyzed in the mid-1990s. (See Brody 1999a.) Versions of some
of these proposals have been perennially reintroduced, and President
Bush's tax reform panel on fundamental tax reform again aired these
issues.[26] The analysis here focuses on the implications of three possible
reform models featured in the final report of the tax reform panel:
(1) a simplified income tax; (2) a simplified income tax with significant
consumption tax features; and (3) a value-added tax.[27]

The baseline proposal put forward by the tax reform panel ("Plan
A: Simplified Income Tax Plan") would affect charitable giving in
several ways (President's Advisory Panel 2005.) It would replace the
current six marginal tax brackets ranging from 10 percent to 35 percent
with four brackets ranging from 15 percent to 33 percent, and would
repeal the alternative minimum tax. Gauging the effects of these

changes on the after-tax cost of giving are complex, though the general effect would be to lower the marginal tax rate many taxpayers face, thereby increasing the after-tax cost of giving. In some cases, the change would be significant (e.g., a decrease in the marginal tax rate from 25 percent to 15 percent, increasing the after-tax cost of giving from $0.75 to $0.85); in others it would be more modest (e.g., a decrease in the top marginal tax rate from 35 percent to 33 percent); and in still other cases, the marginal tax rate would remain unchanged at 25 percent. Based on the modest response to larger changes in the after-tax cost of giving in the 1980s, one might expect these changes by themselves to have no effect, or perhaps a small effect, on giving.

Perhaps more significant than the rate changes, Plan A would retain the current deduction for charitable contributions while modifying and expanding it. The proposal to retain the charitable deduction is symbolically important given that Plan A proposes eliminating a number of other tax deductions. In addition, Plan A would extend the charitable deduction to taxpayers who do not itemize deductions. The revenue cost of extending the charitable deduction to non-itemizers would be offset by limiting all charitable deductions, whether made by itemizers or non-itemizers, to amounts made in excess of 1 percent of a taxpayer's adjusted gross income. This latter proposed change would reduce the after-tax dollar value of the charitable contribution, but it would not affect the "last dollar" or marginal incentive to give of the vast majority of taxpayers.[28]

Additional changes proposed under Plan A, though not explicitly lowering the financial cost of giving, would lower the transactions costs of making certain types of gifts. Taxpayers would be allowed to make charitable deductions directly from their individual retirement accounts, instead of first having to withdraw such funds, include them as taxable income, and then make a charitable contribution. Taxpayers wishing to make gifts of appreciated property to charities would also be allowed to sell such assets and donate the sale proceeds to charities instead of having to donate the asset itself to the charity.

The tax reform panel also offers two suggestions for tightening some aspects of tax-favored charitable giving. The panel suggests that taxpayers be allowed to claim deductions for used clothing and household items only if they receive written documentation of the value of such contributions from the charity.[29] Reflecting recent concerns about greater financial accountability of nonprofits, the reform proposal also recommends that the government take action to "ensure better oversight and governance of tax-exempt organizations," without, however, offering specific proposals for how to implement the recommendation (President's Advisory Panel 2005, 78).

Although the panel does not propose replacing the income tax with a consumption-based flat tax, it does recommend as an alternative to

Plan A that consideration be given to replacing the current income tax with an income-consumption tax hybrid that has many important features of a consumption tax. The treatment of charitable contributions under this option, known as "Plan B: The Growth and Investment Tax Plan," are quite similar to those proposed under Plan A. However, the consumption tax treatment of business enterprises under Plan B would essentially eliminate the benefits of the nonprofit income tax exemption.

To the extent that Plan B might be seen as a precursor to ultimately replacing the personal income tax with a personal consumption tax, one important policy issue would be whether the charitable deduction would be retained under a consumption tax. Unlike the mortgage interest deduction, which is economically incompatible with the "correct" definition of the tax bases under a consumption tax, the charitable deduction could be retained as an explicit means of encouraging a particular type of consumption—charitable contributions.[30] By retaining and actually expanding the charitable deduction in Plan B, the tax reform panel comes down on the side of retaining the charitable deduction.

On the other hand, past proponents of a clean consumption-based flat tax—one that allows no deductions—have argued against retaining the charitable-contribution deduction, asserting, in part, that it provides a subsidy for certain forms of consumption affluent taxpayers favor. In the event that moving toward a consumption tax leads to abolition of the charitable deduction, past estimates suggest that such a move would reduce charitable giving by between 10 and 30 percent.[31]

Finally, the panel also discusses the potential future role that a value-added tax might have in the U.S. tax system. If federal income taxes were scrapped altogether and replaced by a value-added tax, the most visible effect would be the elimination of the charitable-contribution deduction. Moreover, because all capital income would face a zero federal tax rate, much of the relative advantage of the nonprofit tax exemption would be eroded, as would the advantage associated with being able to issue tax-exempt bonds. (If all interest income is excluded from the tax base, then all bonds are tax-exempt). The proposals that would apply tax to inputs purchased by charities would remove exemption from all but their "value added" to goods and services and would require complex accounting and filing obligations to boot. Reform would also eliminate the tax-free treatment of fringe benefits, including health insurance, provided to workers. Finally, the proposals would in general collect a single level of tax on a host of commercial charitable services, notably health care.

It seems unlikely, however, that a value-added tax would be introduced as a complete replacement of existing federal income taxes. A more likely outcome is that future budget deficit pressures might create a political environment in which a VAT would be enacted as a revenue source to supplement federal taxes. In that event, the current individual tax incentives for charitable giving (perhaps as modified by the tax panel's proposed changes in Plan A) would remain intact. Nonprofit organizations would, however, face issues of complying with a value-added tax of the sort discussed above.

STATE AND LOCAL INITIATIVES TO LIMIT THE NONPROFIT PROPERTY TAX EXEMPTION

Three features characterize the current property tax exemption for charities (see Brody 2002, xi). First, the data, although sparse, suggest that exemptions granted to nonprofit organizations constitute only a small fraction of total exemptions (the largest category of exempt property belongs to governments). Second, municipal demands for voluntary payments in lieu of taxes (PILOTs[32]) occur only sporadically, and even where PILOT programs exist, they raise comparatively little revenue. Third, the press treats the charity exemption as front-page news. This is not, it turns out, the paradox it appears.

If "all politics is local," then no tax system is more local than the property tax. Property tax exemptions are enacted at the state level, often in the state constitution. However, property ownership by charities tends to cluster in center cities. Because property tax units are local (municipal, county, or special districts, such as school districts), the burden of exemption is distributed unevenly throughout the state. Worse, the same municipalities that host a disproportionately high share of nonprofit property often suffer a disproportionately high demand for public expenditures. Thus, averages mask the widely varying impact of exemptions on particular communities and of taxes or PILOTs on particular nonprofits. Moreover, the benefits of a particular charity's activities might be enjoyed more broadly than the narrowly defined community that bears the cost of the exemption. Finally, as charities engage in a wider range of activities, including some very commercial ones, public support for exemption crumbles. Much to the nonprofit sector's consternation, tax exemption has come to be viewed as a government subsidy rather than an inherent entitlement of the organizational form. Notably, as states grow increasingly concerned about the health needs of the uninsured, legislatures might be tempted to call upon nonprofit hospitals to spend more on charity care as a condition of property tax exemption.[33]

In applying PILOTs, the charities that look most attractive to local governments are those (1) that have income (excluding, in general, only donations) and (2) whose income comes primarily from patrons outside the taxing jurisdiction. Accordingly, taxing the nonprofit can be viewed as a proxy for taxing the nonresident patrons of the organization. Currently, the practice of challenging exemption or seeking PILOTs focuses on hospitals and institutions of higher education. Under the same theory, municipalities could extend this policy to museums and performing arts organizations—and even to break-even social service nonprofits, thus passing their costs on to government funders, state and federal. (Such a theory might provide a nonconstitutional explanation of why municipalities have not sought to tax churches, which rely primarily on donations, and whose benefits are primarily local.)

USING THE TAX CODE TO IMPROVE NONPROFIT GOVERNANCE

Increasingly, the federal tax regime affects the governance of nonprofit organizations. Currently, the influence is largely passive, taking the form of mandated public disclosures that, in theory, spur good governance (U.S. Government Accountability Office 2005). Today, private foundations face specific prohibitions in the tax code on financial transactions between insiders and the organization. In the future, however, self-dealing prohibitions might be extended to public charities. (See JCT 2005h; SFC 2004.)[34] Other governance proposals—such as a minimum and maximum board size (e.g., between 3 and 15), and standing for private persons to enforce federal tax rules (SFC 2004)—seem more theoretical than genuinely threatening (although Independent Sector [2005] supports a minimum board size of three as a condition of section 501(c)(3) status).

As with state nonprofit law, the tax rules address problems of self-dealing (termed "private inurement" by the Internal Revenue Code) rather than weak management. Since 1969, the tax code has prohibited self-dealing transactions (except for payment of reasonable compensation) between that subset of charities called private foundations and its insiders. For a nonprivate foundation—or public charity—in 1996 Congress adopted intermediate sanctions legislation that imposes a penalty tax of 25 percent on the excess benefits portion of a transaction between an insider and the charity. A smaller penalty applies to fiduciaries that knowingly approved the transactions, and the statute essentially requires restitution of the excess benefit to the charity. The intermediate sanctions regime, however, does not reach other breaches of fiduciary duty. Thus, short of revoking exemption under the poorly understood prohibition against private benefit, the IRS cannot statutorily address such inadequacies of governance as running an indifferent charitable program, accumulating excess income, or paying insufficient attention to investment returns.[35]

As a practical matter, though, the Internal Revenue Service has been able to achieve sometimes fundamental management reforms through negotiation. For example, the IRS can threaten revocation of exemption in order to bring the charity to the bargaining table and then settle for a closing agreement that spells out detailed governance changes (see Brody 1999b).

The recent emphasis on public disclosure of charity tax returns and other filings is nothing less than revolutionary, although sunshine creates both clarity and shadows. Federal tax law obligates a charity to furnish its exemption application and last three tax returns (Forms 990) to any person upon request. Moreover, third parties—notably GuideStar and the National Center for Charitable Statistics—have begun to post information on the Internet that enables donors and other interested parties to compare charities online.

Although the IRS Form 990 is currently the most widely available uniform document on individual charity finances, it is not a complete window into nonprofit operations. Because of exemptions, it can be difficult, if not impossible, to obtain information on churches and on charities with less than $25,000 in gross receipts. Moreover, many of the forms as filed contain errors, some materially misleading. Poor quality filings obviously impede the value of disclosure. Some noncompliance is because of ignorance, some because of a desire to hide costs of fundraising and administrative expenses relative to program expenditures, and some is intentional. It is hoped that compliance will improve as boards recognize that the Form 990 is the public face of the charity. Moreover, the IRS's move to allowing (if not requiring) electronic filing will address problems of omission and accuracy. Substantively, because the Form 990 focuses on finances, it does not provide much insight into the nature and quality of charity activities.

In a congressionally mandated study of the disclosure rules that apply to exemption organizations, the staff of the Joint Committee on Taxation offered options to require disclosure of private letter rulings and audit memoranda without "redaction" of identifying information; business tax returns of exempt organizations and their taxable affiliates[36]; and a description of lobbying activities, including amounts spent on self-defense lobbying and on nonpartisan research and analysis that includes a limited call to action (JCT 2000). The Joint Committee staff asserted that such disclosure allows not only increased public oversight but "also allows the public to determine whether the organizations should be supported—either through continued tax benefits or contributions of donors—and whether changes in the laws regarding such organizations are needed" (JCT 2000, 5). Many of these suggestions have attracted strong criticism by nonprofits asserting privacy rights in information that they are willing to file with the tax collector but not disclose to the public. It should be appreciated, though, that the charity itself can always release identifying information, and so prospective donors remain free to withhold contributions until satisfied with information obtained from the charity.

A charity that violates the private inurement proscription also violates state nonprofit law. Depending on the resources and inclinations of the state attorney general's office, the charity may face investigations on two fronts. Under current privacy law applying to exempt organizations, the state can share information with the IRS, but the IRS cannot share information about its investigation short of notifying the state of revocation of exempt status. The Joint Committee staff's disclosure study contained one well-received suggestion: that Congress would generally require the IRS to inform the appropriate state official of the progress of an exempt organization investigation. Such a proposal, with confidentially obligations on the states, has strong support from nonprofits as well as legislators (see Independent Sector 2005) and was included in the Pension Protection Act of 2006 (Sec. 1224). In a case where both federal and state investigations are proceeding, though, principles of federalism suggest that the IRS should have to defer to the state, or at least stay its hand until the proceedings conclude; such an approach would protect the charity from the risk that different governments would demand inconsistent governance changes

FUTURE POLICY DIRECTIONS

As noted at the beginning of this essay, tax exemption defines an important nexus between government and nonprofit organizations in the United States. Symbolically, in the public's eye conferral of tax-exempt status is seen as legitimating the activities of individual non-profit organizations. At a more practical level, tax exemption expands the financial resources of nonprofit organizations in a variety of important ways. An important consequence to the tax code is that the environment in which charities operate can shift in important ways as tax law changes.

Charities are vulnerable to—or would benefit from—four different types of changes in federal tax law. First, change could come head on, if Congress were to deliberately alter the eligibility rules; for example, Congress might repeal the tax exemption of nonprofit hospitals. Second, change could come indirectly as a result of overall changes to the tax structure that affect the value of the charitable-contribution deduction or of the income-tax exemption; for example, Congress might alter the tax burden on individuals (thus inversely altering the income- or estate-tax price of giving) or on businesses (thus directly altering the relative

tax benefit of income-tax exemption). Third, change could come incidentally through simplifying the tax code of rules that happen to fuel
demand for the types of services charities provide; for example, Congress might strip away the tuition tax credits or eliminate the exclusion
from workers' income for the value of employer-provided health insurance. The fourth potential change could come from a major federalization of the regulation of nonprofit governance.

Their reliance on tax subsidies suggests that nonprofits would not
give them up without a fight. Viewing nonprofits as above the political
fray was always probably an idealized image, and the growing talk of
tax reform is already bringing forth educational efforts by charities.
The increasingly political visibility of nonprofits will, in turn, likely
put increased pressure on the current loose lobbying restrictions. In the
process of defending against fundamental threats to their tax subsidies,
charities risk appearing like any other special interest—and they could
forfeit special claim to subsidies in the process.

Both this chapter and the others in this section suggest that the effects
of eliminating all or some of the tax provisions that currently benefit
nonprofit organizations would certainly not be uniform. For example,
nonprofit organizations that depend on charitable contributions for a
large portion of their financial resources have more reason for concern
about tax changes that raise the after-tax cost of giving than do nonprofits that depend for their financing on fees-for-service paid out of
government spending. Similarly, nonprofit organizations that rely on
subsidies for specific social services that are provided through tax
credits are more apt to be affected by changes in these provisions than
are their counterparts that depend on charitable contributions.

Lastly, anytime two different tax regimes could apply to the same
economic activity, the opportunity for tax arbitrage exists. There is
some evidence that nonprofits have become increasingly aware of these
opportunities and sophisticated at exploiting them. For example, some
nonprofits use unrelated business activities to earn additional revenue
and then shelter that income from tax by overallocating to the taxable
activity the expenses of dual-use assets. Yet the desire of policymakers
to preserve not only the political boundaries between nonprofit organizations and the government but also the economic boundaries between
nonprofit organizations and for-profit enterprises may impose limits
on this trend. As charities grow more sophisticated in operating both
exempt and taxable enterprises, Congress might be unwilling to maintain the existing flexible tax regime. Short of replacing the income tax
with a consumption tax, should it prove too hard to define taxable
income for nonprofits, Congress could instead simply impose a (probably low-level) tax on investment income, making all nonprofit
organizations potentially taxable.

NOTES

1. Under the complicated rate structure now in effect, donors have an incentive to donate "collectibles": Tax on the appreciation is saved at a 28 percent rate instead of the general 15 percent rate on long-term capital gains.

2. In general, the Internal Revenue Code (IRC) limits the current deduction to 50 percent of the donor's adjusted gross income for cash gifts and 30 percent of adjusted gross income for gifts of appreciated property. The limitations for gifts to that subset of charities known as private foundations are 30 percent for cash and 20 percent for appreciated property. Any excess may be carried forward for five years under the same limitations. Moreover, the amount of a gift to a private foundation of property other than publicly traded securities is limited to the donor's basis in the property (IRC sec. 170).

3. As of this writing, estates become taxable only if the value of the taxable estate exceeds $2 million. Under current law, the taxable threshold is slated to rise to $3.5 million in 2009, become unlimited (abolishing the tax) in 2010, and then drop back down to $1 million in 2011. For estates that are taxable, the current marginal tax rate begins at 45 percent and rises to 50 percent.

4. Attempts have also been made to estimate the price elasticity of giving by charitable sector. Most recently, Arthur Brooks (2006) has used data from the 2001 Panel Study of Income Dynamics to estimate sector-specific price elasticities of giving. The estimated price elasticities of giving to religion, education, social welfare, and health are −1.30, −1.18, −1.43, and −0.64, respectively.

5. This factor is arrived at as follows. Assume that an organization receives $1,000 in contributions. Based on data provided in Center on Philanthropy at Indiana University (2005), approximately 75 percent of this amount ($750) can be attributed to private donors, 4.8 percent ($48) to private corporations, and 8 percent ($80) to bequests from estates. The remaining amount is from foundations that, having already received their donations, are assumed not to be directly affected by changes in the tax treatment of charitable contributions. Eliminating the charitable contribution deduction for individual and corporate contributions would raise the cost of giving by 30 percent and 40 percent, respectively, given the assumptions made about tax rates in the text. Eliminating the deduction for charitable bequests would raise the cost of making bequests by 45 percent. Applying price elasticities of giving of −1.0 in the case of individual and corporate giving, and of 2.0 in the case of charitable bequest, results in a reduction in the predicted contribution of just over $300, or 30 percent.

6. This result is obtained by replacing the assumed value of −1.0 for the price elasticity of giving in the calculation described in note 5 with a value of −0.50, while maintaining the assumption that the price elasticity of corporate giving equals −1.0, and the price elasticity of charitable bequests remains at −2.0.

7. Churches are not required to file IRS Form 990. Hence the public charities listed in table 4.5 do not include the churches listed in table 4.2.

8. One might believe that the widely reported real estate boom should have caused the value of the nonprofit property tax exemption to increase considerably since 1999, which is the year on which the estimates in Cordes, Gantz, and Pollak (2002) are based. This perception, however, may not be correct. Although there have been dramatic increases in the prices of *residential* real

estate in recent years, the estimated nationwide increase from July 1999 to July 2004 in the price of office and retail property was 11 percent and 28 percent, respectively. These percentages are calculated from price indexes for commercial and retail property constructed and maintained by the MIT Center for Real Estate (2006).

9. See Graetz (1991), stating that of total national health expenditures in 1989, 38.5 percent was spent on hospital care, and that the one-half of U.S. hospitals that are private, nonprofit institutions account for almost 65 percent of hospital expenses.

10. To use an accounting framework sketched out by Steuerle (1998), the charitable deduction increases the amount of charitable contributions of money and assets, and tax exemption allows nonprofits to capture a higher return on their net assets. Tax-exempt bond financing allows nonprofits to earn arbitrage profits on their investments, and property tax exemption reduces the cost of real-property inputs to charitable activity.

11. The existence of donations uniquely increases the resources of the charitable sector. (The same is true of donations of time.) Henry Hansmann (1981) suggests that the income tax exemption might be designed to compensate nonprofits for their inability to access the capital markets by issuing stock.

12. See Schiff (1990) (describing the "demonstration effects" identified by Feldstein and Clotfelter [1976]; Schiff comments, "as the level of giving by others increases, it may take larger donations to 'buy' prestige and the like via giving, and spending on such goods may rise" (16 n.12)).

13. Recent years have seen a variety of proposals to allow deductions to non-itemizers, but all evidently succumbed to revenue, efficiency, and enforceability concerns. (The proposals would have been offered for only a few years, suggesting that donors would just time-shift, minimizing the IRS's incentive to audit claimed amounts.) See CBO (2002). The Tax Relief Act of 2005, passed by the Senate on November 18, 2005, contains a temporary non-itemizer deduction "paid for" by a uniform floor ($210 for individual and $420 for joint returns) under the charitable deductions of all taxpayers. That non-itemizer deduction proposal, however, is limited to cash gifts. See analysis in Gravelle (2005). This provision was not, however, included in the Pension Protection Act of 2006, PL 109-280 (Aug. 17, 2006).

14. See Clotfelter and Schmalbeck (1996) and the essays in Clotfelter (1992). Because of the different types of charities that high-income and low-income taxpayers favor, though, a tax credit of, 25 percent not only would redistribute taxes from taxpayers with higher marginal rates to those with lower marginal rates, but it also "may result in certain activities, such as education, health care, and the arts, bearing the additional burden nominally imposed on the higher-income contributors. Other activities, such as religion and welfare, might be more likely to benefit from the tax savings given to lower-income contributors" (Bradford 1984, 88).

15. Such premium returns become available to nonprofits because market competition drives up the return that taxable corporations earn before taxes in part to compensate for the corporate taxes. Because nonprofits do not need to pay corporate taxes on related business activities and can easily avoid even unrelated business income taxes, it is possible for nonprofit organizations to capture this premium as additional revenue. For a discussion of this mechanism, see Cordes and Weisbrod (1998), Rose-Ackerman (1982), and Steuerle

(1988). It should also be noted that the exemption from property taxes as distinct from income taxes provides a different kind of financial benefit to nonprofits. See Cordes, Gantz, and Pollak (2002).

16. In *Rensselaer Polytechnic Institute*, the Internal Revenue Service lost an attempt to allow the university deductions only for the marginal costs of renting out a hockey stadium. (*Rensselaer Polytechnic Inst. v. Commissioner*, 732 F.2d 1058 [2d Cir. 1984]). The Treasury regulations permit an allocation of dual-use expenses on "a reasonable basis." Treas. Reg. sec. 1.512(a)-1(c).

17. See, e.g., Wisconsin Statutes sec. 70.11: under subsection (3), up to 80 acres are exempt for colleges and universities; under subsection (4), up to 10 acres for educational, religious, or benevolent associations, but up to 30 acres for churches and religious associations; under subsection (10), up to 40 acres for Y.M.C.A. or Y.W.C.A. training camps or assemblies; under subsection (10m), up to 40 acres for Lions foundation camps for visually handicapped children; and under subsection (11), up to 30 acres for Bible camps.

18. At the federal level, see the testimony presented at the April 20, 2005, hearing "Overview of the Tax-Exempt Sector," of the Committee on Ways and Means, available at http://waysandmeans.house.gov/hearings.asp?formmode= detail&hearing = 400. See generally JCT (2005a).

19. See Christian Broadcasting Network (1998) (announcing a settlement between the Christian Broadcasting Network and the IRS in which, among other terms, CBN loses its tax exemption in 1986 and 1987 "due to the application of the rules prohibiting intervention in political campaign activities," pays a "significant" amount to the IRS, increases the number of outside directors on its board, and makes "other organizational and operational modifications to ensure ongoing compliance with the tax laws").

20. As of this writing, an attempt to abolish the estate tax outright failed in June 2006. Instead, the House of Representatives passed legislation that would raise the taxable threshold to $5 million ($10 million in the case of couples), and slash the estate tax rate to 15% on the first $20 million, and 30% on amounts in excess of $20 million. The legislation approved in the House has yet to be passed in the Senate.

21. Another outcome was that some nonprofits attempted to engage in creative leasing arrangements in which capital tax incentives were effectively sold to for-profit entities through creative leasing arrangements. See Galper and Toder (1983).

22. Note that early state governments made no sectoral distinctions in bestowing or withholding tax subsidies. New England canal, turnpike, bridge, and manufacturing companies enjoyed the same tax exemption extended to eleemosynary institutions such as Yale College (Hall 1992).

23. Enrich (1996) and Hellerstein and Coenen (1996) discuss what has been called the "New Economic War between the States."

24. And things are not always equal: Following a study showing an alarming gap between the claimed value of some donated cars and the amounts that ultimately went to the charity, Congress in 2004 limited the deduction for donated cars to the amount realized by the charity upon resale (IRC sec. 170(f)(12)). Among many other changes affecting exempt organizations and the tax treatment of contributions to them, the Pension Protection Act of 2006, Public Law No. 109-280 (Aug. 17, 2006), provides that no charitable-contribution deduction is allowed for donations of used clothing and household items that

are not in at least good condition, and allows the IRS to deny a deduction for any such item of minimal monetary value (I.R.C. sec. 170(f)(16)). The legislative history cites IRS data that the aggregate amount claimed as deductions for clothing and household items in 2003 exceeded $9 billion (JCT 2006b, 304).

25. The price of giving also increased in 1986 for gifts of appreciated property when the unrealized appreciation became an item of tax preference under the alternative minimum tax (Auten, Cilke, and Randolph 1992). This rule was modified in 1990 and repealed in 1993. Table 7 in Auten, Cilke, and Randolph (2005, 280) shows that between 1979 and 1989, the average contribution (in 1991 dollars) by taxpayers with pretax income of $1 million or more dropped from $133,837 to $82,113, and by taxpayers with between $200,000 and $1 million in income dropped from $11,104 to $8,476.

26. For proposals from the 1990s, see the flat tax as described in Hall and Rabushka (1995) and as introduced in H.R. 2060 (July 19, 1995) by Congressman Armey and S. 1050 (July 19, 1995) by Senator Shelby; for the USA tax, see the USA Tax Act of 1995, S. 722, introduced by Senators Nunn and Domenici (April 25, 1995); for the national retail sales tax, see the National Retail Sales Act of 1996, H.R. 3039, introduced by Congressmen Shaelfer, Tauzin, and others (March 6, 1996). For a summary of recent proposals, see Bickley (2005), describing, among others, Senator Shelby's flat tax proposal (which he reintroduced as The Tax Simplification Act of 2005, S. 1099 [May 23, 2005]); Representative English's Simplified USA Tax, H.R. 269 (in the 18th Congress); Senator Specter's Flat Tax proposal, S. 907 (in the 108th Congress), which would have allowed deductions for charitable contributions up to $2,500; and a version of the national retail sales tax proposal called the Fair Tax Act of 2005, introduced by Senator Chambliss (S. 25, January 24, 2005) and Representative Linder (H.R. 25, January 4, 2005).

27. The tax reform panel also considered adopting a national retail sales tax. However, the introduction of such a measure does not appear feasible either from a tax administration or from a political standpoint.

28. See Cordes, O'Hare, and Steuerle (2000) for an analysis of allowing charitable deductions to be made in excess of a contribution floor.

29. See note 24.

30. Deducting interest expense is inconsistent with the proper definition of a true consumption tax base.

31. Clotfelter and Schmalbeck (1996) calculated that the Armey-Shelby flat tax, which would have denied the deduction for charitable contributions, would result in a 10-percent drop in donations by individuals. A Price Waterhouse study (1997) estimated that had a 21 percent flat tax replaced the income tax in 1996, charitable giving by individuals would have been $71 billion instead of $104 billion. Price Waterhouse conceded that its estimates of the price elasticity of charitable giving are at the high end of studies and its estimates of the income elasticity for charitable giving are low. Using other estimates of the elasticity of giving produced a 24 percent decline rather than a 32 percent decline in giving under the flat tax. A Heritage Foundation study estimated that contributions by individuals to charity, particularly religious congregations, would rise by about 3.8 percent under a 17 percent flat tax without a charitable contribution (Barry 1996).

32. The term has long been in use to refer to payments made to affected municipalities by the federal government. See Advisory Commission on

Intergovernmental Relations (1981). States also pay PILOTs to affected municipalities, but payments often fall short of amounts due. See, for example,
Commonwealth of Massachusetts (1994), estimating that over the last seven
years, cities and towns received about 50 percent of the amount called for in
the statutory formula.

33. Separately, attorney Richard Scruggs, who led suits against the tobacco
industry, recently initiated dozens of suits on behalf of uninsured patients
against nonprofit hospitals, asserting that their tax exemption obligates them
to provide charity care. So far, all of his federal suits have been dismissed,
and he is finding similar lack of success in state courts. (Information about
these suits is maintained on the web site of the American Hospital Association,
at http://www.aha.org/aha/key_issues/bcp/index.html.)

34. Indeed, as this volume was going to press, Congress enacted the Pension
Protection Act of 2006, Public Law No. 109-280 (Aug. 17, 2006), sections 1231
through 1245 of which tighten some of the rules for two types of nonprivate
foundations, donor-advised funds, and supporting organizations. (See JCT
2006b, 330–63.)

35. For private foundations, Congress enacted specific penalty taxes not just
for self-dealing, but also for failure to distribute a minimum payout for charitable purposes, maintenance of excess business holdings, and jeopardizing
investments.

36. Section 1225 of the Pension Protection Act of 2006, Public Law No. 109-
280 (Aug. 17, 2006), requires the public disclosure of UBIT information returns
(Forms 990-T), but not of the returns of taxable affiliates. (See JCT 2006b,
329–30.)

REFERENCES

Advisory Commission on Intergovernmental Relations. 1981. *Payments in Lieu
of Taxes on Federal Real Property*. Washington, DC, Advisory Commission
on Intergovernmental Relations, September.

Andreoni, James. 1989. "Giving With Impure Altruism: Applications to Charity
and Ricardian Equivalence." *Journal of Political Economy* 97(6): 1447–58.

———. 1990. "Impure Altruism and Donations to Public Goods: A Theory of
'Warm Glow' Giving." *Economic Journal* 100(401): 464–77.

Arnsberger, Paul. 2004. "Charities and Other Tax-Exempt Organizations, 2001."
Statistics of Income Bulletin (Fall; Publication 1136). http://www.irs.gov/
pub/irs-soi/01eochin.pdf.

Auten, Gerald E., James M. Cilke, and William C. Randolph. 1992. "The Effects
of Tax Reform on Charitable Contributions." *National Tax Journal* 45(3):
267–90.

Bakija, Jon M., and William G. Gale. 2003a. "Charitable Giving and the Estate
Tax." *Tax Notes*, 101 (December 8), 1233.

———. 2003b. "Effects of Estate Tax Reform on Charitable Giving." Washington, DC: The Urban Institute. *Tax Policy Issues and Options* Brief 6.

Bakija, Jon, William Gale, and Joel Slemrod. 2003. "Charitable Bequests and
Taxes on Inheritance and Estates: Aggregate Evidence from Across States
and Time." *American Economic Review* 93(2): 366–70.

Barry, John S. 1996. "How a Flat Tax Would Affect Charitable Contributions." Washington, DC: Heritage Foundation *Backgrounder*, November 7.

Ben-Ner, Avner, and Benedetto Gui, eds. 1993. *The Nonprofit Sector in the Mixed Economy*. Ann Arbor: University of Michigan Press.

Bickley, James M. 2005. "Flat Tax Proposals and Fundamental Tax Reform: An Overview." Washington, DC: Congressional Research Service, Library of Congress. CRS Issue Brief IB95060.

Bradford, David S., and U.S. Treasury Tax Policy Staff. 1984. *Blueprints for Basic Tax Reform*, 2nd ed. Washington, DC: Tax Analysts.

Brody, Evelyn. 1996. "Institutional Dissonance in the Nonprofit Sector." *Villanova Law Review* 41(2): 433–504.

———. 1997. "Charitable Endowments and the Democratization of Dynasty." *Arizona Law Review* 39(3): 873–948.

———. 1998a. "The Limits of Charity Fiduciary Law." *Maryland Law Review* 56(4): 1400–1501.

———. 1998b. "Of Sovereignty and Subsidy: Conceptualizing the Charity Tax Exemption." *Journal of Corporation Law* 23(4): 585–629.

———. 1999a. "Charities in Tax Reform: Threats to Subsidies Overt and Covert." *Tennessee Law Review* 66(3): 687–763.

———. 1999b. "A Taxing Time for the Bishop Estate: What Is the I.R.S. Role in Charity Governance?" *University of Hawaii Law Review* 21(2): 537–91.

———, ed. 2002. *Property-Tax Exemption for Charities: Mapping the Battlefield*. Washington, DC: Urban Institute Press.

Brooks, Arthur. 2006. "Income Tax Policy and Charitable Giving." Maxwell School of Government, Syracuse University.

Christian Broadcasting Network. 1998. "CBN Press Release in Agreement with IRS." *Tax Notes Today* File 98 TNT 55-78, March 23. Lexis, Fedtax Library.

CBO. See U.S. Congress, Congressional Budget Office.

Center on Philanthropy at Indiana University. 2005. *Giving USA 2005*. Glenview, IL: Giving USA Foundation.

Clotfelter, Charles T. 1990. "The Impact of Tax Reform on Charitable Giving: A 1989 Perspective." In *Do Taxes Matter? The Impact of the Tax Reform Act of 1986*, edited by Joel Slemrod (203–35). Cambridge, MA: MIT Press.

———, ed. 1992. *Who Benefits from the Nonprofit Sector?* Chicago: University of Chicago Press.

Clotfelter, Charles T., and Richard L. Schmalbeck. 1996. "The Impact of Fundamental Tax Reform on Nonprofit Organizations." In *Economic Effects of Fundamental Tax Reform*, edited by Henry Aaron and William Gale (211–46). Washington, DC: Brookings Institution.

Commonwealth of Massachusetts, Auditor of the Commonwealth, Div. of Local Mandates. 1994. *A Review of the Financial Impact of the C.58 Payments-in-Lieu-of-Taxes (PILOT) Program on Massachusetts Cities and Towns*, Oct. 27. Boston: Commonwealth of Massachusetts.

Cordes, Joseph J. 2001. "The Cost of Giving: How Do Changes in Tax Deductions Affect Charitable Contributions?" Washington, DC: The Urban Institute. *Emerging Issues in Philanthropy* 2.

———. 2004. "The Partially Subsidized Muse: Estimating the Value and Incidence of Public Support Received by Nonprofit Arts Organizations." In *City Taxes, City Spending: Essays in Honor of Dick Netzer*, edited by Amy Ellen Schwartz (198–240). Northampton, MA: Edward Elgar Publishing.

Cordes, Joseph J., and Burton A. Weisbrod. 1998. "Differential Taxation of Nonprofits and the Commercialization of Nonprofit Revenues." In *To Profit or Not to Profit: The Commercial Transformation of the Nonprofit Sector,* edited by Burton A. Weisbrod (83–105). Cambridge, England: Cambridge University Press.

Cordes, Joseph J., Marie Gantz, and Thomas Pollak. 2002. "What Is the Property-Tax Exemption Worth?" In *Property-Tax Exemption for Charities: Mapping the Battlefield,* edited by Evelyn Brody (81–112). Washington, DC: Urban Institute Press.

Cordes, Joseph J., John O'Hare, and C. Eugene Steuerle, 2000. "Extending the Charitable Deduction to Non-Itemizers: Policy Issues." Washington, DC: The Urban Institute. *Charting Civil Society* Brief 7.

Enrich, Peter D. 1996. "Saving the States from Themselves: Commerce Clause Constraints on State Tax Incentives for Business." *Harvard Law Review* 110(2): 377–468.

Feldstein, Martin, and Charles Clotfelter. 1976. "Tax Incentives and Charitable Contributions in the U.S.: A Microeconomic Analysis." *Journal of Public Economics* 5: 1–26.

Galper, Harvey, and Eric Toder. 1983. "Owning or Leasing: Bennington College, and the U.S. Tax System. *National Tax Journal* 36(2): 257–61.

Glazer, Amihai, and Kai A. Konrad. 1996. "A Signaling Explanation of Charity." *American Economic Review* 86(4): 1019–28.

Graetz, Michael J. 1991. "Statement of Michael J. Graetz, Dep. Assistant Secretary (Tax Policy), Dept. of the Treasury before the Comm. on Ways and Means" (July 10), *Treasury Official Testifies on Tax-Exempt Status of Hospitals. Tax Notes Today* File 91 TNT 146-10, July 11. Lexis, Fedtax Library.

Gravelle, Jane G. 2005. "Tax Incentives for Charity: An Overview of Legislative Proposals." Congressional Research Service RS21144, December 1. Washington, DC: U.S. Congress.

Hall, Peter Dobkin. 1992. *Inventing the Nonprofit Sector.* Baltimore, MD: Johns Hopkins University Press.

Hall, Robert E., and Alvin Rabushka. 1995. *The Flat Tax,* 2nd ed. Stanford, CA: Hoover Institution Press.

Hansmann, Henry. 1981. "The Rationale for Exempting Nonprofit Organizations from Corporate Income Taxation." *Yale Law Journal* 91: 54–100.

———. 1989. "Unfair Competition and the Unrelated Business Income Tax." *Virginia Law Review* 75: 605–35.

Havens, John J., Mary A. O'Herlihy, and Paul G. Schervish. 2006 [in press]. "Charitable Giving: How Much, By Whom, To What, and How?" In *The Nonprofit Sector: A Research Handbook,* 2nd ed., edited by Walter W. Powell and Richard Steinberg. New Haven, CT: Yale University Press.

Hellerstein, Walter, and Dan T. Coenen. 1996. "Commerce Clause Restraints on State Business Development Incentives." *Cornell Law Review* 81: 789–878.

Hines, James R. 1999. "Nonprofit Business Activity and the Unrelated Business Income Tax." In *Tax Policy and the Economy,* vol. 13, edited by James M. Poterba (57–84). Cambridge, MA: MIT Press.

Independent Sector. 2005. "Report to Congress and the Nonprofit Sector on Governance, Transparency, and Accountability." http://www.nonprofitpanel.org/final/Panel_Final_Report.pdf.

JCT. See U.S. Congress, Joint Committee on Taxation.

Joulfaian, David, 1991. "Charitable Bequests and Estate Taxes." *National Tax Journal* 44(2): 169–80.

———. 2004. "Gift Taxes and Lifetime Transfers: Time Series Evidence." *Journal of Public Economics* 88(9–10): 1917–29.

———. 2005a. "Estate Taxes and Charitable Bequests: Evidence from Two Tax Regimes." OTA Paper 92. Washington, DC: Office of Tax Analysis, U.S. Department of the Treasury. http://www.treas.gov/offices/tax-policy/library/ota92.pdf.

———. 2005b. "Basic Facts on Charitable Giving." OTA Paper 95. Washington, DC: Office of Tax Analysis, U.S. Department of the Treasury. http://www.ustreas.gov/offices/tax-policy/library/ota95.pdf.

MIT Center for Real Estate. 2006. "Transactions-Based Index." http://web.mit.edu/cre/research/credl/tbi.html.

National Center for Charitable Statistics. 2005. http://nccsdataweb.urban.org.

President's Advisory Panel on Federal Tax Reform. 2005. "Simple, Fair, and Pro-Growth: Proposals to Fix America's Tax System." http://www.taxreformpanel.gov/final-report/.

Price Waterhouse LLP and Caplin & Drysdale, chartered. 1997. "Impact of Restructuring on Tax-Exempt Organizations." *Tax Notes Today* file 97 TNT 83-21, April 30, 1997. Lexis, Fedtax Library.

Randolph, William C. 1995. "Dynamic Income, Progressive Taxes, and the Timing of Charitable Contributions." *Journal of Political Economy* 103(4): 709–38.

———. 2005. "Charitable Deductions." In *The Encyclopedia of Taxation and Tax Policy*, 2nd ed., edited by Joseph J. Cordes, Robert D. Bell, and Jane G. Gravelle (51–53). Washington, DC: Urban Institute Press.

Riley, Margaret. 2004. "Unrelated Business Income Tax Returns, Tax Year 2001." *Statistics of Income Bulletin* (Winter; Publication 1136). http://www.irs.gov/pub/irs-soi/01eounrel.pdf.

Rose-Ackerman, Susan 1982. "Unfair Competition and Corporate Income Taxation." *Stanford Law Review* 34: 1017–36.

Salamon, Lester M. 1995. *Partners in Public Service: Government-Nonprofit Relations in the Modern Welfare State.* Baltimore, MD: Johns Hopkins University Press.

Sansing, Richard. 1998. "The Unrelated Business Income Tax, Cost Allocation, and Productive Efficiency." *National Tax Journal* 51(2): 291–302.

Schiff, Jerald. 1990. *Charitable Giving and Government Policy.* New York: Greenwood Press.

SFC. See U.S. Congress, Senate Finance Committee.

Simon, John G., Harvey Dale, and Laura B. Chisolm. 2006 [in press]. "The Tax Treatment of Nonprofit Organizations: A Review of Federal and State Policies." In *The Nonprofit Sector: A Research Handbook*, 2nd ed., edited by Walter W. Powell and Richard Steinberg. New Haven, CT: Yale University Press.

Steinberg, Richard. 1989. "The Theory of Crowding Out: Donations, Local Government Spending, and the 'New Federalism.' " In *Philanthropic Giving*, edited by Richard Magat (143–56). New York: Oxford University Press.

Steuerle, C. Eugene. 1988. "Current Federal Policy Issues for the Nonprofit Sector." Working Paper 88-10. Durham, NC: Duke University Center for the Study of Philanthropy and Voluntarism.

————. 1998. *Just What Do Nonprofits Provide?* Washington, DC: The Urban Institute. http://www.urban.org/url.cfm?ID=1000102.

————. 2005. "A Win-Win Option for Charity and Tax Policy." *Tax Notes* 107(April 18): 361.

U.S. Congress, Congressional Budget Office. 1997. "The Potential Effects of Tax Restructuring on Nonprofit Institutions." *CBO Papers* (February) Washington, DC: CBO.

————. 2002. "Effects of Allowing Nonitemizers to Deduct Charitable Contributions." *CBO Papers* (December). http://www.cbo.gov/showdoc.cfm?index=4008&sequence=0.

————. 2004. "The Estate Tax and Charitable Giving." *CBO Papers* (July). http://www.cbo.gov/showdoc.cfm?index=5650&sequence=0.

————. 2005. "Taxing the Untaxed Business Sector." *CBO Papers* (July). http://www.cbo.gov/showdoc.cfm?index=6567&sequence=0.

U.S. Congress, Joint Committee on Taxation. 1970. *General Explanation of the Tax Reform Act of 1969.* JCS-16-70 (Dec. 3).

————. 1982. *General Explanation of the Revenue Provisions of the Tax Equity and Fiscal Responsibility Act of 1982,* 97th Congress, 2nd Session, H.R. Rep. 97-4961.

————. 1996. *Impact on State and Local Governments and Tax-Exempt Organizations of Replacing the Federal Income Tax.* JCS-4-96. http://www.house.gov/jct/s-4-96.pdf.

————. 1997. *General Explanation of Tax Legislation Enacted in 1997.* Washington, DC: Joint Committee on Taxation.

————. 2000. *Study of Present-Law Taxpayer Confidentiality and Disclosure Provisions as Required by Section 3802 of the Internal Revenue Service Restructuring and Reform Act of 1998, Volume II: Study of Disclosure Provisions Relating to Exempt Organizations.* JCS-1-00. http://www.house.gov/jct/s-1-00vol2.pdf.

————. 2005a. *Historical Development and Present Law of the Federal Tax Exemption for Charities and Other Tax-Exempt Organizations.* JCX-29-05. http://www.house.gov/jct/x-29-05.pdf.

————. 2005b. *Options to Improve Tax Compliance and Reform Tax Expenditures.* JCS-2-05. http://www.house.gov/jct/s-2-05.pdf.

————. 2006a. *Estimates of Federal Tax Expenditures for Fiscal Years 2006–2010.* JCS-2-06. http://www.house.gov/jct/s-2-06.pdf.

————. 2006b. *Technical Explanation of HR 4, the "Pension Protection Act of 2006," as Passed by the House on July 28, 2006, and as Considered by the Senate on August 3, 2006.* JCX-38-06. http://www.house.gov/jct/x-38-06.pdf.

U.S. Congress, Senate Finance Committee. 2004. "Senate Finance Committee Staff Discussion Draft, Tax Exempt Governance Proposals." http://www.finance.senate.gov/hearings/testimony/2004test/062204stfdis.pdf.

U.S. Government Accountability Office. 2005. *Tax-Exempt Sector: Governance, Transparency, and Oversight Are Critical for Maintaining Public Trust.* GAO-05-561T. http://www.gao.gov/new.items/d05561t.pdf.

U.S. Treasury Department. 2005. *Anti-Terrorist Financing Guidelines: Voluntary Best Practices for U.S. Based Charities.* http://www.treasury.gov/offices/enforcement/key-issues/protecting/docs/guidelines_charities.pdf.

U.S. Treasury Inspector General for Tax Administration. 2005. *Review of the Exempt Organizations Function Process for Reviewing Alleged Political Cam-*

paign Intervention by Tax Exempt Organizations. 2005-10-035. http://www.treas.gov/tigta/auditreports/2005reports/200510035fr.html.

Vesterlund, Lise. 2006. "Why Do People Give?" In *The Nonprofit Sector: A Research Handbook*, 2nd ed., edited by Walter W. Powell and Richard Steinberg. New Haven, CT: Yale University Press.

Yetman, Robert. 2001. "Tax-Motivated Expense Allocations by Nonprofit Organizations." *Accounting Review* 76: 297–311.

———. 2005. "Causes and Consequences of the Unrelated Business Income Tax." Paper presented at 2005 National Tax Association meeting, Miami, Nov. 2005.

5

NONPROFITS AND STATE AND LOCAL GOVERNMENTS

Woods Bowman and
Marion R. Fremont-Smith

I n an era of strong federal government, it is easy to forget that the United States was initially a collection of semiautonomous states, and until the mid-19th century, persons seeking to organize a corporation, including those now known as nonprofit, had to apply for permission from the legislature of their state (Roy 1997). Many venerable universities still operate under their original state legislative charters. In this early period, customs duties, excise taxes, and the sale of federal lands were the principal sources of income for the federal government, and property taxes were the principal source of state and local revenue, so tax exemption was tantamount to exemption from state and local property taxes.[1] Programmatically, assistance to aged, poor, and disabled persons had been a local responsibility and an interest of private charity at least as far back as Tudor England. In the United States, the federal government remained aloof from charitable activity well into the 20th century (Axinn and Levin 1975),[2] which helps explain the important role that state and local governments play in health care and social service delivery today.

State governments have a direct impact on nonprofits in three major ways: They regulate them, they exempt them from major taxes, and they use them as vehicles to deliver publicly funded services (Grønbjerg and Child 2004).[3] Local governments are "creatures of the state" and generally have only such powers as are explicitly delegated to them by their respective states.[4] States keep a tight rein on regulatory and tax policies, so the role of local governments is largely limited to funding. This chapter has three parts, each one corresponding to one of these three modes of influence. The first section on state regulation of charities explores the common-law basis of the power of the state attorneys general to police charities, and it reviews statutory efforts to regulate charitable solicitation. The next section makes estimates of the magnitude of the flow of funds from all levels of government to the nonprofit sector to finance service delivery, including federal funds that pass through state and local governments ("pass-through" funds). As service providers, nonprofit organizations receive public money two ways: through grants-in-aid and through fee-for-service on behalf of eligible individuals. We will take account of both in our analysis. The third section estimates the economic value of the property tax, sales tax, and state corporate income tax exemption to the nonprofit sector. Some state and local governments, like the federal government, indirectly assist public charities by exempting their donors and bondholders from income taxes, but discussion of these forms of assistance and their economic impact is beyond the scope of this chapter.[5]

STATE REGULATION OF CHARITIES

State government has two tools of regulation: (1) common law, which is based on tradition and precedent, and (2) statutory law, based on legislation. This section begins with a review of the traditions that shape modern common law and evaluates how state regulation works in practice.[6] The second part examines state regulation of charitable solicitation as the prime example of an issue that has prompted legislative action in states across the country.

Regulation of Fiduciary Duties and Management of Assets

State regulation of charitable nonprofit organizations follows a pattern developed in England under the common law, brought to this country during the Colonial period, adopted after the revolution and currently in effect in every state. Its roots are to be found in the law of trusts as adapted under the common law to deal with trusts established for charitable, as opposed to private, purposes. For a private trust to be valid, it must have trustees competent to administer the trust funds, assets to be administered, and identifiable beneficiaries capable of ensuring that the trustees will fulfill their fiduciary duties. These duties were defined in the law as requiring utmost loyalty to the trust, prohibiting a trustee from receiving any benefit at the expense of the trust and requiring that he exercise reasonable care in the carrying out of his powers. These same duties apply to trustees of charitable trusts. Among the primary differences between them, as explained below, is the fact that a charitable trust may not have identifiable beneficiaries.

One of the benefits granted under the common law to charitable, as opposed to private, trusts was perpetual life. Private trusts could only continue for a finite time. In contrast, charities were intended to last indefinitely. This meant, inevitably, that some charitable purposes would over time become obsolete or incapable of fulfillment. In those instances, the courts were given the power under the doctrine of cy pres[7] to modify the original purposes of a charity and to decree that the funds could be used for purposes similar to those originally specified by their donors. All states have adopted this doctrine, and in almost all jurisdictions the standards for its application have been broadened from those in effect in previous times, so that in many jurisdictions, it is sufficient to modify purposes on a showing that an original purpose is wasteful or impractical.

The common law defined charitable purposes broadly, to include religion, education, health, and relieving the burdens of government. Over time, courts and legislatures have expanded these categories to meet society's changing needs. Today, the definition of charity in the federal tax code is essentially coterminous with laws in the states governing the creation and operation of charities and, although the common law was framed for charitable trusts, these laws apply equally to charities organized as nonprofit corporations, a form that is the most common throughout the country.[8]

An essential element of a charity, whether in the form of a trust or a corporation, is that it is designed for the benefit of an indefinite class of individuals. In this respect, a charity differs from a private trust, which is only valid if it has identifiable beneficiaries capable of acting for their own interests to ensure that the trustees are carrying out their duties. To fill this structural gap and thereby ensure accountability by charitable trustees, the attorney general, representing the king as parens patriae, was assigned the role of enforcing the duties of charitable fiduciaries. As such, he was acting for the general public, which was the ultimate beneficiary of these trusts. The role of the attorney general as regulator, however, was not absolute. His power was confined to a right to demand and receive information about the trust and to bring to the attention of the chancery court breaches in administration. The court, in turn, had broad power to require correction, including the power to remove trustees, to impose fines, demand restitution of funds improperly diverted, appoint receivers, and issue injunctions to prevent further breaches of trust.

Today, the attorneys general in each state, as is the case with their counterpart in England, take on this same role as regulator of charities, and state courts have powers similar to those held under the early common law to correct breaches of trust by trustees and directors of charitable corporations. Similarly, substantive state laws impose the duties of loyalty and care on charitable fiduciaries, although in some states, the directors of charitable corporations are given somewhat more leeway in carrying out their duty of care, and are afforded a higher degree of immunity in the event of breach, unless they are shown to have acted in bad faith or recklessly.

In all but rare instances, suit to enforce fiduciary duties can be brought only by the attorney general. This doctrine of exclusive standing was also developed in medieval England and was based on the rationale that charitable trustees would not serve if they were accountable in court to any member of the general public. Furthermore, as the law has developed in the United States, individual members of the public may not bring suit to force an attorney general to sue a charity or its managers for breach of trust.[9] The attorney general must be given notice of legal proceedings brought by or on behalf of a charity if the suit involves the validity of a gift for charitable purposes; application of the cy pres doctrine to change purposes; or suits to alter methods of administration, disposition of a substantial portion of a charity's assets, or breaches of fiduciary duties. Again, the premise of the requirement is that attorneys general cannot carry out their functions as regulators if they are not informed on matters involving the entities subject to their supervision.

In theory, a state attorney general has a great deal of power to regulate charities; in practice, this power is exercised on a regular, ongoing basis in just a small number of states. In the vast majority of states, the office of the attorney general is rarely involved in regulating the administration of charities, although as noted below, this office, acting in some states with other government officials, will enforce laws governing the solicitation of funds for charitable purposes by charities, professional fundraising personnel, and entities purporting to be charities.

In only 11 states does the attorney general monitor the activities of charities on an ongoing basis: California, Illinois, Massachusetts, Michigan, Minnesota, New Hampshire, New York, Ohio, Oregon,

Rhode Island, and South Carolina. They require certain charities to register and file annual financial reports with the charity division or a registry under the attorney general's jurisdiction. In Minnesota, Rhode Island, and South Carolina, all but certain charitable trusts are exempt from the filing requirements. In contrast, in Massachusetts the registration and filing requirements apply to all charities other than those with religious purposes. California exempts educational institutions, hospitals, and health care service plans, and New York exempts these organizations as well as fraternal and veterans organizations, student alumni associations, historical societies chartered by the state Board of Regents, certain trusts with foreign (i.e., out-of-state) corporate trustees, organizations that support those charities (which are themselves exempt), governmental entities, government-controlled trusts, and certain parent-teacher associations. In each of these states, the annual filing requirement can be met by submitting a copy of the federal information return, Form 990, although some states require certain additional information.

The purpose of these registration and reporting statutes is to provide the attorney general with sufficient information about the charities he is charged with regulating to enable him to carry out his duties. There is no question that enforcement in these 11 states is more active than in any of the others. However, no state is adequately staffed to handle the large volume of matters requiring attention.

As a part of its regulatory scheme, Massachusetts requires charities with gross receipts over a certain amount to have a certified public accountant audit their financial statements. New Hampshire and California joined Massachusetts in January 2006. The threshold for New Hampshire is $1 million; in California, it is $2 million. In Massachusetts, the threshold was $250,000, until it was raised to $500,000 in 2004.[10]

Among the states with active enforcement programs, policing charities is not the sole function of the offices of the attorney general. Rather, many of them conduct educational programs designed to inform fiduciaries of their duties and thereby improve administration of charities. They offer publications and sponsor conferences. Their personnel are available for consultation on questions on the advisability of seeking cy pres application for funds not currently providing public benefit and assist in framing petitions for dissolution. In California, the annual financial reports are available on the Internet (http://ag.ca.gov/charities/index.htm). Since 1960, each Massachusetts attorney general has appointed a citizens committee to advise him how best to meet the needs of the charitable community and the public interest in carrying out his duties. These committees have been of particular assistance in developing and obtaining passage of legislation to improve regulation.

Another area in which state attorneys general have been active in preserving charitable assets has been their role in the conversion of tax-exempt charities from nonprofit to for-profit status, transactions that were fairly widespread in the late 1990s, particularly for hospitals, health care delivery systems, health maintenance organizations, and health insurance providers. Following evidence of a number of instances in the early 1990s in which the assets of converting nonprofits were sold to insiders for below market prices, with the proceeds remaining in private hands, a number of state attorneys general mobilized to ensure that sales were at fair market value and that the proceeds of each sale were held in charitable foundations dedicated to improving health care delivery or supporting hospitals. In a few states, the attorney general interpreted his power to be broad enough to permit his participation in the conversion process. Twenty-five states enacted statutes explicitly granting power to the attorney general to regulate conversions of health care organizations. Another 10 states require approval by the court or the attorney general for the conversion of any charity, and 3 others absolutely prohibit conversions of any charity. These cases demonstrated the ability of an attorney general to protect funds dedicated to public purposes.

The scarcity of states with active enforcement programs has led to a wide variation in the practices of charitable fiduciaries and, inevitably, there is a degree of forum shopping on the part of charities wishing to avoid regulation. By default, therefore, the federal government, specifically the Internal Revenue Service (IRS), becomes the principal source of regulation. Charities look to the standards of behavior defined in the Internal Revenue Code (IRC) and IRS regulations for the rules governing their fiduciary duties. Only secondarily do they consult state law, which in almost every state shields fiduciaries from imposition of penalties except in the most egregious circumstances.

These limitations on state regulation have been compounded by virtue of the fact that, until recent years, the principal sanction for violation of the prohibitions against self-dealing and private benefit in the IRC was revocation of exemption—a sanction that for many charities posed no real threat and, in all events, did nothing to remove fiduciaries who formed charities with intent to violate the law. Managers of charities that are classified as private foundations under federal tax law have been prohibited from entering into self-dealing transactions since 1969, and similar rules prohibiting the provision of excess benefits to insiders have been applicable to managers of publicly supported charities since 1996.

In 2005 the staff of the U.S. Senate Finance Committee proposed far-reaching changes in federal and state regulation of charities. Among them were recommendations to (1) increase federal funding of enforcement at the federal and state levels, (2) increase the ability of the IRS to share information about its enforcement of nonprofits with state charity regulators, (3) mandate electronic filing of information returns and applications for exemption, at the same time increasing the amount of information required to be provided, (4) require financial audits for all charities with gross receipts of $250,000 or more, and (5) give states authority to pursue, with IRS approval, federal tax violations by exempt organizations.

With the encouragement of the Finance Committee's Chairman Grassley and Senator Baucus, the ranking Democratic member, Independent Sector, an association of nonprofit organizations, convened a panel of concerned and involved citizens to consider the staff proposals. After extensive consultations with the nonprofit sector and the broader public, the Panel on the Nonprofit Sector issued reports in March and June of 2005 in which it endorsed the first four of the recommendations, described above, although suggesting that the audit threshold be $1 million. It also expressed a preference for encouraging states to incorporate federal law into their own statutes. A Supplemental Report was issued in April 2006 that addressed, among other issues, state regulation of charitable solicitations and conversion transactions. The Finance Committee Staff had also recommended extending federal regulation to cover charitable fundraising, conversions, and investment of charitable assets as well as increasing the power of the IRS and the federal courts to enforce violations. Draft position papers on these issues were circulated in the spring of 2006 but a final report was not available at the time of this writing.

In summary, the laws in each of the states confer power on government to ensure that charitable fiduciaries act for the benefit of the entities they are entrusted to manage and are not reckless in doing so. In theory, regulation of solicitation affords broad latitude to officers, directors, and trustees to determine the manner in which the purposes of the organization will be carried out. Government does not demand any one type of program, or even any degree of efficiency. Thus the essence of the regulatory scheme is posited on a wide grant of power to individuals to map the ways in which nonprofit organizations carry out their missions.

Regulation of Fundraising

State regulation of charitable fundraising is a separate aspect of government regulation of charities. In some states it is a part of the regulation of charitable fiduciary duties whereas in others it is a component of consumer protection programs under the jurisdiction of a state official other than the attorney general. This aspect of regulation is achieved in the first instance through laws that mandate registration and financial reporting by charities that solicit funds from the general public as well as by individuals and corporations that conduct fundraising activities on a for-profit basis. Charities are required to register with a state office, file certain prescribed information on their proposed activities, and obtain a license to solicit. State officials do not have discretion to deny a license so long as the required information is provided and it indicates that the charity's intended activities will not violate the law.

Statutes with these requirements are in effect in 37 states. Thirty-four of these laws follow to a large extent a Model Act adopted in 1986 by the National Association of Attorneys General and the National Association of State Charity Officials. In 10 additional states, including most recently California, individual and for-profit companies that advise on, or conduct solicitations on behalf of or in the name of, charities are also subjected to these requirements. Many of these statutes define paid solicitors as persons compensated to perform services in connection with the solicitation of charitable funds, whereas in others the term applies only to persons meeting that definition who handle funds during the course of their work. The statutes also extend to "commercial co-venturers"—business organizations that agree publicly to donate a certain percentage of their sales or services to named charities, prohibiting them from undertaking such ventures without a written contract with the charity.

Until the 1980s some of these statutes, and many local ordinances, contained dollar or percentage limits on the amount that charities could spend on fundraising. During the 1980s, the United States Supreme Court, in three separate cases, held that fundraising by charities was subject to the First Amendment protection of free speech. In the case of *Schaumberg v. Citizens for a Better Environment* (444 U.S. 620), decided in 1980, the Court held unconstitutional an Illinois ordinance that placed limits on the amounts a charity could spend on fundraising. In 1984 in *Secretary of State of Maryland v. Munson* (467 U.S. 947), the Court held that a limit on the cost of fundraising similar to that in the Schaumberg case but permitting the state to waive the limit under certain circumstances also violated the First Amendment. In the third case, *Riley v. National Federation of the Blind of North Carolina, Inc.* (487 U.S. 781), decided in 1988, the Court struck down provisions in a North Carolina law that required professional fundraisers to obtain a license before soliciting, contained a presumption that fees exceeding 35 percent of gross funds raised was unreasonable, and required solicitors to disclose at the point of solicitation the amount of their fundraising costs. The states may, and some do, require charities to notify potential donors that information about their expenses for fundraising and for program activities can be obtained from the state, as well as from the charity itself. What the states cannot require is disclosure of fundraising costs as a ratio of total costs.

The office of the attorney general is the situs for registration and reporting in 14 states; in 16 others, the office shares jurisdiction with another state agency; in 4 states, enforcement of charitable solicitations is assigned to the secretary of state, and in 12 it is assigned to another state agency. For example, in Florida it is the Department of Agriculture and Consumer Services; in Connecticut it is the Department of Consumer Protection; and in Mississippi, Oklahoma, and Kansas it is the district or county attorneys. In Pennsylvania, the attorney general, the secretary of state, and the district attorneys share responsibility, although enforcement efforts originate in the office of the secretary of state, which refers matters to the other governmental agencies for prosecution. Substantive state laws governing charitable solicitations are directed at preventing fraud and misrepresentations and apply not just to charities but also to organizations that claim they are charitable, but in effect are for-profit entities.

The most pervasive complaint about state regulation of solicitation is the lack of uniformity in statutory coverage and the consequent burden of meeting numerous, varying filing and disclosure requirements. Religious organizations are exempt from the registration and reporting requirement in all jurisdictions, and there is a wide range of other exemptions, the most common being for educational and political organizations, hospitals, and veterans groups and mutual benefit societies. Some statutes exempt governmental entities, others exclude organizations formed for the relief of a single individual (even though they are not, by definition, charities). Finally, in the majority of states, there is a dollar threshold that has to be reached before the registration requirement applies. In some instances the dollar threshold applies only if unpaid solicitors exclusively conduct the fundraising.

Needless to say, this myriad of exceptions and exemptions makes it extremely difficult for an organization intending to solicit in more than one state to identify the jurisdictions in which it must register and to meet their separate requirements. Attempts to alleviate this burden have been made by state enforcement officials, starting with the 1986 endorsement of the model act described above. In 1998 the National Association of State Charity Officials developed a uniform initial registration statement that is now accepted in 33 states, with 7 of them requiring supplemental information. There is no similar uniformity for the filing of annual financial reports.

For the specific requirements imposed on charities in connection with their fundraising activities, 15 states require an audit if receipts exceed a specified threshold; contracts with solicitors, fundraising counsel, and commercial co-venturers must be filed with the state, and those with solicitors must contain details on the amount the charity is entitled to receive. Safeguards are required for those who will be handling funds, including the posting of bonds. Several jurisdictions require charities to provide written notice to all persons who are solicited of the fact that information about the charity may be obtained from either the state or the charity. Finally, the statutes specifically define prohibited deceptive acts or practices.

There are both criminal and civil sanctions for violation of these laws. Many solicitation statutes specify dollar penalties and possible prison terms for serious violations. The agency assigned the duty of enforcement has broad powers to conduct investigations, subpoena witnesses, and demand documents. In addition, the courts have equity powers to issue injunctions, revoke certain transactions, and ultimately remove fiduciaries and appoint receivers.

State officials charged with regulating charitable solicitation regularly attempt to improve public understanding of charities so that donors may make informed decisions. The web sites for states that have active enforcement programs provide a summary of the state laws and information to assist in compliance. A number of states publish annual reports on the costs of certain fundraising efforts, such as those by telemarketers or professional fundraisers.[11] In 2003, National Association of State Charity Officials and GuideStar, a charitable organization that provides online access to Forms 990 and 990PF, is creating a national online charity information system that will be a common repository of information collected by the various charity regulators.

In 1999, at the annual National Association of State Charity Officials meeting, state charity regulators attempted to deal collectively with the problems raised by the rapid proliferation of solicitations on the Internet. The result was a definition of the circumstances under which charities soliciting funds on the Internet would be required to register and report in a state in which they were not domiciled. Named the Charleston Principles after the site of the meeting at which they were adopted, they require registration if the charity maintains an interactive web site and specifically targets individuals in a particular state or receives substantial contributions from persons in that state on a repeated and ongoing basis as a result of its Internet solicitations. A similar rule was adopted for charities that do not maintain interactive web sites but conduct other activities that generate Internet responses.

The greatest drawback to state regulation of fundraising is the lack of uniformity and the consequent burden on charities soliciting in a number of states. This drawback has led to consideration of federal regulation, under the jurisdiction of the IRS, the Securities and Exchange Commission, and the Federal Trade Commission, among other agencies. The burden of multiple filings will be mitigated with the advent of mandatory electronic filing, which the IRS is in the process of requiring, but unless the states can achieve greater uniformity, federal preemption remains a distinct possibility.

STATE AND LOCAL FUNDING

IRS Form 990, the main source of publicly available financial data on nonprofits, sheds little light on the fiscal relationships between state and local governments and nonprofits. Although it captures information on government grants and fee-for-service payments, it does not identify the source by level of government.[12] Nevertheless, certain characteristics of the system of governmental payments to nonprofits are obvious to anyone familiar with the nonprofit sector. First, public charities receive the bulk of state and local government outlays going to the nonprofit sector either as grants or fee-for-service payments on behalf of individuals. Second, a considerable amount of money passes through state-administered programs that are financed either entirely by the federal government (Food Stamps), or largely by the federal government (Medicaid, Temporary Assistance for Needy Families). Third, in some states, counties and other units of local government act as agents of state and federal government in managing contracts and grants. The analysis in this section includes federal funds passing through local governments and funding originating with local governments in addition to direct payments made by the states.

Direct payments to individuals exceed federal aid to state and local governments, and they are an important determinant of demand for the services of nonprofit organizations. Whether demand is positively or negatively correlated with these payments depends on the program. For example, an increase in Pell Grants or housing assistance will increase demand for nonprofit-provided services, but an increase in income support and food stamps will decrease the demand for services of food pantries and soup kitchens. Unfortunately, sorting out the net effect of these payments is beyond the scope of this chapter.

Figure 5.1 draws on multiple sources to piece together a picture of how governmental funds flow to individuals, nonprofits, and parallel for-profit entities (i.e., for-profits that provide services to the same or similar populations—such as the indigent—, or served by nonprofits for the same or similar policy goals—such as health care). It also shows how funds flow from the federal level through state and local governments on their way to nonprofits and parallel for-profit entities. (See the appendix for information on data sources and estimating techniques.)

In 2001, total federal cash outlays and obligations (i.e., promises to pay) for direct payments and grants were $1.3 trillion, one-fourth of which went to state and local governments for all purposes (table 5.1).[13] Federal cash outlays and obligations on programs of particular importance to nonprofits, such as income maintenance, health, social services, housing assistance, higher education, and arts, was $1.0 trillion. State and local governments expended $475 billion in these same

Figure 5.1. Flow of Funds to the Nonprofit Sector, 2001–2002

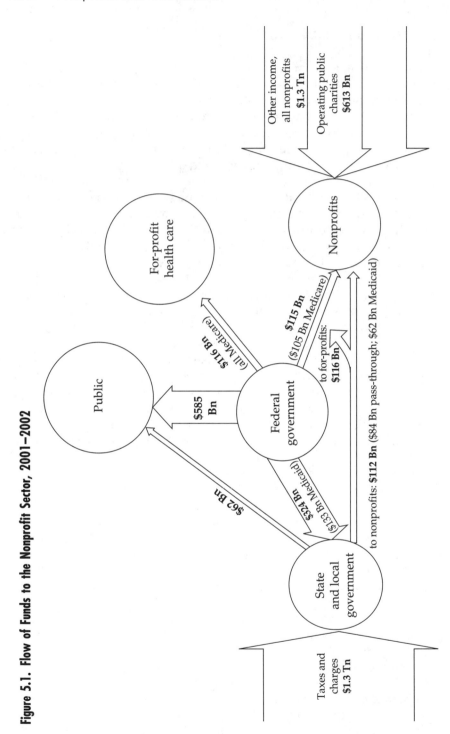

Table 5.1. Federal Payments and Grants, Federal Fiscal Year 2001 (in millions of dollars)

	Direct to all parties	Pass-through to nonprofit organizations
Total federal payments and grants (outlays and obligations)	$1,344,590 [a]	
Social services, health, hospitals, housing, income maintenance, higher education and culture	$1,033,545 [b]	
Directly to persons (outlays and obligations)	$584,727 [c]	
Earned income tax credit	27,257	
Unemployment Insurance	26,196	
Food Stamps	15,539	
Housing assistance	32,301	
Social Security, Survivors, SSI and SSDI	483,434	
Directly to for-profit providers (outlays and obligations)	$115,630 [c]	
Directly to nonprofits (outlays and obligations)	$114,735	
Hospitals (Medicare Part A)	104,861 [c]	
Private higher education appropriations, grants and contracts	9,874 [d]	
Directly to state and local governments (outlays only)	$323,893 [e]	$83,948 [e]
From Department of Agriculture (Food & Nutrition Service)	17,487 [f]	13,748 [f]
From Corporation for National and Community Service	378	378
From Corporation for Public Broadcasting	321	321
From Health and Human Services, including Medicaid & Medicare	205,616	65,815 [g]
Medicare Part A (to public hospitals) and total Medicaid	149,792	33,222 [c]
From Institute for Museum and Library Service	149	149
From Department of Labor (workforce investment)	3,444	3,444
From National Foundation on Arts and Humanities	33	33
From Neighborhood Reinvestment Corporation	60	60
Miscellaneous, all other federal programs	96,405 [h]	0

SSI = Supplemental Security Income; SSDI = Supplemental Security Disability Income.

[a] Data are from U.S. Census Bureau (2002b), table 1: Retirement & Disability + Other Direct Payments + Grants.

[b] Data are from U.S. Census Bureau (2002b), table 2: All SS Payments, table 3: All Medicare Benefits + EITC + Unemployment Compensation + Food Stamps + Housing Assistance, and table 4: HHS + HUD.

[c] Data in this category are from U.S. Census Bureau (2002b), table 3. For method of allocation by ownership type, see appendix.

[d] Data are from *Chronicle of Higher Education*.

[e] Data in this category are from U.S. Census Bureau (2002c), table 1. See also notes f and g.

[f] The difference between columns is reimbursement for food stamp administration. Food stamps are paid directly to eligible persons. Pass-through nutrition programs are Women, Infants, and Children; Child Nutrition; and Commodity Assistance & Need Families.

[g] Department of Health and Human Services spending on child care, foster care, low-income home energy assistance, Temporary Assistance for Needy Families, Medicare/Medicaid, substance abuse, and mental health, per U.S. Census Bureau (2002c), table 1; authors' allocation.

[h] A residual, calculated by subtracting all items in this category from total payments to state and local governments.

program areas (table 5.2). The federal government provided $115 billion directly to nonprofits, and state and local governments provided $112 billion, of which $84 billion is federal pass-through money (tables 5.1 and 5.2). Our estimates of government spending are probably low because data on housing assistance programs broken down by for-profit, nonprofit, and public were unavailable and therefore excluded from our analysis. In the same year public charities had combined revenues from all sources of $840 billion, including $227 billion in public money (see appendix, state and local funding note 7).

Federal spending stimulates state and local spending on certain pro-grams—for example, the federal government on average matches state and local Medicaid spending 57 cents on the dollar, which in federal FY 2001 required state and local governments to put up $81 billion. (See the appendix for a discussion of Medicaid and how federal support varies by state.) We estimate state and local governments spent $28

Table 5.2. Direct Expenditures by State and Local Govenments on Persons and Nonprofit Organizations, 2001–2002 (in millions of dollars)

Expenditure by program[a]	$475,341
Social services and income maintenance[a]	431,058
including Medicaid[b]	*188,959*
Unemployment Insurance	42,166
Private higher education	1,670
Arts	447
Expenditure by recipient[a]	$475,341
To persons (cash assistance payments)	62,290
To for-profit providers (Medicaid, from table 5.3)[b]	115,514
To nonprofit organizations (public welfare vendor payments, higher education, arts)[b,c]	112,127
including Medicaid	*62,477*
For state and local government operations (residual)[d]	185,410
Federal pass-through amount (from table 5.1)	83,948
Expended by state governments for nonprofit organizations in excess of pass-throughs[e]	28,179
including Medicaid	*25,063*

Sources: For all except Medicaid, private higher education, and arts: U.S. Census Bureau (2002a); for Medicaid, Kaiser Commission (2001); for private higher education, Chronicle of Higher Education (2005); for arts, National Assembly of State Arts Agencies (2002).

Note: Detailed source citations can be found in the appendix.

[a] Outlays, including capital, but not veterans' services.

[b] Data from Kaiser Commission (2001).

[c] Public welfare vendor payments are reduced by the amount of Medicaid payments to for-profit entities.

[d] Residual that is equal to total spending minus payments to persons, for-profits, and nonprofits. Includes $16,778 billion in Medicare payments to public hospitals and $10,947 billion of Medicaid payments to public entities.

[e] Expenditures to nonprofit organizations minus federal pass-through.

billion in excess of federal pass-through funds to nonprofits, of which $26 billion is Medicaid. Remarkably, parallel for-profit health care providers received $231 billion from all levels of government—more than government spending on all programs run by all public charities.

Medicare is a $237 billion program administered directly by the federal government for the benefit of the aged, disabled, and dependent survivors (U.S. Census Bureau 2002b). The hospital and physician portion of Medicare (parts A and B) are not means tested; only the new pharmaceutical assistance program (part D) is means tested. About half of Medicare fee-for-service payments flow to the for-profit sector—$18 billion to for-profit hospitals and $97 billion to doctors who, as individuals, are part of the for-profit sector.[14] Medicaid, on the other hand, is a state- and local government– administered, $189 billion means-tested program for medically indigent persons that is funded jointly with the federal government (Kaiser Commission 2001).[15] Hospitals with a high proportion of Medicaid patients receive additional reimbursement under a "disproportionate share formula," and teaching hospitals receive additional funding for medical education. We estimate that of the $189 billion of state and local Medicaid spending, $116 billion flows to for-profits, $62 billion to nonprofits, and $11 billion to public entities. Generally perceived as a program to give poor persons access to doctors and hospitals, the largest share of Medicaid money ($47 million) goes to nursing homes and intermediate care facilities for the mentally retarded, most of which are for-profit (table 5.3). By contrast, a negligible amount of federal Medicare spending goes to nursing homes, mostly for postoperative convalescence.

Within broad national [Medicaid] guidelines established by federal statutes, regulations, and policies, each state (1) establishes its own eligibility standards; (2) determines the type, amount, duration, and scope of services; (3) sets the rate of payment for services; and (4) administers its own program. States share the cost with the federal government. Medicaid is nearly 20 percent of state general funds budgets (Milbank Memorial Fund 2003).[16] Because Medicaid is an entitlement and growing rapidly, and because states share its cost, it strongly influences state budget decisions across the board. During a long period of robust state revenue growth in the 1990s, states tended to expand Medicaid-funded services and the number of persons served. Federal cost sharing results in political gain out of proportion to state budgetary impact. When a fiscal crisis occurs, Medicaid programs are harder for states to cut than programs they finance without federal assistance because achieving one dollar of savings to the state treasury by cutting Medicaid entails cutting two or more program dollars, depending on the cost-sharing formula, and the political cost is out of proportion to money saved (Bowman 2003).

Table 5.3. Allocation of Medicare and Medicaid Spending by Ownership Type (in millions of dollars)

Medicare service	Outlays and obligations[a]	For-profit	Nonprofit	Public
Hospitals (Part A)	139,815.3[b]	18,176.0	104,861.5	16,777.8
Doctors (Part B)	97,454.2[c]	97,454.2	0	0
Total Medicare	237,269.5	115,630.2	104,861.5	16,777.8

Medicaid service	Outlays[d]	For-profit	Nonprofit	Public
Prescribed drugs	23,944.7			
Physicians	11,957.7			
subtotal	35,902.4[c]	35,902.4	0	0
Inpatient hospital	26,121.5			
Outpatient/Clinic	13,300.6			
Mental Health	1,966.7			
subtotal	41,388.8[b]	10,761.1	26,074.9	4,552.8
Managed care	28,105.7[e]	16,975.8	9,471.6	1,658.2
Nursing facilities	37,363.5			
ICF-MR	9,693.9			
subtotal	47,057.4[f]	33,881.3	10,823.2	2,352.9
Home/Personal care	21,373.1[g]	8,763.0	11,114.0	1,496.1
Other	11,954.5			
Unknown	3,176.8			
subtotal	15,131.3[h]	9,230.1	4,993.3	907.9
Total Medicaid	188,958.7	115,513.7	62,477.1	10,967.9
Federal share	107,706.5	65,842.8	35,612.0	6,251.7
State and local share	81,252.2	49,670.9	26,865.2	4,716.2

Note: ICF-MR = Intermediate Care Facilities – Mental Retardation

[a] Data in this category are from U.S. Census Bureau (2002b), table 3.

[b] Data allocated based on proportion of Medicare payments to hospitals by ownership type as provided by American Hospital Association (2002). See appendix for allocation method.

[c] Assumed all for-profit.

[d] Data from Kaiser Commission (2001).

[e] Allocated based on proportion of payments to doctors and hospitals in notes b and c.

[f] Allocated based on proportion of Medicaid certified beds in nursing facilities.

[g] Allocated based on proportion of home visits made by owenership type.

[h] Allocated in the same proportion as all other Medicaid services reported above.

There is considerable variation in the amount states spend on Medicaid as a proportion of direct general expenditures for current operations (table 5.4) as a consequence of having wide latitude under federal Medicaid law to establish eligibility criteria and other program parameters listed above. The amount of state Medicaid spending per capita varies from $304 in Nevada to $1,462 in New York, with the median being $638. Of the 10 lowest ranked states, 6 are located in the Rocky

Table 5.4. State Population and Finances, 2001 (in thousands of dollars)

	Population (1,000s)	Intergovernmental revenue	Total spending[a]	Medicaid spending	Medicaid spending per capita	Medicaid as percentage of spending[a]	Intergovernmental revenue as a percentage of spending[a]
Alabama	4,447	6,263,380	21,446,072	2,952,800	664	13.8	29.2
Alaska	627	1,789,266	6,657,294	560,500	894	8.4	26.9
Arizona	5,131	5,718,580	22,259,308	2,453,200	478	11.0	25.7
Arkansas	2,673	3,645,274	11,340,665	1,684,700	630	14.9	32.1
California	33,872	48,249,715	217,100,387	19,824,900	585	9.1	22.2
Colorado	4,301	4,268,690	22,679,026	2,009,500	467	8.9	18.8
Connecticut	3,406	4,039,357	20,151,685	2,966,900	871	14.7	20.0
Delaware	784	959,029	4,413,505	601,300	767	13.6	21.7
D.C.	572	2,840,094	5,573,064	830,400	1,452	14.9	51.0
Florida	15,982	14,956,257	72,214,648	8,588,400	537	11.9	20.7
Georgia	8,186	9,357,310	38,020,444	4,033,600	493	10.6	24.6
Hawaii	1,212	1,547,487	6,783,055	592,500	489	8.7	22.8
Idaho	1,294	1,415,152	5,786,080	713,500	551	12.3	24.5
Illinois	12,419	12,716,518	60,544,079	8,150,500	656	13.5	21.0
Indiana	6,080	6,282,589	28,868,699	3,355,600	552	11.6	21.8
Iowa	2,926	3,626,235	14,639,298	1,673,600	572	11.4	24.8
Kansas	2,688	3,098,044	12,905,453	1,370,900	510	10.6	24.0
Kentucky	4,042	5,413,584	17,989,820	3,253,600	804	18.1	30.1
Louisiana	4,469	6,484,806	20,732,316	2,881,600	645	13.9	31.3
Maine	1,275	1,900,585	6,843,976	1,460,800	1,146	21.3	27.8
Maryland	5,296	5,927,446	26,543,349	3,918,300	740	14.8	22.3
Massachusetts	6,349	6,175,943	34,977,552	5,786,700	911	16.5	17.7

Table 5.4. State Population and Finances, 2001 (in thousands of dollars) (cont.)

	Population (1,000s)	Intergovernmental revenue	Total spending[a]	Medicaid spending	Medicaid spending per capita	Medicaid as percentage of spending[a]	Intergovernmental revenue as a percentage of spending[a]
Michigan	9,938	12,543,078	52,390,916	5,484,900	552	10.5	23.9
Minnesota	4,919	6,088,091	28,974,667	3,749,100	762	12.9	21.0
Mississippi	2,845	4,625,225	13,655,144	2,181,300	767	16.0	33.9
Missouri	5,595	7,328,511	24,538,654	3,629,700	649	14.8	29.9
Montana	902	1,590,402	4,259,668	475,900	528	11.2	37.3
Nebraska	1,711	1,973,494	9,522,701	1,091,900	638	11.5	20.7
Nevada	1,998	1,632,438	9,670,189	607,700	304	6.3	16.9
New Hampshire	1,236	1,295,929	5,486,593	692,300	560	12.6	23.6
New Jersey	8,414	8,948,972	47,599,071	5,018,500	596	10.5	18.8
New Mexico	1,819	3,123,522	9,690,133	1,482,600	815	15.3	32.2
New York	18,976	36,185,629	139,869,695	27,741,000	1,462	19.8	25.9
North Carolina	8,049	10,240,822	39,414,631	5,502,500	684	14.0	26.0
North Dakota	642	1,156,195	3,185,284	377,100	587	11.8	36.3
Ohio	11,353	13,863,196	56,296,378	8,013,000	706	14.2	24.6
Oklahoma	3,451	4,412,993	15,946,922	2,237,600	648	14.0	27.7
Oregon	3,421	6,437,869	20,616,506	1,889,100	552	9.2	31.2
Pennsylvania	12,281	16,026,341	62,608,610	7,634,300	622	12.2	25.6
Rhode Island	1,048	1,766,157	5,869,470	1,096,100	1,046	18.7	30.1
South Carolina	4,012	5,332,695	20,704,823	3,097,000	772	15.0	25.8
South Dakota	755	1,150,293	3,156,182	425,000	563	13.5	36.4
Tennessee	5,689	7,604,069	29,398,119	4,083,400	718	13.9	25.9
Texas	20,852	22,914,707	93,229,667	9,645,700	463	10.3	24.6

Utah	2,233	2,613,020	11,408,650	1,061,000	475	9.3	22.9
Vermont	609	1,087,106	3,379,582	541,600	889	16.0	32.2
Virginia	7,079	6,234,846	33,140,719	2,716,400	384	8.2	18.8
Washington	5,894	7,041,596	34,845,835	3,977,500	675	11.4	20.2
West Virginia	1,808	2,998,971	8,378,143	1,567,000	867	18.7	35.8
Wisconsin	5,364	6,455,616	28,322,937	3,031,700	565	10.7	22.8
Wyoming	494	1,187,183	3,181,198	242,800	491	7.6	37.3
United States	281,418	360,534,307	1,497,216,362	188,953,500	671	12.6	24.1
Highest	33,872	48,249,715	217,100,387	27,741,000	304	6.3	16.9
Median	4,012	5,332,695	20,616,506	2,453,200	638	12.6	24.8
Lowest	494	959,029	3,156,182	242,800	1,462	21.3	51.0

Source: All except Medicaid: U.S. Census Bureau (2002a); Medicaid: Kaiser Commission (2001).
[a] Spending = direct general expenditure on current operations.

Mountains or farther west. Of the 10 highest ranked states, 8 are east of the Mississippi. States that receive more intergovernmental revenue from the federal government tend to devote a higher proportion of their direct general expenditures for current operations to Medicaid.[17] And these states tend to spend more Medicaid dollars per resident.[18]

In recent years, when states faced fiscal crises, the budget areas they cut most deeply were aid to local governments, higher education, and the arts. State aid to local government is often the first to be cut and to take repeated cuts (Kane, Orszag, and Gunter 2003; Reschovsky 2003), with probable adverse implications for nonprofit groups, but the connections are hard to trace. State spending on higher education goes mainly to public institutions, so cuts here primarily affect public colleges and universities in most states. Direct government support is 11 percent of private higher education revenue—nearly all of it federal grants and contracts. State spending cuts to the arts and cultural institutions fall almost exclusively on nonprofit groups. All levels of government provide only 4 percent of arts and cultural organizations' revenues, one-third of which comes from state and local government. This is not to say that state and local budget cuts have not affected nonprofits in other fields, notably health care, but that the pattern in recent years shows a disproportionate impact on education and arts appropriations.

Political and fiscal circumstances do not remain static for long. The relative strength of the resource flows displayed in figure 5.1 are subject to change. We conclude this section with a brief description of the fiscal situation since 2001 and identify some state-level factors that could shape the future. In the face of a deteriorating economic environment, states actually enacted $5.8 billion in tax cuts in 2001, followed by $0.8 billion more in 2002 (National Association of State Budget Officers 2003).[19] Finally, in 2003 states increased taxes by $8.3 billion, but this infusion of new money barely offset previous tax cuts after allowing for inflation and population growth in the interim (National Association of State Budget Officers 2003). The cumulative effect was painful for nonprofits (Bowman 2003).

Looking ahead, it would be wise to keep an eye on a proposal called the Taxpayers Bill of Rights, which limits annual increases in state spending to the rate of growth in population plus the rate of inflation and refunds to taxpayers any revenue growth in excess of this amount. Colorado adopted it by amendment to its constitution in 1992. Between 2001 and 2003 revenues dropped 16 percent, forcing spending cuts. But when revenues rebounded, this constitutional provision prevented restoration of services to their former levels. To address this problem, Colorado voters in 2005 passed a referendum temporarily suspending it. So far, Colorado is the only state with such a limitation, but Ohio and Maine are expected to put it to referendum in 2006 (Johnson 2005).

In a parallel development, several foundations banded together in 1993 "to strengthen the contributions of state-level non-profit organizations to policy debates by enhancing their ability to provide reliable budget and tax analysis" (Center on Budget and Policy Priorities 2005). They inaugurated the State Fiscal Analysis Initiative, which today consists of 28 state organizations and one national organization—the Center on Budget and Policy Priorities. Some Initiative grantees focus exclusively on fiscal analysis, whereas others have added this capacity to their existing work. The variety of grantee organizations and the different circumstances in which they operate make it difficult to evaluate their effectiveness, but it appears that they have succeeded in achieving "measurably greater influence in the local fiscal policy process," although only a few have achieved "concrete changes in how the game is played" (OMG Center for Collaborative Learning 2005).

STATE AND LOCAL TAX BENEFITS

The three most important state and local tax benefits for the nonprofit sector are exemptions from the property tax, general sales tax, and state corporate income tax.[20] The property tax is predominantly a local tax used extensively in every state. Sales and corporate income taxes are predominantly state taxes utilized secondarily by local governments. As "creatures of the state," local governments are generally unable to tax property, sales, or income unless, and to the extent, state law explicitly permits (see note 4). Every state exempts charitable nonprofits from the property tax and corporate income tax, and most states with a sales tax exempt either the purchases or sales by charities, but the definition of charity varies among the states.

Research on the economic effects of these exemptions has shown that exemption from sales and corporate income taxes gives nonprofits a competitive advantage relative to for-profit firms providing similar services in the same market (Hansmann 1987), but the property tax exemption is neutral in this regard (Chang and Tuckman 1990; Hansmann 1987). The property tax exemption, however, appears to provide an incentive for charitable nonprofits to cluster in central cities where the value of the exemption is high relative to surrounding suburbs (Quigley and Schmenner 1975).

In this section, we estimate the value of the property tax, sales tax, and corporate income tax exemptions from a weighed sample of public charities, other than churches, with Statistics of Income data gleaned from IRS Form 990 made available through the National Center for Charitable Statistics.[21] Because this is not an exhaustive sample, our estimates probably understate the true values, but virtually all of the largest nonprofits, other than churches, are included in the sample.[22] Churches are a major exception, so without a doubt our estimates are a lower bound. We do not, furthermore, estimate government benefits to individuals that indirectly benefit public charities, for example, deductibility of charitable contributions on state and local income taxes, or the financial impact of lower interest rates paid by public charities on bonds that are exempt from state and local income taxes.

Property Tax

Contrary to popular perception, 501(c)(3) federal tax exemption does not automatically confer property tax exemption in any state.[23] The resulting pattern of exemption is a patchwork. Even nonprofit-owned property that is untaxed everywhere—houses of worship, education facilities, hospitals, nursing homes, and social services—are subject to numerous differences in conditions and limitations. Statutes of at least 20 states go so far as to exempt some nonprofits by name. Delaware's three counties have constitutional authority to exempt property. At least 17 states have local option for certain types of property, allowing communities pick and choose which nonprofits to exempt. For some types of institutional property in New York, each unit of local government (i.e., counties, towns, cities, and school districts) enjoys local option, so a parcel may be exempt from taxation by one unit of local government but taxed by a different, overlapping unit.

The property tax exemption is disproportionately important to churches, private schools and colleges, nonprofit housing corporations, and arts organizations, which are the most likely to own significant amounts of property. We estimate the value of charitable property, other than churches, in 2001 to be $570 billion and property tax exemption to be $9 billion to $15 billion—a considerable amount compared with the estimated $28 billion in cash outlays made by state governments out of their own resources (table 5.2). However, the burden of property tax exemption falls almost exclusively on local taxpayers. (See the appendix for an explanation of the calculations.)

Another popular misconception is that a reduction in taxable property necessarily reduces the revenues of local governments (Bowman 2002). The property tax is different from all other taxes in that each year a taxing body decides how much property tax revenue it needs to balance its budget and then calculates the rate necessary to generate the required amount. When property is removed from the tax rolls, the tax base shrinks, but a taxing body need not lose revenue if it has the legal authority to raise its tax rate high enough and fast enough to compensate for base shrinkage. Only where state law is actually limiting will local taxing bodies lose revenue when property is removed from the tax rolls. Raising taxes is always onerous, so removing property from the tax rolls for any purpose, including charity, puts budgets under political pressure.

Constitutions of 26 states mandate exemption for specific classes of property. Sixteen grant discretionary authority to the legislature. Five state constitutions have both mandatory and discretionary provisions. The most common exemptions are, in descending order, with the number of states indicated in parentheses, religious (35, mostly limited to houses of worship), charitable or benevolent (33), educational (33), and cemeteries (27). Nineteen states exempt all four categories. Other exemptions appearing in the constitutions of at least two states are libraries (12), literary and scientific organizations (8), hospitals (4), cultural organizations and museums (4), agricultural and horticultural organizations (3), and patriotic and veterans' organizations (3). Mere ownership by an organization belonging to one of these categories is not sufficient; all states require a parcel of property to be *used* for exempt purposes.

With or without a constitutional mandate, every state exempts charitable property, but only 11 states define charity in the tax statutes.[24] Elsewhere, common law based on the law of trusts is the rule. In at least 27 states, organizations that are primarily social cannot qualify as charities for property tax purposes, even if they perform charitable acts. Several others restrict the ability of charities to serve alcohol as an indirect way of limiting social activity. Nebraska, for example, withholds tax exemption from educational, religious, charitable, or cemetery organizations when property is "owned or used for sale of alcohol more than 20 hours per week" (Nebraska Revised Statutes, section 77-202[d]).

The property tax exemption is controversial because states grant exemptions but local taxpayers pay for them, and the nonprofit hospital exemption is particularly controversial. "The public is increasingly questioning nonprofit hospitals' tax status because of the changed definition of charitable and the decrease in nonprofit hospitals' charity care" (Burns 2004, 670). "Of the 40-odd states whose law in the general area can be discerned, three-fourths expect hospitals to provide at least a minimal volume of services to the poor" (Simpson and Strum 1991, 651). Scholarly criticism of property tax exemption for nonprofit hospitals frequently alleges failure to provide adequate amounts of charity care (Aitsebaomo 2004; Burns 2004; Hyman 1990; Simpson and Strum 1991; an exception is Horwitz 2003). Further, nonprofit hospitals may behave uncharitably by hounding those who cannot pay and charging higher prices to uninsured patients.[25]

Thirty-two nonprofit hospitals lost their property tax exempt status between 1988 and 2000. A statistical analysis suggests that size of fixed assets positively affects and amount of charity care negatively affects the probability of revocation (Barniv, Danvers, and Healy-Burress 2005). In a closely watched case, a local review board voided the property tax exemption of a religiously affiliated hospital in Champaign, Illinois, for not living up to local expectations of its charitable mandate by aggressively pursuing persons who did not meet the hospital's standard for charity but who nevertheless could not pay. At the time of this writing, the case is under review by the Illinois Department of Revenue. In the meantime, the Champaign hospital has taken steps to make the charges against it moot, and the Illinois attorney general has proposed legislation making charity care a precondition for property tax exemption.

Statutes in California, Texas, and Washington illustrate different approaches to the issue of charity care (Sutton and Stensland 2004). Texas law mandates that nonprofit hospitals provide charity care and bases the amount on one of the following: (1) community needs, (2) estimated tax benefits, or (3) net patient revenue. Most Texas hospitals opt to provide charity care according to their net patient revenue (Wood 2001). Washington requires nonprofit hospitals to provide charity care to all uninsured persons whose family incomes are below 100 percent of the federal poverty level and to charge patients between 100 percent and 200 percent of the federal poverty level on a sliding scale. California's approach is process oriented. It requires that nonprofit hospitals do a community needs assessment every three years and develop a community benefits plan annually. Community benefits may include "free care services, wellness and health promotion services, research, medical education, and professional training" (Sutton and Stensland 2004, 238). Statistically controlling for hospital and market characteristics, Texas hospitals provide more than three times more charity care, and Washington hospitals provide 60 percent more charity care, than California (Sutton and Stensland 2004).

Some communities have negotiated payments in lieu of taxes (PILOTs) and services in lieu of taxes with local nonprofits, but they are not the norm among large cities and, where they exist, they tend to be arbitrary, negotiated, and not transparent (Leland 2002). Data, sparse as they are, show PILOTs raise an astonishingly small amount of money (Glancey 2002). It seems that the principle is more important than the payment, although, as a practical matter, local communities have virtually no leverage to force payment. Very few states make payments to local governments to compensate for a reduction in tax base from nonprofit-owned property.[26]

Historically, controversy over property tax exemption has been persistent and occasionally intense, but for the most part, it has been highly localized. The only occasion in recent history where the question of abolishing property tax exemption for most nonprofits was put to statewide referendum was in Colorado in 1996, where it failed by a two-to-one majority.[27] Stephen Diamond observes that attacks on the property tax exemption in different venues have failed to produce significant change and opines that "every outburst of criticism left exemption strengthened" (2002, 117). Pennsylvania illustrates his point. After a long series of lawsuits in Pennsylvania stripped several important nonprofit organizations of their property tax exemption, the legislature intervened. In 1997 it enacted a statute that restored most, if not all, exemptions while substantially broadening the concept of charity to encompass sports activities, open space preservation, summer youth camps, missionary housing, Bible publishing associations, and historic associations (Goodman 2000).

General Sales Tax

General sales tax exemption of nonprofits is no less complicated, although less controversial.[28] By general sales tax, we mean a tax that falls on the gross receipts of a seller, regardless of its statutory name. States differ in the extent of market coverage, however. Some states tax gross receipts from services, whereas others tax only tangible goods. Some tax food, medicine, and clothing, whereas other states exempt these items. This discussion covers general sales taxes, without regard to extent of coverage, except that taxes limited to one specific item, such as motor fuel, alcohol, or cigarettes, are excluded. By this definition, 45 states have a general sales tax. Only Alaska, Delaware, Montana, New Hampshire, and Oregon do not. Alaska permits local taxation of sales, however, and in 30 other states, local governments impose a companion sales tax to their state's tax. In Colorado and Louisiana, local sales tax collections actually exceed state collections (U.S. Census Bureau 2001a).

Exemption on purchases is more common than exemption on sales, perhaps because most general sales taxes do not extend to services, and services generate most charitable program-related revenue. Broad charitable exemptions from collecting taxes on sales can be found in states that broadly tax receipts from services as well as products—Hawaii, for example. Some states exempt fundraising sales and some excuse nonprofit arts and cultural organizations from collecting amusement taxes. The numerical estimates of the value of general sales tax exemption we report do not include fundraising or amusement tax exemptions. (See the appendix for information on data sources and estimating techniques.)

Twenty-four of the 45 states with a general sales tax do not tax purchases by charitable organizations: 10 states use common-law definition of charity, 14 either cross-reference section 501(c)(3) of the federal

Internal Revenue Code or enact a nearly identical description in state law. Sixteen additional states have a limited exemption from the sales tax for purchases by specific categories of charitable organizations and some states even exempt specific organizations by name. In estimating the value of the general sales tax exemption on purchases, we include only the 25 states with a broad charitable exemption. The state general sales tax exemption is worth approximately $2 billion to nonprofits in those states, and the local exemption is worth an additional $400 million. For sales *by* charities, seven states exempt only 501(c)(3) organizations and eight others exempt sales by "charitable" organizations. Common law is the basis for defining "charitable" in the latter group of states. The savings from sales tax exemption on sales by nonprofits are only $100 million.

Corporate Income Tax

Of the 45 states that tax corporate net income, 32 have a flat rate, and the others use graduated rates. States define taxable income differently and use various methods for allocating net income to a particular state for corporations doing business in multiple states or foreign countries. Depending on the assumptions one makes for these factors, the value of the charitable exemption for the state tax on net income for nonprofit corporations ranges between $3.8 billion and $4.0 billion. (See the appendix for information on data sources and estimating techniques.)

CONCLUSION

State and local governments have an impact on nonprofits in at least three important ways: they regulate nonprofits, they use nonprofits as vehicles to deliver public services, and they exempt nonprofits from major taxes. Common law, which grew out of the law of trusts, gives states a broad mandate to regulate charities and gives state courts broad powers to enforce fidelity to the public interest and donor intent. Common law also gives state attorneys general an exclusive right to initiate litigation on the public's behalf. But results are spotty. Attorneys general in only a handful of states attempt to vigorously police local charities, and even they do not have sufficient resources to do a thorough job.

States have the power to regulate organized charity by legislation. States have been particularly active in regulating charitable solicitation, but their efforts suffer from a lack of uniformity and weak enforcement. A myriad of exceptions and exemptions make it extremely difficult for an organization intending to solicit in multiple states to identify the jurisdictions in which it must register and thereafter to meet their separate requirements. The National Association of State Charity Officials has been active in attempting to bring about a degree of uniformity in registration, with modest success.

State and local funding for the nonprofit sector, principally charities, is very important but still secondary to the federal government. All government payments to nonprofits, whether in the form of grants or program service income, total $227 billion—nearly one-third of the combined revenues of public charities. Direct federal funding of nonprofits is $115 billion. An estimated $112 billion flows from state governments to nonprofits, which is $28 billion in excess of federal pass-through dollars. The largest public programs with direct impact on nonprofit organizations are Medicare and Medicaid, and they have been growing faster than spending on other public programs. Government funding makes up more than half of the revenues of nonprofit health care organizations.

The property tax exemption alone is worth $9 billion to $15 billion annually, the general sales tax exemption, $2.5 billion, and the state corporate income tax exemption is worth $3.8 billion to $4.0 billion, for a total of $15.3 to $21.5 billion. There is considerable variation among states in the base to which these taxes apply. Likewise, the requirements and conditions for tax exemption vary considerably. The ratio between the value of property tax exemption and the combined value of sales and state corporate income tax exemptions ranges from a low of 1.4 to a high of 1.6. This is consistent with the 1.4 ratio Kane and Wubbenhorst (2000) estimate for nonprofit hospitals alone.

The property tax exemption is disproportionately important to churches, private schools and colleges, and arts organizations because many of them own large amounts of property. More controversy surrounds exemptions from the property tax than any other exemption. Hospitals are a particular target. Local officials are using the threat of loss of tax-exempt status as a lever to increase the amount of charity care hospitals provide. The tax system has been pressed into service as a supplementary regulatory tool. But, as in the case of formal regulatory tools, the results are uneven.

NOTES

1. The administration of John Adams briefly experimented with a federal property tax.

2. In the mid-19th century mental health crusader Dorethea Dix persuaded Congress to pass a bill granting 10 million acres of federal land for mental hospitals, amended to provide also for institutions for the blind and deaf. President Pierce vetoed it, arguing that the constitution forbade a federal role in such matters.

3. Historically, state officials scrutinized the intended purpose of each applicant for nonprofit corporate status and occasionally denied an application. After a series of legal battles in the 1960s exposing the arbitrary and capricious nature of denials, the courts forced states to abandon their gatekeeper role (Silber 2001). Today, incorporation is a ministerial act.

4. This is an application of Dillon's Rule (*Clinton v. Cedar Rapids & Missouri River R.R. Co.* 24 Iowa 455 [1868]), which has been the common law bedrock of state and local government powers for more than 150 years. However, some states have granted home-rule powers to a limited number of cities and counties. Home rule confers broader powers, which vary from state to state, and it does not exist in every state.

5. Public charities are a subset of organizations that the IRS recognizes as tax-exempt under section 501(c)(3) of the Internal Revenue Code that does not include private foundations.

6. Fremont-Smith (1965, 2004) explores the issues discussed in this section in detail.

7. Cy pres comes from the Norman French phrase, "cy pres comme possible," which has been translated to mean "as near as possible."

8. A nonprofit corporation is established under state law by applying to an appropriate state official, usually the secretary of state, who issues articles of organization to a group of directors. One or more individuals signing a declaration of trust setting forth the terms creates a trust. The duties of directors and trustees of charities are essentially the same. Familiarity with business corporations has led to the popularity of the corporate form for charities.

9. There have been calls to modify this doctrine, based on the failure of the attorneys general in so many states to actively supervise charitable activity. However, to date, the doctrine has not been modified.

10. Mass. Ch. 12 §8F; N.H. Rev. Stat. Title 1, §7:28 IIIa-c; Cal. Code §12586.

11. Access to state citations is available at the Multi-State Filer Project web site, http://multistatefiling.org.

12. The fact that the law requires only tax-exempt organizations other than churches with annual revenue over $25,000 to file 990 forms is less consequential. The overwhelming proportion of revenue from all sources is concentrated in a small proportion of nonprofits. Despite a new emphasis on "charitable choice," very little federal funding flows to churches (Ragan, Montiel, and Wright 2003).

13. Direct payments include Social Security, Supplemental Security Income, Medicare, Earned Income Tax Credit, Unemployment Insurance, Food Stamps, housing assistance, agricultural assistance, and federal retirement and veterans' benefits. Medicaid is classified under grants, despite the fact that the federal government partially reimburses the states for fee-for-service payments. The

federal government spends an additional $400 billion for procurement, wages, and salaries.

14. Some writers (e.g., Bradford Gray, editor of *The Milbank Quarterly*) distinguish two types of for-profits—proprietary, which are locally owned, and investor-owned, which are owned by a corporation that owns multiple facilities.

15. The authors would like to thank Bradford Gray of the Urban Institute, Sara Gooding-Williams of DePaul University, David Carvalho of the Illinois Department of Public Health, and Sara Beazley of the American Hospital Association for consulting on these issues.

16. A general fund is an account that finances goods and services unsupported by a dedicated revenue source. Technically, it is unrestricted. Although a state may maintain many restricted accounts, each one has a single general fund. Most social services are paid out of the general fund.

17. The rank order correlation coefficient between state intergovernmental revenue from the federal government, as a proportion of general revenue, and Medicaid spending, expressed as a proportion of state direct general expenditures for current operations, is 0.39, which is significant at the $p = .05$ level using a one-tail test. State intergovernmental revenue from the federal government includes funding for programs besides Medicaid.

18. The rank order correlation coefficient between state Medicaid spending per capita and Medicaid spending as a proportion of state direct general expenditures for current operations is 0.81, which significant at the $p = .05$ level using a one-tail test.

19. Reported revenue changes are net figures equal to total lost revenue due to tax cuts minus total revenue gained due to tax increases.

20. Throughout this chapter, "property" refers to real property, not personal property. Nothing is lost by this restriction because few states have personal property taxes and none raise appreciable revenue.

21. These include all 501(c)(3) operating public charities other than churches with annual revenues in excess of $10 million and a sample of smaller ones. Weighting the sample provides an estimate for 166,000 nonprofits.

22. "Less than 2,000 organizations with gross receipts over $100 million account for 63% of the income of all the organizations combined. About 11,000 organizations between $10 million and $100 million account for an additional 23%. On the other hand, the 178,000 organizations with income under $1 million account for only 3% of the reported income" (Prives 2006).

23. See for example, the *Chronicle of Philanthropy* ("Taxing Times for Charity," September 18, 2003). Property tax exemptions antedate the federal income tax by at least 60 years. Confusion on this point probably arises because churches, institutions of higher education, hospitals, and nursing homes own most charitable property, all of them are 501(c)(3) eligible, and every state exempts them from property taxes, but for reasons found in state law, not necessarily for their federal tax status.

24. Data on property tax exemptions by state are based on research conducted in 2001 by Woods Bowman supported by the Lincoln Institute of Land Policy (unpublished manuscript).

25. Nonprofit hospitals are exempt in every state but constitutionally exempt in only three. Most states do not exempt them as hospitals per se, but as a subset of charities. As such, they are exposed to a widespread presumption that they have a social responsibility to provide charity care as several recent

cases illustrate (Unland 2004). Charity care is free care given without expectation of compensation. If compensation is anticipated, but subsequently not
forthcoming, the care is de facto free, but it is classified as bad debt.

26. Connecticut and Wisconsin, to name two.

27. The proposition called for "eliminating any property tax exemptions for
real property used for religious purposes, real property used by for-profit
schools, real property used for charitable purposes other than for community
corrections facilities, orphanages, or for housing low-income elderly, disabled,
homeless, or abused persons, and real property used for nonprofit cemeteries;
continuing the property tax exemptions for real property used for nonprofit
schools, community corrections facilities, orphanages, and housing low-income
elderly, disabled, homeless, or abused persons, unless otherwise provided by
general law"(State of Colorado, Secretary of State, Elections Division).

28. Except as noted, this section, up to the last paragraph, is a summary of
Gallagher (1999). Estimates of the economic impact are ours.

REFERENCES

Aitsebaomo, Gabriel O. 2004. "The Nonprofit Hospital: A Call For New
National Guidance Requiring Minimum Annual Charity Care to Qualify
for Federal Tax Exemption." *Campbell Law Review* 26(2): 75–99.

American Hospital Association. 2002. *Annual Survey Database, FY 2001*. Chicago:
Health Forum LLC, an affiliate of the American Hospital Association.

Axinn, June, and Herman Levin. 1975. *Social Welfare: A History of the American
Response to Need*. New York: Harper & Row.

Barniv, Ran, Kreag Danvers, and Joanne P. Healy-Burress. 2005. "An Empirical
Examination of State and Local Revocations of Tax-Exempt Status for
Nonprofit Hospitals." *Journal of the American Taxation Association* 27(2):
1–25.

Bowman, Woods. 2002. "Impact Fees, An Alternative to PILOTs." In *The Property-Tax Exemption for Charities: Mapping the Battlefield*, edited by Evelyn
Brody (301–19). Washington, DC: Urban Institute Press.

———. 2003. *Fiscal Crisis in the States: Its Impact on Nonprofit Organizations and
the People They Serve*. Washington, DC: The Nonprofit Research Fund of
the Aspen Institute.

Brooks, Arthur. 2004. "In Search of True Public Arts Support." *Public Budgeting
& Finance* 24(2): 88–100.

Burns, Jack. 2004. "Are Nonprofit Hospitals Really Charitable?: Taking the
Question to the State and Local Level." *Journal of Corporation Law* 29(3):
665–83.

Center on Budget and Policy Priorities. 2005. "The State Fiscal Analysis Initiative." http://www.cbpp.org/sfai.htm.

Centers for Medicare and Medicaid Services. 2003. *Health Care Financing Review:
Medicare and Medicaid Statistical Supplement, 2003*. http://new.cms.hhs.gov/
apps/review/supp/2003/.

Chang, Cyril F., and Howard P. Tuckman. 1990. "Do Higher Property Tax
Rates Increase the Market Share of Nonprofit Hospitals?" *National Tax
Journal* 43(2): 175–87.

Chronicle of Higher Education. 2005. *Chronicle of Higher Education Almanac Issue, 2004–2005* 51(1).

Cordes, Joseph J., Marie Gantz, and Thomas Pollak. 2002. "What Is The Property-Tax Exemption Worth?" In *The Property-Tax Exemption for Charities: Mapping the Battlefield*, edited by Evelyn Brody (81–112) Washington, DC: Urban Institute Press.

Council of State Governments. 2002. *Book of the States: 2000–2001.* Lexington, KY: Council of State Government.

Diamond, Stephen. 2002. "Efficiency and Benevolence: Philanthropic Tax Exemptions in Nineteenth Century America." In *The Property-Tax Exemption for Charities: Mapping the Battlefield*, edited by Evelyn Brody (115–44). Washington DC: Urban Institute Press.

Fremont-Smith, Marion R. 1965. *Foundations and Government: State and Federal Law and Supervision.* New York: Russell Sage Foundation.

———. 2004. *Governing Nonprofit Organizations: Federal and State Law and Regulation.* Cambridge, MA: Belknap Press of Harvard University Press.

———. 1998. "The Role of Government Regulation in the Creation and Operation of Conversion Foundations." *The Exempt Organization Tax Review* 23(1): 37–54.

Gabriel, Celia S. 2003. *An Overview of Nursing Home Facilities: Data from the 1997 National Nursing Home Survey, Advance Data #311.* Hyattsville, MD: Centers for Disease Control and Prevention, National Center for Health Statistics. http://www.cdc.gov/nchs/products/pubs/pubd/ad/ad.htm.

Gallagher, Janne G. 1999. *Sales Tax Exemptions for Charitable, Educational, and Religious Nonprofit Organizations.* Washington, DC: National Council of Nonprofit Associations.

Glancey, David B. 2002. "PILOTs: Philadelphia and Pennsylvania." In *The Property-Tax Exemption for Charities: Mapping the Battlefield*, edited by Evelyn Brody (211–32). Washington DC: Urban Institute Press.

Goodman, Bert M. 2000. *Assessment Law and Procedure in Pennsylvania.* Mechanicsberg: Pennsylvania Bar Institute.

Grønbjerg, Kirsten, and Curtis Child. 2004. *Indiana Nonprofits: Impact of Community and Policy Changes.* Bloomington: Center on Philanthropy at Indiana University and the School of Environmental Affairs at Indiana University.

Hansmann, Henry 1987. "The Effect of Tax Exemption and Other Factors on the Market Share of Nonprofit Versus For-Profit Firms." *National Tax Journal* 40(1): 71–82.

Horwitz, Jill R. 2003. "Why We Need the Independent Sector: The Behavior, Law, and Ethics of Not-For-Profit Hospitals." *UCLA Law Review* 50(6): 1345–1411.

Hyman, David A. 1990. "The Conundrum of Charitability: Reassessing Tax Exemption for Hospitals." *American Journal of Law and Medicine* 16(3): 327–80.

Johnson, Kirk. 2005. "Colorado Cap on Spending Is Suspended." *New York Times*, November 3, A16.

Kaiser Commission on Medicaid and the Uninsured. 2001. *2001 State and National Medicaid Enrollment and Spending Data (MSIS).* http://www.kff.org/medicaid/kcmu070805oth.cfm.

Kane, Nancy M., and William H. Wubbenhorst. 2000. "Alternative Funding Policies for the Uninsured: Exploring the Value of the Hospital Tax Exemption." *The Milbank Quarterly* 78(2): 185–212.

Kane, Thomas J., Peter R. Orszag, and David L. Gunter. 2003. *State Fiscal Constraints and Higher Education Spending: The Role of Medicaid and the Business Cycle*. Washington, DC: The Urban Institute. Tax Policy Center Discussion Paper 11.

Leland, Pamela. 2002. "PILOTs: The Large-City Experience." In *The Property-Tax Exemption for Charities: Mapping the Battlefield*, edited by Evelyn Brody (193–210). Washington, DC: Urban Institute Press.

Milbank Memorial Fund, National Association of State Budget Officers, and the Reforming States Group. 2003. *2000–2001 State Health Care Expenditure Report*. http://www.milbank.org/reports/2000shcer/index.html.

National Assembly of State Arts Agencies. 2002. *Legislative Appropriations Annual Survey 2001*. Washington, DC: National Assembly of State Arts Agencies.

National Association of State Budget Officers. 2003. *The Fiscal Survey of the States*. Washington, DC: National Association of State Budget Officers and National Governors Association.

National Council of Real Estate Fiduciaries. n.d. "Frequently Asked Questions about NREIF and the NCREIF Property Index (NPI)." http://www.ncreif.com/pdf/Users_Guide_to_NPI.pdf.

OMG Center for Collaborative Learning. 2005. *Assessment of the State Fiscal Analysis Initiative*. Washington, DC: OMG Center for Collaborative Learning.

Prives, Dan. 2006. "IRS Data Shows Largest Nonprofits Have Biggest Economic Impact." http://www.wheremostneeded.org/2006/02/irs_data_shows_.html.

Quigley, John, and Roger Schmenner. 1975. "Property Tax Exemption and Public Policy." *Public Policy* 23(Summer): 259–97.

Ragan, Mark, Lisa Montiel, and David Wright. 2003. *Scanning the Policy Environment for Faith-Based Social Services in the United States: Results of a 50-State Study*. Albany: Roundtable on Religion and Social Welfare Policy, Rockefeller Institute of Government, State University of New York.

Reschovsky, Andrew. 2003. *The Implication of State Fiscal Stress for Local Governments*. Washington, DC: The Urban Institute.

Roy, William G. 1997. *Socializing Capital: The Rise of the Large Industrial Corporation in America*. Princeton, NJ: Princeton University Press.

Silber, Norman I. 2001. *A Corporate Form of Freedom: The Emergence of the Nonprofit Sector*. Boulder, CO: Westview Press.

Simpson, James B., and Sarah D. Strum 1991. "How Good A Samaritan? Federal Income Tax Exemption for Charitable Hospitals Reconsidered." *University of Puget Sound Law Review* 14(3): 633–70.

Sutton, Janet P., and Jeffrey Stensland. 2004. "Promoting Accountability: Hospital Charity Care in California, Washington State, and Texas." *Journal of Health Care for the Poor and Underserved* 15(2): 237–50.

Unland, James J. 2004. "Not-for-Profit Community Hospitals' Exempt Status at Issue in Charity Care Controversy." *Journal of Health Care Finance* 31(2): 62–78.

U.S. Census Bureau. 2002a. *2002 Census of Governments: State and Local Government Finances*. Washington, DC: U.S. Government Printing Office. http://www.census.gov/govs/www/estimate02.html.

———. 2002b. *Consolidated Federal Funds Report for Fiscal Year 2001*. Washington, DC: U.S. Government Printing Office.

———. 2002c. *Federal Aid to States for Fiscal Year 2001*. Washington, DC: U.S. Government Printing Office.

Wood, Kevin M. 2001. "Legislatively-Mandated Charity Care for Nonprofit Hospitals: Does Government Intervention Make Any Difference?" *Review of Litigation* 20(3): 709–42.

Appendix

STATE AND LOCAL FUNDING

The data reported in figure 5.1 and supporting tables are for 2001 because it is the most recent year for which all data sources are available. The most recent *Census of Governments* covered 2001–2002, and data on private higher education are published four years after the fact. Because of methodological differences, data in figure 5.1 only roughly indicate the size of different funding streams. This appendix describes the data sources and definitions of key concepts.

(1) The *Consolidated Federal Funds Report for Fiscal Year 2001* (CFFR) provides information on federal agency outlays to recipients in each state, the District of Columbia, Puerto Rico, and federal territories. The CFFR breaks down outlays by direct payments to individuals, federal salaries and wages, and obligations for grants and procurement contracts. A direct payment is a current cash outlay, whereas an obligation is a promise to pay in the future. CFFR makes no distinction between governmental and nongovernmental recipients. Direct payments of $1.0 trillion include Social Security, Supplemental Security Income, Medicare, earned income tax credit, Unemployment Compensation, Food Stamps, housing assistance, agricultural assistance, as well as federal insurance payments, and veterans' benefits. Grants include Medicaid. The federal government spends an additional $400 billion for procurement and wages and salaries.

(2) *Federal Aid to the States* reports grants made to state and local governments. Unlike CFFR, it excludes payments and obligations to nongovernmental entities, it reports actual expenditures (not obligations), and it reports expenditures at the agency level by major program.

(3) A formula that compares a state's average per capita income level with the national income average determines the federal share of Medicaid. States with a higher per capita income level are reimbursed

a smaller share of their costs. By law, the federal share cannot be lower than 50 percent or higher than 83 percent. In 2001, the actual federal share ranged from 50 percent in 10 states to 77 percent in Mississippi, averaging 57 percent. The $81 billion figure is the average state and local share of 43 percent times Medicaid spending as reported by Kaiser Commission (2001).

A detailed breakdown of Medicaid spending on inpatient hospitals, nursing homes, prescribed drugs, doctors, and outpatient facilities and clinics is found in table 3 of *State and National Medicaid Enrollment and Spending Data*, compiled by the Kaiser Commission on Medicaid and the Uninsured from Urban Institute estimates based on Medicaid Statistical Information System data for federal FY 2001. For consistency we used Medicaid spending data from this source and allocated it by ownership type as described in the following paragraphs.

The American Hospital Association provided unpublished Medicare and Medicaid payments by ownership type from its annual survey for federal FY 2001 on all registered hospitals in the United States from its *Annual Survey Database, FY 2001* (American Hospital Association 2002). Its survey had a response rate of 61 percent on these items. For nonrespondents, the American Hospital Association supplied data from the prior year's survey, if available, or estimated them from payments received by a peer group. Data are actual payments, not billings, and include disproportionate share funding. Payment data were not used in their raw form, but were the basis for calculating a percentage distribution by ownership type that was applied to total payments reported by CFFR and Kaiser Commission (2001) to estimate payments by ownership categories. The American Hospital Association reports Medicare payments to hospitals as $147 billion; the corresponding figure from CFFR is $140 billion.

We estimated governmental payments to nonprofit, public, and for-profit nursing homes by the fraction of Medicaid-certified beds in each group. Nursing home data are from tables 1 and 2 of *Advance Data #311* (Gabriel 2003). Two-thirds of nursing home beds are in for-profit facilities, nearly all of them certified for Medicaid. Only one quarter are in nonprofit facilities, of which 77 percent are certified for Medicaid.

Finally, we allocated the payments to home care and personal care based on the number of home visits by ownership type as reported by Centers for Medicare and Medicaid Services (2003, table 49).

(4) The *Census of Governments* reports intergovernmental revenue from the federal government and actual expenditures made by state and local governments in various programs. In state fiscal years 2000–2001, total state and local general revenues were $1.6 trillion, of which $361 billion was from the federal government, $905 billion was taxes, and $419 billion was charges and miscellaneous. There is a $37 billion (approximately 10 percent) difference in federal aid to the states

between *Census of Governments* and *Federal Aid to the States*. Although both measure actual cash payments, a discrepancy might be expected because *Census of Governments* uses state fiscal years (usually June 30), whereas *Federal Aid to the States* uses a September 30 federal fiscal year.

(5) Because most state/local funding of higher education supports public institutions, we turn to the *Chronicle of Higher Education, Almanac Issue, 2004–2005* (p. 30) for data pertaining to private, nonprofit education. Direct appropriations and contracts from the federal government were $10 billion and from state and local governments, $1.6 billion. Total revenue of all institutions of higher education was $256.7 billion, with private institutions accounting for $82.1 billion, or a one-third share. Pell Grants and student loans are payments and loans to individuals. If we had counted these funds as institutional revenue from federal sources, the federal share would be higher.

(6) There is no *Census of Governments* category for arts funding, so for this information we use the *Legislative Appropriations Annual Survey* of the National Assembly of State Arts Agencies, which reports total state appropriations for the arts of $447 million. This total does not include local funding for the arts. Federal outlays through the Corporation for Public Broadcasting, Institute for Museum and Library Service, and other arts and humanities funding total $764 million and additional state appropriations are $447 million, for a combined total of $1.2 billion. Based on data from the IRS Business Master File, total revenue of the 45,585 public charities in the arts and culture category is $29.4 billion. Arthur Brooks (2004) found that indirect support for the arts through various tax exemptions is 14 times direct federal arts funding. His finding strongly suggests that state and local tax exemptions are far more important than state grants.

(7) For information on total revenues of the nonprofit sector, we use IRS Form 990 data compiled by the National Center for Charitable Statistics (IRS Business Master Files [Exempt Organizations] 2001, available at http://nccsdataweb.urban.org).

STATE AND LOCAL TAX BENEFITS

(1) Property Tax: According to Cordes, Gantz, and Pollak (2002), the market value of tax-exempt property, excluding houses of worship, was $900 billion in 1997. They calculated charitable property, including hospitals, nursing homes, schools, and universities, accounted for about $500 billion of this amount, and the value of the property tax exemption to charitable nonprofits was $8 billion to $13 billion annually. We extrapolated these data to 2001 for consistency with other data in this chapter.

We increased the 1997 valuation data by 14 percent. This increase includes an assumed 1 percent annual addition of new charitable property plus capital appreciation, which was 10.5 percent between 1997 and 2001. The latter estimate is based on the capital component of a commercial real estate index from the National Council of Real Estate Fiduciaries. The properties used in constructing the index are representative of properties in the investment portfolios of tax-exempt entities. The income component of the index was not used in this calculation because owner-occupied property is not an investment, so its income-generating potential is not relevant to calculating value for tax purposes. The property tax is predominantly a local tax. A few states impose property taxes, but only 1 percent of total state tax receipts are from this source (Census of Governments 2002a, table 1). States regulate property tax administration, however, and generally define what is exempt.

(2) Sales Tax: For general sales taxes, we apply the state tax rate to the reported amount of supplies purchased and add an estimate of the local sales tax; this yields an estimate of $3.6 billion. Of the 166,000 charities in the weighted sample, 33,000 reported no purchase of supplies. We use tax rates that were effective on January 1, 2000 (Council of State Governments 2002). Complicating matters, some states permit local governments to impose a general sales tax, and the rate may vary from place to place. To obtain an estimate of the benefit of the local tax exemption, we compute the ratio of state and local general sales tax receipts to the state's tax receipts alone (Census 2002a) and multiply it by the estimate of state sales taxes lost because of the charitable exemption. States with a broad charitable exemption are: Colorado, Connecticut, Illinois, Indiana, Kentucky, Maryland, Massachusetts, Michigan, Minnesota, Missouri, Nevada, New Jersey, New Mexico, New York, North Carolina, Ohio, Pennsylvania, Rhode Island, Tennessee, Texas, Utah, Vermont, Wisconsin, Wyoming, and Washington, D.C. (Gallagher 1999). Some states exempt sales *by* charities. But this amounts to only $98 million, which is swamped by the value of the tax exemption on purchases.

(3) Corporate Income Tax: We use corporate tax rates in effect as of January 1, 2000 (Council of State Governments 2002) applied to nonprofits with positive net operating income. For purposes of calculating the value of charitable exemption from this tax, we define net income as gross income from all sources (except sale of assets) net of costs, and apply the corporate tax rate to only those charities that have positive net income. Some states and the federal government permit losses to be carried forward. For simplicity, our estimates overlook these complications. For those states with a graduated tax, we calculate the value of the exemption, assuming that all organizations are taxed at the minimum rate, and repeat the calculation assuming all are taxed at the maximum rate.

6

GOVERNMENT FINANCING OF NONPROFIT ACTIVITY

Steven Rathgeb Smith

G overnment funding of nonprofit organizations is at a crucial transition stage in the United States. Since the 1960s, funding of nonprofits has been on the rise, although the extent of this increase depends upon the type of nonprofit organization. However, many pending proposals in Congress would significantly alter several major federal programs, such as Medicaid, the Temporary Assistance for Needy Families (TANF) program, and the Section 8 housing voucher program, possibly reducing government funding of a wide array of nonprofit organizations over time. Further, the ongoing debate on the Bush administration's faith-based and community initiative reflects differing views on how much government should support nonprofit organizations as well as the appropriateness of direct government financial support of churches and faith-related agencies. Proposals to devolve responsibility for important federal programs to the states would also fundamentally change the regulatory role of the federal government as it relates to nonprofit agencies receiving federal funds, such as Medicaid, with potentially important consequences for government financing of non-profit services.

The high profile politics of government funding of nonprofits has tended to overshadow the ongoing transformation and diversification of the ways government conducts its business (Salamon 2002; Smith 2002). Government financing of public services has moved well beyond direct government services to include grants, contracts, and, increasingly, tax credits, tax-exempt bonds, tax deductions, vouchers, and fees for services. This diversification tends to mask the extent of public funding of nonprofits and, simultaneously, the increased centralization of government funding at the federal level in many areas, such as health and social services. The variety of policy tools has also had important and far-reaching effects on the operations of nonprofit organizations.

This chapter focuses on the development and diversification of government financing of nonprofits along with its attendant impact on the management and programs of nonprofits. The chapter is divided into five parts. First, an overview of trends in government financing of nonprofit organizations is followed by a discussion of five key tools of government that are central to supporting nonprofit activity: (1) direct grants and contracts; (2) fees from individuals and third party organizations; (3) tax credits and deductions; (4) tax-exempt bonds; and (5) regulations encouraging nonprofit service delivery. The second section assesses the effect of government financing on nonprofit agencies, followed by an examination of private financing alternatives to government funding. The fourth section analyzes five nonprofit organizations receiving public funds: a social welfare agency; an architectural and design firm for other nonprofit organizations serving disadvantaged populations; a low-income housing organization; a community agency for the developmentally disabled; and a new sculpture park affiliated with an art museum. The final section discusses the implications of recent development pertaining to government financing of nonprofits for public policy, the staff and volunteers of nonprofits, and the citizenry.

GOVERNMENT FINANCING OF NONPROFIT ORGANIZATIONS: GROWTH AND DIVERSIFICATION

Government financial support on nonprofit organizations has a long tradition in the United States dating to the colonial period (Hall 1987; Salamon 1987; Smith and Lipsky 1993). Harvard University, the Massachusetts General Hospital, and other leading educational and health institutions received public funding in their formative years. Throughout the 19th early 20th centuries, government funding of nonprofit service agencies continued, although it tended to be most extensive in the urban areas of the Northeast and Midwest. For example, New York City relied almost completely upon nonprofit sectarian agencies, such as Catholic Charities, to provide child welfare services (Young 1979). But these arrangements tended to be the exception. Most nonprofit agencies relied upon donations, fees, and occasional payments from government; this pattern was particularly evident in southern, western, and rural states. Even states, such as New York, with substantial government financing of nonprofits, frequently placed limitations on this government support because of broad concern that nonprofit agencies were receiving excessive public funding (Fetter 1901).

Beginning in the 1960s, government financing of nonprofit organizations increased sharply, fueled by extensive federal spending on many new social and health programs and organizations, including Medicare and Medicaid, community action agencies, community mental health centers, neighborhood health centers, and child protection agencies. In the 1970s, government funding essentially created a national network of mostly nonprofit drug and alcohol treatment programs. Other innovative community agencies receiving federal funds were battered women's shelters, rape crisis programs, and emergency shelters for runaway youth. In the 1980s, the government's principal response to AIDS, homelessness, and hunger was through contracts with nonprofit service agencies (Smith 2002; Smith and Lipsky 1993).

Government funding of nonprofit agencies increased in the 1980s despite a renewed emphasis on policy devolution from the federal government to state and local governments. In particular, President Reagan won passage in 1981 of the Omnibus Budget Reconciliation Act (OBRA), which reduced the growth rate of federal spending and regulations on many federal social and health programs and devolved responsibility for the administration of these programs, at least in part, to the states (Gutowski and Koshel 1984). Some nonprofit agencies, especially other than hospitals and higher educational institutions, experienced sharp reductions in government funding, at least initially.

Even before the end of the second Reagan administration in 1988, government funding of different types of nonprofit agencies recovered and in many cases increased substantially. Many states and localities substituted their own funds for lost federal money, refinanced their contracts with nonprofit agencies, or reconfigured programs to maximize federal assistance to take advantage of federal programs with increasing budgets (General Accounting Office [GAO] 1984; Milroy 1999). This shift was particularly apparent in such policy areas as mental health, developmental disabilities, child welfare, home health, and counseling, where state government increasingly tapped Medicaid to fund services previously funded through federal, state, and local categorical grant programs (GAO 1995).

In addition, federal funding to address urgent public needs, such as low-income housing, immigrant assistance, and community development, rose, often substantially during the late 1980s and 1990s. For example, the George H. W. Bush administration initiated a sharp rise in federal spending on drug and alcohol treatment, prevention programs, and child welfare services. New funding was available for new or expanded child care, foster care, and pre-school, such as Head Start (Executive Office of the President 2005; House Ways and Means Committee 1996). Nonprofit low-income housing agencies proliferated throughout the country, spurred in part by the federal Low-Income Housing Tax Credit (LIHTC) program enacted in 1986.

More recently, the devolution of federal policy entered a new stage with the implementation of welfare reform, signed into law in 1996 by President Clinton. This legislation replaced the Aid to Families with Dependent Children (AFDC) program, enacted in 1935 as a shared federal/state program with wide variations in payment levels and eligibility standards. In place of AFDC, Temporary Assistance for Needy Families (TANF) was established, initially with higher levels of funding than AFDC but with fewer recipients. TANF includes new state block grant programs and greater discretion for states to design income assistance programs, although new strict federal regulations govern the expenditure of federal TANF money by the states, including specific performance targets for states to meet on the number of people on the welfare rolls, rates of teenage pregnancy, and work participation by welfare recipients. The welfare reform legislation also included a "Charitable Choice" amendment to encourage states to fund faith-based agencies providing social services.

The impact of TANF on nonprofit organizations was complex. Almost immediately, many clients of nonprofit social welfare agencies lost their income maintenance support. However, these clients, to greatly varying degrees across the country, were eligible for additional services (funded in part with new federal grants) to help them find permanent employment. Overall, the size and character of welfare rolls and the expenditure of funds on welfare-related programs changed dramatically. A comparison of 1996 AFDC data with 2001 TANF data underscores this transformation: the number of families on welfare dropped 53 percent, the number of teen parents on welfare dropped 50 percent, and the share of AFDC and TANF dollars spent on direct cash assistance declined from 73 to 44 percent (House Ways and Means 2004).

In short, federal funding for income maintenance support for individuals declined sharply; at the same time, federal support for nonprofit (and to a much lesser extent, for-profit) services rose significantly. For instance, in Wisconsin, funding for cash assistance to individuals dropped from $352 million in 1995 to $73 million in 1999, but total expenditures rose from $1.082 billion to $1.239 billion because of a big increase in federal service funding, especially for child care (Boyd and Billen 2003; more generally, see House Ways and Means 2004, 9–56). Overall, the federal share of total human service spending increased in the wake of welfare reform. Indeed, the federal share of total spending on income-tested service benefits, including welfare, climbed substantially. State spending on services dropped from $8.1 billion in 1995 to $4.6 billion in 2002, whereas federal spending rose $7.1 billion to $17.5 billion (in 2002 dollars) (House Ways and Means 2004). A large percentage of this additional service funding was spent in support of nonprofit programs, including day care, welfare to work, job training, and counseling.

The federal share of social welfare services funding has also risen due to sharp escalation in federal expenditures for Medicaid, the shared federal–state health care program. The number of Medicaid recipients has risen from 20 million in 1975 to almost 50 million in 2004 (Behn and Keating 2004; House Ways and Means 2004;). Total spending on Medicaid surged more than one-third between fiscal years 2000 and 2003 from just over $200 billion to more than $275 billion (see Holahan and Ghosh 2005). This rapid increase was due in part to substantial growth in enrollment, especially among the aged and disabled poor who receive long-term care and personal care benefits from Medicaid (Holahan and Ghosh 2005; Kaiser Commission on Medicaid and the Uninsured 2005a, b).

Medicaid, for instance, is critical to funding services for the developmentally disabled, especially community-based programs. In 1980, most public funding for services for the developmentally disabled came from state dollars, but because of the Home and Community Based Services waiver program of Medicaid, state funding represented only 46 percent of community spending in 2002. Total public spending rose from about $8 billion in 1977 to $27 billion in 2002 (in 2002 dollars) (Rizzolo et al. 2004). Medicaid also funds a broad group of programs provided by nonprofit agencies, including child welfare, home care, hospices, counseling, residential foster care, drug and alcohol treatment, and services for the mentally ill (although the extent of coverage varies depending on the state).

The transformation of state child welfare systems underscores the increasing importance of Medicaid. A recent *New York Times* article on the unprecedented improvements in the child welfare system in Alabama noted that in 1990, the state spent a total of $71 million, including $47 million in federal money. By 2004, though, total spending had risen to $285 million, with $179 million of it from the federal government. Medicaid funding, a source the state had not previously tapped, was a key part of this federal funding (Eckholm 2005).

In arts and cultural policy, the reverse pattern is evident: a sharp decline in federal funding and a steady rise in state and local funding for the arts during the 1990s. Between 1992 and 2001, the budget of the National Endowment of the Arts dropped from $175 million to $102 million. But spending by state and local arts agencies rose from approximately $800 million to $1.4 billion (Mulcahy 2002).

The overall rise in government funding of nonprofit organizations spurred substantial growth in the number of nonprofit organizations nationwide. For instance, the National Center for Charitable Statistics (NCCS) reports that the number of 501(c)(3) public charities rose from 535,888 in 1996 to 822,817 in 2004 (NCCS 2005a). And the number of nonprofit social welfare agencies has more than tripled since 1980 (Smith 2002). Arts and cultural organizations have experienced a similar rise in numbers. For instance, the number of nonprofit dance companies nationwide more than doubled between 1995 and 2005 (from 724 to 1576). Similarly, the number of nonprofit theater companies increased from 3,302 in 1995 to 5,719 in 2005 (NCCS 2005b).

The extensive diversification of government financing support of nonprofits is a major contributing factor to this expansion in the number of nonprofit organizations. In the past 25 years, a variety of new financing vehicles has been introduced, including tax credits, government loans, and new and creative uses of tax deductions. For instance, the LIHTC was enacted in 1986 as part of the omnibus tax reform legislation. Since 1986, LIHTC has played a major role in creating thousands of nonprofit, low-income housing organizations throughout the country. In fiscal year 2004, Congress authorized $382 million to fund the LIHTC (House Ways and Means 2004). In the arts and cultural arena, historic preservation tax credits have helped many nonprofit organizations preserve architecturally significant buildings and facades (National Park Service 2005). These historic preservation tax credits are often combined with the LIHTC, and the LIHTC and historic preservation tax credits are sometimes combined with grants, direct contracts, and tax-exempt bonds (Nolden et al. 2003).

Despite this financing growth and diversification, the short and long-term outlook is very unclear. For many years, proposals have been floated at the federal level to rein in the spiraling costs of Medicaid, an increasingly important source of revenues for nonprofit agencies. President Clinton unsuccessfully proposed a voucher-like cap on total Medicaid expenditures per recipient. President Bush has proposed modest changes in the Medicaid program, including a cap on expenditures that could shift a greater burden for controlling costs to the states and away from the federal government (Kaiser Family Foundation 2005). However, overall funding for Medicaid would still grow at a healthy rate. As a result, the growth of state and federal spending on Medicaid is likely to squeeze public spending on other discretionary programs, such as child welfare and drug treatment—programs where nonprofit organizations have a major service delivery role (Behn and Keating 2004; Steuerle 2003).

Adding to the climate of funding uncertainty are the many and varied proposals pending in Congress to reduce government spending. For instance, Rep. Jeb Hensarling (R-TX) has introduced legislation that would essentially cap all nondefense, discretionary spending. The Center for Budget and Policy Priorities estimates that this legislation, if enacted, would require deep cuts in discretionary spending (Carlitz, Kogan, and Greenstein 2005). The impact could be particularly severe for many federal programs that have supported nonprofit agencies in recent years.

Further, state governments are facing serious budget challenges, especially given the growth of such major programs as Medicaid, although budget pressures have eased in the past year (Behn and Keating 2004; National Association of State Budget Officers [NASBO] 2005). Some states, including Missouri, Oregon, and Tennessee, have reduced eligibility for Medicaid for thousands of people, leaving them ineligible for many needed services (even though total state spending on Medicaid continues to rise). State funding for the arts also dropped significantly during recent state budget crises. Thus, the shifts in government spending—for example, toward more spending on health care—have had important effects on the nonprofit sector.

The uncertainty of government funding is likely to lead to additional diversification of tools the government uses to support nonprofit activity, especially since financing tools, such as tax credits and deductions and fees for services, tend to generate much less political opposition and controversy than direct grants and contracts. Given this shift in financing, examining different types of financing on the operations of nonprofit agencies and their effect on nonprofit operations is particularly important. This topic is the focus of the next section.

THE DIVERSIFICATION OF GOVERNMENT FINANCING

Direct government funding of nonprofit agencies often receives most of the attention in the discussion of government financing of nonprofit activity. And direct funding is particularly important for social and health organizations that can sometimes receive millions of dollars in contracts for service. But, as noted, government facilitates nonprofit activity in many ways. This chapter focuses on five of the most important government tools that support nonprofit activity: direct grants and contracts, fees for service, tax credits and deductions, tax-exempt bonds, and regulations. As direct funding and contracts become scarcer and more competitive, the contribution of fees, tax credits and deductions, and bonds to nonprofit revenues has increased substantially.

Direct Grants and Contracts

Before the 1960s, government funding of nonprofit agencies was relatively limited and tended to be restricted to services such as child welfare or high profile institutions like the Metropolitan Museum of Art in New York City. Typically, public subsidies to nonprofit agencies were provided with relatively minimal accountability requirements; nonprofit agencies were assumed to use the money wisely and efficiently, partly because many nonprofits were part of a web of relationships that included the local chapter of the United Way, which offered legitimacy and some measure of accountability to government. Also, state and local governments—the primary source of government funding—tended to maintain little capacity to monitor nonprofit grantees.

Public funding of nonprofit agencies increased sharply in the 1960s, spurred by a wave of new federal legislation providing direct and indirect funding to an array of nonprofit organizations, including arts and cultural organizations, community-based poverty programs, and new health care agencies. Federal funding fueled additional spending by state and local government in support of a variety of nonprofit organizations. In the social and health fields, government contracting tended to be the preferred strategy to fund local nonprofits. In some states, such as Massachusetts, entire state departments contracted out their services to nonprofit agencies.

Initially, many new federal and state grants lacked stringent guidelines and regulations. Over time, though, federal, state, and local agencies discovered that they now were in charge of a very large service system, albeit one delivered by nonprofit agencies. In order to "rationalize" this system, (Brown 1983) and ensure the government agencies were maintaining accountability for the expenditure of public funds, the regulations governing government contracts became increasingly stringent, even to the point of specifying the clients to be served (Gronbjerg 1993; Smith and Lipsky 1993). Increasingly, many government programs explicitly tie reimbursement for services to specified outcome measures through performance contracting arrangements (Behn 2001).

Also noteworthy is the shift to managed care instead of direct contracts. In the early years of widespread contracting, most contracts entailed a direct relationship between government and the nonprofit agency. For example, the federal government would directly contract with a local community mental health center to provide mental health services to the local population. Likewise, a state department of social services would directly contract with a local nonprofit child welfare agency. This government–nonprofit agency relationship tended to be the norm until the late 1980s when a wave of managed care rolled through state and local government.

The advent of managed care made the relationship between government and affected nonprofit agencies more complicated and indirect. For instance, in such states as Kansas, Massachusetts, and New Jersey, the state agency responsible for child welfare services replaced, at least in part, its direct contracts for foster care and related services with private nonprofit agencies with contracts with third-party intermediaries that are paid on a capitated basis to manage the foster care services for the state. This third party agency then subcontracts with private agencies to provide services (Courtney 2000; Mahoney 2000; Wulczyn 2000). Managed care is also prevalent in mental health services and various health care programs, including state Medicaid programs.

Managed care in the context of government contracting for social and health services presents complicated policy tradeoffs. The new managed-care firm may allow greater opportunity to focus on client and program outcomes and introduce efficiencies into the delivery of contract services. Yet managed care can make nonprofit contract agencies uncertain of clients and revenues since agencies now depend on managed-care firms, instead of government, for client referrals. Further, managed-care contracts typically have built-in incentives to reduce service utilization, unlike many previous contracts with government.

Further, by blurring the lines of accountability between state and private agencies, managed-care contracts can create confusion regarding the agency responsible for ensuring the provision of quality service and the judicious use of public funds. As a result, the risk of service delivery outcomes shifts from the state agency (and to an extent the nonprofit agency) to the third party managed-care organization. But these managed-care organizations are usually not very open to outside scrutiny, especially by clients and consumers (see Smith 1993). For example, managed-care firms are typically for-profit or nonprofit organizations not subject to the same rules on disclosure, open meeting laws, and service appeals that are characteristic of government agencies.

Overall, the extent of government contracting with nonprofit agencies varies greatly across the country, reflecting a variety of political and historical circumstances. States in the Midwest and Northeast tend to do more contracting in part because they already had many nonprofit agencies when federal funding arrived in the 1960s and 1970s. Also, many of these states had administrators and elected officials eager to take advantage of the federal social programs that expanded in the 1960s and 1970s (Derthick 1975). The Midwest and Northeast also have longer traditions of local philanthropic support of community organizations, so many nonprofit agencies were able to combine public and private funds to expand services through contracting (especially since some federal programs required matching funds). States in the South and West have tended to do more selective contracting and relied more heavily on public sector service delivery until relatively recently. In these states, the broad interest in reducing costs and supporting community-based organizations is spurring more government contracting with nonprofit organizations, even for services long considered the province of the public sector, such as child protection.

Significantly, the fiscal problems of state government in recent years forced many state and local government agencies to reduce funding or the number of clients for individual agencies. (Overall, spending on contracts continues to increase, however, driven by the escalation in spending for Medicare and Medicaid.)

In sum, contracting between government and nonprofit agencies has increased at the state and local level, but the structure of the contracting relationship has undergone important shifts. To varying degrees, contracts are much more performance oriented, with many contracts tying agency reimbursement to meeting specific performance measures. Further, the competition for resources means that the value of the contract to nonprofit agencies often fails to keep pace with rising costs or increased client demand for service. The increased emphasis on accountability and performance means that contracts are much more specific and project focused, leaving less opportunity for nonprofits to fund administrative infrastructure adequately. (Insufficient financial support for organizational infrastructure is also a broad problem that involves private funders [Hager et al. 2004].)

Fees for Service

The uncertainty of government funding has also increased because government has moved away from a reliance on direct contracts to a greater use of fees for service. Fees have always been a part of the nonprofit revenue mix. Universities, for instance, have historically been very dependent upon tuition revenue. Museums have relied primarily upon admission fees and special event ticket sales. And many long-standing child welfare agencies received per diem payments from government and private individuals from the 19th century through the post–World War II period; only the advent of federal funding in the

1960s substantially decreased the reliance of these agencies on fee income. Indeed, part of the justification of federal funding in the 1960s was that fee income was a barrier to the widespread utilization of needed services by the disadvantaged (Gilbert 1978; Kahn 1972).

In the contemporary period, fees is an umbrella term for diverse revenue collected from individuals and organizations and can include rent payments from residents in community housing programs, reimbursement from public and private health insurance programs, direct payments from clients, income from technical assistance services, tuition, the sale of goods (such as meals from a café), and special event ticket sales.

For social and health organizations, the very consequential shift in the past 20 years has been the increase in fee income directly or indirectly from government funds. The extent of this shift is difficult to discern, even through examining agency program and financial records. For instance, identifying fee income in an audit or the Internal Revenue Service (IRS) Form 990 tax return does not tell us much about the original source of the funds. Rent payments from the disabled could be from a person's Supplemental Security Income rather than private savings or income from employment. Health insurance reimbursement could be from Medicaid or private insurance. On Form 990 tax returns, fees are a separate line from direct government grants and contracts, with the implication that fees are private rather than public revenue. But fee income for many nonprofit social and health agencies is often government funds paid to individuals through Medicaid, vouchers, income maintenance payments, and per diem payments. The government indirectly subsidizes many fees, such as day care fees, subsidized through the Child Care Tax Credit.

Government can also contribute to the fee income of nonprofits by agreeing to use nonprofits' goods and services. Three examples illustrate this point. First, an agency to help the homeless may operate a restaurant staffed by the homeless to earn income and provide training opportunities for agency clients. Government might agree to use the restaurant to cater functions as way of boosting the agency's earned income. Second, the government (or a private company) might contract with this agency for staff and pay fees for these workers' services. (Private companies that hire disadvantaged workers may be eligible for tax credits as well.) And third, a sheltered workshop for the disabled might produce certain goods that government could buy.

Overall, then, fee income for many types of nonprofit organizations, especially in the social and health fields, remains largely government funds, either directly or indirectly, despite efforts to move into earned income activities, such as for-profit ventures. As a result, the increase in fee income has tended to mask the continued importance of government funding and the diversification of the means of government support for these agencies.

Other nonprofits, including arts and cultural organizations and educational institutions, continue to be quite dependent upon fees in the form of ticket or tuition payments from individuals (although the government often subsidizes the latter). But as subsequent pages note, government financing can be important for these organizations as well.

Tax Deductions and Credits

Tax deductions and credits are a critical and growing part of government financial support of nonprofit activity. In particular, individual and corporate tax deductions for cash and in-kind contributions to nonprofit organizations are essentially an indirect subsidy to nonprofit organizations because they reduce the cost of donations to qualifying organizations (Clotfelter 1985). Further, while the cash donations have been particularly important since the creation of the federal income tax in the early 20th century, in-kind donations have become much more important as the value of noncash donations, such as real property, patents, historical facades, and automobiles, has risen. For example, many nonprofit service organizations have instituted car donation programs: individuals donate their used cars to a nonprofit agency, which then resells the autos to third party firms that then sell the car, sharing a portion of the purchase price with the agency. Gifts of property are crucial to the development of many important conservation and cultural projects by nonprofit organizations.

The growing value and contribution of non-cash donations is evident in the concern within Congress on the "loss" to the federal treasury of non-cash donations and the potential abuse of the tax code by individuals who donate goods and property. For instance, Congress enacted legislation in 2004 that limited the value of automobile donations because of widespread concern that the recipient charity realized too little of the value of the deduction. Proposals in Congress would further restrict the value of tax deductions that individuals and corporations could take for noncash donations.

In addition to tax deductions, tax credits are growing in importance as a strategy for government to address important social problems. Two noteworthy examples are the child and dependent care credits and the Low-Income Housing Tax Credit (LIHTC). Individuals and couples can claim the child care credit on their tax returns. This credit partially offsets the cost of child care and dependent care (such as home health services), making nonprofit (and for-profit) services more affordable. The LIHTC allows private investors to reduce their tax liability by purchasing tax credits to build low-income housing with the hope that the tax savings will be passed on to low-income renters in the form of lower rent payments. This tax credit program is vital to the ability of nonprofit community development and housing organizations to build low-income and affordable housing.

The growth in the use of tax credits (and deductions) reflects, in part, the broad interest within public management for more consumer choice in how citizens receive and utilize public services and the popularity of more indirect and hidden expenditures at a time when pressure exists to reduce government expenditures. Tax credits exercised by private individuals and corporations do not excessively create new government bureaucracies (Howard 2002). Tax credits are alternatives to direct grants and contracts, which usually entail more visible and direct government expenditures. Some tax credits, such as the child care tax credits, are exercised by individuals and relatively easy to claim. Deductions for charitable contributions are similar. Other tax credits, though, are very complicated. Indeed, the LIHTC and the historic preservation credits are similar to contracts in that they are subject to detailed government regulations and eligibility requirements. Compliance with the terms of the LIHTC, for instance, requires extensive paperwork and monitoring by the government and the recipient nonprofit agency, just like contracts. (However, in many cases, these tax credits are not monitored well for their programmatic outcomes.)

From the perspective of the nonprofit agency, tax credits such as the child care tax credit boost demand for agency programs by subsidizing the cost of service. The Work Opportunity Tax Credit (WOTC) encourages firms to hire disadvantaged clients of nonprofit agencies, providing in some cases a source of income for nonprofits (Hamersma 2005). But the policy and management dilemma the various tax credits raise is that they are often a less efficient financing strategy than direct government support through grants and contracts. For instance, many consultants and investors share the value of the LIHTC for a particular project, so the total foregone revenue to the U.S. Treasury is far more than the actual money derived from tax credits used to build low-income housing. And, tax credits such as the LIHTC or the WOTC are tied to specific projects or individuals, they lack a capacity to build the nonprofit organizational infrastructure and significantly contribute to program sustainability.

Tax-Exempt Bonds

Large nonprofit institutions, such as hospitals and universities (as well as for-profits), have taken advantage of tax-exempt bonds for decades. These bonds help nonprofit organizations finance the cost of capital improvements, such as a new construction or renovation. What is new is the growing use of tax-exempt bonds by smaller nonprofit organizations including, housing development organizations, child welfare agencies, and mental health centers. This increase in tax-exempt bond financing reflects in part the steady rise in the number of nonprofit organizations, especially smaller community-based organizations. Most of these smaller organizations are undercapitalized so as they develop as organizations, they face substantial challenges in adequately funding their capital costs (Miller 2003). The lack of financing for capital costs within government contracts exacerbates this situation. As a result, nonprofit organizations have turned to policymakers at the federal, state, and local levels to help them address these important capital costs. For example, state housing finance agencies have helped support low-income housing development by issuing bonds. Also, states such as Massachusetts, New Jersey, and Washington have created state agencies for economic development or housing development that offer tax-exempt bond financing programs for qualifying 501(c)(3) organizations. For instance, MassDevelopment (2005) has provided tax-exempt bond financing to nonprofit human service organizations for building purchase and renovation. Bond financing is often combined with various forms of below–market rate loans. The New Jersey Economic Development Authority (2005), for example, issued tax-exempt bonds for many different health and social welfare agencies. The Washington State Housing Finance Commission (2005) has issued tax-exempt bonds on behalf of a wide variety of social, health, and educational nonprofits, including some relatively small community organizations. Tax-exempt bonds are an attractive financing option for nonprofits because they can obtain sizable financing for their capital needs; by comparison, few foundation sources of extensive capital financing exist, although some big national foundations have begun to offer programs specifically targeted to capital needs (Ryan 2001). Targeted fundraising through capital campaigns can be a very labor intensive and expensive process that smaller agencies find especially difficult to undertake.

Regulations

Government regulations also have a major impact on nonprofit financing. Sometimes, regulations give preference to nonprofit organizations over public or for-profit agencies. For instance, many government programs contain set-asides for nonprofit and for-profit agencies. The tax-credit program for low-income housing has a set-aside for nonprofit housing developers in the IRS regulations. In Washington, the state Housing Trust Fund will provide low-income housing funds only to nonprofit organizations. Many other states have their own set-asides for nonprofits.

Government regulations on for-profit businesses can promote various nonprofit-for-profit partnerships. The federal Community Reinvestment Act has been used with varying levels of effectiveness to push banks to provide capital for low-income housing and community development projects, including specific funding for nonprofit, community-based organizations (Gittell and Wilder 1999).

In addition, regulations pertaining to nonprofit expenditures from public contracts grants are very important in determining the internal allocation of funds by nonprofits. Many nonprofits with government contracts complain that the contract requirements greatly limit their flexibility in appropriately meeting client needs and responding to unexpected developments. And as noted, contracts do not adequately fund the infrastructure requirements of nonprofits or their capital needs (Miller 2003). Restrictive regulations also can make it difficult for nonprofit organizations to undertake revenue diversification away from a dependence on government contracts.

Assessing the Impact of Government Financing of Nonprofit Organizations

The effect of government financing on nonprofit organizations is the subject of an ongoing debate with origins dating to the 19th century and the work of de Tocqueville (1835). In *Democracy in America*, he argued that voluntary associations were critical to democracy because they provided an opportunity for citizen participation and the protection of liberties from state infringement. Voluntary associations were alternatives to the state and the individual; by implication, the boundaries between the state and voluntary associations should be quite separate and distinct.

In practice, though, the lines between state and voluntary agencies were already blurred in the 19th century. State and local government often provided cash and in-kind assistance to voluntary associations, such as relief organizations and child welfare agencies. In large urban areas, public funding of social welfare agencies could also be controversial because of the concern about the potential for abuse and corruption. In response, many states eventually outlawed or restricted public subsidies and grants to private charities (Fetter 1901; Fleischer 1914).

Many private social welfare agencies were opposed to receiving public funds during the early decades of the 20th century. They viewed their mission as strictly private; public funds would confuse donors and clients and undermine the distinctive niche within the service system of these nonprofit agencies. Private agencies were also worried that government funds might interfere with their autonomy (Smith and Lipsky 1993).

In the 1960s and 1970s, nonprofit social and health agencies became more accepting of government funding. Even organizations formally entirely dependent on private donations dropped their reluctance to accept government funds. This acceptance of support for government financing reflected the widespread perspective that federal funding was needed to broaden citizens' access to social, health, and cultural services and programs.

Since the 1960s, government funding of nonprofit agencies has shifted from grants with relatively loose accountability to increasingly specific contracts and requirements. More generally, government funding affects the operations of nonprofit organizations in different ways, depending on the type of service, the extent of professionalization, the origins and mission of the organization, and the character of the government–nonprofit relationship. However, among nonprofit social service and health organizations, the response to government funding is rooted in the different approaches nonprofits and government take toward services and clients. Nonprofits emerge out of a desire of a like-minded community of people to address a problem or social need. Examples include battered women's shelters, neighborhood drop-in centers for youth, inter-faith homeless shelters, community health centers, and Lutheran Social Services. All of these organizations represent a community, and, as such, feel a special obligation to their community of interest. Battered women's shelters may view their obligation as primarily to any abused women in a given locality; community health centers may want to serve anyone in a community regardless of their specific problem; and a drop-in center may serve any adolescent who identifies himself or herself as troubled and in need of help. Responsiveness to a particular community is the guiding norm (Smith and Lipsky 1993).

Government, by contrast, tends to approach services and clients from the norm of equity. The ever-present problem facing government officials charged with distributing funds or services is to justify why they provide services to one group rather than another, because government does not have the resources to serve everyone in need. In a democracy, groups can seek redress if they feel they are being unfairly treated; government officials are accountable to these groups and to the citizenry in general for their policy choices (Moe 1990). Equity is a norm consistent with the need of government officials to treat groups and individuals fairly. Equity can be interpreted in a variety of ways, but in social and health services, it usually means defining need in order to allocate resources by criteria deemed to be fair—for example, income, geographic location, and severity of illness or need.

Because of their emphasis on responsiveness, nonprofit agencies may clash with government over policy matters of services, clients, and staff. For instance, a program for troubled youth may prefer to serve any adolescent in the community, but government officials may believe its funds should only serve the neediest clients. Indeed, government staff may accuse the program of "creaming"—taking only the easiest cases and neglecting the more difficult ones. Nonprofit agencies often respond to the creaming charge by arguing that they only provide services within their mission and their services were never designed to serve difficult and expensive clients, such as troubled youth. This same basic disagreement between government and nonprofits can occur when nonprofit agencies favor certain groups such as co-religionists or local neighborhood children.

In addition to programmatic effects, government funding tends to affect the internal organization of agencies. Service agencies started through community initiative often lack, at least initially, highly trained professionals or administrative staff. Some of these agencies emerge from an unincorporated group of like-minded people concerned about a social problem. A clear separation between the board and staff is absent, and many do not have full-time executive directors. Government funding means accountability, which often requires these agencies to adopt new administrative procedures, add professionals, institute new financial management practices, and in some cases, modify physical structures. These organizational changes are often difficult to achieve because many smaller agencies do not have the financial resources. This is a key public policy concern because a disproportionate amount of the growth of the nonprofit sector in the past 20 years has been among community-based agencies that after an initial, start-up phase must undertake complicated and sometimes expensive changes to their management and programs to abide by government expectations.

Administrative and programmatic restructuring in response to government funding is also apparent in other types of nonprofit agencies. More established agencies may sometimes be required to undertake expensive changes in their programs to comply with government regulations. For instance, when government funds arrived in significant amounts in the 1960s and 1970s, many agencies were already formal organizations with large boards and professional social workers and psychologists on staff. Over time, new staff regulations were usually added and the client mix changed in a way that forced these agencies to hire more specialized staff, renovate their buildings, and change their client mix. (In part, these new regulations reflected the lack of attention to accountability, especially programmatic outcomes, by many nonprofits.)

Some agencies are oriented toward government from their inception and may even be a spin-off from government, an increasingly common practice at the local level. These agencies then may be in close agreement with government expectations from the beginning of the organization, and therefore the organizational changes characteristic of agencies with roots in the community may not be evident.

Arts and cultural organizations and 501(c)(4) organizations generally do not receive sizable government grants except for specific projects. Nonetheless, the effects of project-related funding from government on small arts organizations or 501(c)(4) organizations are likely to be similar to the effects of government funding on small social and health organizations. One effect can be to significantly increase the overhead costs of these agencies, requiring them to raise much larger sums of money to fund their basic operations. The need to support higher overhead expenses may then be quite consequential for nonprofit programming and management practices.

NONGOVERNMENTAL OPTIONS FOR REVENUE DIVERSIFICATION

The competition for government funds, prompted by the growth of nonprofits and changes in public policy and management, has predictably encouraged nonprofits to search for alternative sources of support. This section focuses on charitable giving and social enterprise activities as potential options for revenue diversification.

Charitable Giving

Private cash donations from individuals and corporations are an especially important source of revenue for certain types of nonprofit organizations, notably educational institutions, cultural organizations, and many larger social welfare agencies, such as the Salvation Army and the American Red Cross. Older and more established organizations with sizable boards of directors and staff and a diversified base of support can be well positioned to raise private donations. By contrast, smaller community-based and advocacy organizations—the type of nonprofit with the sharpest growth in recent years—face substantial infrastructure and capacity problems that limit their ability to raise significant sums of charitable donations (Light 2004). Indeed, one major policy and practice challenge of contemporary nonprofit organizations is adequately funding the administrative infrastructure, such as professional development staff, so agencies can effectively raise private donations. Moreover, the difficulty of generating private donations tends to increase the vulnerability of smaller nonprofit organizations to the influence of government funders (or large private donors).

In addition to individual philanthropy, nonprofit organizations can benefit from grants and donations from federated funding campaigns—including the United Way, the Combined Federal Campaign, and more specialized campaigns, such as the Black United Fund and Women's Way in Philadelphia (Barman forthcoming). The United Way is especially noteworthy because trends in United Way support of local agencies illustrate the complex relationship between the public and private in financial support for nonprofit service organizations.

Historically, the United Way was organized for the benefit of its member agencies, usually the large agencies, such as the American Red Cross, the Boy Scouts and Girl Scouts, Catholic Charities, and family service agencies. These agencies could depend upon annual allocations that hinged on the success of the annual campaign. Until the 1960s, most member agencies were primarily dependent upon the United Way for their revenues. Many child welfare agencies, for example, typically received more than 50 percent of their revenues from the United Way. For example, Children's Friend, a nonprofit agency founded in 1849 in Worcester, Massachusetts, received $77,721 from the United Way in 1960, or just over 50 percent of their total revenues of $155,004.

In the 1960s and 1970s, the percentage of United Way funds contributed to agency budgets dropped as government contracting expanded. Then, in the 1980s, the United Way was pressed to open membership to a broader array of community agencies, especially the many service agencies created directly or indirectly by the big build-up of federal funds in the previous two decades. Gradually, United Way chapters responded to this new environment of public and private funding and the very different mix of local community agencies. Many chapters, including large chapters in Seattle and Washington, D.C., adopted a project-oriented allocation process that essentially jettisoned the traditional concept of membership and the agency expectation of an entitlement to a certain allocation every year. Instead, these chapters will only fund agencies offering projects that fit the priorities of the local chapter. Thus, United Way chapters are more like local community foundations that give short-term, modest grants for innovation and start-up costs; many chapters are even starting endowments. This shift also reflects a long-term decline in real terms in donations to the United Way (in the aggregate). For instance total nationwide giving to all United Way chapters rose incrementally in constant dollars from $2.06 billion in 1968 to $2.19 billion in 1998 (in constant dollars) (Billitteri 2000). Since 1998, the United Way has struggled to keep pace with inflation, with total giving nationwide actually declining in some years, including fiscal year 2003–04 (Wolverton 2004).

The changes in United Way allocation procedures have other effects as well. Many older social welfare agencies depended on regular allocation every year to fund their operational budget, including administration, and to cross-subsidize money-losing services, such as services to the poor. As government contracting expanded, this United Way funding was particularly valuable because government contracts are project-based and typically do not provide substantial money for cross-subsidization. The changes in United Way funding squeeze these agencies since the effect is to limit the ability of agencies to cross-subsidize or invest in administration.

The funding shifts at the United Way have also been prompted by the well-publicized scandals involving the United Way of America in the early 1990s and, more recently, the United Way of the National Capital Area. The scandals have pushed the United Way to promote donor choice in the selection of agencies as destinations for the charitable contributions, which over time has meant that many member agencies do not receive regular or predictable United Way allocations; some agencies may even have experienced significant decreases.

Overall, then, the transformation of the United Way and its relationship to local nonprofits reflects several trends, including the heightened concern with accountability among nonprofit agencies and the increasingly important financing role of government in social welfare. The central role of United Way as a funder of local nonprofit agencies has greatly diminished. For example, in 2005, Children's Friend received $67,461, or 2.5 percent of its budget, from the local United Way chapter. As a result, the United Way has had to reinvent itself as a funder of program innovation, an agenda setter in identifying urgent community needs, and a leader in mobilizing the community, including public, nonprofit, and for-profit organizations to address these needs.

In addition to federal fundraising organizations, private foundations represent another important part of organized philanthropy. The number of foundations has risen sharply in recent years, fueled in part by the tax deductions available to donors who start foundations or give money to foundations in the form of donor-advised funds and charitable remainder trusts. (For instance, the number of foundations increased from 58,774 in 1996 to 102,881 in 2004 [NCCS 2005a].)

Overall, the universe of foundations is so diverse that it is hazardous to generalize. Many of the large national foundations, such as the Ford Foundation and the Robert Wood Johnson Foundation, have historically played a leading role in funding innovation and social experimentation at the local level. Of late, they are supporting complex, action-oriented initiatives to address such pressing problems as substance abuse, crime, at-risk youth, and maternal and child health. Many local foundations give money for high-priority projects, such as drug prevention or reducing teen pregnancy.

The national and local foundations tend to give preference to project-specific funding or seed money for program innovation. Even new multi-year projects of the Annie E. Casey Foundation and the Robert Wood Johnson Foundation are funded on a declining basis, with the expectation that local sponsors will continue funding. The preference for project and seed grants means that it is very difficult for nonprofits to obtain operational money from foundations, limiting the ability of nonprofits to substitute private foundation funds for declining public operational money. Another consequence is that foundations often help nonprofit agencies get started but then expect the nonprofit to transition to more sustainable financial support from government or other revenues sources when the grant expires. This problem of sustainability has encouraged scholars, foundation staff, and policymakers to urge foundations to rethink policies against funding operational expenses or endowment (Brest 2003; Letts and Ryan 2003; Letts, Grossman, and Ryan 1999; NCRP 2005). While this effort has attracted substantial attention, it remains quite limited as an option for most nonprofits.

Social Enterprise

The competition for funds and the pressure by funders on nonprofits to diversify their revenue base has also encouraged nonprofits to generate higher fee income through "social enterprise" activities. An almost dizzying array of initiatives can be included under the rubric of social enterprise: cause-related marketing, affinity credit cards, gift shops, collaborations between nonprofit agencies and for-profit companies, the creation of for-profit subsidiaries, and separate for-profit companies to tap new markets (Alter 2004; Austin 2000; Dees 1998; Dees, Emerson, and Economy 2001; Lifset 1989). For instance, Plymouth Housing in Seattle, a large nonprofit low-income housing agency, recently created a for-profit catering business to generate more income for the organization. FareStart, a nonprofit agency in Seattle for the homeless, established a restaurant with a staff of previously homeless individuals to help them learn job-ready skills. Many museums around the country have started jazz concert series to increase their overall revenue and help attract a new, younger group of museum members.

These examples illustrate that social enterprise initiatives need not create barriers to entry for the disadvantaged, although the concern remains that greater attention to social enterprise will lead to a shift in mission among nonprofit organizations toward more market-oriented activities and programs. But many nonprofit organizations, especially in the health and social welfare fields, are not well positioned to raise money through social enterprise ventures. Typically, these new earned-income activities are intended to work in combination with government funds (Plymouth Housing and many community development organizations are good examples) or serve as a supplement to current private funding and fee income (museums, for example). Even FareStart, a successful and innovative agency, receives significant support from government and private foundations, in addition to its restaurant revenue.

Nonetheless, social enterprise ventures may help publicize the organization and bring new members or donors into the organization. Even if these ventures do not generate substantial money, agencies may still find them worthwhile in the long-run for the collateral benefits of visibility and reputation. However, social enterprise initiatives can pose complex management challenges because they often represent a departure for nonprofit agencies' missions or services. As a result, these initiatives can entail a huge investment of staff time and resources (depending, of course, on the scope of the project). Thus, many smaller nonprofits may be unable to undertake these social enterprise ventures because they do not have the necessary administrative infrastructure or funding. Consequently, these agencies may remain dependent upon government financing and private donations.

GOVERNMENT FINANCING OF NONPROFITS: FIVE CASES

The diversity and importance of direct and indirect government financing to nonprofits is especially apparent in how nonprofit agencies operate. The following section examines five nonprofit agencies: a social service agency, a nonprofit architectural firm, a community agency for the developmentally disabled, a low-income housing organization, and an art museum and its new sculpture park. Several key policy and practice developments are evident in these organizations: (1) the growing complexity and diversity of government funding of nonprofit organizations; (2) the expansion of government funding and the number of nonprofit organizations in the past 25 years; (3) the current stiff competition for public and private resources; and (4) the difficulty of adequately funding administrative infrastructure.

Catholic Community Services of Western Washington

Catholic Community Services of Western Washington (CCSWW) has a long history in the community and provides an extensive array of social and health services in the Puget Sound region. Its many services include home care, foster care, a homeless shelter for single men, emergency assistance, adoptions, and residential facilities for teen mothers.

This agency is a central component of the overall public service delivery system in the Puget Sound. Its services reflect this orientation. It is a Catholic agency but its services are available to anyone regardless of his or her faith; indeed, 90 percent of its clients are not affiliated with the agency's denomination. It chooses clients based upon criteria established in government contracts. For example, 80 percent of its home care program clients are referrals from the Washington Department of Social and Health Services; thus, clients need to meet the state's criteria for admittance into the program. Many other agency programs are required to use state or city referral criteria. The agency is subject to many different state and federal regulations on wage and hour laws, union representation, immigration and citizenship, non-discrimination, access for people with disabilities, and Drug-Free Workplace rules. Increasingly, the agency is required to track outcomes for its programs.

The agency has also been active in a variety of important social policy issues. It was opposed to the welfare reform legislation of 1996 and for many years subsidized a poverty advocacy organization that used its facilities. In general, though, its legislative priorities focus on obtaining funding increases for its programs either through organizational advocacy by agency staff or through various local and statewide advocacy coalitions.

Overall, the agency has experienced significant budget growth in recent years. In fiscal year 1994, total income was more than $43 million, with approximately $37 million from government. In fiscal year 2003, total revenue was more than $63 million with up to $52 million from government through grants, contracts, and fee revenue, including substantial reimbursement from Medicaid. Underscoring the complexity of the current funding environment, the exact percentage of federal government funding is difficult to discern without individually scrutinizing the myriad of client transactions. (Further, even the agency does not know how much funding is from Medicaid because the state is not required to inform the agency when it is reimbursed for services.) Medicaid has become increasingly important as a funding source because CCSWW serves a primarily poor and disadvantaged population. Many of its clients are Medicaid eligible, allowing the state to seek reimbursement from the federal government for approximately half the cost of services CCSWW delivers to eligible clients. This shift to Medicaid financing is especially noticeable in CCSWW's foster care program, which 25 years ago was financed primarily through state funds, supplemented with some federal funding such as Title XX. Today, though, CCSWW's foster care services are primarily financed through Medicaid, supplemented by other federal and state funds.

The varied and extensive mix of programs is indicative of the valued role of CCSWW in its community and the diversification and expansion of government funding (at least until recently). One indication of this diversity of support is the sheer number of federal agencies and programs supporting CCSWW services. In fiscal year 2003, CCSWW received funding from several funding programs within the federal Departments of Housing and Urban Development, Agriculture, Education, Health and Human Services, Justice, and Homeland Security (for emergency food and shelter) as well as the Corporation for National and Community Service (for foster grandparents and senior volunteer programs). Most of this federal money was pass-through funding initially given to another public or private agency, including the cities of Tacoma and Seattle, the state of Washington, the United Way of King County, and other local nonprofit service agencies, such as the Children's Home Society and the Fremont Public Association. These varied and complex funding arrangements make funds difficult to track and therefore require sophisticated management systems.

Overall, then, CCSWW illustrates the following four key points about government financing typical of many multiservice social welfare agencies: (1) the continued dependence of social welfare agencies on government support; (2) the expansion of large social welfare agencies, such as CCSWW, into a variety of service categories, such as home care, as government funding became widely available; (3) the vital but decidedly secondary role of private donations; and (4) the relative absence of significant private fee income from individuals or earned income from social enterprise activities, such as the sale of goods and services.

Environmental Works

Environmental Works (EW) was founded in the early 1970s during a period when more than 270 similar organizations were created nationwide, primarily through government grants. The mission of EW is to create and improve affordable housing and physical facilities for low-income populations by providing architectural design and technical support to nonprofit agencies. Typical clients include low-income housing developers, child care centers, social service agencies, and community development organizations. Initially, the agency functioned as a "technical assistance" arm of the Seattle Department of Housing and Human Services, but in the last 15 years, the mission and activities of the agency have broadened.

Twenty years ago, the agency relied almost completely on funding from the federal Community Development Block Grant (CDBG). This money was given to the state, which then gave it to the city of Seattle, which then contracted with Environmental Works for technical assistance and design work with local nonprofits. In short, most of its money was "pass-through" federal funding in the form of contracts between EW and the city.

CDBG funding (and many other block grants such as the Social Service Block Grant) have been in decline since the early years of the Reagan administration (Posner 2005). In the mid-1990s, EW experienced a funding crisis when the city notified the agency that it would terminate its funding. This was a particular problem for this agency since, like many agencies dependent upon government contracts, its board and staff had done relatively little fundraising, so the agency did not have ready access to alternative sources of private donations.

As part of a revenue diversification strategy, the agency essentially bought a for-profit architectural firm, Gleason and Associates, which became a for-profit subsidiary of EW in 1997. The agency remained a nonprofit, 501(c)(3) organization with a for-profit subsidiary that provided services to corporations and sometimes to individual homeowners. In 1998, total income was approximately $890,000, with $260,000 from CDBG funds and $225,000 from the for-profit subsidiary. The remaining revenue was composed of small public grants and private donations.

Ultimately, the city decided to continue to fund the agency but the level of CDBG funds has declined steadily. In 2004, CDBG funds were only $120,000, and the for-profit subsidiary revenue was only $42,000. However, total income was $1.425 million, and EW expects to reach $1.7 million in 2005. The increase in revenue has been through fee income from nonprofit agencies, which usually originates directly or indirectly from public funding sources. For example, a low-income housing organization might receive funding from the LIHTC program to build affordable housing. The budget for the housing includes funding for design services that the housing agency directly pays to EW. Local housing agencies have also used money from a state housing trust fund to pay EW for services. Overall, in 2004, almost $500,000 of EW revenues came from fees from nonprofits raised for construction projects. This money represented a combination of public funds (city, county, state, federal, LIHTC) and capital campaigns, with foundations and private individuals donating funds to the agencies, not EW.

EW's success in revenue diversification reflects, in part, the growth in the overall number of agencies as well as the shift away from single source government financing evident in the initial CDBG funding in the 1970s and '80s. This shift in revenue is consequential for EW's allocation and use of funds. In the early 1980s, CDBG funds were distributed with loose accountability standards, offering the recipient agencies broad discretion in terms of clients and services. But increasingly, CDBG funds are very targeted, and the fee income received from local nonprofits (and in turn, from government) is very specific about expectations and objectives. EW has difficulty using the fee income to cross-subsidize other parts of its operations.

Further, the financing trends illustrated at EW demonstrate that including for-profit activity does not inevitably lead an organization away from its mission. Indeed, EW's mission of supporting social welfare agencies and low-income housing organizations has only strengthened and expanded in the past 10 years. Its ability to expand its mission has hinged on the availability of direct and indirect government support, supplemented by an occasional private donation or grant. Consequently, EW's experience indicates that a dependence on fee income does not necessarily lead to the so-called commercialization of nonprofits or move an agency away from its commitment to disadvantaged populations. Instead, EW should be regarded as representative of a new wave of nonprofits—from community development organizations to emergent job training programs to innovative programs for the homeless—that mix direct and indirect public funding complemented by occasional project-specific grants from foundations and corporations.

Banchero Friends Services

Banchero Friends Services (BFS) was founded in 1971 by students at the University of Washington who were volunteering at Fircrest School, a state institution for the developmentally disabled. (At this time, most services for the developmentally disabled were provided through state-funded institutions.) In 1991, the agency decided to focus on adults, focusing on in-home case management and support services. In 1993, the total income of the agency was $365,000; the projected income for 2006 is $1.6 million, reflecting the growth in agency services and the increase in government funding. This expansion also reflects the increase in the number of recipients of the federal Supplemental Security Income (SSI) program. For example, the number of SSI recipients with disabilities nationwide rose from 1.6 million in 1974 to 5.4 million in 2002 (House Ways and Means 2004).

Currently, BFS receives almost 95 percent of its funding from state government. This funding is mostly in the form of fee income from Medicaid. (SSI eligibility triggers eligibility for Medicaid.) So Banchero, which at its inception was completely state funded, is now funded primarily by Medicaid and service costs are split roughly evenly between the state and the federal government.

For BFS, the reliance on Medicaid means compliance with complex regulations that restrict the types of clients the agency serves and how services can be provided. Moreover, Medicaid rates have failed to rise sufficiently to keep pace with increasing costs, so the agency is sometimes simply not able to provide the appropriate amount of services to its clients. In an effort to provide as much direct services as possible, the agency, like many other similar agencies in the region and state, has been cross-subsidizing its low direct service rate from Medicaid with excess funds from its administrative rates from Medicaid. (New state Medicaid policies will prevent this type of cross-subsidization starting in 2007.)

BFS faces significant constraints in trying to diversify its programs or revenues. The policies of the state of Washington Department of Social and Health Services (DSHS) prevent the agency from offering vocational services in addition to current services. The agency has been able to increase its private fundraising modestly in recent years, but the rise in private donations has not been sufficient to compensate for the failure of Medicaid to keep pace with rising costs and client need.

The executive director of BFS is quite active politically at the state level. She is the chair of the statewide association of community-based providers serving people with developmental disabilities. This association has worked closely with state funding agencies to increase rates for its programs and advocate for a higher quality and quantity of services for people with developmental disabilities.

The experience of Banchero Friends Services underscores several important financing trends and their implications for nonprofit organizations. First, Medicaid is vital in supporting nonprofit agencies providing community services for people with developmental disabilities. Second, medium-sized agencies like BFS face serious challenges in their ability to diversify revenues away from dependence on Medicaid, especially given the restrictions involved in receiving Medicaid funds. Third, BFS, like many other similar agencies, remains very mission-driven, so its response to underfunding in Medicaid is to ration services and find funds to cross-subsidize their direct services.

Lutheran Alliance to Create Housing

The Lutheran Alliance to Create Housing (LATCH) was founded in 1990 by a group of Lutheran churches to provide affordable housing opportunities to the poor and disadvantaged in the Puget Sound region. In the 1990s, LATCH successfully developed several housing projects using the Low-Income Housing Tax Credit (LIHTC) program, at least in part. But in recent years, the process of obtaining tax credits has been increasingly difficult and competitive due to the growth in number of low-income housing organizations and the increased demand for affordable housing in many communities around the country. In response, the state Housing Finance Commission—the administering agency for tax credits in the state of Washington—has put in place increasingly stringent rules and regulations, especially for the populations served. The result is a much "needier" population that usually requires agencies to partner with other more specialized agencies. In particular, the state has shifted its scoring system for housing development proposals; it now awards more points to projects that will serve the homeless. Section 8 housing vouchers for the poor and disadvantaged often are used as part of these housing projects to help clients pay the rent once the project is completed. But the number of vouchers is declining, creating profound affordability problems for clients and increasing the amount of public and private financing needed to put together a housing development package.

In short, creating a viable housing deal for low-income and disadvantaged populations has become a daunting task, especially for the working poor at 30 to 50 percent of median income—the market niche for LATCH and many other low-income housing agencies founded in the past 25 years. Resources for development and client services have declined while client need has increased.

A second complicating factor for LATCH (and other community-based housing organizations) is a product of the success of the nonprofit low-income housing "movement." Almost every neighborhood in Seattle now has a low-income housing or a community development organization. As a result, more agencies are seeking a shrinking pool of public and private resources to build housing.

As exemplified in the evolution of LATCH, the LIHTC has had a number of important organizational and political ramifications that go well beyond financing low-income housing. First, tax credit financing has pushed (and forced) nonprofits to create a number of hybrid nonprofit-for-profit structures. For instance, LATCH, like other nonprofit housing developers, has created for-profit, limited partnerships for tax credit projects (so the private investors can receive their tax credits). Sometimes, the nonprofit effectively owns the limited partnership; in other cases, the nonprofit may be a minority partner.

Second, tax credit deals are very complicated and require the specialized services of accountants, lawyers, investment bankers, equity funds personnel, and consultants. This complexity makes it difficult for small agencies to participate and tends to give an edge to skilled professionals with detailed knowledge of the program, rather than community members or lay people who may have an interest in developing more affordable housing.

Third, the structure of tax credit financing tends to unintentionally obfuscate the actual revenue and expenses of a housing development as well as the programmatic and operational situation of nonprofit housing developers. For instance, total revenue for LATCH, as reported on its IRS Form 990, incrementally rose from $706,000 in 1999 to

$850,000 in 2003. But several projects this agency built during this period are not reflected in the Form 990s; thus, one needs to look at the affiliated partnerships to obtain a true picture of the agency (these partnerships are reported elsewhere). Discerning the true costs of a project given the many professionals and organizations involved (in addition to the lead nonprofit agency) is also quite difficult.

Fourth, tax credit financing pushes an agency to be entrepreneurial and to keep building. A child welfare agency with contracts with state government can often depend upon a certain number of children every year and a predictable stream of funding, barring any major budget or program quality problems. But tax credits are unpredictable and uncertain because they are allocated on a project-by-project basis with no assurance of another tax credit package. Especially in recent years, the competition for the federal tax credits allocated at the state level has been especially keen. Thus, agencies specializing in tax credits are pressured to always be thinking of a new deal because new funds come into the organization only through new tax credit deals. The need to partner with for profit organizations as part of the project development and construction further encourages this entrepreneurialism.

Fifth, tax credit financing as well as the tax exempt bonds, loans, and direct grants that are part of housing project have created a political constituency for these financing tools. LATCH participates in the Housing Development Consortium (HDC), which is composed of nonprofit agencies, contractors, architects, and consultants with an interest in low-income housing. Over the years, HDC has become increasingly sophisticated in its political advocacy on behalf of affordable housing and has invested more resources in professional advocacy in support of policies and funding for low-income housing (Housing Development Consortium 2005).

Sixth, the complexity of tax-credit deals and their multiple revenue streams has masked how much these deals depend on indirect and government support not tied directly to tax credits, including (1) local government donations of land to the housing organization at no cost or substantially below market, and (2) the use of Section 8 housing vouchers to support tenants' rent payments. The increase in land values in Seattle (and elsewhere) has meant that local government is no longer in a position to offer bargains on land, and Section 8 vouchers are increasingly scarce. So the economics of tax credits deals as practiced by nonprofit developers like LATCH has shifted substantially.

Due to the vastly altered revenue picture, LATCH is contemplating shifting into new development areas, including specialized programs and projects for individuals with higher incomes (so the public subsidy of the rents would not be as high as currently required) or even market-rate housing that would include affordable units cross-subsidized by the income from the market-rate units. The agency has also successfully increased its private fundraising, although the growth in private donations still is insufficient to address the agency's development and operational revenue needs.

The Seattle Art Museum and the New Olympic Sculpture Park

The Seattle Art Museum (SAM) was founded in 1933 and for many decades was funded through a mix of private donations and fees supplemented with the modest public funding typical of many arts and cultural institutions. However, recent years have brought significant changes for the organization that underscore the shift in financing strategies among cultural organizations. Like the social welfare and health organizations profiled above, the financing of SAM and its many programs has become increasingly diversified and sophisticated. These new financing strategies are exemplified by a major new project on the Seattle waterfront: the Olympic Sculpture Park (OSP), with a grand view of the Olympic Mountains and Puget Sound.

The OSP evolved from the joint efforts of SAM, private donors, a large oil company (Unocal, which is now part of Chevron), and the nonprofit Trust for Public Land (TPL). Unocal had owned a site on the Seattle waterfront for its operations for several decades. SAM staff viewed this site as the perfect location for a new sculpture park that would rival nationally recognized sculpture parks of other museums, such as the sculpture garden at the Walker Art Center in Minneapolis. The Unocal property was appraised for $24 million but Unocal was willing to sell the property to TPL for $16 million (and take a tax deduction for the $8 million difference). TPL, working with SAM, raised the $16 million for the purchase price from private donors, including the project lead donors, Jon and Mary Shirley. TPL then transferred title of the land to the Museum Development Authority, a public development authority (PDA) that owns the land on which the current SAM building resides. (A PDA is a quasi-public institution in Washington that can issue bonds; it possesses more financing flexibility than a traditional nonprofit and is similar to other types of public development authorities that exist in different forms in other states.) The acquisition of the site was only the beginning; the total project cost is projected to be $80 million (including site acquisition costs). This $80 million includes $40 million for the design, construction, and project management and $20 million for an endowment for future maintenance of the park. The site was also polluted from petroleum-related products in the ground and needed serious environmental remediation.

Consequently, the successful development of OSP requires extensive public and private fundraising and creativity on the part of SAM staff. To lead the fundraising effort, the person at TPL responsible for negotiating the deal with Unocal, Chris Rogers, moved to SAM to finish the project. Over the past five years, Rogers, working closely with the SAM leadership and board, has raised public funds from many federal, state, and local agencies, including the National Endowment for the Arts, the Washington State Arts Commission, the state Department of Ecology (for site remediation), and the city of Seattle, including the Seattle Arts Commission. Substantial private funds have also been raised from local private foundations and private donors. While funds still remain to be raised to reach the $80 million target figure, the sculpture park is on track to be completed in the fall of 2006.

Crucial to the success of the fundraising campaign has been a savvy political effort that enlisted the ongoing support of key leaders in state and local government, including the mayor of Seattle, the Seattle City Council, the governor, and high-ranking legislative leaders. Indeed, the OSP hinges on the partnership between the public sector and SAM and its staff. This type of partnership is only nurtured and maintained through skillful political advocacy by the SAM leadership including the board of directors.

The OSP project illustrates a number of important trends in government financing of nonprofit organizations as well as the implications of these trends. First, OSP underscores the emergence of land trusts and the national Trust for Public Land, in particular, as central players in various types of nonprofit-for-profit partnerships (and public-for-profit partnerships). The ability of corporations and individuals to take a tax deduction for a gift of land at its appraised market value is a significant financial incentive (over and above the current incentives for cash contributions) to give appreciated land for public purposes. Also, corporations may save substantial sums in environmental remediation and associated transaction costs. TPL and similar organizations have the expertise and the professional capacity to manage these land deals and facilitate fundraising for the purchase price. Gifts of land have recently received widespread attention in Congress, and various proposals are pending to restrict the value of these gifts due to the perception by members of Congress that some land donations have been overvalued. Based on the OSP experience, severely curtailing the value of the tax deduction available for donations of land would likely reduce the incentive to give such gifts and the ability of TPL and other organizations to complete these deals. However, restrictions on these gifts might lead to more economic activity, which, depending upon the circumstances, may be a better use for the land.

Second, the OSP example also illustrates the positive side of the donation of appreciated property in that it represented a great fit between the needs and incentives of the donors (Unocal and then TPL) and SAM. The problem for public policy is that at least in some instances gifts of appreciated property may not be the best use of funds, but the receiving organization may feel that it must accept the donation. An art museum, for example, might find it difficult to turn down works of art by wealthy donors even if these works do not fit the artistic mission of the organization.

Third, these projects are complicated, not unlike tax credit deals. The OSP has involved many professionals at various stages as well as a full-time staff at SAM to manage the project and bring it to fruition. Large, elite cultural organizations are much better positioned to raise the money necessary to put together these types of projects.

Fourth, the complexity of the deal and the many different pots of money used to support the project largely mask the public role, including the substantial financing role, of government, especially at the state and local levels. This lack of clarity on government's role may be unavoidable in public–private partnerships like OSP, but it does mean that government may not receive credit from the citizens for helping support a world-class sculpture park.

In addition, this financing complexity may also unintentionally obscure the continuing obligations of government once a program is implemented or a new building constructed, especially if other sources of financing do not meet expectations. This scenario is very unlikely in the OSP case; however, it remains a genuine concern in many projects, especially in the arts and cultural arena.

Fifth, the OSP represents the importance of hybrid organizations to help attract the necessary financing for nonprofit organizations. The OSP is technically owned by the Museum PDA. SAM also has created an affiliated Seattle Art Museum Foundation to help attract private donations. In this sense, the OSP and SAM fit with the broader trend evident in housing organizations and many other types of nonprofit organizations (including Environmental Works) to create new organizational structures to gain greater financing and programmatic flexibility.

Finally, the success of SAM in raising public and private funds for OSP illustrates the attractiveness of OSP as a cultural phenomenon *and* a development opportunity. That is, OSP will certainly contain world-class art, but it also will be a destination spot for tourists and help spur economic development along the Seattle waterfront. More generally, it will be another cultural amenity for the city and will attract businesses and an educated workforce (Florida 2002).

CONCLUSION

In the past 25 years, government's relationship to the nonprofit sector, especially in terms of a financing role, has undergone a profound transformation, although the changes in policy and practice are frequently intertwined in complex ways. Indeed, the wide-ranging and ongoing debate about privatization and devolution (see Gilbert 2004; Hacker 2002) has diverted attention from the realities of public policy and street-level practice as reflected in the programs of nonprofit agencies.

At one level, privatization of a sort has certainly occurred. Hundreds of thousands of nonprofit agencies have been established since the 1960s. In some policy areas, such as developmental disabilities and mental health, a substantial shift has occurred from large public institutions to smaller, nonprofit, community-based programs. But most new nonprofits—whether in child welfare, dance, or low-income housing— provide services that were previously unavailable. Many of these organizations might have been at one time completely volunteer-led and financed, but eventually, many of the organizations, especially in the social and health arena, received substantial public funding. These organizations and their programs represent an expansion of the American welfare state. Agencies like Banchero Friends Services, Environmental Works, Catholic Community Services, and LATCH are offering programs that did not previously exist to people in need. So although the organizational auspice might be nonprofit, the funding is substantially public, and the organizations are pursuing public purposes (see chapter 2).

Another perspective on privatization is to consider it a shift away from direct public grants and contracts. Nonprofit social and health agencies that were funded through direct grants in the 1960s, are now funded through a variety of funding sources, including fee for services through Medicaid and private insurance. Housing development agencies, such as LATCH, depend in part on tax credit revenues as opposed to direct grants for low-income housing.

The experience of most nonprofit agencies suggests that increases in fee income, at least among social service and health organizations, are not from private funds from individuals or organizations but instead from public funds, especially through Medicaid but to a lesser extent through other public programs, such as Medicare, Section 8 housing voucher programs, and per diem payments from government. The growth of Medicaid as a funder of social programs for a broad spectrum of the population with very diverse needs—from residential treatment for children to outpatient drug programs or home care for the developmentally disabled—is a largely overlooked story of the growth of government and its funding of nonprofit organizations. To be sure, governors across the country routinely complain about the rapid increase in the budget of Medicaid and the strain it places on state budgets, but little concerted attention is devoted to the emergence of Medicaid as a central funder for social service programs throughout the United States, especially through nonprofit community-based organizations.

Some fear that an abandonment of public goals and objectives in favor of private goals has accompanied the shift to private nonprofit agencies. Whether true or not, most nonprofits receiving public funding, even in the form of fee-for-service revenue, are very tied to public priorities and regulations. Medicaid eligibility, for example, and the rules governing reimbursable services are extensive and elaborate. Low-income housing agencies must use these credits to serve eligible clients to the extent required by the programs, lest the entire project lose its tax credit eligibility. Many government contracts with nonprofit agencies are also controlled through various performance measures and targets. Indeed, the continuing interest in the United States (and elsewhere) in the new public management and its emphasis on accountability and performance measurement has encouraged governments (and private funding agencies) at the state and local level to tie ever more closely the programmatic outcomes of nonprofit contract agencies to public priorities.

Importantly, the rhetoric of privatization tends to minimize the need for additional public resources and thus creates major difficulties for program advocates to successfully press their case for government support. Further, the risks to nonprofit organizations of even incremental adjustments to key funding programs, such as Medicaid or the LIHTC, are largely neglected because the connection between Medicaid and the health of nonprofit community agencies is not immediately apparent.

Finally, the expectations on nonprofit performance have never been higher (see Light 2004). Government financing tends to focus the attention of nonprofit staff, volunteers, government administrators, and policymakers on performance measures of the efficiency and effectiveness of organizational services. Less tangible contributions of nonprofit organizations, such as building community and social capital or encouraging citizen participation in local affairs, tend to be overlooked or minimized. Nonprofit organizations would be well served by keeping these less tangible goals in mind in their governance and strategic planning. These goals will help build broader community support and encourage higher levels of accountability, helping a nonprofit organization build long-term political and funding support from government as well as individuals and corporations.

NOTE

The author is indebted to many individuals for their assistance during the preparation of this chapter. Special thanks to Putnam Barber, Peter Bernauer, Elizabeth Boris, Laura Bullock, CaraLee Cook, Jan Gleason, Helen Landry, Stephen Page, Jennifer Genung Rigg, Chris Rogers, C. Eugene Steuerle, and Sue Yuzer for input and feedback.

REFERENCES

Alter, Kim. 2004. *Social Enterprise Typology*. Washington, DC: Virtue Ventures. http://www.virtueventures.com.

Austin, James. 2000. *The Collaboration Challenge*. San Francisco: Jossey-Bass.

Barman, Emily. forthcoming. *Contested Communities: The Transformation of Workplace Charity*. Stanford: Stanford University Press.

Behn, Robert D. 2001. *Rethinking Democratic Accountability*. Washington, DC: Brookings Institution Press.

Behn, Robert D., and Elizabeth. K. Keating. 2004. "Facing the Fiscal Crises in State Governments: National Problem, National Responsibilities." *State Tax Notes* 20 (September): 833–47.

Billitteri, Thomas. J. 2000. "United Ways Seek a New Identity." *The Chronicle of Philanthropy* 9 (March).

Boyd, Donald J. and Patricia L. Billen. 2003. *The Fiscal Effects of Welfare Reform: State Social Service Spending before and after Welfare Reform*. Albany: The Nelson A. Rockefeller Institute of Government.

Brest, Paul. 2003. "Smart Money: General Operating Grants Can Be Strategic— for Nonprofits and Foundations." *Stanford Social Innovation Review* 1(3): 44–53.

Brown, Lawrence. D. 1983. *New Policies, New Politics*. Washington, DC: Brookings Institution Press.

Carlitz, Ruth, Richard Kogan, and Robert. Greenstein. 2005. "Proposed Appropriations Caps Would Require Deep Cuts in Domestic Discretionary Programs." Washington, DC: Center for Budget and Policy Priorities.

Clotfelter, Charles. T. 1985. *Federal Tax Policy and Charitable Giving*. Chicago: University of Chicago Press.

Courtney, Mark E. 2000. "Managed Care and Child Welfare Services: What Are the Issues?" *Children and Youth Services Review* 22(2): 87–91.

Dees, J. Gregory. 1998: "Enterprising Nonprofits." *Harvard Business Review* 76(1): 54–67.

Dees, J. Gregory, Jed Emerson, and Peter Economy. 2001. *Enterprising Nonprofits: A Toolkit for Social Entrepreneurs*. San Francisco: John Wiley.

de Tocqueville, Alexis. 1835. *Democracy in America*. New York: New American Library, 1995.

Derthick, Martha. 1975. *Uncontrollable Spending for Social Services Grants*. Washington, DC: The Brookings Institution.

Eckholm, Erik. 2005. "Once Woeful, Alabama Is Model in Child Welfare." *The New York Times*, 20 August.

Executive Office of the President. 2005. "Budget of the United States Government, Fiscal Year 2006, Historical Tables." Washington, DC: Government Printing Office. http://www.gpoaccess.gov/usbudget/fy06/pdf/hist.pdf.

Fetter, Frank A. 1901. "The Subsidizing of Private Charities." *American Journal of Sociology* 7(3): 359–86.

Fleischer, Alexander. 1914. "State Money and Privately Managed Charities." *The Survey* 33 (31 October): 110–12.

Florida, Richard. 2002. *The Rise of the Creative Class*. New York: Basic Books

General Accounting Office (GAO). 1984. "States Use Several Strategies to Cope with Funding Reductions under Social Services Block Grant (SSBG)." Washington, DC: GAO. GAO/HRD-84-68.

254 ■ Nonprofits and Government

———. 1995. "Medicaid: Spending Pressures Drive States toward Program Reinvention." Washington, DC: GAO. GAO/HEHS-95-122.

Gilbert, Neil. 1978. "The Transformation of Social Services." *Social Service Review* 51(4): 624–41.

———. 2004: *Transformation of the Welfare State: The Silent Surrender of Public Responsibility.* New York: Oxford University Press.

Gittell, Ross and Margaret Wilder. 1999. "Community Development Corporations: Critical Factors That Influence Success." *Journal of Urban Affairs* 21(3): 341–62.

Gronbjerg, Kirsten. 1993. *Understanding Nonprofit Funding.* San Francisco: Jossey-Bass.

Gutowski, Michael F., and Jeffrey J. Koshel. 1984. "Social Services." In *The Reagan Experiment,* edited by J. L. Palmer and I. V. Sawhill (307–28). Washington, DC: Urban Institute Press.

Hacker, Jacob S. 2002. *The Divided Welfare State: The Battle over Public and Private Social Benefits in the United States.* Cambridge, UK: Cambridge University Press.

Hager, Mark, Thomas Pollak, Kenneth Wing, and Patrick Rooney. 2004. *Getting What We Pay For: Low Overhead Limits Nonprofit Effectiveness.* Washington, DC: The Urban Institute. http://nccsdataweb.urban.org/FAQ/index.php?category=51#311.

Hall, Peter Dobkin 1987. "A Historical Overview of the Private Nonprofit Sector." In *The Nonprofit Sector: A Research Handbook,* edited by W. W. Powell (3–26). New Haven: Yale University Press.

Hamersma, Sarah. 2005. "The Work Opportunity and Welfare-to-Work Tax Credits." Washington, DC: The Urban Institute. http://www.urban.org/url.cfm?ID=311233.

Holahan, John, and Arunabh Ghosh. 2005. "Understanding the Recent Growth in Medicaid Spending, 2000–2003." *Health Affairs* web exclusive 25(2): 52–62. http://content.healthaffairs.org/cgi/reprint/hlthaff.w5.52v1.

House Ways and Means Committee. 1996. *The Green Book.* Washington, DC: U.S. Government Printing Office. http://www.gpoaccess.gov/wmprints/green/1996.html.

———. 2004. *The Green Book.* Washington, DC: U.S. Government Printing Office. http://www.gpoaccess.gov/wmprints/green/2004.html.

Housing Development Consortium (HDC). 2005. *The Future of Nonprofit Affordable Housing.* Seattle, WA: HDC. http://www.housingconsortium.org.

Howard, Christopher. 2002. "Tax Credits." In *The Tools of Government,* edited by L. M. Salamon (410–44). New York: Oxford University Press.

Kahn, Alfred J. 1972. "Public Social Services: The Next Phase—Policy and Delivery Strategies." *Public Welfare* 40(1): 15–24.

Kaiser Commission on Medicaid and the Uninsured. 2005a. *Medicaid: A Primer.* Washington, DC: The Henry J. Kaiser Family Foundation. http://www.kff.org/medicaid/upload/7334%20Medicaid%20Primer_Final%20for%20posting-3.pdf

———. 2005b. "Medicaid 1915(c) Home and Community-Based Service Programs: Data Update." Washington, DC: The Henry J. Kaiser Family Foundation. http://www.kff.org/medicaid/upload/7345.pdf

Kaiser Family Foundation. 2005. "Medicaid: Bush Administration Sends Medicaid Proposal to Congress." 11 August. http://www.kaisernetwork.org/

daily_reports/rep_hpolicy_recent_rep.cfm?dr_cat = 3&show = yes&dr_DateTime = 08-11-05#31960

Letts, Christine A., and William P. Ryan. 2003. "Filling the Performance Gap." *Stanford Social Innovation Review* 1(1): 26–33.

Letts, Christine, Albert Grossman, and William P. Ryan. 1999. *High Performing Nonprofit Organizations.* San Francisco: John Wiley.

Light, Paul C. 2004. "Sustaining Nonprofit Performance: The Case of Capacity Building and the Evidence to Support It." Washington, DC: Brookings Institution.

Lifset, Reid. 1989. "Cash Cows or Sacred Cows: The Politics of the Commercialization Movement." In *The Future of the Nonprofit Sector*, edited by Virginia A. Hodgkinson, Richard Lyman, and Associates (140–66). San Francisco: Jossey-Bass.

Mahoney, Maureen. 2000. "Privatization in Kansas: Where We Were and What Is Our Future?" In *Privatization of Social Services, Conference Proceedings*, edited by S. C. Kinnevy and Ira M. Schwartz (69–81). Philadelphia, PA: University of Pennsylvania. http://www.sp2.upenn.edu/crysp/reports/privatization/index.html

MassDevelopment. 2005. "Financing: Tax-Exempt Bonds." http://www.massdevelopment.com/financing/bond_exempt.aspx.

Miller, Clara. 2003. "Hidden in Plain Sight: Understanding Nonprofit Capital Structure." *The Nonprofit Quarterly* 10(1): 16–23.

Milroy, James B. 1999. "The Impact of Federal Budget Cuts on the Community-Based Nonprofit Service Sector: A Case Study." Ph.D. diss., State University of New York at Buffalo.

Moe, Terry M. 1990. "The Politics of Structural Choice: Toward a Theory of Public Bureaucracy." In *Organization Theory: From Chester Barnard to the Present and Beyond*, edited by Oliver E. Williamson (116–33). New York: Oxford University Press.

Mulcahy, Kevin V. 2002. "The State Arts Agency: An Overview of Cultural Federalism in the United States." *Journal of Arts Management, Law, and Society* 32(1): 67–81.

NASBO. See National Association of State Budget Officers.

National Association of State Budget Officers. 2005. "The Fiscal Survey of States." Washington, DC: National Governors Association and National Association of State Budget Officers. http://www.nasbo.org/Publications/fiscalsurvey/fsspring2005.pdf

National Center for Charitable Statistics. 2005a. "Number of Nonprofit Organizations in the United States, 1996–2004." Washington, DC: The Urban Institute.

———. 2005b. "Registered Nonprofits by Type of Organization." Washington, DC: The Urban Institute.

National Committee for Responsive Philanthropy (NCRP). 2005. "Not All Grants Are Created Equal: Why Nonprofits Need Operating Support from Foundations." Washington, DC: National Committee for Responsive Philanthropy.

National Park Service. 2005. "Federal Tax Incentives for Rehabilitating Historic Buildings. Annual Report for FY 2004." Washington, DC: National Park Service.

NCCS. See National Center for Charitable Statistics.

NCRP. *See* National Committee for Responsive Philanthropy.

New Jersey Economic Development Authority (NJEDA). 2005. "EDA Resources for Not-for-Profit Organizations." Trenton: New Jersey Economic Development Authority. http://www.njeda.com/notforprofits.asp

Nolden, Sandra, Carissa Climaco, Jessica Bonjorni, Meryl Finkel, and Karen Rich. 2003. "Updating the Low-Income Housing Tax Credit (LIHTC) Database: Projects Placed In Service Through 2001." Cambridge, MA: Abt Associates.

Posner, Paul L. 2005. "Community Development Block Grant Formula: Targeting Assistance to High-Need Communities Could Be Enhanced." Washington, DC: GAO.

Rizzolo, Mary C., Richard Hemp, David Braddock, and Amy Pomeranz-Essley. 2004. "The State of the State in Developmental Disabilities." Washington, DC: American Association on Mental Retardation.

Ryan, William P. 2001. "Nonprofit Capital: A Review of Problems and Strategies." Report prepared for The Rockefeller Foundation and Fannie Mae Foundation. http://rockfound.org/Library/Nonprofit_Capital_-_A_Review_of_Problems_and_Strategies.pdf

Salamon, Lester M. 1987. "Partners in Public Service: The Scope and Theory of Government–Nonprofit Relations." In *The Nonprofit Sector: A Research Handbook*, edited by W. W. Powell (99–117). New Haven: Yale University Press.

———, ed. 2002. *The Tools of Government*. New York: Oxford University Press.

Smith, Steven Rathgeb. 1993. "The New Politics of Contracting: Citizenship and the Nonprofit Role." In *Public Policy for Democracy*, edited by Helen Ingram and Steven Rathgeb Smith (198–221). Washington, DC: Brookings Institution Press.

———. 2002. "Social Services." In *The State of Nonprofit America*, edited by Lester M. Salamon (149–86). Washington, DC: Brookings Institution Press.

Smith, Steven Rathgeb and Michael Lipsky. 1993. *Nonprofits for Hire: The Welfare State in the Age of Contracting*. Cambridge, MA: Harvard University Press.

Steuerle, C. Eugene. 2003. "The Incredible Shrinking Budget for Working Families and Children." *National Budget Issues* Brief no. 1. Washington, DC: The Urban Institute. http://www.urban.org/url.cfm?ID=310914.

Washington State Housing Finance Commission. 2005. "Nonprofit Facilities." Seattle, WA: Washington State Housing Finance Commission. http://www.wshfc.org/bonds/npfacilities.htm.

Wolverton, Brad. 2004. "Giving to United Ways Drops for a Second Consecutive Year." *The Chronicle of Philanthropy* 13 May.

Wulczyn, Fred W. 2000. "Federal Fiscal Reform in Child Welfare Services." *Children and Youth Services Review* 22(2): 131–59.

Young, David W. 1979. *The Managerial Process in Human Service Agencies*. New York: Praeger Publishers.

7

NONPROFITS AND FEDERALISM

Carol J. De Vita and Eric C. Twombly

Nonprofit organizations are at the heart of the social service delivery system in the United States, but there is a perennial debate over how best to divide the responsibility for delivering services between the public and private sectors and among the three levels of government—federal, state, and local. Like other functions in the federalist system of government, delivery of social services is a shared responsibility among many players. The lines of authority and delegation of responsibilities are not always clear and are often renegotiated.

In the 1990s, the term "devolution" entered the policy lexicon. Based on the assumption that decisions are best made by the people and governmental units closest to the problem, policymakers often embraced devolution as a way to address local needs. But devolution has also been seen as a strategy to cut the rate of growth of federal program costs, reduce the size of federal budget deficits, and encourage the entry of new providers into the service delivery system. Although devolution may be viewed as a new variant of federalism, with its tension between centralized and decentralized authority, little is known about the effects of devolution on nonprofit organizations and their ability to provide needed and sustained services for local communities.

This chapter explores some of those effects during a period of decentralized decisionmaking (1994 to 2003).

The concept of devolution certainly is not new to the American political scene. Its roots run deep, going back to the framing of the Constitution with its debate over federal versus state responsibilities. Although the Constitution gives the federal government explicit oversight in a number of policy areas, such as national defense, it remains obscure on how to address other issues, such as education, economic development, or environmental protections. This ambiguity has fueled a 200-year debate on the proper role and responsibilities of each level of government in fostering the common good. As a consequence, the policymaking pendulum has swung between periods of more centralized federal leadership to times of dispersed or shared governmental authority. Devolution is simply a new term applied to the latest swing of the policy pendulum, which calls upon states and local governments to assume a greater role in crafting solutions for the country's social and economic ills.

Although the term devolution is widely used in policy circles, it is not well defined and in fact has two popular meanings. It primarily connotes a shift in the locus of responsibility, decisionmaking, or control from the federal government to state or local levels of government. But the term also is used to imply federal expenditure cuts (or savings) that potentially reduce or limit the role of government in particular policy areas. Although states and local governments generally are not restricted from using their revenues to compensate for a loss of federal dollars, they are often unwilling to do so.

The fiscal capacity of states varies widely, and the capacities of urban centers are even more varied. Since the mid-1970s, America's cities have faced persistent budget problems (Fuchs 1998). Many cities, particularly those in the Northeast and Rust Belt areas, have seen their tax bases erode as both middle-class residents and businesses move to the suburbs. Left behind are some of the nation's most persistently poor and vulnerable populations (Berube and Tiffany 2004; Frey 2005). Yet despite fiscal strains, cities must continue to provide basic public services. Faced with stringent budget scenarios, local governments are sometimes left to grapple with tough administrative decisions regarding how to deliver services. As a result, devolution often evokes fears of a zero-sum game, with services as diverse as road repairs, health care, trash disposal, and summer camps for kids pitted against one another in the policymaking and budget processes.

Although devolution connotes shifting responsibility for program decisions and administrative policies to lower levels of government, budget cuts do not always follow. In the social service field, which this chapter highlights, there is ample confusion regarding what constitutes devolution and how best to measure its effects.

While the concept of federalism is as old as the nation, two factors set the current debate apart from earlier ones. First, many more actors, including nonprofits and faith-based organizations, have entered the policymaking arena. These multiple players raise both the complexity of the policymaking process and the stakes in policy outcomes. The debate today is less about which level of government should take the lead in setting policy, but rather how responsibilities for policy implementation should be allocated among various public and private sector players. In the social service field, policymakers routinely use the front-line service delivery capabilities of nonprofit organizations instead of developing new public bureaucracies (Gronbjerg and Smith 1999; Smith and Lipsky 1993). But this implementation strategy raises questions about the ability of private organizations to meet widespread service demands while maintaining their fiscal health. Recent efforts to increase the role of faith-based organizations in providing social services have further expanded and complicated the implementation of service delivery systems at the state and local levels (Kramer et al. 2005).

Second, devolution, with its emphasis on local solutions, unfolds against a counter trend toward national and global interconnectedness. Today's rapid communication and technological changes not only enhance the sharing of information but also create national and international standards and norms. Devolution, with its emphasis on addressing local differences, simultaneously raises questions about equity and fairness across boundaries within a national context. It exposes the continual tension between equity, equality, and uniformity on the one hand, and diversity and experimentation on the other (Steuerle et al. 1998). Can local differences and locally based solutions be harnessed to enhance the sum of the parts? Is there a national standard or are there multiple sets of norms?

This chapter focuses on the effects of devolution on human service nonprofit organizations between 1994 and 2003. This was a period of rapid policy transformation in the human service field, which included state experimentation with Aid to Families with Dependent Children (AFDC) waivers, the passage of the landmark Personal Responsibility and Work Opportunity Reconciliation Act of 1996 (PRWORA)—commonly known as federal welfare reform—and broad economic shifts that changed the demand for human services. The chapter examines the relationship between nonprofits and government in the provision of human services and highlights the tools of devolution used extensively since the mid-1990s to create program and funding flexibility for local policymakers and service providers. The chapter also analyzes the fiscal health of nonprofit human service organizations between 1994 and 2003, and assesses efforts since the passage of PRWORA to bring community- and faith-based providers into the government contracting system. Finally, the chapter discusses the implications of the changing roles, responsibilities, and relationships of government and the nonprofit sector in providing human services.

THE CHANGING SHAPE OF THE GOVERNMENT-NONPROFIT RELATIONSHIP

The passage of federal welfare reform in 1996 was a bold effort to change the way that the welfare system in the United States operated. It also was arguably the most visible and controversial effort at devolution in decades and was viewed as a new way to reshape the government–nonprofit partnership, particularly through new funding and contracting arrangements.

PRWORA fundamentally altered state welfare programs by creating a federal block grant that caps federal aid to the states. In return, states received much more flexibility in running their welfare programs. Under PRWORA, the AFDC program was replaced by a block grant, Temporary Assistance for Needy Families (TANF), which gives states wide latitude for setting program eligibility requirements. In exchange for this flexibility, TANF requires states to adhere to some specific program parameters. For example, welfare recipients are required to find employment within two years of entering the welfare rolls and are subject to a five-year lifetime limit for receiving welfare benefits. Failure to enforce these requirements can jeopardize the state's future funding levels under the TANF block grant.

The legislation did not cut federal funding for welfare programs, as some opponents charged. Instead, it sustained aggregate funding at levels received under the AFDC program and increased funding for some critical ancillary services, such as child care and job training programs. Budget "savings" were obtained by tightening program eligibility requirements for other welfare-related programs, such as Food Stamps and Supplemental Security Income (SSI). Advocates for the poor feared that as individuals became ineligible for government programs, the demand for assistance would overwhelm the services available through private philanthropy.

During the welfare reform debates, many policymakers looked to nonprofit organizations, particularly at the local level, to assume a larger role in building the human, economic, and social capital necessary to bring about change. Nonprofits, especially those that provide services for low-income people, were challenged to find new ways to alleviate poverty, encourage employment, strengthen families, and reduce long-term dependence on welfare. While the public debate generally focused on the goals and objectives of the new government policies, little attention was paid to the role and capacity of nonprofit organizations to respond to these community needs. Could nonprofits meet the rising expectations that accompanied the goals of welfare reform? Could they remain fiscally solvent in the process?

The assumption that private, nongovernmental organizations presented a new alternative to government programs for overcoming the problems of poverty and welfare dependence ignored an important fact—namely, nonprofit organizations were already substantially involved in the delivery of welfare-related services and had been for decades. During the War on Poverty in the 1960s and early 1970s, the federal government used nonprofit organizations as agents for the expansion of the welfare state (James 1987). Many services and programs created and funded by federal statute were delivered at the local level by nonprofit organizations, which helped fuel the growth of the nonprofit sector, particularly in service delivery programs. More than 60 percent of the nonprofit human service providers operating in the early 1980s were founded after 1960 (Salamon 1985). Rather than displacing nonprofits, the growth in government spending on social welfare programs stimulated the expansion of the nonprofit sector—fulfilling the complementary role discussed in chapter 1.

Government, at every level, provides few human service programs directly. Instead, government funds an array of services and programs, such as employment and training, health care, child care, foster care, food and nutrition programs, senior citizen centers, social services, and many others. The actual delivery of services is generally achieved through the use of nonprofit, and sometimes for-profit, providers. This arrangement has enabled government to control some of its personnel costs and overhead expenses while maintaining direction and oversight of social welfare programs.

Although cuts in federal spending for some domestic social programs slowed the growth of related social welfare programs during the 1980s, nonprofits remained extensively involved in providing social services through contracts with state and local governments (Smith and Lipsky 1993). Indeed, the role of nonprofits had become so prominent in the social service delivery system that Salamon (1995) called them "partners" with government in supplying assistance to the poor.

Several administrative tools and funding mechanisms have been used to establish this partnership and foster flexibility in program implementation at the local level. Among the most prominent tools are block grants and program waivers. The Johnson administration introduced block grants in 1966 to consolidate several public health grants into a single grant for public health services. The move came in response to state and local government complaints that categorical grants-in-aid were too narrow and rigid to address local needs effectively.

The Nixon administration's "New Federalism" used the block grant mechanism to decentralize many government services away from Washington, D.C., and toward elected officials in state and local governments. Although nonprofit organizations were not explicitly mentioned as players in this decentralization strategy, they nonetheless became its unintended beneficiaries. The federal government's overall domestic spending rose from 10.3 percent of gross national product in 1969 to 13.7 percent in 1974 (Nathan 1996, 34). The lion's share of that growth went to entitlement programs, such as Social Security, Food Stamps, and Medicaid, but general-purpose funds and broadly based grants-in-aid also saw a steady rise in revenues.

During the 1980s, the Reagan administration also used block grants to consolidate categorical programs, but the intent of the Reagan block grant strategy was to reduce the size of the federal government and privatize some federally supported services. Unlike the Nixon era, which saw a steady increase in domestic spending, the Reagan years slowed the rate of growth in domestic spending and, in some areas, imposed sharp cuts. Excluding Medicare and Medicaid funding, federal spending on social welfare programs declined by roughly 12 percent during the first half of the 1980s and did not return to its 1980 levels until 1991 (Salamon and Abramson 1996). Discretionary programs were hit even harder, falling by as much as 30 percent below 1980 levels between 1980 and 1984. Nonprofits that operated in these service areas often experienced these federal budget cuts as a direct loss of revenue.

Since the 1980s, entitlement programs, such as Medicare, Medicaid, and Social Security, have generally been sheltered from federal budget cuts, but discretionary social service programs are often among the first candidates considered for cutbacks when policymakers trim budgets. According to Abramson, Salamon, and Steuerle (see table 3.3), federal outlays for health programs reached $518.3 billion in 2004, an increase of 132 percent since 1980. In contrast, federal outlays for social welfare programs in 2004 were $63.8 billion and for income assistance $183.3 billion. To retain government support and survive in a climate of changing policy and budget priorities, nonprofits become quite adaptive. For example, many substance abuse providers have recast their services as a medical model rather than a social service model to tap into new lines of federal health expenditures.

States, too, have found ways to adapt to changing federal priorities and continue to seek greater control and flexibility for implementing social welfare programs. The use of waivers from federal statutes, particularly for AFDC and Medicaid, became a prominent tool for addressing this need. By August 1996, before passage of PRWORA,

43 states had received AFDC waivers (Department of Health and Human Services 1997). Fifteen states had Medicaid waivers to conduct managed-care demonstration projects (Holahan and Liska 1997). The use of waivers opened new opportunities for funding and delivering nonprofit services, particularly in the areas of child care, employment and training, and health care.

While previous attempts at streamlining and downsizing government focused on specific grant-in-aid programs, devolution in the 1990s sought to rein in entitlement programs, particularly cash assistance programs, such as AFDC and SSI, targeted at low-income families and individuals. In a historic policy shift, the 1996 welfare reforms ended the guarantee for AFDC assistance as an entitlement to income-eligible families and opened new questions about the structure and viability of America's social safety net.

In the policy environment of the 1990s, government promoted policy tools designed to reduce costs, foster choice among clients, and develop competitive social service and contracting environments. Indeed, government moved in large measure from producer-side subsidies to consumer-side subsidies in the social service field (Gronbjerg and Salamon 2002). It downplayed the direct funding of human service nonprofits through grants and contracts in favor of vouchers, tax credits, and loan guarantees. For example, an increasing number of parents used government vouchers to pay their child care provider directly and used child care tax credits to receive indirect reimbursement for services. In the housing field, the federal government provided low-income housing tax credits, which have been vital to nonprofit community development organizations that build low-income and affordable housing (Gronbjerg and Salamon 2002; Smith 1999).

The momentum toward greater consumer choice and the use of indirect policy mechanisms produced two major issues for nonprofits. First, they increased competition in the human service field. While competition is not new, even in a mission-driven field like the nonprofit human service sector, government actively began to promote the involvement of for-profit firms and faith-based organizations in social service provision (Frumkin and Andre-Clark 2000; Smith and Sosin 2001; Twombly 2002). For example, large defense contractors, such as Lockheed Martin, were encouraged to enter the human service field to manage welfare caseloads and track former welfare recipients who were moving from welfare to work. Government contracting with faith-based organizations was explicitly encouraged through the Charitable Choice provision of PRWORA and later expanded through executive orders issued by the Bush administration.

Second, government demanded more accountability from the non-profit sector. In 1993, Congress passed the Government Performance and Results Act (GPRA) to increase public confidence in governmental programs and related expenditures. Government agencies and their contractors were directed to articulate goals and objectives and measure performance. Because several billion dollars of public funds flow into human service providers annually, many nonprofits are subject to the GPRA rules and regulations. The substantial flow of funding into the sector, the passage of GPRA, and several high profile scandals at the United Way and the American Red Cross,[1] have put a spotlight on the cost and programmatic effectiveness of nonprofit human service organizations (Brody 2002; Lampkin and Hatry 2003; Light 2000, 2002). But empirically measuring the outcomes and effectiveness of human service programs is difficult because outcomes are not easily defined and quantified, and definitions of effectiveness may vary among the different stakeholders (Hatry et al. 2003).

In short, broad shifts in policy, new tools for government action, increased competition, calls for greater accountability and transparency, and economic booms and busts create a dynamic and sometimes turbulent environment for nonprofits. Realignment of roles and responsibilities in a federalist system poses new challenges to nonprofit human service providers. Perhaps the most direct challenge is maintaining an organization's fiscal health whenever the government–nonprofit relationship is redefined.

THE FISCAL HEALTH OF NONPROFITS SINCE WELFARE REFORM

Groundbreaking work by Salamon in the early 1980s showed that government was the single largest source of funding for nonprofit human service agencies and provided roughly half of all revenues for employment and training, social service, and mental health programs (Salamon 1995). Given this heavy reliance on government funding, nonprofits have a vital stake in new partnerships that might result from shifts in welfare policies.

Using data from the National Center for Charitable Statistics at the Urban Institute,[2] the number, average size, and fiscal health of nonprofit human service organizations[3] were tracked between 1994 and 2003 to determine the potential effects of devolution and welfare reform on these community-based service providers. The findings illustrate not only the resiliency of the nonprofit sector but also some unintended consequences of the original policy goals.

Perhaps the most striking feature was the growth in both the number of nonprofit human service organizations and their annual revenues and expenditures (figure 7.1). Despite concerns that the shift in welfare priorities after 1996 might negatively impact nonprofits, the sector

Figure 7.1. Growth in Nonprofit Organizations, Revenues, and Expenditures, 1994–2003 (2003 inflation-adjusted dollars)

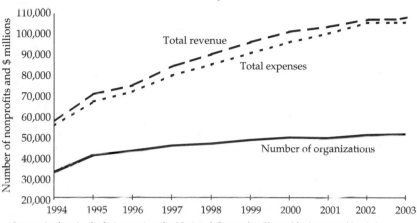

Source: Authors' calculations using the National Center for Charitable Statistics/GuideStar National Nonprofit Database.

expanded dramatically. The number of human service organizations rose from around 32,000 in 1994 to more than 51,000 in 2003—nearly a 60 percent increase. Likewise, aggregate revenues and expenditures (in inflation-adjusted 2003 dollars) also grew steadily, from about $56 billion in 1994 to $106 billion in 2003—a 90 percent upswing. How much of this growth can be attributed to the changing welfare priorities and how much to the robust economy of the mid- and late 1990s cannot be determined from these data, but the trend lines show a leveling off of growth patterns after 2001 when the economy faltered, suggesting that the state of the economy had a major impact on the sector.

Although the overall financial picture of the nonprofit human service sector appears strong during this period, signs of stress are nonetheless apparent. Rather than lifting all boats, this decade of policy change and economic cycles strengthened the largest organizations, leaving smaller nonprofits to navigate more treacherous waters. Four measures are indicative of this trend: (1) large organizations control an increasing share of the revenues in the sector, (2) the average revenues of the largest organizations increased, while they fell for medium-sized and small human service groups, (3) the number of organizations that ended the year with a positive net operating margin declined, and (4) the fiscal cushion between total revenues and total expenses in the human service field closed substantially.

As figure 7.2 illustrates, an increasingly larger share of revenue in the sector is going to nonprofits that comprise the top 20 percent of all human service organizations. Because the bottom 20 percent of organizations controls relatively few dollars, it is the middle range of

Figure 7.2 Distribution of Aggregate Revenue among Nonprofit Human Service Providers, 1994–2003

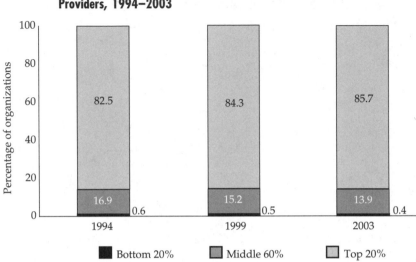

Source: Authors' calculations using the National Center for Charitable Statistics/GuideStar National Nonprofit Database.

human service providers that collectively lost ground. While large nonprofits have always held the vast majority of resources, the concentration of revenue going to the top quintile of nonprofit human service providers increased after 1994. In 1994, these large organizations accounted for roughly 83 percent of all revenues; by 2003, they held almost 86 percent. In contrast, human service providers in the middle range—constituting 60 percent of the human service sector—seem the most affected by the shift in resources to larger nonprofits. Their share of revenues declined from roughly 17 to 14 percent. The smallest organizations—that is, groups comprising the bottom 20 percent—experienced a very modest decrease in their share of the sector's revenue. Because these organizations typically control less than 1 percent of total sector revenues, the decline, while important for individual organizations, is miniscule in the sector's overall financial picture.

A second indicator that the largest, presumably most professionalized, nonprofits became more fiscally dominant over time is the trend in average revenues since 1994. After adjusting for inflation, the average revenue for the largest 20 percent of human service providers grew from $7.3 million in 1994 to roughly $9 million in 2003. For the middle 60 percent of organizations, average revenues dropped a modest 3 percent from $496,000 to $481,000. The bottom 20 percent experienced the sharpest drop, losing more than one-quarter of their average revenues. Average revenues fell from $56,000 in 1994 to roughly $41,000 in 2003. Although nonprofits at the bottom quintile of the sector control relatively few of the sector's overall dollars, these groups, on average, were hit the hardest in the financial realignments between 1994 and 2003.

A third indicator of financial health is the number of organizations able to balance their operating budgets or show a slight profit at the end of the fiscal year. Government substantially increased funding of a number of social service areas in the late 1990s (Smith 2002), which may have had a positive impact on the ability of nonprofits to show positive balance sheets. As table 7.1 shows, the percentage of nonprofits with positive end-of-year operating budgets increased from 61 percent in 1994 to 64 percent by 1999. However, after the economic downturn began in late 2000, these positive gains succumbed to economic pressures. By 2003, fewer than 55 percent of human service providers reported positive operating margins.

Larger nonprofits tended to do better at balancing their annual operating budgets than mid-size and small human service providers, as table 7.1 shows. Between 1994 and 2000, roughly 70 percent of organizations in the top quintile reported having enough revenue to meet their annual expenditures. In contrast, about three in five organizations in the mid-size and small range reported positive operating margins. Because of their size, larger nonprofits may be better positioned to tap into multiple funding streams, develop more extensive community and government connections, and financially weather deferred payments to keep their operating margins in the black. Nonetheless, after 2001, when the economy slowed, nonprofit human service groups found it more difficult to post positive end-of-year balance sheets. In the top quintile, the

Table 7.1. Percentage of Human Service Nonprofits with Positive Operating Margins at the End of the Year, 1994–2003

Year	Largest 20%	Middle 60%	Smallest 20%	All nonprofits
1994	67.2	59.6	56.6	60.5
1995	71.0	60.9	57.0	62.2
1996	70.4	61.3	57.6	62.4
1997	71.6	62.7	56.9	63.3
1998	72.9	65.2	58.1	65.3
1999	70.9	63.6	57.2	63.8
2000	70.8	62.2	56.7	62.8
2001	67.2	58.7	52.7	59.2
2002	63.8	55.3	52.8	56.6
2003	61.4	53.8	50.5	54.7

Source: Authors' calculations using the National Center for Charitable Statistics/GuideStar National Nonprofit Database.

percentage of organizations reporting positive balance sheets dropped from 70 to 60 percent, and in the bottom quintile, only half were able to make ends meet.

A fourth sign of financial stress is the shrinking cushion in operating margins. The annual gap between total revenues and expenses closed between 1994 and 2003. While nonprofits are barred from distributing "profits" to board members and executives, a fiscal cushion—that is, having more revenues than expenses in a given year—can be critical for organizational health. These funds can be put away for a rainy day when the agency has an unanticipated decline in revenues or a spike in demand. Nonprofits built a healthy fiscal cushion between 1994 and 1999, with the aggregate operating margin for the human service sector growing from roughly $2.2 billion to $5.3 billion in inflation-adjusted 2003 dollars. By the end of 1999, total revenues outpaced total expenses by nearly 6 percent in the human service sector. However, starting in 2000, the cushion between revenues and expenses began to narrow, declining to $1.7 billion in 2003, and the operating margin fell to 1.6 percent. Put another way, for every $100 in revenue that flowed into the nonprofit human service sector in 2003, organizations spent nearly $99 on programs, services, labor, and a host of other expenses. As these data show, the economic downturn that began in 2000 posed considerable challenges for the financial health of nonprofit human service providers and made managing these resources more difficult.

FAITH-BASED SERVICE PROVIDERS AND GOVERNMENT CONTRACTING

Because religious congregations are an active and visible part of local community life and an important thread in the fabric of civil society, it is not surprising that some proponents of devolution view the faith-based community as a key player in addressing social issues. To encourage local churches and religious congregations to become more active in welfare reform efforts, Senator John Ashcroft (R-MO) introduced the Charitable Choice provision into PRWORA (Section 104 of P.L. 104-193). Charitable Choice enables religiously affiliated organizations to compete for government contracts (or accept government vouchers) on an equal basis with secular service providers, without giving up the religious character of their faith-based program.

Under Charitable Choice, states cannot discriminate on the basis of the provider's religious character in awarding contracts or establishing voucher systems. Faith-based providers may display religious artifacts and symbols of faith at the service delivery site and in program materials, but they cannot use money from government contracts to proselytize or conduct religious services or instruction. Like their secular counterparts, faith-based providers are subject to financial audits for the funds received under government contracts.

Although the Charitable Choice provisions were passed in 1996, they did not become prominent until 2001, when President George W. Bush made them a core component of his domestic policy agenda. Shortly after taking office, Mr. Bush created a White House Office of Faith-based and Community Initiatives and subsequently created similar offices in eight cabinet departments and two federal agencies. The administration also issued regulations to implement Charitable Choice and created new discretionary grant programs to provide technical assistance for building the capacity of faith-based and community groups. The policies to stimulate the involvement of faith-based organizations have been advanced through executive orders rather than legislation because bills to extend Charitable Choice provisions to other program areas have been stalled in the Senate since 2001.

The administration's faith-based initiatives are predicated on three assumptions: (1) community and faith-based groups face discrimination in seeking public funds; (2) there is a large and untapped resource of faith-based organizations that wants to partner with government to deliver social services to people in need; and (3) these organizations provide more effective services than traditional (secular) providers in transforming an individual's behaviors. In general, the faith-based initiatives are intended to "level the playing field" and encourage small community- and faith-based groups to seek government support for their programs (The White House 2001).

A growing number of studies have examined the implementation of the federal faith-based initiatives and their effects on service delivery, particularly at the state and local levels (De Vita and Palmer 2003; Kennedy and Bielefeld 2003; Kramer et al. 2005; Monsma 2004; Monsma and Mounts 2002; Smith 2005). But a host of factors impedes direct comparison of these studies. For example, there is no consensus among researchers or policymakers on what constitutes a faith-based organization, so identifying and measuring these organizations is problematic and may vary across studies. Also, because jurisdictions have latitude in how the initiatives are implemented, there is considerable variation in program design and implementation strategies. General patterns, however, are emerging from this body of research that shed light on the responses of states and localities to the federal initiatives and the underlying premises of the federal faith-based policies.

First, there is scant evidence that faith-based organizations face discrimination in working with government. Religiously affiliated groups have worked with government for years, and some, such as Catholic Charities and Lutheran Social Services, receive a sizeable share of their revenue from government contracts. Faith-based groups run 70 percent of the food pantries and soup kitchens in the nation (Poppendieck 1998), and some of these programs receive excess federal commodities to feed the poor and needy. Faith-based groups also operate about one-quarter (27 percent) of emergency shelters and transitional housing, and many get funding under the federal homelessness program (Aron and Sharkey 2002).

Surveys of faith-based organizations report that most faith-based groups are satisfied with their interactions with government (Green and Sherman 2002; Monsma and Mounts 2002), and there is evidence suggesting bias in favor of faith-based organizations (Chaves 2003; Farnsley 2001). An Urban Institute study of three cities and four federal funding streams (three block grant programs and one discretionary program) found that state agency officials expressed no hostility toward working with faith-based organizations. Indeed, some welcomed the involvement of the faith community because it often helped them reach populations that were reluctant to seek government assistance (Kramer et al. 2005).

Second, whether there is a large and untapped pool of grassroots and faith-based providers that want to work with government remains unclear. Early studies by Sherman (2000) catalogued the ways that faith-based organizations are working with government, but more recent studies (Kennedy and Bielefeld 2003; Kramer et al. 2005) report a relatively small number of faith-based organizations seeking government contracts. In a study of TANF-funded job training and placement programs in Indiana, Bielefeld (2005) found that although technical assistance workshops on the state's procurement process apparently increased the number of faith-based providers that received contracts from three in 2000 to nine in 2001, the number returned to previous levels in recent years because of reductions in state funding and a shift in contracting priorities.

Similarly, Kramer et al. (2005) found that despite efforts by state agencies to reach the faith community and help faith-based organizations understand the procurement process, only a few submitted applications for public funding. One state agency sponsored a two-day workshop attended by about 20 people—many of whom were already state contractors. Many state agency officials and church leaders believed that the pool of faith-based providers with the capacity and desire to work with government is relatively small. The demands of recordkeeping and program monitoring that accompany government funding may be beyond the capacity of many local congregations (De Vita and Palmer 2003). Other congregations may not want to separate the faith content of their programs to comply with government regulations.

Finally, despite claims of superior results in the delivery of social welfare services, there is little evidence about the greater effectiveness of faith-based services compared with secular providers. Although studies are emerging, the evidence, to date, shows no appreciable differences between faith-based and secular services in the social welfare field. A study of job training programs in Indiana found that while participants in both the faith-based and secular programs had similar characteristics, participants in the secular programs were somewhat more likely to find full-time jobs and receive health insurance (Deb and Jones 2003). These differences were small, however. Similarly, a national study of nursing homes found that faith-based homes had fewer inspection deficiencies and complaints than other nonprofit nursing homes, but the differences were small and attributed to institutional characteristics rather than the religious character of the faith-based homes (Ragan 2004). A study of welfare-to-work programs in Los Angeles found no systematic advantage of one type of service provider over another type (Monsma and Mounts 2002). Each type had its own strengths. For-profit providers, for example, had higher placement rates than other types of providers, but program participants viewed staff of government programs as particularly knowledgeable and helpful and regarded staff at faith-based and nonprofit programs as kind and empathic.

Studies that claim faith-based programs are more effective than other types of providers often lack methodological rigor. For example, they may lack a control group for comparison or do not account for selection bias in terms of who enters or stays in the program. Further, success rates may not adjust for the cost of treatment, including the use of volunteer labor, so it is impossible to know if the success was in response to the faith component of the program or some other factor. Until research using rigorous methods is more plentiful, the jury will be out on whether faith-based programs are more effective than secular social service providers.

IMPLICATIONS OF DEVOLUTION FOR HUMAN SERVICE PROVIDERS

The policy reforms and economic cycles of the 1990s present a unique prism to examine the affects of devolution and decentralized decision-making on the nonprofit human service sector. Changes in federal welfare policies and the devolution of authority to states and local governments did not negatively affect the nonprofit human service sector, as many advocates feared. Instead, there was tremendous growth in the number of organizations and the amount of money flowing to the sector. Overall, nonprofit organizations proved adept at navigating the new social service environment and securing the connections needed to further their work during a time of transition. However, not all nonprofits fared well in this new environment, with mid-size and small groups feeling the brunt of the transition pains.

A close look at the revenues of nonprofit human service providers between 1994 and 2003 presents an interesting paradox about the concepts that underpin devolution. While the intent of devolution was to create more players and diffuse authority, the concurrent demand for greater program accountability resulted in a concentration of resources among the largest human service providers. Smaller nonprofits may be less able to compete in this environment because they often lack the management and technological capacity to monitor revenues, measure client outcomes, and adhere to the accountability demands that today's funders require. Ironically, the unintended consequence of the recent efforts at decentralization and diffusion has led to greater concentration of resources, not less.

One also cannot ignore the economic context in which recent devolutionary changes unfolded. During the robust economy of the mid-1990s, nonprofit human service providers seemed to manage the twists and turns of changing welfare policies. But once the economy took a downslide from 2000 to 2003, the fiscal health of the human service sector began to show signs of strain. The economic turmoil most negatively affected small and mid-size nonprofits. How well and how quickly these groups rebound is still unknown, but the policies of devolution are likely to make this recovery slower and more difficult in economically poor regions of the country.

The current approach to federalism raises important issues to monitor in the nonprofit human service sector. The ever-changing policy and economic environments place nonprofit service providers squarely in competition with one another and with for-profit businesses. The specter of more intense competition has turned up the pressure on nonprofit managers to show that they can deliver their services efficiently and effectively. Management issues, such as staffing patterns, resource allocation, and costs, are scrutinized as measures of efficiency. The debate over faith-based providers rests, in part, on an assumption that the use of volunteers will make faith-based providers more cost-effective than many secular counterparts.

Likewise, discussions of competition also raise questions of quality of care and access to services, particularly in comparisons between nonprofit and for-profit providers. Are corners being cut and is quality sacrificed to obtain a competitive advantage in the marketplace? Do indigent populations have access to needed services? Nonprofit providers are skeptical that for-profits will provide adequate services for low-income and indigent people. For-profit providers counter that the amount of charity care some nonprofits provide does not warrant their tax-exempt status. While these challenges will not directly or adversely affect every nonprofit, competition, particularly with for-profit providers, will stimulate the debate on what constitutes a nonprofit charitable enterprise.

Increased competition also raises the need to monitor how well nonprofits continue to adapt to changing tides in policymaking. Part of this adaptation may require nonprofits to become a stronger voice in articulating public needs and preferences. While only a small share of nonprofit organizations make advocacy and legislative activity their primary concern, almost all are affected by changes in public policies.

As states and local government assumed a larger policy and regulatory role during the 1990s, the focus of policymaking shifted. As a result, nonprofits refocused their attention away from the federal government and established new and stronger lines of communication with state and local officials. This was not always easy to do and led to misunderstandings and frustrations among nonprofit leaders (De Vita and Capitani 1998; Pindus et al. 1998). However, access to the political process and effective communication between the nonprofit sector and all levels of government are essential parts of federalism that help shape the nonprofit–government relationship.

Federalism poses a critical test of the character, structure, contributions, and cohesiveness of the nonprofit sector. It continually challenges the sector to respond to new opportunities and perceived threats, and to be flexible and adaptable in response to change. Because the environment is never static, the relationship between the nonprofit sector and government is constantly in flux, and the outcomes subject to the skill of nonprofit leaders, the fortunes (or misfortunes) of economic times, and the vagaries of politics. It is an unfinished story subject to economic cycles and policy swings. Yet amid the turbulence lies the heart of civil society and the social safety net that the nonprofit human service sector embodies for local communities.

NOTES

1. Jacqueline Salmon, "Given to Skepticism? With Charity Scandals in the News and Less Money to Give, Donors Are Asking More Questions," *Washington Post*, November 3, 2002, p. H-1; Lena H. Sun, "Red Cross to Give All Funds to Victims: Contrite Charity Changes Course on September 11 Donations," *Washington Post*, November 11, 2001, page A-1.

2. The National Center for Charitable Statistics (NCCS) at the Urban Institute is a national repository for Internal Revenue Service Forms 990 on nonprofit organizations in the United States. Form 990 is an annual information return

on the finances of nonprofit organizations that have revenues of $25,000 or more each year. Smaller organizations and religious organizations are not required to file Form 990.

3. Human service organizations provide a variety of services, such as child care, youth mentoring programs, work readiness and job training programs, family counseling, family planning, mental health and substance abuse programs, community clinics, housing assistance and community development, food banks, homeless shelters, foster care, and more. For this study, we have excluded hospitals and schools of higher education from the analysis.

REFERENCES

Aron, Laudan Y., and Patrick T. Sharkey. 2002. "The 1996 National Survey of Homeless Assistance Providers and Clients: A Comparison of Faith-based and Secular Nonprofit Programs." Washington, DC: U.S. Department of Health and Human Services.

Berube, Alan, and Thacher Tiffany. 2004. "The Shape of the Curve: Household Income Distribution in U.S. Cities, 1979–1999." *The Living Cities Census Series*. Washington, DC: The Brookings Institution.

Bielefeld, Wolfgang. 2005. "Investigating the Implementation of Charitable Choice." Paper presented at the annual meeting of the Association for Research on Nonprofit Organizations and Voluntary Action (ARNOVA), Washington, D.C., November.

Brody, Evelyn. 2002. "Accountability and Public Trust." In *The State of Nonprofit America*, edited by Lester M. Salamon (471–98). Washington, DC: Brookings Institution Press.

Chaves, Mark. 2003. "Debunking Charitable Choice: The Evidence Doesn't Support the Political Left or Right." *Stanford Social Innovation Review* (Summer): 28–36.

Deb, Partha, and Dana Jones. 2003. "Does Faith Work? A Comparison of Labor Market Outcomes of Religious and Secular Training Organizations." Paper presented at the Faith-based Social Service Provision under Charitable Choice Conference, Washington, D.C., October.

Department of Health and Human Services, Office of the Assistant Secretary of Planning and Evaluation. 1997. "Setting the Baseline: A Report on State Welfare Waivers." Washington, DC: U.S. Government Printing Office.

De Vita, Carol J., and Jill Capitani. 1998. "Michigan Nonprofits and Devolution: What Do We Know?" Washington, DC: The Aspen Institute.

De Vita, Carol J., and Pho Palmer. 2003. "Church-State Partnerships: Some Reflections from Washington, D.C." *Charting Civil Society* Policy Brief no. 14. Washington, DC: The Urban Institute.

Farnsley, Arthur E. 2001. "Can Faith-based Organizations Compete?" *Nonprofit and Voluntary Sector Quarterly* 30(1): 99–111.

Frey, William H. 2005. "Metropolitan America in the New Century: Metropolitan and Central City Demographic Shifts since 2000." *The Living Cities Census Series*. Washington, DC: The Brookings Institution.

Frumkin, Peter, and Alice Andre-Clark. 2000. "When Missions, Markets, and Politics Collide: Values and Strategy in Nonprofit Human Services." *Nonprofit and Voluntary Sector Quarterly* 29(1): 141–63.

Fuchs, Ester R. 1998. "The Permanent Urban Fiscal Crisis." In *Big Cities in the Welfare Transition,* edited by Alfred J. Kahn and Sheila B. Kamerman (43–73). New York: Cross-National Studies Research Program, Columbia University School of Social Work.

Green, John C., and Amy L. Sherman. 2002. "Fruitful Collaborations: A Survey of Government-funded Faith-based Programs in 15 States." Charlottesville, VA: Hudson Institute.

Gronbjerg, Kirsten A., and Lester M. Salamon. 2002. "Devolution, Marketization, and the Changing Shape of Government-Nonprofit Relations." In *The State of Nonprofit America,* edited by Lester M. Salamon (447–70). Washington, DC: Brookings Institution Press.

Gronbjerg, Kirsten A., and Steven Rathgeb Smith. 1999. "Nonprofit Organizations and Public Policies in the Delivery of Human Services." In *Philanthropy and the Nonprofit Sector,* edited by Charles T. Clotfelter and Thomas Ehrlich (139–71). Bloomington: Indiana University.

Hatry, Harry P., Jake Cowan, Ken Weiner, and Linda M. Lampkin. 2003. "Developing Community-wide Outcome Indicators for Specific Services." Washington, DC: The Urban Institute.

Holahan, John, and David Liska. 1997. "Reassessing the Outlook for Medicaid Spending Growth." Washington, DC: The Urban Institute. *Assessing the New Federalism* Policy Brief A-6.

James, Estelle. 1987. "The Nonprofit Sector in Comparative Perspective." In *The Nonprofit Sector: A Research Handbook,* edited by Walter H. Powell (397–415). New Haven: Yale University Press.

Kennedy, Sheila Suess, and Wolfgang Bielefeld. 2003. "Charitable Choice: First Results from Three States." Indianapolis, IN: Center for Urban Policy and Environment, Indiana University-Purdue University.

Kramer, Fredrica D., Kenneth Finegold, Carol J. De Vita, and Laura Wherry. 2005. "Federal Policy on the Ground: Faith-Based Organizations Delivering Local Services." Washington, DC: The Urban Institute.

Lampkin, Linda M., and Harry P. Hatry. 2003. "Key Steps in Outcome Management." Washington, DC: The Urban Institute.

Light, Paul C. 2000. *Making Nonprofits Work: A Report on the Tides of Nonprofit Management Reform.* Washington, DC: Brookings Institution Press.

———. 2002. *Pathways to Nonprofit Excellence.* Washington, DC: Brookings Institution Press.

Monsma, Stephen V. 2004. *Putting Faith in Partnerships: Welfare-to-Work in Four Cities.* Ann Arbor: The University of Michigan Press.

Monsma, Stephen V., and Carolyn M. Mounts. 2002. "Working Faith: How Religious Organizations Provide Welfare-to-Work Services." Philadelphia: Center for Research on Religion and Urban Civil Society.

Nathan, Richard P. 1996. "The 'Nonprofitization Movement' as a Form of Devolution." In *Capacity for Change? The Nonprofit World in the Age of Devolution,* edited by Dwight F. Burlingame, William A. Diaz, and Warren F. Ilchman (23–55). Indianapolis: Indiana University Center on Philanthropy.

Pindus, Nancy, Randy Capps, Jerome Gallagher, Linda Giannarelli, Milda Saunders, and Robin Smith. 1998. "Income Support and Social Services for Low-Income People in Texas." Washington, DC: The Urban Institute.

Poppendieck, Janet. 1998. *Sweet Charity? Emergency Food and the End of Entitlement.* New York: Viking.

Ragan, Mark. 2004. "Faith-based vs. Secular: Using Administrative Data to Compare the Performance of Faith-Affiliated and Other Social Service Providers." Albany, NY: The Rockefeller Institute of Government.

Salamon, Lester M. 1985. "Government and the Voluntary Sector in an Era of Retrenchment: The American Experience." *Journal of Public Policy* 6: 1–20.

———. 1995. *Partners in Public Service: Government-Nonprofit Relations in the Modern Welfare State.* Baltimore: Johns Hopkins University Press.

Salamon, Lester M., and Alan J. Abramson. 1996. "The Federal Budget and the Nonprofit Sector: Implications of the Contract with America." In *Capacity of Change? The Nonprofit World in the Age of Devolution,* edited by Dwight F. Burlingame, William A. Diaz, and Warren F. Ilchman (1–22). Indianapolis: Indiana University Center on Philanthropy.

Sherman, Amy L. 2000. "The Growing Impact of Charitable Choice: A Catalogue of New Collaborations between Government and Faith-based Organizations in Nine States." Washington, DC: Center for Public Justice.

Smith, Steven Rathgeb. 1999. "Government Financing of Nonprofit Activity." In *Nonprofits and Government: Collaboration and Conflict,* edited by Elizabeth T. Boris and C. Eugene Steuerle (177–210). Washington, DC: The Urban Institute Press.

———. 2002. "Social Services." In *The State of Nonprofit America,* edited by Lester M. Salamon (149–86). Washington, DC: Brookings Institution Press.

———. 2005. "Comparative Case Studies of Faith-Based and Secular Service Agencies: An Overview and Synthesis of Key Findings." Paper presented at the annual Association of Public Policy Analysis and Management (APPAM) meeting, Washington, D.C., October.

Smith, Steven Rathgeb, and Michael Lipsky. 1993. *Nonprofits for Hire: The Welfare State in the Age of Contracting.* Cambridge: Harvard University Press.

Smith, Steven Rathgeb, and Michael R. Sosin. 2001. "The Varieties of Faith-Related Agencies." *Public Administration Review* 61(6): 651–70.

Steuerle, C. Eugene, Edward Gramlich, Hugh Heclo, and Demetra Smith Nightingale. 1998. *The Government We Deserve.* Washington, DC: Urban Institute Press.

Twombly, Eric C. 2002. "Religious versus Secular Human Service Organizations: Implications for Public Policy." *Social Science Quarterly* 83(4): 947–61.

White House, The. 2001. "Unlevel Playing Field: Barriers to Participation by Faith-Based and Community Organizations in Federal Social Service Programs." Washington, DC: The White House.

8

OWNERSHIP FORMS, CONVERSIONS, AND PUBLIC POLICY

John H. Goddeeris and Burton A. Weisbrod

In 1991, the managers and directors of Health Net, a nonprofit California health maintenance organization, proposed to purchase it and convert it to a for-profit firm. Though nonprofits initially dominated the HMO industry, the market share of for-profits was increasing, and a number of nonprofit HMOs, as well as hospitals, had already converted in California and elsewhere. In the evolving market for health insurance and health care, lack of access to equity capital is often believed to put nonprofits at a decided competitive disadvantage.

Insiders offered $108 million in cash and promissory notes for Health Net's assets—to be given to a nonprofit charitable trust. The deal was nearly approved until consumer groups and others protested that the price was too low. A bidding war for the HMO ensued. When the California Department of Corporations approved the conversion in early 1992, the insiders paid $300 million—nearly three times the original offer—but for only 20 percent of Health Net stock; the money and the remaining 80 percent of the stock in the converted HMO went to the new foundation (Hamburger, Finberg, and Alcantar 1995). Assuming that the $300 million was a fair price for 20 percent ownership—it may have understated what the buyers were willing to pay—the entire HMO was worth at least $1.5 billion. Had the original offer been accepted, the new owners would have received assets worth $1.5 billion or more at a cost of $108 million (only a small part of which was in cash). The conversion would have transferred $1.4 billion to the insider group. A massive appropriation of public assets, accumulated with the help of governmental subsidies and tax exemptions, nearly occurred.

In 1994, the national Blue Cross and Blue Shield Association agreed to consider affiliations with for-profit firms. Since that time, Blue Cross plans in 14 states have converted (Conover, Hall, and Ostermann 2005). In a number of these cases, the value of assets to be transferred to a public or charitable purpose at the time of conversion was a subject of dispute. In Georgia, for example, legislators approved a law in 1995 that permitted Blue Cross and Blue Shield of Georgia to convert to for-profit status without paying anything to a surviving foundation.[1] Two years later, however, nine charities sued the new for-profit BCBS (Cerulean), claiming that the public was being deprived of money owed to it because of the public subsidies the insurer had received (Hall and Conover 2003; Marchetti 1997). To settle the suit, a foundation was created and endowed with 20 percent of the firm's assets. In 1994, Blue Cross and Blue Shield of Missouri created a for-profit HMO called Right Choice Managed Care, transferred 80 percent of its assets to Right Choice, and then took the wholly owned firm public by selling 20 percent of the stock. After first approving, the state of Missouri later demanded that the public be compensated because the for-profit had benefited from various tax-related subsidies.[2] Ultimately all of BCBS of Missouri's shares of Right Choice were given to a new charitable foundation. They were valued at nearly $500 million when the agreement was reached in 2000 (Hall and Conover 2003).

The tide has turned, at least temporarily, against Blue Cross conversions, with regulators rejecting conversion proposals in Kansas, Maryland, and Washington and proposals in New Jersey and North Carolina being withdrawn (Conover et al. 2005). But conversion is again under discussion in New Jersey, spurred in part by state officials' interest in capturing Horizon Blue Cross and Blue Shield's assets to help solve budget problems.[3]

In the hospital industry, even larger numbers of nonprofits have shifted to for-profits. The share of community hospital beds for-profit firms control remains relatively small, but grew from 9 percent in 1983 to 11 percent in 1993 to more than 13 percent in 2003 (American Hospital Association 2005). The numbers of conversions spiked in the mid-1990s, with investor-owned firms acquiring at least 84 nonprofits between

1995 and 1997 (Leone, Van Horn, and Wedig 2005). The pace of hospital conversions slowed after 1997 in the wake of federal investigations of Columbia/HCA (now HCA), which had been the nation's most aggressive for-profit hospital chain. State attorneys general and other regulatory bodies also increased their scrutiny of hospital conversions at that time. Hospital conversion activity appears to have reaccelerated, however, with investor-owned firms acquiring 41 nonprofits in 2002 (Galloro 2003).

Conversions are not limited to the health care sector. In another recent case, the nonprofit Minnesota Public Radio (MPR) sold a for-profit subsidiary to a private firm, with multimillion dollar payments made to officials of the subsidiary through a type of phantom stock option (Abelson 1998a, b). While not clearly a conversion—because the subsidiary was already for-profit—the large gains in this transaction by individuals closely linked to MPR made it controversial. The subsidiary, while for-profit, could legally deploy its assets and profit only to benefit the nonprofit parent organization, but its sale to a for-profit firm permitted transferring those resources to private hands. Thus, the price at which the conversion occurred was an appropriate subject of scrutiny.

The dividing line between the nonprofit and for-profit sectors, both in revenue sources and in the way organizations behave, is increasingly blurred (Weisbrod 1997, 2004). Symptomatic of that blurring is the growing prominence of conversions from one organizational form to another. While changes in organizational form occur in all directions, conversions from nonprofit to for-profit have recently drawn much public attention, especially in health care. The examples above illustrate the public policy issues nonprofit conversions, complete or partial, raise.

This chapter begins by considering the concept of conversion and suggest that it is fundamentally a matter of transfer of control over assets between parties that face different incentives and constraints on their behavior. As such, conversion is not an all-or-nothing proposition; the concept encompasses a variety of transfers of control. Next, the chapter discusses what might motivate a nonprofit to convert because understanding the motivation is useful in formulating public policy responses. Events in health care, where most of the current activity is occurring, are examined, as well as conversions in higher education. The chapter then turns to the important policy questions: (1) When is a conversion socially desirable? That is, when is it likely to be economically efficient and distributionally equitable? (2) How can public policy promote desirable conversions and discourage undesirable ones?

Policymakers might wish that a minimal policy role were appropriate—that an "invisible hand" mechanism applied to nonprofit conversions—so that conversions would naturally take place when, and only when, they enhance economic efficiency. However, the transfer of assets from nonprofits to for-profits does not always increase social value. Private gain may motivate conversions, as the Health Net example suggests.

The fundamental point is that converting a nonprofit to an independent for-profit firm involves transferring the assets from an organization legally prohibited from distributing profits or surplus to managers into an organization that faces no such constraint. Thus, some mechanism is needed to prevent nonprofit managers from accumulating assets through the aid of public subsidies and then transferring the assets to a private firm that distributes them without restriction. Fostering an environment that allows for and even facilitates efficient conversions without also encouraging inappropriate transfers of wealth is a significant challenge.

Under current law, conversions of nonprofits normally require regulatory approval. In some cases, as with complete conversions to for-profit status, formal approval is required in advance, although state governmental policies vary. In other, more partial transfers of control, such as in a joint venture with a for-profit firm or a contracting out of the nonprofit management, prior approval is not required, but the regulator may subsequently penalize the nonprofit or require it to cancel the arrangement. For a conversion to occur, therefore, more than a desire to convert must be present. The regulatory agencies must also consent, at least tacitly.

Although this book focuses on relationships between government and nonprofits, a discussion of conversions from nonprofit to for-profit is not out of place. The government is no disinterested bystander with respect to conversions. It is often a major purchaser in markets where nonprofit and for-profit firms compete—such as the health care and higher education markets. Government subsidies and tax abatements also help nonprofits accumulate assets that can be transferred to private firms through conversion. Government regulators rule on conversion proposals. Finally, when the government privatizes—selling assets or contracting functions with the private sector—similar "conversion" issues arise.

WHAT IS A CONVERSION?

Conversion is fundamentally about changes in control over an organization's assets and responsibility for its liabilities. After a change in control, assets may be deployed in different ways and for the benefit of different individuals or groups. Public policy concerns revolve around efficiency—whether a change enhances the social value the assets will produce—and around fairness—whether some parties benefit improperly at others' expense.

What Is Special about Conversions by Nonprofits to For-Profits?

While this chapter primarily focuses on changes from nonprofit to for-profit control, there are many forms of organizations that provide goods and services (Hansmann 1996). Government organizations directly provide services, often in competition with nonprofits and for-profits, as in education and hospital care. In addition to the investor-owned firms, worker-owned or customer-owned cooperatives and mutual organizations provide examples of other forms of private ownership.

Transfers of control, or "conversions," occur across and within all these organization types. The market for for-profit corporate control is often lauded as an important mechanism for disciplining management to seek maximum value for shareholders, thereby enhancing the organization's efficiency. However, even mergers and buyouts within the corporate sector raise concerns about improper private gain by insiders because whether corporate executives' financial incentives coincide with stockholders' interests can be unclear. During the 1990s, a number of large life insurers, including Prudential, MetLife, and John Hancock, converted from mutuals owned by policyholders to shareholder-owned companies (Chaddad and Cook 2004). Debates about demutualization have a familiar ring to those who followed discussions of nonprofit conversions. Management claims a need for access to equity capital, while consumer groups express concern that managers are motivated by private gain at policyholders' expense.

So what, if anything, is special about *nonprofit* conversions that merits particular public policy concern? Three points make nonprofit conversions different and of greater importance to public policymaking than other types of conversions: lack of private ownership, different legal constraints, and different objectives.

Lack of Private Ownership

In a firm with clearly defined private owners, the owners will resist any transfer of control that undervalues their ownership shares. The more diffuse the ownership and the less transparent the value of shares, however, the less effective this check on self-dealing by management insiders is likely to be. The essence of a nonprofit organization is that no individuals have a legal claim to the organization's assets or net income, both of which may be hard to measure but, in some cases, have tremendous value. In the sense that the owners are the public, owners' incentives to exercise oversight are extremely diffuse in a nonprofit. Managers and directors have both the control needed to arrange conversions and a potential incentive to do so, as the Health Net case suggests, although board members' moral and legal fiduciary responsibilities are important countervailing influences.

Different Legal Constraints

When organizations operate under different legal constraints, transactions among them may exploit the difference for private gain without a corresponding social benefit.[4] While this problem can exist for transactions between various forms of private organizations facing different rules, it is a particular concern for conversions of nonprofits (Cordes and Weisbrod 1998). Nonprofits have often benefited from preferred tax treatment, including the tax deductibility of donations, and other subsidies not available to for-profits. The largest benefits generally go to nonprofits that are tax exempt under section 501(c)(3) of the Internal Revenue Code. Other nonprofits generally receive only the exemption from corporate profits taxation. Public policies that give any advantage to nonprofits thereby provide a "wedge" that disadvantages for-profit competitors and creates opportunities for nonprofit managers to accumulate assets that, if conversion were arranged, could lead to private benefit.

Different Objectives

Although problems of managerial incentives exist in all complex organizations, those that are privately owned are generally expected to seek maximum value for their owners. Conversion from one type of privately owned organization to another may then only modestly affect how the organization behaves. Whether an insurance company is a mutual—owned by its policyholders—or a stock company may not matter greatly for the products it offers or its responsiveness to customers, despite the formal difference in ownership. In a reasonably competitive insurance market, stockholders' interests are strongly linked to satisfying policyholders. Thus, the public policy case for limiting conversions is weaker when both the selling and acquiring organizations pursue the owners' private interests than when the selling organization has broader social goals than the acquirer. If nonprofits behave differently than for-profits—an issue discussed later in this chapter—conversion from nonprofit to any form of privately owned firm could change the organization's objectives in policy-relevant ways. Note that for this reason, the privatization of governmental assets through transfer to for-profit ownership—or even for-profit management—presents problems similar to the conversion of nonprofits to for-profits.

Complete and Partial Conversions

The extreme case of nonprofit conversion occurs when an entire organization changes its legal form from nonprofit to for-profit or is sold to a for-profit. Even such a seemingly clear change of organizational form, however, is complicated by the fact that the assets of the nonprofit do not belong to individuals. If the nonprofit sells its assets and ceases to exist in its previous form, where do the proceeds of the sale go? Normally, that value is passed to another nonprofit organization, frequently a newly created foundation. Valuing the assets to be transferred, however, is often a contentious issue, as the Health Net case and a number of Blue Cross conversions exemplify.

Transfers of control can also occur in other ways and to varying degrees. For example, joint ventures between nonprofit and for-profit firms are common. In arrangements between the for-profit HCA and various nonprofit hospitals, the hospital became a for-profit venture, jointly owned by HCA and the original nonprofit (or a new foundation) but managed by HCA, which exercised substantial control over the use of core assets. Attorneys general in California and Michigan recognized the transfer of control over nonprofit assets in this type of joint venture and successfully opposed such a transfer in well-publicized cases (Whitehead, Johnson, and Moore 1997). The Internal Revenue Service (IRS) also reviewed the question of whether joint ventures between nonprofits and for-profits should retain tax-exempt status and concluded that control is the key issue.[5] Similarly, the formation by a nonprofit of a for-profit subsidiary can lead to a transfer of control because a major motivation for creating such a subsidiary is to gain access to equity capital by selling part ownership to the public. When that happens, the assets the subsidiary holds shift at least partially to for-profit control.

When the full range of any organization's activities is considered, that some elements can be converted without the entire organization converting is easy to see. When this occurs, the same issues arise as when an entire organization converts. In a recent case of partial conversion by a quasi-government agency—a community college proposed to sell its public television station—a California state appeals court rejected the college's sale to a buyer other than the highest bidder. The Coast Community College District (Orange County) approved the sale to a local (nonprofit) foundation even though a Texas religious television network had offered a higher price. The court ruled that the college district could not legally accept a lower bid because it wanted to avoid selling to a religious broadcasting group, a decision that is still under review.[6]

Yet another form of partial conversion occurs when a nonprofit contracts with a for-profit firm for management services. Whether such a contract involves significant public policy issues depends on how much control is transferred—that is, the degree to which the for-profit firm is effectively constrained—and on the reward structure for the for-profit, which affects its incentives to use its discretionary authority in various ways. While transfers of managerial control have been happening frequently in the hospital industry, similar conversions by delegation are occurring in the public sector. Firms such as the Edison Project and Apollo Group, Inc., have put public schools in Minneapolis, Hartford, and elsewhere under private sector management, and prisons have been increasingly privatized through management contracts with firms like Corrections Corporation of America and Behavioral Systems Southwest. In those cases, the nonprofit (or public) organization was neither sold nor formally converted; instead, control was transferred to a private firm for a finite period and with a variety of contractual constraints.

One might argue that contracting with a for-profit does not necessarily imply a transfer of control if the contract is sufficiently well-specified. Theoretically, the for-profit contractor could be provided with incentives to pursue the nonprofit's social goals, however complex and subtle those goals might be. But while nonprofit institutions are most valuable, and most common, where socially important dimensions of performance are difficult to define in a contract and to monitor (Weisbrod 1988), transferring managerial authority to a for-profit often alters performance away from those hard-to-monitor dimensions. That will be the case as long as the difficulty of writing a complete contract allows the for-profit contractor to discreetly alter how the nonprofit's goals are realized.

Because transfers of control to for-profits can take many forms, the complete nonprofit conversions and sales now drawing attention in health care are likely only the tip of a much larger iceberg of shifts toward for-profit control over nonprofit assets and activities. Moreover, such shifts may be occurring in other industries but less visibly than in health care. That possibility carries a major implication for public policy: if an increasingly strong searchlight of public attention focuses on particular forms of conversion, the goals that motivate transfers of control over assets (examined below) are likely to be pursued through other, more subtle means. There will be more joint ventures, partial buyouts, and complex interorganization contracts that preserve the apparent independence of each nonprofit organization but actually shift control and financial benefits to for-profits.

State Regulation of Health Care Conversions

While the IRS exercises some regulatory oversight on nonprofit conversions, state regulators play a particularly central role. Their authority to oversee health care conversions has traditionally derived from state nonprofit corporation law and common law that applies to charitable trusts, as well as law specific to particular types of health care institutions. However, the extent of this authority and how it applies to complex transactions between nonprofits and for-profits have often been unclear. As Shriber (1997) notes, "Regulators have too many authorities and too little guidance" (see also Butler 1997).

In the wake of heightened interest in health care conversions, at least 27 states and the District of Columbia have passed, since the mid-1990s, legislation dealing specifically with the conversion of hospitals, health insurers, and health maintenance organizations (Community Catalyst 2003). While the legislation generally casts a broad net in requiring prior regulatory approval of conversions, usually by a state's attorney general, the extent and form of oversight vary across states in important ways. Some differences are indicated below.

Precisely what transactions should be deemed "conversions"? The National Association of Attorneys General (NAAG) in its 1997 resolution on "Conversion of Nonprofit Health Care Entities to For-Profit Status," calls for written notice "before a voluntary health care entity sells, leases, conveys, exchanges, transfers, or otherwise disposes of all or substantially all of its assets" (Volunteer Trustees Foundation for Research and Education 1998). This formulation appears to permit disposition of assets that are less than "substantially all," which could permit a series of partial dispositions that, over time, would constitute an almost total transfer.

Most state legislation has included a broad list of the types of transactions that trigger regulatory review, as in the NAAG resolution. Definitions vary in how much control may be transferred before approval is required. For example, regulatory approval is required in California, Connecticut, and Oregon, if a "material" or "significant" amount of control is involved; in Arizona, for any disposition of assets of $1 or more; in Wisconsin, Nebraska, and Ohio, for any change of at least 20 percent of "ownership or control"; in Louisiana and South Dakota, for any change in ownership or control of at least 30 percent of voting rights or assets; in Colorado and Georgia, for a transfer of 50 percent or more of assets over a five-year period; and in Virginia, for a disposition of "all or substantially all of the assets."

(continued next page)

State Regulation (cont.)

With respect to the valuation of assets in a conversion, state require-ments are more alike, focusing on payment of fair market prices for the nonprofit's assets, with some relatively minor variation in language. For the most part, the laws reflect the common-law doctrine of cy pres, directing that conversion proceeds be used for a charitable purpose as near as possible to that of the converting nonprofit. The New York State legislature has, however, attracted attention—some highly critical—for passing a law that designated 95 percent of the proceeds from the conversion of Empire Blue Cross to go to a fund within the state budget earmarked for health programs, much of it to pay for wage increases for health care workers (Horwitz and Fremont-Smith 2005; Robinson 2003). Empire converted to the for-profit WellChoice in 2002, but the disposition of the assets has been a subject of litigation.

What Motivates Conversions?

Economists usually view individuals as maximizing their well-being subject to the constraints their environment imposes, including the legal system and their wealth. Modeling organization behavior in the same way—as the pursuit of some objective or set of objectives subject to constraints—is often useful. From that perspective, the choice of organizational form, nonprofit or for-profit, is a choice of constraints under which an organization will operate because these constraints differ between nonprofits and for-profits. A particular form is pre-sumably chosen because it is the most conducive to attaining the founders' goals.

Both the legal system and the market impose constraints. As noted, nonprofits receive certain tax advantages relative to for-profit firms but also face a legal "nondistribution constraint" not imposed on private firms—a restriction against distributing any profits or surplus to man-agers or others connected with the organization (Hansmann 1980). Nonprofits are restricted from access to equity capital because they may not grant private ownership shares in the organization. However, they have greater access to tax-exempt bond financing than do for-profit firms. While generally only state and local governments are eligible to issue such bonds, many types of nonprofits have been able to use the proceeds of tax-exempt bonds issued on their behalf (Davis and Davis 2002).

Market conditions also constrain behavior. Demand conditions—buyers' willingness to pay—constrain both for-profit and nonprofit firms when they sell output, though not necessarily identically. In some cases, buyers might prefer to purchase from nonprofits, perhaps because buyers regard them as more trustworthy. Trust is particularly important for goods with essential attributes that are difficult to monitor directly (e.g., the "tender loving care" provided in a nursing home or day care center), leaving buyers concerned that sellers will exploit this informational advantage for personal gain. If some buyers regard nonprofit status as a signal of trustworthiness, demand will differ between the two types of organizations, even if all the observable characteristics of their services are identical.

Suppliers of resource inputs may also treat nonprofits differently from for-profits. As previously noted, volunteer time appears to be more readily supplied to nonprofit firms, and paid employees sometimes offer to work for nonprofits at lower wages, according to several empirical studies (Preston 1989; Roomkin and Weisbrod 1999; Weisbrod 1988; but see Goddeeris 1988). Some employees appear willing to sacrifice monetary compensation to work for a nonprofit organization, perhaps because they identify with its goals and derive satisfaction from working to achieve them.

In light of the numerous differences in constraints between nonprofits and for-profits, some providing advantages to nonprofits, others to for-profits, the optimal choice of organization form depends on the organization's objectives as defined by the founder, top management, and directors, subject to IRS approval. Suppose, for example, that the founding managers of a new medical clinic care about two things, their own monetary compensation and the provision of some collective service, such as subsidized health care for the poor.[7] In either the nonprofit or for-profit sector, some tradeoff is likely between the goals of compensating managers and providing services. But maximum monetary rewards to the founders may be higher in the for-profit sector because the nondistribution does not limit compensation. Nonprofits may have larger collective good output, however, due to tax advantages and the ability to attract donations and volunteer labor. Entrepreneurs who place little value on the collective goods would then organize as for-profits, but those who prefer providing services would choose the nonprofit form. Thus, the two forms may coexist; even when for-profits and nonprofits compete head-to-head in the same markets, the differential constraints permit nonprofit and for-profit managers to pursue different goals.

Potential Conflict of Interest for Nonprofits with For-Profit Subsidiaries: The Case of Minnesota Public Radio

A case involving Minnesota Public Radio (MPR) illustrates the complex relationships that can exist between nonprofits and for-profits. The nonprofit American Public Media Group owns both MPR, also a nonprofit, and a for-profit subsidiary called Greenspring. William H. Kling is president of both MPR and Greenspring, and his compensation at Greenspring included value performance units (VPUs), similar to stock options often provided to private sector executives. Greenspring sold its Rivertown catalogue business—originally launched to market products related to MPR's "Prairie Home Companion" program—to the Dayton Hudson Corporation (now Target Corporation) for $120 million, of which about $90 million was added to MPR's endowment. Mr. Kling personally received $2.6 million in the deal through the sale of his VPUs, and about two dozen other Greenspring executives similarly received a total of $4.7 million. It appears that the VPUs could only be "cashed out" through a sale to a private for-profit firm. MPR "fought the release of the salary and bonuses of its top executives, saying that it hurt the ability of the for-profit operation to recruit talent," but the state of Minnesota passed a financial disclosure law requiring their release (Levy 1998). The board of directors regarded the VPUs, referred to as "phantom stock options," as essential for attracting outstanding managerial leadership in competition with for-profit firms (personal communication, Steven M. Rothschild, 1998).

The decision to permit the sale may be a sensible one for MPR. It is certainly possible that the Rivertown business is more valuable as a part of Target, so that the income the endowment increase generates exceeds the expected income the business would produce if the sale did not take place. MPR may also prefer the more stable endowment income stream. The compensation package for the executives may have motivated the creation of Rivertown, which now provides substantial revenue for MPR. Nonetheless, the sale and the prior close relationship between MPR and Greenspring raise questions. When top executives of a nonprofit have a significant financial interest in a closely related for-profit, is the conflict of interest in the management of the nonprofit too great?

Sources: Reed Abelson, "At Minnesota Public Radio, a Deal Way Above Average," *New York Times*, March 27, 1998, C3; Reed Abelson, "Nonprofit Work Gets Profitable," *New York Times*, March 29, 1998, C1; Terry Fiedler and Deborah C. Rybak, "Bill Kling, Public Radio King; MPR Chief 'Sings His Own Song' in Creating a National Powerhouse,"*Minneapolis Star Tribune*, October 24, 2004; Mellissa Levy, "Dayton Hudson to Acquire Rivertown Trading Co. Catalogs," *Minneapolis Star Tribune*, March 24, 1998; and James P. Miller, "Public Radio Outlet in Minnesota Reaps $120 Million in Sale of Direct Marketer," *Wall Street Journal*, March 24, 1998, B10.

Why Would a Nonprofit Want to Convert?

Why would an organization that has chosen to form in one way later decide to convert? A conversion decision is in some ways like the original decision about organization form. If either the objectives of the firm's decisionmakers or the constraints the firm faces have changed, it may wish to reconsider its original choice. For example, since most nonprofits are exempt from the property taxes that private firms must pay, if the government cut property taxes, the advantage of the nonprofit tax exemption would be reduced. Thus, lower property taxes could induce an organization with a sufficiently weak preference for the nonprofit form to switch status (Hansmann 1987; Cordes and Weisbrod 1998). If the ability of a nonprofit to attract donations declines relative to its costs of operations, the attractiveness of nonprofit status also falls.

Given that conversion has particularly accelerated in one sector of the economy, health care, the cause likely involves changes in constraints—the legal, regulatory, and market environment—rather than changes in organizational objectives. Why organizational objectives would shift systematically, but only in this one field, is not clear. Below, we will discuss briefly how changes in the health care marketplace may contribute to interest in conversions and whether such changes can be expected in other industries.

The distinction between objectives and constraints is not entirely tidy. In the absence of operational measures of "success" analogous to profit or share prices, key decisionmakers within the nonprofit significantly determine its goals. Those goals often change over time, sometimes in *response* to changes in constraints imposed on the organization. Goals may change as a nonprofit, in pursuing its original mission, encounters budgetary constraints and takes on board members who represent sources of actual or potential finance. As an example, in the early 1980s, a nonprofit food bank in Phoenix that, at first, had local volunteers as directors, witnessed a struggle in which food manufacturers—such as Beatrice Foods and Kraft, and food marketers, including the Grocery Manufacturers of America and the Food Marketing Institute—rather than the volunteers, came to exert control.[8] If financial constraints become more stringent, an organization's goals might change considerably over time as managers with greater concern about, and skills with, fundraising and finance replace those whose visions were of public service outputs. Such a change in organization goals could contribute to a decision to convert, as the altered goals became less compatible with the constraints under which the nonprofit operates.

There are also some important differences between a decision to convert and the initial choice of organizational form. A desire to convert may evolve naturally over an organization's life cycle, even if the environment and goals of the organization do not change. For a newly established nonprofit with few assets, the nondistribution constraint may be of little consequence because the nonprofit has little or nothing to distribute.[9] If the organization is successful, however, and the market value of its assets grows, its managers and board face an increasing opportunity and temptation to distribute some of that market value to themselves. At the same time, the organization's success may increase opportunities for it to exploit the equity capital market as a for-profit firm.[10] In addition, if public policy effectively subverts or even weakens the nondistribution constraint, a conversion may occur. Within such a policy regime, some organizations may even pursue a long-range strategy of forming as nonprofits and converting to for-profits.

On the other hand, if the nondistribution constraint is effectively enforced during the conversion process, as state and federal laws intend, the firm could not siphon off the assets it accumulated as a nonprofit. That diminishes the private gain motivation for converting. At the same time, if the conversion does occur and the for-profit firm's behavior shifts toward maximizing market value and away from providing collective goods, this does not *necessarily* mean that collective goods are lost in the process. The income from the accumulated assets could be redirected toward the continued provision of collective goods—and the government could also direct the additional revenue from increased taxes that the firm now pays as a for-profit entity toward collective goods.

In concluding this section, it is worth emphasizing that conversions do not go only from nonprofit to for-profit.[11] Indeed, firms near the margin in the initial selection of the for-profit sector might convert if an environmental change increased the attractiveness of the nonprofit sector. There is, however, a possible asymmetry between conversions in the two directions. To the extent that the conversions are part of a long-term strategy motivated primarily by private gain, the more financially successful nonprofits would seek conversion to for-profit status (to escape the nondistribution constraint), while the for-profits that seek conversion would be relatively unsuccessful ones. For those for-profits that have done less well than their initial expectations and that are only marginally viable, accepting the nondistribution constraint may matter little, while the tax advantages and subsidies available to nonprofits look attractive.

Conversions in Health Care

The incentive to convert exists for any nonprofit organization that has accumulated valuable assets, assuming its leaders could then capture part of the nonprofit's value for their own financial gain. Why, then, has health care been such a focus of conversion activity compared with other industries in which nonprofits play a prominent role, such as museums and day care? Why within the health care sector have so few nonprofit nursing homes and home health care agencies converted?

A full analysis of these issues is beyond the scope of this chapter.[12] It is plausible, however, that conversions of nonprofit hospitals, HMOs, and Blue Cross plans have been influenced heavily by changes in the legal and regulatory environment, as well as in the nature of market competition, that have made surviving competition with for-profits more difficult. In other words, changes in constraints may be leading health care nonprofits to reconsider which organizational form is optimal, and many are opting for conversion.

A number of policy changes have reduced advantages for health care nonprofits, making it more difficult for them to finance collective goods while surviving in the market. For HMOs, the end in 1983 of federal grants and loans for HMO development coincided with, and perhaps stimulated, the shift toward for-profit status. For the Blues, tax advantages have eroded over time. The Tax Reform Act of 1986 finally ended exemption for them from the federal corporate income tax; many states have also limited special tax treatment of Blue Cross plans. Changes in tax policy in the 1980s also reduced advantages of nonprofit hospitals over for-profits with regard to issuing tax-exempt bonds (Sloan 1988).

While government legislated these changes in tax policy, the nature of competition in the health care marketplace changed. An era in which third-party payers passively reimbursed hospitals for their self-reported costs or charges gave way to one of standardized payment rates and even active price competition for patients. The public and private health care financing system and government policies of the first decades after World War II (including the Hill-Burton Act of 1946, which subsidized construction of hospital beds) encouraged an enormous buildup of hospital capacity. As the total number of hospital admissions began to fall in the early 1980s (as a result of technological changes and economic pressures to rein in hospital spending), average occupancy levels fell.

The occurrence of hospital and health insurer conversions coincides with and surely relates to a drive toward consolidation in these industries. Some analysts have stressed a link between excess capacity in health care, particularly in hospitals, and these movements. As the market for hospital services became more price competitive, hospitals often affiliated with larger organizations to survive. The most attractive suitors have often, though not always, been for-profits (Hollis 1997; Coye 1997), and a large number of hospital conversions have been sales to or joint ventures with large for-profit chains, such as HCA and Tenet Healthcare.

Similarly, as government and employers have sought to become more prudent purchasers of health care, health insurers have found an increasing need to compete for enrollees on the basis of price and to embrace managed-care principles. In turn, insurers have felt pressure to expand, whether to achieve economies of scale or gain market power. Increased emphasis on cost containment has decreased the degree to which market competition tolerates differences in behavior between nonprofit and for-profit insurers, including HMOs. In addition, the perceived need to grow has made access to capital seem increasingly critical for health insurers' survival.[13]

Access to equity capital, one advantage that investor-owned for-profits clearly enjoy over nonprofits, appears consistently in arguments for conversions—including, for example, the demutualizations of Prudential and other life insurers, and MPR's decision to sell its for-profit Rivertown subsidiary. While more research is needed, we remain somewhat skeptical of the importance of this advantage, including its application to health insurers. Nonprofits have access to the debt market and often even to tax-exempt bonds as well as their earnings as funds for investment. Some have questioned whether lack of access to equity capital is a serious problem for a well-established health insurer that is not rapidly expanding (Johnson 2003). For example, in rejecting CareFirst's proposal to convert, the Maryland insurance commissioner also rejected CareFirst's claim of needing access to equity capital, citing evidence that CareFirst was already investing at rates comparable to for-profit plans (Larsen 2003).

With the merger of Anthem and WellPoint and their announced acquisition of WellChoice,[14] all 14 Blue Cross plans that have converted to for-profits likely will be combined into a single organization. Motives for conversion are therefore also difficult to disentangle from motives for consolidation, although there are no particular impediments to consolidating nonprofits.

It is difficult to determine how many conversions in health care are socially efficient responses to changes in the environment in which hospitals, HMOs, and Blue Cross plans operate and how many are opportunistic behavior by insiders. Dramatic changes in those markets, changes not matched in other markets where nonprofits operate, have made both avenues possible. Personal financial enrichment of key nonprofit officials has often been present in conversions, particularly of nonprofit HMOs and in some proposed conversions of Blue Cross plans.[15] It is widely alleged that in many HMO conversions, insiders purchased ownership shares at low rates before the converted organizations were valued in the stock market and then profited enormously when the organizations "went public" and a true market value was established (Hamburger et al. 1995; Fox and Isenberg 1996). The possibility that private financial gain, through subversion of the nondistribution constraint, has motivated some health care conversions cannot be ruled out. Leonard Schaeffer, the chairman of the board of WellPoint and former head of California Blue Cross, which converted to a for-profit in a highly controversial deal, was convinced of such self-interested behavior:

> Before the conversion of WellPoint, the value of every single company that converted to for-profit status was significantly underestimated. What was granted to charity turned out to be much less than was realized a week, a month, or a year later, when Wall Street placed a true market value on the for-profit HMO that resulted from the conversion. Almost all of the value created went to the management and boards of these companies . . . FHP International, Foundation Health, Pacificare, TakeCare, you name it.These are companies that today are led by multimillionaires who achieved that status by virtue of receiving stock that was dramatically undervalued at the time of conversion. (Iglehart 1995, 142)

With regard to hospitals, however, evidence from case studies (Collins, Gray, and Hadley 2001; Cutler and Horwitz 2000) and broader statistical analyses (Mark 1999; Sloan, Ostermann, and Conover 2003) cast considerable doubt on insider enrichment as the primary motivator for nonprofit conversions, although it still might be important in individual cases. The typical nonprofit hospital converting to for-profit status had been under financial duress for at least several years prior to conversion. Not surprisingly, for-profits converting to nonprofits had also typically been experiencing financial difficulties.

Conversions in the Higher Education Industry

Although conversions in higher education have attracted far less attention than in health care, large numbers have occurred. Table 8.1, column 1, shows the number of conversions each year from 1988 through 2002 (omitting 1999, for which data are unavailable). We tabulate conversions by identifying institutions that change their reported ownership form from one year to the next while retaining the same identification number.[16] Columns 2 through 7 display the pattern of conversions between all six possible pairs of the three ownership forms—from public to nonprofit, from public to for-profit, from nonprofit to public, from nonprofit to for-profit, from for-profit to public, and from for-profit to nonprofit. There are significant numbers of conversions in every direction—a pattern similar to that in the hospital industry. Of particular note is that 36 percent of all conversions were to the for-profit form from either public or private nonprofit schools.[17] These conversions pose the greatest potential problems, reflecting the transfer of assets out of organizations subject to a nondistribution constraint. At the same time, an even larger number of schools have converted away from the for-profit form.

The large majority of post-secondary schools that have converted to for-profit were two-year schools, such as career academies or "trade schools." Many conversions, however, have involved four-year, degree-granting colleges or professional schools, and all ownership types:

- *From public to private nonprofit:* In 1988, the public Nova University, in Ft. Lauderdale, Florida, converted to a private nonprofit, as did the Martin Luther King, Jr., Charles R. Drew Medical Center, in Los Angeles.
- *From public to for-profit:* In 1990, Southern Ohio College, a two-year public institution in Fort Mitchell, Kentucky, converted to for-profit ownership. We find no evidence, however, of a four-year school conversion of this type.
- *From nonprofit to for-profit:* In 1992, the nonprofit Walden University, in Naples, Florida, converted to a for-profit university. In 2004, the nonprofit Grand Canyon University, a self-described Christian school in Phoenix, Arizona, became a for-profit school.
- *From nonprofit to public:* In 2001, the nonprofit University of Pittsburgh Medical Center converted to a public organization.
- *From for-profit to nonprofit:* In 1995, the for-profit John Marshall Law School, in Chicago, converted to a nonprofit.
- *From for-profit to public:* Si Tanka Huron University, in Huron, South Dakota, converted in 2001, as did Sanford-Brown College, in Fenton, Missouri, in 2003.

(continued next page)

Conversions (cont.)

Higher education clearly offers another laboratory for studying the conditions under which conversions occur and their economic and social consequences.[18]

The basic issues in higher education conversions are the same as in health care conversions. A for-profit school converting to a non-profit is accepting a constraint on its freedom to distribute profits to its owners in return for the subsidies and tax exemptions available to nonprofits. A nonprofit struggling financially may find conversion to for-profit status opens new doors to investment funds from stock sale. This, together with strengthened incentives for cost-cutting and revenue-enhancing innovation, may help the organization survive. But questions arise about improper financial gains and the former nonprofit's mission to provide such public goods as basic research and scholarship aid for deserving but poor students—analogous to hospitals' charity care. Issues regarding change of mission were controversial in the 2004 conversion of the Grand Canyon University from nonprofit to for-profit status. The new owners saved the finan-cially failing school and promised to sustain its Christian mission (Broida 2004), but whether the new private ownership, cost cutting, faculty firings, and massive enrollment increase are consistent with the former tax-exempt organization's mission remains unclear.

Table 8.1. Conversions of Ownership Form, Post-secondary Schools in the U.S., 1988–2002

Year	All Conversions (1)	Public to Nonprofit (2)	Public to For-profit (3)	Nonprofit to Public (4)	Nonprofit to For-profit (5)	For-profit to Public (6)	For-profit to Nonprofit (7)
1988	162	13	34	9	43	8	55
1989	123	9	33	4	30	18	29
1990	172	14	24	16	51	17	50
1991	191	23	38	9	50	24	47
1992	334	32	87	12	98	21	84
1993	179	24	48	9	38	19	41
1994	190	20	56	10	40	12	52
1995	86	10	25	6	15	11	19
1996	588	14	37	97	30	369	41
1997	94	4	18	9	18	27	18
1998	68	9	12	6	12	10	19
2000	111	9	13	8	33	19	29
2001	82	6	5	6	26	7	32
2002	83	6	11	6	21	12	27
All years	2,463	193	441	207	505	574	543

Source: Burton A. Weisbrod, Jeffrey Ballou, and Evelyn Asch, "Commercializa-tion of Higher Education," research in progress, utilizing data from the U.S. National Center for Education Statistics, Integrated Postsecondary Education Data System (IPEDS)

APPROPRIATE PUBLIC POLICY: GUIDING THE INVISIBLE HAND

When is Conversion Socially Desirable?

The conversion of a nonprofit clearly can be financially advantageous to the buyers and the managers representing the sellers. Less clear are the conditions under which a conversion is socially beneficial. From the point of view of a conventional benefit–cost analysis, a conversion is desirable if it leads to a higher social value of production. Social value is ordinarily thought of as the aggregate of what society members are willing to pay for what the organization produces (Haveman and Weisbrod 1975). Such an analysis attempts to set aside issues of equitable distribution, that is, of whether the gains and losses from a change are distributed fairly. This division between efficiency issues—or maximizing social value—and equity issues, while often not fully tenable, has proven highly useful in organizing thought about the consequences of economic changes.

Conversions can have consequences for both efficiency and equity, affecting resource allocation and output distribution; so, whether concerned citizens and policymakers will regard a particular conversion as desirable depends on both effects. Efficiency issues are easier to analyze. Analysts are generally less comfortable making strong value judgements about "equity" because there is no widely shared definition of what the term implies. We offer the following principle, however, which encompasses both efficiency and equity considerations. *To warrant regulatory approval, a conversion should make all affected parties better off, or at least none worse off, compared with what would happen if the conversion did not occur.* In economic jargon, conversions should be "Pareto-improving."

We recognize that Pareto improvements are, in practice, hard to come by. In almost any organizational restructuring, even without a conversion, some managers and workers lose while others gain. We do not mean to treat each individual associated with a nonprofit as a distinct affected party. In invoking the Pareto principle, we emphasize not only that a conversion should create net social gains, but that it should not harm the beneficiary groups that constitute the nonprofit's mission—for example, the medically indigent in the case of a hospital. Our principle is in keeping with the common law doctrine of cy pres, which requires that the assets of a converting charitable nonprofit be dedicated to purposes as close as possible to those for which the nonprofit was originally set up.

Notice that the Pareto-improvement principle does not preclude private gain for individuals who organize the conversion; in a free enterprise economy, the pursuit of private gain is an essential driving force motivating growth and efficient change. A Pareto improvement requires only that other groups also gain in the process. Indeed, it is desirable that those who control a nonprofit's assets seek out Pareto-improving conversions and respond favorably when such opportunities arise. A useful, though not necessarily essential, mechanism is one in which nonprofit officers share in the greater price that they negotiate for the sale of the organization—thereby encouraging an efficient principal–agent relationship. MPR, for example, apparently provided its executives with an incentive to build up the profitability and hence the sales value of the for-profit subsidiary, and maximize the sales price. While such incentives always have the potential to go too far, their total absence would lead to lost opportunities for social gains.

The Pareto improvement concept should be interpreted in a forward-looking way. The relevant consideration is not, for example, the charity care a nonprofit clinic has provided in the past, but what it can give in the future should it remain a nonprofit. External forces, such as decreased government grants or private donations, could cause such prospects to change.

Turning to the efficiency question, can the conversion of a nonprofit to a for-profit ever increase social value? A "no" answer is difficult to defend. Because private ownership and control of assets provide stronger incentives for minimizing costs and responding to consumer demands, and perhaps greater flexibility associated with access to equity capital, the same resources may often produce greater value in the for-profit than the nonprofit sector. If this were not the case, for-profits would not be the primary form of organization in most industries.

The root issue involves a central question confronting researchers who study the nonprofit sector: do nonprofits and for-profits operating in the same industry behave differently, and if they do, in what ways? If they do not, conversions should have few efficiency consequences, and the key issues are all distributional. But if organization form does influence behavior, then a change of form may lead the surviving organization to act differently, which could influence efficiency in either direction. It might enhance efficiency, as already noted, through the stronger incentives for efficient production coming from private ownership and the flexibility associated with access to equity financing. Alternatively, it could reduce social value because the increased emphasis on what is privately profitable can lead to neglecting services valued collectively but difficult to sell profitably—for example, indigent care in hospitals, basic research at universities, and cultural and species preservation activities by museums and zoos.

As an empirical matter, we submit that because of measurement difficulties, the nature and extent of differences between nonprofits and for-profits remains an open question, with both systematic differences and similarities found in many industries (Weisbrod 2005). Direct measurement of outputs and their differences across institutional forms is difficult. In part, this difficulty reflects the problems of measuring outputs in the social service sector, where most nonprofits operate. In part, it also reflects the complexity and subtlety of the outputs society expects from nonprofits. As with governmentally provided outputs, nonprofits are typically utilized precisely in markets where private enterprise is least promising—where, for example, "tender loving care" in nursing homes and day care centers is difficult for consumers to monitor; where the presence, and value, of aid to the poor is similarly hard to monitor; and where, in general, consumers are asymmetrically underinformed relative to providers. In such markets, nonprofits often supplement governmental services, as consumers are skeptical of the unbridled incentives of profit-oriented firms.

Even in the case of hospitals, where the question has been most extensively studied and the differences in legal and regulatory constraints between nonprofits and for-profits seem relatively small, evidence is insufficient to reject the possibility of subtle but important differences between nonprofit and for-profit behavior (see, however, Sloan 1998 for a survey that emphasizes evidence of similarity between for-profit and nonprofit hospitals in the provision of services to the poor). Indirect indicators of comparative institutional behavior in various industries have sometimes shown substantial differences. Among nursing homes, nonprofits often have lower prices, higher staff–patient levels, higher patient satisfaction, and longer waiting lists (Weisbrod 1998). Among hospitals, CEOs in for-profits receive a substantially greater share of their compensation as performance-based bonuses and receive substantially greater overall compensation (Roomkin and Weisbrod 1999). Among day care centers, nonprofits have been found to have higher ratios of staff to children and better-educated staff (Mauser 1993). A recent review of over 250 published empirical studies comparing for-profit and nonprofit performance in health care concludes that there is a good deal of evidence of differences in performance (Schlesinger and Gray 2005).

Competitive Bidding

If a nonprofit is to be sold to a for-profit buyer, how *should* the price be determined? An obvious suggestion is to open the process for bids and sell to the highest bidder (presuming selling is appropriate, a key issue discussed below), but this approach is not without problems. The process can be costly and time-consuming (Schaeffer 1996), and is less straightforward than it appears. Consider the ambiguity of precisely what is to be transferred from the nonprofit to the for-profit purchaser. A sale would naturally include the items that appear on the organization's balance sheet, its assets and financial liabilities. But what of the organization's obligation, which may be more or less formal, to provide collective goods—those valued by the community but not profitably sold in the market? Suppose a nonprofit hospital has been providing charity care for poor and uninsured patients, basic scientific research, medical training, or community health education. Suppose also that this hospital is considering a sale to a private, for-profit hospital chain. Would a sale require the new owner to provide those services at the same level? Clearly, the value of the nonprofit to the for-profit firm would be greater if that obligation could be avoided, so comparing offers solely on price would not be appropriate if they differ in the dimension of commitment to charity care or other public service outputs. Conversion agreements now frequently specify that the for-profit buyer will provide the same level of charity care as the former nonprofit hospital (Claxton et al. 1997). A central problem with such a contract, however, is the difficulty of defining, monitoring, and enforcing the agreement, especially over time. The precise measure of "charity care" for example, is by no means clear, nor are the measures of "basic research" or "community education."

If competitive bidding is to be used, defining terms carefully and ensuring that offers being compared are truly comparable is thus important. This point is one argument for preferring "complete" conversions to partial ones in which, for example, a formerly nonprofit hospital becomes a joint venture between a for-profit and a successor to the nonprofit. Different suitors will undoubtedly prefer different terms for a joint venture deal, making offers difficult to compare. HCA has participated in joint ventures in which it receives, in addition to its ownership share, a fee for managing the new organization. Clearly, a higher management fee increases the price HCA would willingly pay for its share of the joint venture. Such issues exist whether the selling price is determined by a bidding process or by an investment banking firm that attempts, on the basis of its knowledge and experience, to estimate what a competitive bidding process would generate.

For these reasons, the nonprofit's decisionmakers—formally and legally the board of trustees—should have flexibility to choose among bids and not necessarily accept the highest. Even in the context of a complete conversion or outright sale, difficulties of specifying all the relevant terms of the contract should not be underestimated. Another reason that the highest bid may not be the best is the social interest in maintaining competitive pricing in product markets. In a community with just two hospitals, hospital A may be in a position to offer the highest bid for hospital B because the combined hospitals could engage in monopoly pricing, an advantage that other potential buyers of hospital B would not have. A's advantage does not come from an ability to use resources more efficiently, but from being better positioned to extract payment from consumers. In this case, antitrust considerations might rule out hospital A as a potential buyer, but the issue can exist in less extreme circumstances.

Can a regulator scrutinize a proposed conversion to determine whether it is efficient? The regulator may be able to approximate the surplus generated in the for-profit sector by taking the offered sale price and adding expected taxes and any losses (marginal revenue minus marginal cost) the for-profit is expected to generate on any collective goods obligations it has agreed to take on. The last element assumes that the social value of those community obligations is equal to their cost of production. That assumption is reasonable if society's best alternative is to purchase these services at cost from that vendor or another whose costs would be similar.[20] The more difficult problem for the regulator is to estimate the social surplus generated if the firm continues to operate as a nonprofit. Valuing the collective goods a nonprofit produces is particularly difficult. Market values are not directly relevant, though in some cases regulators can draw inferences from them.[21] Decisionmakers at the nonprofit are likely to be better informed about the organization's future possibilities than a regulator would be. While they may better understand their organization's collective good outputs, they may not know how the rest of society values these goods. Thus, they will more likely overestimate value than understate it, creating another bias against conversions.

The analysis in this section relied on an assumption that private gain does not motivate nonprofit decisionmakers. However, we highlighted earlier the bias of nonprofits toward conversion growing from the potential for private gain. There is still considerable danger of inefficient conversions that produce private gains but social losses (and unfairly redistribute wealth) without careful, but expensive, regulatory scrutiny. The social policy challenge is how best to provide an incentive for managers and trustees to seek efficient conversions, while guarding against inefficient and inequitable transfers of wealth. This is an important and complex question that merits further attention.

Comparing Value as Nonprofit and For-Profit

From an efficiency perspective, an organization should convert if the net present value of the services it could produce with its current assets (tangible and intangible) is higher as a for-profit than as a nonprofit. By *net* present value, we mean net of the opportunity costs of *other* resources (labor, new capital and other productive inputs) that the organization will employ to produce output. Ideally, the organization should choose the sector in which

$$\text{(value of services produced)} - \text{(costs of additional resources used)} \quad (1)$$

is maximized. (In the expression above and those that follow, flows that continue over time should be converted to present values.) Conversions for which (1) is higher in the for-profit sector are at least potentially Pareto-improving because, in principle, the "surplus" value could be used to compensate groups that would otherwise lose, and thus make everyone better off. How close are the decisionmakers in a nonprofit likely to apply this rule in their own considerations about conversion?

A nonprofit considering conversion, if motivated by service to its constituents rather than the private gain of its decisionmakers (clearly a key assumption, the validity of which depends in part on the regulatory environment surrounding conversions), would compare the surplus it generates *for its "constituents"* if it continues to operate as a nonprofit with what it would generate if it converted (sold to a for-profit). By constituents, we mean anyone who benefits from the services the organization provides, including paying customers and anyone benefiting indirectly from collective goods.[19] Organizational survival, while perhaps important for the management and employees of the nonprofit, is not, in itself, a social goal. The surplus for constituents from continuing to operate as a nonprofit is

$$\text{(value of services produced)} - \text{(revenue from sales)} \quad (2a)$$

The difference between expression (2a) and the socially relevant expression (1) is that we have assumed that the nonprofit counts only the costs its constituents bear, which we have equated with its revenues from sales.

If the nonprofit sells to a for-profit, the surplus that can serve its constituents is

$$\text{(sales price)} + \text{(value of services produced)} - \text{(revenue from sales)} \quad (2b)$$

This expression captures the idea that the proceeds of the sale can also serve the constituents of the old nonprofit. Because the converted

(continued next page)

Comparing Values *(cont.)*

firm may behave differently than if it had not converted, future services and sales revenues will likely take different values in expression (2b) than in expression (2a). However, if the for-profit agrees to subsidize certain services, it may continue to provide some surplus value to constituents of the nonprofit who value those services.

If we make some additional assumptions, we can arrive at expressions more directly comparable to the efficiency criterion of expression (1). In the long run, a nonprofit must generate sufficient revenue—through sales, government subsidies, and donations—to cover the payments it makes to obtain resources. If we assume that the payments it makes for resources equal their opportunity costs, then (2a) can be rewritten as

$$\begin{array}{r} \text{(value of services produced)} \\ - \text{ (costs of additional resources used)} \\ + \text{ (subsidies and donations)} \qquad \text{(3a)} \end{array}$$

Our treatment of donations in this analysis warrants some comment. Clearly, nonprofits use donations—as well as government subsidies—to support the provision of services, substituting for other sources of revenue, as expression (3a) implies. From a social perspective, donations to a specific organization are not costless, for they displace either donations to another organization or another form of spending of value to the donor. Our analysis assumes that the nonprofit does not consider these opportunity costs of donations in making its decisions.

The most a for-profit should be willing to bid to obtain the nonprofit's assets is the future revenue it expects to generate minus the costs of additional resources and the taxes it will need to pay. In a competitive bidding process, the sale price offered for the nonprofit should approach the maximum any bidder is willing to pay. Making the simplifying assumption that sales price equals maximum bid, we may rewrite (2b) as

$$\begin{array}{r} \text{(value of services produced)} \\ - \text{ (costs of additional resources used)} - \text{ taxes} \qquad \text{(3b)} \end{array}$$

Comparing (1), (3a), and (3b), we see that if the nonprofit's decisionmakers value services in the same way that society does (aggregate willingness-to-pay) but do not treat subsidized or donated inputs as costs, or value the taxes that a for-profit pays, there would be some bias *against* efficient conversions. That is, the prospect of lost subsidies and donations and increased taxes could deter an organization from converting even when doing so would increase social value. It follows that the smaller the difference in tax treatment between the two sectors and the lower the nonprofit's expectations are about future donations, the closer its incentives to convert are to unbiased.

CONCLUSION: WHICH INDUSTRY IS NEXT?

A nonprofit conversion will only occur if two conditions are met: the nonprofit's decisionmakers request it *and* the public regulators approve. The relatively intense burst of conversion activity in HMOs, Blue Cross plans, and hospitals could, therefore, have come from an increase in nonprofits' desire to convert, from regulators' willingness to approve conversions, or from some combination of the two. This chapter identified two main types of motivation a nonprofit might have for conversion: (1) a perception of *social* benefit—a decision that its mission is now better served by reorganizing as a for-profit and passing the value of its assets to a new charitable organization, and (2) *private* benefit to executives and board members without commensurate social gains. As external circumstances change, the first motivation may arise at about the same time for many similarly situated organizations, such as occurred in the health care market.

The private gain motive is clearly much stronger for a wealthy organization than for, say, a small neighborhood day care center struggling to stay afloat. Consider a major art museum that, through donations, has amassed collections worth hundreds of millions of dollars. If its managers could arrange to purchase it at a price well below its true value and begin selling paintings, they could benefit enormously at public expense. Arguably, something like this happened in the early HMO conversions. So why did Health Net convert but not the Art Institute of Chicago?

We hypothesize, first, that other things being equal, a nonprofit is more likely to *propose* a conversion when the potential for private gain is greater, and this depends on the organization's wealth. Second, the probability of regulatory *approval* depends on how effectively the case can be made that a conversion would be socially efficient. The case is easier to make the greater the extent to which the industry is one in which nonprofits already compete with for-profits; the stronger the evidence that because of changing circumstances, the for-profits are enjoying increasing success; and the greater the public acceptance of the proposition that the industry's output, at least in the geographic region involved, should not be contracted. Resistance to the idea of for-profit ownership, especially of a failing nonprofit, is then likely to be weaker, and the organization may be able to credibly claim that conversion is necessary for its survival. The greater the informational advantage the nonprofit insiders have over the regulators in assessing the value of the nonprofit, the greater their opportunity for arranging a conversion in a way that benefits them privately. Such an advantage will be greater in a fast-growing industry in which the value of an organization is changing rapidly, as are the relative advantages of the nonprofit and for-profit forms. That scenario much better describes the HMO industry in the 1980s and early 1990s than the world of art museums or higher education, where massive wealth also provides fertile ground for private gain.

Regulators, of course, should learn to be wary of insiders' claims of the social virtue of conversion to for-profit. It may be that regulators were "asleep" during early HMO conversions, but increasing public attention to the issue will make appropriating public assets through conversion more difficult for nonprofit insiders (or savvy for-profit buyers). By underscoring regulators' watchdog role, we do not mean to imply that top managers and trustees of nonprofits are generally self-serving and unconcerned with the public's interest. Nonetheless, understanding the incentives confronting those leaders to balance public and private interests is important.

Aside from attempts to subvert the nondistribution constraint, upon which regulators can be expected to cast an increasingly wary eye, we expect more interest in conversions in industries where changes have occurred that reduce advantages that nonprofits formerly held while increasing the apparent advantages of the for-profit form—access to equity capital being the most obvious one. Growth in the for-profit market share in an industry—through new entrants and the growth of existing for-profits—may indicate that some nonprofits will think about conversion. In this regard, higher education is an industry worth watching.

Although still a small segment of the entire industry, for-profit higher education appears to be growing rapidly. Between 1980 and 2003, the percentage of all undergraduates at institutions of higher education offering at least a four-year degree who were enrolled in for-profit schools increased from 1.0 percent to 4.7 percent.[22] Echoing arguments heard in the health care industry for some time, for-profit higher education firms claim that their access to equity capital allows them to respond more quickly to changing demand (Strosnider 1998).

The for-profit University of Phoenix is establishing new campuses around the country and advertising low tuition made possible by disdaining the collective good, research, and promising only the private good, coursework for paying consumers. A plausible speculation is that colleges will find, as many nonprofit hospitals have already found, that competition from for-profit firms will force prices—in this case, tuition—down to levels that will increasingly constrain colleges' ability to finance research and offer student financial aid that displaces full-pay students. Nonprofit colleges not among the elite schools could be placed in the competitive position of either converting to a for-profit—in order to obtain access to capital to finance expansion and take advantage of scale economies in marketing and, perhaps, production—or restricting expenditures on student aid or on other programs as tuition revenue falls. Maintenance of tuition levels under increased competition from for-profits would be a recipe for failure, as student clientele might wither away. That scenario, while highly speculative, provides food for thought as we consider whether another industry will join hospitals and HMOs in the conversion derby.

NOTES

1. Like some other BCBS plans, the Georgia plan could argue that it was organized as a mutual company—that is, for the benefit of its policyholders—and had no charitable obligation.

2. James P. Miller, "Blue Cross Missouri Agrees to Settle Legal Fight on Creating For-Profit Unit," *Wall Street Journal*, April 23, 1998, B2.

3. Josh Benson, "When Will the State Cash In on Horizon?" *New York Times*, June 19, 2005, 14NJ.

4. A case in point involved the nonprofit Bennington College (Galper and Toder 1983). The college sold its buildings to a private firm and then leased the buildings back. This changed nothing in the way the buildings were used but was advantageous to both parties because of differences in their liability for taxes. Congress later removed the tax advantage from this particular maneuver.

5. Judith Burns and Lucette Lagnado, "IRS Rules Threaten Alliances Made by For-Profit and Nonprofit Hospitals," *Wall Street Journal*, March 5, 1998, A2-3.

6. Jeff Gottlieb, "Courtroom Drama Ahead for KOCE?" *Los Angeles Times*, July 10, 2005, B3.

7. Such a set of objectives has been hypothesized and termed "bonoficing" (Weisbrod 1988).

8. Jeffrey H. Birnbaum, "Charity That Delivers Surplus Food to Needy Is Split by Accusations," *Wall Street Journal*, October 25, 1982, A1, A20.

9. The nondistribution constraint could be a crucial one even for a new firm if it is important that the firm be able to attract investment capital, and if equity capital is more easily obtained than alternative sources of funds, such as loans or donations (Robinson 2000).

10. Its ability to borrow in the bond market may also improve even if it remained a nonprofit. The key issue is the changing relative attractiveness of debt and equity finance.

11. Hospital conversions among nonprofit, for-profit, and publicly-owned institutions occur in all directions (Ferris and Graddy 1996; Needleman, Chollet, and Lamphere 1997; Sloan, Ostermann and Conover 2003). Sloan and colleagues find, for example, that between 1986 and 1996, 148 for-profit hospitals converted either to non-profit or public institutions.

12. The March/April 1997 issue of *Health Affairs*, devoted to hospital and health plan conversions, is a good source of additional discussion.

13. A few illustrative examples, of many that could be cited, of the emphasis placed on access to equity capital: Leonard Schaeffer, then of Group Health of Minnesota, "In order to [protect our traditional markets and expand to new markets], we must have large amounts of capital. Capital markets are only interested in for-profit entities" (Iglehart 1984); Norwood Davis of Virginia

Blue Cross and Blue Shield, "We want the same access to the capital market as the other players" (Milt Freudenheim, "Blue Cross Lets Plans Sell Stock," *New York Times*, June 30, 1994); Michael Stocker of Empire Blue Cross of New York, "We have to have the potential to raise capital. . . . We can't raise it as a not-for-profit" (Milt Freudenheim, "As Blue Cross Plans Seek Profit, States Ask for a Share of the Riches," *New York Times*, March 25, 1996).

14. Milt Freudenheim, "WellPoint' Blue Period May Be Over," *New York Times*, September 28, 2005, C1.

15. The issue of improper enrichment emerged again as a key reason for the recent denial of CareFirst's proposed conversion. The Maryland insurance commissioner wrote, "The initial attempt by corporate officers to take over $68 million [of the value of CareFirst] for themselves as part of the original Proposed Transaction was, and is, outrageous" (Larsen 2003).

16. We therefore very likely miss some conversions—for example, those where a school is purchased by an institution of a different ownership type and ceases to exist as an independent entity.

17. These data were developed from information in IPEDS as part of an ongoing study of "Commercialization of Higher Education." A book on that work is in progress, coauthored by Burton Weisbrod, Jeffrey Ballou, and Evelyn Asch, who thank John Parman for his research assistance.

18. Undoubtedly, there is also growing involvement of public and nonprofit universities and colleges in joint ventures with for-profit firms that do not rise to the level of a total change in organizational form.

19. One element of value that may exist only as long as the firm remains a nonprofit is any special contribution of nonprofits to civil society, emphasized elsewhere in this book.

20. A case in point is a for-profit hospital that agrees to support some level of indigent care for which marginal cost exceeds revenue. If the relevant alternative is for government to purchase that care at cost from the same hospital, the social value of taking on the obligation is the same as the present value of the government spending that it replaces.

21. For example, as noted with regard to community obligations for-profits take on, if a service, such as indigent care, can be purchased from another vendor, the purchase price provides at least an upper bound on its value.

22. Integrated Postsecondary Education Data System (IPEDS), accessed at http://nces.ed.gov/ipedspas on February 8, 2006, using the data set cutting tool (DCT), described at http://nces.ed.govipedspas/dct/intro.asp.

REFERENCES

American Hospital Association. 2005. *Hospital Statistics*. Chicago: Healthcare InfoSource.

Broida, Bethany. 2004. "Private Firm Buys Grand Canyon U." *Chronicle of Higher Education* 50(24): A27.

Butler, Patricia. 1997. "State Policy Issues in Nonprofit Conversions." *Health Affairs* 16(2): 69–84.

Chaddad, Fabio R., and Michael L. Cook. 2004. "The Economics of Organization Structure Changes: A U.S. Perspective on Demutualization." *Annals of Public and Cooperative Economics* 75(4): 575–94.

Claxton, Gary, Judith Feder, David Shactman, and Stuart Altman. 1997. "Public Policy Issues in Nonprofit Conversions: An Overview." *Health Affairs* 16(2): 9–28.

Collins, Sara R., Bradford H. Gray, and Jack Hadley. 2001. "The For-Profit Conversion of Nonprofit Hospitals in the U.S. Health Care System: Eight Case Studies." New York: The Commonwealth Fund. http://www.cmwf. org/usr_doc/collins_convstudies_455.pdf.

Community Catalyst, Inc. 2003. "Conversions: A Compendium of State Laws." Boston: Community Catalyst. http://www.communitycatalyst. org/resource.php?doc_id = 191.

Conover, Christopher J., Mark A. Hall, and Jan Ostermann. 2005. "The Impact of Blue Cross Conversions on Health Spending and the Uninsured." *Health Affairs* 24(2): 473–82.

Cordes, Joseph J., and Burton A. Weisbrod. 1998. "Differential Taxation of Nonprofits and the Commercialization of Nonprofit Revenues." In *To Profit or Not to Profit: The Commercial Transformation of the Nonprofit Sector*, edited by Burton A. Weisbrod (83–104). New York: Cambridge University Press.

Coye, Molly J. 1997. "The Sale of Good Samaritan: A View from the Trenches." *Health Affairs* 16(2): 102–7.

Cutler, David M., and Jill R. Horwitz. 2000 "Converting Hospitals from Not-for-Profit to For-Profit Status." In *The Changing Hospital Industry: Comparing Not-for-Profit and For-Profit Institutions*, edited by David M Cutler (45–79). Chicago: University of Chicago Press.

Davis, Roger L., and Alexandra Davis. 2002. *Nonprofit Corporations: Borrowing with Tax-Exempt Bonds*. San Francisco: Orrick, Herrington & Sutcliffe. http://www.orrick.com/fileupload/172.pdf.

Ferris, James M., and Elizabeth A. Graddy. 1996. "Structural Changes in the Hospital Industry and the Nonprofit Role in Health Care." In *Nonprofit Organizations as Public Actors*, edited by Astrid Merget, Ed Weaver, and Virginia Hodgkinson. San Francisco: Jossey-Bass.

Fox, Daniel M., and Phillip Isenberg. 1996. "Anticipating the Magic Moment: The Public Interest in Health Plan Conversions in California." *Health Affairs* 15(1): 202–9.

Galloro, Vince. 2003. "Advantage: For-Profits." *Modern Healthcare* 33(11): 52.

Galper, Harvey, and Eric Toder. 1983. "Owning or Leasing: Bennington College and the U.S. Tax System." *National Tax Journal* 36: 257–61.

Goddeeris, John H. 1988. "Compensating Differentials and Self-Selection: An Application to Lawyers." *Journal of Political Economy* 96:411–28.

Hall, Mark A., and Christopher J. Conover. 2003. "The Impact of Blue Cross Conversions on Accessibility, Affordability, and the Public Interest." *Milbank Quarterly* 81(4): 509–42.

Hamburger, Eleanor, Jeanne Finberg, Leticia Alcantar. 1995. "The Pot of Gold: Monitoring Health Care Conversions Can Yield Billions of Dollars for Health Care." *Clearinghouse Review* (August–September): 473–504.

Hansmann, Henry. 1980. "The Role of Nonprofit Enterprise." *Yale Law Journal* 89(5): 835–901.

———. 1987. "The Effect of Tax Exemption and Other Factors on the Market Share of Nonprofit versus For-Profit Firms." *National Tax Journal* 40:71–82.

———. 1996. *The Ownership of Enterprise*. Cambridge, MA: Belknap.

Haveman, Robert H., and Burton A. Weisbrod. 1975. "Defining Benefits of Public Programs: Some Guidance for Policy Analysts." *Policy Analysis* 2:169–96.

Hollis, Stephen R. 1997. "Strategic and Economic Factors in the Hospital Conversion Process." *Health Affairs* 16(2): 131–43.

Horwitz, Jill R., and Marion R. Fremont-Smith. 2005. "The Common Law of the Legislature: Insurer Conversions and Charitable Funds." *The Milbank Quarterly* 83(2): 225–46.

Iglehart, John K. 1984. "HMOs (For-Profit and Not-For-Profit) on the Move." *New England Journal of Medicine* 310: 1,203–8.

———. 1995. "Inside California's HMO Market: A Conversation with Leonard D. Schaeffer." *Health Affairs* 14(4): 131–42.

Johnson, Susan R. 2003. "Nonprofit Health Insurers: The Story Wall Street Doesn't Tell." *Inquiry* 40(4): 318–22.

Larsen, Stephen B. 2003. "Report of the Maryland Insurance Administration Regarding the Proposed Conversion of CareFirst Inc. to For-Profit Status and Acquisition by WellPoint Health Networks, Inc." Baltimore: Maryland Insurance Administration. http://www.mdinsurance.state.md.us/documents/FinalMIAReport-CareFirst3-5-03.pdf.

Leone, Andrew J., R. Lawrence Van Horn, and Gerard J. Wedig. 2005. "Abnormal Returns and the Regulation of Nonprofit Hospital Sales and Conversions." *Journal of Health Economics* 24(1): 113–35.

Marchetti, Domenica. 1997. "Georgia Charities Sue to Recover Millions in Blue Cross Deal." *Chronicle of Philanthropy* 9: 36.

Mark, Tami L. 1999. "Analysis of the Rationale for, and Consequences of, Nonprofit and For-Profit Ownership Conversions." *Health Services Research* 34(1): 83–101.

Mauser. Elizabeth. 1993. "Comparative Institutional Behavior: The Case of Day Care." Ph.D. diss. Madison: University of Wisconsin.

Needleman, Jack, Deborah Chollet, and JoAnn Lamphere. 1997. "Hospital Conversion Trends." *Health Affairs* 16(2): 187–95.

Preston, Anne E. 1989. "The Nonprofit Worker in a For-Profit World," *Journal of Labor Economics* 7:438–63.

Roomkin, Myron, and Burton A. Weisbrod. 1999. "Managerial Compensation and Incentives in For-Profit and Nonprofit Hospitals." *Journal of Law, Economics, and Organization* 15(2): 740–81.

Robinson, James C. 2000. "Capital Finance and Ownership Conversions in Health Care." *Health Affairs* 19(1): 56–71.

———. 2003. "The Curious Conversion of Empire Blue Cross." *Health Affairs* 22(4): 100–18.

Schaeffer, Leonard D. 1996. "Health Plan Conversions: The View from Blue Cross of California." *Health Affairs* 15(4): 183–87.

Schlesinger, Mark, and Bradford H. Gray. 2005. "Why Nonprofits Matter in American Medicine: A Policy Brief." Nonprofit Sector Research Fund Working Paper Series Washington, DC: Aspen Institute. http://www.nonprofitresearch.org/usr_doc/final_hc_brief_8_15_05.pdf.

Shriber, Donald. 1997. "State Experience in Regulating a Changing Health Care System." *Health Affairs* 16(2): 48–68.

Sloan, Frank A. 1998. "Commercialism in Nonprofit Hospitals." In *To Profit or Not to Profit: The Commercial Transformation of the Nonprofit Sector*, edited by Burton A. Weisbrod (151–68). New York: Cambridge University Press.

Sloan, Frank A., Jan Ostermann, and Christopher J. Conover. 2003. "Antecedents of Hospital Ownership Conversions, Mergers, and Closures." *Inquiry* 40(1): 39–56.

Strosnider, Kim. 1998. "For-Profit Higher Education Sees Booming Enrollments and Revenues." *The Chronicle of Higher Education*, January 23.

Volunteer Trustees Foundation for Research and Education. 1998. "The Sale and Conversion of Not-For-Profit Hospitals: A State-By-State Analysis of New Legislation." Washington, DC: Volunteer Trustees Foundation for Research and Education. http://www.volunteertrustees.org/hospitals/hospitals_toc.html

Weisbrod, Burton A. 1988. *The Nonprofit Economy.* Cambridge, MA: Harvard University Press.

———. 1997. "The Future of the Nonprofit Sector: Its Entwining with Private Enterprise and Government." *Journal of Policy Analysis and Management* 16(4): 541–55.

———. 1998. "Institutional Form and Organizational Behavior." In *Private Action and the Public Good,* edited by Walter W. Powell and Elisabeth Clemens (69–84). New Haven, CT: Yale University Press.

———. 2004. "The Pitfalls of Nonprofits." *Stanford Social Innovation Review* 2(3): 40–47.

———. 2005. "Why Private Firms, Governmental Agencies, and Nonprofit Organizations Behave Both Alike and Differently: Application to the Hospital Industry." Working Paper. Evanston, IL: Northwestern University, Department of Economics.

Whitehead, Roy, Clint Johnson, and Michael Moore. 1997. "Avoiding State Intervention in Not-for-Profit/For-Profit Affiliations." *Health Care Financial Management* 51(12): 56–62.

9

CLASH OF VALUES: GOVERNMENT FUNDING FOR THE ARTS AND RELIGION

Robert Wuthnow

Two recent episodes of government funding for nonprofit organizations have raised competing concerns among leaders of nonprofit organizations and government agencies, as well as in the public, that basic values were being violated. The first emerged in the early 1990s as cultural conservatives mobilized against the National Endowment for the Arts (NEA) and succeeded in sharply reducing its appropriations. The second occurred more recently as initiatives to expand government funding of faith-based service organizations generated support from some segments of government and the population and opposition from others. In both instances, the resulting controversies involved deep questions about the responsibilities of government, the role of nonprofit organizations, and trade-offs among the values being served. Many existing theories of nonprofit organizations focus on the gains and costs from various mixtures of government and private funding but do not give sufficient consideration to the concerns of taxpayers and public officials when they feel their values are under attack. This chapter examines the NEA controversies and faith-based initiatives with the aim of shedding light on the role of values in determining policies toward nonprofit organizations and identifying a number of issues requiring consideration by policymakers and non-profit administrators. Although it is easy to imagine that controversies involving basic societal values are regrettable, I argue that public discussion of these values is actually one of the significant ways in which their importance is reinforced.

CLASH OF VALUES

For some time, social observers have written about a clash of values or "culture war" that sharply divides the American public along political and religious lines (e.g., Bolton 1992; Hunter 1991, 1994; Nolan 1996; Williams 1997). The language of bellicosity is probably overstated. As critics of the culture wars thesis have argued, a sizable share of the American public identifies with neither the extreme right nor the extreme left and shares common values, including the value of tolerance, and is no more divided on some issues than was true in the 1970s (DiMaggio, Evans, and Bryson 1996; Evans 1996; Fiorina 2004; Wolfe 1999; Wuthnow 1996a). Nevertheless, the fact that activists have mobilized on different sides of a range of issues, from abortion to gay marriage to free trade agreements, is indisputable, and by some indications is reflected in public opinion polls and in the voting patterns that separate "red" and "blue" states (Baker 2004; Greenberg 2004; White 2002). The current conflict is sometimes characterized as a clash between liberal and conservative world views—the first favoring tolerance, diversity of opinion, and a more relativistic orientation toward values, and the other emphasizing conformity to absolute values and truths. Whatever the underlying differences, the clash of values surfaces in debates about a variety of public issues, including abortion, homosexuality, prayer in public schools, and the teaching of creationism or evolution.

One arena in which this clash of values bears directly on nonprofit organizations and their relationship with government is the arts. Government funding for nonprofit arts organizations and individuals has evoked reactions from cultural conservatives who felt their tax dollars were being used inappropriately to support exhibits and performances that violated standards of public decency and morality. The debate has focused on questions about the appropriateness of public funds being channeled to local and regional nonprofit arts associations by the NEA, especially when some of these funds were used for artistic projects that dealt with controversial subjects (Dorf 1993; McLeod and MacKenzie 1998; Rice 1997). Critics have also charged that public monies could be better used for social services and for health care. The NEA's supporters have defended the arrangement on the grounds that the arts are not only intrinsically worthwhile but also contribute to the general good in a way that merits support from society as a whole. They also argue that public support for the arts is minuscule compared with national budgets for defense and entitlement programs. Although government funding accounts for only 10 to 15 percent of total funding for the arts (with less than one third of that amount from the NEA), many in the arts community consider NEA support critical because it symbolizes public commitment to the arts and helps to support innovative projects that might not draw the interest of private donors (Americans for the Arts 2002; Scheff and Kotler 1996). The NEA's critics have been especially concerned that taxpayers were being asked to support projects that violated their standards of decency and morality (Adler 1993; Balfe 1993; Bolton 1992). Exhibits of visual art depicting sexual themes or accused of treating religious subject matter in inappropriate ways have been flashpoints for efforts to curb government funding for the arts (Arthurs and Wallach 2001; Brooks 2005).

Social service provision has become another contested arena because of government funding to support nonprofit organizations that are "faith based," thus raising questions about separation of church and state and the free exercise of religion (Black, Koopman, and Ryden 2004; Formicola, Segers, and Weber 2003; Wuthnow 2004). By 1997, the social and legal services subsector of the nonprofit sector had grown to approximately $76 billion in annual revenue, half of which came from government, whereas the health services subsector had annual receipts of $326 billion, of which 41 percent came from government, and if tax subsidies are considered, this proportion would be higher (Hodgkinson and Weitzman 1996; Independent Sector 2001; Salamon 1995; Smith and Lipsky 1993; Wolch 1990). Meanwhile, observers have long recognized religious organizations' potential for serving the needy in their communities. Approximately 6,700 distinct religion-related organizations exist in the United States, receiving a total of $1.7 billion in public support, whereas more than 340,000 congregations that were not eligible for public support took in approximately $58 billion in annual revenue from private sources. The Charitable Choice legislation of the mid-1990s reflected and reinforced debates in Washington and in the wider public about the relative advantages and disadvantages of religious organizations (compared with secular nonprofits and government agencies) being able to express their implicit and explicit values (Bartkowski and Regis 2003; Watt 1991). To some, the growth of secular nonprofits and their increasing levels of support from government put religious organizations at a competitive disadvantage. For others, the autonomy of religious congregations in government funding was a privilege that needed to be protected vigilantly. Government funding of faith-based service providers has been supported, opposed, and debated at many levels, including among public officials, nonprofit administrators, and religious leaders, and in the courts (Greenberg 2000; Kearns 2003; Minow 2003; Sider 2005).

The current clash of values is often interpreted in the popular press as evidence of the growing power of politically conservative evangelical Protestants and traditional Catholics (Green, Rozell, and Wilcox 2003; Kaplan 2004; Linn 2004). In this interpretation, religious conservatives and their allies amassed political influence in recent decades through the efforts of powerful leaders (such as television preachers Jerry Falwell and Pat Robertson) and as a kind of backlash against the liberalizing and egalitarian reforms that began during the civil rights era in the 1960s. This conservative religiopolitical movement is now seeking to impose its distinctive views about morality and public policy on the wider society. It is doing so, on the one hand, by *opposing* government funding for arts projects it finds objectionable and, on the other hand, by *promoting* government funding for faith-based service organizations (Horton 1994; Nolan 1996; Sine 1996). For those who do not agree with this agenda, the upshot is that religious conservatives are the problem, and this problem will go away only if these activists can be debunked, disallowed through litigation from having their way, or defeated during national and local elections. In short, the clash of values is primarily a political issue that calls for opponents of the so-called Christian Right to mobilize themselves more effectively.

Interpreting the current clash of values as a product of religious mobilization is consistent with *some* of the facts of empirical studies. For instance, it is the case that the American public is divided in many of the ways that the culture wars argument suggests: surveys show that public opinion is divided on such specific issues as abortion and school prayer, and that people also identify themselves as, for example, religious and political conservatives or religious and political liberals (Wuthnow 1996b). Studies also show that underlying differences in religious identities and in world views are the ways in which people think about social welfare and their preferences in music and the arts (Bryson 1996; Wuthnow 2003, 2004).

An exclusive focus on the culture war between liberals and conservatives, however, fails to take into consideration the distinctive roles that nonprofit organizations play, both in the arts and in social service provision, and the issues that arise when a growing share of funding for these organizations comes from government. In this chapter, I argue that the clash of values is indeed an important context for understanding the recent controversies about government funding for arts and service organizations, but that we also need to consider basic questions about the relationships between values and the nonprofit sector, as well as questions about the administration of nonprofit organizations. I develop this argument in four parts: first, by showing that theories of the nonprofit sector point to the likelihood of fundamental conflicts about values when government becomes a significant source of funding for the nonprofit sector; second, by tracing the ways in which these conflicts emerged concerning funding for the arts and for faith-based service provision; third, by describing the strategies that nonprofit managers and policymakers have used in the midst of these conflicts; and finally, by suggesting that cultural conflicts, though often viewed negatively, may be *beneficial* for civil society.

THE ROLE OF VALUES IN THEORIES OF THE NONPROFIT SECTOR

Theories of the nonprofit sector hold that values are not just incidental or pertinent in particular cases but are fundamental to how we understand the very existence of the nonprofit sector. According to these theories, the nonprofit sector is inherently different from the public or governmental sector and from the market or for-profit sector—and thus has a unique raison d'etre—because of the distinctive ways in which nonprofit organizations permit values to be pursued. Three distinctive relationships between nonprofit organizations and values have been identified.

The first emphasizes the unique role of nonprofit organizations for government. Whereas government provides the ideal means of pursuing values the entire society (or a large majority) shares or that are so-called public goods that can only be attained through collective action by the entire society, nonprofit organizations are better suited to the pursuit of values that are *not shared* but indeed vary from group to group and are perhaps held only by a minority (Hansmann 1986; Weisbrod 1988). National defense is the clearest example of the former. If a society is to be militarily secure, it cannot rely on voluntary contributions of money and labor from those who merely happen to value security the most or are the most altruistic about sacrificing for the common good. National security is best achieved through the coercive means of taxation and conscription that only government can command. In contrast, nonprofit organizations can be relied upon when a particular set of values that may not be shared throughout the society is at issue. For instance, citizens of Polish descent might wish to commemorate their ethnic origins and provide scholarships to children sharing their heritage, and it would be appropriate for them to initiate a nonprofit organization to solicit contributions for this purpose, but it would not be appropriate to pass laws requiring citizens of all ethnic and racial backgrounds to support this cause. Nonprofit organizations are thus voluntary, rather than coercive, and they function best when values are important enough to one constituency to generate voluntary support but lack the broad mandate necessary to warrant governmental intervention.

A second argument holds that nonprofit organizations are particularly well suited to facilitate values that cannot be easily monitored (DiMaggio and Anheier 1990; Hansmann 1986, 1987). Missionaries are an example. Baptists in the United States may wish to send missionaries to a remote part of the world to "save souls." In keeping with the voluntaristic principle, this is an activity better conducted by a nonprofit organization than by government because it is a value held by Baptists but presumably not by American Jews or Muslims or atheists. In addition, it results in activities that are difficult to monitor. A missionary thousands of miles away from his or her sponsoring organization may not engage as actively in the task of saving souls as the donors supporting that missionary would hope (Hutchison 1987). The problem is compounded by the intangibility of the values at issue: how exactly does one determine if a soul has been saved? In contrast, government-supported activities or for-profit organization activities require more precise monitoring. Taxpayers and shareholders want to know if their money is being used in the most efficient and effective way possible. Nonprofit organizations provide a buffer, as it were, between such demands for short-term accountability and longer-range objectives.

The third argument suggests that certain values would intrinsically be compromised if they were pursued through government or the market, rather than through the nonprofit sector (Wuthnow 1991). Altruism is probably the clearest example. If the law requires me to pay taxes to support social welfare programs, my payment of these taxes can hardly be considered altruistic (Nagel 1979; Post 2003). Similarly, I can hardly be considered a person who selflessly gives of my time and money if I work for a for-profit organization or buy stock in a company in hopes of securing a profit. Altruism is better suited to an organization that depends heavily on voluntary contributions of time and money and that is not expected to produce profits for its owners or shareholders. Another value that is often associated in this manner with the nonprofit sector, at least in the United States, is freedom of religious expression. We assume that worship should be engaged in voluntarily and for this reason consider it somehow less authentic and diminished if government mandates it. Many people also regard worship as an intrinsic good that is engaged in for no ulterior motives, such as economic gain, and thus would likely be bothered if the sanctuary in which people worshipped was plastered with signs advertising Pizza Hut and Wal-Mart.

Although students of nonprofit organizations have criticized and refined these arguments, they bear directly on controversies about government funding of the arts and for faith-based service organizations. Proponents of government funding for the arts would argue that high quality aesthetic expression is a public good of such importance that its support cannot be left in the hands of the few who might value it enough to support it voluntarily (Alexander 1996; Ivey 1999). In this view, beauty enriches everyone and is a kind of national treasure. The opposing view would hold that art is essentially a matter of taste and is thus subject to so many different standards of judgment that it should be supported voluntarily or through the marketplace (Brubaker 1994). Art could also arguably be considered the kind of value that cannot be monitored easily or that government intervention or profit motives would compromise. Faith-based social services raise similar considerations. If policies emphasize *faith*, then voluntary support through nonprofit organizations is attractive because it permits those of other faiths (or no faith) to opt out. But if programs emphasize *service*, then it might be argued that everyone should pay, including through government initiatives, and services provided in whatever way is most effective. The other two arguments also come into play. If service is difficult to measure and requires long-term personal care, then nonprofit organizations may be the most desirable venue, whereas if service is considered measurable, then considerations of effectiveness and efficiency of the kind expected in government programs and for-profit organizations are appropriate. Similarly, a person who regarded faith as an intrinsic value might worry that government or market involvement would compromise this value, whereas a person who considered faith differently might think it so important that it should be promoted by any means possible, including government support.

It is worth noting that these arguments about values and the nonprofit sector do not take into consideration other factors that influence whether activities are pursued in one sector or another. For instance, historical factors are also involved. For that matter, many activities, including the arts and social services, are pursued through a combination of nonprofit, government, and for-profit support (DiMaggio and Anheier 1990). The point is simply that when government becomes involved in the support of nonprofit activities, as it has in the arts and social service provision, questions often arise about whether this support is conducive to the values involved or is in some way incompatible with those values. This is an important point because it shifts attention from the particular controversies that have focused on the

Christian Right and the culture wars to the more general issues that arise from government support of nonprofit activities. Had the Christian Right never existed, these issues would still be present. Questions would still need to be addressed about art being a public good meriting support through the coercive means of government or being a matter of taste better supported voluntarily, and about art being difficult to monitor or an intrinsic value as opposed to art being subject to measurable standards of quality and efficiency. In the social service arena, similar questions would be present about which sector is in a better position to advance such values as altruism and whole-person care, about the relative availability of voluntary and public funding, and about standards of accountability. To see how these questions have emerged, it will be helpful to consider the specific controversies that have been at issue in the case of government funding for the arts and for faith-based social services.

FUNDING FOR THE NEA AND FOR FAITH-BASED INITIATIVES

The NEA controversy occurred amidst public concern about government expenditures, but funding itself was less the issue than the controversial uses of these funds. In 1981, budget director David Stockton proposed cutting the NEA's budget by 50 percent, resulting in an actual reduction that was considerably smaller (from $158.8 million in 1981 to $143.5 million in 1982), and during the remainder of the Reagan administration, NEA funding (like that of the National Endowment for the Humanities and some educational programs) rose modestly (to $167.7 million in 1988). In 1989, following a widely publicized event involving a controversial photograph by Andres Serrano (of a plastic crucifix immersed in urine) that was part of an NEA-sponsored exhibit, some conservative groups called for abolishing the NEA (McGee 1995). During the summer of 1989 members of Congress frequently referred to Serrano's work and to Robert Mapplethorpe's homoerotic photographs while debating budget allocations for the NEA. In 1990 Congress passed a law that required the NEA to take account not only of artistic excellence in making grants but also considerations of decency and respect for public values. Although the law appears to have had relatively little impact on NEA activities in the years immediately following its approval, it was challenged in 1992 by performance artist Karen Finley, overturned in 1996 by the Ninth U.S. Circuit Court of Appeals, and subsequently upheld by the U.S. Supreme Court in 1998 (Van Camp 1997; Wong 1998).

Having already cut appropriations by 40 percent in 1995, opponents of the NEA renewed their efforts to cut all funding for the agency. On

July 11, 1997, the House of Representatives passed by a one-vote margin a bill to replace the NEA with block grants to state arts councils and local school boards. Senators Ashcroft and Helms sponsored a similar bill, arguing that the NEA was, among other things, helping elitist organizations rather than supporting country musicians or artists who might appeal to "people driving pickup trucks" (Trescott 1997). The Senate defeated the Ashcroft-Helms proposal and several others, however, thus averting elimination of the NEA but leaving its long-term future the subject of continuing controversy. Between 1992 and 2000, annual appropriations for the NEA , according to the NEA, dropped from $176.0 million to $97.6 million. By 2005, the NEA's budget of $121.3 million was still lower than it had been in 1978, and with inflation would be even lower (National Endowment for the Arts, 2005; http://www.americanartsalliance.org/americanartsalliance/NEA_issue_brief.html).

Senator John Ashcroft, a Republican from Missouri, also played a key role in what would become known as Charitable Choice and subsequent efforts to ease restrictions on government funding of faith-based nonprofit service organizations (Denny 1996; Goode 1997). These efforts emerged in a climate of antigovernment sentiment that had been prominent during the Reagan administration and then became more pronounced during the 1994 congressional election (Dionne 1992; Robinson and Colliau 1995). Republican candidates called for sweeping reforms of the welfare system on grounds that it was inefficient, costly, and ineffective. The funding that government would provide for social services should be smaller, they argued, and thus would need to be administered more efficiently, a task that was widely considered to be done best by nonprofit organizations. These organizations were also expected to help accomplish the legislation's aim of promoting self-sufficiency among welfare recipients and incorporating them into the workforce. The idea that churches and other faith-based nonprofits could shoulder more of the burden of providing social services gradually gained support in both parties. Lawmakers expressed hope that churches would provide a wide range of services, from temporary food and shelter to voluntary day care, transportation, job training, counseling, tutoring, and low-income housing. In speeches following the bill's signing, President Clinton suggested that congregations consider creating jobs for unemployed members of the community. House Speaker Newt Gingrich made similar pleas (Rodrigue 1996). Senator Ashcroft's Charitable Choice legislation reflected the premise that churches and faith-based nonprofits could help not only through their own contributions and volunteering but by receiving public funding as well. The legislation was meant both to recognize that some churches and separately incorporated tax-exempt faith-based organizations were receiving government support and to remove some of the barriers preventing more organizations from doing so.

Lawmakers recognized the potential for this legislation to result in religious discrimination or to promote the establishment of religion if some faith-based organizations were given an advantage over others. They were also concerned that existing arrangements sometimes made it difficult for faith-based providers to deliver services without altering their basic mission and administrative structure. The wording of "Charitable Choice" in Section 104 of the Personal Responsibility and Work Opportunity Reconciliation Act of 1996 offered detailed rules about the conditions under which faith-based organizations could receive federal funding. The act gave states the option of excluding all nongovernmental entities from the use of funds they received through federal block grants for assisting the needy. But if states dispensed any of these funds through nonprofit organizations, then faith-based nonprofits could not be excluded. Faith-based nonprofits included congregations, nonprofit service providers affiliated with religious organizations, and nonprofit service organizations that may have been founded on the basis of religious beliefs and teachings. The legislation distinguished between two ways in which such organizations might receive federal funds: "direct" funds consisted of a contract with the government to provide services; "indirect" funds consisted of remuneration from the government in return for vouchers that clients might submit to a nonprofit organization in return for a service rendered. Because indirect funds came from situations in which clients presumably were able to choose between faith-based and other providers, somewhat looser conditions were imposed than in cases where faith-based nonprofits contracted directly with government. In both cases, however, an attempt was made to balance and protect the rights of providers and those of clients.

Providers were permitted to apply religious tests (such as being a member of a particular denomination or vowing to abstain from alcohol) in hiring personnel but were prohibited from discriminating on other grounds, such as race, gender, disability, or national origin. They were permitted to maintain the religious environment of their organization, rather than having to remove religious icons, art, or publications to be eligible. They were not required to alter their administrative structure to comply with government standards, because this structure was sometimes derived from theological and ecclesiological considerations, and they could isolate the portion of funds received from government for reporting purposes rather than having to disclose all sources and distributions of funds. Clients were given the right to choose among religious and nonreligious providers and could not be refused services on the basis of their religion, religious beliefs, or religious practices. Clients who felt they had been discriminated against could bring civil suits against providers (Gilman 2002).

The NEA reductions and Charitable Choice legislation were sometimes interpreted as controversies simply about ways to reduce government spending. Opponents of the NEA argued, for example, that its elimination would be a major boon to taxpayers who were already struggling to make ends meet, whereas NEA supporters claimed the agency's budget amounted to only 37 cents per taxpayer per year (Ivey 1999). Yet the two debates were also about the values represented when public support was channeled to nonprofit organizations. In the case of Charitable Choice, interest groups that perceived religion to be under siege by secular social institutions quickly rose to support Senator Ashcroft's proposal on grounds that congregations should not be discriminated against in receiving federal funds. Efforts to abolish the NEA alarmed museums and local artist associations that had been recipients of NEA funding, partly because of its financial implications but also because the very value of artistic expression appeared to be in question. As writer Madeleine L'Engle remarked, "I don't often write letters, but I wrote one to Mr. Gingrich. 'Dear Mr. Gingrich. A great country has always been noted by the attention it pays to the arts. Does your present point of view indicate that you no longer think we are a great country? Sincerely yours'" (quoted in Wuthnow 2001b, 140).

As each debate developed, aspects of it focused on broad questions about the ways in which deeply held values in the public at large were being reinforced or undermined by government's support of nonprofit organizations. But the values under consideration were not only about whether or not to help the needy or how much to support the arts; the debates raised broader questions about freedom, religion, morality, and how best to preserve core American values. Charitable Choice sparked debate about the rights of religious communities to express their beliefs and teachings. Proponents of the legislation argued that religious communities were inhibited in what would otherwise be a natural inclination to serve the needy because their leaders feared government regulation would follow if they accepted federal funds. Opponents expressed a similar concern about government intrusion but perceived the legislation as an invitation for greater intrusion rather than less. Charitable Choice was contested on grounds that it would infringe on individuals' religious freedom as well. Whereas the concerns expressed about religious communities emphasized the likelihood that government regulation would impose uniform standards on otherwise diverse traditions, the concerns about individual religious freedom stressed the likelihood that government funding would inevitably favor some traditions more than others and thus make it harder for individuals to pick and choose on the basis of conscience alone. Another concern was that in some locales people might be forced to be served by organizations that did not reflect their religious values because no alternatives were available. Still another concern was when to apply nondiscrimination rules in hiring workers. Apart from the issues it raised about religion, the emerging debate about faith-based initiatives included more general concerns about the character of local communities. On the one hand, both its supporters and opponents saw merit in strengthening the capacity of local community organizations to dispense services in ways consistent with their diverse traditions, needs, and lifestyles. On the other hand, both sides recognized the need for federal involvement if services were to receive adequate funding and if potential inequities were to be avoided.

The NEA case revolved around a similar set of issues. Although Serrano's *Piss Christ* offended the religious sensibilities of many of the NEA's opponents (just as Robert Mapplethorpe's homoerotic art did), the controversy took on broader importance because it raised issues about the relationship between government funding and the uses of tax dollars for the activities of artists and arts organizations. In response to the works of Serrano, Mapplethorpe, Karen Finley, and others being denounced from pulpits and in newspapers, members of Congress passed legislation requiring the NEA to pay attention to decency and public values. Amid congressional investigations of individual artists and widespread publicity, NEA's director wrote that works depicting lesbian, gay male, and other explicit sexual activities would no longer be funded (McLeod and MacKenzie 1998).

Finley and three other plaintiffs' suit against the NEA focused on charges that the NEA's denial of their request for grants to support their work as artists had violated their rights to freedom of speech. Their lawyers argued the case on grounds that the NEA had treated their applications unfairly by taking into consideration political pressures and that parts of Finley's application had been released to the media without her permission. The case, however, included the more general argument that public subsidization of art, like public funding of the press and university activities, demands government neutrality (Sabrin 1993, 1224).

The neutrality argument asserts the value of artistic expression, like that of scientific or other scholarly activity, and thus calls on government to provide support for artists. Yet it recognizes that professional expertise is required to make judgments about art and asks government to allow the allocation of public funding to be made by representatives of the artistic community itself. In its ruling on the Finley case, the appellate court determined that Congress's requirement that the NEA take into account considerations of decency and public morality opened

the door for potential violations of neutrality because ideas ab\
decency and other values were too varied to be defined objectively. It
explicitly sought to exclude any possibility that government procedures
would infringe on artists' freedom to express their own values, however
unpopular they might be with the general public.

In his dissenting opinion Judge Andrew J. Kleinfeld drew a distinction between government censorship and government's right to influence the content of activities it subsidizes, and he argued that the latter
consideration should prevail. Although this distinction failed to be
persuasive to the other justices, Kleinfeld argued that, funding aside,
government should not censor or interfere in the activities of artists.
Noting that a cross immersed in urine is likely to offend the religious
beliefs of most Americans, Kleinfeld cited numerous other examples,
ranging from Lenny Bruce's monologues to Allen Ginsberg's poetry
to Modigliani's nudes, as similar examples and argued that none should
be subjected to censorship.

The court's decision that Congress could not impose standards of
decency and morality on the NEA left its critics with no apparent
recourse other than reducing or eliminating its funding entirely. Providing funding to states for use by regional arts councils and local school
boards was a way to devolve responsibility to other jurisdictions where
other legal precedents and concerns about community norms might
prevail. Like the Charitable Choice legislation, the NEA decision made
it possible for nonprofit organizations to receive federal funding but
also demonstrated that there would be continuing controversies about
which organizations would be eligible and which would not.

The debates about government funding for the arts and religion
continued in episodic fashion. Research showed that arts controversies
appeared frequently in newspapers and that some of these controversies, such as that over the 1999 *Sensation* exhibit at the Brooklyn
Museum of Art, attracted widespread interest across the nation
(DiMaggio et al. 2001; Halle 2001). A 1998 survey showed that the
public was evenly split between those who favored and those who
opposed federal funding for the arts (Marsden 2001). Relatively speaking, the debate about faith-based initiatives commanded considerably
more attention. During the 2000 presidential campaign, Al Gore and
George W. Bush both expressed support for greater involvement of
religious organizations in social service delivery. In January 2001, President Bush launched the White House Office of Faith-Based and Community Initiatives and pressed for legislation to expand Charitable
Choice. Although this legislation was defeated, funding for faith-based
organizations increased as a result of various executive orders. By
2004, official estimates suggested that approximately $2 billion, or 10
percent of all federal spending for social programs for which individual

groups could compete, had been granted to faith-based organizations (Bumiller 2005).

IMPLICATIONS

Controversies about NEA support for the arts and federal funding for faith-based service organizations raise a number of issues for nonprofit managers and policymakers. These issues pose practical questions for nonprofit administration but also point to topics in need of further thought and investigation in the scholarly literature (see also Smith and Lipsky 1993; Wolch 1990). Space permits a brief discussion of nine such issues.

Devolution

In recent decades federal policymakers have increasingly favored shifting greater administrative control of domestic welfare programs to state and local governments through block grants and other strategies of devolution (Winston 2002). Although proponents of devolution cite various reasons for these shifts, the most common explanations are that "big government" at the national level is a blunt instrument for dealing with human needs, whereas state and local jurisdictions can more effectively take account of differences in community cultures and needs. Charitable Choice was left largely in the hands of state officials to implement (Green and Sherman 2002). Since the mid-1990s, NEA funds have also been channeled increasingly to state and local arts councils, and these agencies have significantly increased their own contributions to the arts (Lowell 2004; Seaman 2002). These policies furthered devolution, but of course also reflected the fact that state and local agencies were already quite active in arts programs and social services.

For nonprofit organizations, devolution has had mixed consequences. On the negative side, devolution has *sometimes* resulted in reduced levels of government support as federal spending has shrunk or remained constant while already-strapped state and local governments were unable to make up the difference. As far as cultural clashes are concerned, controversial projects may have also experienced setbacks as local jurisdictions assumed greater responsibility for making decisions; for instance, about public arts projects. On the positive side, devolution has put funding decisions closer to final points of delivery (food banks, homeless shelters, neighborhood arts programs) where local nonprofit organizations could play a greater role both in influencing these decisions and in implementing them. Localization has perhaps also had the inadvertent consequence of reducing the likelihood of public outcry about controversial projects by limiting the affected population to a particular community or state, rather than involving the pocketbooks of all Americans.

Public Morality

Most of the controversies that have arisen in recent years about public arts projects—government-sponsored or otherwise—have focused on "morality," particularly the morality or immorality of homoerotic art, other sexual themes, gay and lesbian issues, and the profanation or desacralization of religious symbols. Beyond the particular substantive issues that have been debated, the broader question that pertains to nonprofit organizations concerns their role in *framing* issues as moral issues (or in some other way) in the first place. As numerous studies have shown, what counts as a moral issue in one context may be regarded differently in another context. For instance, gay marriage may be regarded as a moral issue by some but not by others, whereas the minimum wage is viewed as an economic issue by some but as a moral issue by others. Going back a bit more into history, the 19th-century Comstock laws against the distribution of "obscene" materials and contraceptive devices were associated with a stronger sense of public morality in some cities than in others; fetal alcohol syndrome came only recently to be defined as a moral issue; and drinking alcohol has more generally been viewed through quite different moral lenses in different eras (Armstrong 2003; Beisel 1993, 1997; Gusfield 1963). Nonprofit organizations play a role in these processes of public definition; for instance, by helping to frame activities as artistic, medical, religious, and so on.

Meanwhile, artists and directors of arts organizations typically framed artistic work by aesthetic modes of evaluation, and secondarily by "free expression," whereas religious leaders (especially conservative Protestants and Catholics) were more likely to emphasize the potential moral implications of art (Wuthnow 2003). In most instances, venue considerations also influenced these frames, meaning that aesthetic frames were selected if art were located in galleries or museums more often than if it appeared in public parks or newspapers. Where arts leaders and religious leaders largely agreed was that art in the wrong context could be morally offensive, even though arts leaders were often more willing to regard offensiveness itself as a cultural benefit.

The question of how best to strike a balance between artistic freedom and popular definitions of morality has been the focus of considerable discussion and remains in need of empirical inquiry. A hypothesis that emerges from comparing arts controversies with faith-based initiatives is that the more an issue is currently framed in moral terms, the less likely it is that the issue will be resolved through legislation and the courts rather than through executive order or self-monitoring. This is probably a counterintuitive hypothesis in view of the fact that "legislating morality" is such a familiar phrase and does in fact correspond with many such efforts in American history. However, legislators and courts have found it difficult in recent years to define morality in ways that were both clear and exempt from concerns about freedom of speech, whereas FCC regulations of network television content or the motion picture industry's self-ratings provide examples of working definitions of public morality being implemented. Whether or not this hypothesis has merit is less the issue, though, than the fact that non-profit organizations are routinely faced with difficult decisions about competing definitions of morality.

Religious Special Interest Groups

The clash of values influences and in turn is influenced by the nonprofit sector itself. These influences occur not only because nonprofit organizations may be implicated in the values that are being debated, but also because new nonprofit organizations have emerged to promote particular issues. It is wrong to think of the nonprofit sector as an entity that is somehow under siege by forces alien to it (as if civilization itself were under attack by barbarians). The reality is that other organizations within the nonprofit sector are initiating attacks on some activities within the nonprofit sector (Wuthnow 1989). A powerful voice within the Christian Right, for instance, is James Dobson's Focus on the Family, which is a nonprofit organization. On a smaller scale, nonprofit organizations have been established to oppose abortion, defend traditional Catholics against discrimination, promote heterosexual marriage, and conduct advertising campaigns for and against various reforms of Social Security.

I will return later to the potentially positive benefits of this proliferation of nonprofit organizations for the well-being of civil society and American democracy. The negative implications are likely to be more self-evident. One is that mobilization tends to generate counter-mobilization and thus requires greater expenditures on waging attacks and counter-attacks at the expense of pursuing other objectives, such as social services or promoting the arts. Another is that nonprofit organizations become divided into warring factions that mistrust each other and conform more to ideological agendas than they otherwise would. Perhaps most important, the attempt to persuade often obscures and even attacks efforts at dispassionate analysis, accurate presentation of facts, and the search for common ground.

Partnerships and Coalitions

Research on nonprofit organizations has increasingly been pointing to the growing importance of partnerships and coalitions within the nonprofit sector (Boguslaw 2002; Reisch and Sommerfeld 2003). Such partnerships and coalitions are particularly evident among social service organizations and appear to be one of the ways in which nonprofit administrators are adapting to the new climate of government funding that has emerged with Charitable Choice. Whereas the academic and policy literature sometimes suggests that funding is being directed to faith-based organizations *or* nonsectarian organizations, the reality is that these organizations are often working cooperatively as part of larger coalitions that also include governmental organizations and for-profit organizations. For instance, one of the urban housing development programs I studied a few years ago was a coalition involving churches that raised money through individual donations and denominational grants, a separate faith-based ecumenical organization that administered public and private funds, several nonsectarian nonprofit organizations that dealt with legal and administrative details, state and local government agencies, banks, and construction companies (Wuthnow 1998). Other research shows that local religious congregations are increasingly partnering with nonreligious service organizations in their communities and, more generally, that networking is becoming increasingly important as a way for nonprofit organizations to adapt to the fluid economic and political environments in which they currently work (Ammerman 2005). In the case of faith-based initiatives, government funding has also been directed explicitly toward clearinghouses and coordinating agencies that can play a role in building coalitions among small nonprofit organizations.

My research among arts organizations and with religious congregations suggested that directors of arts organizations were beginning to recognize the value of working through partnerships with congregations (Wuthnow 2001a). Congregations have long supported the arts through programs within houses of worship themselves, such as hymn singing, choirs, and musical instruction for children (Chaves 2004). As "megachurches" have grown in size and numbers, some congregations are now sponsoring their own symphony orchestras, ballet companies, theater guilds, video libraries, and artist-in-residence programs. In major metropolitan areas, such as New York, San Francisco, and Dallas, arts leaders have been working with interfaith religious councils and large urban congregations to cosponsor performing arts events and advertise or host community arts programs (Wuthnow 2003). These coalitions and partnerships also serve as bridges between the arts and religious communities and thus can provide countermeasures against attacks on controversial arts programs that may come from some quarters of the religious population.

Advocacy

One of the more frequently expressed concerns about government funding of the nonprofit sector is that this funding may come with explicit or implicit strings attached such that public advocacy is diminished. These concerns are particularly worrisome when clashes of values are present. Directors of nonprofit organizations may be tempted to increase their chances of receiving government funding by siding with current administration perspectives on values or at least refraining from siding with the opposition. For instance, a religious organization might be less likely to speak in favor of a redistributive tax policy if its leaders feel their own government-funded day care program might be jeopardized. Or an art gallery might avoid showing the work of a controversial artist for fear of losing a grant from the state arts council. These concerns are aggravated when nonprofit organizations become vested interests that argue to protect or increase their own funding, rather than promoting the broader good of society. The same may be true when nonprofit organizations simply accept the status quo, rather than challenging it (Berry and Arons 2003).

A research study based on information from two large surveys—one of religious congregations and one of nonprofit organizations in Minneapolis and St. Paul—found no evidence that receiving government funding reduced the likelihood of nonprofit organizations engaging in public advocacy (Chaves, Stephens, and Galaskiewicz 2004). However, more research is needed before definitive conclusions can be drawn. Other research and anecdotal evidence suggests that public advocacy is probably not distributed across a wide cross-section of religious and nonreligious organizations but is more likely to be concentrated among particular organizations, for instance, faith-based community organizations or ones that specialize in monitoring lawmakers or the courts. Specialization of this kind has complex implications for the possible relationships between government funding and public advocacy by the nonprofit sector. On the one hand, specialization arguably helps to insulate advocacy organizations from concerns about political fallout. On the other hand, advocacy organizations are sometimes directly involved in raising money for other nonprofit organizations or are aligned with a particular part of the nonprofit sector. For instance, a service organization such as Prison Fellowship that is closely aligned with the Christian Right might find its fortunes improving as the Christian Right's influence in government circles increases, whereas Planned Parenthood might experience greater tension between making public statements and quietly maintaining its services in local communities.

Nongovernmental Resources

When government funding for nonprofit organizations results in public controversy, an option that remains open for some nonprofit organizations is to work more creatively to secure resources that do not derive from government. Examples include appealing to the public for donations through television advertising and direct-mail solicitations. It may be assumed that such appeals hold limited potential if the overall pool of available dollars and volunteer hours for nonprofit activities is constant. This assumption is belied by the fact that philanthropic giving and volunteering appears to have increased during the same period that the number of nonprofit organizations has grown and by research showing that one of the main predictors of giving and volunteering is having been asked (Wuthnow 1998). In addition, the NEA and faith-based service examples suggest another possible strategy for increasing nongovernmental resources.

This strategy involves recognizing the considerable potential within the religious arena of the nonprofit sector. Religiously involved people give and volunteer at higher rates than nonreligious people do, and some research suggests that this giving and volunteering extends beyond religious organizations themselves. In the case of social services, faith-based and nonsectarian organizations alike draw heavily on volunteers recruited through religious congregations (Wuthnow 2004). Similar potential exists for arts organizations. Leaving aside the few instances in which congregations and arts organizations may be at odds over moral controversies, the larger pattern of relationships between religion and the arts is complementary and mutually reinforcing. Research shows that people who learned to sing in religious settings as children are more likely to be involved in the arts more broadly as adults, and that many other relationships between religion and the arts also are present. People who are involved in the arts are more likely to be interested in spirituality, for example, than people who are not involved in the arts, and this interest in spirituality is typically associated with actually participating in religious activities (Wuthnow 2003). In addition, congregations provide social capital that encourages the arts: people say they go with friends from their congregations to museums and performing arts events and have friends at their congregations who work as artists. As mentioned previously, congregations also provide space for artistic events, host artists-in-residence, and expose children to the arts through music programs (Chaves 2004; Walker 2004; Walker and Sherwood 2003). The relevance of these considerations to government funding is not only that nongovernmental resources may be available, but also that government funding itself may be more likely for organizations that can leverage this funding by drawing on volunteers or making use of available space.

Organizational Specialization

The issues that have arisen in conjunction with government-funded faith-based initiatives have been particularly instructive in revealing the extent to which values clashes can be mitigated or circumvented altogether by adopting innovative organizational strategies. When the Charitable Choice legislation passed, some policymakers spoke as if local congregations were the most likely recipients of this funding (Mitchell 1996). This rhetoric may have been politically advantageous because it suggested that the funding would be dispersed widely and avoided the fact that large organizations (such as Catholic Charities) had already been receiving government funds for years. However, it also resulted in worries that, in retrospect, were probably exaggerated about churches using government money to put in new pews, pay preachers' salaries, and proselytize in their neighborhoods. The reality that emerged was quite different. Although surveys of pastors and laity found large proportions saying they would accept government money, more careful research showed that relatively few actually did and, when confronted with the possibility of red tape and government auditors, most pastors interviewed almost immediately expressed doubts about the attractiveness of applying for government grants (Wuthnow 2004). Instead, faith-based service organizations that were separately incorporated as 501(c)(3) nonprofit agencies applied for grants. In addition, congregations that applied for grants also set up separate tax-exempt organizations to administer the funds. In short, religious leaders adapted to concerns about the potential impact of government funding on their congregations by setting up new and legally distinct faith-based service organizations.

Religious organizations have increasingly used this strategy. It effectively reduces the problems associated with separation of church and state by legally separating the religious component of their activities from social service components that receive government funding. It may not eliminate the danger of public funds being used for religious purposes, especially when the same boards of directors supervise the separate organizations. However, it at least permits separate accounts to be kept and regulations (about nondiscrimination, for instance) to be applied to the service component without also being applied to the religious component. Separate organizations also create a legal firewall that protects the congregation's assets in the event of liability suits or business losses incurred by the service agency (Campbell 2002).

The more general point is that government funding may be a source of increasing specialization within the nonprofit sector (Barman 2002). What was at one time a multipurpose organization that received funding from multiple sources may in the future be several organizations that specialize in different activities, partly in response to different funding streams. This pattern is already evident in instances where a profitable wing of a hospital becomes a for-profit corporation, but a research arm that relies mostly on government funds is organized separately as a nonprofit entity, and another unit that receives generous donations from the public may be another separate entity. What appears as organizational diversity, though, may also be subject to processes that encourage greater homogeneity. For instance, a faith-based organization that aspires to be a caring community, like congregations of the past, and devoted to distinctive religious teachings may increasingly conform to expectations about efficiency and effectiveness and develop professional norms and reporting procedures to the point that it is indistinguishable from a nonsectarian service agency (Chambre 2001).

Professional Autonomy

In the past, norms of professional autonomy typically provided a buffer between government and the nonprofit sector. If funds were received from government, nonprofit administrators insisted that professionals within their own organizations be the ones to decide how those funds would be used and their uses evaluated. Peer review was the most common way in which professionals exercised this control. Scientists made the decisions about how scientific projects would be evaluated; doctors, social workers, educators, and artists made similar decisions within their particular domains. These practices may be eroding for a variety of reasons, including the recent clashes of values.

A study by Lewis and Brooks (2005) suggests the possible connection between clashes of values and the decline of professional autonomy. Their study compared the values, opinions, and religious orientations of people working in various artistic occupations who were included in national General Social Surveys with those of people not employed in these occupations. The results showed that fewer artists than nonartists were fundamentalists (17 percent versus 31 percent), that more were nonreligious (30 percent versus 11 percent), and that more regarded themselves as political liberals (44 percent versus 27 percent). By a margin of 24 percentage points, fewer artists than nonartists thought homosexual sex was always wrong and fewer artists disapproved of art that mocked religion (24 percent versus 45 percent). Because of these differences, the authors concluded that peer review among artists to allocate grants to artists would undoubtedly result in projects being funded that would be unsavory to the general public. They predicted that policymakers and artists alike might opt for a different way of deciding on government funding to avoid controversial outcomes.

Several caveats must be mentioned. First, the differences between artists and the general public were relative, not absolute. For instance, although the proportion of artists who expressed no religious preference was higher than in the general public, 70 percent of artists *did* adhere to a religious tradition—a finding similar to that shown by a separate analysis of the data in which a majority of artists also participated in religious services (Wuthnow 2001b). Thus, the kind of statement that sometimes appears in the mass media about all artists being atheists or secular humanists is as false as similar allegations that *all* journalists are Democrats. Second, the fact that artists differ from the general public says nothing distinctive about artists. Were comparisons made between the general public and scientists, professors, social workers, clergy, or bankers—indeed, any "elite" group—there would also be differences. It is not the presence or even the size of these differences that renders controversies likely. It is, rather, the existence of values controversies and the means to mobilize these controversies that threaten the autonomy of peer review. It is also the case that professional autonomy depends greatly on the degree to which professions are embedded in social institutions that have gained legitimacy with the wider public. Universities provide such institutional insulation for educators and scientists. In the business world, despite hugely expensive scandals such as those involving Enron and WorldCom officials, the power of corporate America provides similar insulation. In comparison, artists work largely without such institutional protection and therefore are more vulnerable if accusations of producing morally offensive work arise.

Client-Based Strategies

During the period in which the debates about NEA grants and government funding for faith-based organizations were taking place, a growing preference for what might be called client-based strategies—for example, vouchers—became evident. Charitable Choice legislation emphasized client choice among various faith-based, nonsectarian, or government options as a way of avoiding the charge that clients might be forced to participate in religious activities against their will. In response to criticism that some faith-based organizations were using government funds to provide life transforming faith experiences (i.e., make people into religious believers), proponents of faith-based initiatives have suggested a voucher system, similar to proposed school voucher programs in which the government does not make payments to organizations but to clients who then use them at the organization of their choice (Loconte et al. 2000; Sherman 2000). A somewhat different strategy has been evident in the arts. NEA director Dana Gioia has argued that the NEA's objective should not be to facilitate the supply of art, but to reinforce demand by helping children and lower-income residents gain access to the arts (Weber 2004). In recent years, a significantly larger share of the NEA budget has been devoted to community arts programs, school programs, and projects in disadvantaged communities.

Client-based strategies have an important ideological advantage: they appear to be egalitarian and appeal to the widely held American value of freedom of choice. In a sense, these strategies solve the problem of balancing public goods with personal preferences. Emphasizing people with needs for social services and people in poor communities who cannot otherwise benefit from the arts satisfies the public goods part of the equation. Whether these are public goods in the same sense as national security is not the issue. It is that helping the needy is valued widely enough that the public is generally willing to consider it legitimate for some government funding to go to this purpose. Giving clients options, rather than dictating the particular organizations or programs that will receive funding, satisfies the personal preference part of the equation.

There are, however, some complex considerations. Client-based arts programs may stimulate and broaden demand, but critics question whether these programs can be designed in a way that facilitates the production of high-quality art. This question in turn is difficult to answer because of varying definitions of quality and different views about the role of artists, policymakers, and the marketplace in promoting quality. Vouchers for social services pose other considerations. Although they may be more attractive than vouchers for schooling (because schooling is intended to promote a *common* culture that would be undermined by separate school systems, whereas social services do not have this objective), vouchers for social services may be more difficult to administer (Glenn 2000). Unlike an annual voucher for tuition that might be paid once a year and determined entirely on the basis of a child's age and eligibility, vouchers for social services would have to be made available in the middle of the night when someone had an accident and decided to enter a detox program or whenever a homeless claimant needed shelter or a hungry child needed a meal. Although it might be conceivable to hand out vouchers on short notice under such varied circumstances, it is likely that the administrative process would result in precisely the kind of large government-run program that the proponents of vouchers have been most intent on opposing. For client-based programs to function effectively, therefore, care needs to be given to designing them in ways that are both fair and administratively practical.

THE CONTRIBUTION OF VALUE CLASHES TO CIVIL SOCIETY

It is easy to imagine that the kinds of controversies that have arisen over NEA projects and faith-based initiatives are inimical to the common good and thus a regrettable instance of problems that should be solved if nonprofit organizations are going to contribute positively to civil society. The assumptions behind this concern, though, require scrutiny. The central assumption is that nonprofit organizations are connected to civil society and that this connection is positive. The related assumption is that conflicts over values are somehow bad for civil society.

That there is a positive connection between nonprofit organizations and civil society is well established, although not without qualifications (Cohen and Arato 1992). In some views, the nonprofit sector and civil society are nearly identical, both referring to all forms of social organization other than government and economic enterprises (with the possible exception of private activities pursued within the family); in other views, the nonprofit sector is more delimited, consisting of such entities as 501(c)(3) organizations that are formally excluded from having to distribute profits or pay taxes. In either view, nonprofit organizations are regarded as a principal source of such beneficial activities as social solidarity, social services, volunteering and altruistic values, civic skills, community participation, and trust (Boris 1999). The qualifications to these assertions focus on the possibility that some nonprofit organizations function more as letterheads and sources of fundraising than as places in which members actually congregate and on the possibility that some nonprofit organizations are too thoroughly professionalized or commercialized to promote the kind of informal interaction that might have happened in days gone by at lodges, clubs, and dinner parties (Putnam 2000). Another criticism of nonprofits is that they become vested interests serving themselves rather than the general public.

The assumption that clashes of values are bad for the nonprofit sector and perhaps for the functioning of civil society rests in the idea that civic harmony should prevail. When society divides into warring factions it becomes more difficult to achieve national goals. People spend more time within their own homogeneous groups, bicker more with people in other groups, and are more likely to take hostile action toward the other groups (Dionne 1992; Elshtain 1995). Misunderstanding and discrimination result. For nonprofit organizations, conflict of this kind can result in reduced government funding, mistrust, and leaders having to spend more time fighting opponents and protecting their turf than focusing on more important activities. These concerns are legitimate, but they miss one important consideration.

That one consideration is the fact that controversies about values may also reinforce values, especially if a public discussion encourages people to think more deeply about their convictions or to express them with greater clarity. This inadvertent reinforcing of values may be true especially for those who feel their own values are threatened by another group or by the wider culture and for this reason rededicate themselves to the preservation of their particular values—a reaction that has been observed among evangelical Christians, for instance (Smith 1998). It may also be true, though, for people who may otherwise be bystanders to the controversies themselves. In sociological theory since Durkheim (1992, originally published in 1915), it is widely recognized that the health of civil society depends on periodic renewal of the population's commitment to core values, and such renewal comes about through rituals and controversies as much as through more routinized mechanisms (such as schooling). Closely contested national elections in which issues of character and morality are debated reinforce the idea that character and morality are important. In these political campaigns candidates are forced to articulate their values, demonstrate that these stem from the heart, and defend themselves against opponents who may hold different values. The same has been true on a smaller scale when controversies have arisen about funding for the arts or for religious organizations. The resulting debates become occasions for talking publicly about such issues as freedom of expression, standards of aesthetic evaluation, the public roles of the arts and of religion, decency, morality, and a variety of other issues. One can see this in instances where progressive groups have been offended by ethnic slurs passing as art or where officials who believe strongly in government-funded welfare programs have had to defend their views against religious leaders who argue that faith-based charities are more effective. In a pluralistic democracy, it is unnecessary for these debates to result in agreement. It is nevertheless important that they happen, for without them the likelihood that life would be shaped entirely by economic calculations or self-interest would increase.

CONCLUSION

The NEA controversies of the 1990s and more recent efforts to promote faith-based initiatives have certainly had direct consequences, such as ificant reduction in the NEA budget, a redirection of NEA programs, and a significant expansion of government funding for faith-based service organizations and impending litigation about the propriety of this funding. In both instances, public debate led, at least initially, to the perception that the nation is experiencing a fundamental cultural war and that political operatives may be exploiting the current clash of values for their own purposes.

The NEA and faith-based service examples point to a wider range of issues that policymakers and nonprofit leaders must understand. Too often the nonprofit sector is depicted in the academic literature as a quiet space, largely shielded from the intrusions of government and market forces and functioning internally to achieve a kind of equilibrium that serves the common good. In this view, the nonprofit sector takes up the slack when government falters and rises above the self-interestedness of for-profit organizations. Its component agencies more or less exist in happy mutual accommodation based on adherence to professional norms and a division of labor. Practitioners know the nonprofit sector is much messier than this. It is subject to the fluctuating priorities of policymakers, which are in turn influenced by public opinion and by special interest groups. Nonprofit management increasingly includes efforts to shape public opinion and build strategic alliances as well as providing goods and services. Nonprofit organizations compete for scarce resources and sometimes find themselves on different sides of major policy debates.

The two examples I have examined here demonstrate clearly that religion is an important aspect of the nonprofit sector. Seemingly minor (in dollar amounts) investments of government funding in controversial arts projects can be seized upon by religious leaders who, however sincere their intentions, lead to symbolic battles that confer additional visibility on these leaders. Having become watchdogs of government policy, religious organizations can mobilize more easily around new issues that their leaders may choose to emphasize. In some instances, this mobilization may emerge in opposition to programs favored by nonsectarian nonprofit leaders, but in other instances there may be greater congruence of interests. It should also not be assumed that only conservative religious groups are capable of mobilizing in this way, although examples of progressive religious mobilization have been relatively infrequent (Wuthnow and Evans 2002).

It would be wrong to leave the impression, though, that the relationships among nonprofit organizations, government, and values are compounded only by the mobilization of religious groups. The larger conclusion to be drawn from considering the examples of the NEA and faith-based initiatives is that nonprofit organizations are often concerned with values and, as such, are subject to the ways in which the political process shapes values. Nonprofit organizations are not passive in this process. By engaging in such activities as sponsoring arts exhibits or organizing neighborhood crime watch programs or tutoring children, the leaders and constituencies of nonprofit organizations dramatize to the public that certain values are important. When government funding or legislation is involved, the likelihood of public debate emerging is higher than when nonprofit organizations work only with their own constituents. What counts as "public goods," "special interests," "morality," "indecency," and the like is not inherent in the activities themselves but is a result of public negotiation. Leaders of nonprofit organizations are thus engaged in a process of defining the meaning and public significance of the activities in which they engage and of negotiating these meanings. In this larger sense, clashes of values are inevitable.

NOTE

I wish to thank Stan Katz, Elizabeth Boris, and C. Eugene Steuerle for comments on an earlier draft of this chapter.

REFERENCES

Adler, Amy M. 1993. "Why Art Is on Trial." *Journal of Arts Management, Law, and Society* 22(4): 323–34.

Alexander, Jane. 1996. "Our Investment in Culture." *Vital Speeches of the Day* 62(7): 210–12.

Americans for the Arts. 2002. *National and Local Profiles of Cultural Support: Summary Report.* Philadelphia, PA: Pew Charitable Trusts. http://www.pewtrusts.com/pdf/culture_policy_profiles.pdf.

Ammerman, Nancy Tatom. 2005. *Pillars of Faith: American Congregations and Their Partners.* Berkeley: University of California Press.

Armstrong, Elizabeth M. 2003. *Conceiving Risk, Bearing Responsibility: Fetal Alcohol Syndrome and the Diagnosis of Moral Disorder.* Baltimore, MD: Johns Hopkins University Press.

Arthurs, Alberta, and Glenn Wallach, eds. 2001. *Crossroads: Art and Religion in American Life.* New York, NY: New Press.

Baker, Wayne E. 2004. *America's Crisis of Values: Reality and Perception.* Princeton, NJ: Princeton University Press.

Balfe, Judith Huggins. 1993. *Paying the Piper: Causes and Consequences of Art Patronage.* Urbana: University of Illinois Press.

Barman, Emily A. 2002. "Asserting Difference: The Strategic Response of Nonprofit Organizations to Competition." *Social Forces* 80(4): 1191–1222.

Bartkowski, John P., and Helen A. Regis. 2003. *Charitable Choices: Religion, Race, and Poverty in the Post-Welfare Era.* New York, NY: New York University Press.

Beisel, Nicola. 1993. "Morals Versus Art: Censorship, the Politics of Interpretation, and the Victorian Nude." *American Sociological Review* 58(2): 145–62.
———. 1997. *Imperiled Innocents: Anthony Comstock and Family Reproduction in Victorian America*. Princeton, NJ: Princeton University Press.

Berry, Jeffrey, and David F. Arons. 2003. *A Voice for Nonprofits*. Washington, DC: Brookings Institution Press.

Black, Amy E., Douglas L. Koopman, and David K. Ryden. 2004. *Of Little Faith: The Politics of George W. Bush's Faith-Based Initiatives*. Washington, DC: Georgetown University Press.

Boguslaw, Janet. 2002. *Social Partnerships and Social Relations*. New York, NY: Routledge.

Bolton, Richard, ed. 1992. *Culture Wars: Documents from the Recent Controversies in the Arts*. New York, NY: New Press.

Boris, Elizabeth T. 1999. "Nonprofit Organizations in a Democracy: Varied Roles and Responsibilities." In *Nonprofits and Government*, 1st ed., edited by Elizabeth T. Boris and C. Eugene Steuerle (3–30). Washington, DC: Urban Institute Press.

Brooks, Arthur C. 2005. "Are Culture Wars Inevitable in the Arts?" *Cultural Comment* (March). http://www.culturalcommons.org/comment-print.cfm?ID=23.

Brubaker, Stanley C. 1994. "In Praise of Censorship." *Public Interest* 114: 48–64.

Bryson, Bethany. 1996. "'Anything But Heavy Metal': Symbolic Exclusion and Musical Dislikes." *American Sociological Review* 61(5): 884–99.

Bumiller, Elisabeth. 2005. "Bush Says $2 Billion Went to Religious Charities in '04." *New York Times*, March 2: A17.

Campbell, David. 2002. "Beyond Charitable Choice: The Diverse Service Delivery Approaches of Local Faith-Related Organizations." *Nonprofit and Voluntary Sector Quarterly* 31(2): 207–30.

Chambré, Susan M. 2001. "The Changing Nature of 'Faith' in Faith-Based Organizations: Secularization and Ecumenicism in Four AIDS Organizations in New York City." *Social Service Review* 75(3): 435–55.

Chaves, Mark. 2004. *Congregations in America*. Cambridge, MA: Harvard University Press.

Chaves, Mark, Laura Stephens, and Joseph Galaskiewicz. 2004. "Does Government Funding Suppress Nonprofits' Political Activity?" *American Sociological Review* 69(2): 292–316.

Cohen, Jean L., and Andrew Arato. 1992. *Civil Society and Political Theory*. Cambridge, MA: MIT Press.

Denny, Doreen. 1996. "Landmark Welfare Law Reforms." *Congressional Press Releases*, October 23.

DiMaggio, Paul, and Helmut K. Anheier. 1990. "The Sociology of Nonprofit Organizations and Sectors." *Annual Review of Sociology* 16(1): 137–59.

DiMaggio, Paul, John Evans, and Bethany Bryson. 1996. "Have Americans' Social Attitudes Become More Polarized?" *American Journal of Sociology* 102(3): 690–755.

DiMaggio, Paul, Wendy Cadge, Lynn Robinson, and Brian Steensland. 2001. "The Role of Religion in Public Conflicts Over the Arts in the Philadelphia Area, 1965–1997." In *Crossroads: Art and Religion in American Life*, edited by Alberta Arthurs and Glenn Wallach (103–38). New York, NY: New Press.

Dionne, E. J., Jr. 1992. *Why Americans Hate Politics*. New York, NY: Touchstone Books.

Dorf, Michael C. 1993. "The Battle Over the National Endowment for the Arts." *Brookings Review* 11(1): 32–35.

Durkheim, Emile. 1915. *Professional Ethics and Civic Morals*. Translated by Cornelia Brookfield. London, England: Routledge, 1992.

Elshtain, Jean Bethke. 1995. *Democracy on Trial*. New York: Basic Books.

Evans, John. 1996. "'Culture Wars' or Status Group Ideology as the Basis of U.S. Moral Politics." *International Journal of Sociology and Social Policy* 16(1): 15–34.

Fiorina, Morris P. 2004. *Culture War? The Myth of a Polarized America*. New York, NY: Longman.

Formicola, Jo Renee, Mary C. Segers, and Paul Weber. 2003. *Faith-Based Initiatives and the Bush Administration: The Good, the Bad, and the Ugly*. New York: Rowman and Littlefield.

Gilman, Michele Estrin. 2002. "'Charitable Choice' and the Accountability Challenge: Reconciling the Need for Regulation with the First Amendment Religion Clauses." *Vanderbilt Law Review* 55: 799–888.

Glenn, Charles Leslie. 2000. *The Ambiguous Embrace: Government and Faith-Based Schools and Social Agencies*. Princeton, NJ: Princeton University Press.

Goode, Stephen. 1997. "Secular Faith Fails: God Is King of the Hill." *Washington Times*, March 31: 10.

Green, John Clifford, and Amy L. Sherman. 2002. *Fruitful Collaborations: A Survey of Government-Funded Faith-Based Programs in 15 States*. Washington, DC: Hudson Institute.

Green, John Clifford, Mark J. Rozell, and Clyde Wilcox, eds. 2003. *The Christian Right in American Politics: Marching to the Millennium*. Washington, DC: Georgetown University Press.

Greenberg, Anna. 2000. "Doing Whose Work? Faith-Based Organizations and Government Partnerships." In *Who Will Provide? The Changing Role of Religion in American Social Welfare*, edited by Mary Jo Bane, Brent Coffin, and Ronald Thiemann (178–97). Cambridge, MA: Harvard University Press.

Greenberg, Stanley B. 2004. *The Two Americas: Our Current Political Deadlock and How to Break It*. New York, NY: Thomas Dunne.

Gusfield, Joseph. 1963. *Symbolic Crusade: Status Politics and the American Temperance Movement*. Urbana: University of Illinois Press.

Halle, David. 2001. "The Controversy Over the Show *Sensation* at the Brooklyn Museum, 1999–2000." In *Crossroads: Art and Religion in American Life*, edited by Alberta Arthurs and Glenn Wallach (139–88). New York, NY: New Press.

Hansmann, Henry. 1986. "The Role of Nonprofit Enterprise." In *The Economics of Nonprofit Institutions: Studies in Structure and Policy*, edited by S. Rose-Ackerman (57–84). New York, NY: Oxford University Press.

———. 1987. "Economic Theories of Nonprofit Organization." In *The Nonprofit Sector: A Research Handbook*, edited by W.W. Powell (27–42). New Haven, CT: Yale University Press.

Hodgkinson, Virginia A., and Murray S. Weitzman. 1996. *Nonprofit Almanac, 1996–1997: Dimensions of the Independent Sector*. San Francisco, CA: Jossey-Bass.

Horton, Michael S. 1994. *Beyond Culture Wars*. Chicago, IL: Moody Press.

Hunter, James Davison. 1991. *Culture Wars: The Struggle to Define America*. New York, NY: Basic Books.

———. 1994. *Before the Shooting Begins: Searching for Democracy in America's Culture Wars*. New York, NY: Free Press.

Hutchison, William R. 1987. *Errand to the World: American Protestant Thought and Foreign Missions*. Chicago, IL: University of Chicago Press.

Independent Sector. 2001. *The Nonprofit Almanac in Brief*. Washington, DC: Independent Sector.

Ivey, Bill. 1999. "The Benefits of the Arts." *Vital Speeches of the Day* 65 (6): 181–84.

Kaplan, Esther. 2004. *With God on Their Side: How Christian Fundamentalists Trampled Science, Policy, and Democracy in George W. Bush's White House*. New York, NY: New Press.

Kearns, Kevin P. 2003. "The Effects of Government Funding on Management Practices in Faith-Based Organizations: Propositions for Future Research." *Public Administration and Management: An Interactive Journal* 8(3): 116–34.

Lewis, Gregory B., and Arthur C. Brooks. 2005. "A Question of Morality: Artists' Values and Public Funding for the Arts." *Public Administration Review* 65(1): 8–17.

Linn, Jan G. 2004. *What's Wrong with the Christian Right*. Orlando, FL: Brown Walker.

Loconte, Joe, Marvin Olasky, Eli Lehrer, Amy Sherman, and Robert Sirico. 2000. "Compassionate Conservatism Ahead." *American Enterprise* 11(4): 26–35.

Lowell, Julia F. 2004. *State Arts Agencies 1965–2003: Whose Interests to Serve?* Santa Monica, CA: RAND Corporation.

Marsden, Peter V. 2001. "Religious Americans and the Arts in the 1990s." In *Crossroads: Art and Religion in American Life*, edited by Alberta Arthurs and Glenn Wallach (71–102). New York, NY: New Press.

McGee, Celia. 1995. "A Personal Vision of the Sacred and Profane." *New York Times*, January 22: Sec. 2, 35.

McLeod, Douglas M., and Jill A MacKenzie. 1998. "Print Media and Public Reaction to the Controversy Over NEA Funding for Robert Mapplethorpe's 'The Perfect Moment' Exhibit." *Journalism and Mass Communication Quarterly* 75: 278–91.

Minow, Martha L. 2003. "Public and Private Partnerships: Accounting for the New Religion." *Harvard Law Review* 116(5): 1229–70.

Mitchell, Alison. 1996. "Clinton Urges a Jobs Role on Churches." *The New York Times*, September 7: 10.

Nagel, Thomas. 1979. *The Possibility of Altruism*, rev. ed. Princeton, NJ: Princeton University Press.

Nolan, James L., Jr., ed. 1996. *The American Culture Wars: Current Contests and Future Prospects*. Charlottesville: University of Virginia Press.

Post, Stephen G. 2003. *Unlimited Love: Altruism, Compassion, and Service*. Philadelphia, PA: Templeton Foundation Press.

Putnam, Robert. 2000. *Bowling Alone: The Collapse and Revival of American Community*. New York, NY: Simon & Schuster.

Reisch, Michael, and David Sommerfeld. 2003. "Interorganizational Relationships among Nonprofits in the Aftermath of Welfare Reform." *Social Work* 48(3): 307–19.

Rice, William Craig. 1997. "I Hear America Singing: The Arts Will Flower Without the NEA." *Policy Review* 82: 37–45.

Robinson, James W., and Russ Colliau. 1995. *After the Revolution: A Citizen's Guide to the First Republican Congress in Forty Years*. Washington, DC: Prima.

Rodrigue, George. 1996. "Gingrich Aims for Kinder Image." *Dallas Morning News*, August 14: 20A.

Salamon, Lester M. 1995. *Partners in Public Service: Government-Nonprofit Relations in the Modern Welfare State*. Baltimore, MD: Johns Hopkins University Press.

Sabrin, Amy. 1993. "Thinking about Content: Can It Play an Appropriate Role in Government Funding of the Arts?" *Yale Law Journal* 102(5): 1209–34.

Scheff, Joanne, and Philip Kotler. 1996. "Crisis in the Arts: The Marketing Response." *California Management Review* 39(1): 28–59.

Seaman, Bruce A. 2002. *National Investment in the Arts: Art, Culture and the National Agenda*. Washington, DC: Center for Arts and Culture. http://www.culturalpolicy.org/pdf/investment.pdf.

Sherman, Amy L. 2000. "Churches as Government Partners: Navigating 'Charitable Choice.'" *Christian Century* 117(20): 716–21.

Sider, Ronald J. 2005. "Evaluating the Faith-Based Initiative: Is Charitable Choice Good Public Policy?" *Theology Today* 67(4): 485–98.

Sine, Tom. 1996. *Cease Fire: Searching for Sanity in America's Culture Wars*. Grand Rapids, MI: Eerdmans.

Smith, Christian. 1998. *American Evangelicals: Embattled and Thriving*. Chicago, IL: University of Chicago Press.

Smith, Steven Rathgeb, and Michael Lipsky. 1993. *Nonprofits for Hire: The Welfare State in the Age of Contracting*. Cambridge, MA: Harvard University Press.

Trescott, Jacqueline. 1997. "Senate Spares NEA: Bids to Eliminate Agency's Funding Are Defeated." *Washington Post*, September 18: B2.

Van Camp, Julie C. 1997. *Freedom of Expression at the National Endowment for the Arts: An Interdisciplinary Curriculum Project Funded by the American Bar Association, Commission on College and University Legal Studies through the ABA Fund for Justice and Education*. Long Beach: California State University, Department of Philosophy.

Walker, Chris. 2004. *Arts and Non-arts Partnerships: Opportunities, Challenges, and Strategies*. Washington, DC: The Urban Institute.

Walker, Chris, and Kay Sherwood. 2003. *Participation in Arts and Culture: The Importance of Community Venues*. Washington, DC: The Urban Institute.

Watt, David Harrington. 1991. "United States: Cultural Challenges to the Voluntary Sector." In *Between States and Markets: The Voluntary Sector in Comparative Perspective*, edited by Robert Wuthnow (243–87). Princeton, NJ: Princeton University Press.

Weber, Bruce. 2004. "Endowment Chairman Coaxes Funds for the Arts." *New York Times*, September 7: E1.

Weisbrod, Burton A. 1988. *The Nonprofit Economy*. Cambridge, MA: Harvard University Press.

White, John Kenneth. 2002. *Values Divide: American Politics and Culture in Transition*. Boston, MA: Chatham House.

Williams, Rhys, ed. 1997. *Cultural Wars in American Politics: Critical Reviews of a Popular Myth*. New York, NY: Aldine de Gruyter.

Winston, Pamela. 2002. *Welfare Policymaking in the States: The Devil in Devolution*. Washington, DC: Georgetown University Press.

Wolch, Jennifer R. 1990. *The Shadow State: Government and Voluntary Sector in Transition*. New York, NY: Foundation Center.

Wolfe, Alan. 1999. *One Nation, After All: What Americans Really Think about God, Country, Family, Racism, Welfare, Immigration, Homosexuality, Work, the Right, the Left and Each Other*. New York, NY: Penguin.

Wong, Shun Ning. 1998. "Determining Decency." *Princeton University Law Journal* 3(1). http://www.princeton.edu/~lawjourn/Fall98.

Wuthnow, Robert. 1989. *The Restructuring of American Religion: Society and Faith Since World War II*. Princeton, NJ: Princeton University Press.

———. 1991. "Tocqueville's Question Reconsidered: Voluntarism and Public Discourse in Advanced Industrial Societies." In *Between States and Markets: The Voluntary Sector in Comparative Perspective*, edited by Robert Wuthnow (288–308). Princeton, NJ: Princeton University Press.

———. 1996a. *Christianity and Civil Society: The Contemporary Debate*. Philadelphia, PA: Trinity Press International.

———. 1996b. "Restructuring of American Religion: Further Evidence." *Sociological Inquiry* 66(3): 303–29.

———. 1998. *Loose Connections: Joining Together in America's Fragmented Communities*. Cambridge, MA: Harvard University Press.

———. 2001a. "Arts Leaders and Religious Leaders: Mutual Perceptions." In *Crossroads: Art and Religion in American Life*, edited by Alberta Arthurs and Glenn Wallach (31–70). New York, NY: The New Press.

———. 2001b. *Creative Spirituality: The Way of the Artist*. Berkeley: University of California Press.

———. 2003. *All In Sync: How Music and Art Are Revitalizing American Religion*. Berkeley: University of California Press.

———. 2004. *Saving America? Faith-Based Services and the Future of Civil Society*. Princeton, NJ: Princeton University Press.

Wuthnow, Robert, and John Evans, eds. 2002. *The Quiet Hand of God: Faith-Based Activism and the Public Role of Mainline Protestantism*. Berkeley: University of California Press.

10

ADVOCACY AND THE CHALLENGES IT PRESENTS FOR NONPROFITS

Elizabeth J. Reid

Americans have a long-standing tradition of association and expression on political issues (Barber 2002; Reid 2003). Today, they largely organize their voices through a variety of nonprofit organizations— for example, large membership organizations, unions, locally based civic action groups, political organizations, issue-oriented lobbies, and social service organizations. In fact, nonprofit organizations are a familiar institutional force in American politics on almost every side of every issue. They promote the interests, values, and preferences of a diverse civic culture that includes the mainstream and minority, social service providers and their clients, businesses and employees, and the religious and secular. Indeed, nonprofits themselves have become a well-organized lobby on policy issues affecting the nonprofit sector.

Along with elected officials and formal institutions of government, nonprofits are part of the system of representation in American democracy (Boris and Krehely 2002; Reid 2000, 2003; Reid and Montilla 2001, 2002). They monitor policy, put forward policy positions, agree and disagree with government, and support and challenge public officials. Their influence is not limited to the legislative process, but includes court and executive appointments and agency rule-making. Nonprofits are also part of broader social movements that mobilize volunteers and resources to voice widespread social concerns and push for government reforms (Reid and Montilla 2001; Zald and McCarthy 1987). They educate and mobilize voters during elections (Green and Gerber 2004; Magleby 2000) and often play significant roles in the initiation and advancement of ballot initiatives (Reid 2003). Many look beyond government to address issues of corporate responsibility both here and abroad and to improve accountability of international financial institutions and multilateral organizations.

Until recently, government regulation of nonprofit advocacy was primarily concerned with charitable lobbying expenditures. New organizational practices by nonprofits and recent changes to federal campaign finance laws have created a need for additional clarification of current regulations and have stimulated discussion about additional reform. The Internal Revenue Service (IRS), the federal agency charged with oversight of tax-exempt organizations, remains concerned that charitable donations not be diverted to partisan purposes. However, clarifying the proper role for regulation and defining the boundaries between public education and political intervention is challenging for tax regulators when nonprofits use sophisticated media messages to influence voter behavior, skirting the traditional definitions of partisanship. Complex organizational structures and a lack of detailed reporting on political activities make it difficult to understand the full extent of political engagement by groups.

Additionally, the Federal Election Commission (FEC), charged with oversight of the financing of federal elections, wants individuals, political parties, and political organizations, including nonprofits, to reveal sources and amounts of partisan contributions and stay within appropriate election spending limits. Recent passage of federal campaign reforms raised public awareness about the extent of soft money[1] in the political system, banned its use by national political parties in federal elections, and limited its use for certain types of highly partisan broadcast advertising close to election days. However, the law did not address the use of soft money expenditures for a range of election-oriented activity by nonprofit organizations, generating questions about the adequacy of current FEC regulation and reporting standards to capture the full extent of partisan campaign activity and expenditures in federal elections.

Nonprofits face organizational challenges in this changing regulatory environment. Most nonprofit organizations occasionally engage government on issues and find lobbying and political regulations at best confusing and at worst a deterrent to political engagement (Berry with Arons 2003). Generally speaking, nonprofits frequently resist proposed regulatory and reporting reforms as a form of government overreaching, potentially threatening their autonomy to openly exchange ideas, overburdening their organizations administratively, and impinging on their right to freely associate and speak with one voice. Charitable organizations concerned about protecting donor anonymity, a major incentive for charitable giving, are cautious of the potential impact on organizational funding from calls for greater financial transparency. Nonprofit-sector advocates fiercely protect the right of individuals to associate privately and of their organizational leaders to speak freely on policy issues and on the performance of pubic officials. Issue-oriented membership organizations, labor unions, and trade associations with voting members and elected leaders are particularly sensitive to constraints on their organization's ability to represent member interests.

This chapter updates topics on advocacy practices and lobbying regulation of nonprofits introduced in the first edition of *Nonprofits and Government* (Boris and Steuerle 1999). During the last 10 years, the Internet has transformed communications, government priorities have shifted, and nonprofits have developed new organizational forms and strategic capacities that make them prominent actors in elections. Regulation of nonprofit advocacy is in flux as groups take on new political roles and practices. These changes and others have occurred during a period of heightened partisanship, federal campaign finance reform, and greater public scrutiny of nonprofit practices. The chapter discusses these conditions and identifies areas needing greater accountability in organizational governance and advocacy practices and greater clarity in regulatory policies. Better accountability and clarity can engender public confidence in nonprofits, build public engagement in democratic processes, and improve the relationship among citizens, civil society organizations, and government.

Nonprofit Advocacy in a Highly Charged Political Environment

Even the best prepared organizations recognize the limits of their influence in the political system. Nonprofit advocacy efforts can influence the speed at which the political system addresses problems, and, by framing issues, the way in which policies are designed and attract support. Advocacy can also shape democratic procedures, such as voting rules, legislative procedures, or nonprofit political regulation, sometimes increasing and encouraging greater civic participation.

Advocacy can shape how policy is implemented by influencing the approaches and mechanisms used to put new policy into practice. And advocacy can increase voter engagement, animating constituencies on issues that increase registration rates and voter turnout during elections.

Organizations and Their Structures

The array of nonprofit organizations shaping public understanding of issues and attempting to influence government policy is diverse in size and scope. Nonprofits referred to as interest groups are large organizations and highly visible in Congress and state legislatures as they try to shape budget and policy priorities in areas such as taxes, reproductive health, the environment, health care, education, and human services. Smaller civic-minded organizations tend to be more intermittent in their policy advocacy, becoming active when decisions at the state and local level of government affect, for example, public services, development, jobs, or education (Minkoff 2002).

Civil rights and civil liberties organizations have advocated for federally guaranteed nondiscrimination, establishing norms that have broadened the social contract between government and its citizens (Axelrod 2002; Skrentny 2002). Think tanks bring information to bear on policy choices and approach policy engagement from a range of tactical perspectives, some as impartial technical experts, others as ideologues (Rich 2004). Many nonprofit organizations are global in reach and advocate before national and foreign governments and multilateral institutions on issues such as environmental degradation, human rights, trade, peace and security, and foreign aid (Florini 2000; Keck and Sikkink 1998; Lindenberg and Bryant 2001).

Organizations use a variety of organizational arrangements and structures to align support and enlarge resources for their advocacy campaigns. They form policy networks and coalitions as a way to coordinate scarce resources and reduce political competition (Hula 1999). Organizational affiliations are particularly important for small organizations that lack the capacity to wage policy campaigns on their own. Coalitions and networks coordinate media expertise, mobilize constituencies, and build political connections into unified campaigns for change. Policy entrepreneurs and skilled organizational leaders expand the exchange of information on and resources for policy influence (Kingdon 1995).

Nonprofits structure and govern themselves in a variety of ways to carry out their political roles. Large interest groups may employ multiple tax-exempt entities to deal with different tax and political regulations and permit a wider range of political activity (Reid and Kerlin

2003), a trend discussed in the next section of this chapter. Board structures may also facilitate advocacy activity. Board members may work on political affairs committees or take responsibility for moving forward resolutions on policy positions, prioritizing policy issues, budgeting for advocacy, coordinating community input, and shaping staffing for policy action (De Vita et al. 2004).

Scholars examining structures, membership, and democratic practices in organizations note how democratic processes and communication structures inside of organizations in turn shape the character of civic voice in the political system (Barakso 2005; Rosenblum 1998; Shaiko 1999; Skocpol 2003; Warren 2000). Some nonprofits are membership organizations and weigh member interests and opinions before advocating organizational positions in public and before elected officials, acting more or less as a conveyor of constituency interests. Others have few ties with members or constituencies and act independently, attracting donors and employing experts to seed new policy ideas, promote policy positions, or monitor program performance. Some have paid professional staff with political skills, whereas others rely primarily on board members and community leaders and volunteers to generate interest and support for policy initiatives.

Some nonprofit forms are more controversial. "Astroturf" organizations are commonly run by political consulting firms and act as conduits for fundraising and use market techniques to generate support or opposition on policy issues from niche constituencies. Some charities are closely connected with elected officials, raising questions about whether they operate in the interest of the charity or the politicians (Reid and Montilla 2001).

Nonprofit Advocacy Activities

Nonprofits use a wide range of advocacy activities to affect how policy is made (Reid 1999). Many are familiar activities in the nonprofit toolbox, such as public education, media exposure, and lobbying, but advocacy activities have also been changing in recent years in response to corporate practices, globalization, technology, political pressure, close elections, and regulatory reforms. A popular way for groups to bring issues directly before voters is for citizens organizations to place initiatives on the ballot. Partisans, who initially saw ballot initiatives as citizen challenges to officials and political parties, are increasingly viewing ballot initiatives as useful for mobilizing voters. For example, in 1996 the Republican Party infused Americans for Tax Reform with $4.5 million to sponsor antitax initiatives and paycheck protection in California to increase conservative voter turnout in elections, which, if passed, would have affected the political voice of unions and other nonprofit organizations, such as the United Way, that are reliant on paycheck deductions (Smith and Tolbert 2004).

In the face of government reluctance to regulate, nonprofit campaigns for greater corporate responsibility focus on corporate accountability to shareholders on fiscal matters, greater responsibility in social and environmental matters, and improved labor practices with living wages and health benefits. Some groups have made strides in urging corporations to adopt voluntary industry standards on social and environmental issues. For example, a broad coalition of faith organizations, the Interfaith Center on Corporate Responsibility, raised concerns with corporations about the inappropriate marketing of violent video games to youth and urged retailers, game developers, and marketers to conform with standards that limit the exposure of youth to videos with violence and strong sexual content.

Globalization has widened the scope of activities and issues in which U.S. nonprofits are involved (Reid and Kerlin 2005). U.S. nonprofits or nongovernmental organizations have always played a strong role in delivering development and assistance services, but globalization has increased awareness about the consequences across borders of national government action or inaction on environmental, trade, and human rights issues, spawning nongovernmental organization growth and action around the world (Anheier, Glasius, and Kaldor 2002; Brinkerhoff and Brinkerhoff 2002). To be effective advocates, U.S. nonprofits have become active in networks with nongovernmental organizations from other countries, with foreign governments and multilateral institutions. The International Campaign to Ban Landmines, for example, is based in the United States but works on a global problem. Although 464 of the 1,300 member organizations that signed onto the campaign to ban landmines are U.S. religious and civil society organizations, the U.S. government does not support the Mine Ban Treaty. To leverage the support needed for the ban, the organization secures endorsements for the ban and financial and volunteer support from foreign governments, organizations, and individuals from around the globe.

From a tactical point of view, new communication technologies have transformed the ability of advocates to find new recruits and money, communicate quickly, and inspire action toward specific ends (Bennett and Fielding 1999). The Internet has become an indispensable tool for nonprofit advocates, expanding their capacity for information dissemination to the public and contact with elected officials; providing improved fundraising opportunities; facilitating networking with allies; deepening the reach of organizations to unaffiliated individuals; and strengthening communication among staff, boards, members, and donors. In the health subsector, for example, new Internet-based advocacy organizations stress individual rights in the health system, transforming an institutional landscape once populated by organizations that focused on health services, funding, and research for specific diseases. Using the Internet as a flexible tool for advocacy, these new health nonprofits spread their messages broadly and adapt their communications quickly to changing conditions (Brainard and Siplon 2002).

The Policy Environment

In a positive model for civil society and democracy, nonprofits would anchor representative government in the values and interests of the citizenry. Civic organizations would affiliate citizens and deliberate public issues so that government could glean a broad spectrum of views and experiences from civil society to construct responsive public policy. Organizational affiliations would motivate citizens to engage in politics by participating in parties and other political organizations, voting in primaries and elections, shaping candidates for public office, and running for office themselves. Nonprofits would open democratic processes to new voices and voters—for example, by promoting the inclusion in policy deliberations of underrepresented voices of immigrants or the poor. In short, organizations would contribute to keeping American democracy popular, open, and just, and their advocacy would serve to enlarge the public consensus for the general welfare.

In reality, nonprofits face a fragmented consensus about the extent of the roles and responsibilities of government, business, civil society, and individual citizens in providing for the general welfare. Nonprofits must work hard to be heard and to strike political bargains with governments that are partisan, divided, and often stalemated. They must operate in an environment where private interests, including the funding of nonprofits, may trump common interests. Political dollars may outweigh civic voice, bureaucracies may stifle expression and action, and government priorities—such as defense, terrorism prevention, and deficit reduction—may overshadow other pressing public concerns. Sometimes nonprofits, like other institutions, can be faulted for fragmenting and polarizing the electorate on policy issues.

Nonprofits working in challenging political environments are faced with adapting their advocacy to policy shifts. Established nonprofits must navigate the ascent and descent from power of politicians and parties during political transitions. Policy priorities shift with the party in power, pressing events, and budgets. New groups form; some rise to prominence with the development of new policy; other groups live on to resist, adapt, or reorganize; and others disappear (Minkoff 1999; Reid and Montilla 2002). In the past 25 years, nonprofits have helped build and unravel liberal majorities and policy priorities and now play prominent roles in the conservative majority and its issue agenda.

On the one hand, an era of conservatism has meant a sea change in political conditions for many nonprofits that were formerly ascendant, diminishing opportunities for action and funding. Some social service groups, environmental organizations, reproductive rights organizations, minority rights groups, labor unions, women's organizations, and others have been put on the defensive about the values underpinning policies they promote and the availability of public resources for these policy priorities. The federal system, where substantial authority rests with states and localities, encourages policy innovation and change at all levels of government, but constant shifts in government priorities, spending reductions, and federal and state budget deficits have created organizational crises, particularly for charitable, social service organizations that built a presence on policy issues when government grants and spending on social services were increasing or stable. They must answer hard questions: What strategies will build long-term public and political support for programs that serve their constituents when priorities change? How can innovative programs and reforms be brought to scale?

On the other hand, nonprofits advancing conservative social and economic values—such as limited government and reduced taxation, education reform, tort reform, right-to-life issues, conservative court appointments, and faith-based social services—have used political openings to advance their ideas, policies, and programs and have helped build conservative majorities in Congress and on the courts. Religious organizations, think tanks, foundations, businesses, and trade organizations illustrate the power of organizations to coalesce for policy and electoral gains and collaborate with coordinated research, public messages, political donations, and constituency mobilization to elect majorities (Micklethwait and Wooldridge 2004).

The contested 2000 presidential election and 2001 federal campaign finance reform, the first federal reform in 25 years, were grounds for nonprofits from both ends of the political spectrum to evaluate their contributions to voter engagement and operate under a new regulatory framework (Boatwright et al. 2003). In anticipation of the federal elections, nonprofits coalesced and launched issue campaigns. They revamped their operations to inform voters about candidate positions, to improve election laws and procedures, and to register voters and generate voter turnout that would benefit candidates they favored. Charitable organizations adhered to strict nonpartisan outreach strategies required by law. Other types of nonprofits under more liberal political regulations—such as 501(c)(4) membership organizations, unions, and trade associations—made political endorsements and sent partisan messages to members to motivate them to act as a voting bloc.

Large nonprofit interest groups, such as the National Rifle Association or the Sierra Club, often favor one party over another as the standard-bearer for their cause. More recently, observers have come to understand the key role of think tanks and foundations in shaping the agenda for policy change that is then more aggressively pursued by interest groups. Several studies have examined ideological preferences and partisan alignment in think tanks and foundations to discover the nexus between funding and the promotion of ideas that gain popular currency and are advanced through the political system (Krehely, House, and Kernan 2004; Rich 2004).

Conservative and liberal preferences can be discerned in patterns of foundation support for nonprofits. The National Committee for Responsive Philanthropy, an outspoken critic of underspending by liberal foundations for groups engaged in advocacy, has documented patterns of giving among conservative foundations that benefit the advancement of conservative policy agendas (Krehely, House, and Kernan 2004). A recent study found the largest U.S. foundations provided about 11 percent of their grant dollars to support structural changes aiding those least well off economically, socially, and politically by promoting economic development in distressed areas; ensure access to health care for disadvantaged populations; and encourage diversity in education (Independent Sector and The Foundation Center 2005).

Though policy advocacy is often portrayed as adversarial, collaborative arrangements between government and nonprofits based on shared ideology and mutual self-interest also shape government–nonprofit relations in the policy process, particularly at the state and local levels of government. The T.E.A.C.H. (Teacher Education and Compensation Helps) Early Childhood Project exemplifies how partnership with government can facilitate change (Kerlin, Reid, and Auer 2003). This model program, initiated in North Carolina, provides financial support for training and improves certification standards and compensation for child care workers. Once the idea for T.E.A.C.H. spread throughout the nonprofit community, groups lobbied to have it funded. Often nonprofits were able to gain the support of key state legislators and agency administrators to facilitate funding. Once funded, nonprofits partnered with agencies and community colleges to make sure child care workers would take advantage of the program's benefits.

Government Funding and Advocacy

Scholars and nonprofit managers often differ as to whether financial interdependency with government is a plus or minus for advocates. Advocacy organizations with government grants and contracts can face criticism as self-interested organizations when calling for policy reform. In some instances, groups forgo government funding altogether, as is the case with Oxfam America, to maintain independence of action.

Many groups report a dampening effect on advocacy when they are entwined with government through grants and programs. Yet some research suggests otherwise. One study suggests that financial support by government does not necessarily constrain political activity (Chaves, Stephens, and Galaskiewicz 2004). Organizational size may be a factor. Nonprofit lobbying expenditures reported on the IRS Form 990 indicate government grants and lobbying appear to be compatible, at least for large organizations. Forty-two percent of lobbying organizations receive government grants, and 64 percent of the lobbying organizations with government grants are large (National Center for Charitable Statistics 2002).

Organizational Capacity

Given the political challenges advocates face in promoting their causes, it is not surprising that many nonprofits, especially small charitable organizations, opt out of politics altogether. With narrowly defined service missions and competing organizational priorities, they are unlikely to dedicate precious resources to advocacy. For example, advocacy to improve client conditions through better public policy may take a back seat to daily obligations to clients and donors. Deficits in organizational capacity, such as a lack of money, time, and leadership, can discourage organizations from pursuing advocacy activities. When they advocate, organizations must contend with tax and political regulations about the permissibility of legislative and political activities and expenditures. In fact, many nonprofits do not lobby on policy issues even though they are permitted to lobby under current regulations (National Council of Nonprofit Associations 2005).

In spite of the political and organizational obstacles, advocates often persist and sometimes succeed (Reid and Montilla 2001). Strategies for surmounting difficulties include training organizations to be advocates (and providing incentives or funding for participating in the training); building strategic cooperation among potential allies; engaging organizational entrepreneurs with political networks; and developing sound policy information and dissemination strategies.

Organizational preparation and resources, the execution of an influential political strategy, and a clear regulatory framework can help groups enter politics and shape public outcomes in ways that are transparent and accountable to citizens and democratic processes. And groups that use their collective voice to strengthen public awareness, policy development, program implementation, and voter participation rightly stake a claim in the initiatives they have helped to advance.

Organizational successes in a political system with multiple opportunities for influence mean groups see their impacts through a different lens. Success is sometimes elusive, for example, in long-standing campaigns to eradicate AIDS (Chambre 1997) or in the ongoing campaign to alleviate poverty in the United States and abroad. Sometimes success is defensive, when groups are able to prevent budget cuts, tax increases, or legislation they deem harmful to their constituencies. Sometimes success is small and targeted to specific constituencies—for example, cajoling local government for basic neighborhood services or preventing a damaging cut in an essential social service program for children (De Vita and Mosher-Williams 2001). Sometimes success is large and the effects of change widespread, such as when groups align in broad political coalitions that can ultimately alter policy approaches, political parties, and the terms of the social contract between government and citizens.

To summarize, nonprofits that advocate are a diverse group of organizations with a variety of structures, capacities, resources, tactics, constituencies, and alliances. To be successful advocates, they must overcome four organizational challenges: securing sufficient organizational capacity; devising a strategic direction that will advance their cause in a crowded and changing political environment; using resources in efficient, effective, and accountable ways; and navigating a complex regulatory framework. In the next section, we turn to the regulatory framework.

Nonprofit Advocacy in a Complex and Fluctuating Regulatory Framework

Nonprofit advocates must abide by regulations from multiple authorities, depending on the advocacy activities and tax status of their organizations. Lobbying by charities and some political expenditures are subject to IRS limits, taxation, and reporting requirements. Federal election contributions and expenditures are subject to federal election law, reviewed by the FEC, with the sources and amounts of contributions and expenditures disclosed regularly to the FEC. Nonprofits that lobby and engage in election-related activities at the state and local levels face additional regulations from states in which they operate. Further, nonprofits that receive government grants and contracts are subject to oversight by the Office of Management and Budget (OMB), are not permitted to use federal funds for lobbying, and may face additional restrictions by agencies responsible for the specific programs.

Finally, regulations in some areas, such as Internet lobbying and issue advocacy, are changing, so nonprofits need to keep a close eye on new regulatory developments.

In this section, I examine some prominent areas of federal regulation for policy and electoral advocacy activities of charitable and other types of exempt organizations, such as social welfare organizations, unions, and trade associations, along with related Section 527 political organizations. The discussion focuses on the interaction between nonprofit advocacy practices and advocacy regulations. Table 10.1 provides a brief overview of lobbying and election regulation for 501(c)(3), social welfare 501(c)(4) organizations, and Section 527 political organizations. The following discussion is not intended to be a guide for advocates.[2]

Regulation of Lobbying by Charities

The IRS limits lobbying of charitable organizations to approximately 20 percent of their annual expenditures. The rationale for limits on lobbying expenditures stems from the revenue forgone by the government when donors deduct their charitable contributions from their income taxes. This tax subsidy benefits charitable organizations by providing an incentive for donors to contribute. This rationale was articulated in *Regan v. Taxation with Representation of Washington* when the Supreme Court, in upholding advocacy limits, ruled that free speech does not mean subsidized speech. The IRS collects financial information on lobbying expenditures, defined narrowly as expenditures on direct or grassroots contact with elected officials on specific legislation or judicial appointments, and levies financial penalties on organizations that exceed the expenditure limits.

Most nonprofit advocates accept the logic in *Regan* but still argue that lobbying limitations and other restrictions are infringements on fundamental First Amendment rights of speech and association. (See the argument by Brody in Reid [2003].) Given the low level of lobbying engagement overall, they question whether the subsidy rationale has had the unintended consequence of further suppressing engagement in a democracy that espouses popular expression and action as a center-piece of legitimate government. Rates of lobbying in the nonprofit sector and some recent studies may give credence to their concerns.

With IRS Form 990 data from the NCCS Guidestar National Nonprofit Research Database (National Center for Charitable Statistics 2002), it is possible to approximate the scope of lobbying by charitable organizations and to observe some variation in lobbying by size and type of tax-exempt organization. These data indicate that few charitable organizations report lobbying on federal or state legislation. In FY 2002, 1.9 percent of charitable organizations with more than $25,000 in annual revenues reported lobbying expenditures. The percentage has remained steady at around 2 percent for the past 10 years. In FY 2002, a higher percentage of environmental groups and civil rights and liberties organizations lobbied than did other categories of nonprofits.

These data also confirm the important role of financial resources among lobbying organizations. Thirty-two percent of lobbying organizations were small, with less than $500,000 in annual revenue; 19 percent are medium sized, with $500,000 to $2 million in annual revenue; and 48 percent were large organizations, with more than $2 million in annual revenue. Large or small, most organizations that lobby do not spend up to their permissible expenditure limits for lobbying. Only 1 percent of the lobbying organizations had spent between 15 and 20 percent of their total expenditures on lobbying, though small organizations were more likely to reach or exceed their lobbying limits.

To determine effects of existing regulations on charitable lobbying and advocacy, Jeff Berry with David Arons (2003) studied more than 2,000 groups and found that nonprofits viewed the rules as overly complex and that reporting requirements were a deterrent to action. Berry and other nonprofit sector watchdog organizations make the case for full implementation of simplified reporting of lobbying expenditures, or the 501(h) election,[3] as a way to remove a regulatory barrier to lobbying by charitable organizations.

Several organizations help charitable organizations become more engaged in lobbying. Independent Sector and OMB Watch provide training for nonprofits on what is permissible activity and how to report it. They have also sponsored campaigns to urge foundations to remove restrictive language on lobbying from their grant agreements with organizations. Alliance for Justice, a coalition of politically active nonprofits, trains groups about the most strategic and efficient ways to structure and finance their organizations within the tax-exempt legal framework and trains lawyers and accountants that represent nonprofits in the Advocacy Lawyers and Accountants Network (Alliance for Justice 2005). These nonprofit-sector trade organizations and coalitions represent a formidable lobby on behalf of the nonprofit sector, defending the advocacy of nonprofits as critical public input to developing policies responsive to communities and opposing government regulation that might further dampen nonprofit advocacy activity.

Whether or not the limits are appropriate, constraints on the political activities of public benefit organizations are becoming more common around the world. As they become more integrated into legal and tax systems, public benefit organizations are increasingly subject to registration, reporting, and political restrictions.[4] Lester Salamon makes the point in chapter 12, however, that in most countries there are fewer legal constraints on nonprofit advocacy and lobbying than in the United States.

Attempts to further constrain advocacy, such as the discourse and hearings over the proposed Istook amendment, and IRS investigations of advocacy activities by certain groups have not produced convincing evidence of the need for further regulation of charitable lobbying. Nonprofit organizations often consider more restrictive measures to be politically motivated efforts to eliminate resistance to policy change. At a time when social service organizations were lobbying against federal budget cuts, proponents of the Istook amendment argued that the government was subsidizing the lobbying of charitable organizations with political interests and moved, unsuccessfully, to draw a line between advocacy and charitable activity.

A report by OMB Watch has documented how restrictive rule-making and revenue cuts can be used to target certain kinds of social service programs, most recently family planning, health assistance for AIDS, and housing (Bass, Guinane, and Turner 2003). In 2005, a group of conservative House members persuaded the sponsors of the Federal Housing Finance Reform Act (a bill designed to reform certain government-sponsored housing enterprises), such as Fannie Mae and Freddie Mac, to add provisions that would bar organizations that lobby or engage in nonpartisan election-related activities from applying for grants from the new fund.

Nonprofit Election-Related Advocacy and Regulation

Elections provide citizens the opportunity to exercise their fundamental and sovereign right to vote to constitute their government. One way or another, nonprofits are taking advantage of their connections with citizens and their knowledge of the issues to influence voter preferences through raising and spending private dollars for broadcast ads during elections, voter information on candidate positions, candidate forums, and coordinated, targeted voter turnout operations. Competitive national elections in 2000 and 2004 brought to light the important roles that different forms of tax-exempt organizations play in elections.

Charitable organizations, though mindful of their need to remain nonpartisan in their outreach to voters, have nevertheless found highly strategic ways to provide information to their members and constituents at election time. In 2004, the Center for Community Change partnered with 53 organizations in 26 states to launch the Community Voting Project to make a difference in community awareness on issues and to increase voter turnout among low turnout populations, such as the poor, immigrant, and Native American communities throughout the country (Bhargava 2004). Churches and religious organizations also joined in the chorus of organized expression, with moral issues front

Table 10.1. Lobbying and Election Regulation for Tax-Exempt Organizations

	501(c)(3) charitable organizations	501(c)(4)–(6)	Section 527 political organizations
Key tax rules	Tax-exempt and contributors may deduct contributions	Tax-exempt, but contributors do not receive deduction	No tax on contributions spent on permitted politial activity
	No federal gift tax on contributions	Federal gift tax on donors for contributions over $10,000	Business and investment income is taxed
		Tax on investment income to the extent of electioneering expenditures	No federal gift tax
General permitted activities and reporting	Charitable and educational activities, including all forms of public education on policy issues	Activities primarily for social welfare, including any activities permitted by charitable organizations, plus any activity that serves public purposes	Must be primarily involved in activities to influence elections. Electioneering activities include all forms of partisan-oriented voter influence except express advocacy
	Files IRS Form 990 annually; indicates lobbying expenses; no public disclosure of donors	Lobbying and election-related advocacy permitted	Nonpolitical activities may give rise to tax
		Files IRS Form 990; indicates political expenditures; no public disclosure of donors	If 527 is PAC or political committee conducting express advocacy on behalf of candidates or donating to campaigns and parties, it reports financial transactions and donors to FEC
			If 527 is a political organization engaged in electioneering, it reports to IRS; also reports BCRA-defined broadcast electioneering communications to the FEC

(continued)

Table 10.1. Lobbying and Election Regulation for Tax-Exempt Organizations *(cont.)*

	501(c)(3) charitable organizations	*501(c)(4)–(6)*	*Section 527 political organizations*
Lobbying activity and reporting Defined by IRS as direct or grassroots support for or against specific legislation	Lobbying is allowed to a limited extent. May not be "substantial," generally interpreted to be approximately 20% of expenditures. Or may be defined by 501(h) election limits for simplified reporting. Report expenditures on Schedule A of IRS Form 990 Register and report state lobbying as required by state law No lobbying by private foundations	May lobby without restriction, so lobbying may be the exclusive activity of the organization No separate reporting of lobbying required on IRS Form 990, but combined lobbying and political expenditures are reported Register with House clerk and secretary of Senate; report semiannual lobbying expenses Register and report state lobbying as required by state law	For IRS, lobbying is not an exempt function (i.e., not a political activity) and may give rise to tax
Nonpartisan election-related activity and reporting IRS regards communications on issues that do not promote, support, attack, or oppose a federal candidate as nonpartisan issue advocacy. Uses six part "facts and circumstances" test to determine if activity is nonpartisan or partisan. Nonpartisan activities financed by soft money	IRS permits nonpartisan voter registration, voter education, candidate forums and candidate education, and get-out-the-vote activities. Permits nonpartisan issue advocacy. No reporting required for nonpartisan election-related activity	IRS permits same activities as 501(c)(3) IRS permits nonpartisan issue advocacy. No reporting required for nonpartisan election-related activity	Issue advocacy, as defined by the IRS, is a nonexempt activity Nonpartisan activities may give rise to tax

(continued)

Table 10.1. Lobbying and Election Regulation for Tax-Exempt Organizations *(cont.)*

	501(c)(3) charitable organizations	*501(c)(4)–(6)*	*Section 527 political organizations*
Partisan activity or express advocacy and reporting Defined as use of language for or against a candidate for elected office Must be financed through hard money	Outright prohibition on campaign intervention, including endorsing or opposing a candidate—implicit or explicit; coordinating activities with a candidate; contributing money, time, or facilities to a candidate; setting up, funding, or managing a PAC. Partisan communications and expenditures prohibited by IRS	IRS permits express advocacy communications with members, but not with public Political expenditures reported to IRS, but must not be a primary organizational activity	Permitted and unlimited for 527s that are not political committees, provided organization registers and files disclosure reports with FEC 527 PACs and political parties, subject to FEC limits for hard money contributions and expenditures.
Other electioneering activity and reporting Evolving area of law and regulation. In BCRA, FEC defines electioneering communications as broadcast ads directed at a candidate's constituents and distributed for a fee that *refer to* a candidate for federal office aired within 30 days of a primary or 60 days of a general election	IRS generally prohibits issue advocacy that promotes or criticizes particular candidates by prohibiting issue advocacy that is electioneering or partisan activity.	Electioneering may not be a primary organizational activity Reported to the IRS as a political expenditure when activity promotes or criticizes particular candidates. No donor disclosure required When electioneering is consistent with FEC definition of broadcast electioneering, no corporate or union financing is permitted and organizations must report donors, contributions, and expenditures to FEC	All forms of electioneering permitted 527s regularly disclose donors, contributions, and expenditures to IRS Broadcast electioneering communications regularly disclosed to FEC Qualified state and local organizations report to state campaign finance agencies

(continued)

Table 10.1. Lobbying and Election Regulation for Tax-Exempt Organizations *(cont.)*

	501(c)(3) charitable organizations	*501(c)(4)–(6)*	*Section 527 political organizations*
Federal campaign contributions and reporting Donations and expenditures to candidates for federal office and national political parties. State laws vary for state and local campaigns and parties	Prohibited	FEC prohibits campaign expenditures directly from organization, but permitted by a connected PAC May solicit members for contributions to the PAC and pay for administration of PAC and PAC solicitations. FEC limits on size of individual donations to PACs and parties and expenditures to campaign or party Donors and expenditures reportable to FEC	Restrictions on size of individual donations to PACs and parties and expenditures to campaigns and parties

BCRA = Bipartisan Campaign Reform Act; FEC = Federal Election Commission; IRS = Internal Revenue Service; PAC = political action committees

and center in the 2000 and 2004 presidential elections. Republican activists, nonprofit leaders, and religious organizations backed citizens' initiatives to ban gay marriage in 11 states, conducting intense voter contact campaigns. The issue of abortion was further highlighted when some Catholic bishops professed their unwillingness to allow 2004 presidential candidate John Kerry to participate in communion because of his pro-choice platform (Hillygus and Shields 2005). Many political observers consider moral issues to have had a positive influence on Republican victories, though scholars of voter behavior have questioned the real impact of voter value preferences on election outcomes (Smith 2005).

Social welfare organizations (501[c][4]), unions (501[c][5]), and professional and trade organizations (501[c][6]) may lobby without restriction and engage in issue advocacy and some forms of electioneering as long as it is not the primary focus of their organizational operation (Reid 2004). Further, many are structured as membership organizations and are permitted to have partisan communication with members and solicit donations from them for hard money contributions to their connected political action committees (PACs). These more liberal rules make the 501(c)(4) social welfare organization a popular organizational form for public interest, environmental, tax, pro-choice, pro-life, gun, and other advocacy organizations with regular lobbying and political operations.

Section 527 organizations are the most partisan of the tax-exempt organizations. They are chartered as tax-exempt organizations and report to either the IRS or the FEC, depending on the nature of their activities. The more traditional form of the Section 527 political organizations are PACs and political parties that raise and expend money in election campaigns. Federal campaign finance reforms in the 1970s required nonprofit organizations to form separate segregated accounts, or connected PACs, and defined limits on donations to PACs and their contributions to campaigns and national political parties. Connected PACs report donations and expenditures to an oversight authority, the FEC. Initially, the definition of partisanship or express advocacy was elaborated on in *Buckley v. Valeo*, establishing a bright-line test for partisan communications as those using the specific words "for or against" a named candidate.

A hybrid Section 527 organization came to public attention in the 2000 presidential election, with practices that challenged existing regulation of political activity. Initially, hybrid Section 527 organizations fell between the regulatory cracks, with neither the IRS nor the FEC having jurisdiction or mechanisms to provide for a public accounting of their finances. The new tax-exempt form was used for electioneering in the form of paid broadcast communications and voter contact campaigns. During the 1990s, issue advertising financed by individuals and soft money contributions became a regular part of elections. Political parties and groups used issue advertising to gain support for candidates favorable to their causes or to tarnish opponents. The ads provided information on candidates, using highly suggestive language linking policy issues to candidates, often in a negative light, and left no doubt in the voters' minds about who to support or defeat.

Some Section 527 political organizations were highly influential in launching broadcast advertising in the last two national elections. In a close 2000 presidential primary in South Carolina, the defeat of Senator John McCain was credited to last-minute negative advertising financed by a Section 527 organization backed by two wealthy brothers interested in securing a primary victory for George W. Bush. After the 2000 presidential election, Congress sought to remedy regulatory shortcomings, passing legislation to provide for regular disclosure of donors to Section 527 organizations and reporting of their electioneering expenditures to the IRS. Then, in 2001, Congress moved to control soft money in federal elections, passing the first substantial federal campaign finance reform legislation in 25 years.

Reform organizations, such as Common Cause, Public Citizen, and Center for Responsive Politics, had long pressed for campaign finance reform, concerned that huge infusions of soft money into the political system were fueling negative advertising, violating prohibitions on partisan activity by corporations and unions. With voter turnout lagging and the public wary of special interests, negative advertising, and unchecked money in elections, Congress passed the Bipartisan Campaign Reform Act (BCRA). BCRA sought to control soft money from the treasuries of nonprofits and businesses by prohibiting its use by national political parties and for electioneering broadcast advertising just prior to federal elections. In doing so, it created a working definition of electioneering as broadcast advertising near elections and required that the sponsors of these ads be clearly identified and that their financing be reported to the FEC.

Regulation and disclosure notwithstanding, new Section 527 organizations blossomed and increased their activity in the 2004 election, reporting to the IRS under the new disclosure guidelines and to the FEC under new broadcast electioneering guidelines. Again, Section 527 organizations proved flexible enough to organize and influence elections. For example, Swift Boat Veterans for Truth financed messages designed to create public doubt about Democratic presidential nominee John Kerry's leadership role as a combat veteran in Vietnam, and MoveOn.org raised millions of dollars to air ads attacking the record of George W. Bush. More reform of Section 527 organizations is likely as reformers argue that it is necessary to define electioneering with more rigor, bring Section 527 groups fully under the jurisdiction of the FEC, and further rein in soft money donations used to influence federal elections.

Another nonprofit practice, the use of multiple tax-exempt organizations, has become a common way of structuring organizations to conduct policy advocacy and electoral activity. Stand-alone tax-exempt organizations can run up against regulatory limits on permissible activities due to their tax status. If structured with multiple tax-exempt entities, the organization has more opportunities to compete for scarce resources and build political leverage. One of the more familiar arrangements is a combination of a 501(c)(3) charity, a 501(c)(4)–(6) lobbying arm, a connected PAC, and a 527 organization. The Sierra Club, for example, is a 501(c)(4) membership organization and the main governance and lobbying body for the national environmental organization. The Sierra Club Foundation is its charitable, educational arm, whereas the Sierra Club PAC is its connected PAC for political contributions. The Sierra Club Voter Education Fund is another related Section 527 that conducts electioneering get-out-the-vote activity. These complex organizations can conduct nonstop political operations and are equipped to stay up and running during legislative and election cycles. They are legal, efficient, and flexible operations.

Individual tax-exempt organizations that are part of a complex organizational structure cannot share control of day-to-day activities, but they can have overlapping boards, share advocacy goals, collaborate on strategies of action, and manage their resources in ways to best achieve their political ends. When social welfare advocacy organizations team up with charitable organizations, limited advocacy activities engaged in at the greatest tax benefit can be combined with the most aggressive advocacy activities to obtain the broadest menu of advocacy tactics at presumably the most efficient cost (Reid and Kerlin 2003). This efficiency in funding advocacy activities can be achieved through the transfer of organizational resources from one nonprofit to another as long as resources are not used to subsidize activities elsewhere that the nonprofit itself cannot conduct.

Complex organizational arrangements may be legal, efficient ways to work within the regulatory framework, but their operations lack transparency under current regulation and reporting requirements by the IRS and the FEC. It is difficult to determine which organizations are related to each other and how money moves between organizations for various political purposes. Insufficient information on IRS Form 990 creates concerns about who is really behind an organization and how individual tax-exempt entities are related to one another for political purposes (Weissman 2003). Organizational donors and members may be concerned about whether their contributions are going for intended purposes and organizational leaders may face concerns about fiscal and operational accountability among organizations. Further, regulators may have a difficult time determining whether funds have been diverted to purposes not consistent with tax status or whether political activities have been financed with improper donations.

To conclude, nonprofit organizations use many organizational forms and strategies of action in the political system, and the regulations and reporting they must abide by are specific to their tax status and advocacy activities. Lobbying by charitable organizations with occasional interests in budget and policy issues contrasts with the complex organizational structures of large advocacy organizations with regular, visible, and strategic political operations. Charitable organizations face tax regulation that requires they spend most of their charitable donations on charitable activities, and as a whole, they show little inclination to lobby legislatures. For them, regulation can be an additional barrier to political engagement.

Large, politically active nonprofits with multifaceted political operations face more regulation but navigate the system by building organizational structures that provide opportunities to raise, spend, and transfer deductible and nondeductible donations among related entities for use on a range of regulated and unregulated influential activities, including public education, lobbying, issue advertising, and electioneering. As nonprofits become more visible players in policymaking and elections, they face greater scrutiny by the public and regulators interested in a full accounting of their political roles, and a clearer picture of how organizational finances are used in policymaking and elections emerges, to which this chapter now turns.

Organizational Practices and Public Accountability

Nonprofit advocacy practices are changing in a host of ways; the financial structuring of political activity into legally separate but coordinated exempt organizations, the use of nonprofit organizations by politicians and parties, new technologies for political action, new venues for political action, and the restructuring of campaign finance laws at the federal level all pose new challenges for government regulators and nonprofit organizations. These practices test current regulatory definitions of political activity, expose conflicts and loopholes in the authority of regulating agencies, reveal the complex interface of tax and political regulation, generate questions about disclosure and transparency of current reporting standards, and expose contradictions in representational claims by organizations with purportedly public purposes.

In the past several years, federal campaign finance reform created new dynamics in election advocacy that forced nonprofits into the public spotlight. Campaign finance reformers and the media tried, with limited success, to keep watch on social welfare organizations, trade and professional organizations, unions, and Section 527 organizations in the 2002 and 2004 elections to determine whether soft money, now prohibited in national political parties, would flow to nonprofit organizations for partisan purposes, particularly in instances where nonprofits were not required to disclose their donors or political expenditures. After the 2004 election, the Campaign Finance Institute concluded that Section 527 organizations have thus far replaced part, but not the majority, of soft money banned by the McCain-Feingold law. Of $591 million in 2002 party soft money, $337 million was not replaced by 527 contributions in 2004. Democrats, hoping to stay financially competitive in a system increasingly reliant on hard money, have favored Section 527 groups; they received nearly four times as much 527 money as Republicans in 2004—$321 million to $84 million (Weisman and Hassan 2005).

In contrast, hard money[5] became the most traded political currency of the 2004 election, dominated by business donations and favored by Republicans who took advantage of higher limits allowed under BCRA to raise record amounts of it, outpacing the Democrats in party and candidate hard money contributions. The Center for Responsive Politics, which tracks campaign spending, calculated that business interests were responsible for 74 percent of the PAC and individual contributions to candidates in the 2004 federal election, with nearly every sector of the economy favoring Republicans. Nonprofit labor organizations were responsible for 3 percent and heavily favored Democrats, whereas ideological groups were responsible for 3.6 percent and slightly favored Democrats (Center for Responsive Politics 2005).[6]

The BCRA solved some problems, opened awareness about others, and left many unresolved issues for the courts, Congress, and agency regulations to address. Organizations in the nonprofit sector are divided over the proper role for regulation in a post-BCRA environment. Concerned about the impact on social welfare organizations, conservative and liberal nonprofit organizations and their trade associations have stood firmly behind the notion that intrusive restrictions, enhanced disclosure, or reporting by 501(c)(4)s to the FEC or the IRS could violate basic speech and privacy rights of members and donors and impede the ability of organizations to represent their members and the public to the fullest. In contrast, reform-minded campaign finance advocates have questioned whether there is sufficient rigor in the definition of electioneering and sufficient transparency of organizational donations to permit monitoring of attempts to influence federal elections.

The definition of electioneering activity and appropriate levels of reporting and disclosure are thorny issues for nonprofits. Currently, a lack of transparency of soft money in and out of these nonprofits obscures the role of soft money in social welfare organizations, unions, and trade associations. Contributions from businesses, individuals, and other nonprofits are consolidated as private revenue in one line on the IRS Form 990, so it is not possible to determine sources of soft money. Further, the line between public education and partisan electioneering is not clear, except in BCRA, which more narrowly defines it as broadcast electioneering communications and requires disclosure and reporting of those expenditures to the FEC, making it impossible to decipher how groups are spending their finances for lobbying and political activity. The IRS attempts to capture electioneering expenses as political expenditures on Form 990, but its guidance on calculating expenditures includes a broad range of election-related activities that must meet a series of confusing tests to distinguish expenditures that are political from those that are for public education. Even if activities meet the test and groups report political expenditures, no additional disclosure of organizational donors is required.

At the same time, some groups fear that more of their activities, now considered to be public education, will fall under the BCRA definitions of electioneering and trigger additional disclosure and reporting. One of the most controversial practices is issue advertising, and some nonprofits want to insure that interpretations of BCRA do not further constrain nonprofits' communication by narrowing the definition of public education or grassroots lobbying communications in favor of a more rigorous definition of electioneering. For example, a coalition of 35 charities from across the political spectrum have joined an amicus brief in *Wisconsin Right to Life v. the Federal Election Commission*, a case yet to be decided. The coalition argues that the BCRA electioneering communications rule—which bans corporations, both nonprofit and for-profit, from running broadcast ads that refer to a candidate for federal office within 30 days of a primary or 60 days of a general election—unconstitutionally restricts nonprofit grassroots lobbying ads. The coalition stresses the importance of allowing the full participation of nonpartisan voices in the public debate of important policy issues. The case involved ads run in 2004 by Wisconsin Right to Life that urged Senators Russ Feingold (D-WI) and Herb Kohl (D-WI) to oppose filibusters of judicial nominees. At the time, Senator Feingold was campaigning for reelection, but the ads did not refer to his candidacy or the elections (Independent Sector 2006).

In coming years, regulators will likely seek to clarify the disparity between the need for public transparency in elections and the right to associate in private nonprofit organizations with political ends without disclosure of individual members or donors. The Supreme Court has recognized the need to disclose individual donors to PACs and political campaigns, holding that disclosure is constitutional if "narrowly tailored" to advance a "compelling public interest." In key cases such as *Buckley v. Valeo*, *Nixon v. Shrink*, and *Missouri Government PAC and Colorado Republican Party v. FEC*, the Court found that combating "corruption or the appearance of corruption" was compelling enough to limit contribution levels and in some cases require public disclosure of contributor information.

Still, the issue is complicated. Member privacy or the right to associate without disclosing the names of members to government authorities is also a protected element of civic participation, valued as the right of citizens to associate to place demands on government without fear of retribution (Reid 2003). The Supreme Court in *NAACP v. Alabama* held that the State of Alabama could not require NAACP to disclose its members as a condition for registering as a corporation under state law. Contributor anonymity, nonprofit sector leaders have argued, has allowed individuals and institutions to give substantial sums of private money to tax-exempt organizations without incurring public notoriety.

In conclusion, institutional legitimacy and organizational accountability are necessary for nonprofits that engage in politics. Advocacy organizations can expect to have their public missions, tax benefits, and organizational practices questioned if these functions are not sufficiently transparent to the public, lawmakers, and regulators. Nonprofit sector umbrella organizations have defined and promoted best practices for organizations, but proposals for formal accreditation standards and oversight by government generate debate within the nonprofit sector about whether additional government oversight will result in improved public trust or government overreaching, as well as more or less politicization of the sector. Some nonprofits have opted for voluntary disclosure of donors and activities to assure the public and their donors that their organizational activities and finances are representative of civic interests and that their political messages are rooted in the preferences and sentiments of their members and consistent with their missions. Voluntary disclosure is a step that will begin to isolate those who find organizational opacity, not civic participation, the most attractive feature of the nonprofit forms they are adapting for their own uses.

Increased media, congressional, and agency scrutiny of nonprofits has created an aura of uncertainty for nonprofits about the risks associated with advocacy, including greater demands on nonprofits to justify their tax privileges. In some cases, the oversight is justified, but government scrutiny of organizational affairs and the threat of sanction, either real or perceived, can chill political engagement and political criticism. For example, the IRS—convinced a speech by NAACP CEO Kweisi Mfume that criticized President Bush was evidence of overstepping— opened an investigation of the NAACP in the waning days of the 2004 election. In the end, the investigation could not substantiate the charges, provided little clarification or precedent for nonprofit organizations, and left many to suggest, fairly or not, that political harassment was the motivation for the investigation (Hill 2005). Undeterred, the IRS has promised to step up its controversial Political Intervention Program with renewed investigations of nonprofits and religious organizations during the 2006 election. Nonprofits are concerned that the distinction between political criticism and political intervention are not clear enough to prevent politically motivated harassment by officials.

In the future, nonprofit organizations will need to examine their advocacy practices in light of new opportunities, perceptions, and constraints. The demand for greater private sector accountability will continue to draw public attention to politically active nonprofits. Response to demands for financial accountability will likely require greater transparency of organizational finances to better inform the public about sources of money influencing the political system. Tax accountability will require that organizations favored by subsidies apply resources for a clear public benefit that includes a balance between their historic role as advocates and their charitable purposes. Organizational accountability will challenge groups to govern themselves with sufficient internal checks and balances and in ways that lend legitimacy to their representational roles in politics. Ideally, the principles can guide advocacy practices and shape interaction between government institutions and nonprofits that will be reflected in a higher level of public discourse, a more informed electorate, and sounder public policy.

NOTES

1. Soft money refers to unregulated expenditures by political parties and organizations in conjunction with elections.

2. Readers new to the subject matter should consult official government websites, such as the Internal Revenue Service and the Federal Election Commission, and watchdog organizations, such as OMB Watch, Independent Sector, Alliance for Justice, National Council of Nonprofit Associations, and Center for Responsive Politics, for more detailed descriptions and definitions of terms.

3. The 501(h) election permits charitable organizations to use a formula to calculate the limit for lobbying expenditures instead of relying on the indefinite "not substantial" criterion. Total lobbying limits are currently set at 20 percent for the first $500,000 of exempt-purpose expenditures for organizations that make the 501(h) election. After 20 percent of the first $500,000, lobbying limits are then calculated on a sliding scale based on total exempt-purpose expenditures, up to a cap of $1 million for total lobbying expenditures. See Alliance for Justice (2003) for a discussion of the 501(h) election.

4. International Center for Not-for-Profit Law web site, http://www.icnl.org.

5. Hard money refers to contributions that are made directly to political candidates from individuals, organizations (especially PACs), and political parties.

6. The remaining amount was split between "Others" at 12.9 percent and "Unknown" at 6.5 percent.

REFERENCES

Alliance for Justice. 2003. *Worry-Free Lobbying for Nonprofits—How to Use the 501(h) Election to Maximize Effectiveness.* http://www.allianceforjustice.org/images/collection_images/Worry-Free%20Lobbying%202003.pdf.

———. 2005. "Advocacy Lawyers and Accountants Network." http://www.afj.org/nonprofit/lawyers_accountants/index.html.

Anheier, Helmut, Marlies Glasius, and Mary Kaldor, eds. 2002. *Global Civil Society 2001.* New York, NY: Oxford University Press.

Axelrod, Alan. 2002. *Minority Rights in America.* Washington, DC: CQ Press.

Barakso, Maryann. 2005. "Civic Engagement and Voluntary Associations: Reconsidering the Role of the Governance Structures of Advocacy Groups." *Polity* 37(July): 315–34.

Barber, Lucy G. 2002. *Marching on Washington*. Berkeley: University of California Press.

Bass, Gary, Kay Guinane, and Ryan Turner. 2003. "Attack on Nonprofit Speech: Death By 1000 Cuts." Washington, DC: OMB Watch.

Berry, Jeffrey M., with David F. Arons. 2003. *A Voice for Nonprofits*. Washington, DC: Brookings Institution Press.

Bennett, Daniel, and Pam Fielding. 1999. *The Net Effect: How Cyberspace Is Changing the Political Landscape*. Merrifield, VA: E-advocates Press.

Bhargava, Deepak. 2004. "Community Organizations and the 2004 Election. The Poor at the Polls." *NFG Reports* 11(4): 1, 4–5.

Boatwright, Robert G., Michael J. Malbin, Mark J. Rozell, Richard M. Skinner, and Clyde Wilcox. 2003. "BCRA's Impact on Interest Groups and Advocacy Organizations." In *Life After Reform*, edited by Michael J. Malbin. Lanham, MD: Rowman and Littlefield Publishers, Inc.

Boris, Elizabeth T., and Jeff Krehely. 2002. "Civic Participation and Advocacy in the Nonprofit Sector." In *The State of Nonprofit America*, edited by Lester M. Salamon. Washington, DC: Brookings Institution Press.

Boris, Elizabeth, and C. Eugene Steuerle, eds. 1999. *Nonprofits and Government: Collaboration and Conflict*, 1st ed. Washington, DC: Urban Institute Press.

Brainard, Lori A., and Patricia D. Siplon. 2002. "The Internet and NGO-Governmental Relations: Injecting Chaos into Order." *Public Administration and Development* 22(1): 63–72.

Brinkerhoff, Jennifer M., and Derick W. Brinkerhoff. 2002. "Government-Nonprofit Relations in Comparative Perspective: Evolution, Themes and New Directions." *Public Administration and Development* 22(1): 3–18.

Center for Responsive Politics. 2005. "The Business-Labor-Ideology Split in PAC and Individual Contributions to Candidates and Parties, 2004 Cycle." http://www.crp.org/bigpicture/blio.asp.

Chambre, Susan. 1997. "Civil Society, Differential Resources, and Organizational Development: HIV/AIDS Organizations in New York City, 1982–1992." *Nonprofit and Voluntary Sector Quarterly* 26(4): 466–88.

Chaves, Mark, Laura Stephens, and Joe Galaskiewicz. 2004. "Does Government Funding Suppress Nonprofits' Political Activity?" *American Sociological Review* 69(2): 292–316.

De Vita, Carol J., and Rachel Mosher-Williams, eds. 2001. *Who Speaks for America's Children? The Role of Child Advocates in Public Policy*. Washington, DC: Urban Institute Press.

De Vita, Carol, Maria Montilla, Elizabeth J. Reid, and Omolara Fatiregun. 2004. *Organizational Factors Influencing Advocacy for Children*. Washington, DC: The Urban Institute.

Florini, Ann M, ed. 2000. *The Third Force: The Rise of Transnational Civil Society*. Washington, DC: Carnegie Endowment for International Peace.

Green, Donald P., and Alan S. Gerber. 2004. *Get Out the Vote! How to Increase Voter Turnout*. Washington, DC: Brookings Institution Press.

Hill, Frances R. 2005. "Auditing the NAACP: Misadventures in Tax Administration." *Tax Notes Today* 147–21.

Hillygus, D. Sunshine, and Todd G. Shields. 2005. "Moral Issues and Voter Decision Making in the 2004 Presidential Election." *PS: Political Science and Politics* 38(2): 201–9.

Hula, Kevin W. 1999. *Lobbying Together.* Washington, DC: George Washington University Press.

Independent Sector. 2006. "Supreme Court Sends Issue Advocacy Case Back to Lower Court." http://www.independentsector.org/programs/gr/ WRTLamicus.html.

Independent Sector and The Foundation Center. 2005. "Social Justice Grantmaking: A Report on Foundation Trends." Washington DC: The Foundation Center.

Keck, Margaret E., and Kathryn Sikkink. 1998. *Activists Beyond Borders.* Ithaca, NY: Cornell University Press.

Kerlin, Janelle, Elizabeth J. Reid, and Jennifer Auer. 2003. *The Transfer of Child Care Worker Education and Compensation Policy Across States: The T.E.A.C.H. Early Childhood Model.* Washington, DC: The Urban Institute.

Kingdon, John W. 1995. *Agendas, Alternatives, and Public Policies.* New York, NY: Longman.

Krehely, Jeff, Meaghan House, and Emily Kernan. 2004. *The Axis of Ideology: Conservative Foundations and Public Policy.* Washington, DC: National Committee for Responsive Philanthropy.

Lindenberg, Marc, and Coralie Bryant. 2001. *Going Global: Transforming Relief and Development NGOs.* Bloomfield, CT: Kumarian Press.

Magleby, David B., ed. 2000. *Outside Money, Soft Money and Issue Advocacy in the 1998 Congressional Elections.* Lanham, MD: Rowman and Littlefield Publishers, Inc.

Micklethwait, John and Adrian Wooldridge. 2004. *The Right Nation: Conservative Power in America.* New York, NY: Penguin Press.

Minkoff, Debra C. 1999. "Bending with the Wind: Strategic Change and Adaptation by Women's and Racial Minority Organizations." *American Journal of Sociology* 104(6): 1666–1703.

Minkoff, Debora C. 2002. "The Emergence of Hybrid Organizational Forms: Combining Identity-Based Service Provision and Political Action." *Nonprofit and Voluntary Sector Quarterly* 31(3): 377–401.

National Center for Charitable Statistics. 2002. Core and Digitized Datasets.

National Council of Nonprofit Associations. 2005. "BCAPP: Building Capacity for Public Policy."

Reid, Elizabeth J. 1999. "Nonprofit Advocacy and Participation." In *Nonprofits and Government: Collaboration and Conflict*, 1st ed., edited by Elizabeth Boris and C. Eugene Steuerle (291–326). Washington, DC: Urban Institute Press.

———, ed. 2000. Structuring the Inquiry into Advocacy. Nonprofit Advocacy and the Policy Process Seminar Series, Vol. 1. Washington, DC: The Urban Institute.

———, ed. 2003. *In the States, Across the Nation, and Beyond.* Nonprofit Advocacy and the Policy Process Seminar Series, Vol. 3. Washington, DC: The Urban Institute.

———. 2004. "Social Welfare Organizations, Politics, and Regulation." In *In Search of the Nonprofit Sector*, edited by Peter Frumkin and Jonathan B. Imber. New Brunswick, NJ: Transaction Publishers.

Reid, Elizabeth J., and Janelle Kerlin. 2003. "More Than Meets the Eye: Structuring and Financing Nonprofit Advocacy." Paper presented at the annual conference of the American Political Science Association, Philadelphia.

———. 2005. "Dimensions of U.S. International Nonprofits." *Nonprofits in Focus.* Washington, DC: The Urban Institute.

Reid, Elizabeth J., and Maria Montilla, eds. 2001. *Exploring Organizations and Advocacy.* Nonprofit Advocacy and the Policy Process Seminar Series, Vol. 2, Iss. 1. Washington, DC: The Urban Institute.

———, eds. 2002. *Exploring Organizations and Advocacy.* Nonprofit Advocacy and the Policy Process Seminar Series, Vol. 2, Iss. 2. Washington, DC: The Urban Institute.

Rich, Andrew. 2004. *Think Tanks, Public Policy, and the Politics of Expertise.* New York, NY: Cambridge University Press.

Rosenblum, Nancy L. 1998. *Membership and Morals: The Personal Uses of Pluralism in America.* Princeton, NJ: Princeton University Press.

Shaiko, Ronald G. 1999. *Voices and Echoes for the Environment: Public Interest Representation in the 1990s and Beyond.* New York, NY: Columbia University Press.

Skocpol, Theda. 2003. *Diminished Democracy: From Membership to Management in American Civic Life.* Norman: University of Oklahoma Press.

Skrentny, John D. 2002. *The Minority Rights Revolution.* Cambridge, MA: Belknap Press of Harvard University Press.

Smith, Daniel A. 2005. "Was Rove Right? The Partisan Wedge and Turnout Effects of Issue 1, Ohio's 2004 Ballot Initiative to Ban Gay Marriage." Presented at Initiative and Referendum Institute Conference, Newport Beach, CA, Jan. 14–15.

Smith, Daniel A., and Caroline J. Tolbert. 2004. *Educated by Initiative: The Effects of Direct Democracy on Citizens and Political Organizations in the American States.* Ann Arbor: University of Michigan Press.

Warren, Mark E. 2000. *Democracy and Association.* Princeton, NJ: Princeton University Press.

Weissman, Steve. 2003. "Comments of the Campaign Finance Institute Re: Proposed IRS Form 990 Changes." Announcement 2002-87. January 23, 2003.

Weissman, Steve, and Ruth Hassan. 2005. "BCRA and the 527 Groups." Washington, DC: Campaign Finance Institute.

Zald, Mayer N., and John D. McCarthy, eds. 1987. *Social Movements in an Organizational Society.* New Brunswick, NJ: Transaction Books.

11

U.S.-BASED INTERNATIONAL NGOs AND FEDERAL GOVERNMENT FOREIGN ASSISTANCE: OUT OF ALIGNMENT?

Janelle A. Kerlin

International humanitarian and development nongovernmental organizations (INGOs)[1] based in the United States have, as a group, an ambivalent relationship with the U.S. government. Although they are often in agreement on the basic goals of saving and improving lives abroad, INGOs are at times out of alignment with government in ideology and approach to international work. With foreign assistance becoming a greater tool of foreign policy after September 11, 2001, INGOs are facing increasingly difficult questions about their autonomy, legitimacy, and ability to advocate when accepting government funding. Issues of accountability also become complex when diverging goals of the government as donor and INGO as service provider come into conflict. This chapter examines the financial relationship between INGOs and the U.S. government and consequences for INGO autonomy, advocacy, and accountability in the context of shifts in policy for foreign assistance.

United States–based INGOs currently embrace a growing spectrum of nonprofits. Their activities include financial, physical, or educational assistance to foreign individuals, institutions, or communities in the areas of disaster relief, agriculture, economy, health, education, human rights, immigration, and, more recently, democracy and civil society. INGOs are also increasingly part of a global activist agenda that includes—in addition to human rights—women's rights, workers' rights, AIDS prevention and assistance, environmental protection, and other transnational issues. Examples of INGOs include World Vision International, Physicians for Human Rights, Freedom House, Hungarian American Enterprise Fund, India Literacy Project, Agricultural Services International, and the Global Fund for Children's Vaccines.

THE EMERGENCE OF THE INGO–U.S. GOVERNMENT RELATIONSHIP

INGOs first appeared in the United States between the two world wars to provide relief to war victims in Europe. They continued to increase in number after World War II as countries under colonial rule were decolonized and new independent states emerged. During this time INGOs raised most of their money through small private donations and remained on the "periphery of the foreign aid establishment" (Dichter 1999, 44). However, the cold war, the movement for economic development assistance, and heightened concern with poverty reduction all played into their continued growth in the 1960s and 1970s, a period that also saw a growing contractual relationship between INGOs and the U.S. government. Realization of the failure of direct government-to-government foreign assistance spurred on government contracting to INGOs as a more reliable, effective, and efficient alternative (Forman and Stoddard 2002). By the 1980s, INGOs began to fill gaps in assistance arising from public fiscal crises, such as foreign government cutbacks in services, privatization, and other forms of structural adjustment in foreign countries (Lindenberg 1999).

As the cold war came to a close in the 1990s, client states of the former Soviet Union and African states with unstable regimes faced refugee problems, violence, and other humanitarian crises. INGOs partnered with the U.S. government and multilateral organizations such as the United Nations to respond to need in Bosnia, Chechnya, Armenia,

Rwanda, Somalia, and Sierra Leone. In some cases, foreign governments asked INGOs to respond as a substitute for their own government services (Lindenberg 1999). The growing trend in INGO-delivered humanitarian assistance and development projects was reflected in the use of INGOs by the U.S. government and world and regional development banks for building roads, bridges, and water systems in addition to traditional assistance tasks.

Approximately 50 U.S. government organizations are currently involved in overseas assistance (box 11.1), with the actual number changing from year to year. However, the majority of U.S. foreign assistance is still routed through the United States Agency for International Development (USAID)[2], which, as a consequence, works with more INGOs in international humanitarian relief and development than any other agency. In the 1970s, USAID changed its approach to implementation from hands-on USAID staff to third-party intermediaries such as for-profit and nonprofit contractors (including INGOs), universities, and recipient governments. In the 1980s, USAID increased the number of contracts and grants it made to large INGOs in particular, such as CARE and World Vision, and in the 1990s cuts in the USAID budget led to a reduction in staff and the contracting out of more services. Overall, the number of organizations registered with the agency rose dramatically from 52 in 1970 to 458 in 2002 (Lindenberg 1999; Lindenberg and Bryant 2001; OECD 2002; USAID 2002a).

Not only has there been a shift to private organizations for the implementation of foreign assistance, but the funding of foreign assistance has shifted dramatically toward the private sector as well. USAID reports that in 1970 the U.S. government provided 70 percent of foreign aid but today "provides only 20 percent [of U.S. foreign aid] and American citizens and corporations provide 80 percent" (USAID 2005b, 1). Indeed, private giving, including worker remittances to developing countries, has grown substantially over the past 25 years. Whereas in 1970 U.S. official development assistance accounted for 0.30 percent of gross domestic product, in 2003 it stood at only 0.15 percent. However, when both official development assistance ($16.3 billion) and estimates for private contributions ($62.1 billion) are figured in, total U.S. foreign aid made up 0.71 percent of gross domestic product[3] in 2003 (Adelman, Norris, and Weicher 2005). Though experiencing a slow start, new funds from the millennium challenge account called for by President George W. Bush in 2002 may raise government spending on development assistance by a few billion dollars over the next couple of years.[4] To qualify for these funds countries must first show good governance, investment in their people, and policies that support economic growth (Millennium Challenge Corporation 2005).

Historically, the percentage of USAID budget going toward INGOs or private voluntary organizations[5] (as USAID refers to them) has

Box 11.1. U.S. Government Organizations Involved in Overseas Assistance in Fiscal Year 2003

African Development
   Foundation
Department of Agriculture
   Agricultural Research Service
   Cooperative State Research
   Education and Extension
   Service
   Foreign Agricultural Service
Department of Commerce
   U.S. Patent and Trademark
   Office
Department of Defense
   Counter-Narcoterrorism
   Technology Program Office
   Defense of Israel Against
   Terrorism
   Defense Security Cooperation
   Agency
   Defense Threat Reduction
   Agency
   Foreign Military Sales
   HIV/AIDS Prevention
   Program
   International Military
   Education Program
   Overseas Humanitarian,
   Disaster and Civic Aid
   U.S. Army Corps of Engineers
Department of Energy
Department of Health and
   Human Services
   Center for Disease Control
Department of Interior
   Compact of Free Association
   U.S. Fish and Wildlife Service
Department of Justice

Department of Labor
   International Labor Affairs
   Bureau
Department of State
   Democracy, Human Rights,
   and Labor
   Educational and Cultural
   Affairs
   European and Eurasian
   Affairs
   International Information
   Programs
   International Narcotics and
   Law Enforcement Affairs
   Oceans and International
   Environmental and
   Scientific Affairs
   Political-Military Affairs
   Population, Refugees, and
   Migration
Department of Treasury
Department of Transportation
Export-Import Bank
Federal Trade Commission
Foreign Agricultural Service
Inter-American Foundation
National Endowment for
   Democracy
Overseas Private Investment
   Corporation
Peace Corps
U.S. Trade and Development
   Agency
U.S. Agency for International
   Development

Source: USAID (2003).

ranged between 14 and 19 percent.[6] However, this figure can vary dramatically by individual office. In 2000, for example, the Office of U.S. Foreign Disaster Assistance within USAID reported that more than 70 percent of its aid was channeled through private voluntary organizations (Office of U.S. Foreign Disaster Assistance 2000). The actual amount of USAID funding going to private voluntary organizations is likely higher because the percentages noted here do not reflect USAID funding that is initially given to U.S. government agencies and multilateral organizations that then channel it to private voluntary organizations (U.S. General Accounting Office 2002). Among numerous examples, in October 2005 USAID contributed $2 million to the United Nations World Food Programme to assist victims of Hurricane Stan in Guatemala (United Nations World Food Programme 2005).

As discussed below, changes in foreign policy after September 11 calling for an increase in foreign assistance are the most recent round of events to affect the relationship between INGOs and the U.S. government. After hovering around $10 billion or less for a decade, U.S. official development assistance jumped from $9.9 billion in 2000 to $16.2 billion in 2003 (USAID 2005a). Although INGOs have more government resources to draw on, the situation raises some questions about whether or not government funding preferences and program requirements are shaping the work of INGOs. This chapter revisits concerns that scholars first raised in the 1990s about INGO autonomy, legitimacy, and accountability (Commins 1997; Edwards and Hulme 1996a, 1996b; Salm 1999). While their studies grew out of concern for an increase in the number of contracts between INGOs and government, these same issues come to the fore when government provides more overall funding to INGOs.

Scope of Federal Government Financing of INGOs

The full scope of federal government financing of INGOs and how it changes over time has generally been difficult to estimate. With different government agencies providing international assistance in different areas, numbers of organizations involved and financial amounts have been hard to determine. However, newly analyzed data from the Urban Institute's National Center for Charitable Statistics (NCCS) show that, while both numbers of INGOs receiving government funding and actual funding amounts are relatively low, there has been a rise in government funding of INGOs since 2001. The data also indicate a shift in the types of INGO activities the government funded after 2001.

Of the 4,124 INGOs in the NCCS 2003 dataset of international organizations,[7] only 391 (less than 10 percent) show they received government grants.[8] Moreover, figure 11.1 shows that only 20 percent of aggregate INGO revenue comes from government grants (a small amount of government funding may also be found in program service revenue though not on a scale to influence this analysis). Nonetheless, there was an increase in government dollars when looking across years 2001–2003.[9] Table 11.1 shows a relatively large increase in government

Figure 11.1. Sources of Revenue for INGOs by Percentage, 2003

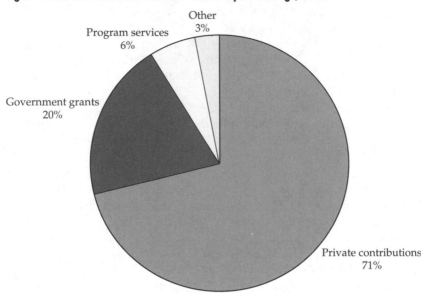

Source: National Center for Charitable Statistics/GuideStar National Nonprofit Database.

Table 11.1. Government Grants to INGOs, 2001–2003

Form 990 filers[a]	2001	2002	2003
INGOs with government grants	350	360	391
Government grants to INGOs (in thousands of dollars)	$2,334,337	$2,493,948	$3,142,256
Government grants as a percentage of total INGO revenue	17	18	20

Source: National Center for Charitable Statistics/GuideStar National Nonprofit Database.

INGO = International humanitarian and development nongovernmental organizations.

[a] Table does not include 990 EZ filers because they do not have to provide information on specific sources of revenue. (Organizations with gross receipts of less than $100,000 and total assets of less than $250,000 at the end of the year are eligible to file form 990 EZ.)

funding of INGOs, especially from 2002 to 2003, a rate of increase that was not found in other sources of funding.[10]

The NCCS international dataset also shows that income from government grants can vary considerably by type of INGO (see table 11.2). Democracy and civil society INGOs, as a group, are the most highly reliant on government grants, with 54 percent of revenue coming from

Table 11.2. INGO Sources of Revenue by Type of INGO, 2003

		Source of revenue (% of total)			
Type of INGO	n^a	Private contributions	Government grants	Program services	Other revenue
International relief	854	85	13	1	1
General	636	69	25	5	1
Health	528	70	20	8	3
Education	351	51	30	12	7
Environment, population, sustainability	174	56	21	21	3
Economic	173	29	39	19	14
Human rights, migration, refugees	171	71	24	1	3
Democracy and civil society	79	31	54	12	4
Agriculture	56	16	39	42	5
Science and technology	39	64	10	23	4
Total	3,061	71	20	6	2

Source: National Center for Charitable Statistics/GuideStar National Nonprofit Database.

INGO = International humanitarian and development nongovernmental organizations.

Note: Rows may not total 100 percent because of rounding.

[a] Table does not include 990 EZ filers because they do not have to provide information on specific sources of revenue. (Organizations with gross receipts of less than $100,000 and total assets of less than $250,000 at the end of the year are eligible to file form 990 EZ.)

government grants. Even so, only about one third of these organizations actually receive government grants, with three getting the lion's share of government funding: the National Democratic Institute for International Affairs ($48 million), the International Republican Institute ($19 million),[11] and the International Foundation for Election Systems ($27 million). These three organizations account for 82 percent of the government grants in this category.

At times, high levels of private funding hide high absolute levels of government spending for several types of INGOs. The international relief category provides the best example, where government grants accounted for only 13 percent of total revenue, making it appear that the government channels relatively few relief funds through INGOs. In fact, in absolute terms, government grants for this category were the highest, totaling more than $820 million and accounting for 26 percent of all government grants to INGOs. As mentioned previously, the Office of U.S. Foreign Disaster Assistance within USAID channels more than half of its funding for relief assistance through INGOs (Development Initiatives 2000). In this case, huge private donations for international relief offset large government grants as a percentage of revenue for these INGOs.

The data also indicate that a shift occurred between 2001 and 2003 in the types of activities the government funds. Table 11.3 shows not only the large increase in government funding from 2002 to 2003, but also that the largest rate of increase (62 times) occurred with organizations involved in international relief rather than with other, more long-term, development-based INGOs. Many large multiservice INGOs are clustered in both the international relief and general development and assistance categories, the type of organization that USAID tends to fund (Forman and Stoddard 2002).

Table 11.3 also shows that 2002 saw a decrease in funding of democracy and civil society organizations, which was then reversed in 2003 when aid for this category increased by 20 percent. This turnaround may be attributed to a 2002 withdrawal of democracy and civil society development funding for Eastern and Central Europe, followed by new funding for this activity elsewhere (perhaps particularly in Afghanistan) in 2003. Other analysis of the NCCS international dataset indicates this may be the case, showing a decrease in government grants to INGOs supporting democracy and civil society in Central and Eastern Europe from 2001 to 2003 (Reid and Kerlin 2006).

As alluded to, the NCCS international dataset shows an interesting trend in the size of INGOs working with government. Among INGOs receiving government funds in 2003, 24 percent had less than $500,000 in annual revenue, another 24 percent had annual revenue of $500,000 to $2 million, and 52 percent received more than $2 million in revenue annually. Comparison with the size distribution for all INGOs shows

Table 11.3. Types of INGOs with the Greatest Rates of Increase in Government Grants, 2002–2003

	Increase over previous year (millions of dollars)		Percent rise in total amount
Selected types of INGOs[a]	*2002*	*2003*	*2002–2003*
International relief	5	310	60
Health	76	114	30
Education	17	40	21
Democracy and civil society	−2	23	20
Environment, population, sustainability	22	49	19
All INGOs	160	648	26

Source: National Center for Charitable Statistics/GuideStar National Nonprofit Database (2002, 2003).

INGO = International humanitarian and development nongovernmental organizations.

[a] Table does not include 990 EZ filers because they do not have to provide information on specific sources of revenue. (Organizations with gross receipts of less than $100,000 and total assets of less than $250,000 at the end of the year are eligible to file form 990 EZ.)

there is a clear bias of government funding for larger INGOs. Forman and Stoddard (2002) confirm this finding based on their analysis of more than 400 organizations registered with USAID in 1999. They attribute USAID preference for large organizations to prior work relationships, an established track record, and fewer problems with coordination when working with a smaller number of large organizations. It is also likely that the high, fixed costs of administration and proposal development for government grants work against smaller organizations.

GOVERNMENT–INGO FINANCIAL ARRANGEMENTS

The federal government arranges financial support for INGOs to carry out many of its international programs in the areas of services (i.e., the shipment of humanitarian supplies), project planning, implementation, consulting, research, and technical assistance. Funding for INGOs from the government most often comes in the form of contracts, grants, and cooperative agreements. Contracts are used when purchasing or leasing property or services for the direct benefit of the federal government (in the NCCS international dataset these funds are most often listed under program service revenue). Grants are used to transfer resources where there is considerable freedom for the recipient to pursue an agreed-upon program and substantial involvement (participation or intervention) of the sponsoring government agency is not expected. Cooperative agreements are also a means to transfer resources to a recipient provider, though recipients can expect involvement of the sponsoring government agency during project implementation (funds from both grants and cooperative agreements are categorized as grants in the NCCS international dataset) (USAID 2002b).

Many of the funding relationships that INGOs enter into with USAID are in the form of grants and cooperative agreements, the two mechanisms that delegate some control to the implementing organizations (U.S. General Accounting Office 2002). With some exceptions, USAID solicits grants and cooperative agreements through either an annual program statement that invites proposals with creative approaches to meet broadly outlined strategic objectives or a request for applications that solicits proposals for more narrowly specified projects (USAID 2002b). USAID generally awards grants and cooperative agreements on a competitive basis, evaluating applications for their technical merit, cost-effectiveness, and the past performance of the applicant (USAID 2002b). Though USAID adheres to rules for the awarding of contracts, there is an informal network of INGO lobbyists regularly in contact with USAID staff. Moreover, USAID project officers informally contact staff at organizations they know and encourage them to respond to particular requests for proposals. Many organizations have relocated to the Washington, D.C., area so they can be in a position to develop and maintain close relationships with donors, especially USAID. Increasingly, both nonprofit and for-profit contractors compete for the same USAID projects (Dichter 2003).

Problems that INGOs have found with these types of financial arrangements are short submission time for proposals, award and approval delays, inflexibility for project modifications, and short-term expectations for outcomes that can only be achieved over the long term (Robinson 1997). USAID bureaucratic regulations and paperwork can overwhelm even experienced INGOs, many of which add staff to deal with the burden of applications. Part of the blame lies in the large number of congressional mandates built into each project:

> In the United States, by the 1980s, so many different concerns and sensibilities about development were being effectively voiced to Congress that USAID has to make sure that these myriad "thou shalts" and "thou shalt nots" are built into each RFP [request for proposals] and consequently each overseas project. (Dichter 2003, 78)

Indeed, an OECD report stated that in 2001, USAID identified 270 separate provisions and earmarks in legislation dealing with development (OECD 2002). Nonetheless, among a certain set of INGOs, government grants and contracts remain a highly sought after form of funding for their ability to contribute to an organization's capacity, track record, and the geographic expansion of activities. Thus, organizations are willing to put in the time, money (often drawn from limited unrestricted funds), and effort to apply for funding, which some observers note seems to require as much work as implementing the project itself (Dichter 2003).

While some western governments tend to distribute much of their aid directly to foreign governments, USAID prefers to work through INGOs. USAID has found there is greater risk of corruption and that aid will not reach the desired recipients when assistance is channeled through foreign governments. From USAID's perspective INGOs are more reliable, have more financial integrity, and allow USAID more say in the types of programming that receive U.S. funds. Indeed, USAID requires that organizations it funds have adequate financial resources, a satisfactory performance record, and accounting, recordkeeping, and management systems that are in keeping with current government standards (U.S. General Accounting Office 2002). A 2002 report from the General Accounting Office determined from a limited review that "the risk of USAID contractors and grantees misusing funds was relatively low" (18).

Autonomy

U.S. foreign assistance policy guides the strategic objectives behind the projects that USAID funds INGOs to undertake. Such policy at times prescribes and limits the activities of the INGOs involved. The Foreign Assistance Act of 1961, though periodically amended, continues to be the main legislation that governs U.S. foreign aid. Language in the legislation clearly spells out both a foreign policy and a humanitarian purpose behind foreign assistance (box 11.2). The subsequent history of the act reveals that more often than not, foreign assistance is closely tied to foreign policy goals. Indeed, during the cold war the United States provided much foreign assistance to shore up fragile democracies against communist influences. Henry Kissinger remarked in 1976 that "disaster relief is becoming increasingly a major instrument of our foreign policy" (de Waal 1997, 625).

After the terrorist attacks of September 11, 2001, the foreign policy emphasis in foreign assistance turned decidedly to national security. President Bush established international development as the "third pillar" of U.S. foreign policy alongside diplomacy and defense and created new institutions and policies to ensure alignment of the three strategies. The National Security Strategy, introduced by President Bush in September 2002, underscores that although poverty, poor health, and lack of economic opportunity do not lead directly to unrest

---

Box 11.2. Excerpt from the Foreign Assistance Act of 1961

"The Congress finds that fundamental political, economic, and technological changes have resulted in the interdependence of nations. The Congress declares that the individual liberties, economic prosperity, and security of the people of the United States are best sustained and enhanced in a community of nations which respect individual civil and economic rights and freedoms and which work together to use wisely the world's limited resources in an open and equitable international economic system. Furthermore, the Congress reaffirms the traditional humanitarian ideals of the American people and renews its commitment to assist people in developing countries to eliminate hunger, poverty, illness, and ignorance."

Foreign Assistance Act of 1961, P.L. 87-195, §101

and terrorism, they can be their precursors. It states, "America is now threatened less by conquering states than by failing ones" (U.S. Department of State 2004, 2). Andrew Natsios, then head of USAID, elaborated that, "these fragile states are characterized by a growing inability or unwillingness to provide even basic services and security to their populations. Our goal is to stabilize, reform, and help these states recover to a point where they are better able to provide for their own further development" (U.S. Department of State 2004, 2).

USAID was the target of a number of reforms reflecting the shift in foreign policy. These reforms included the creation of a joint State Department–USAID Strategic Plan, the State Department–USAID Joint Policy and Management Councils,[12] and the establishment of the Bureau of Democracy, Conflict, and Humanitarian Assistance at USAID (U.S. Department of State 2004; U.S. Department of State and USAID 2003). USAID was also provided with a large increase in funding to fulfill its new mandate. As noted above, U.S. official development assistance jumped from $9.9 billion in 2000 to $16.2 billion in 2003 (USAID 2005a).

The encroachment of foreign policy goals on humanitarian and development assistance has often sat uneasily with INGOs and has raised some difficult situations for INGOs working with USAID. Indeed, some development experts and other governments often criticize the U.S. government for using assistance as a foreign policy tool (Beattie 2003). One criticism is that foreign assistance is based more on U.S. strategic interests than need in a given country (Center for Global Development 2004). Figures showing the distribution of aid reveal that, historically, the largest recipient countries of U.S. development assistance have been U.S. strategic allies. Thus, whereas middle-income countries such as Russia, Egypt, and Israel receive a respective $6, $13, and $121 per person in assistance, the poorest countries such as Bangladesh, Ghana, and Kenya receive on average only $3 per person per year (Center for Global Development 2004).[13] INGOs have advocated for a reallocation of aid from middle- to lower-income countries with little success (Commins 1997). As a result, INGOs drawing on U.S. government funding must either look elsewhere for resources to support their work in the poorest countries or focus their activities on regions where there is government interest.

The issue of accepting much-needed government funding versus the need to maintain autonomy from government prerogatives has long divided the INGO community and forced some hard decisions. Some organizations are concerned with maintaining their responsiveness to those in need rather than to the government as donor. Others worry about being able to remain true to their organization's mission and approach to providing assistance if public funds are used. Indeed, one of the dangers in becoming overly reliant on government funding is that an organization will slowly align itself with government goals and drift from its mission to retain government funding. Hulme and Edwards find the risks to an organization's autonomy are widespread when government funding is accepted:

> The acceptance of increasing volumes of foreign aid involves entering into agreements about what is done, and how it is to be reported and accounted for. This fosters an emphasis on certain forms of activity at the expense of others, on upward accountability (rather than downward accountability to members and beneficiaries), and on particular techniques and donor definitions of "achievement" throughout the organization. (1997, 8)

The NCCS dataset of international organizations shows that, in 2003, 27 percent of those INGOs receiving government grants received 75 percent or more of their revenue from government grants, an indication that these organizations may be vulnerable to some compromise in their autonomy as stated above. Future research is needed to determine the actual impact on organizational autonomy under these circumstances, including beneficial returns (other than financial) to the organization.

Organizations deal with the autonomy issue in different ways. Oxfam America, for example, has refused to take government money to ensure it can be responsive to the needs of its clients (Brown and Moore 2001). Some well-funded service organizations, such as World Vision, strive to maintain a critical distance while receiving public sector funds (Commins 1997). Sometimes organizations pick and choose among federal foreign assistance projects and only apply for those that agree with their mission and operational approach. An example is the decision in 2003 of three major INGOs not to apply for USAID Iraq reconstruction grants. International Rescue Committee, CARE, and World Vision cited objections to working under the military, promoting democracy before basic services were in place, and providing assistance to Iraq when other countries were more in need (Read 2003).

Others give up parts of their programming to be eligible for restricted government funds. The Mexico City Policy, reinstated in January 2001, mandates that "no U.S. family planning assistance can be provided to foreign NGOs that use funding from any other source to: perform abortions in cases other than a threat to the woman's life, rape or incest; provide counseling and referral for abortion; or lobby to make abortion legal or more available in their country" (Global Gag Rule Impact Project 2005). As a result of this policy, EngenderHealth, a global women's health organization, discontinued its support of some of its foreign nongovernmental family planning partners to continue receiving millions of dollars in U.S. government grants (EngenderHealth 2005). Clearly, government funding and the policies tied to it have an impact on which countries or regions some INGOs operate in and their responsiveness to beneficiaries, though the extent of that impact is not known.

Legitimacy

Autonomy from government can also be an important issue in the public perception and legitimacy of an INGO. Many INGOs realize that who funds their work in part determines their legitimacy in the public eye. Lindenberg and Bryant (2001) discuss how organizations that are pulled away from their missions by government funding may lose their credibility as operators connected at the grassroots level. Even if an organization is known to work closely with the U.S. government, the public, including potential private donors, might question the organization's ability to maintain its connection to its own objectives and the people it says it is serving (Edwards and Hulme 1996b).

Recent shifts in policy on foreign assistance are making it more difficult for some INGOs to maintain their autonomy from government when accepting public funds. The U.S. government is increasingly using foreign assistance to improve the image of the United States internationally and is asking USAID in particular to tell its story as it assists foreign nations (U.S. Government Accountability Office 2005). It appears this public relations campaign has also been extended to INGOs. In 2003, Andrew Natsios, then head of USAID, described INGOs as "an arm of the U.S. government" and cautioned that "unless they improved their performance and did a better job of promoting their contacts to the U.S. administration, the government would cut off funding" (Beattie 2003).

Many INGOs working in areas that are antagonistic to the United States, however, are wary of directly connecting themselves to the American government for reasons other than just donor fallout. As an example, in December 2001, USAID requested that INGOs operating in the West Bank and Gaza collect detailed information on their local partners, including names, home addresses, identification numbers, birth dates, and places of birth for staff and board members. The request immediately chilled INGO relations with local partners precisely because locals began to perceive American INGOs as branches of the U.S. government. The local alarm was great enough that it led to a public campaign to boycott American INGOs and USAID funding. The crisis was resolved with the assistance of InterAction (an alliance of U.S.-based INGOs) and when USAID agreed to a more limited information request. Indeed, groups representing INGOs say that such data collection in the name of the U.S. government would "compromise the independence and integrity of our members, expose their staff to great personal risk, alienate local partners, and chill charitable activity" (InterAction and Independent Sector 2003, 12).

In the post–September 11 world there is also greater pressure on all INGOs to maintain their legitimacy with the U.S. government. In accordance with new U.S. laws, United States–based INGOs must comply with the requirements of Executive Order 13224 and the Patriot Act or face certain consequences. With Executive Order 13224, INGOs shown to have transactions (including financial support, in-kind support, and technical assistance) with individuals and entities associated with terrorism can have their assets frozen by the government. The Patriot Act imposes stiff fines and imprisonment on any entity that "provides material support or resources knowing or intending that they are to be used in terrorist acts or by foreign terrorist organizations" (Ramos et al. 2004, v).

To ensure compliance, INGOs must repeatedly check a number of terrorist lists from different government agencies. The most comprehensive is the "specially designated nationals" list maintained by the Treasury Department, which includes about 2,000 names of individuals and organizations. In addition, organizations are encouraged to consult the Department of States "terrorist exclusion list" and lists maintained by the United Nations and the European Union (Ramos et al. 2004). The difficulty of checking multiple lists that are continually changing has led to recommendations by INGO groups that the government maintain a consolidated list that is updated on a regular schedule. Trainings and new software, though an added financial burden on INGOs, have helped ease compliance. Organizations with funding from USAID must additionally certify that they have not and will not provide resources to any individual or entity involved in terrorist activity (InterAction and Independent Sector 2003; Ramos et al. 2004).

To assist organizations in complying with these new laws, the Treasury Department issued voluntary Treasury guidelines, which, although not mandatory, offer best practices for antiterrorist planning (Ramos et al. 2004). INGO representatives, however, advocated for the withdrawal of the guidelines because many of the recommendations were unfeasible or inadvisable given the conditions many INGOs work under or because the guidelines would cost more for organizations to implement than the actual assistance they provide is worth. There was even concern that costs for suggested data collection would cause some INGOs to discontinue their overseas work altogether (InterAction and Independent Sector 2003). In December 2005, the Treasury Department released revised guidelines that take into consideration recommendations made by the INGO community, improving their usefulness as an aid for INGOs (U.S. Department of the Treasury 2005).

ACCOUNTABILITY

The preceding discussion shows that at the root of an organization's autonomy and legitimacy are questions about accountability. To whom is an INGO most responsible? With whom should its allegiances lie? Questions of accountability for INGOs have become increasingly important as many of the stakeholders they are involved with require they show they are meeting expectations for their work. Sponsors, partners (including governments, multilateral organizations, businesses, and other NGOs), beneficiaries, and even an organization's own staff all have expectations for how and what an organization accomplishes and how it uses its resources. Finding the right balance between the multiple stakeholders INGOs are involved with is a critical task with important implications for the organization's functioning and aid efforts.

Reflecting a growing interest in accountability in nonprofits generally, the INGO literature has seen increased discussion on the topic of accountability (Brown and Moore 2001; Ebrahim 2003; Edwards and Hulme 1996a; Lindenberg and Bryant 2001; Smillie et al. 1999). Lindenberg and Bryant (2001) in *Going Global* devote an entire chapter to INGO accountability and evaluation. They find that, in addition to the multiple stakeholders listed above, organizations hold themselves accountable to their own core values, mission, and standards of performance. Organizations attempt to answer to each of the audiences they are responsible to, including public funders. Interestingly, the authors find that organizations with strong "accountability cultures" are not necessarily those with the greatest amounts of public funding. Their proposed "contingency model of accountability" takes into consideration the multidimensional and multidirectional quality of accountability that INGOs must face. The model reflects the idea that the reporting process for accountability is "necessarily contingent upon both the demander and the context of the demand" in content and type of product (Lindenberg and Bryant 2001, 218). Thus, for example, certain donors might require formal evaluations whereas others request only financial reports. Meanwhile, beneficiaries may be interested in a set of on-the-ground outcomes that differ from donors' interests entirely.

According to some observers, the challenge for INGOs is not simply to try to equally balance the various accountabilities they juggle, but to discover the right stakeholder emphasis for the type of work they do. Brown and Moore write that "accountability choices should advance the strategy an INGO is trying to execute" (2001, 570). As an example they suggest that organizations involved in service delivery, capacity building, and policy influence (i.e., international human rights organizations) should emphasize different stakeholders to most effectively move forward their type of work. Most INGOs are service delivery organizations that Brown and Moore say should be placing more emphasis on donors because they are indispensable to an organization's ability to complete its mission. When holding themselves accountable to donors, INGOs typically invest more in establishing the efficiency and effectiveness of their work as well as their integrity. Although requiring more work of the INGO, it is likely that in some situations such accountability has improved the work of INGOs and corrected or prevented activities that would have been harmful or wasteful. Indeed, many institutional donors now require that organizations clearly demonstrate project results through impact measurement.

When USAID is the donor each grant and cooperative agreement must include three elements:

- a results-oriented program description that is tied to USAID strategic objectives and overall agency strategic plan;
- a performance management system that includes performance indicators for measuring results at different stages; and
- responsibility for performance that holds the funding recipient accountable for the achievement of results within their sphere of control (USAID 2002c).

To help organizations accomplish these three requirements, USAID developed a method that brings together project objectives and goals in a timeline and connects them with indicators to measure progress. Other aspects built into USAID projects also ensure there is a process for holding INGOs accountable for their work. These include lengthy, detailed project proposals, systematic evaluations of projects, and relatively short time frames within which specified, tangible activities must be accomplished.

Service delivery INGOs often find that these and other donor priorities may require they put other stakeholders such as staff, partners, and even beneficiaries in second place when they come in conflict with donors. Thomas Dichter argues that such program requirements, done in the name of accountability to the donor, contribute to the lack of successful development projects (Dichter 2003). Lindenberg and Bryant explain that the emphasis on accountability to donors can "lead NGOs to focus on their immediate projects without examining the broader economic, social, and political realities having an impact on communities," all factors that play into the long-term success of development work (2001, 220). On the other side of the coin, USAID has a feedback process through which it is able to justify existing and future programming by showing that current programs are meeting policy objectives and are working in the national interest.

Brown and Moore suggest that, unlike service delivery INGOs, capacity-building INGOs should hold themselves more accountable to beneficiaries, the clients of their programs. The capacity-building focus of these organizations "implies a commitment to strengthening clients' abilities to carry out their own purposes and aspirations rather than to achieving those purposes specified by the INGO or its contributors" (Brown and Moore 2001, 581). Rather than providing assistance in a paternalistic fashion, these organizations shape their intervention to the skill-building activities clients request. Organizations committed to this strategy face dilemmas when clients request capacity-building assistance that is not in line with priorities of donors, other clients, and even the INGO itself. Because of these kinds of pressures, some capacity-building programs revert to service delivery accountabilities, although they risk losing the gains of the capacity-building approach including client trust, project flexibility, and innovation. Given the service delivery model followed by USAID, few, if any, government-funded projects appear to allow much discretion for client-driven services.

Nonetheless, the movement in the field is toward more beneficiary accountability (Forman and Stoddard 2002). In 2003, Humanitarian Accountability Partnership International (n.d.) started in Geneva, Switzerland, to bring together INGOs interested in humanitarian work that is more focused on listening and responding to beneficiaries. Service delivery INGOs receiving government funding may, however, find it difficult to reconcile donor-driven programming with pressure from the INGO community to allow for exclusive beneficiary input into service provision.

Brown and Moore suggest that a third type of INGO, those that influence policy,[14] may want to emphasize their accountability to their political constituencies and advocacy targets. INGOs, particularly those with an active membership making up part of their political constituency, may choose to align themselves more with their members than with other stakeholder groups. Political constituencies might also include other institutions and individuals with approaches to policy that align with those of the INGO. These political constituencies hold policy influence INGOs accountable for establishing and maintaining the legitimacy of the organization in policy debates. To achieve this, INGOs may show that their advocacy is rooted in widespread values or concern for an issue, that they have access to expertise and information on given issues, and that they are representing a strong base of constituents (Brown and Moore 2001). Though their numbers are growing, there are relatively few INGOs that focus solely on policy influence. A lot of advocacy occurs through organizations for which policy influence is only a component of their work, creating complex accountability issues. One of the most complex is where INGOs both receive government funds to deliver services and advocate for or against government policies, a topic examined in the following section.

ADVOCACY

A common public assumption is that government-funded INGOs refrain from advocacy efforts for fear they will lose their government support. Edwards and Hulme even suggest the emergence of "a widening rift between well-resourced service providers and poorly funded social mobilization organizations" because government funding was thought to hinder advocacy activities (1996b, 966). In reality, a number of large service delivery INGOs with government funding are prominent advocates for issues that are not always in line with the current government administration. Organizations such as Save the Children, CARE, and World Vision all actively participate in advocacy efforts (Lindenberg and Dobel 1999) while receiving sizable amounts of government funding (Forman and Stoddard 2002). Moreover, fears that INGO advocacy would decrease as government funding of INGOs increased are unfounded. Commins (1997) finds that organizations involved in InterAction, an alliance of more than 160 United States–based INGOs begun in 1984, have continued to be active in their advocacy efforts even as government funding of their work has increased.

Yet public perception, even on the international level, persists in the expectation that government funding will influence INGO advocacy. Forman and Stoddard state, "Despite international criticism over the large portion of their funding that comes from U.S. government sources, and the expectation that this would inevitably hinder independence in programming and policy stance, the major U.S. NGOs for the most part have not behaved in thrall to their largest benefactor and client" (2002, 259). As evidence, they cite strong opposition by some INGOs to the government's proposal to target assistance to Sudanese rebels and to the U.S. Export-Import Bank's lending program that only provided resources for more expensive U.S.-made AIDS drugs in African countries.

There may, however, be limitations to the extent to which government-funded INGOs are willing to advocate. Though advocacy occurs, some critics argue that it focuses too much on specific aid priorities while ignoring wider government-supported macroeconomic policies that contribute, in some cases, to the need for INGO poverty relief in the first place (Commins 1997). Moreover, with the war in Iraq, some large United States–based INGOs with U.S. funding for their humanitarian relief work in Iraq have been criticized for "fail[ing] to condemn the war outright" because they did not want to risk cuts in their funding (Brown 2004). This avoidance of large issues may be explained by the fact that some organizations feel advocacy on big policy issues is simply not their raison d'être. Lindenberg and Dobel (1999) point out that INGO advocacy is most successful when it is based on the organization's immediate experience in the field, draws on examples of real people and their stories, and makes use of sound analysis, an approach that also works to maintain the organization's legitimacy and reputation in the eyes of funders.

Certain types of INGOs are more likely to advocate than others. Analysis of the NCCS dataset of international organizations shows an interesting divergence in government funding between small and large organizations that report formal lobbying activity.[15] Twelve percent of small INGOs (those with less than $2 million in revenue) that lobby receive government funding, whereas 59 percent of larger lobbying organizations (those with $2 million or more in revenue) have government funding.[16] Why large government-funded organizations appear to lobby more than small ones may be because of funding and organizational capacity factors as well as differences in knowledge about lobbying regulations, though further research is needed.

One of the more influential ways INGOs indirectly advocate government is through the media. In what has become known as the CNN effect, media coverage of humanitarian crises raises public sympathy and support for victims that pressures government officials to send increased aid to distressed areas (Robinson 2000). An example of this effect is the response generated after the BBC aired news reports of the 2005 famine in Niger. While the world's attention was focused on helping victims of the December 2004 tsunami, the growing food crisis in Niger was overlooked for months until the BBC stepped in and aired reports of emaciated and dying children. Other news media picked up the story, and governments and others pledged an average of $1 million a day between mid-July and early August. All told, the U.N. World Food Programme's emergency campaign expanded from $2.9 million to $57.6 million (Timberg 2005).

Although apparently less influential in determining the initial decision to provide aid, media coverage has been shown to have a very strong impact on the amount of official aid allocated. Drury, Olson, and Van Belle (2005) show in their study on politics and U.S. disaster assistance that for each *New York Times* article printed about a disaster an additional half million dollars in government aid is provided. Demonstrating the power of the media, they showed that the severity of the disaster had less impact on the amount allocated than the level of media coverage, "with one *New York Times* article being worth more disaster dollars than 1,500 fatalities" (Drury, Olson, and Van Belle 2005, 470). Realizing the connection between media coverage and political action, Alexander de Waal states, "aid agency staff and journalists try to make the magic formula work, so that they can obtain the funds and recognition that will follow" (1997, 637).

CONCLUSION

INGOs working to implement humanitarian and development programs may, at times, find themselves out of alignment with the U.S. government when it comes to aid distribution, approach to international work, and policy objectives. While INGOs are interested in basing aid levels on degree of need in a foreign country, the government often bases foreign assistance on strategic interests. INGOs are also increasingly moving toward client-driven services, while the USAID model is directed at service delivery to meet top-down program objectives. Also, whereas INGOs may be interested in achieving certain policy objectives (such as the family planning at issue in the Mexico City Policy), the U.S. government at times opposes their implementation.

Recent shifts in foreign assistance to include more foreign policy objectives have increased the tension between some INGOs and government. Certain INGOs are opposed to what they see as the government promoting democracy before basic services in Iraq. Some are also finding it difficult to maintain a level of autonomy from government when receiving public funds. This is particularly the case where INGOs are being asked to work under the military in Iraq or where USAID has pressured INGOs to advertise their connection to the U.S. government for public relations purposes.

Despite these areas of misalignment, the INGO community seems to have found a working compromise. For many organizations there is still fundamental agreement with government when the basic purpose of aid is to assist victims of disasters and help poor regions develop, even if the end objective of new official aid is national security. In those situations where organizations feel their mission would be compromised, some condition their use of public funds on whether a particular project agrees with their aid philosophy or adjust their programming. Among these are INGOs that walk a tenuous line between receiving government money and influencing government policy. Still, an unexpectedly sizable number (a full 90 percent of all INGOs in the NCCS international dataset) refrain from all government funding on political grounds or simply lack the interest or administrative structure to pursue government contracts and grants.

Although government-nonprofit relationships are found in many sectors, the relationship between INGOs and government can be more intense precisely because the stakes are higher. For INGOs the struggle with government arises when there are disagreements over priorities and best approaches to helping those in need beyond U.S. borders. However, as evidenced by the growing number of organizations working with government, it appears INGOs are increasingly willing to navigate these areas of misalignment.

NOTES

1. The term INGO in this chapter means international nongovernmental organizations working in the areas of international humanitarian assistance and development. These types of organizations have also been referred to as development NGOs, transnational NGOs, Northern NGOs, or simply NGOs as well as PVOs (private voluntary organizations, a label used by the U.S. Agency for International Development).

2. An OECD Development Cooperation Review of the United States found that USAID disbursed 50.2 percent of U.S. development assistance dollars in 2002, followed by the State Department at 18.6 percent, and the Treasury Department at 10.7 percent (OECD 2002).

3. This percentage meets the 0.7 percent of gross domestic product that the United Nations has established as a target for development assistance.

4. The Millennium Challenge Corporation established in January 2004 administers the millennium challenge account. Congress allocated nearly $1 billion in initial funding for FY 2004 and $1.5 billion for FY 2005. President Bush requested $3 billion for FY 2006 and is seeking to increase annual funding to $5 billion (Millennium Challenge Corporation 2005).

5. Private voluntary organization is a USAID term for "tax-exempt, nonprofit organizations that receive voluntary contributions of money, staff time, or in-kind support from the general public and are engaged in voluntary, charitable, or development assistance activities. They can be U.S. based, international, or locally based in the host country" (U.S. General Accounting Office 2002, 4). Their scope is broader than INGOs because they include locally based non-profits in foreign countries.

6. This is the percentage range found between 1995 and 2000 and includes aid to both domestic and foreign private voluntary organizations. About two-thirds of the percentage for 2000 was for domestic private voluntary organizations alone.

7. The NCCS international dataset contains data from IRS Form 990 that 501(c)(3) INGOs filed with the Internal Revenue Service in years 1999–2003.

8. Not all private voluntary organizations registered with USAID are in the NCCS international dataset. For example, only about half of the private voluntary organizations registered with USAID in 2000 show year 2000 records in the international dataset. This low figure is attributed to the fact that a number of organizations registered with USAID are not international in scope as defined for inclusion in the international dataset. Also, many religious INGOs are not required to file an IRS Form 990 and thus are not included in the dataset.

9. Datasets for individual years in this section are based on circa years, that is, each dataset includes INGO IRS forms for the given year supplemented with records from previous years when organizations failed to file in the given year.

10. As a cautionary note, analysis of the NCCS dataset of international organizations does not reflect the entire proportion of official U.S. government aid administered through INGOs. See note 8.

11. The National Democratic Institute for International Affairs and the International Republican Institute are closely affiliated with the National Endowment for Democracy, which receives congressional funding. They receive much of their government support from the National Endowment for Democracy.

12. Released in August 2003, the joint State Department–USAID Strategic Plan for Fiscal Years 2004–2009 outlines a strategy for aligning diplomacy and development assistance in support of policy positions set forth in the 2002 National Security Strategy. It established the State Department–USAID Joint Policy and Management Councils to coordinate each agency's work in this area and oversee the management of joint policies and projects (U.S. Department of State and U.S. Agency for International Development 2003).

13. Numbers from the Center for Global Development reflect data from the Development Assistance Committee published by the Organisation for Economic Co-operation and Development in 2001.

14. Examples of INGOs that influence policy are Amnesty International, the Center for International Environmental Law, and Rainforest Action Network.

15. The Internal Revenue Service defines lobbying as direct and grassroots action to promote specific legislation at the local, state, and national levels of government and regulates nonprofit lobbying activity by limiting the amount of lobbying a nonprofit can engage in to approximately 20 percent of its expenditures.

16. Where numbers of small to medium government-funded organizations are comparable to numbers of large government-funded organizations.

REFERENCES

Adelman, Carol, Jeremiah Norris, and Jean Weicher. 2005. "America's Total Economic Engagement with the Developing World: Rethinking the Uses and Nature of Foreign Aid." Washington, DC: The Hudson Institute.

Beattie, Alan. 2003. "NGOs Under Pressure on Relief Funds." *Financial Times*, June 13.

Brown, Ian. 2004. "This Fatal Compromise." *The Guardian*, Nov. 19.

Brown, L. David, and Mark H. Moore. 2001. "Accountability, Strategy, and International Nongovernmental Organizations." *Nonprofit and Voluntary Sector Quarterly* 30(3): 569–87.

Center for Global Development. 2004. "Why Global Development Matters for the U.S." Rich World, Poor World: A Guide to Global Development Series. Washington, DC: Center for Global Development.

Commins, Stephen. 1997. "World Vision International and Donors: Too Close for Comfort?" In *NGOs, States and Donors: Too Close for Comfort?* edited by David Hulme and Michael Edwards (140–55). New York, NY: St. Martin's Press.

Development Initiatives. 2000. *Global Humanitarian Assistance 2000*. Geneva, Switzerland: Inter-Agency Standing Committee Office for the Coordination of Humanitarian Affairs.

de Waal, Alexander. 1997. "Democratizing the Aid Encounter in Africa." *International Affairs* 73(4): 623–39.

Dichter, Thomas W. 1999. "Globalization and Its Effects on NGOs: Efflorescence or a Blurring of Roles and Relevance?" *Nonprofit and Voluntary Sector Quarterly* 28(suppl. 1): 38–58.

———. 2003. *Despite Good Intentions: Why Development Assistance in the Third World Has Failed*. Boston: University of Massachusetts Press.

Drury, A. Cooper, Richard Olson, and Douglas Van Belle. 2005. "The Politics of Humanitarian Aid: U.S. Foreign Disaster Assistance, 1964–1995." *The Journal of Politics* 67(2): 454–73.

Ebrahim, Alnoor. 2003. "Accountability in Practice: Mechanisms for NGOs." *World Development* 31(5): 813–29.

Edwards, Michael, and David Hulme. 1996a. *Beyond the Magic Bullet: NGO Performance and Accountability in the Post-Cold War World*. West Hartford, CT: Kumarian Press.

———. 1996b. "Too Close for Comfort? The Impact of Official Aid on Nongovernmental Organizations." *World Development* 24(6): 961–73.

EngenderHealth. 2005. "The Fourth Anniversary of the Global Gag Rule." http://www.engenderhealth.org/news/whatsnew/gag_rule.html.

Forman, Shepard, and Abby Stoddard. 2002. "International Assistance." In *The State of Nonprofit America*, edited by Lester Salamon (240–74). Washington, DC: Brookings Institution Press.

Global Gag Rule Impact Project. 2005. "Access Denied: U.S. Restrictions on International Family Planning." http://www.globalgagrule.org.

Hulme, David, and Michael Edwards. 1997. "NGOs, States and Donors: An Overview." In *NGOs, States and Donors: Too Close for Comfort?* edited by David Hulme and Michael Edwards (3–22). New York, NY: St. Martin's Press.

Humanitarian Accountability Partnership International. n.d. Home page. http://www.hapinternational.org/en/.

InterAction and Independent Sector. 2003. "Public Comment on 'International Grantmaking and International Activities by Domestic 501(c)3 Organizations.'" http://www.independentsector.org/programs/gr/intlactivities.html.

Lindenberg, Marc. 1999. "Declining State Capacity, Voluntarism, and Globalization of the Not-for-Profit Sector." *Nonprofit and Voluntary Sector Quarterly* 28(suppl. 1): 147–67.

Lindenberg, Marc, and Coralie Bryant. 2001. *Going Global: Transforming Relief and Development NGOs*. Bloomfield, CT: Kumarian Press.

Lindenberg, Marc, and Patrick Dobel. 1999. "The Challenges of Globalization for Northern International Relief and Development NGOs." *Nonprofit and Voluntary Sector Quarterly* 28(suppl. 1): 4–24.

Millennium Challenge Corporation. 2005. "The Millennium Challenge Account." http://www.mcc.gov/about_us/overview/index.shtml.

National Center for Charitable Statistics/GuideStar National Nonprofit Database. Center on Nonprofits and Philanthropy, The Urban Institute.

OECD. See Organisation for Economic Co-operation and Development.

Office of U.S. Foreign Disaster Assistance. 2000. "OFDA Annual Report 2000." Washington, DC: Office of U.S. Foreign Disaster Assistance, U.S. Agency for International Development.

Organisation for Economic Co-operation and Development. 2002. "United States Development Cooperation Review." Paris, France: Development Assistance Committee, Organisation for Economic Co-operation and Development.

Ramos, Edgardo, Timothy R. Lyman, Patricia Canavan, and Clifford Nichols III. 2004. "Handbook on Counter-Terrorism Measures: What U.S. Nonprofits and Grantmakers Need to Know." Washington, DC: Day, Berry & Howard Foundation.

Read, Richard. 2003. "Aid Agencies Reject Money Due to Strings." *Oregonian*, June 6.

Reid, Elizabeth J., and Janelle A. Kerlin. 2006. "The International Charitable Nonprofit Subsector in the United States: International Understanding, International Development and Assistance, and International Affairs." Washington DC: The Urban Institute. http://www.urban.org/publications/411276.html.

Robinson, Mark. 1997. "Privatising the Voluntary Sector: NGOs as Public Service Contractors?" In *NGOs, States and Donors: Too Close for Comfort?* edited by David Hulme and Michael Edwards (59–78). New York, NY: St. Martin's Press.

Robinson, Piers. 2000. "The Policy-Media Interaction Model: Measuring Media Power During Humanitarian Crisis." *Journal of Peace Research* 37(5): 613–33.

Salm, Janet. 1999. "Coping with Globalization: A Profile of the Northern NGO Sector." *Nonprofit and Voluntary Sector Quarterly* 28(suppl. 1): 87–103.

Smillie, Ian, Henny Helmlich, Tony German, and Judith Randel. 1999. *Stakeholders: Government-NGO Partnerships for Development.* London, England: Earthscan.

Timberg, Craig. 2005. "Global Aid System Stalled as Niger's Crisis Deepened." *Washington Post*, Aug. 17.

United Nations World Food Programme. 2005. "WFP Thanks U.S. Military and USAID for Help in Guatemala." http://www.wfp.org/english/?ModuleID=137&Key=1885.

United States Agency for International Development. 2002a. "2002 PVO Executive Contact List." Washington, DC: Office of Private and Voluntary Cooperation, U.S. Agency for International Development.

———. 2002b. "Grants and Cooperative Agreements to Non-Governmental Organizations." Automated Directives System, Acquisition and Assistance Chapter 303. Washington, DC: U.S. Agency for International Development.

———. 2002c. "Results-Oriented Assistance: A USAID Sourcebook." http://www.usaid.gov/pubs/sourcebook/usgov/index.html.

———. 2003. "U.S. Overseas Loans and Grants, Obligations and Loan Authorizations (The Greenbook)." http://qesdb.cdie.org/gbk/USG%20Organizations.html.

———. 2005a. "USAID Primer: What We Do and How We Do It." Washington, DC: U.S. Agency for International Development.

———. 2005b. "USAID's Global Partnerships." http://www.usaid.gov/our_work/global_partnerships/.

U.S. Department of State. 2004. "USAID's Natsios Links Global Development, National Security." Washington, DC: Bureau of International Information, U.S. Department of State.

U.S. Department of State and U.S. Agency for International Development. 2003. "FY 2004–2009 Department of State and USAID Strategic Plan." Washington, DC: U.S. Department of State and U.S. Agency for International Development.

U.S. Department of the Treasury. 2005. "U.S. Department of the Treasury Anti-Terrorist Financing Guidelines: Voluntary Best Practices for U.S.-Based Charities." Washington DC: U.S. Department of the Treasury.

U.S. General Accounting Office. 2002. "Foreign Assistance: USAID Relies Heavily on Nongovernmental Organizations, but Better Data Needed to Evaluate Approaches." Washington, DC: U.S. General Accounting Office.

U.S. Government Accountability Office. 2005. "U.S. Public Diplomacy: Interagency Coordination Efforts Hampered by the Lack of a National Communication Strategy." Washington, DC: U.S. Government Accountability Office.

12

GOVERNMENT– NONPROFIT RELATIONS FROM AN INTERNATIONAL PERSPECTIVE

Lester M. Salamon

The debate over the appropriate relationship between government and private, voluntary institutions in the United States is hardly taking place in a vacuum. To the contrary, similar issues are being debated in other parts of the world. Regrettably, however, solid information about nonprofit organizations and the relationships between these organizations and the state has long been even more limited abroad than in the United States. This has given rise to a variety of misconceptions—some ideologically inspired—that have materially influenced U.S. policy. A careful examination of international experiences can therefore not only improve our understanding of nonprofit realities elsewhere but usefully inform the American debate.

This chapter's purpose is to provide such an examination. To do so, the discussion falls into five major parts. The first section takes up the basic conceptualization that has long framed American understanding of the relationship between government and the nonprofit sector. Against this backdrop, the second section examines the realities of overseas experiences, focusing particularly on the overall scale of nonprofit activity and the extent of government financial support for it. The third section examines the causes of what turn out to be varying patterns of government–nonprofit relationships and the trends that affect them in different parts of the world. The fourth section explores the implications of these trends for both government and the nonprofit sector. Finally, a concluding section outlines lessons that emerge from international experiences for American government–nonprofit ties.

Although this chapter attempts to outline the major contours of international experience with government–nonprofit relations, completely covering so vast a topic in a single chapter is impossible. For one thing, the span of relationships between government and the nonprofit sector is quite broad, as the chapters in this book attest. For another, solid international information on these relationships has only recently begun to be available and only on some countries. Under these circumstances, it will be necessary to draw with rather broad brush strokes and to focus on a few facets of this complex and often contradictory set of relationships. Still, enough information is now available to identify a number of important, if somewhat tentative, conclusions:

- First, the nonprofit sector is a far more substantial presence abroad than Americans tend to recognize, even in countries where the prevailing theories would lead us to expect otherwise;
- Second, while government–nonprofit relations range across a wide spectrum, they are far more collaborative abroad than is often assumed.
- Third, the nonprofit sector's relationship with government has been critical to its growth and development. Where this relationship is positive and supportive, nonprofit organizations have prospered. Where it is not, they have struggled.
- Finally, key facets of government–nonprofit relationships are in flux abroad just as they are in the United States, with competing pressures strengthening and undermining collaborative ties.

The balance of this chapter reviews the evidence that undergirds these observations.

THE PARADIGM OF CONFLICT: THE AMERICAN CONCEPTION OF GOVERNMENT–NONPROFIT RELATIONS

For much of the past century or more, a powerful "paradigm of conflict" has influenced much of American thinking about the relative roles of government and the nonprofit sector and the relationships between them. Central to this paradigm has been a belief in an inherent conflict between nonprofit institutions and the state. According to this line of argument, nonprofit organizations are a preferred vehicle for addressing social and economic problems because they protect individual liberty and encourage personal initiative. The growth of government, in this view, weakens private, nonprofit institutions, displacing voluntary activity and "crowding out" private charitable contributions.

This line of thinking provided a strong rationale for resisting efforts to establish government social policies in the period prior to the New Deal. More recently, it surfaced as the conceptual foundation for the new conservative movement of the 1980s. Writing as early as the 1950s, such conservative theorists as Robert Nisbet made defense of the nonprofit sector against the encroaching power of the state a central tenet of their philosophy. "The real struggle in the modern era," Nisbet wrote in 1954 in his influential *Power and Community*, "is not between state and individual, but between state and voluntary group" (Nisbet 1953, 109). A principal goal of the conservative movement that brought Ronald Reagan to power in 1980, therefore, was to shrink the state and restore the primacy of the voluntary sector. As Reagan put it soon after his 1980 electoral victory: "We have let the state take away the things that were once ours to do voluntarily." Though muted in part, this sentiment was also evident in President George H.W. Bush's championship of the "thousand points of light" and President George W. Bush's "faith-based charities" initiative. Each justified cuts in government-funded social programs in terms of the salutary effect this would have on American traditions of voluntarism.[1]

According to this theory, what distinguished the American experience from its overseas counterparts, at least through the Great Society era of the 1960s, was that Americans resisted the growth of government and relied instead on private, voluntary groups. By contrast, other countries, particularly advanced industrial ones, turned toward an expansive welfare state that supposedly squeezed out the nonprofit sector. From this it followed that the countries of Western Europe, like those in the developing world, would lack a significant nonprofit sector. By the same token, this conceptualization left little room for expecting extensive cooperation between government and the nonprofit sphere. To the contrary, the "paradigm of conflict" essentially acknowledges only two dominant models for organizing efforts to cope with public problems: a "voluntary-sector model" featuring limited government action and primary reliance instead on the third sector; and a "government-dominant model" featuring extensive government action—either benign or authoritarian—and limited opportunity for a flourishing nonprofit sphere (Gidron, Kramer, and Salamon 1992). In the popular mythology, America adhered to the first of these models and Western Europe and much of the developing world to the second.

THE PREVAILING REALITY

To what extent does reality conform to what this paradigm suggests? Elsewhere I have argued that this paradigm of conflict has never fit the American reality (Salamon 1987, 1995; Salamon and Abramson 1982). Behind the rhetoric of conflict, the relationship between government and the nonprofit sector in America has more often been one of collaboration and mutual support, with results that have generally been beneficial to both.[2]

What now seems clear, however, is that this mythology does not fit reality overseas either. The nonprofit sector turns out to be a far more significant presence in countries throughout the world than this mythology would suggest, particularly in countries where government social welfare provision is extensive and the conflict theory would lead us to expect only a limited nonprofit presence. Similarly, government–nonprofit cooperation is quite extensive, especially in countries where the nonprofit sector is most developed.

The Scale of Nonprofit Activity Abroad

In terms of the scale of nonprofit activity, nonprofits constitute a massive social and economic force well beyond the borders of the United States. Focusing just on their service role, nonprofits account for 40 percent of all hospital patient days in Germany, 55 percent of all residents in residential care facilities in France, three-fourths of all students in higher education institutions in Japan, and much of the social service provision in Italy (Salamon and Anheier 1996a, 24). Indeed, at least four countries of the 38 with systematic, comparative data have nonprofit workforces proportionally larger than America's (Salamon and Sokolowski and Associates 2004). All of these countries have high levels of government social welfare spending (the Netherlands, Belgium, Ireland, and Canada) (see figure 12.1). This suggests that the popular conception of an inherent conflict between government and the nonprofit sector is seriously overdrawn.

Figure 12.1. Civil Society Organization Workforce as a Share of the Economically Active Population, by Country

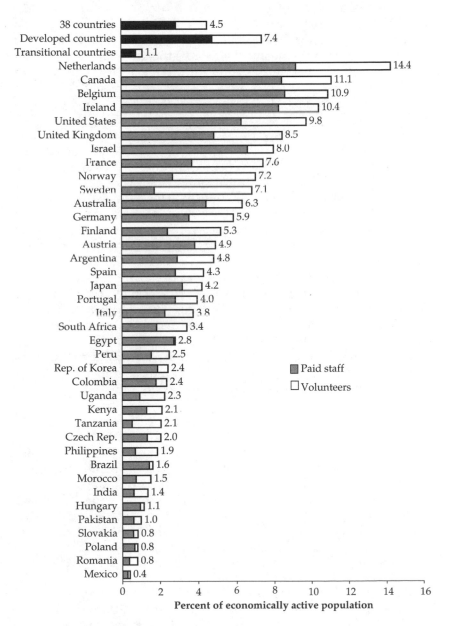

Source: Johns Hopkins Comparative Nonprofit Sector Project

Illustrative of this surprising nonprofit presence abroad is the situation in Germany, where government spending on social welfare accounts for 35 percent of gross domestic product, compared with just over 20 percent in the United States (OECD 1997; Bixby 1997). To conclude from the significant level and range of government social welfare activity that Germany is a case of the government dominant model, however, is to misread significantly the character of the German welfare state. To the contrary, side by side with government is a massive network of private, nonprofit organizations that share important social welfare functions (Anheier and Seibel 2001; Salamon and Anheier 1993).

At the center of this network are six large conglomerates, the "free welfare associations" (freie Wohlfahrtsverbande), which include the Catholic and Protestant social welfare agencies—Caritas and Diakonisches Werk, respectively. These are massive federations of local welfare agencies spread throughout the country. These religiously oriented social welfare networks have, in turn, helped inspire the creation of three others: the Arbeiterwohlfahrt (Workers' Welfare Association), founded in 1919 as a vehicle for reconciling workers with the capitalist state and historically linked to the Social Democratic party (Bauer 1978); the Zentralwohlfahrtsstelle der Juden in Deutschland (the Central Welfare Association for Jews in Germany), created in 1917 to coordinate numerous Jewish local welfare committees and activities and reestablished after World War II to provide assistance to concentration camp victims; the Deutscher Paritätischer Wohlfahrtsverband, a consortium of nondenominational, nonpartisan private welfare organizations founded in 1920; and the Deutsches Rotes Kreuz (German Red Cross), which functions both as a relief organization and a social service organization.

These free welfare associations represent a major presence in the German social welfare scene, with an estimated 650,000 full-time equivalent employees and 1.5 million volunteers (Anheier 1991; Spiegelhalter 1990). Taken together, they run 68,466 institutions in health care, youth and family services, as well as services for the handicapped, elderly, and the poor (Bundesarbeitsgemeinschaft 1990). As table 12.1 shows, these organizations account for over 60 percent of the employment in such fields as family services, services for the elderly, services for the handicapped, nursing home care, and child day care.

Nonprofit institutions are even more powerfully present in the Netherlands. Seventy percent of all elementary and secondary school pupils in the Netherlands attend private, nonprofit institutions. Nonprofit institutions also dominate the provision of health care and welfare services. Recent estimates put the nonprofit workforce in the Netherlands, paid and volunteer, at 14.4 percent of the economically active population, nearly 50 percent higher than the comparable U.S. figure (see figure 12.1) (Burger et al. 1997; Salamon, Sokolowski, and List 2004).

Table 12.1. Nonprofit, For-Profit, and Public Shares of Social Service Employment in Germany, by Field

Industry	For-profit sector (%)	Nonprofit sector (%)	Public sector (%)	Total employment in industry
Family services	9.4	73.1	17.5	28,566
Services for the elderly	17.7	67.6	14.7	67,140
Services for the handicapped	9.5	83.7	6.9	96,518
Nursing homes	20.2	63.0	16.8	128,510
Child day care	1.0	62.3	36.7	155,874
Vocational training	17.6	21.5	60.9	202,898
Clinics and hospitals	14.2	34.2	51.0	722,734
Other health institutions	47.6	36.2	16.2	91,586

Source: Anheier 1991.

Even in Sweden, perhaps the classic welfare state, nonprofit institutions exist in profusion, though they take a slightly different form, functioning less as service providers than vehicles for social advocacy and social integration. Thus, an official 1987 report identified close to 200,000 membership associations in Sweden, and the country's 9 million people account for 30 million separate memberships in various voluntary groups. Beyond this, nearly half of the Swedish population is active as volunteers, roughly comparable to the proportions in the United States (Lundstrom and Wijkstrom 1997a). As figure 12.1 shows, Sweden and Norway rank close behind the United Kingdom, Israel, and France in the scale of their nonprofit workforces. So much for the theory that government involvement "crowds out" voluntary groups.

Perhaps not surprisingly, nonprofit organizations are considerably less prominent in the developing world and in the transitional countries of Central and Eastern Europe. Even when informal organizations and volunteer activity are taken into account, in the late 1990s, the nonprofit workforce averaged only 1.1 percent of the economically active population in developing and transitional countries, compared with 7.4 percent in developed countries (Salamon, Sokolowski, and List 2004) (see figure 12.1). Nevertheless, a global associational revolution seems to be under way in many of these countries, a massive upsurge of organized private, voluntary activity that is significantly boosting the scale and diversity of nonprofit institutions nearly everywhere (Civicus 1994; Salamon 1994). Evidence of this phenomenon is apparent in widely disparate areas:

- In the more than 1 million registered nonprofit organizations recent research has uncovered in India (Sen 1998);

- In the more than 210,000 nonprofit organizations operating in Brazil, representing over 2 . percent of the employed workforce (Landim 1998);
- In the large nonprofit conglomerates, such as BRAC and the Grameen Bank, functioning in Bangladesh, and the Rural Reconstruction Movement operating in the Philippines;
- In the 250,000 civil society organizations formally registered in China and the 2 million widely thought to exist there.[3]

In short, a sizable and vibrant nonprofit sector is not a monopoly of the United States. On the contrary, nonprofit organizations are present in substantial numbers in other countries. Though nonprofits seem to have expanded considerably in recent years, the presence of voluntary organizations is hardly new. In fact, the tradition of nonprofit activity outside the United States stretches back at least as far as America's experience with these organizations, and in many cases much farther. Finally, the prevalence of nonprofits does not seem to vary inversely with the size of government social welfare spending, as the paradigm of conflict would suggest. Rather, sizable nonprofit sectors seem to be highly consistent with large-scale government social welfare activity, as has increasingly been the case in the United States as well. Indeed, of the countries for which reliable data are available, the ones with the highest government social welfare spending (e.g., Belgium and the Netherlands) often have the largest nonprofit sectors.

Partners in Public Service: Government–Nonprofit Cooperation

That sizable nonprofit sectors exist in many countries where government social welfare spending is extensive is hardly accidental. On the contrary, the nonprofit sector in these countries is so large because government and the nonprofit sector cooperate—often to an extent that the paradigm of government–nonprofit conflict fails to acknowledge. Indeed, the Johns Hopkins Comparative Nonprofit Sector Project showed that, in the 35 countries for which data were available, government support (including grants, contracts, and reimbursements) accounted on average for 35 percent of all nonprofit revenue as of the late 1990s, nearly three times more than the share private philanthropy provides (Salamon, Sokolowski, and List 2004) (figure 12.2).

Government support was particularly evident in the core social welfare fields of health, education, and social services, which together account for nearly 60 percent of all nonprofit activity (Salamon, Wojciech, and List 2004). As figure 12.3 shows, the public sector accounted on average for over half of all nonprofit revenue in these three fields.

Figure 12.2. Sources of Civil Society Organization Revenue, by Country

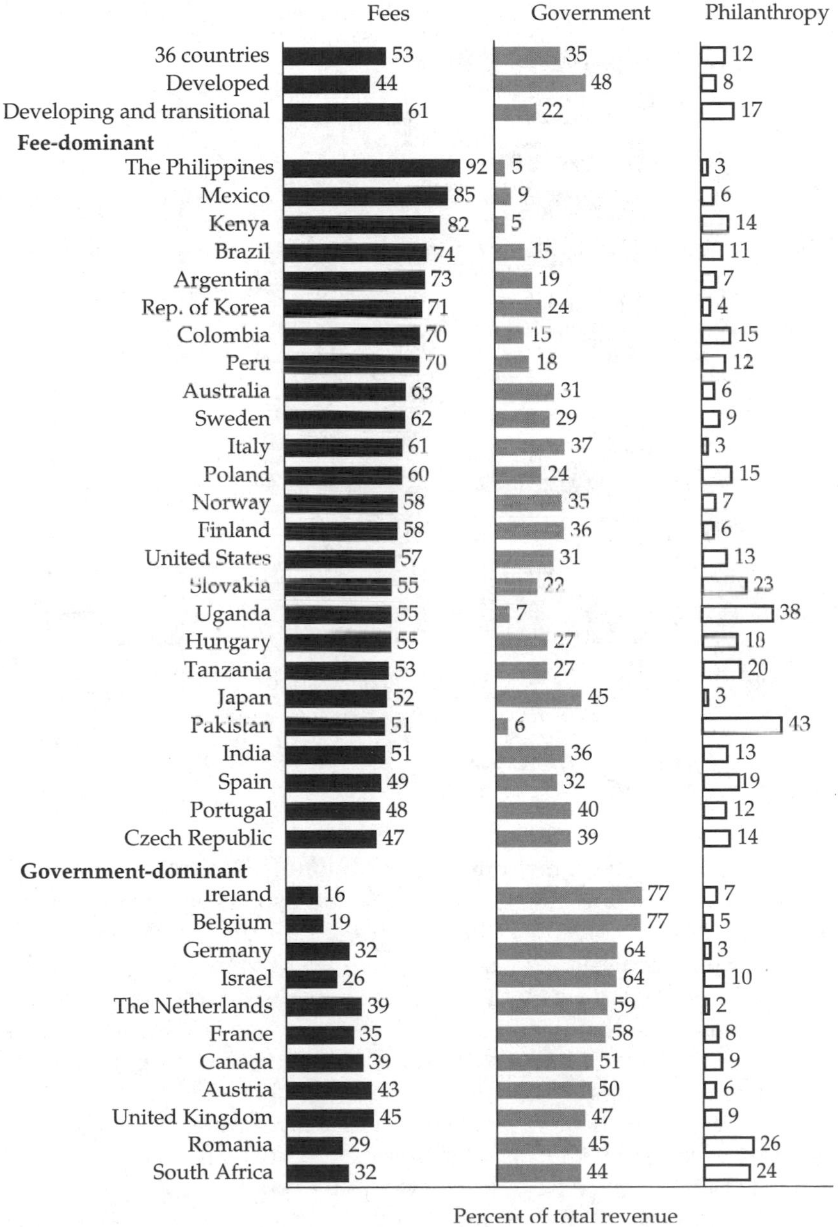

	Fees	Government	Philanthropy
36 countries	53	35	12
Developed	44	48	8
Developing and transitional	61	22	17
Fee-dominant			
The Philippines	92	5	3
Mexico	85	9	6
Kenya	82	5	14
Brazil	74	15	11
Argentina	73	19	7
Rep. of Korea	71	24	4
Colombia	70	15	15
Peru	70	18	12
Australia	63	31	6
Sweden	62	29	9
Italy	61	37	3
Poland	60	24	15
Norway	58	35	7
Finland	58	36	6
United States	57	31	13
Slovakia	55	22	23
Uganda	55	7	38
Hungary	55	27	18
Tanzania	53	27	20
Japan	52	45	3
Pakistan	51	6	43
India	51	36	13
Spain	49	32	19
Portugal	48	40	12
Czech Republic	47	39	14
Government-dominant			
Ireland	16	77	7
Belgium	19	77	5
Germany	32	64	3
Israel	26	64	10
The Netherlands	39	59	2
France	35	58	8
Canada	39	51	9
Austria	43	50	6
United Kingdom	45	47	9
Romania	29	45	26
South Africa	32	44	24

Percent of total revenue

Source: Johns Hopkins Comparative Nonprofit Sector Project

Figure 12.3. Sources of Civil Society Organization Revenue, by Field, 35 Countries

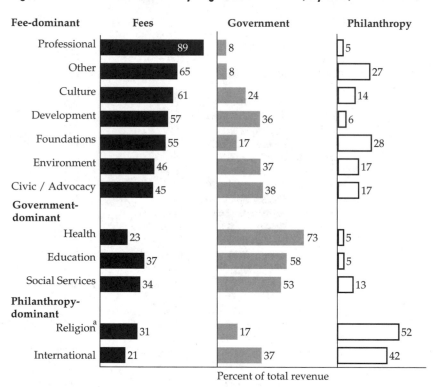

Source: Johns Hopkins Comparative Nonprofit Sector Project.
[a] 29-country unweighted average

The extent of government financing of nonprofit activity is not uniform across the world. Significantly, however, such support is particularly extensive in precisely the countries with the largest nonprofit sectors. Thus, as figure 12.2 shows, in all four countries in which the nonprofit workforce was larger than in the United States (the Netherlands, Canada, Belgium, and Ireland), government provided over half of all nonprofit income. This pattern was widespread throughout Western Europe and suggests that the classical Western European "welfare state" is really a welfare *partnership* in which government relies heavily on private, nonprofit groups (Salamon, Sokolowski, and List 2004). More generally, government accounts on average for 48 percent of nonprofit income among the developed countries for which systematic data are available.

Other studies confirm these findings. Thus, an examination of nonprofit agencies serving the handicapped in four Western European countries revealed that government support averaged 87 percent of agency income in Italy, 50 percent in the United Kingdom, over 90 percent in the Netherlands, and over 40 percent in Norway (Kramer et al. 1993). Even in Sweden, perhaps the classic welfare state, the nonprofit sector has close, cooperative ties with the state in culture, adult education, and sports. Further, extensive cooperation exists between nonprofit organizations and government in the traditional social service fields at the local level (Lundstrom and Wijkstrom 1997a).

In addition to extending financial support to the nonprofit sector, government has also frequently accorded nonprofit organizations an expanded role in the formation, not just the execution, of public policy. Perhaps the classic example of this practice is in Germany, where the government expanded support to nonprofit agencies and gave nonprofits input into state decisionmaking through a formal consultative arrangement. In a sense, Germany's free welfare associations enjoy a position in social welfare similar to the position business and labor groups enjoy in economic policy: they not only have a seat at the table, they often have a virtual veto over policy initiatives. In France, similar provisions giving nonprofits a seat on the prestigious Economic and Social Council accompanied expanded government funding of nonprofits (Ullman 1998). Indeed, far from inhibiting nonprofit advocacy, expanded government support to nonprofits in France seems to have stimulated it:

> Once nonprofits became involved in implementing the government-funded poverty plans, they were politicized. They began to question the government's definition of the problems of the new poor and les exclus and to develop their own policy demands. Through their lobbying, nonprofits extended their involvement in the welfare state from the social service programs at its periphery to the social insurance role at its core. (Ullman 1998, 170)

The recent adoption of a "compact" between the new Labor Government and the voluntary sector in the United Kingdom similarly signaled a move "from a contract culture to a partnership culture" in which nonprofits enjoy a broader policy role (Taylor 1997, 21).

Government support has also been a highly dynamic source of nonprofit income around the world. In the United Kingdom, for example, statutory fees and grants rose from one-third to two-thirds of agency income between 1975 and 1987. Government support to nonprofit organizations in Italy increased by 40 percent between the mid-1970s and the mid-1980s (Kramer et al. 1993). And in France, a veritable revolution occurred in the early 1980s as the socialist government of Francois Mitterand turned decisively to nonprofit organizations to revitalize an increasingly bureaucratized welfare state (Ullman 1998). More generally, recent efforts to reform government social welfare programs in Europe by shifting additional responsibilities to the nonprofit sector, far from reducing government support, have substantially increased it. As one analysis of recent European experience noted, "there is no competition between public and private or nonprofit sectors in the social care field, but an increasing interdependence of roles and responsibilities" (Ascoli and Ranci 2002, 230).

As a general rule, governments in the developing world have been suspicious of nonprofit organizations, at least those committed to fundamental social and political change. At times, authoritarian regimes in Egypt, Brazil, Argentina, Chile, and Ghana have thus severely restricted the right to associate, provoking antagonism from nongovernmental organizations that has often been difficult to diffuse. Reflecting this, among the developing and transitional countries for which data have been assembled, government support accounts on average for only 22 percent of nonprofit revenue, compared with 48 percent for the developed countries. Government support of nonprofit activity is particularly limited in Latin America and parts of Africa (e.g., Kenya and Uganda), which also happen to be places where the overall scale of nonprofit activity is especially constrained. In only a few developing countries, most notably India and South Africa, does government account for as much as 30 percent of nonprofit revenue, though important changes are under way elsewhere, as noted more fully below.

Patterns of Government–Nonprofit Relations

In short, the relationships between government and the nonprofit sector are considerably more complex than the paradigm of conflict, which has dominated much American thinking on these questions until relatively recently, suggests. In addition to the third-sector dominant and government-dominant models this paradigm depicts, a third route seems to be available for coping with public problems (Salamon 1995; Salamon and Anheier 1993, 1998a)—a partnership model featuring extensive cooperation between government and the nonprofit sector. Interestingly, these models correspond closely with the liberal, social democratic, and corporatist models, respectively, identified in welfare state literature (Esping-Andersen 1990). Further, a fourth broad pattern is evident on the international scene—an authoritarian model characterized by both limited government social welfare provision and limited nonprofit provision.

As table 12.2 shows, these models can be differentiated in terms of the relative scale of government social welfare spending and the relative size of the nonprofit sector. In authoritarian regimes, both government

Table 12.2. Nonprofit Regime Types

Nonprofit workforce as a percentage of labor force	Government social welfare spending as a percentage of GDP	
	Low	High
Low	Authoritarian	Government-dominant/ social democratic
High	Third-sector dominant/ liberal	Partnership/ corporate

social welfare spending and the nonprofit sector are tightly constrained. By contrast, in the corporatist and partnership regimes, both government social welfare spending and the nonprofit workforce are large. In between are the liberal and social democratic regimes, in which either the third sector workforce or government social welfare spending are above average, but usually not both.

But these different models differ not only in terms of the relative scale of the third sector and government social welfare provision, but in terms of the types of relationships between these sectors. As Young suggested in chapter 1, these relationships can take different forms, including supplementation, contestation, and cooperation. Supplementation refers to government and the nonprofit sector operating in separate spheres, going about their business with relatively little interaction, although often implicitly filling in for each other. Contestation refers to nonprofit organizations actively contesting the policies that governments advance or neglect to advance. Finally, cooperation characterizes situations where nonprofits and government actively cooperate in carrying out social functions.

While these three modes of government–nonprofit interaction are in some sense alternatives, all three can be present in varying degrees. In fact, as table 12.3 shows, different combinations of these three modes can characterize different nonprofit regime types. Thus, for example, in liberal regimes, supplementation is the dominant mode of govern-

Table 12.3. Modes of Government–Nonprofit Relations under Different Nonprofit Regime Types

Regime Type	Supplementation	Contestation	Cooperation
Third-sector-dominant/liberal	High	Low	Low
Government-dominant/ social democratic	High	High	Low
Partnership/corporatist	Medium	High	High
Authoritarian	Medium	Low	Low

ment–nonprofit interaction. In such regimes, government social welfare spending is relatively low and heavy reliance is placed on nonprofits and private philanthropy to generate social protections. While the government often permits nonprofits to engage in contestation in such regimes, nonprofits often choose not to, preferring to fit the prevailing pattern of government action and supplement state action. This produces what some have termed an "assistentialist" pattern of nonprofit activity. The mode of government–nonprofit interaction in the partnership or corporatist model is very different. Here nonprofits play a supplementary role in some fields but a more cooperative one in others. As suggested above, moreover, an active nonprofit role in policymaking in such regimes often accompanies the partnership role in service delivery.

Explaining the Patterns: The Social Origins of Government–Nonprofit Interaction

How can these variations in patterns of government–nonprofit relations in different parts of the world be explained? And what implications do they have for the health and vitality of the nonprofit sector and for the contributions it can make to social, economic, and political life?

One factor is the balance of substantive advantages and disadvantages that each model is believed to possess. Thus, the third-sector-dominant, or liberal, model is most likely to preserve nonprofit independence and encourage individual initiative in solving public problems. Its drawback is that it often fails to mobilize the support needed to overcome serious social, economic, and environmental problems or direct resources to where they are needed most. Further, it leaves control in the hands of those with resources and is therefore prone to paternalism. The government-dominant model, by contrast, overcomes the paternalism of the liberal model by establishing citizens' rights to assistance but sacrifices, in the process, some of the liberal model's flexibility. Finally, the partnership model combines many advantages of the other two approaches (Salamon 1987, 1995) but at the potential cost, if not handled carefully, of undermining the sector's independent political voice (Smith and Lipsky 1992).

But more is involved in the choice of social and political arrangements than their relative effectiveness in promoting programmatic goals. Questions of power and influence are also at work. The nonprofit sector is firmly embedded in the cultural, religious, political, and economic realities of different countries. Choices about the relative roles of the market, the state, the third sector, and of the relations among them are therefore heavily constrained by prior patterns of historical development, and particularly by the relative power of social groups, which have significant stakes in the outcomes of these decisions. To understand the current nature of the nonprofit sector and of government–nonprofit relations, it is therefore necessary to delve into the sector's social origins (Moore 1966), the pattern of relations among social classes, the character and role of the state, and organized religion (Salamon and Anheier 1996b, 1998b; Salamon and Sokolowski 2002a).

For example, recent economic theories of the nonprofit sector attribute what I have termed the "third-sector dominant" model to circumstances where substantial social heterogeneity exists and, consequently, majority support for government action to address social ills is unlikely (Weisbrod 1977). However, the social origins theory attributes this result to more complex circumstances—a strong commercial middle class that has neutralized landed elites and working class protest, and can consequently resist demands for expanded government social welfare benefits. Where these circumstances coexist with religious influences stressing individualism and institutionalization (e.g., Christianity, Catholicism, and Judaism as contrasted with Hinduism), government-sponsored social protections likely will be limited and the state will rely instead on private, nonprofit groups to provide the services people need. While legal opportunities to form nonprofits are typically open in such regimes, government often restricts the political activities of nonprofits and encourages them to supplement state action, not to alter or expand it. Examples of this liberal model include the United Kingdom and Australia through the end of World War II and the United States until the Great Society of the 1960s.

The social democratic, or "government-dominant," model, by contrast, arises where the working class and its allies are organized and can press for universal rights to social protections against weakened or divided landed elites and the commercial middle class, particularly when church and monarchical power are limited. While the upshot is a limited service-providing nonprofit sector, such circumstances do not necessarily imply a limited nonprofit sector overall. Rather, the nonprofit sector can be quite strong in social democratic regimes, but as a force for advocacy and personal expression rather than as a direct provider of social-welfare services (Salamon and Sokolowski 2002b). This pattern surfaced in Sweden, Norway, and Finland, and, to a lesser extent, in France and Italy prior to the 1980s. In Sweden, for example, working class political parties gained significant power early in the 20th century in the context of a state-dominated Church and a limited monarchy. In Italy, a slightly different route produced the same social outcome. Church-dominated social welfare institutions had been placed firmly under state control since the mid-19th century as part of the effort to achieve national unification. In the 1920s, the Fascist regime of Benito Mussolini established a state-centered system of social welfare protections, which the democratic governments of the postwar era then extended. The upshot was a strong tradition of state-provided welfare assistance with little room, until recently, for an independent, non-profit sector.

A far different pattern of government–nonprofit interaction is evident in what I have termed "welfare partnership" regimes. The distinguishing feature of such regimes is the extensive cooperation they exhibit between nonprofit organizations and government. Prevailing economic theories have not explained this model,[4] but the social origins theory sees its roots in social forces that contain working class pressures for expanding state-provided social welfare protections. In Germany, for example, a monarchical government, backed by powerful landed elements and a relatively weak urban middle class, responded to the threat of worker radicalism in the 19th century by forging an agreement with the major churches to create a state-dominated social welfare system that nevertheless maintained a sizeable church, and hence nonprofit, presence. This agreement was ultimately embodied in the concept of "subsidiarity" as the guiding principle of social policy (Anheier and Seibel 2001). The result has been a close working relationship between the state and voluntary organizations—both secular and religious—and the resulting coexistence of extensive government social welfare spending and a large nonprofit sector. In the process, this model preempts more radical demands for state-delivered social welfare and ensures a greater degree of social control. However, this pattern is consistent with nonprofit involvement not just in delivering welfare services, but also in developing them, albeit through an intricate system of consultations that pacifies the nonprofit sector even while granting it a voice. In the Netherlands, conflict between secular and religious elements over control of schools early in the 20th century resulted in a similar outcome. To resolve this conflict, an agreement was reached that guaranteed Dutch citizens free universal education, but at a school of each citizen's choosing. The resulting pattern of publicly financed and privately provided services was replicated in other fields, producing a system known as "pillarization," the division of society into separate religious and ideological groups, or pillars, each served by its network of nonprofit organizations but heavily subsidized by the state (Burger et al. 1997; Kramer 1981).

Finally, in authoritarian, or statist, regimes, powerful political or economic elites thwart the emergence of significant nonprofit institutions or keep such institutions pacified through legal and extra-legal controls. While nonprofits can often still play a supplementation role in such settings, they cannot counter state power or insist on a cooperative role in setting or executing state policy. The result is limited government social welfare protections and limited nonprofit development.

This outcome is likely in countries where industrialization is limited and significant portions of the population remain on the land, where the urban middle and working classes consequently remain weak, and where external colonial influences are strong.

This authoritarian pattern has been evident in a wide assortment of countries, particularly in the developing world. Until recently, in much of Latin America, for example, dominant social classes have allied with colonial powers to limit the growth of state-provided social welfare and sizable nonprofit sectors. Combined with a Catholic religious apparatus firmly allied with government officials and limited or nonexistent peasant or working class mobilization, the result has been a classic authoritarian outcome until relatively recently. In Kenya, Tanzania, Uganda, and other African nations, strong communal traditions organized along tribal lines, modern charitable institutions introduced by foreign missionaries, and independence movements spearheaded by militant political groups (such as the Kenya Land Reform Movement and the Mau Mau peasant movement) have partially muted authoritarian impulses (Kanyinga et al. 2004). Few of these groups developed the strength to resist the powerful authoritarian tendencies that emerged in the wake of independence from colonial control, however, limiting the development of an independent nonprofit sector.

To be sure, these nonprofit regime types are heuristic devices intended to demarcate broad tendencies (Salamon and Sokolowski 2002a). Further, the social origins theory treats these development paths not as predetermined outcomes but as likely contingencies. Developments in one epoch are viewed as "stacking the cards" in favor of one line of evolution, but discontinuities can occur that change the course of events. Indeed, a number of crucial trends are now shaping and reshaping these basic patterns. Six such trends in particular deserve attention.

Recent Trends

Expanded Government Action. The past fifty years have witnessed a dramatic growth of government involvement in social and economic life in almost all countries, significantly altering historical patterns of government–nonprofit relations. This has had particular implications for the evolution of the liberal regimes, which have changed dramatically as a consequence. Thus, in the United Kingdom, returning World War II veterans mobilized sufficient political power to overwhelm conservative resistance to government social protections and shifted the country away from the liberal and toward the social democratic pattern. In the United States, worker pressures remained fragmented and conservative resistance was more effective. Not until the Great

Society era of the 1960s did sufficient political support move the federal government beyond basic social security protections to establish broader health and welfare protections. In addition, the form that resulted differed significantly from that in the United Kingdom, leaving far more responsibility in the hands of private nonprofits. The result is a pattern much closer to the partnership model than the social democratic one.

The "Global Associational Revolution." Side by side with expanding government activity, particularly during the past 20 years, however, has come the dramatic global associational revolution mentioned earlier, a massive upsurge of organized, private, nonprofit activity throughout the world (Salamon 1994). This development is the consequence of a unique coalescence of historical forces—rapidly expanding communications technologies that have made forming grassroots nonprofits easier; growing doubts about the capabilities of government to solve the interrelated problems of poverty, development, and environmental degradation and the search for alternative mechanisms; the emergence of cadres of educated professionals increasingly frustrated by a lack of economic and political opportunities and therefore willing to create such alternative mechanisms; and the appearance of outside sources of support from international organizations, foundations, and others to help underwrite and nurture the resulting nongovernmental organizations. The result has been the blossoming of private, nonprofit organizations dedicated to improving the environment, overcoming poverty, and seeking greater political freedom through private rather than public agencies (Fisher 1993; Ritchey-Vance 1991; Salamon 1994).

This development has had particular implications for the evolution of authoritarian regimes. Newly formed civil society organizations have played crucial roles in the break-up of the Soviet empire in Central and Eastern Europe, in the fall of the apartheid regime in South Africa, and in the democracy movements that toppled dictatorships in the Philippines, Brazil, Argentina, and Chile, to name a few. While these organizations have not always been able to follow up on breakthroughs with sustained political involvement, important progress has been evident. Thus, for example, Brazilian associations, which once stood outside the political process during the dictatorship period of the 1960s and 1970s, have increasingly taken an active role, significantly stretching the boundaries of political acceptability (Landim 1998, 331). Citizen movements in South Africa and the Philippines have also motivated greater political engagement by nonprofits. Indeed, the Asia-Pacific region has been credited with having "some of the most potent citizens' movements of this century," particularly in Thailand, India, Nepal, and the Philippines (Morales and Serrano 1997).

In response to these developments, authoritarian regimes have evolved into various "transitional" arrangements. Nonprofits in these transitional settings have not progressed into full-blown partnerships with government but have clearly established some legitimacy and, in many cases, have begun to challenge authoritarian control.

Expanded Government–Nonprofit Cooperation. While governments may look to nonprofits and philanthropy as a way to relieve the pressures on public budgets, one of the most salient consequences of the recent global associational revolution has been to expand government–nonprofit cooperation. The partnership model, not the third-sector dominant model, in other words, seems to be the one gaining ground internationally. Fiscal considerations have played a part; governments have increasingly looked to voluntary institutions and private philanthropy for help in responding to public demands for services. Equally important, however, has been what Ascoli and Ranci (2002, 225) have termed "an organizational crisis" caused by disappointments with the bureaucratic rigidities and administrative constraints of publicly delivered services. Inspired by neoliberal economic concepts emphasizing the importance of consumer choice and market-like competition among service providers, governments have increasingly turned to indirect tools of action, such as grants, contracts, and vouchers that turn the delivery of publicly financed services over to nongovernmental actors, including private nonprofits (Ascoli and Ranci 2002; Evers and Svetlick 1992; Salamon 1981, 2002; Smith and Lipsky 1992).

This development has had striking implications for the evolution of the social democratic regimes described above. The past two decades have witnessed a rediscovery of nonprofit institutions and a significant elaboration of their partnerships with the state (Kuhnle and Selle 1992; Lundstrom and Wijkstrom 1997b). Nowhere, perhaps, has this development been more striking than in France, which outlawed nonprofit institutions from the French Revolution until the 20th century and which has long frowned on them as the expressions of the "partial will" of particular groups as opposed to the "general will" of all the people. This situation changed dramatically in the early 1980s, however, when the government of Socialist President Francois Mitterand adopted a bold program of government decentralization to cope with a perceived crisis of state capacity that threatened popular support for the French welfare state. Lacking the capacity to deliver human services, local governments throughout France were encouraged to turn to private voluntary associations for help in the hope that these associations could revitalize stagnant welfare bureaucracies. The result was a rapid growth of local nonprofits and the rapid transition of France from a social democratic to a welfare partnership model of government–nonprofit relations (Archambault 1996; Ullman 1998). As Ullman (1998, 164) notes,

The Socialist government offered nonprofits unprecedented roles in the administration of welfare state programs, delegating to them significant new responsibility for the implementation of public programs and providing them with substantial public funding. Indeed, every major poverty policy initiative of the 1980s in France relied on nonprofits for its implementation, including a campaign against hunger and homelessness, a law implementing a national right to housing, and, more important, major legislation creating a guaranteed minimum income.

Similar developments were evident in Italy and other Western European welfare states, including Scandinavia, where commitment to the principles of universal, state-guaranteed welfare services were perhaps most deeply entrenched (Barbetta 1997; Eikås and Selle 2002; Kramer et al. 1993).

This trend has found pronounced echoes in the developing world as well. Such partnerships have a long history in numerous places, such as India and Pakistan (Sen 1998; Salamon 1995), and have begun to develop elsewhere. This is particularly true in countries like South Africa, the Philippines, and Chile, where regimes sympathetic to the nonprofit sector came to power on the backs of citizen movements in which civil society organizations were prominent actors (Cariño et al. 2004; Swilling et al. 2004). This may explain the especially prominent role of government support in the funding base of South African nonprofit organizations (Salamon, Sokolowski, and List 2004). Also at work has been the "new policy agenda" among northern development agencies, which has encouraged governments to engage civil society and channeled an increasing share of development assistance to both northern and southern nongovernmental organizations to stimulate private initiative (Hulme and Edwards 1997). Chile's FOSIS program and Argentina's CENOC agency stand as examples of government efforts to enlist grassroots nonprofits in the development process.

Rise of the "Contract Culture." Not only have government–nonprofit partnerships expanded in scale, they have increasingly changed form. In the classic "welfare partnership" regime, government tended to provide general support grants to nonprofits as if they were part of the state apparatus. In Germany, for example, the government relied on four tools to subsidize nonprofit activities (Anheier 1992): direct subsidies and block allocations to support basic organizational operations; grants for special projects; reimbursements for services provided to specially eligible recipients; and fee-for-service contracts for particular services. However, in general, direct subsidies and reimbursements dominated the fiscal flows. When contracts were used, they tended to last for decades and to take on the character of permanent subsidies. This pattern has also characterized government–nonprofit relationships in other welfare partnership and social democratic settings, such as the Netherlands, Norway, and the United Kingdom (Burger et al. 1997; Eikås and Selle 2002; Taylor 2002).

Since the 1980s, however, a decided shift has occurred in the nature of government–nonprofit ties. One impetus for this shift has been the growing influence of new public management, which has sought to inject business notions of accountability, performance measurement, efficiency, competition, and choice into the relations between government and the nonprofit sector. As Taylor (2002, 78) notes in the United Kingdom, the big change in recent years is "not the introduction of government funding to the third sector, but a potential change in the nature of that funding . . . from a gift or investment based on services specified largely by the third sector organization, to a purchase, with the service and the terms and conditions under which it is provided specified by the government purchaser." This was the thrust of the Thatcher government's National Health Service and Community Care Act of 1993, which turned much of the responsibility for health care and social services over to local governments and empowered these authorities to enter into competitive contracts with nonprofit and for-profit groups. The hope was that contracting out the provision of human services and requiring nonprofits to compete for the resulting contracts would increase the efficiency of the system and decrease the cost. Further, by forcing decisions about the appropriate level of human services down to levels of government closest to the taxpayers, conservative politicians hoped to reduce the overall level of public spending on social welfare (Wistow et al. 1996). Government contracting with nonprofit providers was thus part of a broader strategy to reduce government social welfare activity.

Similar changes are under way, moreover, in other welfare partnership regimes, with varying paces and impacts from country to country (Ascoli and Ranci 2002). Reflecting this change, formal contracts increasingly replaced informal grant and reimbursement arrangements as the basic form of public sector support to nonprofits, even in social democratic regimes (Eikås and Selle 2002). In the process, the provision of basic welfare services has been opened not only to nonprofit providers but to for-profit ones as well, stimulating an even more competitive welfare service market.

Institutionalization of Third Sector Policy Involvement. While the movement toward a contract culture has reduced the formal discretion left to nonprofit service organizations even as public sector support expands, nonprofits have responded by seeking and achieving more structured avenues for influencing government policy. This is not an entirely new development. Many European and Latin American countries have a long tradition of "corporatist" arrangements, structured mechanisms for sharing power among major social institutions, and in some countries, nonprofit organizations operate as integral parts of corporatist structures. Indeed, this feature has been characteristic of the welfare partnership pattern.

Thus, in Germany, long-standing partnerships between state authorities and free welfare associations were not simply left to administrative discretion. Rather, they were firmly implanted in public law. Between 1950 and 1975, three separate laws were passed implementing the principle of government support to nonprofit institutions as a cornerstone of German social policy (Anheier 1992; Salamon and Anheier 1993). The Social Assistance Act of 1961, Germany's basic social welfare law, thus obliges the "public bodies responsible for social assistance" to "collaborate with the public law churches and religious communities and with the free welfare associations" and to do so in a way that acknowledges "their independence in the targeting and execution of their functions." Furthermore, in Section 3, the act requires the public bodies to "support the Free Welfare Associations appropriately in the field of social assistance." Finally, the act almost guarantees a local monopoly to the nonprofit providers by forbidding public agencies from establishing offices at the local level "if suitable establishments of the free welfare associations . . . are available, or can be extended or provided." These principles have since been reinforced in the context of specific fields, such as youth services or employment and training, and in the basic Social Code, enacted in 1976 to codify and systematize various bodies of social legislation, and which reasserts in Article 3 the obligation for the public and nonprofit sectors to "effectively complement one another for the benefit of those receiving assistance" (Deutscher Verein 1986).

Interestingly, other countries have begun recently moving in a similar direction, establishing legal requirements or informal agreements that stipulated governments must consult with nonprofits in designing public programs, and establishing special liaison offices between the voluntary sector and the state. One of the most well-known of these is the "compact" that Tony Blair's New Labor government entered with the United Kingdom's voluntary sector (Her Majesty's Government 1998). This document establishes the principle of "shared values and mutual respect" between government and the voluntary sector and commits the government to "meaningful consultation" with the voluntary sector on policy and program design issues. Canada has moved in a similar direction with its voluntary sector initiative, and even France and Japan, long known for their state-centered approaches to policy development, have recently established formal liaison offices for civil society or "social economy" institutions. In addition, such entities have appeared in the developing world.[5]

Emergence of Global Nonprofit Networks. Finally, in addition to the internal shifts in government–nonprofit relations, a significant change has also occurred in the relations between nonprofits and states at the international level. Global nonprofit networks have emerged, capable of mobilizing citizen attention and action on a global scale. Such networks now operate in a wide range of fields—human rights, biodiversity hot spots, child labor, environmental protection, gender equality, children's services, land mine protection, fair trade, and many more (Clark 2003; Florini 2000; Keck and Sikkink 1998). Transparency International, for example, is a network of over 100 national organizations with a governing council that attracts top corporate and government leaders from around the world. Greenpeace and Amnesty International span dozens of countries and claim hundreds of thousands of members. By mobilizing press and political contacts on a global scale, such networks pressure unresponsive national governments and multinational companies from international organizations, foreign governments, and the global marketplace. Countries and companies alike have therefore found shielding their behavior from these non-state actors on the international stage increasingly difficult, adding another crucial dimension to the relationships between government and nonprofits.

IMPLICATIONS OF RECENT TRENDS IN GOVERNMENT-NONPROFIT RELATIONS

What are we to make of these trends in government–nonprofit relations? What has been their impact on nonprofits and on the governmental institutions with which nonprofits interact? Although the evidence is still incomplete, some tentative observations seem possible.

Growing Government–Nonprofit Cooperation

First, growing evidence at the international level indicates a general expansion of government–nonprofit cooperation. Nonprofits have long existed in most countries around the world, often on a scale greater than in the United States. Moreover, many countries boast rich histories of government–nonprofit cooperation, even if these histories have not been widely recognized or researched. Still, the past thirty years have witnessed a substantial growth in nonprofit organizations and a further intertwining of government and nonprofit roles. The collaborative model seems to be on its way to becoming the international norm though deep suspicions remain on both sides in many parts of the world.

Generally Benign Development

Despite important tensions and dangers, growth of government–nonprofit cooperation appears to be a positive development, making it possible to combine what governments do best—namely set broad societal directions and mobilize resources for their implementation—while calling on nonprofit organizations for what they do best—respond flexibly to human needs and adjust general policies to the circumstances of particular groups.

These relationships bring enormous risks. Excessive dependence on state support can rob the nonprofit sector of cherished qualities—its independence and ability to advocate on behalf of the powerless. Over time, the collaborative model can distort the mission of nonprofits and transform them into agents of the state. Particularly vulnerable is their advocacy function, their role in contesting state policy and providing a voice to unrepresented perspectives or groups. In addition, nonprofits can lose their flexibility as the demands of state contracting induce them to become administratively more cumbersome and bureaucratic. The "nonprofitization" of service delivery can also harm the state, undermining efforts to establish state capacity.

But sole reliance on private revenue is no better guarantee that nonprofits will be able to defend disadvantaged groups since those in control of these revenues may be every bit as hostile as government officials to nonprofit advocacy. Further, a number of factors potentially protect nonprofit organizations from the dangers of excessive government control. One factor is the presence of alternative sources of nonprofit support—for example, from private philanthropy, earned income, or external support. When such supports are available, the prospects that nonprofits can enter cooperative arrangements with government without surrendering their independence or changing their mission increases considerably. What is more, multiple sources of government support can also have the same effect. Governments are not monoliths, after all, and nonprofit agencies can often achieve a degree of autonomy by playing one level of government against another, or balancing support from one ministry or agency against others (Grønbjerg 1991).

Cultural traditions concerning the state are also important. Where habits of deference to state authority are strong, nonprofits are at greater risk in dealing with government. Where such habits are less evident and nonprofits enjoy some moral status, the same government support can yield less government control. This factor may help explain the significant difference between the treatment of nonprofits in Germany or the Netherlands and Japan. Germany and the Netherlands have strong traditions of decentralization, reinforced by long histories of religious resistance to central control. The result has been a fairly solid base for protecting the integrity of private initiative organizations and free welfare associations that deliver many state-financed services. Public authorities in Germany are required by law to consult the free welfare associations in matters of social policy, and an elaborate consultative apparatus has been established to implement this requirement.

A different relationship between government and the nonprofit sector has evolved in Japan (Yamamoto 1998). Here, as well, a far larger nonprofit sector exists than traditional accounts tend to acknowledge, and these organizations receive extensive governmental support.[6] In addition, formal laws stipulate the roles nonprofits can play in different fields. Unlike in Germany and the Netherlands, however, where the laws operate to constrain the state and empower the nonprofit providers, in Japan, the opposite comes closer to the truth. Nonprofits require the explicit approval of the government ministry in their respective fields in order to be incorporated, and those that accept government support must also accept extremely close governmental supervision and control. Indeed, a provision of the Japanese Constitution of 1949 (originally inserted by the allied victors in World War II to protect nonprofits by forbidding government from establishing and financing them) has come to be interpreted as permitting such financing only when the recipient organizations function essentially as quasi-public institutions (Amenomori 1997).

Also limiting the impact government funding has on the nonprofit sector are the information asymmetries emphasized in "principal–agent theory." According to this theory, the principal in a contractual relationship faces a difficult dilemma in ensuring that its agent adheres to the terms of the contract since the agent—in this case the nonprofit agency—always knows more about how the contract is being implemented than the principal (Kettl 1993; Moe 1984; Pratt and Zeckhauser 1985). To exercise effective control, the principal must therefore gather and process information, which can be costly and time consuming. The more complex and ambiguous the task, the more information the principal needs, and the more costly it is to collect. Governments have been especially negligent in putting in place the evaluation and information-gathering mechanisms needed to monitor and control agents (DeHoog 1985). The new public management precepts that have recently gained popularity in government circles have sought to avoid this problem by specifying target outcome measures explicitly, formalizing contract relationships, and promoting competition, but they have hardly eliminated the problem (Ascoli and Ranci 2002). Therefore, in the complex principal–agent relationships that governments often enter into with nonprofit organizations, "he who pays the piper" often does not "call the tune."

Whether for these reasons or others, the record to date suggests many fears surrounding increased nonprofit cooperation with government have been overstated. For example, Ralph Kramer and colleagues, in their study of contracting relationships in four Western European countries (the United Kingdom, Italy, Norway, and the Netherlands), found little support for the thesis that government contracting distorts the mission of nonprofit agencies or robs the agencies of their autonomy (Kramer et al. 1993). "Financial dependence," Kramer notes, "does not mean organizational dependence" (Kramer et al. 1993, 65).[7]

Recent studies in the United Kingdom reach a similar conclusion: fears about nonprofit loss of independence with the growth of a contract culture have proved "unduly pessimistic" (Taylor 1997, 11). While problems certainly exist in some quarters, the growth of local authority contracting with nonprofit providers has been far more positive than many nonprofit agencies feared, clarifying objectives, strengthening management systems, evening the playing field, and improving the quality of information available to users. The major difficulty appears to be calibrating reimbursement rates so that they cover agencies' core administrative costs in addition to direct service costs (Taylor 1997, 2002).

While little evidence indicates that expanded government–nonprofit cooperation has distorted the missions of nonprofits, there is evidence that it has encouraged the formalization and bureaucratization of the sector. Government grants and contracts tend to be large in scale, causing recipient organizations to expand and, in some cases, favoring already large organizations (Taylor 1997). Further, government grants and contracts typically contain formal stipulations and monitoring requirements that necessitate professionalization of agency management structures. These developments are not, of course, wholly or even mostly negative, but they do contribute to nonprofit providers losing some flexibility. Moreover, the more formal the collaborative arrangement with government, the more likely these bureaucratization effects are. Thus, in Germany, where collaboration is both highly developed and extremely formal, the free welfare associations have become highly bureaucratized institutions with complex management structures and staffing systems that closely mirror those of the state agencies with which they interact (Anheier and Seibel 2001). A similar pattern is evident in the officially sanctioned and state-supported health, education, and social service nonprofits in Japan (Yamamoto 1998). In Scandinavia, where voluntary control and membership engagement have remained salient features of the nonprofit sector until recently, these changes have been forcefully felt (Eikas and Selle 2002).

Expanding Policy Role

Interestingly, this sanguine finding carries over to the advocacy function of nonprofit agencies. To be sure, in many parts of the world, governments have made determined efforts to keep nonprofits, and the citizens they represent, excluded from effective participation in government policymaking. Indeed, a prime motivation for the surge in nonprofit formation in many parts of the world has been citizens' determination to secure more effective participation (Howell and Pearce 2001). Not surprisingly, therefore, nonprofits have been wary about having too close an embrace with government, fearing it may compromise their independence and undermine their ability to represent those in greatest need. Even some newly democratic governments have resisted nonprofit policy involvement on the grounds that nonprofits have less claim to legitimacy as representatives of "the people" than do newly elected governments.

Persuasive as these arguments are, it is hard to escape the conclusion that expanded nonprofit presence and growing nonprofit–government cooperation has increased the policy presence of nonprofits. This has occurred even when nonprofits have become full partners with government and significant recipients of government financial support. Thus, Kramer and colleagues note, "Reliance on public funding . . . did not seem to inhibit either [voluntary nonprofit] advocacy and political lobbying efforts, or their self perception as being autonomous from the state" (Kramer et al. 1993, 167). On the contrary, nonprofit cooperation with government has frequently stimulated nonprofit advocacy. In France, for example, the decentralization policies instituted in the early 1980s led to increased government reliance on nonprofit institutions. One important byproduct, as noted above, was that French nonprofits were more thoroughly engaged in the policy process. Similarly, research in the United Kingdom has found "little evidence that advocacy is squeezed out by contracts" (Taylor 1997, 14). In fact, many new contracting provisions in the United Kingdom, particularly under the New Labor government, have established joint planning arrangements between local governments and voluntary organizations, giving nonprofits the opportunity to shape the design of public programs and not just participate in their execution (Taylor 2002). Indeed, concerns about the potential negative effects of government contracting on nonprofit advocacy has given way in some countries, particularly in conservative circles, to concerns about the formation of unholy alliances between nonprofits and government bureaucrats in support of expanded public sector spending.

The persistence and growth of the advocacy function of nonprofit organizations internationally also likely reflects the position that advocacy has played in the nonprofit sector's historical development around the world. Advocacy and political involvement have long been more central and legitimate features of nonprofit activity in many other developed democracies than they have been in the United States. In

Sweden, for example, more than 40 percent of nonprofits identify them-selves as mass movement organizations (Lundstrom and Wijkstrom 1997a). These popular mass movements developed in the late 19th and early 20th centuries in Sweden in the form of powerful labor, temperance, and "free church" movements, and they have been reflected more recently in environmental, women's rights, consumer cooperative, sports, and adult education movements, not to mention the powerful antiwar movement that made Sweden well-known in America during the Vietnam War. In other words, far from abjuring a policy role, nonprofits in Sweden have specialized in it, creating a distinctive definition of themselves as "schools for democracy" rather than simple service providers. Similar conceptualizations are evident elsewhere in Scandinavia.

Reflecting this, nonprofit advocacy is often better protected legally in other developed countries than in the United States, where government allows more favorable charitable contribution deductions—raising the possibility that government will indirectly subsidize advocacy activity by nonprofits. Whatever the rationale, where American law proscribes charitable nonprofits from engaging in political campaign activity and limits their lobbying, or attempts to influence legislation (Hopkins 1992), few such restrictions are placed on the political and policy activi-ties of nonprofits in most other advanced industrial democracies (Sala-mon 1998). Sweden, for example, has no legal restrictions on the politi-cal or policy activities of nonprofits. Such activity is taken as a natural function of nonprofit institutions, more natural than the delivery of services, which is viewed as the state's responsibility (Lundstrom and Wijkstrom 1997a). In France, nonprofits are permitted to lobby, actively participate in political campaigns, and even raise money for political candidates, with the only limitation being that such political activities be identified in the organization's by-laws as part of its general aims (Salamon 1998). The provisions of German law are more restrictive, but only partially so. Thus, German nonprofits cannot engage directly in political campaign activities. However, they may, without limitation, lobby for legislation furthering their missions (Salamon 1998). Only in the United Kingdom, in fact, do restrictions on nonprofit political activ-ity approach American restrictions in severity. However, British restric-tions appear more loosely drawn. Thus, charitable status is not available in the United Kingdom to organizations whose principal purpose is to promote a political party or seek changes in government policy. However, organizations can still secure charitable status—that is, access to deductible contributions—if they use political means for pursuing another principal purpose.

This same perspective on the policy advocacy role of the nonprofit sector has also gradually emerged in developing countries. By providing vehicles for citizen action, nonprofits are increasingly seen as guarantors of a new kind of governance that not only makes the state more responsive and accountable, but creates greater space for citizen "self-organization" (Clark 1992; Morales and Serrano 1997, 99). Nonprofit policy advocacy is thus a useful complement to the free market and a way to promote liberalization (Hulme and Edwards 1997).

Implications for the State

The trends in government–nonprofit relations outlined above have significant consequences for the state beyond the impact they may or may not have on nonprofits. As private, nonprofit groups increasingly deliver state-financed services, citizens can easily forget the real source of the benefits they receive. In the process, public support for government can atrophy (Salamon 2002). In addition, where suitable private providers are not available, government may have to purchase what the private agencies can provide rather than the mix of services it considers most needed (Barlett 1993; Salamon 1995; Starr 1987; Wistow et al. 1996). This problem seems to be developing in several European countries where efforts to foster competition among service providers is a priority but where the array of providers is insufficient (Ascoli and Ranci 2002). Finally, government can find itself without the capability to monitor, let alone deliver, the services it finances, creating far larger possibilities for inefficiencies than direct action often entails.

Fortunately, however, many countries have substantial experience in dealing with these challenges. Thus, for example, joint planning and execution mechanisms have long been in place in the Netherlands and other welfare partnership regimes to coordinate government and nonprofit activity (Ringeling 2002). Similar efforts to rationalize government–nonprofit relationships are evident in the United Kingdom, Italy, and Canada (Ascoli and Ranci 2002; Government of Canada 1999; Taylor 2002). These experiences hold potentially important lessons for how to improve on the far more chaotic and ad hoc relationships that have evolved in the United States.

The Need to Preserve Nonprofit Distinctiveness

Although the patterns of government–nonprofit cooperation evolving internationally may extend the reach of the nonprofit sector and merge the advantages of both government and nonprofits in addressing complex problems, the ultimate assessment of these arrangements may depend on their ability to preserve the very qualities that make the nonprofit sector an attractive partner to the state. Historically, the substantial cooperative ties between the state and the nonprofit sector in

Western Europe have respected the distinctive character of nonprofits. Assistance tended to be accommodating, reaching nonprofits in the form of open-ended block grants for basic organizational support. By contrast, recent changes inspired by new public management endanger these distinctive features by injecting business-like discipline through tighter targeting, monitoring, and performance measurement. Norwegian scholars already are noting a subtle transformation in the character of Norwegian voluntary organizations, which are reducing the role of membership and of internal democratic controls and are transforming into "mere" service providers (Eikås and Selle 2002).

This suggests a need to pay particular attention to the mission critical activities and functions of nonprofits in the design and execution of partnership programs with government. This need is particularly critical in settings such as those in the developing world, where the legitimacy and institutional viability of nonprofits is less fully established and where habits of deference to state authority are more firmly entrenched. In particular, infrastructure organizations need to be strengthened. Such organizations have generally been relatively underdeveloped internationally, though they have evolved significantly in the past decade.

CONCLUSIONS AND IMPLICATIONS

Contrary to many American preconceptions, the nonprofit sector constitutes a more substantial presence in many countries outside the United States than it does within the United States. Further, this sector operates not as an alternative to the state, but as a partner with it, and often a significant partner. Government plays a major role in financing nonprofit activity in almost every country with a sizable nonprofit sector, and the resulting state support outdistances the support these organizations receive from private charity. In a sense, the nonprofit sector has enlisted the state as its chief fundraiser in many parts of the world, and this collaborative model is fast becoming the international norm.

Most evidence indicates that nonprofits have found ways to enter cooperative relationships with the state at far less risk to their missions or purposes than has long been feared. This is not to say that strains do not exist. In some countries, such as Japan, long traditions of government dominance have limited the autonomy and advocacy activity of nonprofit organizations. But in many places, nonprofits have retained considerable autonomy vis-à-vis public authorities even while relying heavily on public resources. Indeed, in Germany and the Netherlands, public authorities are under a political and legal obligation to support nonprofits, giving these organizations a distinct bargaining advantage. In addition, as nonprofits are drawn more heavily into cooperating with government, their policy activism increases rather than declines, contrary to widespread expectations.

Still, immense uncertainties attend the expansion of government contracting with nonprofit providers, and enormous risks confront both parties. Nonprofits can subtly surrender the flexibility and grass-roots involvement that make them a useful alternative to large-scale state bureaucracies, while governments can lose the in-house capability to monitor nonprofit performance and the attachment to citizens needed to keep democratic government vibrant. However, these risks, while real, are far from certain, and the balance of benefits and costs appears to favor the continuation and extension of these collaborative ties.

At the same time, significant changes are under way in the design and operation of government–nonprofit collaboration around the world. The basic thrust of these changes is to inject more business discipline into government–nonprofit relationships and open them to competition from private businesses. Hopefully, these changes will improve the responsiveness and efficiency of service delivery without surrendering the special contributions that nonprofits can offer, but it is by no means certain that the results will be this benign.

The implications of these findings for the evolution of public policy toward the nonprofit sector in the United States are serious. Although far more widespread collaboration characterizes government–nonprofit relationships in the United States than is frequently recognized, the resulting partnerships are less explicit and structured than they are elsewhere, at least in the developed world (Salamon 1995). No overarching principle governs the relationships between nonprofit organizations and government in the United States. Many relationships are worked out at the local level, on a program-by-program basis, with little overall structure or coherence. Further, the role different partners play varies from program to program. Indeed, this structure is so loose, most Americans are unaware of its existence even though government human service spending is often managed in this way. Under these circumstances, the risks of popular misunderstanding are immense, and the strains on nonprofit providers are great.

U.S. policymakers could therefore learn from overseas experience about how to make the new model of government–nonprofit cooperation work more effectively. At a minimum, this approach would require explicit acknowledgment of the partnership that exists and the disavowal of a paradigm that stresses conflict between government and nonprofits. Beyond this, more explicit channels of communication need to be opened between government agencies at all levels and nonprofit providers at the design stage of public policy, as the Labor Government in the United Kingdom has promoted with its compact with the nonprofit sector. Finally, concrete steps need to be taken to improve current contracting and reimbursement arrangements—especially through enhancing the training of personnel on both sides, simplifying procedures, and facilitating coordinated approaches to complex social problems.

By enshrining the ideal of an "independent" nonprofit sector in its national iconography, Americans are in danger of turning their back on one of the most important developments strengthening the nonprofit sector internationally: the growing partnership between the nonprofit sector and the state. A better understanding of international experience, therefore, may be needed to help Americans preserve the institutions they have long considered their unique contribution to the world.

NOTES

1. This "paradigm of conflict" also finds support in some recent economic theories of the nonprofit sector that explain the existence of a nonprofit sector in terms of inherent limitations of the market and the state. Thus, nonprofits exist even in a democracy, according to this line of theory, because democratic governments can only respond to those demands for collective goods that enjoy majority support. Where great diversity exists in a society, making it difficult to reach agreement on the range of collective goods to supply publicly, nonprofits are more likely to exist in order to fill the gaps. This suggests, however, that the size of the nonprofit sector in a country is likely to be inversely related to the size of the government sector: where government is large, the nonprofit sector will likely be small, and where government is small, the nonprofit sector will likely be large (Weisbrod 1977).

2. For further detail on this history, see Nielsen (1979, 25–48) and Warner (1894). See also chapter 3.

3. Ming Wang, personal interview, Beijing, July 6, 2005.

4. Two recent adaptations of the basic "market failure/government failure" economic theory of the nonprofit have sought to take account of this model. The first is the "voluntary failure" concept formulated by Salamon (1987); the second is the public sector preferences concept formulated by James (1987). According to the voluntary failure concept, close cooperation between government and the nonprofit sector is a natural byproduct of two characteristics of the nonprofit sector: (a) its ability to respond more quickly than government to newly recognized social needs because it faces fewer transaction costs in mobilizing a response; and (b) its inability to generate sufficient resources to address serious social ills on its own. Hence, cooperation between government and the nonprofit sector emerges as a way to take advantage of the respective strengths of the two sectors while minimizing their respective weaknesses. The public sector preferences concept, by contrast, emphasizes the similarity in objectives between public and nonprofit organizations, which makes it possible for government agencies to contract with these organizations with fewer oversight costs.

5. The relevant office in France is the Délégation a l'économie sociale. In Japan, it is the Civil Activities Division of the Cabinet Office. CENOC plays a similar role in Argentina, while responsibilities for promoting cooperation between government and the third sector is vested in the Planning Department in both Chile and India.

6. Nonprofit institutions deliver much of the higher education, social services, residential care, and medical services in Japan. They do so, moreover, with significant government support. In the fields of health and social services, for example, Japanese nonprofits receive 95 percent and 65 percent of their income, respectively, from government sources (Salamon and Anheier 1996a).

7. The one exception appears to be the Netherlands, where government reliance on nonprofits is perhaps the most extensive, but the complaints that nonprofits have recently voiced about undue governmental interference must be viewed against a context of past governmental willingness to finance nonprofit providers without asking much in return (Kramer et al. 1993).

REFERENCES

Amenomori, Takayoshi. 1997. "Japan." In *Defining the Nonprofit Sector,* edited by Lester M. Salamon and Helmut K. Anheier (188–214). Manchester, U.K.: Manchester University Press.

Anheier, Helmut K. 1991. "Employment and Earnings in the German Nonprofit Sector: Structure and Trends." *Annals of Public and Cooperative Economics* 62(4): 673–94.

———. 1992. "An Elaborate Network: Profiling the Third Sector in Germany." In *Government and the Third Sector: Emerging Relationships in Welfare States,* edited by Benjamin Gidron, Ralph M. Kramer, and Lester M. Salamon. San Francisco: Jossey-Bass Publishers.

Anheier, Helmut K., and W. Seibel. 2001. *The Nonprofit Sector in Germany.* Johns Hopkins Nonprofit Sector Series, edited by Lester M. Salamon and Helmut Anheier. Manchester, U.K.: Manchester University Press.

Archambault, Edith. 1996. *The Nonprofit Sector in France.* The Johns Hopkins Nonprofit Sector Series, edited by Lester M. Salamon and Helmut K. Anheier. Manchester, U.K.: Manchester University Press.

Ascoli, Ugo, and Costanzo Ranci. 2002. "Changes in the Welfare Mix: The European Path." In *Dilemmas of the Welfare Mix: The New Structure of Welfare in the Era of Privatization,* edited by Ugo Ascoli and Costanzo Ranci (225–43). New York: Kluwer Academic/Plenum Publishers.

Barbetta, Paolo, and Associates. 1997. *The Nonprofit Sector in Italy.* Johns Hopkins Nonprofit Sector Series, edited by Lester M. Salamon and Helmut K. Anheier. Manchester, U.K.: Manchester University Press.

Bauer, Rudolph. 1978. *Wohlfahrtsverbände in der Bundesrepublik, Materialien und Analysen zu Organisation, Programmatik und Praxis, Ein Handbuch.* Weinheim: Basel.

Bixby, Ann Kallman. 1997. "Public Social Welfare Expenditures, Fiscal Year 1994." *Social Security Bulletin* 60 (3): 40–45.

Burger, Ary, Paul Dekker, Tymen van der Ploeg, and Wino van Ween. 1997. "Defining the Nonprofit Sector: The Netherlands." *Working Papers of the Johns Hopkins Comparative Nonprofit Sector Project* no. 23, edited by Lester

M. Salamon and Helmut K. Anheier. Baltimore: Johns Hopkins Institute for Policy Studies.

Bundesarbeitsgemeinschaft der Freien Wohlfahrtspflege. 1990. *Gesamtstatistik 1990*. Bonn: Bundesarbeitsgemeinschaft der Freien Wohlfahrtspflege.

Cariño, Ledevina V., Rachel H. Racelis, Ramon L. Fernan III, S. Wojciech Sokolowski, and Lester M. Salamon. 2004. "The Philippines." In *Global Civil Society*, edited by Lester M. Salamon and S. Wojciech Sokolowski (185–99). Bloomfield, CT.: Kumarian Press.

Civicus. 1994. *Citizens: Strengthening Global Civil Society*. Washington, DC: Civicus.

Clark, John. 1992. *Democratizing Development: The Role of Voluntary Organizations*. Hartford, CT: Kumarian Press.

Clark, John, ed. 2003. *Globalizing Civic Engagement: Civil Society and Transnational Action*. London: Earthscan.

DeHoog, Ruth Hoogland. 1985. "Human Services Contracting: Environmental, Behavioral, and Organizational Conditions." *Administration and Society* 16:427–54.

Deutscher Verein für öffentliche und private Fürsorge. 1986. *Voluntary Welfare Services*. Frankfurt: Deutscher Verein.

Eikås, Magne, and Per Selle. 2002. "A Contract Culture Even in Scandinavia." In *Dilemmas of the Welfare Mix: The New Structure of Welfare in the Era of Privatization*, edited by Ugo Ascoli and Costanzo Ranci (47–76). New York: Kluwer Academic/Plenum Publishers.

Esping-Andersen, Gosta. 1990. *The Three Worlds of Welfare Capitalism*. Princeton: Princeton University Press.

Evers, Adelbert, and Ivan Svetlick, eds. 1992. *Balancing Pluralism: New Welfare Mixes in Care for the Elderly*. Averbury: Aldershot.

Florini, Ann, ed. 2000. *The Third Force: The Rise of Transnational Civil Society*. Tokyo and Washington, DC: Japan Center for International Exchange and Carnegie Endowment for International Peace.

Fisher, Julie. 1993. *The Road from Rio: Sustainable Development and the Nongovernmental Movement in the Third World*. Westport, CT: Praeger.

Gidron, Benjamin, Ralph M. Kramer, and Lester M. Salamon. 1992. "Government and the Third Sector in Comparative Perspective: Allies or Adversaries?" In *Government and the Third Sector: Emerging Relationships in Welfare States*, edited by Benjamin Gidron, Ralph M. Kramer, and Lester M. Salamon (1–30). San Francisco: Jossey-Bass Publishers.

Government of Canada. 1999. *Working Together: A Government of Canada–Voluntary Sector Joint Initiative*. Ottawa: Government of Canada.

Grønbjerg, Kirsten. 1991. "Managing Grants and Contracts." *Nonprofit and Voluntary Sector Quarterly* 20(1): 5–24.

Her Majesty's Government. 1998. *Compact: Getting It Right Together: Compact on Relations between Government and the Voluntary and Community Sector in England*. London: The Home Department.

Hopkins, Bruce R. 1992. *The Law of Tax-Exempt Organizations*, 6th ed. New York: John Wiley and Sons, Inc.

Howell, Jude, and Jenny Pearce. 2001. *Civil Society and Development: A Critical Exploration*. Denver: Lynne Rienner.

Hulme, David, and Michael Edwards. 1997. "NGOs, States, and Donors: An Overview." In *NGOs, States, and Donors: Too Close for Comfort?* edited by David Hulme and Michael Edwards (3–22). London: Macmillan, Ltd.

James, Estelle. 1987. "The Nonprofit Sector in Comparative Perspective." In *The Nonprofit Sector: A Research Handbook,* edited by Walter W. Powell (397–415). New Haven: Yale University Press.

Kanyinga, K., W. Mitullah, W. Odhiambo, S. Wojciech Sokolowski, and Lester M. Salamon. 2004. "Kenya." In *Global Civil Society,* edited by Lester M. Salamon and S. Wojciech Sokolowski (95–109). Bloomfield, CT: Kumarian Press.

Keck, Margaret E., and Kathryn Sikkink. 1998. *Activists Beyond Borders: Advocacy Networks in International Politics.* Ithaca: Cornell University Press.

Kettl, Donald F. 1993. *Sharing Power: Public Governance and Private Markets.* Washington, DC: Brookings Institution Press.

Kramer, Ralph. 1981. *Voluntary Agencies in the Welfare State.* Berkeley: University of California Press.

Kramer, Ralph M., Håkon Lorentzen, Willem B. Melief, and Sergio Pasquinelli. 1993. *Privatization in Four European Countries: Comparative Studies in Government–Third Sector Relationships.* Armonk, NY: M.E. Sharpe.

Kuhnle, S., and P. Selle. 1992. "Government and Voluntary Organizations: A Relational Perspective." In *Government and Voluntary Organizations,* edited by S. Kuhnle and P. Selle. Bristol: Avebury.

Landim, Leilah. 1998. "Brazil." In *The Nonprofit Sector in the Developing World,* edited by Helmut K. Anheier and Lester M. Salamon (53–121). Manchester, U.K.: Manchester University Press.

LeGrand, Julian, and Will Barlett. 1993. *Quasi-Markets and Social Policy.* London: Macmillan.

Lundstrom, Tommy, and Philip Wijkstrom. 1997a. *The Nonprofit Sector in Sweden.* The Johns Hopkins Comparative Nonprofit Sector Project Series, edited by Lester M. Salamon and Helmut Anheier. Manchester, U.K.: Manchester University Press.

———. 1997b. "Sweden." In *Defining the Nonprofit Sector: A Cross-National Analysis,* edited by Lester M. Salamon and Helmut K. Anheier (215–48). Manchester, U.K.: Manchester University Press.

Moe, Terry M. 1984. "The New Economics of Organization." *American Journal of Political Science* 28(November): 739–77.

Moore, Barrington, Jr. 1966. *Social Origins of Dictatorship and Democracy: Lord and Peasant in the Making of the Modern World.* Boston: Beacon Press.

Morales, Horatio, and Isagani Serrano. 1997. "Finding Common Ground in Asia-Pacific Development." In *NGOs, States, and Donors: Too Close for Comfort?* edited by David Hulme and Michael Edwards (93–103). London: MacMillan.

Nielsen, Waldemar. 1979. *The Endangered Sector.* New York: Columbia University Press.

Nisbet, Robert. 1953. *The Quest for Community: A Study in the Ethics of Order and Freedom.* New York: Oxford University Press.

OECD. *See* Organisation for Economic Co-operation and Development.

Organisation for Economic Co-operation and Development. 1997. *National Accounts.* Paris: OECD.

Pratt, John W., and Richard J. Zeckhauser. 1985. "Principals and Agents: An Overview." In *Principals and Agents: The Structure of Business,* edited by John W. Pratt and Richard J. Zeckhauser (1–35). Cambridge, MA: Harvard Business School Press.

Ringeling, Arthur. 2002. "European Experience with Policy Tools." In *The Tools of Government*, edited by Lester M. Salamon (585–99). New York: Oxford University Press.

Ritchey-Vance, Marion. 1991. *The Art of Association: NGOs and Civil Society in Colombia.* Country Focus Series, vol. 2, edited by Diane B. Bendahmane. Washington, DC: Inter-American Foundation.

Salamon, Lester M. 1981. "Rethinking Public Management: Third-Party Government and the Tools of Government Action." *Public Policy* 29 (Summer): 255–75.

———. 1987. "Of Market Failure, Voluntary Failure, and Third-Party Government: Toward a Theory of Government-Nonprofit Relations in the Modern Welfare State." *Journal of Voluntary Action Research* 16(1–2): 29–49.

———. 1994. "The Rise of the Nonprofit Sector." *Foreign Affairs* 73(4): 111–24.

———. 1995. *Partners in Public Service: Government-Nonprofit Relations in the Modern Welfare State.* Baltimore: Johns Hopkins University Press.

———. 1998. *International Guide to Nonprofit Law.* New York: John Wiley and Sons, Inc.

———. 2002. "The New Governance and the Tools of Public Action: An Introduction." In *The Tools of Government: A Guide to the New Governance,* edited by Lester M. Salamon. (1–47). New York: Oxford University Press.

Salamon, Lester M., and Alan J. Abramson. 1982. *The Federal Budget and the Nonprofit Sector.* Washington, DC: Urban Institute Press.

Salamon, Lester M., and Helmut K. Anheier. 1993. "The Third Route: Subsidiarity, Third-Party Government, and the Provision of Social Services in Germany and the United States." Report to the OECD.

———. 1996a. *The Emerging Nonprofit Sector.* Johns Hopkins Nonprofit Sector Series, edited by Lester M. Salamon and Helmut K. Anheier. Manchester, U.K.: Manchester University Press.

———. 1996b. "Social Origins of Civil Society." Paper presented at the Second Annual ISTR Conference, Mexico City, Mexico, July.

———. 1998a. "The Third Route: Government-Nonprofit Collaboration in Germany and the United States." In *Private Action and the Public Good,* edited by Walter W. Powell and Elisabeth S. Clemens (151–62). New Haven, CT: Yale University Press.

———. 1998b. "Social Origins of Civil Society: Explaining the Nonprofit Sector Cross-Nationally." *Voluntas* 9(3): 213–48.

Salamon, Lester M., and S. Wojciech Sokolowski. 2002a. "Social Origins of Civil Society." *Working Papers of the Johns Hopkins Comparative Nonprofit Sector Project.* Baltimore: Johns Hopkins Center for Civil Society Studies.

———. 2002b. "Volunteering in Comparative Perspective." Paper prepared for delivery at the International Association of Volunteer Executives, Amsterdam.

Salamon, Lester M., S. Wojciech Sokolowski, and Regina List. 2004. "Global Civil Society: An Overview." In *Global Civil Society: Dimensions of the Nonprofit Sector,* vol. 2, edited by Lester M. Salamon and S. Wojciech Sokolowski (3–60). Bloomfield, CT: Kumarian Press.

Salamon, Lester M., S. Wojciech Sokolowski, and Associates. 2004. *Global Civil Society: Dimensions of the Nonprofit Sector.* Bloomfield, CT: Kumarian Press.

Sen, Siddhartha. 1998. "The Nonprofit Sector in India." In *The Nonprofit Sector in the Developing World,* edited by Lester M. Salamon and Helmut K. Anheier (198–293). Manchester, U.K.: Manchester University Press.

Smith, Steven R., and Michael Lipsky. 1992. *Nonprofits for Hire*. Cambridge, MA: Harvard University Press.

Spiegelhalter, Franz. 1990. *Der Dritte Sozialpartner*. Bonn: Lambertus.

Starr, Paul. 1987. "The Limits of Privatization." *Proceedings of the Academy of Political Science* 36(3): 124–37.

Swilling, Mark, Bev Russell, S. Wojciech Sokolowski, and Lester M. Salamon. 2004. "South Africa." In *Global Civil Society: Dimensions of the Nonprofit Sector*, vol. 2, edited by Lester M. Salamon and S. Wojciech Sokolowsi (110–25). Bloomfield, CT: Kumarian Press.

Taylor, Marilyn. 1997. *The Best of Both Worlds: The Voluntary Sector and Local Government*. York, U.K.: Joseph Rowntree Foundation.

——. 2002. "Government, the Third Sector, and the Contract Culture: The U.K. Experience So Far." In *Dilemmas of the Welfare Mix: The New Structure of Welfare in the Era of Privatization*, edited by Ugo Ascoli and Costanzo Ranci (77–108). New York: Kluwer Academic/Plenum Publishers.

Ullman, Claire F. 1998. "Partners in Reform. Nonprofit Organizations and the Welfare State in France." In *Private Action and the Public Good*, edited by Walter W. Powell and Elisabeth C. Clemens (163–176). New Haven: Yale University Press.

Warner, Amos G. 1894. *American Charities: A Study in Philanthropy and Economics*. New York: Thomas Y. Crowell.

Weisbrod, Burton. 1977. *The Voluntary Nonprofit Sector: An Economic Analysis*. Lexington, MA: D.C. Heath.

Wistow, Gerald, Martin Knapp, Brian Hary, Julien Forder, Jeremy Kendall, and Rob Manning. 1996. *Social Care Markets: Progress and Prospects*. Buckingham: Open University Press.

Yamamoto, Tadashi. 1998. *The Nonprofit Sector in Japan*. Johns Hopkins Nonprofit Sector Series, edited by Lester M. Salamon and Helmut K. Anheier. Manchester, U.K.: Manchester University Press.

ABOUT THE EDITORS

Elizabeth T. Boris is the founding director of the Center on Nonprofits and Philanthropy, which she has led since 1996, at the Urban Institute in Washington, D.C. She is the author of many research publications and articles on philanthropy and nonprofits, coeditor with C. Eugene Steuerle of the first edition of *Nonprofits and Government: Collaboration and Conflict* and *After Katrina: Public Expectation and Charities Response*, and coauthor of *Working in Foundations: Career Patterns of Women and Men*. Dr. Boris was the first director of the Nonprofit Sector Research Fund at the Aspen Institute from 1991 to 1996. She serves on many boards and is past president of ARNOVA.

C. Eugene Steuerle is a senior fellow at the Urban Institute, a columnist for *Tax Notes* magazine, and a codirector the Urban–Brookings Tax Policy Center. Among other positions, he has served as deputy assistant secretary of the Treasury for tax analysis (1987–1989), president of the National Tax Association (2001–2002), chair of the 1999 technical panel advising Social Security on its methods and assumptions, economic coordinator and original organizer of the 1984 Treasury study that led to the Tax Reform Act of 1986, and a columnist for the *Financial Times*. He is the author, coauthor, or coeditor of close to 1,000 articles and briefs and 14 books. His research on charity and philanthropy includes studies on the patterns of giving by the wealthy, the effect of taxes on charitable giving, payout rates for foundations, and ways of simplifying and reforming tax rules for charitable contributions and charitable giving.

ABOUT THE CONTRIBUTORS

Alan J. Abramson is director of the Nonprofit Sector and Philanthropy Program at the Aspen Institute in Washington, D.C. In this capacity, he oversees the Nonprofit Sector Research Fund and other research and leadership initiatives that focus on critical issues for nonprofits and philanthropy. He has served on many local and national nonprofit boards and advisory committees, and has been an adjunct faculty member at Georgetown, Johns Hopkins, and George Washington universities. His research has focused on the impact of government budget cuts on nonprofits, the challenges facing nonprofit infrastructure organizations, and the operation of the federal budget process. He is currently the editor of the *Aspen Philanthropy Letter*.

Woods Bowman is an associate professor of public service management at DePaul University. An economist with 18 years of experience in state and local government finance, he has published numerous articles on nonprofit finance. Prior to coming to DePaul, Mr. Bowman has served as the chief financial officer of Cook County and was also a member of the House of Representatives in the Illinois General Assembly. In addition to his work at DePaul, Mr. Bowman also writes a column for the *Nonprofit Quarterly* on ethics.

Evelyn Brody is a professor at Chicago-Kent College of Law, Illinois Institute of Technology, having visited at Penn, Duke, and New York University. She teaches courses on tax and nonprofit law. Evelyn is the reporter of the American Law Institute's *Project on Principles of the Law of Nonprofit Organizations*. From 2003 to 2005, she served as secretary of the American Bar Association's Tax Section and has worked in the U.S. Treasury Department and in private practice. An associate scholar with The Urban Institute's Center on Nonprofits and Philanthropy, she edited *Property-Tax Exemption for Charities: Mapping the Battlefield* (2002) and is writing the chapter on legal boundaries problems for the forthcoming volume *Nonprofits and Business*.

Joseph J. Cordes is professor of economics, public policy and public administration, and international affairs in the School of Public Policy and Public Administration at George Washington University, and serves as its director. An associate scholar in the Center on Nonprofits and Philanthropy at the Urban Institute, he is coeditor of the *Encyclopedia of Taxation and Tax Policy* (Urban Institute Press) and *Democracy, Social Values, and Public Policy* (Greenwood Praeger). He has also published numerous articles and chapters in books on tax policy, the economics of nonprofit organizations, government regulation, and government spending.

Carol J. De Vita is a senior research associate at the Urban Institute's Center on Nonprofits and Philanthropy in Washington, D.C., where she studies the role and financial capacity of nonprofit organizations. Her research focuses on the relationship between nonprofits and government and the availability of nonprofit services in local communities, especially in low-income neighborhoods. She also has examined the capacity of faith-based organizations and their ability to work with government. Dr. De Vita is the co-editor of *Who Speaks for America's Children* and *Building Capacity in Nonprofit Organizations*.

Marion R. Fremont-Smith is an adjunct lecturer at the Kennedy School of Government at Harvard University and a principal of its Hauser Center for Nonprofit Organizations. She is currently directing a research study on governance and accountability of nonprofit organizations. She has published numerous studies and papers on government regulation of nonprofit organizations. Her book, *Governing Nonprofit Organizations: Federal and State Law and Regulation*, was published in 2004 by Harvard University Press. Prior to coming to Harvard in 1998, Mrs. Fremont-Smith was a partner in the Boston law firm Choate, Hall, and Stewart for 30 years, focusing on nonprofits.

J ohn H. Goddeeris is professor of economics and associate dean of the College of Social Science at Michigan State University. His primary research interests are in the economics of health care and government finance. He has published numerous articles in journals such as the *Journal of Political Economy*, the *Journal of Health Economics*, *JAMA*, *Economic Inquiry*, and the *National Tax Journal*, as well as a number of chapters in edited volumes.

V irginia A. Hodgkinson is an adjunct professor of public policy at the Georgetown University Public Policy Institute, where she founded and formerly directed the Center for Public and Nonprofit Leadership and the Center for Democracy and Civil Society. She is the author and editor of numerous articles and papers on the nonprofit sector, including *The Nonprofit Almanac: Dimensions of the Independent Sector, 1996–1997*. She has coauthored six volumes in the Jossey-Bass Publishers' *Nonprofit Sector Series* and served as associate editor of the *Nonprofit and Voluntary Sector Quarterly* from 1985 to 1990.

J anelle Kerlin is an assistant professor in the Andrew Young School of Policy Studies at Georgia State University, where she conducts research on politics and policy related to nonprofit development and operation. Her present areas of interest include social enterprise and international nonprofit organizations. She is the author of several book chapters on social enterprise and international nonprofits and of the book, *Social Service Reform in the Postcommunist State: Decentralization in Poland*.

E lizabeth J. Reid has 20 years of experience in labor and community organizations, grassroots political education, leadership training, and involvement in civic and political affairs. At the Urban Institute's Center on Nonprofits and Philanthropy, she was an expert on nonprofit advocacy and on U.S. tax-exempt international organizations. She served as national political director for the American Federation of Government Employees and taught courses in society and politics at the Corcoran School of Art in Washington, D.C.

L ester M. Salamon is a professor at the Johns Hopkins University and director of the Johns Hopkins Center for Civil Society Studies. He previously served as director of the Center for Governance and Management Research at the Urban Institute in Washington, D.C. and as deputy associate director of the U.S. Office of Management and Budget. Author of more than a dozen books, Dr. Salamon's most recent publications include *The Tools of Government: A Guide to the New Governance* and *The Resilient Sector: The State of Nonprofit America*.

S teven Rathgeb Smith is professor of public affairs at the Daniel J. Evans School of Public Affairs at the University of Washington. He is also associate dean of the Evans School and director of the Nancy Bell Evans Center on Nonprofit Organizations and Philanthropy. He is coauthor of *Nonprofits for Hire: The Welfare State in the Age of Contracting* and coeditor of *Public Policy for Democracy*. He was the editor of *Nonprofit and Voluntary Sector Quarterly*, the journal of the Association for Research on Nonprofit Organizations and Voluntary Action (ARNOVA), from 1998 to 2004. He is also the president-elect of ARNOVA. His recent publications examine government financing of nonprofit organizations, the role of faith-related service agencies in social welfare policy, and government–nonprofit relationships in the United States and abroad.

E ric C. Twombly is an assistant professor in the department of public administration and urban studies in the Andrew Young School of Policy Studies at Georgia State University. His current research focuses on social service provision by nonprofit organizations. He has also written widely on the determinants of charitable giving in metropolitan areas, the fiscal capacity of nonprofit organizations, and wage setting in the nonprofit sector

B urton A. Weisbrod is John Evans Professor of Economics at Northwestern University, and is a faculty fellow of its Institute for Policy Research. He is the author of nearly 200 articles and author or editor of over a dozen books on such subjects as the interaction of insurance and technological change in medical care, benefit-cost analysis, and the economic behavior in mixed industries. His book, *To Profit or Not to Profit* (Cambridge University Press, 1998), focused attention on the causes and consequences of commercial activity by nonprofits in many industries. He is currently completing work on a book, *Markets, Missions, and the Business of Higher Education*, (coauthored with Jeffrey Ballou and Evelyn Asch), that examines the activities of various ownership forms of schools.

R obert Wuthnow is the Gerhard R. Andlinger 1952 Professor of Social Sciences and director of the Center for the Study of Religion at Princeton University. He has served as president of the Society for the Scientific Study of Religion and as president of the Eastern Sociological Society, and he is currently chair of the sociology department. He has written extensively about religion, nonprofit organizations, philanthropy, volunteering, and civil society. His recent books include *Saving America? Faith-Based Services and the Future of Civil Society* (2004), *America and the Challenges of Religious Diversity* (2005), and *American Mythos:*

Why Our Best Efforts to Be a Better Nation Fall Short (2006). He is currently conducting research about the role of U.S. religious organizations in global humanitarian and relief efforts.

Dennis R. Young is Bernard B. and Eugenia A. Ramsey Professor of Private Enterprise and director of the nonprofit studies program at the Andrew Young School of Policy Studies at Georgia State University. He is also president of the National Center on Nonprofit Enterprise and founding editor of the journal *Nonprofit Management and Leadership*. His research interests include the management and economics of nonprofit organizations. His recent books include *The Music of Management: Applying Organization Theory* (2004), *Wise Economic Decision-Making in Uncertain Times: Using Nonprofit Resources Effectively* (2006), and *Financing Nonprofits: Putting Theory into Practice* (2006).

INDEX